International Economics: A Policy Approach

SECOND EDITION

International Economics: A Policy Approach

SECOND EDITION

MORDECHAI E. KREININ
Michigan State University

HARCOURT BRACE JOVANOVICH, INC.
New York   Chicago   San Francisco   Atlanta

ISBN: 0-15-541545-X

Library of Congress Catalog Card Number: 74-24699

Printed in the United States of America

To my daughters:
Tamara
Elana
Miriam

Preface

Much has happened in the international economic arena since the appearance of the first edition of *International Economics* four years ago. The international financial system has gone through a succession of crises, including two devaluations of the dollar, which led to the abandonment of the Bretton Woods system in favor of a mixture of fixed and fluctuating exchange rates. The outline of a new system is under deliberation among the world's central bankers. The European Economic Community has been enlarged from six to nine members, with an attendant maze of special trading arrangements having far-reaching implications for many nations. In the United States, the administration is seeking enactment of the Trade Reform Act of 1973, which would open the way to a new round of tariff negotiations under the General Agreement on Tariffs and Trade (GATT). Various other industrial countries have introduced special tariff preferences in favor of the developing countries.

These and many other policy changes have been incorporated into this new edition. A separate chapter (Chapter 17) is now devoted to the trade problems of developing countries, and most chapters contain new material. While the analytical sections have been strengthened and extended, the theoretical level of the book is unaltered. The fundamental objective remains the same: to extract maximum policy insights out of a minimum use of theoretical constructs. The original arrangement, which enabled the uninitiated reader to skip over the technical sections without loss of continuity, has been retained. In this edition, each technical section is indicated with a short horizontal line at the beginning and end, and each paragraph within the section begins with an open square ($\square$).

The Appendix section has been expanded for those students interested in more complex theoretical formulations. Also, a bibliography has been added at the end of the book for the benefit of readers wishing to pursue further any of the topics covered.

Chapter 9 is a new chapter dealing with the international financial upheavals of 1970 through 1974. It is not merely a historical survey; rather, it exemplifies how theory works in reality. Chapter 9 may be assigned as independent reading, as may Chapter 14 and parts of Chapters 7, 16, and 17.

My deep gratitude is due to the many professors who used the first edition and took the trouble to write words of encouragement and constructive criticism. Special thanks go to Professor Max Corden of Oxford University for very helpful comments on the first edition, and to Professors Gerald Meier of Stanford University and Robert Baldwin of the University of Wisconsin at Madison for reading and commenting on an early draft of the second edition.

MORDECHAI E. KREININ

From the Preface
to the First Edition

Since World War II, a large segment of our society has become at least superficially familiar with the functioning of the economy and with the way in which it can be influenced by government polcy. Partly because they are believed to affect everyone's daily life, and partly because of the excellent interpretive work of journalists and economists, terms such as "gross national product," "cost of living index," and "rate of unemployment" have almost become household words. Economic understanding in general has become rather widespread.

But this increased awareness of economic problems has reached the international field to only a limited extent. In part this is because international trade occupies a fairly minor role in the American economy and is therefore less likely to interest most Americans directly. In some measure it results from the mystique associated with international finance and trade. However, in recent years the frequency with which such problems have occupied the financial headlines has brought a growing recognition of their importance.

Traditionally, international trade and finance has been taught only at the senior level in college, with considerable economics as prerequisite. As a result, even those preparing for a career in international relations and international business often have no exposure to international economics beyond the smattering offered in the introductory economics course.

This volume provides a simplified yet comprehensive analysis of international economic relations, with a formal prerequisite of only one course in economics. Designed primarily as a basic text for a one- or two-term undergraduate course in international economics, it necessarily contains certain analytical tools. However, material has been chosen and arranged to serve a dual purpose. The analytical sections that are basic course material are fully integrated into the general discourse. . . . The more advanced technical material is included as appendixes. Without loss of continuity, these analytical sections may be omitted and the main text used in policy-oriented courses for non-economics majors. The volume will also be useful supplementary reading for students of international relations and business administration (especially those majoring in international business) and for economics students in money and banking courses.

The overwhelming emphasis is on analytical content rather than on technique. Each subject is expounded verbally before any use is made of analytical tools beyond simple supply and demand curves. Whenever technical terms and tools are needed to gain new insights or to clarify old ones, they are carefully explained. This also introduces the reader to economic parlance. Domestic economic policies are included only to the extent that they are inseparable from their international counterparts. Although the focus is on policy, the necessary theoretical underpinnings are fully presented. The book also attempts to dispel some common misconceptions about international economic relations. Finally, selected sources of relevant statistics are cited for each topic under discussion.

I wish to thank William J. Baumol of Princeton University, Robert W. Gillespie of the University of Illinois, Harry G. Johnson of the University of Chicago, and Norman N. Mintz of Columbia University for their valuable comments and advice during the preparation of the manuscript.

M.E.K.

Contents

1. Foreign Trade in the American Economy   1

Part 1   International Financial Relations

Introduction: The Alleged Mystique of International Finance   7

2. The Balance of International Payments   11

The Meaning of Deficit and Surplus   11
Uses and Misuses of Balance-of-Payments Statistics   18

3. The International Financial System and How It Functions   26

Market-Determined Exchange Rates   27
Exchange Stabilization under the Gold Standard   31
Exchange Stabilization under the Bretton Woods System: 1944 to 1973   33
Market Forces and the Determination of Fixed Exchange Rates   35
The Foreign Exchange Market   38
The Role of the Dollar in the Bretton Woods System   44
The International Currency System Since March 1973   50

4. Balance-of-Payments Adjustment Policies under
      Fixed Exchange Rates   56

Short-Run Imbalances   56
"Automatic" Processes   58
Summary of the "Automatic" Balance-of-Payments Adjust-
    ment   79
Government Policy   80
Foreign Repercussions   87
The Balance of Payments in the Context of General Policy
    Objectives   91

5. Exchange-Rate Adjustment   97

Relative Price Effect   98
Domestic Income and Price Effects   109
Redistribution of Domestic Resources   111
Another View of Devaluation—The Absorption
    Approach   112
A Third Approach—Emphasis on Money   115
Summary   116
Balance-of-Payments Adjustment under Fluctuating Ex-
    change Rates   120

6. Further Analysis of the Adjustment Process and
      Some Unanswered Questions   126

Domestic Policies   127
Exchange-Rate Adjustment   131

7. Exchange Control and Currency Inconvertibility   135

Exchange Control   135
Bilateral Clearing Agreements   140
Concepts of Currency Convertibility   142
The European Payments Union (EPU)   143
Historical Survey   146

8. Steps Taken to Increase International Liquidity   156

Ad Hoc Measures   156
Gold Policy   157
Special Drawing Rights   161

9.   From the Smithsonian Agreement to the Collapse of Bretton Woods   168

Events Leading to the U.S. Measures of August 15,
   1971   168
Policy Measures Announced on August 15, 1971   171
The Smithsonian Agreement   178
Post-Smithsonian Developments   181
The Second Devaluation of the Dollar   184
March 1973—The Collapse of Bretton Woods   187

10.   Proposals for Reform of the International Monetary System   193

A Dollar Exchange Standard   193
Centralization of Reserves and Establishment of an Inter-
   national Reserve-Creating Institution   195
Freely Fluctuating (Floating) Exchange Rates   198
Conclusion   209

Part 2   International Trade Relations

Introduction: Data on International Commodity Trade   213

11.   Why Nations Trade   217

The Principle of Comparative Advantage   218
Comparative Opportunity Cost   225
Absolute Advantage and Wage Rates   236
Summary of Policy Implications   237
Dynamic Gains from International Trade   238
More Advanced Analysis of the Static Gains from
   Trade   242

12.   The Commodity Composition of Trade   256

Introduction   256
The Factor Proportions Theory   258
Empirical Testing   263
Alternative Theories   265
Economic Adjustment to Changing Circumstances   269

13. **Protection of Domestic Industries: The Tariff**   272

Some Institutional Considerations 272
Economic Effects of the Tariff 276
How Protective is the Tariff? 294
Arguments for Protection 303
Approaches to Free Trade 306

14. **U.S. Commercial Policy**   313

Political Considerations in U.S. Commercial Policy 313
Reciprocal Trade Agreements Legislation 314
The 1962 Trade Expansion Act 320
The Trade Reform Act of 1973 321

15. **Other Barriers to Trade**   325

Import Quotas 325
International Commodity Agreements 330
Administrative, Technical, and Other Regulations 335
Cartels 337
Dumping 340

16. **International and Regional Trade Organizations among Developing Countries**   345

The European Communities 347
The European Free Trade Association 356
Special Trading Arrangements of the EEC with Developing
    Countries 359
The General Agreement on Tariff and Trade 361
Some Issues in East-West Trade 368

17. **Selected Trade Problems of Developing Countries**   373

Alternative Trade Approaches to Development 373
The United Nations Conference on Trade and Development
    (UNCTAD) 375
The Generalized System of Preferences (GSP) 380
Regional Integration among Developing Nations 384
International Currency Reform 387

18. International Mobility of Productive Factors 388

Introduction 388
Motives for Direct Investments Abroad 390
Foreign Investments and Economic Welfare
    (Real Income) 394
Effect on the U.S. Balance of Payments 402
International Trade Theory and the Multinational
    Corporation 403
International Migration of Labor 407

Appendix I 409

A Formal Proof of the Domestic Multiplier Formula 409
Foreign-Trade Multiplier with Foreign Repercussions 410

Appendix II 414

Stability of the Foreign Exchange Market 414
Elasticity Conditions with Less Than Infinite Supply
    Elasticities 417
Effect of Devaluation on the Terms of Trade 424

Appendix III 428

Elasticity of Import Demand and the Domestic Demand
    and Supply Elasticities 428
Elasticity of Export Supply and the Domestic Demand
    and Supply Elasticities 428
A Country's Share in World Export Markets and the Elas-
    ticity of Demand for its Exports 429
Import-Demand and Export-Supply Elasticities and the
    Incidence of a Tariff 430
Economic Cost of the Tariff 431
Static Effects of a Customs Union 433

Appendix IV 435

U.S. Balance of Payments, 1972 and 1973 435
U.S. International Investment Position in Selected Years,
    1950 to 1972 437

Appendix V   438

Forums for Trade and Monetary Talks   438

Appendix VI   440

The Factor Proportions Theory   440
A Domestic Monopolist Under a Tariff and a Quota   443

Bibliography   445

445

Index   461

461

International Economics:
A Policy Approach
SECOND EDITION

1
Foreign Trade in the American Economy

The past two decades witnessed a phenomenal and uninterrupted expansion of international trade. The value of world exports grew from $108 billion in 1958 to $240 billion in 1968, and to $413 billion in 1972. Most rapid was the growth of trade in manufactured products (from $64 billion in 1960 to $257 billion in 1972), followed by minerals (from $21 billion to $65 billion) and agricultural products (from $40 billion to $83 billion over the same twelve-year period). Particularly remarkable was the expansion of trade among the score of industrialized nations who are members of the Organization of Economic Cooperation and Development—Western Europe, North America, Japan, and Australia. Intra-OECD trade amounts to half of total world trade.

As the analysis of international economic relations unfolds in subsequent chapters, the United States will be seen as a pivotal country in the world trading and financial community. Two features of its economy make this country ideally suited for such a central role. It is a giant among nations and a "closed economy" at one and the same time. The first appellation refers to the fact that the U.S. gross national product (GNP)[1] exceeds that of all other industrial countries combined and that the United States is by far the leading importing and exporting nation. As a consequence, whatever occurs here may have profound implications for the rest of the world. For example, a recession in the United States lowers our demand for imported materials and other goods and may thereby cause problems for the exporting countries for which we are such an important market. Thus American economic policies that affect our trade position are important not only to us but also to our trading partners.

On the other hand, the term "closed economy" refers to the fact that the United States is relatively independent of foreign trade; quantitatively, ex-

[1] Total value of final goods and services produced during a one-year period.

ports (or imports) occupy a relatively small proportion of total economic activity. Because of its size and the diversity of its resources, the American economy can satisfy consumer wants and national needs with a minimum of reliance on foreign trade. This is in contrast to other industrial economies in which foreign trade plays a significant, if not a dominant, role. Thus the U.S. gross national product in 1972 amounted to $1,155 billion. Exports of goods and services were $73 billion, or 6.3 percent of GNP, while imports amounted to $78 billion (see Table 1-1). In 1973, both imports and exports increased to 7–8 percent of the U.S. GNP. By comparison, exports amount to one-half of GNP in some small European countries and to over 15 percent in the large ones. Comparatively speaking, therefore, the United States is immune to disturbances originating abroad.

This should not be construed to mean that the American economy is completely independent of foreign trade, in either a quantitative or qualitative sense. The quantitative importance of foreign trade cannot be judged solely on broad aggregative measures, because its impact is not spread evenly over all sectors of the economy. A substantial portion of GNP is made up of such items as construction activities and various services—many of which never enter international trade and are therefore termed "nontraded goods"— and is not directly affected by changes in trade policies. Most of the direct effects of such changes are concentrated in the commodity-producing sectors. Exports appear to be most important in the agricultural sector, while imports are most significant among mineral commodities.

But even these figures are too aggregative. Foreign trade among industrial nations is extremely specialized, and the manufacturing sector in particular contains variations that are not reflected in the sectoral average. In assessing the role of foreign trade in individual industries, it is customary to examine

Table 1-1

Gross National Product of the United States, 1972 and 1973
($ Billions)

		1972		1973
Personal Consumption Expenditures		$726.5		$804.0
Gross Private Domestic Investments		178.3		202.1
Government Purchases of Goods and Services		255.0		277.1
Net Exports of Goods and Services		−4.6		+5.8
Exports:	$73.5		$102.0	
Imports:	78.1		96.2	
Total GNP		$1,155.2		$1,289.0

SOURCE: *Survey of Current Business,* March 1973.

the ratio of exports to output and the ratio of imports to apparent consumption, where apparent consumption is measured as output plus imports minus exports. There are numerous industries in which one or the other of these ratios is very high, at times upward of 15 percent. Such industries are often termed, respectively, export and import-competing industries. Thus, although most American manufacturing industries are relatively independent of foreign trade, there are a few industries in which foreign trade plays an important role.

A second sense in which this country cannot be considered independent of foreign trade is qualitative. To say that imports of goods and services amount to 7 percent of the gross national product is to understate their importance in several respects. American imports contain important primary commodities that cannot be produced domestically but are crucial for numerous productive processes. Their absence would considerably curtail domestic production, lower consumer satisfaction, and interfere with our ability to meet national goals. Over 70 percent of U.S. agricultural imports are "complementary commodities"—commodities such as tropical products that cannot easily be grown in the United States. Likewise, the absence of imported fuel could have severe effects on the nations' output and/or environment, as the experience of 1973–1974 has shown. The same may apply in the future to shortages of other basic materials, such as aluminum. While most manufacturing imports compete directly with domestically produced substitutes, foreign trade widens consumer choice through diversification of available products, and it expands the producer's horizons in marketing his products and investing his capital. Opening the economy to the fresh winds of foreign competition also adds to its viability by spurring technological progress and other advances. And foreign imports can also be used to curtail inflationary pressures at home. Countries often relax import restrictions to cope with domestic inflation by increasing supply. Moreover, the external payments position of the country, of which merchandise trade is the major component, influences aggregate output and income indirectly through its effect on government fiscal and monetary policies. Finally, American imports constitute an important source of dollar earnings for many underdeveloped countries, whose stability is vital to the United States. Similar considerations can be articulated with respect to exports. Thus it would be misleading to suggest that the elimination or diminution of foreign trade would work no hardship on the American economy.

These are important qualifications, but they do not change the position of the United States *relative* to that of other countries. Comparatively speaking, this country is indeed a giant among nations and a closed economy. Whatever happens in the American economy has important repercussions abroad, but the reverse is not the case. And this dual characteristic qualifies this country to play a pivotal role in the world economy.

This book is concerned with the functioning of the international economy. It analyzes general principles and avoids the listing of factual details except to document and apply these principles.

In line with the traditional approach, the book is in two parts. Part 1 (Chapters 2 through 10) is devoted to international financial relations. It explains the present-day currency arrangements, dwells at length on the policies of individual countries within the framework established by the community of nations, and concludes with a discussion of reform plans for the international financial system. The analysis is accompanied by examples of financial episodes of the 1960s and early 1970s.

However, it should be borne in mind that a smoothly functioning international financial system is not an end in itself. Rather, it is designed to lubricate the wheels of international trade and investments, to ensure that these activities—conducted by a multitude of profit-seeking individuals and private corporations—can be carried on unobstructed in the interest of the trader and the investor as well as the community at large.

Part 2 lays down the principles that govern world trade and investment and discusses the factors that determine the direction of that trade. It then analyzes the effect of various policies that obstruct the free flow of trade, and it deals extensively with regional and international organizations designed to promote the orderly functioning of the trading system and to increase the welfare of their member states. A list of the major international organizations dealing with trade and financial problems is offered in Appendix V.

A few words concerning what this book is *not* about are in order. Except for a short section in Chapter 16, we shall not be concerned with the system of state trading evolved and practiced in the socialist countries. Our focal point is that part of international trade which is conducted by private interests guided by the profit motive. It is an interesting question, to which economists have failed to provide an adequate answer, whether in the final analysis the trade pattern of the socialist countries conforms to what would have been the case in a free-enterprise setting.

Finally, this is not a book on economic development. The development problem raises a host of sociological, political, and economic questions, none of which will be treated here. We shall, however, devote attention in Chapter 17 to the special trade problems of the underdeveloped world and to the demands that these problems place on the industrial countries.

1
International Financial Relations

Introduction

The Alleged Mystique of International Finance

Recurrent crises in international finance have often captured the news headlines in recent years: The pound sterling devaluation in November 1967; the revaluations of the German mark in 1961, 1969, and 1971; the French financial crises of November 1968 and March 1969; U.S. balance-of-payments deficits; the float of the Canadian dollar since June 1970, and the Special Drawing Rights (paper gold) introduced by the International Monetary Fund in January 1970; the two devaluations of the dollar in 1971 and 1973; and the floating of the major world currencies jointly or individually beginning March 1973—all occurred within a span of one decade. Neither the meaning nor the implication of these matters is understood clearly by even well-informed citizens. The baffled reader of news reports regards them all as part of the "mystique" of international finance understood only by highly specialized experts, and he usually skips over to the next story. Yet there is nothing mysterious or bewildering about these occurrences. They all reflect the periodic adjustments of the international financial system and have at their root the fact that each country must, over the long run, live within its means.

A country must balance its international financial accounts in much the same way as a family deals with its finances. In the short run, any deficit in a family budget can be financed by depletion of previously accumulated assets (spending from savings) or by accumulation of liabilities (buying on credit or obtaining a loan). But this process cannot go on forever. Sooner or later the family must adjust its behavior: either lower its expenditures or raise its income. The inability to go on financing deficits forever acts as a constraint on the economic behavior of the family. An analogous rule applies to a country in its relations with the rest of the world. In short run, an external deficit can be *financed* by drawing down previously accumulated assets, such as gold, or by accumulating debts to other countries. In time, however, an *adjustment process* must set in to eliminate the deficit.

But a country is not a family, and the analogy cannot be carried to the point of equating the adjustment processes. Family decisions concerning income and outgo are made by a single decision-making unit with reasonably full information and control over its position at any given time. The action involved is both direct and prompt. No elaborate mechanism is required to balance the accounts. By contrast, millions of individual decision-makers affect a country's international accounts. They include importers and exporters who in turn must be responsive to the demands of consumers and producers, all individuals engaged in overseas travel, and all companies involved in the transfer of investment and other capital across national boundaries. Even this list is not exhaustive. With such diverse interests represented, it would indeed be a miracle if the accounts exactly balanced on their own (although there is some tendency in the direction of balance). Balancing them necessarily becomes an objective of national policy, which differs considerably from family decisions.

In a free market economy the government has no direct control over individual decisions. Most policies subject to government jurisdiction are aggregative in nature, in the sense that they are aimed at the overall performance of the economy. They work through indirect effect on individuals and organizations, who are the actual decision-makers. While the individual family balances its accounts by direct action, all the government can do is press one or more policy buttons. It thereby sets in motion a sequence of internal (*endogenous* in economists' parlance) processes as the various economic agents, individuals as well as institutions, react to the external (*exogenous*) policy push. The hope is that the series of interactions will lead the economy toward the prescribed goal.

What in the individuals' case is a direct action with immediate and certain effects becomes a cumbersome and lengthy process with uncertain results in the case of government policy. Consequently, the study of economic policy is rather complex; it calls for full understanding of what happens in the economy between the adoption of a certain policy and the time when its impact is felt. The mechanisms involved in this process may be cumbersome, they may have conflicting effects, and they may be slow in working their way through the economy.

Not only that, unlike a family, a nation has no automatically generated information about its position at any given time on which to base policy decisions. Therefore, each government must establish an elaborate reporting mechanism to compile the necessary statistics and perform the analysis needed to guide the policy-makers. Moreover, if the policies of trading nations are not to conflict with one another, those nations must act in concert to set up a framework within which their policies are to be formulated. Such a framework is known as an international monetary or financial system.

In a sense, a nation operating within the system of state trading as it is practiced in Eastern Europe is more like a family than a free-market country. That system requires no elaborate national and international mechanisms. International transactions are handled on a barter basis by a state trading authority, which can balance the external accounts at whatever level suits the national economic plan. The government can determine the degree of autarky under which it chooses to operate. However, a system so divorced from the workings of the market mechanism can result in an inefficient allocation of resources. Equally important, it deprives the consuming and producing public of personal freedom, by denying it the right to deal in foreign markets.

Thus the periodic crises such as those enumerated in the first paragraph above are the price that the Western countries pay for the freedom of persons to trade and speculate coupled with the freedom of the nation-states to pursue their national objectives. The elaborate system that is required can be viewed as a means of having this freedom and at the same time minimizing international financial crises. The function of the monetary system is to provide a well-lubricated mechanism by means of which a multitude of traders and investors can each pursue his own goal and yet result in one harmonious whole. On the national level, each country must compile detailed statistics on international transactions on which to base policy decisions, and such decisions are subject to the constraints imposed by the international system. The nature of the statistical compilations involved and the policy options open to a country under various conditions are the subject of Chapters 2 through 6. Chapters 7 through 10 apply some of the principles to actual situations and consider possible improvements in the system.

2
The Balance of International Payments

A statement of all the transactions between one country and the rest of the world, usually reported annually, is known as that country's *balance of international payments* or simply its *balance of payments*. The transactions included are merchandise trade, exchange of services (sometimes referred to as *invisible* items), and transfers of capital in both directions. In order to facilitate the understanding of the various items appearing in the statement, it is useful to divide them into two groups: those giving rise to dollar *inpayments* (plus or credit items) and those resulting in dollar *outpayments* (negative or debit items). This dichotomy should be kept in mind throughout the exposition.

The Meaning of Deficit and Surplus

In the explanation that follows we shall make use of the U.S. balance-of-payments statement for 1972, as published by the U.S. Department of Commerce. A highly condensed version of this statement appears in Table 2-1, and the discussion in this section should be read in conjunction with this statement. It will be observed that the bulk of all transactions is export and import of goods and services. Commodity or merchandise trade[1] accounts for two-thirds of the total in both lines 1 and 2, with the remaining third consisting of service transactions. On the exports (inpayments) side, these services include such items as income receipts on U.S. investments abroad and foreign tourist expenditures in the United States; the corresponding items on the imports (outpayments) side are foreign investment income and American travel expenditures in foreign countries.

---

[1] The difference between merchandise exports and imports—not shown separately but amounting to —$6.9 billion in 1972—is called the *balance of trade*.

Table 2-1

U.S. Balance of Payments, 1972 ($ Billions)

1.	Exports of goods ($48.8 billion) and services ($24.7 billion)	+73.5
2.	Imports of goods ($55.7 billion) and services ($22.4 billion)	−78.1
3.	Balance of Goods and Services	−4.6
4.	Private remittances and government grants	−3.7
5.	Balance on Current Account	−8.3
6.	Long-term capital, U.S. and foreign, net	−1.5
7.	Balance on Current Account and Long-term Capital	−9.8
8.	Private short-term capital, U.S. and foreign, net[a]	−0.5
9.	Official Reserve Transactions Balance	−10.3
Means of Settlement (or Financing)		
10.	U.S. official liabilities to foreign monetary authorities	+10.3
11.	U.S. official reserve assets holdings (gold, convertible foreign currencies, SDRs, position in the IMF)	0

[a] Includes errors and omissions and allocation of Special Drawing Rights (SDRs).

SOURCE: *Survey of Current Business,* March 1974.

While in most years in the 1950s and 1960s the United States had an excess of exports over imports of goods and services,[2] the situation was reversed in 1971 and 1972. In 1972 the balance on goods and services was negative, showing an excess of imports (outpayments) over exports (inpayments) to the tune of −$4.6 billion. Another reversal, to a surplus of $6.9 billion, took place in 1973 (see Table 2-3). The most dramatic improvement occurred in merchandise trade, within which the worldwide shortages of agricultural products and the improved competitive position of the United States following the devaluations of the dollar both played important roles in promoting American exports. However, the deficit on merchandise trade is expected to reappear in 1974 as a result of the increase in the price of imported oil.

Returning to 1972, and Table 2-1, outpayments resulting from private remittances abroad and government grants under the foreign aid program amounting to $3.7 billion added to the deficit and resulted in a "current account" deficit of $8.3 billion, shown in item 5.

Item 6 nets out all long-term capital transactions. On the outpayments side these include direct investments abroad by U.S corporations, purchases of foreign stocks by Americans, and American investments in foreign bonds and bank accounts with over one year maturity. On the inpayments side they

[2] The balance on goods and services is one of the four main expenditure components of gross national product (see Table 1-1).

include foreign direct investments in the United States, foreign purchases of U.S. stocks, and foreign investments in U.S. bonds and bank accounts of over one year duration. While all items reporting the transfer of capital are included in the capital account component of the balance of payments (items 6 and 8), the income on foreign investments—whether interest, dividends, or repatriated profits—is part of the goods and services section. These earnings, of course, are a result of investments made in previous years.

It should be noted that U.S. corporations generally prefer direct investments, such as the establishment of foreign subsidiaries, which give the American investors control over the overseas operations. By contrast, most foreign investments in the United States have traditionally been of the portfolio variety, such as stock ownership, not involving a controlling interest in American enterprises. This preference on the part of foreign corporations appears to be changing in the 1970s, as an increasing number of them are establishing branch plants in the United States. Most notable was the spurt in European and Japanese direct investments in the United States following the second devaluation of the dollar in early 1973.

Item 8 of Table 2-1 nets out all private transfers of short-term capital during the year; the distinction between short- and long-term is often arbitrary, one year being the cutoff point for bonds and bank deposits, with stock transactions and direct investments considered long-term flows. For some purposes the short-term transactions are further classified into liquid transfers (for example, checking accounts) and nonliquid transfers (such as certificates of deposit).

All the entries covered thus far constitute a response to general economic or political factors. Trade in goods and services is mainly a result of relative prices in different countries, the relative purchasing power of their populations, and the geographical distribution of natural resources around the globe. It is also affected by such intangible factors as taste and marketing ability. Foreign investments reflect relative profit opportunities at home and abroad, which in turn can be traced to a number of economic (and political) factors. Also, short-term capital may be attracted to the financial centers that pay the highest interest rate, although not all flows can be so explained.

Items 1–8 (with the possible exception of the last one, or part of it) are therefore known as the *autonomous* items, transactions whose existence (and size) is not caused by the state of the balance of payments. And because they are motivated independently of each other by a multitude of traders and investors, they cannot be expected automatically to produce a balance. When these items do not add up to zero, the balance of payments is considered out of balance, or out of equilibrium. It is in *deficit* when their sum is negative and in a *surplus* when it is positive. This difference between the inpayments and outpayments must somehow be settled, and the means for settling it—gold and foreign currency transfers and official debt—are known as the *balancing* or *accommodating* items. These entries are brought into being by the very existence of imbalance in the autonomous transactions. Their total must equal the imbalance but bear the opposite sign, making the entire statement add up to zero.

More specifically, it will be noted in items 10 and 11 that the accommodating or financing items include changes in official liabilities to foreign official authorities, or exchange of official assets that are acceptable means of payments to all countries. These assets, known as "official reserves," include gold, convertible foreign currencies, and Special Drawing Rights—assets created by the International Monetary Fund (IMF) and distributed to its member countries which the official monetary institutions of these countries accept from each other in settling debts. (Special Drawing Rights, or SDRs, will be explained in greater detail in Chapter 8.) If in 1972 the United States autonomous transactions resulted in a $10.3 billion excess of outpayments over inpayments (deficit), then one of two things must have happened: either we paid up with an internationally accepted means of payment (line 11), or we owed the money to our trading partners (line 10). In 1972 the entire deficit was settled by an increase in U.S. official liabilities to foreign monetary institutions. The dollar amount of American official reserve assets did not change, although there was a change in the composition of these assets.

In sum, a deficit in the balance of payments occurs when there is an excess of outpayments over inpayments on autonomous transactions; a surplus occurs when the opposite is true. Reserve assets and official debt instruments constitute the means of *financing* that imbalance. In the case of a deficit, such financing can go on only as long as the reserve assets last or as long as foreign countries are willing to accept the IOUs of the deficit country, permitting it to pile up foreign liabilities. In the case of a surplus, there is no limit to financing, as long as the surplus nation is willing to accumulate reserve assets and claims on foreign countries. Since a deficit cannot be financed forever, sooner or later an adjustment process must be instituted to eliminate the imbalance.

Clearly, the size of the country's external imbalance depends on which items in the statement are considered autonomous and which balancing (or accommodating). Although the conceptual distinction between the two categories is clear-cut, in practice it is difficult to determine under which heading to classify certain transactions. For that reason, experts can look at the same set of figures and reach different conclusions concerning the balance-of-payments position of the country. In particular, the treatment of private short-term capital movements is a source of dispute among students of the problem. Part or all of these flows may be balancing rather than autonomous in character. Depending on how these flows are classified, we get alternative definitions and measurements of the imbalance.

When private short-term capital movements are considered autonomous, the resulting imbalance is known as the "official reserve transactions balance" (line 9 in Table 2-1). Under it the balancing items, appearing *below the line,* are official reserve assets and official debt. On the other hand, if private short-term flows are regarded as balancing (along with government capital), the resulting imbalance is known as the "balance on current account and long-term capital" or the "basic balance" (line 7 in Table 2-1). According to this concept, only items 1 through 6 would be considered autonomous, yielding a deficit of $9.8 billion in 1972. Thus the "basic" balance shows the underlying long-run external position of the country, while the official reserve transactions balance incorporates also the more transitory elements by including short-term capital transfers among the autonomous transactions. In reporting the statistics, the Department of Commerce usually publishes the imbalance measured according to both these concepts as well as the "net liquidity balance." The *net liquidity* balance places nonliquid short-term private capital *above* the line and liquid short-term private capital *below* the line; that is, the first element is considered autonomous and the second, balancing. But in fact none of the alternatives provides a foolproof distinction between autonomous and accommodating transactions, and therefore none can be regarded as absolutely satisfactory.

Several terms incorporating the word "balance" are frequently used in the financial press in describing a country's external position. They often serve to bewilder and mislead the reader. The following glossary of terms is offered in the interest of clarification.

The Balance of Payments   This is no balance at all; it is the statement of all international transactions as defined earlier in this chapter. The fact that the word "balance" is included in the term is a source of much confusion.

The Balance of Trade   Exports of merchandise (commodities) minus imports of merchandise.

The Balance of Goods and Services   Exports of goods and services minus imports of goods and services.

The Current Account Balance   Exports of goods and services minus import of goods and services and unilateral transfers.

The Balance on Current Account and Long-Term Capital   Inpayments arising from exports of goods and services and inflow of long-term capital minus outpayments arising from imports of goods and services, unilateral transfer, and outflow of long-term capital.

The Net Liquidity Balance   Inpayments arising from exports of goods

and services and inflow of long-term and private nonliquid short-term capital
(plus allocation of SDRs by the IMF), minus outpayments arising from
imports of goods and services, unilateral transfers, and outflow of long-term
and private nonliquid short-term capital.

The Official Reserve Transactions Balance Inpayments arising from exports of goods and services and inflow of long-term and private short-term
capital (and allocation of SDRs by the IMF), minus outpayments arising
from imports of goods and services, unilateral transfers, and outflow of long-
term and private short-term capital. In other words, the official settlement
balance is the change in U.S. official reserve assets plus the change in liquid
and nonliquid liabilities to foreign official agencies.

With the exception of the first, all terms defined above can be positive
(surplus) or negative (deficit). The balance of trade, the balance on goods
and services, and the balance on current account are considered "partial"
balances, while the last three represent *alternative* means of describing the
country's total external position. No single statistic can faithfully summarize
the U.S. balance-of-payments position, and the choice between the various
"balances" must vary with circumstances. At times several measures must be
used to obtain an accurate representation of the American external position.
For further clarification, Table 2-2 shows how the last three "balances" are
related, while Table 2-3 calculates the accounts for 1969–1973. A detailed

Table 2-2

Grouping of U.S. International Transactions under Three
Balance-of-Payments Concepts

Goods and services
Remittances and pensions
U.S. government grants and capital movements
Private long-term capital, U.S. and foreign

Balance on current account and long-term capital

Nonliquid short-term private capital
Allocations of Special Drawing Rights
Errors and omissions

Net liquidity balance

Liquid private capital, U.S. and foreign

Official reserve transactions balance

Foreign official liquid and nonliquid dollar
   holdings in the United States
U.S. official reserve assets

---

statement of the balance of payments for 1972 and 1973, as reported in the official statistics, is presented in Table IV-1 of Appendix IV.

In most years during the 1950s and 1960s, the United States had sizable surpluses on goods and services, but these were more than offset by the outflows of investment capital and unilateral transfers. This situation changed dramatically late in the 1960s, when the decline in the competitive position of the United States resulted in the shrinking of the goods and services surplus to a level below $1 billion in 1971 and a sizable deficit in 1972. In 1973 the surplus reappeared, and the "balance on current account and long-term capital" also showed a surplus for the first time in several years, with the

Table 2-3

U.S. Balance of Payments, 1969–1973 ($ Billions)

	1969	1970	1971	1972	1973[b] (prelim.)
Goods and Services					
Merchandise exports	36.5	42.0	42.8	48.8	70.3
Merchandise imports	−35.8	−39.9	−45.5	−55.7	−69.6
1. Trade Balance	+0.7	+2.1	−2.7	−6.9	+0.7
Military transactions (net)	−3.3	−3.3	−2.9	−3.6	−2.2
Investment income (net)	+5.9	+6.2	+8.0	+7.9	+9.7
Other services (tourism, etc.)	−1.3	−1.4	−1.6	−2.0	−1.3
2. Balance on Goods and Services	+2.0	+3.6	+0.8	−4.6	+6.9
Unilateral transfers	−2.9	−3.2	−3.6	−3.8	−3.9
3. Balance on Current Account	−0.9	+0.4	−2.8	−8.4	+3.0
Long-term capital (net)	−2.0	−3.4	−6.8	−1.4	−1.8
4. Balance on Current Account and Long-Term Capital	−2.9	−3.0	−9.6	−9.8	+1.2
Nonliquid private short-term capital (net)[a]	−3.2	−0.8	−12.3	−4.1	−9.0
5. Net Liquidity Balance	−6.1	−3.8	−21.9	−13.9	−7.8
Liquid private short-term capital (net)	+8.8	−6.0	−7.8	+3.6	+2.5
6. Official Reserve Transactions Balance	+2.7	−9.8	−29.7	−10.3	−5.3
Financed by changes in:					
U.S. Official Liabilities to Foreign Monetary Authorities	−1.5	+7.3	+27.4	+10.3	+5.1
U.S. Official Reserve Assets Holdings	−1.2	+2.5	+2.3	+0.0	+0.2

a Including, where appropriate, allocations of SDRs and errors and omissions.
b Goods and services entries do not jibe with those of Table 1-1 because of the preliminary nature of the 1973 balance-of-payments figures. They will undoubtedly be revised.

turnaround from 1972 amounting to 9.8 + 1.2 = $11.0 billion. However, because of the large increase in the outflow of nonliquid private capital, the net liquidity and official settlement balances remained in deficit, albeit smaller than in 1972. In 1973 the official reserve transactions balance was financed mainly by an increase in liabilities to foreign official agencies, and by a $0.2 billion decline[3] in U.S. official reserve assets.

Uses and Misuses of Balance-of-Payments Statistics

In attempting to simplify the exposition, we have glossed over many vexing problems embodied in the balance-of-payments statistics. Readers who may have occasion to seek more detailed information will find the U.S. statement published in the Department of Commerce monthly *Survey of Current Business* and reproduced in the *Federal Reserve Bulletin,* a Federal Reserve Board monthly publication. The annual *Economic Report of the President* contains data and analysis of developments in international finance and trade. For other countries, information may be found in *International Financial Statistics* and the *Balance of Payments Yearbook,* both published by the International Monetary Fund. Balance-of-payments statistics are reported annually, but quarterly data for the United States are also available.

Little or no credence should be given to the occasional news reports that draw conclusions from monthly trade returns, for these data may result from special circumstances. Even quarterly statistics can be unrepresentative and misleading. Normally an imbalance must persist for several years before it can be determined whether it is in some sense a fundamental rather than a temporary phenomenon, likely to reverse itself in due course. A warning against some common misuses of balance-of-payments statistics is in order.

Interrelationships Among Items

It is misleading to single out of the balance-of-payments statement one item that happens to approximate in size the total imbalance and attribute the imbalance to it, the implication being that if that item were eliminated the deficit or surplus would disappear. The impropriety of such an assertion arises from the intricate network of relationships among the various items. Only after these have been fully explored can the balance-of-payments implications of a particular action be evaluated. Correspondingly, government policy should be aimed at the overall position of the country. It should at-

---

[3] The positive sign attached to the 0.2 figure in the official statement may be a source of confusion. To avoid it, the reader might think of the last row in Table 2-3 as showing U.S. export of official assets such as gold. This leads to a decline in U.S. gold holdings, but conceptually it is an export transaction that gives rise to inpayments in return for the gold.

tempt to eliminate a deficit or a surplus *in toto* through appropriate general economic measures and not control individual balance-of-payments items by administrative means.

A few examples will illustrate the point. It was contended in the 1960s that restrictions of direct investments made abroad by American corporations would reduce the U.S. deficit to manageable proportions. Indeed, this was the thrust of government policy in the past decade (controls terminated in 1974). But such an argument loses sight of several facts. First, a large amount of American exports in the form of capital equipment, raw materials, and semiprocessed goods is associated with the outflow of investment capital. The amount varies from one recipient nation to another but tends to average around one-fourth of total foreign investments. Consequently, it is quite likely that the imposition of government restrictions on foreign investments in the mid-1960s impaired our export performance. Second, capital investments in a given year result in repatriated earnings several years later. Earnings on U.S. investments abroad amounted to $13.8 billion in 1972, far exceeding the outflow of long-term capital that year and constituting a powerful positive factor in our external position. (Foreign earnings on investments in the United States in 1972 were $6 billion.) To be sure, repatriated earnings would be curtailed only several years after any restriction on investments outflow. But the payback period on such investments has been estimated at only 5–10 years, and therefore the restrictive program that was in effect for a decade could not fail to hurt more than it helped. Finally, direct foreign investments affect the balance of payments through the sales of foreign subsidiaries in the United States, the host country, as well as in third countries, but the magnitude and direction of this effect cannot be estimated.

A second example concerns the U.S. foreign economic assistance program, whose opponents have often used the balance-of-payments deficit as a powerful argument in support of their position. But most of the foreign-aid money is spent in the United States, partly because the grants contain a stipulation that ties them to purchases of American products (known as tied aid). Thus, any curtailment of aid would reduce United States exports by a nearly equal amount; the improvement in the balance of payments would be minimal.

Finally, any reduction in specific expenditures by some form of government intervention runs the risk of foreign retaliation, which would be detrimental to all countries involved.

Long-Run Shifts in the Balance on Merchandise Trade

Because of its importance in the total payments position, the balance on merchandise trade merits special attention. In Table 2-1, commodity trade constitutes about two-thirds of items 1 and 2, making it the largest single category in the balance of payments. Yet, in line with the previous section, the trade balance should not in and of itself be a cause for alarm or jubilation, nor should it serve as the sole guide to policy making. In what follows, we attempt to place the balance on commodity trade in its proper perspective, particularly as it relates to the balance on capital account.

For more than twenty years following World War II, the United States mounted huge surpluses on its balance of trade—so much so that the financial press used to refer to the trade position as the strongest component or the brightest spot in the U.S. balance of payments. These surpluses, to the tune of several billion dollars, occurred practically every year. At the same time, the capital account showed substantial outflows of investment funds, often exceeding the surplus on merchandise trade.

This relationship between the two subaccounts is not accidental; it is characteristic of a capital-exporting nation. Although the causal relation is rather complex and cannot be fully explored here, we can say that a capital-exporting country must generate large trade surpluses in order to offset the deficit on capital account. In part, these surpluses are a direct result of the capital export, because overseas investment projects use American materials and equipment and thereby foster exports. But mainly there is an indirect process, internal to the economic system (see Chapter 4), through which capital export generates trade surpluses. By the same reasoning, one would expect a capital-importing country, as the United States was a century ago and Australia and Canada have been in the recent past, to have a deficit on merchandise trade. Here we may say either that the deficit is financed by the import of capital or that the import of capital generates the trade deficit. Whatever the line of causation, these tend to be companion phenomena that offset each other so as to yield an overall balance.

What does that relation imply for the U.S. trade position, past, present, and future? It should come as no surprise that, during the era of large inflows of investment capital into this country, the United States experienced continuous deficits on merchandise trade. As the importation of capital subsided and gradually declined below the annual outflow of repatriated earnings as well as debt servicing and repayment to Europe, the trade deficit diminished and slowly gave way to surpluses. For it is only through trade surpluses that foreign debts can be paid and earnings can be remitted abroad. Those surpluses grew to huge proportions as the United States became the world's major exporter of capital. Certainly this situation prevailed in the period 1944–1970. But sooner or later this country will approach the stage of the "mature economy"—namely, a stage in which repatriated earnings in all forms will far exceed the outflow of capital. And to accommodate large net inflows of such earnings, the trade balance will have to transform into a deficit position.

When that time comes, there will be some American private citizens and public officials who will view the trend with alarm. For some reason, large trade surpluses are popularly regarded as "healthy." But so are net inflows of repatriated earnings. The fact that the two are internally inconsistent escapes many observers. There is nothing inherently healthy or unhealthy about trade surpluses; it all depends on the circumstances surrounding them.

Just to drive home the point that a trade surplus is not necessarily *a* favorable phenomenon, think of the country giving up more goods than it receives in return and ask yourself, What is so favorable about that? The term "favorable balance" as applied to a surplus is a leftover from the mercantilist period when one overriding objective of nations was to accumulate gold. Because countries that do not possess gold mines can acquire the yellow metal only through balance-of-payments surpluses, having such a surplus came to be regarded as favorable. But it is easy to realize that by giving away goods we lose the pleasure or satisfaction of consuming them, while little gain accrues to the citizenry from having stocks of gold buried in Fort Knox. However, all this should not be construed to mean the reverse—that a trade surplus is necessarily unhealthy.

Neither a surplus nor a deficit on merchandise trade should be viewed with concern as long as it accommodates and offsets capital movements of similar size flowing in the opposite direction. Both components are a result of millions of transactions that, if carried on unobstructed, are beneficial to the world trading community. Thus, when the time comes for the traditional American surplus on merchandise trade to give way to a deficit so as to accommodate a net inflow of earnings, it should be viewed more with satisfaction than with alarm.

A similar analysis can be applied to other major components of the balance of payments. For example, it makes little sense to impose war reparations on a vanquished country and at the same time prevent it from earning the funds with which to pay them (by developing a surplus on merchandise trade) by raising tariff rates on imports from that country. Such a surplus constitutes the only way in which the reparation transfer can be effected. This is nonetheless what victorious powers often insist on.

Public policy ought to be concerned with the overall position of the balance of payments and not with any one component of it, or with partial balances, important as that component may be. In Chapters 4 and 5 we discuss the means by which authorities may bring about balance in the external accounts. Such a balance need not exist monthly or even annually but should persist over a period of a few years, covering at least one business cycle. In other words, there is nothing wrong with balance-of-payments deficits in two successive years if they are approximately matched by surpluses in the two or three succeeding years. When such an external balance exists over a period of several years, we say that the balance of payments is in *long-run equilibrium*.

Placing Balance-of-Payments Considerations in Proper Perspective

A country as wealthy, diversified, and productive as the United States, in which foreign trade occupies only 7 percent of GNP should not hasten to subject domestic and foreign policies to the requirements of the balance of payments. To be sure, these requirments cannot be totally overlooked; the balance of payments always exercises a restraining influence on any country's actions. But all too often a stand is taken in public debates that is based soley on balance-of-payments grounds, almost to the complete exclusion of other considerations. Exactly the opposite should be the case. Within limits (which we have not yet approached), policy objectives should be formulated on the basis of national priorities, and the balance of payments should be made to adjust through an economic mechanism to be discussed later.

A few examples will again serve to illustrate the point. In our discussion of the interrelationships among items in the balance-of-payments statement, we attempted to refute the proposition that the elimination of foreign aid would reduce the payments deficit by a corresponding amount. But the point can be carried further. Decisions concerning foreign aid and its distribution among donor nations should not be based on balance-of-payments considerations. Rather, they ought to relate to overall national priorities and to what the country can afford to spend. And it is per capita and total national income, not the balance of payments, that best indicate our ability (or any country's ability) to engage in foreign assistance. Likewise, only the income criterion can properly be used in any attempt to arrive at an equitable distribution of the aid burden. The fact that Ghana may have a balance-of-payments surplus and Great Britain a deficit does not mean that Ghana should initiate a foreign aid program to the United Kingdom. Assuming that we are able and willing to pursue a certain national objective, the balance-of-payments position should not stand in the way.

Another example concerns the U.S. commitments abroad, such as the maintenance of troops in Europe and direct involvement in foreign conflicts. Any such commitments must be decided in terms of the ranking of national objectives. Even the strongest opponents of military action should not base their opposition strictly on the grounds of the balance of payments. This is not to suggest that cost considerations play no role in decisions of war and peace. They must certainly be weighed alongside any noneconomic costs and against whatever potential benefits can be expected from a given policy. The only positive contribution that the economist can make, in his capacity as an economist, is to tell the policy-maker what the costs of the policy would be and what economic consequences are likely to follow from various courses of action.

The major economic burden resulting from war or foreign commitments is in the form of annual domestic budgetary expenditures. The pressure on the balance of payments resulting from any conflict is subsidiary in nature and consists of the following elements: (1) direct spending by American personnel abroad, part of which is drained into the coffers of foreign monetary authorities, (2) U.S. government procurement of materials in foreign countries, (3) imports of raw materials into the United States to support war production, and (4) the effect of inflationary pressures in the United States, generated by the war,[4] in encouraging imports and retarding exports. These costs can be estimated for any given conflict. In most cases the economy can be made to adjust to the external drains so as to remove the resulting deficit.

This type of reasoning is necessary to the assessment of the impact of any massive foreign involvement. A complete balance sheet of potential benefits and costs must be prepared, with the economic burden constituting only one element on the negative side of the ledger, the others being political and social costs. The best measure of the economic burden is the required budgetary outlay. This is particularly true for the United States, where foreign trade is a very small portion of the national economy. Provided we are willing to defray the budgetary cost, the balance of payments should be made to accommodate our other socioeconomic and political needs. Of course, competing national needs must be weighed against each other in deciding on budgetary allocations.

Limitations of Balance-of-Payments Information

Like any statistics collected from a great variety of reporting sources, the balance-of-payments data are far from perfect. Without going into the methods of gathering the figures, we might mention that the merchandise component is allegedly the most reliable, since traders are required to make detailed reports on both volume and value when goods cross national boundaries. Probably the least dependable are accounts of private capital flows.

But even if it were thoroughly accurate, the balance-of-payments statement does not contain all the useful information about a country's international position. The merchandise account, for example, which is by far the largest item, appears in an aggregative form. If an investigator wished to discover the commodity composition of this trade, he would have to turn elsewhere. One source of such data for all countries is the United Nations *Commodity Trade Statistics,* in which a standard classification of commodities (known as SITC) is employed.[5] More important, the balance of payments only shows changes in a country's positions, not the positions themselves. All

---

[4] It should be noted, however, that defense expenditures may be more inflationary than equivalent government expenditures on domestic projects. Both types generate the same amount of effective demand, but defense spending does not contribute anything to the domestic supply of goods and services, while domestic expenditures do make such a contribution.

[5] This is formally called the Standard International Trade Classification.

items in the statement refer to flows of goods, services, and capital over the one-year period covered. Total American holdings of overseas investments at a point of time, which are the product of flows over many previous years, are not given. Nor are the sales of foreign subsidiaries reported. Since these activities have important bearing on the strength of the dollar, information about them is collected and published separately by the U.S. Department of Commerice. The international investment position of the United States for selected years is shown in Table 2 of Appendix IV.

Finally, although the balance of payments is a global statement, it is often subdivided into the country's relations with separate continents. But the common belief that there is somehow a need to balance the external accounts vis-à-vis individual countries or groups of countries is erroneous. One often sees reference to the fact that our exports to a certain European country exceed our imports from it or vice versa. Such concern would be valid only if currencies were subject to government control and were not freely convertible to each other. Under the conditions of currency convertibility prevailing among the industrialized countries today, the United States can use its surplus with one country to pay for a deficit with another. It is only the overall external position that matters. And even that need not be in balance all the time. Just as a family can run into short-run deficits and cover them out of previous savings or by borrowing, so a country can finance temporary deficits out of reserves or by incurring foreign debts. It is only if the deficits persist over a period of years that they provide a cause for concern.

A Nation Versus a State

Why, it may be asked, is a country the smallest unit to have a balance-of-payments statement? Every region, state, and other subdivision conducts transactions with the world outside it: Why does one never hear of a balance-of-payments deficit of the state of West Virginia or the Rocky Mountains Region? A superficial difference is that there exist no comprehensive data on the economic transactions of a state with the world outside. Only countries, with political boundaries through which goods and services must pass, collect such information.

More important is the way the problem manifests itself in the context of a state. Let us suppose that because of a technological change or a shift in consumer taste, there occurred a sharp decline in demand for the products of West Virginia. That state's exports would drop sharply, and in all probability it would develop a balance-of-payments deficit. Yet there would be no press reports to that effect. Instead, public discussion would emphasize the fact that workers in the export industries were thrown out of work and that production and income declined all around. If the situation persisted and nothing were done to rectify it, the state would become a depressed area, and eventually people would start migrating to other parts of the country where jobs were more plentiful—that is, to states producing the type of products for which national and world demand were booming. Such migration is much more difficult, if not impossible, betwen countries. In other words, whereas an independent country is said to have an external deficit or surplus, a state with a similar trade position is said to be depressed or flourishing.

But the difference does not stop here. A country has its own currency and a national government that can pursue fiscal, monetary, and commerical policies aimed at curing the external imbalance. If nothing else works, it is reasonably free to impose import controls or exchange restrictions. By contrast, a state government can take few measures to alleviate a depression within its borders; its ability to act is much more limited. A state cannot pursue independent fiscal and monetary policies. It does not issue its own currency or control the supply of money; neither can it impose restrictions on "foreign" trade and payments. In a more general way, regions of the same country are subject to uniform economic policies affecting income and prices and therefore the balance of payments. Such uniformity does not exist between countries that pursue independent policies. Finally, a country can change the exchange rate of its currency, and in the present system of fluctuating exchange rates such changes occur every day. In contrast, the ratio, say, of the New York to the California dollar is immutably fixed at one to one.

On the other hand, the national government of which the state is a part can take steps to help the state by direct government assistance, by a variety of transfer payments, or by encouraging private capital to move in. In general, given the proper business environment, capital is more mobile between states than between countries and can be counted on to offset imbalances on current account to a much larger extent. Certainly, in the short run, the existence of an integrated capital market within a nation makes it easier to finance imbalances within itself than between nations. And if such financing is not adequate, the adjustment can take the form of outflow of labor from the deficit (depressed) region. Thus a deficit in a state is more easily financed and adjusted to than a deficit in a country. The upshot of this comparison between a country and a political subdivision such as a state is that in the context of a state an external deficit is differently manifested; it is more likely to be offset by movement of the factors of production such as labor and capital, and it cannot be handled by policy measures, which are the prerogative of the central government.

When a country experiences a persistent imbalance in its external accounts, the government is called upon to pursue policies that bring into action an economic adjustment mechanism designed to restore balance. Before examining what these policies are, we need to inquire into the international framework within which they are exercised.

3
The International Financial System and How it Functions

Unlike the situation in the period immediately following World War II, the currencies of most industrialized countries are today freely convertible to each other, some at a fixed ratio and others at a ratio subject to daily fluctuations. This ratio—the number of units of one currency that are exchangeable for a unit of another—is known as the *exchange rate*.[1] Thus, at a recent date, the British pound sterling (£) was worth $2.40 in American currency, the West German mark was valued at $0.40, the French franc at $0.24, the Belgian franc at $0.027, and the Japanese yen at $0.033. The fact that every exchange rate has a corresponding inverse is frequently a source of confusion. The dollar–mark rate can be expressed by saying that 1 mark = $0.40 or, equivalently, that $1 = 2.5 marks. An *increase* in the value of the mark to $0.50 is equivalent to a *decrease* in the value of the dollar to 2 marks. Consequently, a statement that the exchange rate has gone up (or down) requires further clarification, because its meaning depends on how the exchange rate is defined. To avoid confusion, one can use such phraseology as "the exchange value of the dollar went up" (or "down") in terms of other currencies. In general, extreme care is necessary in making and interpreting statements concerning variations in exchange rates.

Exchange rates by themselves tell us nothing about the relative strength of the currencies involved or the economies behind them. The fact that the pound sterling is set at $2.40 and the West German mark at $0.40 is not to be construed as an indication that the first currency is six times as strong as the second. It may simply reflect the difference between the denominations into which the two countries have chosen to divide their respective currencies.

[1] Exchange rates are published monthly in the *Federal Reserve Bulletin*.

When first decreed, the external value of each currency presumably reflected the country's economic conditions in general, and the purchasing power of the currency (that is, the internal costs and prices) relative to that of other currencies in particular. This relative position changes over time, and such changes may either weaken or strengthen the currency vis-à-vis other currencies. A currency is considered externally weak if the government is having difficulty maintaining the predetermined exchange rate under a fixed rate system, or if the currency declines in value on the foreign exchange market under a fluctuating exchange-rate system.

For nearly thirty years following World War II, world currencies were maintained at a fixed ratio to each other (a system of fixed exchange rates). But this system broke down in March 1973 and was replaced by a mixture of fluctuating and fixed exchange rates. The alternative exchange-rate regimes will be explained in the following sections, leading up to the system that has prevailed since 1973.

Market-Determined Exchange Rates

When the exchange value of a currency is permitted by the government to fluctuate freely on the foreign exchange markets, with its value determined daily by supply-and-demand conditions, it is known as a *freely fluctuating* or a *floating* exchange rate. The Canadian dollar floated from 1951 to 1964 and began its current float in May 1970; several major currencies, including the U.S. dollar, the Japanese yen, and the British pound sterling have been floating since March 1973. In such a situation, market forces determine each exchange rate at the level that clears the market. A floating currency is said to *appreciate* when its exchange value increases and to *depreciate* when its exchange value decreases.

To illustrate how the exchange rate of a floating currency is determined, Figure 3-1 shows the German foreign exchange market, where marks are traded for dollars, which for simplicity are taken to represent all foreign currencies as far as Germany is concerned. The two intersecting curves show the demand for and supply of dollars at various mark prices. They exhibit "normal" slopes: as the mark price of the dollar declines, more dollars are demanded and fewer are supplied. The equilibrium exchange rate for this particular set of curves is 2.4 marks = $1; it would vary with shifts in either demand or supply. The quantity axis indicates the number of dollars changing hands. This is similar to the price determination mechanism in the market for any commodity.

But the analysis begs the more fundamental question of what gives rise to such supply and demand. For foreign currencies are not commodities. A

Figure 3-1
Supply and demand curves for dollars in Germany

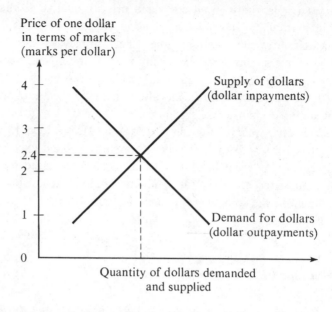

commodity is demanded by consumers for its own sake, to enhance consumer satisfaction, and is supplied by producers through the use of productive factors. By contrast, people do not normally require foreign currencies for their own sake, and foreign currencies are not manufactured in the same manner as commodities. Rather, the demand for dollars in our illustration reflects German desire to purchase foreign goods, to travel abroad and buy other foreign services, or to transfer capital abroad for investment and other purposes. Together these items constitute the *outpayments* side of the German balance of payments. On the other hand, the supply of foreign currencies is derived from commodity and service exports and from the inflow of foreign capital. These entries make up the inpayments side of the German balance of payments. Thus, the demand curve in Figure 3-1 is tantamount to a German dollar outpayments curve, and the supply curve, to a German dollar inpayments curve. Since the exchange rate is determined by the intersection of the two curves, it ensures equality between inpayments and outpayments. A shift in one or both curves will also change the exchange rate to a new level, which again clears the market. In other words, in contrast to a fixed exchange rate, a freely fluctuating rate will ensure equilibrium in the balance of payments.

At any given point in time, the supply-and-demand forces emanating from international transactions exert their influence on the foreign exchange market to determine the exchange rate. Thus, a currency is fundamentally "strong," and its value may be pushed upward, when the country's autonomous inpayments (exports of goods and services plus inflow of long-term capital) exceed outpayments (imports plus outflow of capital)—that is, when it has a surplus in the balance of payments. It is "weak" when this situation is reversed and the country's balance of payments is in deficit. In turn, the country's trade position is determined largely by the relative price of its goods compared to the rest of the world (that is, by its competitive standing) and by the relative changes in money income in it and other countries—changes that affect the demand for goods in general and for imports in particular. Similar considerations apply to trade in services. Likewise, the direction of net long-term capital flows is determined by expected relative profitability of investments at home and abroad, which in turn depends largely on relative income movements, while short-term capital flows respond to interest rate differentials between financial centers at home and abroad, as well as other factors. In other words, the demand and supply of foreign currencies depends on economic conditions and policies of the home country relative to the rest of the world. Anything that affects prices, incomes, interest rates, and so forth, at home and abroad influences the position of the supply and demand curves and therefore affects the exchange rate. The exchange rate is deeply rooted in the country's economic conditions; in no way can it be divorced from its own and other countries' general economic policies. The entire constellation of economic circumstances exerts its influence on the exchange rates through its effect on internationally traded items.

A general rise in wage rates in one country, for example, raises production costs and undermines that country's competitive trade position; it also raises money incomes, thereby encouraging commodity purchases in general and purchases of imports in particular. On both scores the country's balance of payments is adversely affected, and the exchange value of its currency will move downward. Besides the price and income factors, the trade position is affected by such imponderables as international shifts in taste, and the quality and design of the country's products and the service that goes with them. Practically any economic change, such as the lengthening of workers' coffee breaks, an increase in the price of fuels, a deficit in the government budget, or a rapid expansion in the money supply would affect the exchange rate through its impact on costs, prices, interest rates, and incomes, which in turn influence inpayments and outpayments.

It bears emphasizing that in all cases it is the changes inside the country *relative* to changes in the rest of the world that count. If prices and income rise commensurately on both sides of the border, then outpayments and inpayments may be similarly affected, with no change in the exchange rate. As an example consider the 1973 energy crisis and the quadrupling of oil prices by the producing countries during that year. This was expected to generate inflationary pressures and cause economic dislocations in the consuming countries, thereby weakening the balance of payments. But since Europe and Japan are more dependent on foreign oil than the United States, the dollar appreciated late in 1973 relative to the European and Japanese currencies.

☐ On a more technical level, this discussion raises an important question: If the demand and supply for foreign currencies is not the same phenomenon as the demand and supply for a product but is rather "derived" from a desire to operate on foreign markets, how can we be sure that the curves have the usual slopes of supply and demand, as shown in Figure 3-1?

☐ Suppose for the sake of simplicity that all international transactions consist of commodities. Then the German demand for dollars represents indirectly German demand for American goods. If the price of one dollar rises from 2 to 4 marks (moving upward along the price axis), then an American product costing one dollar would double in price to the German consumer (from 2 to 4 marks), shrinking Germany's volume of imports and with it the amount of dollars required to finance such imports. Thus a rise in the mark price of a dollar is associated with a decline in dollar outpayments, and conversely a reduction in the mark price of a dollar is associated with a rise in dollar outpayments. This explains the negative slope of the "demand for dollars" curve.

☐ By the same token, the supply of dollars is derived from German merchandise exports to the United States. An increase in the price of one dollar from 2 to 4 marks means that American consumers of German imports would find that by spending one dollar they can now get 4 marks worth of German goods instead of 2. If as a result of this price reduction they would spend more dollars to increase their purchases in Germany, German dollar inpayments would rise. This explains the (positive) slope of the "supply of dollars" or inpayments curve. This last point is subject to certain qualifications, which will be explored in Chapter 5.   ■

In direct contrast to floating exchange rates is the *fixed exchange-rate* system. As the name implies, fixed exchange rates are not permitted to fluctuate freely on the market or to respond to daily changes in demand and supply. Rather, the government fixes the exchange value of the currency, and it remains at the same level until such time as the government decides to change it. Such changes normally occur in discrete infrequent steps, as distinguished from the very small daily changes under a fluctuating exchange-rate system. A government-decreed decrease in the value of a fixed-rate currency is known as *devaluation,* and an increase, *revaluation.* Exchange stabilization under two systems of fixed exchange rates are described in the following sections.

Exchange Stabilization under the Gold Standard

During the days of the gold standard, before World War I, the external value of all currencies was maintained by fixing their prices in terms of gold. Each government or central bank stood ready to buy and sell unlimited quantities of gold at a fixed price in terms of its currency. Since the price was set at a predetermined level, it could not be expected to "clear the market"—a function performed by the price system when prices are allowed to vary continuously. In other words, at the given price there were periods during which the supply of gold exceeded the demand; the difference was then purchased by the central bank and retained in its vaults as reserves for future contingencies. Conversely, there were periods when demand exceeded supply, and the shortage in private supply was met out of the reserves of the central authorities; the country was then losing gold reserves. Indeed, it is to meet such unforeseen contingencies that central bankers insist on accumulating and maintaining large amounts of reserves in a form (such as gold) acceptable to all countries. Were it not for the fixed price of gold, there would be no need for gold reserves, since unlimited fluctuations in the price of gold would equate supply and demand on a daily basis.

Under the gold standard, the price of each currency in terms of gold was known as its *par value,* and each currency could fluctuate by a very small amount around that par, the degree of fluctuation being determined by the cost of shipping gold. Assume, for example, that the United States fixed the price of gold at $3 for each one-tenth of an ounce, that the United Kingdom fixed its price at £1 for each one-tenth of an ounce, and that the cost of shipping gold across the Atlantic was $0.02 for each one-tenth of an ounce. Each government would then stand ready to buy and sell gold in unlimited quantities at the fixed price. In that case, the exchange rate between the dollar and the pound sterling could vary only between $2.98 and $3.02; that is,

$$\pounds 1 = \begin{cases} \$3.02 \text{ (known as the "gold import point" for the United Kingdom)} \\ \$2.98 \text{ (known as the "gold export point" for the United Kingdom)} \end{cases}$$

We demonstrate this by showing that it was impossible for the pound value to be outside this range. Suppose that on some foreign exchange market a situation developed where the pound equaled only $2.50. Then it would pay an American to convert $2.50 into £1 on that market, purchase one-tenth of an once of gold from the Bank of England (Great Britian's central bank), ship it to the United States, and sell it to the U.S. Treasury for the fixed price of $3. He would make a profit of $0.48 (50¢ minus the 2¢ cost of shipping gold). In doing so he would demand pounds and supply dollars, thereby pushing up the value of the pound. The process would go on as long as it was profitable or until the value of the pound was pushed to $2.98, where the cost of shipping gold was equal to the gold price differential between the two markets. Indeed, the price of the pound could hardly go below $2.98 without bringing forth this process of shipping gold from London to New York.

Conversely, the upper limit of the pound's value would be maintained at $3.02 by a reverse procedure, involving gold shipment from New York to London. To demonstrate this, assume that a freak market developed somewhere, in which £1 equaled $4. Then it would pay an Englishman to convert £1 into $4, purchase .13 ounce of gold from the U.S. Treasury, ship it to the United Kingdom, and sell it to the Bank of England for £1.3. He would make a profit and in the process he would have supplied pounds and demanded dollars, thereby depreciating the value of the pound in terms of dollars. The process would go on until £1 was equal to $3.02, when profit opportunities would cease to exist (because the cost of shipping the gold is 2¢).

In either case, the shipments would be executed by *private arbitragers,* who would stand to make riskless profit, and not by an official institution such as the government or the central bank. Unlike a speculator, an arbitrager assumes no risk. He makes his profit by taking advantage of price differentials existing between geographical locations or points of time. The lower limit of the pound ($2.98) is shown as the gold export point for the United Kingdom, while the upper limit ($3.02) is the United Kingdom gold import point, indicating the prices at which gold is exported or imported as a result of the fixed price. The difference between them is the *spread;* in our example it is 2¢ on either side of par, for a total of 4¢. The same mechanism would work for all other currencies so defined in terms of gold, with the spread setting the limits to exchange fluctuations.

Since under the gold standard gold was a common denominator in terms of which all currencies were fixed, it also served to maintain fixed exchange ratios among the currencies themselves. For example, if one ounce of fine gold was worth £14.6, $35, 140 German marks, and 175 French francs, then the exchange rates would be fixed at £1 = $2.40 =9.6 marks = 12 francs. Only small fluctuations could occur around the exchange rates, with the spreads determined by the cost of shipping gold between the financial centers involved.

An alternative system for maintaining fixed exchange rates was introduced after World War II. (The various exchange regimes that were in force during and between the two world wars will be outlined in Chapter 7.)

Exchange Stabilization under the Bretton Woods System: 1944 to 1973

After World War II, gold no longer reigned supreme; it shared the spotlight with the dollar. True, gold still played a reference role, and a large portion of currency reserves was maintained in gold. But the stabilization operations of central banks were no longer conducted by buying and selling gold, and it was not usually shipped across the ocean.[2] The U.S. dollar had become the more meaningful standard in terms of which all other currencies were fixed and the major asset, along with gold, in which most countries maintained their international reserves.

Foreign central banks were not committed to redeem their currencies in gold. Only the United States maintained (until August 1971) a commitment to exchange dollars for gold, at $35 an ounce, when the dollars were presented for redemption by foreign central monetary authorities.[3] This system, under which other countries settled their debts in dollars, which could then be exchanged for gold, was known as the *gold exchange standard*. It grew out of an international conference in Bretton Woods, New Hampshire, immediately after World War II (in 1944), which established the International Monetary Fund as the central instrument to develop and oversee the ground rules of an international financial system.

Each central bank maintained the value of its currency in terms of the dollar by standing ready to buy and sell unlimited quantities of dollars on its money market at fixed buying and selling rates.[4] The pound sterling, for example, was valued at $2.40, but the Bank of England permitted a range of fluctuations between $2.38 and $2.42—approximately 1 percent on either side of par:

$$£1 = \$2.40 \begin{cases} \$2.42 & \text{(the dollar buying point)} \\ \$2.38 & \text{(the dollar selling point)} \end{cases} \Bigg\} \text{spread}$$

[2] Much of the gold belonging to foreign monetary authorities is kept "earmarked" for them at the Federal Reserve Bank of New York.

[3] It is illegal for an American citizen to own gold, except for industrial or medical purposes. But this prohibition is expected to be repealed in 1974.

[4] A noted exception was the Sterling Area, which consisted mainly of British Commonwealth countries (except Canada). It became a semiformal organization after the devaluation of the pound sterling in 1930 and a formal one when exchange control was practiced by Great Britain during and after World War II. The countries of the Sterling Area pegged their currencies to the pound sterling and maintained much of their reserves in pounds. In turn, they relied on the Bank of England to maintain the fixed rate between the pound sterling and the dollar. A similar arrangement was maintained by France with respect to its former colonies in Africa.

Whenever the pound became weak under selling pressure and its price dropped to $2.38, the Bank of England sold as many dollars as necessary, in exchange for sterling, to maintain the lower limit. The limit was so maintained because no private trader would sell his sterling for less than the $2.38 he could get from the central bank. Conversely, whenever the pound became strong under buying pressure and its value reached $2.42, the Bank of England purchased dollars in exchange for sterling to maintain the upper limit. No private trader would purchase sterling for more than $2.42 if he could get it for that price from the central bank. It might be noted that since the Bank of England bought pounds (for dollars) when the pound was weak and sold pounds when the pound was strong, its stabilization operations were profitable.

The two support limits, the floor and the ceiling, were known as the *dollar selling and buying points,* respectively. The difference between them, the spread, was no longer determined by the cost of shipping gold but by the central bank's decision concerning the support limits. Under the original regulations of the International Monetary Fund (IMF), support prices could not be more than 1 percent on either side of the currency's par value, for a total spread of 2 percent. Some countries, such as Germany, did not employ even this full range and restricted themselves to 0.75 percent on either side of par. At the end of 1971 the permissible spread was widened to 2¼ percent on either side of par, for a total spread of 4½ percent between each currency and the dollar.

It should be noted that if each currency was allowed to vary 2 percent with respect to the dollar, the total permissible variation between any two non-dollar currencies was 4 percent. To see this, assume two arbitrarily selected exchange rates, designed to make the calculations easy: £1 = $4 and 1 mark = $1. Permit each nondollar currency to fluctuate 1 percent on either side of its dollar value, to obtain the following ranges of fluctuations vis-à-vis the dollar:

$$£1 = \$4 \begin{cases} \$4.04 \\ \$3.96 \end{cases} \quad \text{and} \quad 1 \text{ mark} = \$1 \begin{cases} \$1.01 \\ \$0.99 \end{cases}$$

Then the range of fluctuations between the pound sterling and the mark becomes

$$\text{\textit{Strongest position of mark}} \quad \text{to} \quad \text{\textit{Strongest position of sterling}}$$

$$\frac{\$3.96}{\$1.01} = 3.92 \qquad\qquad \frac{\$4.04}{\$0.99} = 4.08$$

In other words, the sterling fluctuates in terms of marks from $£1 = 3.92$ marks to $£1 = 4.08$ marks, a spread of 0.16 mark:

$$£1 = 4 \text{ marks} \left\{ \begin{array}{l} 4.08 \text{ marks} \\ \\ 3.92 \text{ marks} \end{array} \right\} \quad \text{Spread} = 0.16 \text{ mark}$$

To convert this spread into percents we need a base, and the most reasonable base to use is the midpoint of the range, 4 marks. Thus the percent sterling–mark fluctuations was $0.16/4 = 4$ percent. The *dollar,* by reason of its role as the common denominator, was *the only currency whose spread was 2 rather than 4 percent.*

Figure 3-2 illustrates the system by showing the exchange rates and the range of fluctuation of the major European currencies during 1968–1970.

It was through such stabilization measures in the marketplace that all exchange rates were kept fixed (except for the very narrow range of fluctuations), with the dollar serving as the *intervention currency* as well as a common denominator and a standard of value. For example, if one dollar equalled 4 marks, 5 francs, and 300 yen, then the mark must have equalled 1¼ francs or 75 yen, while the franc was worth 60 yen. A large portion of world trade was (and still is) financed or denominated in dollars. The United States, in turn, was in a unique position; it did not as a rule intervene in the foreign exchange market but only stood ready to buy and sell gold (from and to foreign central banks) at a fixed price. Whatever intervention took place was designed to avoid gold losses or to counter short-term capital movements rather than to keep the exchange rates stable. When the United States was in deficit, it was the surplus countries that were obligated to buy the excess dollars so that their currencies would not appreciate above the upper limit. Conversely, during an American surplus, it was the deficit foreign countries that sold dollars to keep their currencies from depreciating. And in order to accomplish this, all countries had to maintain central reserves in the form of dollars.

The United States did not hold large amounts of foreign currencies, for each such currency could be used only for unilateral settlement with the specific country involved. The dollar came to play a role similar to that occupied by gold in an earlier period. All currencies were tied to the dollar, which itself was tied to gold. The United States was thus placed in a central position, which we shall pursue later in the chapter.

Market Forces and the Determination of Fixed Exchange Rates

Thus far, discussion has concentrated on the mechanical aspects of exchange stabilization. The reader may reasonably ask several interrelated questions:

Figure 3-2

Exchange rates, January 1968–March 1970. Graphs indicate weekly averages of New York daily rates. Upper and lower boundaries of panels represent official buying and selling rates of dollars against the various currencies. The Bank of Canada has informed the market that its intervention points in transactions with banks are $0.9324 (upper limit) and $0.9174 (lower limit). The horizontal rules in each panel indicate the par values of currency. SOURCE: *Federal Reserve Bulletin,* March 1969, p. 215; March 1970, p. 229

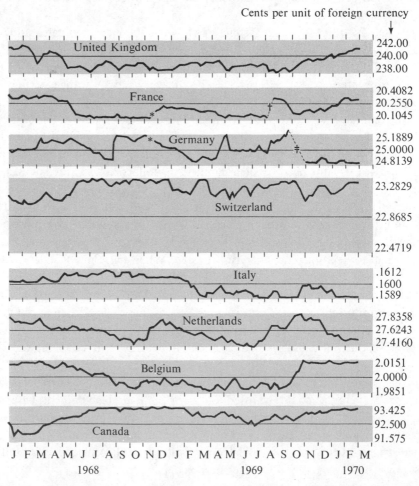

Cents per unit of foreign currency

* No rate is shown for the week of November 22, 1968, because the average of daily data for that week was severely distorted by abnormal or nominal rates during the Bonn meeting on November 20–22, when several major European markets were closed.
† Par value of the franc was changed August 10, 1969 to 18.0044¢ with buying and selling rates of 18.1406 and 17.8699.
‡ Par value of the mark was changed October 26, 1969 to 27.3224¢, with buying and selling rates of 27.5482 and 27.1003.

Can the government choose any exchange rate it wishes? What determines the exchange value of a currency within the limits set by a central bank's intervention (or, in the old days, the gold points)? What forces can push a currency all the way to its upper or lower support limits?

The answers take us back to the first section of this chapter. Under a fixed rate system a government cannot pick an exchange rate or a par value for its currency "out of a hat," for such a value may be artificial and cannot be defended. Only "realistic" exchange rates are sustainable over the long run. To be "realistic," an exchange rate must reflect supply and demand conditions on the foreign exchange markets and the whole constellation of economic circumstances that affect the country's international transactions. Thus the exchange rate must be rooted in the economic conditions of the country relative to conditions prevailing elsewhere.

This point is so important that it bears repeating. The supply-and-demand relation is fundamental, for it shows that the exchange rate cannot be determined arbitrarily by any government. To be realistic it must reflect economic conditions in the country compared to those in the rest of the world. In particular, it must reflect relative prices and income levels as well as other factors that affect dealings in foreign exchange. Any change in the underlying conditions would make the exchange rate either weak or strong and would affect the government's ability to defend it. In the final analysis the exchange rate is a price, albeit a unique price, of one currency in terms of another. Like any other price, it cannot be divorced from supply and demand conditions. Government intervention to maintain a fixed price can succeed only if in the long run the exchange rate reflects these basic influences and is rooted in the country's economic position.

It is apparent that within the intervention limits the exchange rate is governed by supply and demand for goods and services, international long-term capital movement, and transfers of short-term capital. If the exchange rate hits the lower support limit, the government can support it only as long as its international reserves and possible lines of credit last (hence the need for reserves). Once those are exhausted, it may have to devalue the currency to a level that better reflects the country's competitive standing. The upper limit can be supported as long as the government wishes to accumulate reserves.[5] If it wishes to stop the accumulation it may have to revalue the currency (increase its value in terms of other currencies) or take some other steps.

Only an exchange rate that balances the country's external accounts over the long run, under acceptable domestic conditions, can be supported by the

---

[5] Such accumulation of reserves is also inflationary at home. For the government pays for the dollars it buys in domestic currency, thereby increasing the money supply (a multiple increase under a fractional reserve banking system). Often it is the inflationary pressures that induce a surplus country to stop accumulating reserves.

government. Such a rate is known as the *equilibrium exchange rate*. Seasonal or even cyclical fluctuations in the balance of payments, and therefore in the exchange rate, can be ironed out by the government through accumulation or decumulation of reserves and by granting or receiving international loans. This is not so if the imbalance persists over several years and appears to be fundamental in nature. That can easily mean that the exchange rate is not in equilibrium and needs to be adjusted along with the support limits.

The Foreign Exchange Market

In our discussion of both fluctuating and fixed exchange-rate systems, many references have been made to the foreign exchange market. It is therefore useful to interrupt the narrative for a short institutional description of this market.

Market Organization

International transactions call for the use of the foreign exchange market. Although the market is highly competitive and provides traders with full information at all times, it is not to be equated with the stock exchange in terms of its organization. There is no "Big Board" on which instant price quotations (that is, exchange rates) are posted for all currencies. The foreign exchange market consists of the foreign exchange departments of the large New York banks as well as a number of specialized traders. They keep in instant communication with each other by telephone, continuously exchanging price and quantity information. It is therefore useful to think of this market as a network of telephone lines and cables. In addition, each of the large New York banks maintains correspondent banks in all major cities throughout the world, and it is through this relationship that the network of foreign exchange transactions is conducted.

This communication insures that the foreign exchange markets will be orderly: that the value of one currency in terms of another will be the same in all major financial centers. If the franc is worth 20¢ in Paris and 21¢ in London, any financier can purchase francs in Paris, sell them immediately in London, and realize a 1¢ profit on each franc. In doing so he demands francs in Paris, thereby exerting an upward pressure on their price, and supplies them in London, with a resulting downward pressure. The process goes on as long as there are profits to be realized—that is, until the price differential disappears. The transactions described here are called *arbitrage,* for they involve no risk. Profit is realized simply by taking advantage of the geographical price differential. But the arbitrager performs the useful function of insuring that each currency has the same value on all financial markets.

An equally important feature of this arrangement is the existence of "orderly cross rates." By this we mean that if at a given instant the franc is worth $0.20 and the pound sterling is valued at $2.40, then the pound is worth 12 francs. We prove this by showing that no deviation from this price is sustainable. Suppose that a freak situation developed on the Swiss foreign exchange market, and the pound dropped to 10 francs in value (but with the ratios of 1 franc = $0.20 and £1 = $2.40 maintained in Paris and London, respectively). Then it would pay a financier with 10 francs to convert them into one British pound on the Swiss market, exchange the pound for $2.40 in London, and for that sum purchase 12 francs in Paris. Disregarding transaction costs, he makes 2 francs in profit by taking advantage of existing price differentials between geographical locations. In the process he demands pounds and supplies francs on the Swiss market, thereby pushing up the pound–franc ratio. This process, known as triangular arbitrage, goes on as long as there is a profit to be made—that is, until the pound is pushed up to 12 francs and the profit opportunities cease to exist.

If, on the other hand, the pound were by chance equal to 15 francs on the Swiss market, it would pay our financier to do the reverse. He would convert a pound into 15 francs, use them to buy $3.00 in Paris, and exchange this for £1.25 in London, thereby realizing a profit of one-fourth of a British pound. In the process he supplies pounds and demands francs, thereby pushing down the franc value of the pound on the Swiss market. The process will continue as long as it provides an opportunity for profit, or until the value of the pound declines to 12 francs. Simple arithmetic will convince the reader that no further profits could then be realized. Figure 3-3 offers a visual summary of the process.

Figure 3-3
CASE 1

	Exchange rate	Transactions		Profit	Result
Paris	1 franc = 20¢	10 francs	12 francs	2 francs	Pound value (in Zurich)
London	£1 = 240¢		240¢		raised in terms
Zurich	£1 = 10 francs	10 francs→£1			of francs

CASE 2

	Exchange rate	Transactions		Profit	Result
London	£1 = 240¢	£1	£1.25	£0.25	Pound value (in Zurich)
Paris	1 franc = 20¢		300¢		reduced in terms
Zurich	£1 = 15 francs	£1→15 francs			of francs

The Forward Exchange Market

Institutionally, however, the story does not end here. Partly because of the large distances involved, international transactions are not usually consummated in a short time. Months elapse between the time that a London importer of automobiles places an order in Detroit and the time that the goods are delivered. Because of this and other factors, the conduct of foreign trade necessitates the use of special payment instruments not normally employed to finance domestic transactions.[6] But more important for our purposes, it often calls for making future payments. The British importer deals in cars and assumes the normal risks involved in the automobile trade. However, inasmuch as there is a lapse of several months between the time the order is placed and the time he must make payment, additional uncertainty may arise from exchange fluctuations in the intervening period.

When the order for cars is placed, the importer undertakes to pay a certain dollar sum upon delivery. But in the meantime the dollar value of the pound sterling may change—either because of fluctuations under a regime of floating currencies or by government action under a regime of fixed exchange rates—affecting the sterling cost of the merchandise on which his calculations

---

[6] Here is an example of the financing of foreign trade. Assume that exporter A in New York exports $2,400 (£1,000) worth of merchandise to importer B in London. The exporter loads the merchandise on ship and obtains the shipping documents from the ship's officer. He draws a draft for $2,400 on B, attaches the shipping documents, and sells these papers to his bank in New York. Exporter A gets paid immediately by his bank. The New York bank airmails the entire documents package to its London correspondent, which in turn notifies importer B of their arrival. B signs ("accepts") the draft to indicate that he accepts the obligation of payment when it falls due, and in return he receives from the bank the shipping documents that will enable him to get control of the merchandise when the freighter finally arrives. Once the draft is signed, it becomes an "acceptance." The London bank credits the account of its New York counterpart and sells ("discounts") the acceptance on the local money market. The investor who purchases the acceptance thus actually finances the transaction while the goods are in transit. Upon its maturity he will present it to B for payment. Availability of funds to finance acceptances is a prerequisite for a city to become an international trade center.

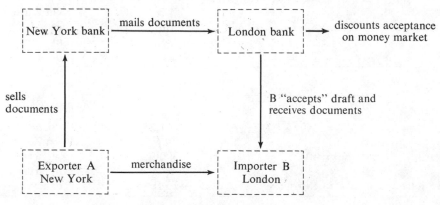

are based. For example, if Great Britain changes the exchange value of the pound sterling from $3 to $2, then the sterling cost of a $3,000 car rises from £1,000 to £1,500. The importer would wish to insure against this contingency. Such insurance, known as *hedging,* is available to him in the *forward exchange market*. This market allows him to determine, at the time he orders the merchandise, what the sterling price of dollars will be when payment falls due. And he can therefore fully account for this price in his original calculations.

In particular, the trader would approach his bank and purchase *x* number of dollars for delivery, say, six months hence. The price of dollars in terms of sterling is agreed upon immediately, but the transaction on both sides—the exchange (or delivery) of dollars for sterling—does not take place until six months later. The price involved here is known as the *forward exchange rate,* as distinguished from the *spot exchange rate,* which applies to transactions consummated the folowing day. In a well-developed financial center there are always markets for forward dealings, and therefore market-determined forward exchange rates, for thirty and ninety days hence, as well as for other periods.[7] It bears repeating that, were it not for the risk of exchange variations, the spot and forward exchange rates would be the same, as they are between California and New York dollars. In other words, with complete certainty, there would be no forward exchange market.

Under orderly market conditions, the forward and spot exchange rates are related to one another in a way that reflects the interest-rate differential in the two financial markets. To see this, let us further pursue the case of the British importer, purchasing from his bank six-month-forward dollars. The selling bank is not a speculative institution; it would normally wish to make sure not only that it is in possession of the dollars on delivery date but that it does not lose money on the transaction from exchange fluctuations. The bank can *cover* itself by immediately purchasing spot dollars and then holding them in New York for six months, when they are scheduled for delivery to the importer in exchange for pounds. In doing so, the British bank earns the New York interest rate instead of the London rate on these funds for the period under consideration. If the interest rate in New York is lower than that in London, the importer would have to pay the differential; forward dollars would sell at a premium compared to spot dollars, the premium being equivalent to the interest differential. On the other hand, should the New York interest rate exceed that of London, it is actually advantageous for the bank to keep the funds there, and under competitive pressure the gain would be passed on to the importer. Forward dollars would sell at a discount com-

[7] These are the most common delivery dates for which daily quotations are readily available. But bankers and dealers supply quotations for other periods (up to four years) on special request.

pared to spot dollars, the discount equaling the interest differential between London and New York. In other words, the importer's demand for forward dollars makes it possible for the bank to enjoy a higher interest return, and these extra earnings are passed on to the importer. Without this demand the bank would not shift the funds to New York for fear of exchange losses in case of revaluation of the pound sterling in terms of the dollar.

As long as orderly conditions prevail, information is complete, and fluid funds are abundantly available, the ratio of forward exchange rate to spot exchange rate would reflect the interest differential. Any divergence between them opens up an opportunity for riskless profit, and arbitragers would operate until the relation is restored. Here the arbitrage equalizes prices over time, instead of between geographical centers at a given point of time, but the principle is the same.[8]

In reality the expected relationship does not often exist. This is due partly to market imperfections (such as imperfect knowledge of the type that accounts for differences in interest rates on savings accounts paid by two banks in the same town). Also, because of such risks as the possible imposition of exchange control by foreign governments, domestic and foreign assets are not perfect substitutes. Another important reason is the desire of people to diversify their asset holdings in order to minimize risk. We might think of every financier as having a portfolio of various financial assets, consisting of stocks, bonds, commercial papers, and the like. If he is a "risk averter" (likes to avoid risk), then he will choose to diversify his portfolio as much as possible to minimize risk of default (which is to say, he will not put all his eggs in one basket). Purchasing foreign assets, as we shall see later on, is one way of accomplishing this. Thus, pepole can move in and out of foreign assets (so as

---

[8] An alternative way of looking at this relationship will clarify the principle of "equalization through time." Each currency's future value is equal to its present value plus the interest that can be earned on assets denominated in that currency over the period under consideration. (Conversely, to convert a future monetary value into its present equivalent, we *discount* it by the interest rate.) Thus, if the annual interest rate in London is labeled i_L, then the value of the pound sterling one year in the future (denoted $£_f$) is its present value ($£_p$) plus the added interest:

$$£_f = £_p(1 + i_L)$$

The same relation applies to the dollar with respect to the interest rate prevailing in New York:

$$\$_f = \$_p(1 + i_{NY})$$

Dividing the second equation by the first, we obtain the relation

$$\frac{\$_f}{£_f} = \frac{\$_p}{£_p} \times \frac{1 + i_{NY}}{1 + i_L}$$

The two currency ratios shown are the future and spot dollar-to-sterling exchange rates, respectively, and they can be denoted r_f and r_p. Thus:

$$r_f = r_p \frac{1 + i_{NY}}{1 + i_L}$$

to reduce risk) and thereby cause international capital flows even when no interest differentials exist.

Speculation

In contrast to the arbitrager, the speculator does not take covered positions (as did the bank in our example). Instead, he sells forward dollars, hoping to deliver cheaper dollars at the future date should the value of the dollar decline in the intervening period. Specifically, a speculator is said to take a *short position* when he sells foreign currency forward without at the same time owning an equivalent amount of this currency (that is, he sells what he does not have), in the expectation of buying it at a lower spot rate when the contract matures. He is said to take a *long position* when he purchases foreign currency forward without incurring an obligation to make a spot payment at the time of delivery (he buys what he does not need), in the expectation that a spot sale of the foreign currency at that time will produce a profit. Because a speculator does not take a covered position, the relationship between interest rates is of no concern to him. What is most important to the speculator is the relation between the forward exchange rates prevailing on the market and his personal expectation about the spot rate at some future date[9] Indeed, speculative funds may create interest differentials that can then be covered by arbitrage funds if they are available in sufficient quantity and if market conditions are not so unsettled (such as under expectations of an immediate exchange-rate adjustment) that they are completely dominated by speculative activity.

Speculators demand and supply currencies in anticipation of changes in their price. If a currency is weak and the government's ability to defend it is suspect, speculators can exert additional pressure by selling the currency en masse in exchange for other currencies. Short-run capital, sometimes referred to as "hot money,"[10] would then leave the country for other financial centers that were thought to have strong and therefore desirable currencies. These currencies would be purchased by the speculators. The only way to combat such a run on currency is by massive intergovernmental assistance or by the imposition of controls. This is the type of pressure that often created grave disturbances on the international financial markets during the 1967–1973 period. Speculative activities were carried out not only by professional speculators but also by the large international corporations, who adjusted their transactions to accommodate anticipated changes in the exchange rates,

---

[9] Since expectations are uncertain, the government can affect speculative activity by floating rumors and otherwise influencing expectations.
[10] Strictly speaking, the term "hot money" is capital flowing against the dictate of interest rate differentials. But the financial press often uses the term to refer to any type of speculative flow.

and by the corner shopkeeper in Europe, who converted his surplus cash to the currencies considered strong.

Thus, as distinguished from traders and investors, speculators purchase foreign currencies and hold them for their own sake. Their demand is derived not from a demand for goods and services but from a desire to profit from changes in the price of the currency itself, and is therefore an exception to the statement made in the first section that people do not usually demand foreign currencies for their own sake.

So much for the institutional digression. We now return to the international financial system, with the next two sections devoted to further elaboration of the Bretton Woods system.

The Role of the Dollar in the Bretton Woods System

It will be recalled that from 1944 to 1973 the dollar served as the intervention currency and international standard of value. How did this situation, involving such a pivotal role for the dollar, come about? Mainly it evolved out of a constellation of circumstances prevailing after World War II and in some measure was established by design. The "design component" of the system was the creation in 1944 of the International Monetary Fund (IMF),[11] which today has a membership of 126 nations. Following the international financial chaos of the 1920s and 1930s, the Western nations yearned for order and cooperation—order that would make possible a smoothy functioning trading system. By the mid-1940s the world had still not recovered from the breakdown of the gold standard during World War I. A return to that system in its strict sense, with all the rules governing the financial behavior of governments, was thought to be neither possible nor desirable. However, the IMF charter contained some of the features of the gold standard; for example, it provided for fixed exchange rates and outlawed exchange control except when a currency was subject to massive speculative attack. The exchange system prevailing during 1944–1973 was often referred to as the *adjustable peg* system, for under it currencies were pegged to each other but each exchange rate was allowed to adjust by discrete amounts whenever it moved out of its long-run equilibrium position. The main functions of the IMF were to lay down ground rules for the conduct of international finance; to serve as an instrument of consultation, advice, and cooperation between countries; and to provide short- and

---

[11] Also established at that time was the International Bank for Reconstruction and Development (sometimes referred to as the World Bank) to extend reconstruction and development loans to needy nations. Over the years the Bank developed into the main agency for extending development loans out of subscription capital, as well as money raised on the international capital markets. It also has a "soft-loan" subsidiary known as the International Development Association.

medium-term financial assistance to countries in external deficit. In recent years one function of the IMF has been to create and distribute international reserves (in the form of SDRs).

Turning now to the evolutionary process through which the dollar emerged into a new central role, we will recall that immediately after World War II there were intense "dollar shortages." Most European countries were engaged in intensive efforts to reconstruct their war-ravaged economies, for which they needed large amounts of materials and equipment. The only source for such materials at the time was the United States, so the dollar was in great demand to finance the necessary purchases. Consequently, most countries saw absolutely no reason to hold gold. Instead, whenever they managed to run an external surplus, they were extremely happy to accumulate dollar balances. The dollar was a much better asset than gold. It was the asset most sought after, and therefore enjoyed full confidence. Like gold, it gave holders access to the vast American market where all the necessities of life were abundantly available, but as a reserve asset *dollars earned interest*[12] *while gold reserves did not.*

Many private international transactions not involving the United States— transactions in goods, services, and capital—began to be financed in dollars. Indeed, a major market known as the *Eurodollar market* developed in Europe in the 1960s, under which European banks and European branches of American banks accepted deposits and finance transactions in American dollars. The Eurodollar market consists mainly of short-term funds with maturities of less than half a year. There is a counterpart long-term market for "Eurobonds"—bonds offered in Europe but denominated in dollars.

———

☐ Eurodollars come into being when an American or a foreign owner of a dollar deposit with a bank in the United States transfers these funds and places them on deposit with a foreign bank or a foreign branch of an American bank. Normally such transfers are prompted by higher interest rates on short-term deposits prevailing abroad, and foreign banks accept the deposits because they can in turn lend them at still higher rates. Often these funds belong to corporations which intend to use them in short order to finance international trade or investments; they are kept in dollars (rather than converted to local currencies) because of the general acceptability of the U.S. dollar in settling international transactions. The phenomenal growth of the Eurodollar market was in part a result of various U.S. credit restrictions, inducing corporations to move funds to Europe.

———

[12] Because foreign holders of dollars invest them in U.S. treasury bills, U.S. bank accounts, and similar instruments.

☐ Once Eurodollars come into being in the form of an interest-bearing dollar deposit having a stated maturity in a foreign bank, they may be lent out and redeposited in a succession of banks before being ultimately used to finance a business transaction. Eurodollar deposits thereby multiply just as the domestic money supply does under a fractional reserve banking system. (For a system of T accounts detailing this process of expansion, see R. L. Reierson, *The Eurodollar Market,* New York: Bankers Trust Co., 1964.) The multiplier effect depends on the magnitude of leakage at each stage (similar to reserve requirements on the domestic banking scene). Generally speaking, the deposits and redeposits are of large sums of money at rather narrow interest rate margins (the interest rate is related to rates prevailing in New York, such as the treasury bill rate) involving some credit and other risks.

☐ Finally, the term Eurodollars is somewhat deceptive. It is true that most of the market consists of dollars held in Europe (estimated at over $100 billion). But European banks also accept deposits denominated in nondollar currencies other than their own, and Japanese banks hold deposits in currencies other than the yen (mainly, but not exclusively, dollars).[13]   ■

Along with the emergence of the dollar as the *reserve, transaction,* and *intervention* currency, New York has become the major capital market of the world. Funds in large sums can be obtained on the New York market for a great variety of purposes, and by reason of its size, fluidity, and flexibility, traders and investors from all over the world are drawn to it to supply their capital requirements. The vast array of financial assets available on the New York capital market makes it possible to accommodate diverse tastes for varying degrees of risk and return on investments. Concomitantly, the New York foreign exchange market has emerged as the major one in the world. Unlike similar markets on the other side of the Atlantic, it has always been reasonably free of government regulation and has afforded its users an opportunity to deal in practically all currencies in both spot and forward transactions.

This pivotal role of the dollar under the Bretton Woods system in effect made the United States the world's central banker and thus sometimes referred to as the "center country." American balance-of-payments deficits supplied

---

[13] Banks in the Eurocurrency markets carry on arbitrage operations between the (dominant) dollar and nondollar markets. Thus if Euromarks loans are in excess demand relative to Euromark deposits, the Eurocurrency banks would convert dollars obtained from Eurodollar deposits into marks and lend the marks thus obtained. To cover the exchange risk, the banks would purchase a forward contract in dollars. Each nondollar Eurocurrency interest rate is determined by the dollar rate and the forward premium on the nondollar currency. Arbitrage is so extensive that interest parity is maintained. Thus, a sizable inflow of capital into, say, Euromarks will not induce a large drop in its interest rate, because the Euromarks will be exchanged for other currencies.

dollar assets, and therefore international reserves (liquidity), to the surplus countries that cared to hold them. In much the same way as in family finances, a country's deficit can be financed by owing the money. The United States accumulated dollar liabilities to foreign countries, the counterpart being that these surplus countries accumulated dollar assets. As long as the dollar was generally acceptable as a means of settling international imbalances, central bankers went on holding dollars as a reserve asset along with gold.

Why Do Countries Need Reserves?

Central bankers accumulate international reserves for a variety of reasons. In some cases, such as in the United States until 1968, national law requires that gold or foreign currency be held as a cover for domestic currency issue. In other cases, it is a matter of prestige or a belief that large international reserves (especially gold) inspire confidence. But *under a system of fixed exchange rates* the most rational reason for a country to hold reserves is so that it can tide itself over a period of external deficits. This is analogous to a family holding reserves against a "rainy day." It should be emphasized, however, that reserves only buy time; they postpone but do not obviate the need for balance-of-payments adjustment.

The amount of reserves, or liquidity, that the international system required under the Bretton Woods system was the sum total of the reserve requirements of individual countries. Most, though not all, reserves were accumulated by the two dozen developed countries, for less developed countries (with the exception of some oil-producing nations) tended to spend their foreign exchange earnings in the markets of the developed countries for the equipment needed in their development programs. Thus, most foreign exchange earnings of most of the countries of Africa, Asia, and Latin America usually found their way back to Western Europe, North America, Japan, and sometimes Australia. When it comes to the reserve needs of the developed countries, there is no clear-cut rule for determining the adequacy of such reserves. In a very real sense, reserves are adequate if the central bankers deem them to be adequate under the given circumstances. The reserve holdings of each country are published monthly by the IMF in *International Financial Statistics*. They will be explored further in Chapter 8.

☐ Judged in a rational way, the amount of reserves needed should depend on the expected size of external payment imbalances, on the fluctuations (or variability) in these imbalances, on the ease or the cost of balance-of-payments adjustment, and on the cost of tying up resources in reserves. The ease of adjustment would vary positively with the priority assigned by the government to the maintenance of balance-of-payments equilibrium over other objectives of economic policy, with the degree of permissible variations in the exchange rate, and with the share of foreign trade in the domestic economy. In turn, the average size of the imbalance may rise with the volume of trade, and perhaps with the proportion of capital movements (relatively more volatile than trade in goods and services) in total transactions.   ■

Under the system of fixed exchange rates, the consequences of a shortage of reserves—a "liquidity" shortage—could be severe. For what can a country do when it is short of international reserves and fears an impending deficit? In much the same way that a family faced with this situation may wish to curtail its consumption, so would the country desire to reduce its imports. But a country is not a family; not being a decision-making unit, it must influence the spending decisions of millions of individuals by aggregative measures that affect all units in the economy. In the first place, it can impose direct restrictions on imports, but if many nations were to impose exchange control and quota restrictions, then the entire international trading system could disintegrate, and the thirty-year trend toward trade and exchange liberalization would be reversed. Disintegration in this form contributed to the spread of the depression in the 1930s.

A second alternative open to a country is the limitation or curtailment of the income of its population. The less income is, the less the citizens can spend on either domestic or foreign goods and services, which reduces imports and leaves more goods free for export. Such an income cut may be achieved by contractionary fiscal and monetary policies. On the fiscal side the government would attempt to build up a budgetary surplus—by raising taxes and lowering expenditures—siphoning off purchasing power from the private sector. Monetary measures include raising the rate of interest, thereby limiting purchases of homes and other equipment that depend on the rate of interest. In addition, the central bank can restrict the lending power of commercial banks by raising reserve requirements or by selling government bonds on the open market. When the lending power of commercial banks is reduced, they inject less money into the income stream, thereby reducing consumption and investment expenditures. But if many countries followed such contractionary policies, a strong deflationary bias would be imparted to the international economy, perhaps leading to a worldwide recession. In sum, a shortage of reserves in a fixed exchange-rate system may have dire consequences.

Under the Bretton Woods system, reserves were held in gold and foreign currencies, mainly in dollars. For the world as a whole, dollar reserves held an advantage over gold because the mining of new gold is wasteful of resources engaged in the mining and transport activities. For the United States, the main advantage of a currency system based on the dollar was the ability to mount huge cumulative balance-of-payments deficits and pay for them with IOUs (U.S. liabilities) that the world accepted as reserves. Against this benefit there were several disadvantages: First, there was interest cost, for foreign nationals and official institutions held their dollar balances in interest-bearing money-market instruments and demand deposits in the United States. Not only that, but large-scale transfers of such funds in and out of the center country may cause disturbances in its money markets. But the main drawback of the system was in depriving the U.S. government of the ability to change the exchange value of the dollar. For when all foreign currencies were pegged to the dollar, the value of the dollar in terms of these currencies was determined (as a residual) by the foreign monetary authorities. And even the width of the *spread* of fluctuations of the dollar in terms of other currencies was only half that of any two other currencies. It was this inability to change the value of the dollar that became increasingly irksome to U.S. policy makers and led to growing American dissatisfaction with the system and finally to its demise. As will become clear in subsequent chapters, the inability to change the exchange rate imposes a severe constraint on the pursuit of economic policy objectives.

For the countries that maintain dollar reserves, the main advantage (compared to gold reserves) lies in the ability to earn interest on reserves. The risk is that the United States may lower the value of the dollar in terms of gold. In that case, if they were holding gold, they would be protected. Foreign countries would go on accumulating dollar reserves only as long as they were confident that the value of the dollar would not decline.

Over a long period after the war, confidence in the dollar was abundantly in evidence, and for good reasons. The dollar was widely used in international transactions[14] and had general acceptability. It was free of government controls. It was and still is backed by the strongest economy in the world, as the U.S. GNP exceeds that of all other western countries combined. Also, the United States was and still is a net creditor on the long-term investments account, as American holdings of direct and portfolio foreign investments far exceed foreign long-term investment holdings in the United States. And for the first twenty years of the Bretton Woods system, the rate of inflation in the United States—which measures the purchasing power of the dollar—fell short of the rate prevailing in other countries. Finally, the United States had a wide and diversified internal capital market, which offered foreign central banks a variety of liquid, low-risk commercial instruments (such as U.S. Treasury bills) in which to invest their dollar reserves.

But as the 1960s wore on, confidence in the dollar was gradually eroded.

---

[14] Only an asset or currency that is widely used in the private sector can serve as an "intervention currency" for stabilizing the exchange rate.

Continual U.S. balance-of-payments deficits, which grew to massive proportions by the end of the decade, resulted in a gradual decline of the U.S. gold
stock (from $25 to $11 billion dollars at the official price) and in massive
increases in foreign official holdings of dollars. Western Europe and Japan
were becoming satiated with dollar assets and increasingly unhappy about
having to finance the American balance-of-payments deficits under the Bretton
Woods system, indirectly enabling American corporations to accumulate large
foreign investments. Thus, Europe and Japan had their own reasons to push
for a change in the system.

Although the need for such a change was widely recognized on both sides
of the Atlantic, the change was not brought about by an orderly deliberative
process. It will be seen in Chapter 9 that the demise of Bretton Woods came
about only after three years of upheaval on the international currency markets.
In March 1973 a new system went into operation.

The International Currency System Since March 1973

Since March 19, 1973, the international currency system has been a mixture of
fixed and floating exchange rates: the pound sterling, Japanese yen, Italian
lira, Canadian dollar, Swiss franc, Austrian schilling, and (beginning in January 1974) the French franc are allowed to float on the market, with their
exchange rates determined by demand-and-supply conditions. Often the monetary authorities of each country intervene in the foreign exchange market in
order to smooth out certain fluctuations, to maintain orderly conditions, or to
prevent their currency's exchange rate from moving upward or downward to
a degree that they consider "excessive."

When an excess of inpayments over outpayments or an inflow of speculative capital pushes up the exchange value of the currency by an amount
the authorities consider excessive, the central bank sells its country's currency
in exchange for foreign currencies to moderate the rise. Conversely, when,
say, an outflow of capital pushes the exchange value of the currency downward, the central bank may moderate the decline by selling foreign currencies
in exchange for the country's currency. In the first year following the breakdown of Bretton Woods, major central banks intervened on the exchange
markets to the extent of $36 billion,[15] to moderate fluctuations in exchange
rates. Such floats are known as *managed* or "dirty" floats, as distinguished
from *free* or "clean" floats, which occur when no official intervention takes
place. At times a float can be so "dirty" as to keep the exchange value of the

[15] Reports on exchange rate movements and on governments' intervention on the foreign
exchange markets are published in the *Federal Reserve Bank of New York Monthly Review*.

currency constant for an extended period and give the impression of a fixed exchange rate. But even under heavily managed floats there is no official commitment to maintain fixed limits to the fluctuations.

Two differences between free and managed floats should be noted. While under a free float the exchange rate is presumed to settle at or around its equilibrium value (barring destabilizing speculation), yielding equilibrium in the balance of payments (that is, equalizing inpayments and outpayments), there is no such presumption in the case of managed floats. For central bank intervention may lead the exchange rate away from its equilibrium value rather than toward it. Secondly, no reserves are accumulated or needed when the exchange rate floats freely, for the exchange rate will always clear the foreign exchange market. By contrast a country whose floating currency is continuously managed, accumulates reserves when the central bank moderates an increase in the value of the currency, and needs reserves to moderate a decline in its value. These points will be further clarified in Chapter 5.

Figure 3-4 shows the fluctuations of the individually floating currencies vis-à-vis the dollar over a six-month period in 1973.

Six European currencies—the West German mark, Belgian franc, Danish kroner, Netherlands guilder, Norwegian kroner, and Swedish kronor—are pegged to each other. They float jointly against the dollar, with a maximum spread of 2¼ percent between the dollar rates of the strongest and weakest participants. Their internal pegging is accomplished by *multiple currency intervention:* Each central bank intervenes in its own market with the currencies of all five other countries to maintain the peg. A central fund of gold and currencies equivalent to $10 billion was established as a source of credit to countries subscribing to this *joint float;* short-term loans are extended to member countries whose currencies become weak and need to be supported within the float. Because the resulting movement of the jointly floating currencies produces a "snake-like" pattern, the arrangement is sometimes referred to as the "snake." Figure 3-5 illustrates the movement of the "snake" vis-à-vis the dollar over a six-month period in 1973.

It will be noted that the French franc was a part of the joint float arrangement during 1973. However, on January 21, 1974, fearing renewed pressure on its balance of payments (as a result of the quadrupling of oil prices), France withdrew from the joint float (officially only a six-month suspension) and began to float independently (see Figure 3-6).

Two features of the joint float arrangement are worth noting: First, the jointly floating currencies do not coincide with the membership of the European Economic Community (EEC) or Common Market (see Chapter 16). Italy, the United Kingdom, Ireland, and France, who are members of the EEC, do not subscribe to the joint float, and their currencies float independently, whereas Norway and Sweden, not members of the EEC, do subscribe to the

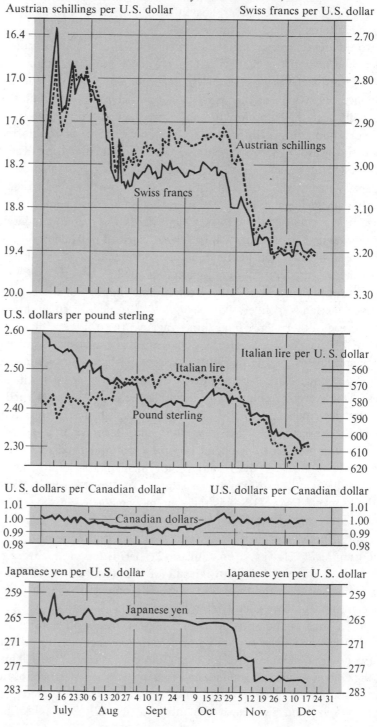

Figure 3-4
Spot exchange rates, July–December 1973
SOURCE: *IMF Survey,* December 17, 1973.

Figure 3-5
Spot exchange rates, July–December 1973:
the European "snake"
SOURCE: *IMF Survey,* December 17, 1973.

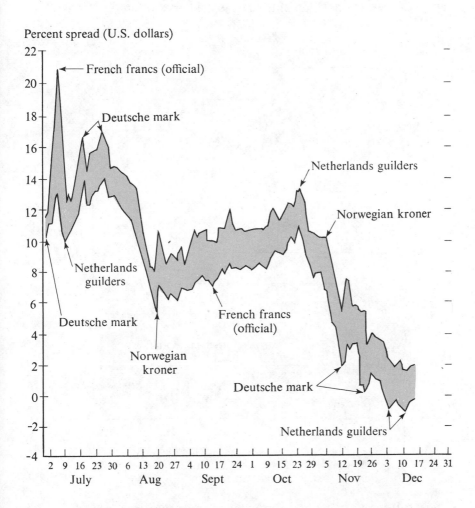

Percent spread (U.S. dollars)

joint float. Second, although the joint float was intended as a scheme of immutably fixed exchange rates, there have already been adjustments of individual currencies within it—such as a 5½ percent revaluation of the mark at the end of June 1973, a 5 percent revaluation of the Netherlands guilder in September 1973, and the withdrawal of France in 1974. Further strains on the joint float may be expected in the future.

Most of the world currencies, namely those of the developing countries, are pegged by government action to one of the major currencies—the dollar, the pound sterling, or the French franc. However, as a general rule, dealing

Figure 3-6

Exchange rates of European float currencies, March 1973–March 1974. The dashed curve for the French franc shows its rate fluctuations following the free float effective January 21, 1974. The lower panel shows the position of the Deutsche mark within the "snake." SOURCE: *IMF SURVEY*, April 22, 1974.

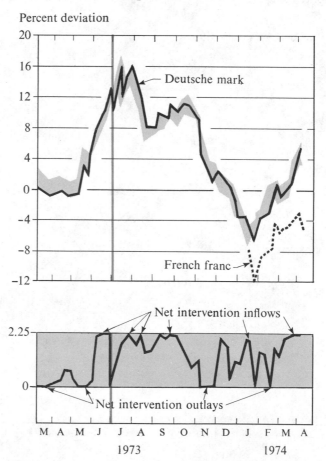

in these currencies is not free but subject to government regulations (see Chapter 7).

Under the present currency arrangements, European and Japanese currencies are no longer pegged to the dollar. That makes the dollar *a fluctuating currency,* free of the constraints imposed by the Bretton Woods system; yet even without the official pegging the dollar continues to play an important role. It remains the major currency for financing international transactions by the private sector of all countries, and the Eurodollar market is both vast and active. It retains its *reference role* for exchange rates, as countries measure their fluctuations vis-à-vis the dollar and often use dollars to *intervene* on the market to affect these fluctuations (managed floats). And many international statistics, such as those relating to commodity trade and published by the United Nations, are still measured in dollars. Such data now embody the fluctuations in the value of the dollar in terms of other currencies. On the other hand, the IMF now uses SDRs (see Chapter 8) and the EEC members use their own unit of account in their statistics.

There are abundant indications that the world central bankers regard this system as transitory and wish to return to a fixed exchange rate system. A committee of twenty members of the IMF (with a composition corresponding to that of the IMF executive board) has been charged with the responsibility of developing a new international currency system.

But the bankers' desire to return to fixed exchange rates has been set back by the worldwide 1973–74 increases in oil prices. Because of the varying degrees of dependence on imported oil, the huge increase in its price was expected to have a differential impact on the balance of payments of various countries and therefore on the strength of currencies. These expectations led to substantial international currency flows and some severe fluctuations in exchange rates. While the floating rate system weathered the period without too much difficulty, there is little doubt that under fixed exchange rates several severe crises would have been triggered. The general recognition of this fact has led to an indefinite postponement of any decision to return to fixed rates.

Because the international currency system is at present a hybrid of floating and fixed exchange rates, and because it is regarded by the world's central bankers as transitory, it is necessary to explain the balance-of-payments adjustment mechanism under both fixed and fluctuating rates. This is done in the next two chapters.

4

Balance-of-Payments Adjustment Policies under Fixed Exchange Rates

Short-Run Imbalances

What policy options are open to a country with a fixed exchange rate that is subject to a deficit in its balance of payments? If the deficit is strictly seasonal or short run in nature, likely to reverse itself in due course, little action need be taken. As long as there is full confidence in the ability of the government to maintain the exchange rate, private short-term capital can be relied upon to bridge the gap. Suppose that the British pound became weak in the fall, because of a seasonal balance-of-payments deficit, and dropped toward the lower support limit of $2.38.

$$\pounds 1 = \$2.40 \begin{cases} \$2.42 \\ \$2.38 \end{cases}$$

Individual financiers would be certain that there was only one way the pound could go: up. After all, it was only temporarily depressed and the lower support limit could not possibly be penetrated. They would act accordingly. Foreigners owing money to Britons could accelerate debt payments to take advantage of the "unusually low" pound price, while Britons having debts denominated in foreign currencies would postpone payments whenever possible, until dollars became somewhat cheaper in terms of pounds.

In general, financiers would be induced to buy and hold pounds, expecting a profit when the "normal" price was restored. They would be certain that they could not lose by such action. Thus, a downward movement in the value of the pound generates inflow of short-term funds, which itself tends to arrest and reverse that movement. Since the expectations of people differ, one might expect the inward flow of these funds to accelerate as the pound moves gradually downward, until at some point the decline in the value of the pound is arrested.

A precisely reverse phenomenon occurs when the pound is seasonally strong and reaches toward the upper support limit. Since everyone knows that it cannot rise in value above $2.42, there is a potential gain and no risk from selling pounds for other currencies, thereby generating an outflow of funds.

These are *stabilizing* short-run capital movements. Caused by public expectations with respect to exchange-rate variations, they offset temporary deficits in the balance of payments, and narrow the range of exchange fluctuations to something less than the official spread.

Variations in interest rates also bring about stabilizing capital movements. An external deficit is an excess of autonomous outpayments over inpayments. But this net excess implies that, on balance, Britons are withdrawing sterling deposits from their bank accounts to convert them into foreign currencies in order to make overseas payments. Temporarily, at least, there is a decline in the British domestic money supply and a stiffening of short-run interest rates. As interest rates rise, foreign capital is attracted to Great Britain to take advantage of higher earning opportunities. Conversely, an external surplus means an excess of inpayments over outpayments and a rise in the money supply. Interest rates are nudged downward, and short-term capital tends to leave the country.

On both counts, therefore, private short-term funds bridge temporary imbalances and stabilize the exchange rate. But it is worth repeating that all this is contingent upon confidence in the long-run value of the currency. If the government's ability to maintain the exchange rate is suspect when the pound hovers around its lower support limit, precisely the opposite movement can occur. Fearing devaluation, say to £1 = $2, the possible small gain of two or three cents from an appreciation within the official spread no longer looms important. The same may be said about small interest gains. Instead, the feared loss from a sizable devaluation may drive people away from the pound to strong currencies, as they were driven away from the pound in 1967, from the franc to the mark during the French crises of 1968 and 1969, and away from the dollar in successive crises from 1970 to early 1973. Conversely, if revaluation is expected when the currency is at its upper support limit, short-term funds tend to flow inward instead of outward. These capital movements are *destabilizing* in nature and usually occur when confidence in the currency is shattered. Whether speculation is stabilizing or destabilizing depends on people's expectations with respect to future movements of the currency, which in turn depend on their confidence in the economy.

Returning to the stable case, the inflow of private capital can be reinforced by official action. The government may raise interest rates or manipulate the forward exchange market to attract short-term funds from abroad, or it can fall back on its accumulated reserves. If necessary, recourse might be sought in borrowing from other countries or from international organizations such as the International Monetary Fund. However, should the deficit last for several years and prove fundamental in nature, a deliberate course of action would have to be pursued. Even so, the more international reserves the country has, the less is the pressure on it to act. But much the same as in the case of a family, reserves can only buy time; if they dwindle, an adjustment mechanism must be set in process to eliminate the deficit.

The first option open to the country is the classical prescription of inducing domestic contraction by monetary and fiscal means. Indeed, some contraction in the level of economic activity (in employment, production, and income) will occur automatically in the deficit country, because external trade and domestic economic activity are intricately interrelated. Specifically, the contractionary effect will operate through both the expenditures and monetary mechanisms, leading to a curtailment in imports and perhaps an expansion of exports, thereby reducing the deficit. Since the purpose of government adjustment policy is to reinforce these tendencies, a detailed explanation of the processes involved will help clarify the mechanism through which government domestic policies affect the balance of payments.

"Automatic" Processes

Direct Effect on Private Expenditures

Income Changes   Consider the case in which a deficit appears in a country's balance of payments, and assume that the deficit is brought about by a reduction in exports as foreign buyers shift to alternative sources of supply. The immediate consequence on the home front is a decline in production, employment, and income in the export industries. But that decline tends to spread throughout the economy in a multiple fashion. Workers and officials in the export industries, who suffer the original impact, have less money to spend on consumption of goods and services produced by other industries. To be sure, they are unlikely to reduce consumption by the full amount of the decline in their purchasing power, for it is just for such a circumstance that they have accumulated savings. But some reduction would undoubtedly occur. In turn, as income and employment decline in the "second round" of industries, their wage-earners spend less elsewhere. And so the process spreads throughout the economy in a wavelike fashion, with its force declining as it becomes further removed from the primary impact areas. At every stage at which the decline occurs, income recipients lower their consumption by something less than the cut in purchasing power, simply because it is human nature to cushion the impact of income reduction on the standard of living by drawing on one's savings. The extent of the total effect is positively related to two factors: the size of the original reduction in income in the export industries and the proportion of any reduction in income that is translated into reduced spending by the citizens (what economists call the *marginal propensity to consume*), at each "round." This multiplier process obviously takes time to work its way through the economy.

When the deficit is caused by an increase in imports (rather than a reduction in exports) the process is somewhat analogous. There is a direct effect on income and employment in the domestic import-competing industries only to the extent that the new imports are substitutes for domestically produced goods (imports that are not financed out of a reduction in the rate of consumer saving). Production of such commodities declines, and the attendant reduction in income and employment spreads throughout the economy in the manner just described. In turn, the multiple reduction in the income of the community produces a cut in the imports of goods and services.

It is an integral part of economic theory, verified time and again in empirical investigations, that imports vary positively and closely with variations in income. In other words, income is an important determinant of imports (though not the only one). Thus the income effect induces a reduction. in imports; it also brings about a cut in the consumption of domestically produced goods, thereby leaving more of them available for exports and exercising greater pressure on producers to market abroad. The upshot of this income–expenditures mechanism is that part of the original decline in exports is offset by an induced reduction in imports and an increase in exports. These automatic tendencies narrow the balance-of-payments deficit by, say, as much as one-fourth (to 75 percent of its original size). They certainly are unlikely to close it altogether. Also, it takes time before their full impact is felt.

Precisely the reverse process takes place in the surplus country, which experiences an increase in world demand for its exports. The primary impact occurs in the export industries, where employment and income expand to satisfy the increasing world demand. Income recipients save part of their additional earnings but spend a large share of it, which leads to an expansion of employment, production, and income in the industries producing the goods that they purchase. In turn, part of the incremental income is translated into purchases elsewhere, channeling purchasing power into a "third round" of industries. And so the process spreads in a declining sequence throughout the economy, where at each round, part of the added income is withdrawn from the spending stream into savings. It is sometimes useful to liken this sequence to the effect of a stone dropped into a pond of water, where the initial splash in the area of impact is followed by a series of waves, which spread in concentric circles throughout the pond in ever-declining intensity. This is how the expansion of income spreads throughout the economy. The total effect on income is likely to be much greater than the primary impact; the ratio between them (total effect/primary impact) is known as the *multiplier*. Its magnitude varies inversely with the proportion of the added income withdrawn (or leaked) from the income stream at each stage.

If the surplus is brought about by a reduction in imports, then the primary impact area consists of the industries producing domestic substitutes (to the extent that domestically produced goods, rather than savings, take the place of imports). From there, successive rounds of consumer spending carry the expansion into other sectors of the economy. If the suplus is brought about by the investment of foreign capital in new plants and equipment, the expansionary effect is virtually the same.

The increase in income produced through the expenditure mechanism raises imports; it also brings about an increase in the consumption of domestically produced goods, thereby leaving less available for export and reducing the pressure on producers to export. On both counts—the induced rise in imports and the decline in exports—the initial surplus would be reduced, again exhibiting an automatic tendency toward partial adjustment of the balance of payments.

To sum up, a disequilibrium in the balance of payments contains the seeds of its own partial reversal. A newly developed surplus increases income by a multiple of that surplus, and the rise in income brings about an increase in imports (and a cut in exports) that partly offsets the original surplus. Conversely, a newly developed deficit results in a multiple reduction in income, which in turn lowers imports (and expands exports) and offsets part of the deficit.

☐ In the years since World War II, economists have developed a body of analysis based on the ideas of John Maynard Keynes that provides a more precise formulation of the relationships outlined above. This is useful for two reasons: it sharpens our understanding of the processes involved, and it makes possible at a subsequent stage measurement of the magnitude of each effect. In what follows we set out the more formal analysis. Although the discussion starts from fundamentals (which accounts for its length), it assumes some familiarity with national-income analysis.

☐ For the sake of simplicity we deal with an economy in which there is only a private sector and no government. Also, in order to focus attention on income changes, prices (and interest rates) are assumed to be constant, a situation that obtains when there is significant unemployment in the economy.

We begin by considering the case of a closed economy (one in which there is no foreign trade) and introduce foreign trade at a later stage.

☐ *Domestic Income Determination*   During any one-year period the economy produces a given value of goods and services known as the gross national product (GNP). (Since under our simplified assumptions of fixed prices and no government this is roughly equal to real national income, it will be denoted by Y.) Output can be in the form of investment goods (I) or consumption goods (C):

$$Y = C + I \tag{1}$$

Over any given period, the value of goods produced must equal the income generated in their production. This is easy to see in a Robinson Crusoe economy. If Robinson Crusoe catches ten fish each day, then ten fish is both his output (production) and his income. In a complex society this relation is less visible, but it remains valid nonetheless. The value of any good produced in the economy equals all incomes—in the form of wages and salaries paid for labor, rent paid for resources, interest paid on capital, and *profit* (which for convenience may be regarded as a residual)—generated in its production. (The reader having difficulty seeing this should think of a good going through the productive stages and add up all incomes generated at every stage. He will come up with the final value of the product.) What is true of one product is equally true of all goods and services put together. Output and income are two sides of the same coin. In other words, income produced (output) equals income earned by all productive factors in the economy.

☐ The income earned in the productive process can be either spent on consumption (C) or not spent. The residual part that is not spent is called savings (S). Thus, by definition,

$$Y = C + S \tag{2}$$

Combining (1) and (2) we obtain the famous accounting identity:

$$Y = C + I = C + S \tag{3}$$

Hence,

$$I = S$$

This relationship will be seen to hold over any period; at the close of the period, realized savings must always equal realized investment. However, it does not necessarily reflect what people intended or wished to do at the beginning of the period, for there is no guarantee that savers and investors, who are two distinct groups of people, would have identical plans. At the end of each period, therefore, many individuals may find that their initial plans

Figure 4-1

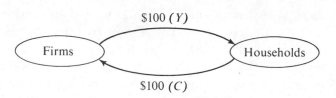

have been frustrated. That is, realized savings and investment are not generally equal to planned savings and investment. The relationship between plans and realization is explained next.

☐ The circular-flow diagram of Figure 4-1 portrays a simple economy in which firms produce goods and services, employing members of households in the productive process. If the firms produce $100 worth of goods and services, then this is the income earned by the households. If the households spend it all on consumption and save nothing, the $100 returns to the firms in the form of purchases, and the circle is complete. No saving and no investment take place, and the economy cannot grow in productive capacity or increased future output. All its capacity is employed in producing for current consumption.

☐ But suppose that, at the beginning of the period, firms planned some investments while households intended to save some of their income. If the two plans were identical (intended $S = I = \$20$), then both plans could be realized, as shown in Figure 4-2. This would always be the case in a Robinson Crusoe economy, where the same person decides how much to save and how much to invest. Suppose this individual has been catching 10 fish a day and now decides to cut his daily consumption down to 8 fish. He can transform his savings (2 fish not consumed) into a productive investment by using the resources freed from producing for consumption (time freed from fishing) in producing for investment (constructing a fishing net). The net will enable him to save even more time from fishing, which can then be invested in other productive activities. This is how savings are transformed into investments,

Figure 4-2

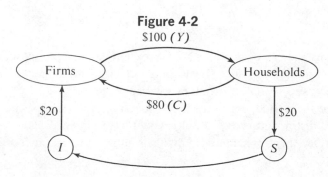

Figure 4-3

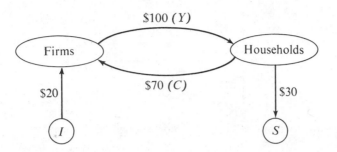

making possible greater production (economic growth) in subsequent periods.
☐ But when millions of individuals are involved in making these decisions, the two sets of plans (the aggregate plans of all persons saving and the plans of all persons investing) are unlikely to match. Let us assume that at the beginning of the period households planned to save $30 of the $100 earned but firms intended to invest only $20. In other words, firms set their production schedules to manufacture $80 worth of consumer goods and $20 worth of investment goods, while consumers planned to consume $70 and save $30. (These intentions are depicted in Figure 4-3.) The outcome of this set of plans must be that some businessmen in the economy are stuck with "unplanned" inventories of consumer goods of $80 − $70 = $10, because they would find customers for only $70 of the goods that they had sent out to market. Since the national-income accounts include inventory changes as part of investments, the realized savings–investments identity is preserved, at $30. But the investments part includes $10 in unwanted inventories (with only $20 in desired or intended investments). The natural reaction of businessmen would be to cut down orders from the factories, thereby reducing production, employment, and income.
☐ Conversely, if firms plan to invest $20 while households intend to save only $10 (as shown in Figure 4-4), then the result would be a decumulation

Figure 4-4

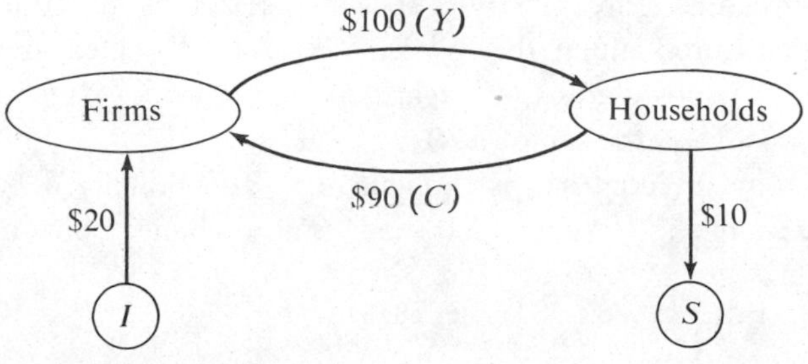

$100 (Y)

Firms   Households

$20 $90 (C) $10

I   S

Figure 4-5

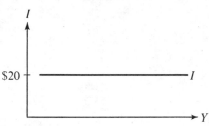

of inventories through which realized savings and investments would be equalized (at $10). For firms produce $80 worth of consumer goods while housholds purchase $90 worth. But this would lead businessmen to raise orders from the factories, with the attendant increase in output and employment. It is the difference between what is planned and what is realized that brings about adjustments in the economy.

☐ Clearly, only the case portrayed in Figure 4-2 is an example of equilibrium, inducing no change in the level of output (Y). Intended expenditures on C ($80) and I ($20) equals planned output ($100), which is equivalent to saying that intended S equals intended I. By contrast, in Figure 4-3, planned output ($100) exceeds the sum of intended C ($70) and I ($20), or planned S exceeds planned I. And in Figure 4-4, the opposite is true: planned expenditures on C ($90) and I ($20) exceed planned output ($100), or intended S ($10) falls short of intended I ($20). Although *realized* savings and investment are always equal, it is the relationship between *planned* savings and *planned* investment that determines the course of the economy. And this relationship is analogous to that between Y on the one hand and $C + I$ on the other.

☐ Because of its analytical importance, we proceed with a diagrammatic representation of the relation between the "intended" magnitudes. In equation (1) we postulated that income produced is made up of consumption and investment. But there is an important difference between these two. At least as a first approximation, investments are often assumed to be independent of current income. Thus, although changes in I definitely bring about changes in Y, the reverse is not true; changes in Y are assumed not to induce changes in I. This is shown in Figure 4-5 by a straight horizontal investment function. Relating I (measured along the vertical axis) to Y (measured along the horizontal axis) it postulates that regardless of the level of income, intended investments are always the same ($20).

☐ Consumption, by contrast, is thought to be functionally dependent upon income. Any change in income[1] (ΔY) is bound to change consumption (ΔC)

---

[1] The Greek letter Δ, read "delta," denotes change.

Figure 4-6

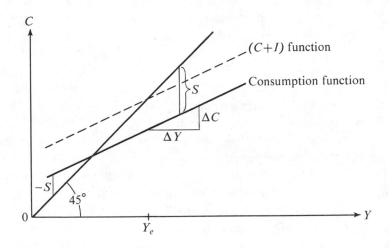

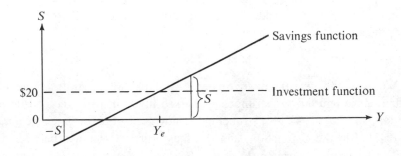

in the same direction, though by a smaller magnitude. This is a central theoretical proposition, demonstrated time and again in empirical studies.[2] It is shown graphically in the upper part of Figure 4-6, where consumption is plotted against income. The line labeled "consumption function" shows that as Y rises so does C but by a lesser amount. For simplicity it is drawn here as a straight line (linear relation). The consumption function shows how much is consumed (vertical axis) out of various levels of income (horizontal axis). From this it follows that savings (the part of income not consumed) is also determined by income. The relation between them, known as the savings

---

[2] As a matter of fact, consumption has a component that is independent of income in addition to the one that is dependent on income. Mathematically this is expressed by the relationship: $C = C_0 + cY$. But for simplicity, we neglect the C_0 and concentrate on $C = cY$.

function, is depicted in the lower part of the figure. It shows the amount saved (vertical axis) out of various levels of income (horizontal axis). This function is derived from the consumption function in the upper part as follows: an imaginary reference line is drawn to bisect the 90° angle between the axes. Known as the 45° line, it has the geometrical property of being at equal distances from the two axes. In other words, it is the locus of points for which $C = Y$ and therefore $S = 0$. Thus, for any level of income the vertical distance between the consumption function and the 45° line indicates savings. It is by transposing these distances to the lower part of the chart that the savings function is formed. Note that $S = 0$ at the level of Y at which the consumption function intersects the 45° line.

☐ Two terms must be defined for each relation: the *average propensity to consume* (APC) is the ratio of total consumption to total income (C/Y), and the *marginal propensity to consume* (MPC) is the ratio of change in consumption to the change in income ($\Delta C/\Delta Y$). Analogously, the *average propensity to save* (APS) is S/Y, and the *marginal propensity to save* (MPS) is $\Delta S/\Delta Y$. For straight-line consumption (and saving) functions, the MPC and MPS are the constant slopes of the functions. Also, since any additional income (ΔY) must be added either to consumption (ΔC) or to savings (ΔS), the sum of the marginal propensities equals 1:

$$\text{MPC} + \text{MPS} = 1$$

☐ We next add investment to Figure 4-6. This can be done in the upper portion of the figure by superimposing a fixed investment on the consumption function, so that the ($C + I$) function (shown as a broken line) becomes a line parallel to the C function, and the fixed vertical distance between them equals investment. Alternatively, it can be done by superimposing Figure 4-5 onto the lower part of Figure 4-6 (broken line). The two methods give identical results. The level of income at which $S = I$ is also the one at which ($C + I$) intersects the 45° line—that is, intended C plus intended investment equals planned output. As the discussion of the circular-flow diagrams indicated, this is the equilibrium level of income, Y_e. At points to the left of Y_e, intended investment exceeds intended saving, and forces will come into action to raise income, while the converse is true of points to the right of Y_e. Level Y_e corresponds to income in our circular-flow chart of Figure 4-2, in which equilibrium prevails.

☐ *The Domestic Multiplier*   Suppose now that the annual level of investment is doubled from $20 to $40, as shown in Figure 4-7. Then the equilibrium level of income will rise from Y_1 to Y_2 (for the sake of simplicity we omit the upper part of Figure 4-6, although the analysis is analogous). Clearly, given the increase in investment (ΔI), the increase in income (ΔY) depends on the slope of the savings function, or MPS, the marginal propensity to save.

Figure 4-7

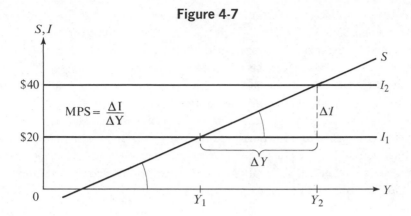

In fact, the geometrical definition of a slope shows that $\Delta I/\Delta Y = \text{MPS}$, or that

$$\Delta Y = \Delta I\, \frac{1}{\text{MPS}} = \Delta I\, \frac{1}{1 - \text{MPC}}$$

Since the MPS is a fraction (say 0.2), the increase in income is several times (five times in this example) the rise in investments. The ratio between the change in income and the change in investments which brought it about ($\Delta Y/\Delta I$) is known as the *domestic multiplier* and is represented by k. It is equal to $1/\text{MPS}$ or $1/(1 - \text{MPC})$. It can also be derived directly from equation (1):

$$k = \frac{\Delta Y}{\Delta I} = \frac{\Delta Y}{\Delta Y - \Delta C}$$

Dividing through by ΔY:

$$k = \frac{\Delta Y}{\Delta Y - \Delta C} = \frac{1}{1 - \Delta C/\Delta Y} = \frac{1}{1 - \text{MPC}} = \frac{1}{\text{MPS}} = \frac{1}{\text{leakage}} \qquad (4)$$

☐ To gain further insight into the economic behavior underlying this relation, we can reformulate our earlier discussion. Suppose, starting from equilibrium income Y_1, annual investment were to rise by $20. The immediate impact is to raise by $20 the incomes of the newly hired workers and sellers of materials used in the new projects. In other words, $20 is *injected* into the income stream in the first period. But the recipients of the added income will raise their level of consumption by spending part of these receipts. They will increase their consumption by $\text{MPC} \times \Delta Y$ (and raise their savings by $\text{MPS} \times \Delta Y$), which in our numerical example (where $\text{MPS} = 0.2$ and $\text{MPC} = 0.8$) equals $0.8 \times \$20 = \$16$. The balance of $4 ($= \text{MPS} \times \Delta Y$)

leaks out of the income stream into savings. Next, the recipients of the $16 in the second round of spending will consume 0.8 of that, or $0.8 \times \$16 = \$12.8$. And so the increase spreads through the economy in successive rounds of new spending, which can be represented by a declining series. This succession, which carries the economy from the initial equilibrium to the new one, takes an infinite length of time to complete. Even to approach the end of the series is a lengthy process. The relationship obtained in equation (4) shows only the change in income between the initial point of equilibrium and the final point of equilibrium after successive rounds of the multiplier process have been completed. This total change in equilibrium income resulting from the initial investment change, ΔI, is given by

$$\Delta Y = \Delta I \frac{1}{\text{MPS}}$$

(Appendix I contains another formal proof of this relation that highlights the time lag involved in the process.)

□ *Introduction of Foreign Trade: The Foreign-Trade Multiplier*   This analysis can be readily extended to incorporate foreign trade. In an open economy, exports as well as investments constitute an injection into the income stream, while imports, like savings, form a leakage out of that stream. Income produced, or output, now consists of consumption (C) and investment (I) of domestically produced goods, as well as exports (X). Equation (1) becomes:[3]

$$Y = C + I + X \tag{1a}$$

Correspondingly, income received is spent on consumption of domestic goods or on imports (M), or it is saved:

$$Y = C + S + M \tag{2a}$$

From these two equations we derive the identity:

$$I + X = S + M \tag{3a}$$

An alternative formulation of this identity is:

$$S = I + (X - M) \tag{3b}$$

If we think of the foreign-trade surplus $(X - M)$ as representing accumulation of foreign assets and label it net foreign investments (NFI), then (3b) underscores the fact that it is the savings–investment identity, with I extended to include NFI.

---

[3] If consumption and investments are defined to include imported as well as domestically produced goods, we write $Y = C + I + (X - M)$. Then imports can be netted out of C and I as well as $(X - M)$ to obtain (1a).

Figure 4-8

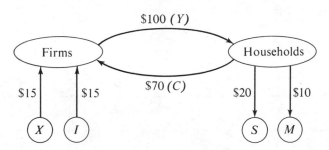

☐ In a "realized" (sometimes referred to as "*ex post*") sense, identity (3a) holds at all times. But it need not obtain in the "intended" sense, for there is no reason for the plans of investors and exporters to match those of savers and importers. When they do coincide, the open economy is at an equilibrium level of income, as depicted in Figure 4-8, which is an extension of Figure 4-2. Whenever equality (3a) in the "intended" sense does not hold, forces will come into action to change the level of income.

☐ The analysis is analogous to that of a closed economy, and it can be demonstrated by an extension of Figure 4-6. To the three functional relations postulated there, we add an export and an import function. Exports (X), like investments, are assumed to be independent of the country's income[4] (see Figure 4-9). They affect that income but are not affected by it, and as such are shown as a horizontal line: regardless of the level of income, exports are the same. By contrast, imports (like savings) depend on income: the higher the country's income is, the higher its imports (M) are. This relation appears in Figure 4-9 as a straight-line import function. We define the average propensity to import (APM) as the ratio of imports to income (M/Y) and the marginal propensity to import (MPM) as the portion of any additional income spent on added imports $(\Delta M/\Delta Y)$.[5] A straight-line import function

Figure 4-9

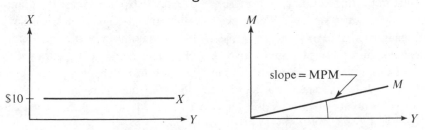

---

[4] Rather, they are a function of income in the importing country.
[5] Another concept often used is the income elasticity of demand for imports η_Y. *It is* defined as a ratio:

$$\eta_Y = \frac{\text{percentage change in imports}}{\text{percentage change in income}} = \frac{\Delta M/M}{\Delta Y/Y} = \frac{\Delta M/\Delta Y}{M/Y} = \frac{\text{MPM}}{\text{APM}}$$

Figure 4-10

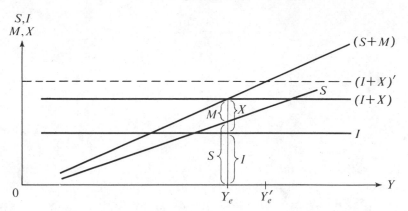

portrays constant MPM, which is equal to the slope of the function. From equation (2a) we infer that in an open economy MPC + MPS + MPM = 1; any addition to income must be spent on consumption of domestic goods, spent on imports, or saved.

☐ We now add the export function to the investment function and obtain the $(I + X)$ function. It is horizontal, indicating constant $(I + X)$ at all levels of income. We also add imports to the saving function to obtain the $(S + M)$ function, the slope of which equals MPS + MPM. These modifications can be introduced into the lower part of Figure 4-6, or into Figure 4-7.[6] They are shown in Figure 4-10, where Y_e represents the equilibrium level of income; that is, $I + X = S + M$. At points to the left of Y_e, forces will come into action to raise Y, and at points to the right, forces would operate to lower income. It can be seen from Figure 4-10 that $S - I = X - M$.

☐ The equilibrium depicted here is characteristic of a capital-exporting country; we saw in Chapter 2 that such a country typically has an export surplus. It now appears that the export surplus is embedded in the domestic economy; it equals the excess of saving over investment. Conversely, in a capital-importing country, imports exceed exports by the excess of domestic investments over savings. We might say that the foreign countries' savings are channeled into investment projects in the capital-importing country by means of an excess of imports over exports. The reader can redraw Figure 4-10 to represent this situation by making $(S + M)$ steeper so that it intersects the $(I + X)$ schedule at a point to the left of the intersection of S and I. If the two points of intersection happen to coincide at the same level of income, then $S = I$ and trade is in balance.

---

[6] We omit discussion of the upper part of Figure 4–6. It can be modified to incorporate foreign trade by superimposing exports upon the $(C + I)$ function. The resulting $(C + I + X)$ function is parallel to $(C + I)$, and its intersection with the 45° line gives the equilibrium level of income.

☐ If exports are raised to a new level $(I + X)'$ (broken line), then equilibrium income rises to Y_e'. Clearly it is the slope of the $(S + M)$ function that
determines the ratio between the autonomous increase in exports and the
increase in income:

$$\frac{\Delta X}{\Delta Y} = \text{slope of } (S + M) = \text{MPS} + \text{MPM} \qquad (4a)$$

or inversely,

$$\frac{\Delta Y}{\Delta X} = \text{multiplier } k = \frac{1}{\text{MPS} + \text{MPM}}$$

This is the formula for the foreign-trade multiplier. Its economic meaning is
analogous to the multiplier in a closed economy. There we saw that a given
increase in the level of expenditures (in that case, investments) resulted in
successive rounds of consumption spending with declining increments. At
each round, part of the added income is leaked away into savings. The difference now is that at each round another part is leaked into imports. Thus
the result that $k = 1/(1 - \text{MPC})$ still holds. But since now MPC + MPS +
MPM = 1, the multiplier becomes

$$k = \frac{1}{1 - \text{MPC}} = \frac{1}{\text{MPS} + \text{MPM}} = \frac{1}{\text{leakage}}$$

☐ This formula adequately describes what happens in a small country whose
income changes have little or no effect on its trading partners that may reflect
back onto itself. For a large country, such foreign repercussions may be significant and must be allowed for in the multiplier formula. (This is done in
Appendix I for a two-country world.) In such a scheme, the exports of each
country are equivalent to the imports of its trading partner, and instead of
being treated simply as exogenous (like investments) they are made a function
of the importing country's income.[7]
☐ *Implications of the Multiplier Formula*   Let us assume that the economy we are considering has an MPS of 0.3 and an MPM of 0.1. Its foreign-
trade multiplier will be

$$k = \frac{1}{0.3 + 0.1} = 2.5$$

This means that any exogenous change in spending, be it investment or ex-

---

[7] By an *exogenous change* we mean a change that is not itself a result of a change in the
country's own income. It includes a shift in the entire consumption function (as opposed
to movement along the fuction) and changes in investments or government expenditures. Government spending (usually labeled G) is excluded from the discussion in the
text but could be incorporated without undue difficulty.

ports, will change the income of the community in the same direction, by 2.5 times the original change. In turn, the variation in income induces a change in imports of $\Delta M = \Delta Y \times \text{MPM}$. Thus, any rise or fall in domestic expenditures must produce changes in the balance of payments. In other words, the country's internal and external positions are intricately interrelated by the income (and other) mechanism, and at no time can they be regarded as separate.

☐ There is a difference between the effect on the balance of payments of an exogenous change in domestic spending such as investment or government expenditures on the one hand, and the effect of a change in exports, on the other. A $100 rise in domestic expenditures will raise income by $100k = $250 once the multiplier process has worked itself out. This will increase imports by $250 × MPM = $25, causing a balance-of-payments deficit of like magnitude. This is an important reminder that any domestic expenditures program, governmental or private, not only raises income but also results in an external payments deficit. By contrast, if the exogenous increase in expenditures is in the exports sector (foreigners demanding more of the country's products), then the immediate result is a balance-of-payments surplus of $100. The rise in domestic income of $250 follows as before, but the $25 induced increase in imports will not cause a $25 deficit. Instead it partly offsets the original surplus, lowering it to $75. Since our main interest is the second case, we shall pursue it step by step.

☐ A $100 increase in exports (X), everything else remaining the same, produces immediately a surplus of $100 in the balance of payments. Next there is a gradual effect on domestic income through the multiplier mechanism:

$$\Delta Y = \Delta X \times k = \Delta X \times \frac{1}{\text{MPS} + \text{MPM}} \tag{1}$$

With an MPM of 0.1 and an MPS of 0.3 as before, this becomes

$$Y = \$100 \times \frac{1}{0.3 + 0.1} = \$100 \times \frac{1}{0.4}$$

$$= \$100 \times 2.5 = \$250$$

(It takes a very long time to approach the new equilibrium.) Given the rise in income (which may be further magnified by the acceleration principle), there will be an induced increase in imports[8] of:

---

[8] Other induced effects of the increase in income will be on savings (S) and domestic consumption (C):

$$\Delta S = \Delta Y \times \text{MPS} = \$250 \times 0.3 = \$75$$

And since MPC + MPS + MPM = 1,

$$\Delta C = \Delta Y \times \text{MPC} = \$250 \times 0.6 = \$150$$

Thus, the increase in imports, savings, and consumption adds up to the rise in income of $250.

$$\Delta M = \Delta Y \times \text{MPM} = \$250 \times 0.1 = \$25 \qquad (2)$$

The original balance-of-payments surplus, $\Delta X = \$100$, is now partially offset by $\Delta M = \$25$, the difference being $\Delta X - \Delta M = \$75$. In other words, the increase in imports induced through the domestic expenditures–income mechanism will, after a lengthy process, reduce the balance-of-payments surplus from $100 to $75. This is a movement in the "right" direction but is not sufficient to restore balance-of-payments equilibrium.

☐ Equations (1) and (2) can be combined to describe fully the effects of income on imports:

$$\Delta M = \Delta Y \times \text{MPM} = \Delta X \times k \times \text{MPM}$$

$$= \Delta X \times \frac{1}{\text{MPS} + \text{MPM}} \times \text{MPM} \qquad (3)$$

In our example this becomes

$$\Delta M = \$100 \times \frac{1}{0.3 + 0.1} \times 0.1 = \$25$$

The induced effects of a $100 increase in exports with MPM = 0.1, but with alternative values of the MPS, are tabulated below[9] all calculated in the same way as the figure of $25 we have just obtained. (The reader can experiment with other numerical examples by selecting alternative marginal propensities.)

ΔX	MPM	MPS	k	ΔY	ΔM	ΔS	ΔC
$100	0.1	0.4	2	$ 200	$ 20	$80	$100
$100	0.1	0.3	2.5	$ 250	$ 25	$75	$150
$100	0.1	0.1	5	$ 500	$ 50	$50	$400
$100	0.1	0	10	$1,000	$100	0	$900

As we lower the MPS, the induced increase in imports (ΔM) rises. But only at zero MPS does it completely offset the $100 original increase in exogenous exports. This is a general result, for when MPS = 0,

$$\Delta M = \Delta Y \times \text{MPM} = \Delta X \times \frac{1}{0 + \text{MPM}} \times \text{MPM} = \Delta X$$

That is, $\Delta M = \Delta X$. In other words, if MPS is zero, the induced change in imports equals the original change in exports. In all other cases the induced movement will stop short of restoring balance.

☐ If the first change is a $100 *reduction* of exports, where a *deficit* of $100 is created, then under our original assumptions income would *decline* by

[9] MPC = 1 − MPS − MPM.

$250 and imports by $25. Again there is an automatic income mechanism that pulls the balance of payments toward equilibrium. But the induced change in imports is less than the original change in exports, leaving some imbalance in the external accounts.[10] The imbalance is eliminated only in the extreme case of zero MPS. In all other cases the income mechanism induced by changes in expenditures constitutes only a partial correction to the imbalance. Additional, though probably still insufficient, automatic help may come from other areas. ∎

Price Changes In today's industrial economies, variations in the level of economic activity are usually accompanied by price movements. Thus, in the deficit country, the reduction in the level of income and employment has the side effect of curtailing the rate of price increases. When jobs are scarcer, unions tend to be more restrained in their wage demands, thereby holding production costs down; and as sales decline, producers are more likely to "hold the line on prices." It is true that since World War II, industrial wages and prices have become rather rigid or sticky in a downward direction, considerably weakening the effectiveness of the price-adjustment mechanism under fixed exchange rates. But since our main concern is with the country's position *relative* to other countries, even a decline in the rate of price increase helps make the country more competitive, assuming that no such reduction occurs in other countries. This decline encourages exports and discourages imports, thereby contributing to automatic adjustment. The strength of this effect depends on the degree of response of trade flows to variations in relative prices.

Precisely the reverse happens in a surplus country, where the expansion of income and output is likely to be accompanied by an acceleration of domestic price increases. And this has the salutary effect of reducing the original surplus. In sum, these price changes reinforce the income mechanism in partially offsetting payment imbalances caused by autonomous factors.

The Monetary Mechanism and its Impact on Income and Prices

The level of economic activity will be affected, in the directions described in the previous section, not only through the expenditure mechanism but also

---

[10] The cause of the deficit can also be a $100 exogenous increase in imports (an upward movement of the entire import function). To the extent that these imports substitute for the consumption of domestically produced goods, there will be a primary reduction in domestic expenditures. This reduction will be short of the rise in imports to the extent that they are financed out of savings rather than substituted for domestic consumption. In terms of the example in the text, the primary impact could be, say, $80 instead of $100. It would cause a decline in income of $80 × 2.5 = $200 and an induced reduction in imports of MPM × $200 = $20. This would partly offset the original increase in imports.

through a set of monetary factors. Money affects the level of real production and employment through its availability and cost (the rate of interest) to producers and consumers alike. Indeed, the direct real impact of an external deficit or surplus on the economy, discussed in the previous section, is generally confined to cases where the imbalance originates in the current account sector or when foreign investments—in the physical sense of plants and equipment—are involved. By contrast, regardless of its source, whether it is the current account or the capital account, an external imbalance affects the economy indirectly through the monetary route in a manner that tends to remove the imbalance.

A surplus or deficit in the balance of payments, whatever its source, means that autonomous outpayments do not equal inpayments. Inpayments are received in foreign currencies either in return for exports or in the form of capital inflow. Their local recipients exchange them for domestic currency, which in turn is deposited in local banks, mainly in checking accounts, thereby creating new demand deposits. In a modern economy these deposits (that is, checking accounts) constitute the bulk of the money supply. And in a banking system that operates on the fractional reserves principle, new deposits serve as a basis for a multiple expansion of the money supply. Thus, unless *offset* by deliberate action of the central bank, a net inflow of foreign exchange (currencies) results in a multiple expansion of the domestic money supply. The reverse process takes place as a result of outpayments. The buyer of foreign goods and services or the exporter of capital acquires the foreign currency necessary to make payment in exchange for his domestic currency. And the latter is usually drawn out of his demand deposit, thereby causing a multiple contraction in the money supply.

Since in the case of a deficit, outpayments exceed inpayments, the net effect is that of contraction in the domestic money supply. Much spending in the economy, and therefore employment and income, depends on the availability of bank loans. As money becomes "tight," or less readily available, it is reasonable to expect certain marginal business-investment projects and consumer purchase plans to go unrealized. Additionally, inasmuch as the rate of interest is determined by the demand and supply of money, the effect of monetary stringency is to raise interest rates on the money markets, thereby adding to the cost of investment, home construction, and other economic activities that depend on borrowed funds. The resulting curtailment of such activity reduces employment and income in the community, and any such reduction spreads through the economy through the multiplier mechanism. As before, the restraint in the level of economic activity also checks the rate of price increase. Both the *income and price* changes have the effect of reducing imports and encouraging exports, thereby partly offsetting the balance-of-payments deficit.

In the case of the surplus country, inpayments exceed outpayments, leading to a multiple expansion of the money supply. This eases the supply of bank credit and lowers interest rates—both factors contributing to increased income and employment and to a higher rate of price increase. In turn, these increases curtail the original surplus.

☐ **The Specie-Flow Mechanism**   In the preceding paragraphs, the equilibrating effect of changes in the money supply was said to operate through the domestic income and price channels. Classical economic doctrine—the body of economic doctrine in vogue before the appearance in 1936 of John Maynard Keynes' *General Theory of Employment, Interest, and Money*—placed primary emphasis on the money supply–price approach. Indeed, this was an integral part of the way the classical economists viewed the aggregate level of economic activity.

☐ One convenient way of looking at the economy is through the so-called equation of exchange:

$$MV = PO$$

M is the quantity of money in circulation, consisting of bank notes, coins, and demand deposits, and V is the income velocity of circulation, the number of times per year the average dollar changes hands to finance transactions in *final* goods and services (excluding goods in intermediate stages of production). Therefore, MV equals the aggregate annual monetary expenditures designed to finance all transactions in final goods and services.

☐ P is the aggregate price level (index), and O is the real volume of final goods and services produced during the year. Thus, PO is the money value of goods and services produced during the year, or the gross national product (GNP).

☐ This equation is in fact a truism. It is true by definition, for it states that the number of dollars spent on purchases of all goods and services equals their money value (GNP). The classical economists, however, proceeded a step further and made two important assumptions (that may or may not be true): First, that the velocity of circulation (V) is constant, for it depends on the payment habits of the community, which rarely change. And second, that the volume of final output is fixed in the short run at the full-employment level.[11] With V and O constant, any changes in M must produce proportional variations in P.

☐ All this is immediately applicable to the balance-of-payments adjustment

---

[11] Strictly speaking, the full-employment condition is not an assumption but a result of other postulates in the classical model: complete price and wage flexibility, and saving as well as investment considered a function of the rate of interest.

mechanism. Under the gold standard a deficit country lost gold. And since the domestic money supply was based on fractional reserve requirements held in gold, the country experienced a multiple contraction in its money supply and a consequent reduction in prices. This improved the country's competitive standing by encouraging exports and discouraging imports, and thereby partly redressed the deficit. Precisely the reverse happened in a surplus country, where the expansion of the money supply raised prices, thereby impairing the country's competitive position and reducing the surplus. This process came to be called the *specie-flow mechanism.* In short, the classical specie-flow mechanism focused on variations in relative prices (variations in the price ratio between two countries), which under a system of fixed exchange rates must be brought about through domestic price changes.

☐ These ideas were first challenged after World War I in connection with the transfer of reparations. Germany at the time needed to generate an export surplus to be able to effect the payment of huge reparations imposed by the victorious powers. In the ensuing debate on how this could be accomplished, Keynes took a classical position: the money-supply–price-change mechanism would bring about the necessary adjustment. On the other hand, the Swedish economist Bertil Ohlin took what fifteen years later would become a Keynesian position. He emphasized the transfer of purchasing power (income) from Germany to the United Kingdom as the main regulatory device but, lacking the post-Keynesian analytical tools, his exposition was not fully convincing.

☐ In a totally different context, various empirical studies convinced economists that as often as not the adjustment mechanism worked too fast and too smoothly to be satisfactorily explained by the money supply–price forces. In short, when the "Keynesian revolution" came in 1936, economists were receptive and ready to apply the new ideas to the international trade field. These adaptations came after World War II.

☐ In particular, some of the classical assumptions were questioned. It was asked: Can it be assumed that gold gains and losses produce multiple changes in the money supply? The central bank can easily *neutralize* their effect by what are called *offsetting policies.* Instead of reinforcing any loss (gain) of gold by contractionary (expansionary) monetary policy, as was required under the *rules of the game* of the gold standard, the central banks could and often did precisely the reverse. In such cases, gains and losses of gold reserves would not produce the expected changes in the money supply. Another classical assumption that came under scrutiny was the constancy of V. Keynes held that money is used either for transactions or for speculative purposes. In the transactions sphere, velocity does indeed depend on the payment habits of the community and is therefore roughly constant. But speculative funds are kept idle by those who expect to benefit from an increase in the value of money in terms of other financial assets (that is, by those who expect the prices of these assets to decline). The amount so held depends on the cost of idle funds in terms of earning opportunities forgone elsewhere. This cost can be measured by the rate of interest; the higher the interest rate, the more costly it is to maintain idle speculative balances. The velocity of these balances is zero, for they do not circulate. Total velocity is a weighted average of the zero and constant velocities in the two sectors, and thus it changes as funds are switched between speculative and transactional balances. Since the rate of interest determines the division of balances between the two sectors, it also affects the velocity of circulation. Thus, changes in the money supply (M) may affect the interest rate and produce offsetting variations in V. Indeed, when M rises (declines) there is a tendency for the interest rate to decline (rise), thereby increasing (decreasing) speculative balances and lowering (raising) V. Total spending (MV) and therefore PO need not be affected at all.

☐ Keynes challenged the idea that physical output is constant at the full-employment level, by questioning the constructs of the classical model that led to this result.[12] Instead, he advanced the proposition that in industrial economies wages and prices are rigid in a downward direction. Thus, even if MV did vary, the impact might be on physical output (O) rather than on prices (P).

☐ Finally, it was said, even if prices do move in the desired direction, this is not a guarantee of success. A decline in the relative prices of the deficit country means that it will sell more goods abroad. But since each unit of the commodity sold now brings a lower price, there is no assurance that total in-payments (price times quantity) will rise. That depends on whether the increase in the quantity sold is proportionately larger than the decline in price— whether the increase is large enough to offset the fact that now every unit sells for less. This would be the case only if the demand for the country's exports is responsive to price change.[13]

☐ Not only did these criticisms run deep, but economists had an alternative explanation of the adjustment mechanism. It was rooted in the Keynesian ideas that became widely accepted after World War II. Instead of the money supply–price approach, the focus was shifted to the expenditures–income

---

[12] In particular, he made savings a function of income rather than of the rate of interest, introduced rigidity into money wages in a downward direction, and added a "liquidity trap" that set a lower limit to the rate of interest.

[13] Economists measure the degree of response in terms of *price elasticity* (η_p), which is defined as the ratio

$$\eta_p = \frac{\text{percentage change in the quantity purchased}}{\text{percentage change in price}} = \frac{\Delta Q/Q}{\Delta P/P} = \frac{\Delta Q}{\Delta P} \times \frac{P}{Q}$$

It is negative, because price and quantity move in opposite directions. However, it is common practice to ignore the negative sign and discuss elasticity in terms of its absolute value. Thus, the necessary condition of response described in the text is such that $\eta_p > 1$, and is known as relatively elastic demand. Chapter 5 offers a more extensive discussion of this concept.

approach, utilizing the marginal propensities and the multiplier as analytical tools. The role of the money supply in affecting domestic income and prices, and therefore imports, was downgraded.

□ Today economists are no longer so sure. One school of thought maintains that velocity is a more stable and predictable relationship than the multiplier and that the money supply affects economic activity more than expenditures.[14] Indeed, there is a heated and important debate going on among economists concerning the relative effectiveness of aggregate expenditures and the money supply in influencing the course of the economy. Consequently, it is necessary to take a balanced view of the adjustment mechanism, and to incorporate both the money and expenditure approaches as they affect income as well as prices. Advanced economic theory devotes considerable attention to the process of interaction between income and price movements, although under present-day conditions of price rigidity the income mechanism is probably more powerful in most cases.   ■

Summary of the "Automatic" Balance-of-Payments Adjustment

The automatic adjustment mechanism under fixed exchange rates is a function of aggregate expenditures and the money supply, both operating in the same direction and both affecting the economy through the income and price mechanisms. The four linkages involved may be diagrammed as:

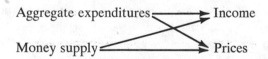

A deficit in the balance of payments automatically brings about a slowdown in the country's economic activity and a slowdown of the rate of price increase through both monetary and nonmonetary (sometimes referred to as "real") factors, while a surplus increases economic activity and accelerates the rate of price increase.

The economic slowdown resulting from a deficit contains the seeds of a mechanism that reverses the deficit in part, for it is primarily the income of the community that determines imports. A reduction in national income means

---

[14] However, the quantity theory has been replaced by the real balance effect in producing external equilibrium. Households and firms are assumed to attempt to maintain a certain level of *real balances*. Lacking money illusion (that is, the belief that a given amount of money is unchanged in value when the price level changes), spending units are believed to increase (reduce) their spending when their real balances rise (fall), either by an increase in nominal balances or by a decrease in prices. Keynes made spending a function of income; in the monetarists' view it is a function of real balances.

that consumption of goods and services is curtailed, including the consumption of imported goods. Likewise, there is a decline in the importation of materials used in the production process. The proportion of a change in national income translated into a change in imports is known as the *marginal propensity to import* (MPM). The higher the MPM, the larger the effect on imports of a given reduction in national income. In the United States the MPM is approximately 0.05. Furthermore, the reduction in the level of aggregate demand in the country means that a larger portion of its productive capacity is freed to produce for export markets. The lower the level of demand is at home, the greater the pressure will be on producers to market their products overseas, for when home demand is high producers have little incentive to seek overseas markets.

Complementing the increased availability of productive resources, and continuously interacting with it, is the improved competitive position of the country on both its own and world markets. For it is the relative behavior of prices at home and abroad that determines a country's competitive standing, and the deficit country normally experiences a slowdown in the rate of price inflation. The extent to which the improved competitive position lowers imports and raises exports depends on the degree of community response to price change (or what economists call *price elasticity*). The greater the response is, the greater will be the improvement in the balance of payments that can be expected from a given reduction in relative prices. In sum, the income–price mechanism set in motion by the deficit tends to reduce the deficit.

Accompanying the expenditure mechanism is the money supply mechanism. Unless the monetary authorities act to offset it, the money supply of the deficit country is reduced. That causes a decline in the rate of inflation as well as a reduction in the level of income or at least in its rate of growth. On both counts, imports decline and exports rise, thereby reversing the external deficit at least in part.

By the same token, it has been shown that surplus countries experience expansion in income and money supply and deterioration in competitive standing caused by the acceleration of price increases. Both lead to higher imports and lower exports. Thus, a surplus as well as a deficit contains in it the seeds of its own reversal. Furthermore, if the surplus and deficit countries are important trading partners, the changes occurring in them reinforce each other. Figure 4-11 presents a schematic illustration of the processes just described.

Government Policy

The automatic income and price mechanisms interact and reinforce each other in the direction of restoring balance. Since they may be insufficient in magni-

Figure 4-11

Automatic processes that reverse external imbalance

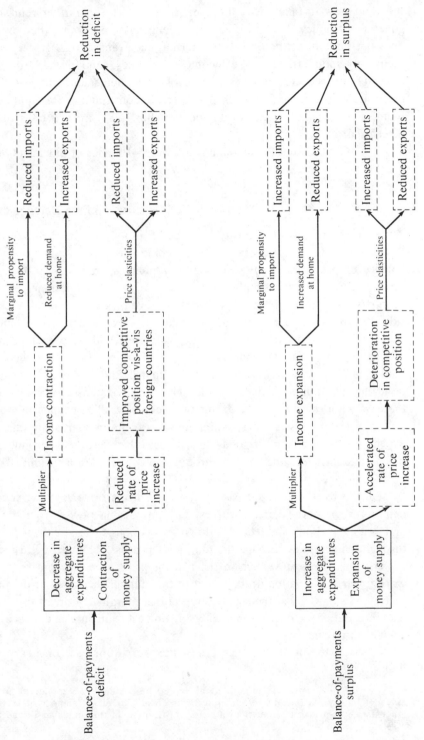

tude and slow to take effect, however, they need to be further reinforced by government policy. But in a free private enterprise economy, the government does not have direct control over international transactions. It can influence them only indirectly. Because income and prices (and perhaps the rate of interest) are the crucial determinants of inpayments and outpayments, the government must use measures that affect income and prices and, through them, influence the balance of payments. Thus there are two links that must be crossed:

Government Policy→Income, prices→Balance of payments

Domestic Measures and the Balance of Trade

Two sets of policy instruments are available to the government to affect the level of economic activity (that is, income and prices) and through it the balance of payments. They are monetary policies, influencing the economy through control of the supply of money, and fiscal policies, influencing the economy through changes in government revenues and expenditures. Consider first the case of a deficit in the balance of payments. On the monetary side the central bank can raise the rate of interest,[15] thereby making borrowing more costly; it can increase reserve requirements of the commercial banks, making less money available for loans; and it can sell government bonds to the public and the banks (known as open-market operations), thereby withdrawing money from the economy. These measures restrict public access to funds for spending purposes and render such funds more expensive. As spending for goods and services declines, so do production and income. And the decline spreads through the economy in a magnified fashion through the multiplier process.

On the fiscal side, the treasury can raise taxes or lower government expenditures, or both, thereby withdrawing purchasing power from the public and bringing about a direct slowdown in economic activity, which spreads through the economy through the multiplier process. The decline in income is accompanied by a slowdown in the rate of price increase, and both factors work toward elimination of the deficit in the manner described in the previous sections. In fact, given the size of the various marginal propensities, one can compute the effect of a given policy on domestic income and hence on the balance of payments.

Precisely the opposite policies are called for in the case of a surplus. Ex-

---

[15] In an open economy with international capital movements, the monetary authorities may not have full control over the rate of interest. Therefore, some writers treat the interest rate as a target rather than a policy instrument in the hands of the authorities.

pansion of the money supply and an increase in the budgetary deficit inflate the economy, with both the income and price effects leading to the removal of the surplus. The processes described in the previous section are merely reinforced, and need not be modified, when the government takes action. The so-called British "stop–go" policies pursued during the 1950s and 1960s constitute an excellent example: contractionary monetary and fiscal measures in response to a balance-of-payments crisis (that is, recurring deficits) and expansion when the crisis passed.

Effect on Direct Investment Capital

There is a possibility that the equilibrating mechanism brought about by government policy may be partly offset by international movement of investment capital. Not much is known of the forces that motivate such capital to move across national boundaries. But certainly it responds to relative profit opportunities at home and abroad, being attracted to high-profit locations.

The expected level of profit on investments is related positively to the degree of prosperity prevailing in the economy—that is, to the level of income and employment. When a surplus country experiences automatic expansion, reinforced by government policy, the effect on the balance of trade is to reduce the surplus. But the expansion also attracts foreign investment capital, an inpayment item that increases the surplus. The converse is true of the deficit country, where domestic contraction reduces the deficit but may also encourage outflow of long-term capital (or discourage inflow), thereby aggravating the deficit. Although the strength of these influences is not known, there is little doubt that they offset part of the equilibrating effect of domestic policies.

Effect on Other Capital Movements

Direct investment is not the only type of capital that moves across international boundaries. People also invest in foreign bonds, stock, commercial paper, bank accounts, and the like. Such funds are referred to as portfolio capital, as distinguished from direct investments. They are considered long-term when they involve stock purchases, but the acquisition of bonds and bank accounts can be either short-term or long-term depending on whether the maturity is less than or more than one year.

A large share of this capital, especially the short-run variety, is sensitive to interest differentials between financial centers. If interest rates in London exceed those in New York by more than the discount on forward pounds (that is, if a covered interest differential exists), then it pays to transfer funds to London. Consequently, the British government can deal with a temporary balance-of-payments deficit by raising the rate of interest and attracting short-term capital.[16] How helpful this might be, even in the short run, depends on the sensitivity of capital movements to interest differentials. Empirical studies on the question have yielded mixed and rather inconclusive results, to the extent that economists have been led to reformulate their thinking on the subject. It used to be thought that barring undue disturbances in the foreign exchange markets (such as expected devaluation), the existence of a *fixed* interest differential would result in a *continuous flow* of funds until the differential was eliminated. The "portfolio approach" developed in recent years leads to a different conclusion.

This approach views each financier as holding a portfolio of financial assets, the composition of which is designed to maximize his return subject to minimum risk. A major determinant of this composition (besides the level of national income) and therefore of its distribution between domestic and foreign assets, is the constellation of interest rates prevailing on domestic and foreign money markets. This portfolio grows each year as additional assets are acquired, but these increments are very small in comparison to the total assets already in the portfolio; their distribution between foreign and domestic assets is governed by the same considerations as that of the entire portfolio and is therefore in the same proportion. For example, a New York financier may have a portfolio worth $1,000, divided half and half between domestic and foreign assets, with an annual increment of $100 also equally divided between the two types of assets.

If the foreign central bank (for example, the Bank of England) raises the rate of interest, two things happen. First and foremost, the financier readjusts his portfolio to account for the fact that foreign assets now have a higher yield (assuming no increase in risk). He may now decide to hold $400 in domestic and $600 in foreign assets. This is the major impact, but it is a one-time rather than a continuous effect. Second, the small annual flow into new assets will also be adjusted to account for the new level of foreign interest and divided on a 40:60 percent basis. This is a continuous effect, but it is rather small. All it does is increase the annual flow into British securities by $10. Summarized, these changes are:

	Before foreign-interest increase		After foreign-interest increase	
	Domestic assets	Foreign assets	Domestic assets	Foreign assets
Portfolio	$500	$500	$400	$600
Annual increments	50	50	40	60

[16] This can be quite costly to the British government because it means higher interest payments on the internal public debt (that is, on government bonds). To avoid this cost and still achieve the same result, the government can manipulate the forward exchange market.

Generalizing from the behavior of this financier, we see that a rise in the rate of interest has a substantial one-time effect in attracting foreign capital and only a minor continuous effect in the same direction. Empirical studies indicate that most of the portfolio adjustment occurs within one year of the change in the interest rate (or national income) that brought it about, and that the annual flow effect is less than one-tenth of the one-time portfolio adjustment. Therefore, a country wishing to attract large amounts of foreign capital continuously will have to keep raising its rate of interest to ever higher levels. A one-time increase can produce only a one-time sizable infusion of foreign capital.

But suppose a country wanted to attain just that type of infusion—say, because its deficit was expected to be reversed within one year. How could that be accomplished with the policy tools under discussion? In other words, what are the effects of monetary and fiscal policies on the rate of interest?

Monetary contraction (assuming no fiscal change) *raises* the rate of interest both because of direct action of the central bank—as it raises the rediscount rate and as it sells government bonds on the market, thereby depressing their price (which means higher interest)—and because of the reduction in the money *supply*. On the other hand, fiscal contraction (assuming no monetary change) brings about a reduction in aggregate expenditures (both private and public) and therefore a reduction in the *demand* for money. Assuming that nothing is done on the monetary side to offset it, this *lowers* the price of money —that is, the rate of interest.[17] For the country in deficit, therefore, monetary

---

[17] This distinction can easily be understood by those readers familiar with the Hicks-Hansen *IS* and *LM* functions, which determine equilibrium combinations of interest rate (r) and national income (Y). Starting from equilibrium (Y_1, r_1), *monetary contraction*

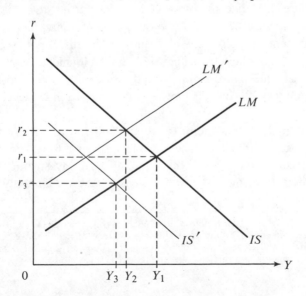

Table 4-1

Policies for Dealing with External Imbalance

Economic processes at work	Deficit country	Surplus country
1. Fiscal measures	Contraction	Expansion
2. Monetary measures	Contraction	Expansion
3. Implications for production, income, and employment	Contraction	Expansion
a. Effect of 3 on trade in goods and services	Imports down, exports up	Imports up, exports down
b. Implication of 3 for long-term capital movements	Outflow	Inflow
4. Implication for rate of domestic price increase	Slowdown	Acceleration
a. Effect of 4 on the country's competitive position	More competitive	Less competitive
b. Effect of 4 on the current account balance	Imports down, exports up	Less competitive Imports up, exports down
5. Implication of 2 for interest rates	Up	Down
a. Effect of 5 on short-term (mainly one-time) capital flows	Inflow	Outflow

contraction helps restore balance in two ways: exports of goods and services rise relative to imports, and there is a one-time influx of foreign capital in response to an increase in the rate of interest. Only the first salutary effect, not the second, is present in the case of fiscal policy.

An equally important difference between them is that monetary policy does not require legislative approval, while under our institutional arrangement fiscal measures are less flexible; on the tax side, especially, they require a long time for enactment. It is also generally believed that fiscal policy is more effective than monetary policy in dealing with unemployment. More specifically, some economists question the ability of the Federal Reserve to fully control the money supply and through it short-run fluctuations in the level of economic activity.

Consequently, many economists recommend the use of monetary policy for dealing with external imbalances while reserving fiscal measures for internal stabilization objectives.[18] Indeed, empirical investigations show that changes in the rate of interest are the measure most commonly used by in-

---

is shown by shifting the *LM* function to *LM′*, leaving the *IS* curve unchanged. The effect is to lower income to Y_2 but raise the interest rate to r_2. Next we show *fiscal contraction* by shifting the *IS* function downward to *IS′*, leaving the *LM* curve unchanged. In this case both income and interest rate are reduced, to Y_3 and r_3.

dustrialized countries for dealing with external imbalances. But the portfolio approach suggests that it is a less effective instrument than it was once thought to be.

Table 4-1 summarizes the economic processes described above. It is clear from lines 3a and 4b that fiscal and monetary measures bring forth an income–price mechanism that works in the direction of restoring balance to the goods-and-services account. This process is partly offset by the effect of the very same mechanism on long-term capital movement, indicated by item 3b. Monetary policy has a further equilibrating effect on the balance of payments through the rate of interest and its impact on short-term capital movement as seen in 5a.

Foreign Repercussions

The analysis can be pursued further. Whenever nations are tied to each other by fixed exchange rates, any action taken in one country affects economic conditions in the rest of the world, especially in the countries that trade heavily with that country. And these effects reverberate back to the original country, with the changes in employment, income, and trade coming full circle (though in diminished strength).

Consider a country (country A) that for reasons of its own pursues contractionary fiscal and monetary policies. The reduction in its income lowers imports,[19] implying reduced exports of its trading partners, countries B and C. This in turn lowers income and employment in the export industries of countries B and C, and the reduction spreads in them through the multiplier mech-

---

[18] Since fiscal and monetary policies are often handled by two separate government agencies (the treasury and the Federal Reserve, respectively, in the case of the United States), each agency should be assigned a policy objective most amenable to the policy instrument under its control. The allocation of such objectives is known as the "assignment problem."

[19] If the country's MPS and MPM are 0.3 and 0.1, respectively, its multiplier is:

$$k = \frac{1}{\text{MPS} + \text{MPM}} = 2.5$$

A cut in government expenditures of $100 would lower income by $250, imports by $\Delta M = \Delta Y \times 0.1 = \$25$. This creates a balance-of-payments surplus of $25. Notice the difference between this case and that on pages 72–73. There the initial (exogenous) action was a reduction in exports of $100, creating a corresponding deficit. The induced repercussions on income and their effect on imports improved the balance of payments by $25, reducing the deficit to $75. Here the initial action is by the government, and therefore the only impact on the balance of payments is an induced surplus of $25. Conversely, an exogenous increase of government spending by $100 would raise income by $250 and induce a $25 increase in imports, creating an initial balance-of-payments deficit of the same magnitude.

anism. This has the further effect of lowering their imports from A, which accentuates the reduction in its national income. Precisely the reverse process holds if country A pursues domestic expansionary measures. It would be a useful exercise for the reader to trace the influences on the community of trading nations emanating from alternative policies of an individual country. These effects clearly indicate that a system of fixed exchange rates links together the economic fates of countries that have close trade relations. Both depression and inflation spread from one country to the next, and no one is isolated from outside disturbances.

What are the implications of this circular mechanism? In the first place, it gives additional responsibility to the leading industrial nation, if it wishes to concern itself with the fate of others. After World War II it used to be said that when the United States sneezed, Europe caught pneumonia; in other words, Europe was so dependent on the American market for the export of goods and services that each deep recession on this side of the Atlantic brought about severe economic contraction on the other. While today this is no longer true, there are still vast areas of the world, notably Latin America, dependent on American prosperity for the maintenance of a high level of exports and therefore national income. Of course, these relations hold among units of any closely knit trading system, such as members of the European Common Market. In recent years the main concern of countries such as West Germany and Switzerland has been over inflation imported from other countries. This occurs when inflation in, say, France improves the West German competitive position and thereby raises West Germany's exports and lowers its imports. (This is often accompanied by influx of capital into West Germany, in anticipation of revaluation of the mark.) The result is a multiple domestic expansion in West Germany, which would be inflationary if the economy functioned at full employment to begin with. It is through this process that inflation spreads from one country to the next.

The second implication is that, to properly calculate the multiplier effect of any policy, one must allow for foreign repercussions as they complete the circuit and affect the country in which the policy originated. The multiplier formulas given earlier ignore these repercussions and to that extent are applicable only to small countries. A more complete derivation is given in Appendix I.

A third implication of the interdependence under fixed exchange rates is that no country is completely free to pursue independent domestic policies: all countries are subject to outside discipline exercised through the balance of payments. When a country gets out of line, a crisis can easily result. Thus, when the French labor unions demand and get higher money wages, as they did in the spring of 1968, a general weakening of the franc is signaled, because a rise in wage rates increases production costs, making French products less competitive, and at the same time raises French money incomes, thereby encouraging imports and discouraging exports. If all its trading partners faced the same wage demands, these factors might roughly cancel each other out. But when it happens only in France, the franc is weakened and may become subject to further pressures exerted by alarmed speculators. Similar crises may follow from such actions as the British trade unions demanding and obtaining a doubling of their tea break, British workers engaging in a "go-slow" work policy or wildcat strikes on a large scale, the Dutch government embarking on a policy of huge new expenditures to reclaim the ocean, or the West German central bank doubling the country's money supply.[20]

What is common to all these measures is that they disturb the price and income relationships between countries and through them affect the balances of payments and the stability of currencies. Under a system of fixed exchange rates, the world is linked by exchange rates, but governments desire or are forced to pursue policies that are independent of other countries while at the same time they wish to preserve the freedom of private citizens to trade and speculate. These three features of the system are not always compatible and they need not lead to one harmonious whole. It is impossible to be completely linked yet completely independent and free at the same time, all the time. To put it differently, we may say that a combination of fixed exchange rates, currency convertibility, and imperfect harmonization of national economic policies that affect incomes, prices, and interest rates cannot work well. When these features clash, a crisis results. It spreads from the country that triggered it to other countries, for all nations are linked together by fixed exchange rates. "International financial crises" are the periodic adjustments of the system to these conflicting forces. It was this kind of clash that produced the recurrent crises during 1967–1973 and finally led to the demise of the Bretton Woods system of pegged exchange rates in March 1973.

In fact, the issue of interdependence can be carried further. Since the advent of currency convertibility in Europe late in the 1950s (see Chapter 7), a truly international capital market has developed. One important feature of this integrated market is the $100 billion or so of so-called Eurodollars. These come into existence in various ways, such as when the United States is losing dollars as a result of balance-of-payments deficits and the dollars are deposited by their owners in foreign banks. Being a fully convertible and universally acceptable asset, such dollars know no national boundaries; they move from one country to another in search of higher interest return, which in turn reflects the needs of commerce.

[20] Even the normal process of economic growth disturbs the balance of payments because it raises income and therefore imports. Of course, other countries also grow and import more from any country in question, but growth rates differ among nations and so does their effect on trade. Even if growth rates of all countries were equal, the resulting effect on trade would be unbalancing, because the marginal propensity to import differs among nations.

If a country wishes to pursue domestic contractionary policies by raising the rate of interest, the higher rates may simply attract Eurodollars into the domestic money market, thereby providing new liquidity and negating the intent of the policy, at least in part. The opposite may occur when a central bank lowers the rate of interest to promote expansion and all that happens is that Eurodollars leave the country in search of higher rates elsewhere, thereby contracting domestic liquidity. This simply demonstrates the limitations that an integrated capital market imposes on the conduct of an independent national monetary policy. In order to gain more independence, some European countries have found it necessary to impose certain controls on the movement of Eurodollar funds and short-term capital in general. Restrictions on the inflow of funds—such as taxes on foreign-held bank accounts—were common in Switzerland, West Germany, and Holland, among others, in the 1969–1973 period. There is, of course, another side to this story. The existence of Eurodollars has provided some countries with a new monetary tool for the pursuit of domestic stabilization policies. For example, if West Germany wishes to bring about contraction in its money supply, its central bank sells on the market not only government bonds but also dollars in exchange for marks. Such sales are normally accompanied by an agreement to repurchase these dollars from their holders (usually commercial banks) at a future date, so as to eliminate the risk from possible exchange fluctuations.

In 1969 the limitations imposed by the integrated capital market were felt even in the United States. The Federal Reserve Board was pursuing restrictive monetary policy to stem inflationary forces. Interest rates and bank reserve requirements were raised in an effort to make funds both more costly and less available. However, there is a legal upper limit to the interest rates that banks can offer savers in the United States to attract deposits (Regulation Q), and in 1969 American short-term interest rates moved well above the Regulation Q ceiling, providing a strong incentive for American depositors to transfer funds to the Eurodollar market. Often these funds flowed to Europe via Canada, which was exempt from U.S. government restrictions on outflow of funds (see Chapter 8).

In order to offset these conditions and to cushion the effect of Federal Reserve policy, American banks bid for Eurodollar funds that at the time were not subject to legal reserve requirements or to legal interest limitations. In the first half of 1969, American banks raised their European borrowings from $4 to $12 billion. This strengthened the international position of the dollar by increasing demand for it in Europe, stopped the outflow of gold from the United States, and raised interest rates on Eurodollar funds to the 12–14 percent range. But such repatriation of funds to the United States increased the liquidity of domestic banks, counteracting the tight money policy of the Federal Reserve. In mid-1969 the Federal Reserve moved to correct the situation by imposing reserve requirements on intra-bank transfers from abroad.

Another example of the effect of currency flows on the American money market arises from the fact that foreign monetary authorities invest their dollar assets in U.S. financial instruments such as U.S. government bonds. At times when foreign monetary authorities are accumulating reserves, the demand for U.S. Treasury bills tends to rise, depressing their yield and with it U.S. money market interest rates.[21] Conversely, as in the fall of 1973, when foreign central banks lose dollars because of U.S. balance-of-payments surpluses, they cash in their Treasury bills. This lowers prices and raises yields on such bills, thereby raising U.S. interest rates. Such changes in interest rates may be a variance with the domestic policy objectives of the Federal Reserve system.

It should not be concluded from all this that an integrated capital market is a bad phenomenon. In fact it is far superior to a system beset by an assortment of controls over international capital movements. What the foregoing examples show is that the degree of interdependence that exists today and, it is hoped, will develop in the future calls for regular policy coordination among central bankers. "We are all in this together," one might say, and the economic navigators of nations, especially of small open economies, must take account of outside restrictions in formulating their policies. With this short but important digression completed, let us return to the vantage point of the individual country.

The Balance of Payments in the Context of General Policy Objectives

Since every economic measure taken by the government affects both the balance of payments and domestic conditions, the economist needs to concern himself with the total situation. If a country suffering from a balance-of-payments deficit happens to be subject to domestic inflationary pressures at the same time, it is in a relatively fortunate situation, for the domestic remedies required to cure the domestic inflation are also those needed to cope with the external deficit. In both cases contractionary fiscal and monetary policies are called for, and the situation is known as "consistent." Such was the situation confronting the United States late in the 1960s and Denmark in early 1970.

Similarly, when a country experiences a domestic recession and a balance-of-payments surplus at the same time, it is in a consistent situation, because

---

[21] In 1974–75 it was expected that the oil-producing countries would invest up to $10 billion of their accumulated oil earnings in U.S. government securities and thereby help the U.S. government finance its budgetary deficit.

Table 4-2

Possible Combinations of Internal and External Economic
Conditions and their Policy Requirements

Internal conditions	Domestic policies called for	Balance of payments	Domestic policies called for	Nature of situation
Unemployment	Expansion	Surplus	Expansion	Consistent
Inflation	Contraction	Deficit	Contraction	Consistent
Unemployment	Expansion	Deficit	Contraction	Inconsistent
Inflation	Contraction	Surplus	Expansion	Inconsistent

both predicaments call for expansionary policies. On the monetary side, the central bank should lower the rate of interest, lower the reserve requirements to which commercial banks are subject, and purchase government bonds on the open market. These actions make money more easily and more cheaply available to the consuming and investing public. Once translated into additional spending, they have a multiplied effect throughout the economy, raising income and employment. On the fiscal side, the government should curtail taxes or raise expenditures, or both, pumping purchasing power into the economy and raising the level of economic activity. The increases in income and employment, and most probably the companion increase in prices, have the effect of increasing imports and lowering exports, thereby eliminating the balance-of-payments surplus. Thus, the same set of policies can be used to deal with both internal and external problems.

But a country can also find itself in an "inconsistent" combination of circumstances. It may have a balance-of-payments deficit and domestic unemployment at the same time, or a balance-of-payments surplus along with domestic inflation. In the first case the deficit calls for contractionary policies while the unemployment necessitates expansionary measures. In the second case the surplus requires internal expansion, while the inflation necessitates domestic contraction. Table 4-2 should help clarify the four combinations.

While the first two situations can be handled by proper domestic policies, the second two are problematical. Thus, the United States late in the 1950s, the early 1960s, and again in 1970, was plagued by a combination of unemployment and deficit. On the other hand, during most of the 1960s and early 1970s, West Germany confronted a combination of an external surplus and an inflationary boom, and during the years 1967–1972, Japan was in a similarly inconsistent situation, registering 11–14 percent growth rates in real GNP and large surpluses in the balance of payments.[22]

---

[22] One reason for the development of such situations is the differential in income elasticities of demand for a country's imports and exports. Empirical studies have shown

Under the "rules of the game" of the gold standard, the guide to government policy was the balance-of-payments position of the country. Policy-makers were expected to subjugate internal stabilization needs to the requirements of balance-of-payments adjustment. But with the depression of the 1930s and the advent of Keynesian economics, governments began to assume increasingly greater responsibility for domestic employment and prices. This brought the conflict within inconsistent situations into sharper focus. This conflict is said to have been partly responsible for the breakdown in the international financial system in the 1930s. In particular, with respect to the United States, it is often claimed that it is unreasonable to expect an $1150 billion economy to be subservient to the needs of the relatively small external sector one-twentieth its size.

It is this conflict of policy goals that was foremost in the minds of the 1944 Bretton Woods conferees, who established the International Monetary Fund and hammered out the rules by which the world's financial system was thereafter governed for almost thirty years. Their objective, not quite successfully met, was to strike a compromise between the two goals, leaving countries scope for independent domestic action while at the same time helping to finance external imbalances out of reserves and loans. On the whole, however, it is the adjustment mechanism that has suffered in the process.

Readers familiar with domestic economic problems will recognize that this inconsistency is superimposed upon another troublesome conflict: that between inflation and unemployment. Contractionary measures designed to combat inflation often create unemployment, while expansionary measures designed to cure a recession can easily bring about or accelerate inflation. In large measure this conflict results from the fact that labor unions and corporations are not perfect competitors but possess varying degrees of market power. Under perfect competition, so many units operate in the marketplace that no one of them has any control over the conditions of sale or purchase, including price. When the demand for a certain product or a whole range of products slackens, the price necessarily declines as sellers bid down their prices to dispose of supplies in the face of shrinking markets. However, in our modern economy, not only have prices become rigid or sticky in a downward direction, but unions and corporations use their market power (not necessarily an absolute monopoly) to push up wages and prices at times of underutilized productive capacity. To be effective (or "to stick"), such price increases—known as cost-push inflation—must be "validated" or accommodated by the Federal Reserve increasing the money supply.

---

that if Japan's income grew at the same rate as that of the rest of the world, the world's demand for Japanese exports would grow three times as fast as Japanese demand for imports. The reverse is true for the United Kingdom.

Judging by the experience of the past thirty years, it takes a fairly deep recession to convince unions and management to hold the line on wages and prices (for example, to confine wage demands to increases in productivity). This point highlights the thorny issue often referred to as the trade-off between price stability and unemployment.[23] It has become impossible to stop inflation altogether, or to reduce it to a socially acceptable level of 2 percent a year, and at the same time have full employment. At one end of the spectrum lies the possible combination of considerable unemployment and reasonable price stability (as occurred early in the 1960s), while at the other end it is possible to have nearly full employment along with a rapid rate of inflation (as happened in 1969 and again in 1969–1972).[24] Between the two extreme positions lie various attainable combinations of unemployment and inflation.

By adding the international dimension, a further source of possible inconsistency between policy objectives emerges. This includes the need to deal with such combinations as an external deficit, unemployment, and cost inflation all occurring at one and the same time. A broad discussion of such conflicts is beyond the scope of this volume. We merely wish to emphasize that at no time should the balance-of-payments objective be viewed in isolation. There is no such thing as a single, isolated policy goal. At any given time the government has several targets, relating to the domestic and external performance of the economy. They may include full employment, high growth rate, price stability, external balance, and the like. The government also has an arsenal of policy instruments, including monetary, fiscal, exchange rate, and other measures.

Application of each instrument would have different effects on each of the policy goals. The rational policy-maker would view the situation in its totality and select a proper mix of instruments to deal with his set of targets. The greater the number of policy objectives (or targets), and the larger the potential conflict between them, the larger the number of instruments that must be employed to meet them. Indeed, the economist's tool kit may not contain enough instruments to meet all the objectives. More realistically, the policy-maker may avoid using any one of the instruments at his disposal

---

[23] This close inverse relationship between inflation and unemployment is often described on a chart called the Phillips curve, named after its developer, the British economist A. W. Phillips. He constructed a "trade-off curve" between the unemployment rate and wage changes that indicated that wages in Great Britain rose rapidly when unemployment was declining, slowly when unemployment was rising. The Phillips curve was drawn to reflect a relationship between wages and unemployment, but other analysts have maintained that a similar relationship holds between prices and unemployment.
[24] In 1974 the United States was facing both high inflation and high unemployment—an undesirable combination indeed.

(exchange-rate adjustment, for example), for political or other reasons, or a country may not have the capacity to use domestic instruments in the required mixes. (Thus, the OECD recently criticized several industrial countries for what it termed excessive reliance on monetary policy.) If a government's hands are tied in this fashion it may also have to choose among conflicting objectives or strike a compromise between them. In short, the importance of viewing a situation in its totality cannot be overemphasized.

Having said this, let us return to the inconsistent positions described in Table 4-2. Assume that a country is faced with unemployment and a deficit at the same time. If the situation is permanent, it cannot be handled by domestic instruments alone and may call for exchange rate adjustment. But should the balance-of-payments deficit be temporary, a remedy can be found in a proper combination of domestic measures. It will be recalled that monetary contraction has a dual effect on the balance of payments: not only does it improve the current account balance but it also attracts short-term capital from abroad by raising the rate of interest. Suppose the government combines a policy of monetary contraction and fiscal expansion. Depending on the relative size of the doses applied, the fiscal measure can more than offset its monetary counterpart in its effect on the domestic economy. We thereby obtain a net expansionary effect, desirable for internal purposes but increasing the current account deficit. On the other hand, the increase in the rate of interest embodied in the monetary contraction attracts funds from abroad, more than offsetting the adverse impact on the current account position. This combination of measures is particularly attractive if the country has a current account surplus less than its normal capital outflow, yielding (under full employment) a total external deficit—a situation typical of the United States in the early 1960s. Thus, in the first half of 1974, large inflows of short-term funds into the United Kingdom—attracted by high interest rates—partly offset the large current account deficit and helped prop the external value of the (floating) pound sterling. A similar inflow into the United States helped strengthen the dollar in June 1974. A precisely reverse combination of measures can be pursued in the case of inflation coupled with surplus, especially when the surplus is a result of a current account deficit smaller than the capital inflow.

In recent American history there was even an episode when the government tried to cope with an inconsistent situation by using only one monetary instrument: the rate of interest. At any given time there is not just one interest rate in the market but a whole structure of rates that apply to various financial instruments, depending on their maturity and risk. Early in the 1960s, faced with external deficits and internal unemployment, the Federal Reserve attempted to raise short-term interest rates by selling short-term bonds on the market and to lower long-term rates by buying long-term bonds.[25] This attempt to manipulate the interest-rate structure was dubbed Operation Twist.

The intent of the policy was to attract short-term funds from abroad—responsive to short-term interest differentials between financial centers—and at the same time promote domestic investments by depressing long-term rates. But the measure was crowned with less than complete success because the two financial markets are not really separate. Private investors can respond to such a policy by shifting funds from the long-term market with its relatively low yields to the short-term market. By doing so they push long-term rates up and short-term rates down, thereby negating the government's intention. The Federal Reserve must continuously keep abreast of private activity to effect a wider differential in the rate structure.

But even if the policy is successful, its impact on internal and external balance turns on several questions that are far from settled: To what extent do short-term funds respond to interest differentials? The empirical evidence on this is mixed, and the portfolio approach suggests that at best the response is a "one-shot" affair. Is domestic investment activity responsive enough to changes in long-term interest rates so as to expand much when rates decline? And, third, are not certain domestic investments, such as the accumulation of inventories, responsive to short-term interest, so as to decline when rates go up?

Be that as it may, with the policy combinations described above the authorities may hope to deal only with highly temporary conditions of deficit and unemployment. If the inconsistent situation was brought about by deeply rooted causes and cannot therefore be considered temporary, such domestic measures are not likely to constitute a sufficient remedy, for they do not contain a mechanism to realign the country's prices (under full employment) with those of the rest of the world. More drastic action is needed. One step in the arsenal of the policy-maker is exchange-rate adjustment.

[25] The price of a bond and the rate of interest are inversely related. A bond carrying a $50 coupon pays 5 percent interest if its price is $1000, 10 percent if its price is $500. Thus by buying bonds and raising their price, the Federal Reserve in effect lowers the rate of interest.

5
Exchange-Rate Adjustment

During the reign of the Bretton Woods system there were many revisions in the par value of currencies, despite the articles of agreement of the International Monetary Fund, which called for exchange-rate stability, and the professed aversion of policy-makers to exchange-rate adjustments. The major changes in exchange rates in the industrial countries during this period were:

(1) The sterling devaluations of 1949 and 1967, when the value of the pound was reduced from $4 to $2.80 and later from $2.80 to $2.40. Both times the British action was accompanied by devaluation of other currencies closely tied to the sterling.

(2) The 11 percent devaluation of the French franc in August 1969.

(3) A 5 percent revaluation of the German mark and Netherlands guilder in 1961 and further revaluations of the mark in 1969, 1971, and 1973.

(4) The 23.8 percent devaluation of the Finnish mark (from 31 to 24 cents) in October 1967.[1]

(5) The "floating" of the Canadian dollar during the 1950s and again beginning in June 1970.

(6) Two devaluations of the U.S. dollar, in December 1971 and February 1973, with the 1971 devaluation being accompanied by widespread exchange realignment of practically all major currencies.

The term "devaluation" refers to a decrease in the value of a currency in terms of other currencies, while "revaluation" describes an increase in that value. Both concepts are used in connection with a system of fixed exchange rates, where the government changes the value of the currency by decree and

---

[1] The contrast in size of the 1967 British and Finnish devaluations (15 and 24 percent, respectively) is a demonstration of the importance of being unimportant. Being a small trading nation, Finland could devalue substantially without retaliation and without causing severe repercussions in the financial world. This is not possible for an important reserve currency like the British pound sterling.

usually by a considerable fraction at a time. Any consideration of a change in the exchange rate is usually shrouded in secrecy and denied publicly, in order to prevent unbearable speculative pressure against the currency. Public suspicion of an impending devaluation inevitably invites speculative activity, as holders of the currency try to avoid losses or realize gains by shifting to other currencies. Therefore, a finance minister cannot be called to task for publicly denying any consideration of devaluation just hours before he officially announces such an action on behalf of his government.

When the exchange rate is not fixed but is left to fluctuate freely in response to market supply and demand, changes in it are not referred to as devaluation or revaluation. Rather, we speak of "depreciation" or "appreciation" when the value of the currency declines or increases. Such changes are usually continuous, involving very small movements each day, but their effects on the economy are similar in nature to those of discrete adjustments. For the sake of clarity of exposition, this chapter deals with discrete adjustments.

In order to understand what can be accomplished by changing the exchange rate, we must inquire into its economic effects. It is instructive to discuss four separate effects, assuming in each case that all other things are held *constant*. In fact, of course, various influences continuously interact with each other. Let us approach the problem by way of a hypothetical, but easily possible, situation. Let us imagine that the United Kingdom, facing a persistent balance-of-payments deficit and sizable unemployment, devalues the pound from $3 to $2, or equivalently raises the price of the dollar from one-third to one-half pound sterling. (The corresponding event under a managed float is for the government to permit the currency to depreciate from the old to the new level; under a free float, market forces would bring about the decline.) What will be the effects of such an action?

Relative Price Effect

The immediate impact of the devaluation is to lower the prices of goods and services produced in the United Kingdom relative to prices in other countries, making British products more competitive both at home and on foreign markets. In other words, British imports become more expensive in terms of pounds, making the home-produced substitutes relatively cheaper, while British exports become cheaper in terms of the foreign currencies in which they are sold. Thus a $3,000 American automobile will cost the British customer £1,500 instead of £1,000 as a result of the devaluation, while the price to the American consumer of a £10 English shirt declines from $30 to $20 as the pound is devalued from $3 to $2. Likewise, an American tourist to the United Kingdom must now spend only $400 instead of $600 on a £200 package tour. Conversely, the cost to a British traveler of a $900 trip to the United States rises from £300 to £450 as a result of the devaluation. Finally, a potential American investor in the United Kingdom finds his dollar cost of a given pound expenditure reduced by one-third, while the converse is true for an Englishman who contemplates buying American securities. The same change applies to all traded goods and services as well as to capital flows. The reader may wish to work out other examples. In sum, relative U.K.–U.S. prices decline even when domestic prices remain the same in both countries.

Becoming more competitive by lowering relative prices is not an end in itself, however. It is a means toward eliminating the external deficit, which is usually measured in terms of dollars, the internationally accepted medium for settling imbalances. In other words, the aim of British policy is to *reduce* the dollar value of *imports* (total dollar inpayments) and *raise* the dollar value of *exports* (total dollar outpayments). It is to that end that prices are reduced. The effect of the relative price change on the value of trade flows depends on the degree of quantity response to price change. But since the results in the case of inpayments and outpayments are not symmetrical, each flow will be considered separately.

Before proceeding with the analysis we need to define more precisely the meaning of "degree of response to price change," a term we used loosely in the previous chapter. Consider the demand curve shown in Figure 5-1. It shows the quantities (on the horizontal axis) that would be purchased at alternative prices (on the vertical axis). It slopes downward and to the right (that is, it has a negative slope) in accord with the inverse relation between prices and quantities: the lower the price the greater the quantity purchased. In the present case, as price declines from P_1 to P_2 quantity increases from Q_1 to Q_2. This inverse relation between price and quantity is assumed to hold for most products. But the dollar value of purchases may or may not increase.

Figure 5-1

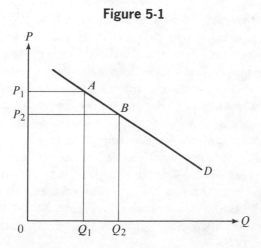

That value is price times quantity ($V = P \times Q$), and since price has fallen while quantity has risen we cannot say, in general, whether their product ($P \times Q$) has risen or fallen. This product is represented by the rectangular area under the relevant point on the demand curve, since that area is $0P \times 0Q$, or price times quantity. In our case this area has changed from $0P_1AQ_1$ to $0P_2BQ_2$. Since the area ($P \times Q$) corresponds to dollar payments by the importer or, equivalently, to dollar receipts of the exporter, we are concerned with the manner in which it changes as a result of the price changes.

The effect of a given price change on $V = P \times Q$ depends on how large the quantity response is. Clearly, the flatter the demand curve is, the greater will be the quantity response that it represents. The standard measure of the degree of response is called the *price elasticity of demand* (η_p). It is the ratio

$$\frac{\text{Percentage change in quantity purchased}}{\text{Percentage change in price}}$$

which may be symbolized by

$$\frac{\Delta Q/Q}{\Delta P/P} = \frac{\Delta Q \times P}{\Delta P \times Q}$$

where Q and P are used as bases to convert the absolute changes ΔQ and ΔP into percentage terms. Since price and quantity normally move in opposite directions, the elasticity will usually have a negative value. However, it is common to ignore the negative sign and measure elasticity of demand in terms of its absolute value.

Consider the value $\eta_p = 1$. By definition this means that any given percentage change in price will exactly equal the resulting percentage change in quantity purchased. In other words, the increase in quantity is exactly sufficient to offset the reduction in the amount for which each unit now sells. This leaves dollar value $P \times Q$, the area under the demand curve, unchanged. When the demand elasticity is greater than 1, the percentage increase in the quantity purchased is larger than the percentage decrease in price, so that a decline in price yields an increase in the dollar value of purchases. Precisely the opposite is true when the elasticity is smaller than 1. In that case a price reduction produces a less-than-proportionate increase in the quantity purchased, so that the dollar value (the area under the curve) declines. We call the first case *demand of unitary elasticity,* the second case *relatively elastic demand,* and the third case *relatively inelastic demand.*

The value of the elasticity changes as one moves along a straight-line demand curve (see Figure 5-2). In particular, for a demand curve that stretches from the price axis to the quantity axis, the midpoint ($\eta_p = 1$) represents unitary elasticity; points above it represent the relatively elastic segment of the curve, and points below it, the relatively inelastic segment.

Figure 5-2

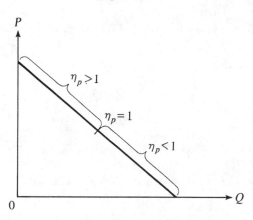

This the reader can verify for himself by changing the price in each of the two segments and examining what happens to the value (the area under the curve). The value attains its maximum at the point of unitary elasticity. A demand curve along which $\eta_p = 1$ at all points is a rectangular hyperbola (Figure 5-3), under which the area is the same at all points. Finally, when economists draw two straight-line demand curves and characterize the flatter one as more elastic, such a statement must be construed as a loose description of the situation. (Note that if a "flat" demand curve is continued on both sides to intersect the axes, it is likely to lie above the midpoint of a straight line drawn between the points of intersection, whereas a "steep" demand curve will generally lie below the midpoint.) Demand is said to be infinitely elastic ($\eta_p = \infty$) when the demand curve is horizontal, because in that case the percentage change in price is zero. On the other hand, a vertical demand curve, where quantity is unchanged, portrays zero elasticity.

We are also interested in the response of suppliers to price change. The

Figure 5-3

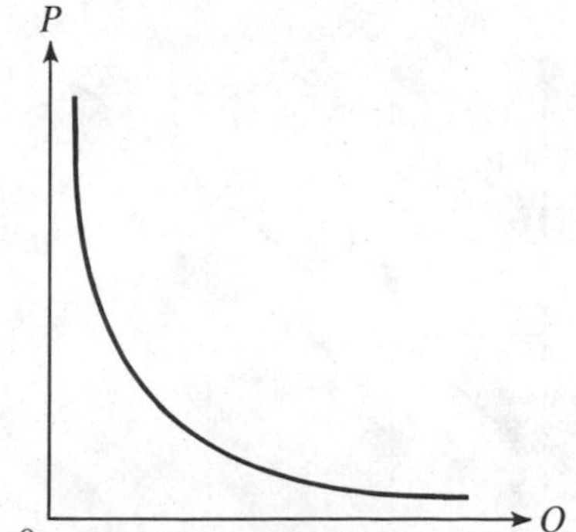

supply curve slopes upward and to the right (positive slope), indicating a direct relation between price and quantity: as price rises so does the quantity supplied, and vice versa (Figure 5-4). The elasticity of supply is therefore positive; it is defined in the same manner as the demand elasticity, except that Q refers to the quantity supplied:

$$\eta_s = \frac{\Delta Q/Q}{\Delta P/P}$$

Loosely speaking, the flatter the supply curve is, the higher is the elasticity that it implies. A horizontal supply curve indicates infinite elasticity of supply, while a vertical curve shows zero elasticity. The shape of the supply curve is determined by the cost conditions (that is, the shape of the marginal cost curves) of the firms that comprise the industry.

The intersection of the supply and demand curves (or schedules, as they are also called), determines the price prevailing in the market and the quantity exchanging hands. A shift in one of the curves, say an upward movement of the demand curve, means that at each and every price more of the product is demanded (for example, because of higher income). It is not to be confused with a movement along that curve. The shift from D_1 to D_2 (Figure 5-5) causes a movement along the supply curve from A to B, and it establishes a higher price as well as a greater quantity. The reader can experiment by shifting one of the two schedules (S or D) in either direction and moving along the other to determine the effect on price and quantity.

We are now in a position to analyze the effects of sterling devaluation upon the dollar inpayments and outpayments of the United Kingdom. Note, however, that in this discussion the supply schedules refer to each country's supply of exports to its trading partner and the demand schedules refer to each country's demand for imports from its trading partner.

Figure 5-4

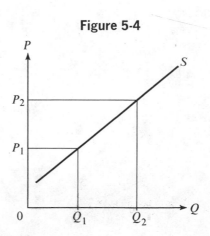

Figure 5-5

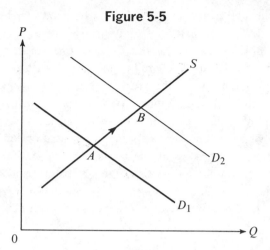

Effect on Dollar Outpayments

Sterling devaluation has made British imports (an American automobile in our earlier example) more expensive in terms of pounds, with *dollar* prices remaining the *same*. Since English consumers deal in pounds, the volume[2] of imports inevitably declines, and dollar outpayments (volume of imports times the constant dollar price) must also decline. The amount by which out-payments are reduced is determined only by the decline in the volume of imports, since dollar prices are unchanged. In turn, the extent of this decline depends on how responsive British consumers are to the increase in the pound price of imports, or what economists call the price elasticity of demand for imports. The more responsive they are, the greater the reduction is. One factor that invariably affects the degree of responsiveness is the availability of accept-able substitutes produced at home. The more readily available they are, the more likely it is that consumers will shift to home-made goods and thereby reduce outpayments. Thus, other things being equal, the import demand elasticity of a large country is likely to be greater than that of a small country because the large country tends to produce adequate substitutes for most of its imports.

Similar reductions in outpayments occur as British tourists are discouraged from going abroad by the fact that they must pay more pounds for the dollars they need, and as British companies contemplating overseas investments are held back by the increase in the pound cost of such ventures. In short, *dollar outpayments* in all forms *necessarily decline,* the extent of the reduction being determined by the degree of responsiveness to price change.

---

[2] The words *volume* and *quantity* are used interchangeably to refer to the physical amount of goods measured by units or aggregated by the use of index numbers. *Value,* on the other hand, is volume times price.

The simple analytical tools of supply and demand can be used to demonstrate the point. The two halves of Figure 5-6 are the usual price–quantity diagrams. They differ from one another in only one respect: prices are expressed in dollars on the upper chart but in pounds on the lower chart. We begin by observing the curves that represent the predevaluation situation. American supply to the United Kingdom ($S_{U.S.}$) is assumed, for the sake of simplicity, to be infinitely elastic, or horizontal. (A small country normally faces an infinitely elastic supply curve.) Its predevaluation level is $3 or £1. British demand for imports from the United States ($D_{U.K.}$) assumes the normal shape. The volume of British imports from the United States is Q_1 and is shown on both charts.

Devaluation of the pound does not affect American supply in terms of

Figure 5-6
Effect of devaluation of the pound on dollar outpayments

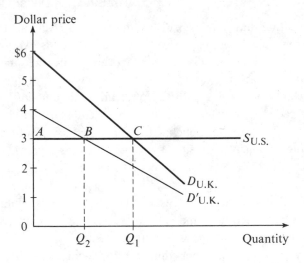

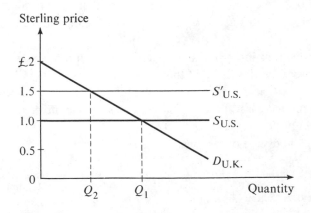

dollars or British demand in terms of pounds. This is not so for the U.S. supply expressed in terms of pounds, however, or the British demand expressed in terms of dollars. The fact that the pound is now at $2 means that the $3 supply price translates into £1.5 instead of £1, indicated by the postdevaluation $S'_{\text{U.S.}}$ shown in the lower diagram. It results in reduced volume of imports—from Q_1 to Q_2. Since the dollar price remains unchanged, the reduced quantity *necessarily* translates into a reduction in *dollar* outpayments. The size of this reduction depends only on the change in quantity, which in turn is a function of the British demand elasticity; the more elastic the demand the larger the decline in dollar outpayments.[3]

Only in the extreme case of zero elasticity of British demand (when $D_{\text{U.K.}}$ is a straight vertical line) will the quantity imported, and therefore outpayments, remain unchanged. In that case sterling prices rise exactly in proportion to the devaluation, and dollar prices reman unchanged. In other words, there is no competitive gain for British products.

Precisely the same result can be demonstrated on the upper diagram. Although $S_{\text{U.S.}}$ remains at $3, $D_{\text{U.K.}}$ must change when expressed in terms of dollars. The British demand curve shows the quantities that consumers are willing to buy at various hypothetical sterling prices. These remain unchanged. But each such sterling price now translates into one-third fewer dollars than before the devaluation. Consequently, the British demand curve on the dollar price scale (upper diagram) must be lowered to $D'_{\text{U.K.}}$, yielding import volume Q_2.

Dollar outpayments—the volume of imports times their dollar price—is the area under the equilibrium point. It declines from $0ACQ_1$ to $0ABQ_2$. The only case in which no such reduction occurs is where the demand curve is of zero elasticity (it is vertical) and does not shift. In general, the larger the elasticity of demand, the greater the decline in outpayments.

Effect on Dollar Inpayments

When it comes to the inpayments side, the picture is less clear cut. British exports become more competitive because their *dollar* prices to foreign customers are down one-third. This decline is certain to induce American consumers to purchase more English goods. But the interest of the British government is not in selling more goods in the United States per se; it lies in earning more dollars. And, as a result of the devaluation, each unit of British exports sells for fewer dollars than before. The total inflow of dollars into the United Kingdom is made up of the volume of British exports *times* the unit dollar price they fetch abroad. Since that price has declined by one-third,

---

[3] Note that total outpayments expressed in sterling may increase (but by proportionally less than the devaluation) or decrease, depending on the elasticity of $D_{\text{U.K.}}$. But the main interest attaches to *dollar* outpayments.

the quantity sold would have to increase by *more* than a third in order for dollar inpayments to rise. More generally, inpayments rise only if the increase in the volume of sales is more than proportional to the decline in price—more than sufficient to compensate for the fact that each unit now sells for less.

In turn, that condition depends on the degree of foreign response to the decline in prices of British goods. If foreign customers are responsive enough to offset the decline in price (if the foreign demand for British goods is relatively elastic), then dollar inpayments rise. The same principle holds with respect to foreign tourists visiting the United Kingdom and foreign users of all British services. It also applies to foreign corporations wishing to invest in the United Kingdom. They all find it possible to purchase each pound neces-

Figure 5-7
Effect of devaluation of the pound on dollar inpayments

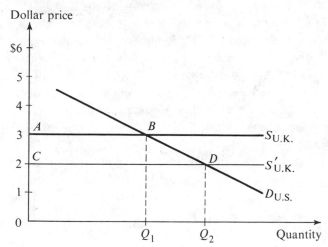

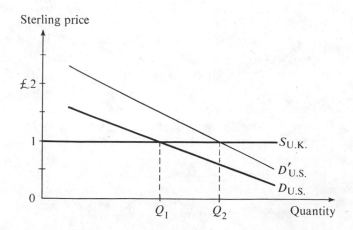

sary for their transactions for fewer dollars. But whether they spend more dollars in the United Kingdom depends on their response to the decline in price. Only if they increase the purchases of British services more than proportionately to the decline in their dollar price will the flow of inpayments increase. (This is the qualification hinted at in the first section of Chapter 3 in connection with the slope of the German inpayments line.)

As before, this conclusion can be clarified by simple demand-and-supply analysis, except that in this case the United Kingdom is the supplier, with an infinitely elastic supply curve ($S_{U.K.}$), and the United States is the demanding country. The curves labeled $S_{U.K.}$ and $D_{U.S.}$ in Figure 5-7 show the predevaluation situation in terms of dollar prices on the upper chart and sterling prices on the lower chart. $S_{U.K.}$ and $D_{U.S.}$ appear in both charts at the predevaluation exchange rate of £1 = $3. The quantity traded is Q_1.

Dollar inpayments, which are our main concern, are shown on the upper chart as the area under the equilibrium point, $0ABQ_1$. They equal price ($3) times quantity: $\overline{0A} \times \overline{0Q_1}$. Devaluation does not affect the American demand relationship $D_{U.S.}$ when it is expressed in terms of dollar prices. But $S_{U.K.}$, which remains unchanged with respect to sterling prices (lower chart), is affected when expressed in terms of dollar prices (upper chart). Specifically, the £1 supply price was equivalent to $3 before devaluation, but it is equal to $2 after devaluation. Correspondingly, $S_{U.K.}$ is shifted downward to $S'_{U.K.}$; that is, the devaluation has made British goods cheaper for American consumers. The new equilibrium point is D. The quantity traded rises to Q_2. Total dollar inpayments are now equal to the area $0CDQ_2$. They are larger than the predevaluation inpayments ($0ABQ_1$) if the U.S. demand elasticity is greater than 1 over the relevant range, smaller if the elasticity is smaller than 1.[4] In general, the more elastic the American demand for British imports, the greater will be the increase in dollar inpayments into the United Kingdom following devaluation.

Outpayments and Inpayments Combined

To recapitulate, while U.K. dollar outpayments are certain to decline, the impact of the devaluation on dollar inpayments to the United Kingdom is uncertain. Here not only the size of the increase but its very occurrence depend on the responsiveness of American consumers to the reduction in the dollar prices of British goods. The reason for the difference is as follows. Because of

[4] The reader may notice that on the bottom chart in Figure 5-7, where prices are expressed in terms of pounds, British supply ($S_{U.K.}$) remains unchanged. But the American demand curve is shifted upward as a result of the devaluation, reflecting the fact that a given number of dollars now buys more pounds. The quantity traded rises to Q_2, and so total sterling inpayments necessarily rises. But whether this rise translates into an increase in *dollar* inpayments depends on whether it is proportionately larger than the devaluation.

the increase in sterling prices of British imports, the volume of these imports declines. Since their dollar prices remain unchanged, their total dollar value (outpayments) is also certain to decline, the size of the reduction depending on the response of British consumers. On the inpayments side, the increase in the quantity of British exports results from a *decline* in their *dollar* prices. Their total dollar value rises only if the percentage increase in quantity is larger than the percentage decline in price. And whether that happens depends on the response of American consumers to the reduction in price.

Of course the British government is interested in the net effect of devaluation on its foreign exchange position. Its target is an *increase* in *inpayments minus outpayments,* both expressed in terms of dollars. While ideally outpayments should decline and inpayments should rise, the two components of the equation can compensate for each other. Even if inpayments actually decline, the reduction may be more than offset by a larger cut in outpayments, thereby benefiting the balance of payments.

Economists have worked out complicated formulas for the conditions that must prevail if devaluation, in its immediate impact, is to reduce the excess of outpayments over inpayments.[5] In the case where the two supply elasticities are infinite, the condition for success is that the sum of the demand elasticities of the two countries must exceed unity[6] When supply elasticities are less than infinite, the formula becomes more complex. Also, in realistic situations, the sum of the elasticities must exceed the bare minimum so as to allow for reversal factors (discussed in the next section). It bears emphasizing that this entire discussion relates to the size of the elasticities necessary to move the balance of payments in the *desired direction,* and not to the degree of impact that a given devaluation would have or to the time lag between devaluation and its effects.

There is abundant empirical evidence to suggest that in the case of industrial countries these conditions are indeed met. The response to price change is large enough to ensure that the relative price change would have the salutary effect of both raising inpayments and lowering outpayments. Devaluation or depreciation of the currency is likely to decrease the country's external deficit. Whether the shift in the balance-of-payments position is sufficiently large to eliminate the deficit altogether depends on the size of the devaluation itself

[5] Known as elasticity conditions or stability conditions of the foreign exchange market.
[6] This can be seen intuitively by referring to Figures 5-6 and 5-7. Assume that the elasticity of $D_{\text{U.K.}}$ is zero. Then nothing happens on the outpayments side, and the only possible salutary effect is a rise in inpayments. This would occur if the elasticity of U.S. demand ($D_{\text{U.S.}}$) is 1 or more—that is, if the sum of the elasticities is 1 or more. If we now raise the elasticity of $D_{\text{U.K.}}$ above zero, some help can come from the outpayments side, correspondingly reducing the absolute need to raise inpayments in order to insure success. Thus it is the sum of the two demand elasticities that counts, and that sum must exceed 1. (For further discussion see Appendix II.)

and on factors to be considered next. (Under a freely fluctuating exchange rate, the depreciation will continue until the deficit is eliminated.)

☐ The analysis of the relative price effect of devaluation can be expanded in several directions, and the more advanced student is urged to study Appendix II for the following extensions:

(1) Figures 5-6 and 5-7 relate price to the quantity of a traded commodity. The upper diagrams can be translated into a relationship between the exchange rate and total foreign currencies demanded and supplied (as in the first section of Chapter 3) by transforming (or "mapping") the area under the equilibrium point (price times quantity) onto the horizontal axis. The horizontal axis then shows quantity of foreign exchange (dollars). Figure 5-6 would then illustrate the outpayments, or demand for dollars, while Figure 5-7 would show the inpayments, or supply of dollars.

(2) The analysis of Figures 5-6 and 5-7 can be extended to the more general case in which the supply curves are less than infinitely elastic.

(3) A similar analysis can be employed to show the effect of devaluation on the commodity terms of trade of the devaluing country (that is, the price of exports divided by the price of imports).   ■

Domestic Income and Price Effects

On the domestic front, the result just obtained implies an expansion of output, and therefore of employment and income, in the industries producing export goods and import substitutes. This expansion is brought about by an increase in demand from foreign and domestic sources, respectively, with the initial impact on output amounting to the rise in exports plus the decline in imports[7] $(\Delta X - \Delta M)$. This expansion spreads throughout the economy through the multiplier mechanism, generating a multiple increase in gross national product. As before, the multiplier is $1/(\text{MPS} + \text{MPM})$, so that the increase in income is

$$\Delta Y = (\Delta X - \Delta M) \times \frac{1}{\text{MPS} + \text{MPM}}$$

Once full employment of resources is aproached, a likely companion to the increased level of economic activity is a rise in domestic prices. In fact,

---

[7] Or rather the portion of the decline in imports that translates into expanded output of domestic substitute products.

an increase in the domestic price level can be anticipated independently of the income expansion, dissipating part of the competitive edge gained by the devaluation. The very fact of a 33⅓% devaluation raises sterling prices of all imported commodities by 50 percent. And, since many imports enter as raw materials into the productive process, while others (like food) enter into the cost of living, which partly determines wage rates, a wage–price inflationary spiral might be triggered as producers attempt to pass on the increase in production costs to consumers in the form of higher prices. The extent of inflation depends on the degree of "openness" of the devaluating country— that is, on how dependent it is on foreign imports whose prices must rise—and on the success of the government in controlling the inflationary trends by contractionary policies. Intransigent labor unions that insist on tight escalator clauses (tying wage rates to the cost of living) and other benefits can negate many of the benefits of devaluation.

Both income expansion and increases in the domestic price level have the effect of encouraging imports and discouraging exports, thereby offsetting or reversing part of the relative price effect discussed in the previous section. For that reason they are sometimes referred to as *reversal* factors. The income reversal factor depends on the change in income and on the MPM, while the price reversal factor depends on the change in prices and the response to that change (elasticity). On the other hand, this offsetting effect may be mitigated if the income expansion attracts capital from abroad. Thus the elasticity conditions necessary for the success of devaluation are actually more exacting than those outlined in the previous section, for the buyers' response to price change must be high enough to allow for the offsetting influences of domestic income and prices.

For this reason it is incumbent upon government to contain domestic expansion, primarily the increase in prices, to the extent possible. Spiraling inflation can wipe out the entire competitive gain and lead to successive but useless devaluations. There is even a danger of the development of an inflationary psychology that feeds upon itself. People begin to expect prices to rise every year, and they purchase commodities as a hedge against inflation. By that very act, they push prices up and add to the inflationary flame. In time, money may even lose its usefulness as a store of value, which harms not only the balance of payments but also the domestic growth rate, as people are induced to curtail their rate of saving. The experience of some Latin American countries is a case in point; such a situation should be guarded against at all costs.

After the 1967 devaluation of the pound Great Britain was unable to curb wage and price increases through a vigorous income policy, and some signs of inflationary psychology were visible in 1968. By contrast, the success of the French devaluation of 1958 was attributable in no small measure to the political ability of the de Gaulle regime to impose restrictive measures. Similarly, internal belt-tightening measures and incentives to modernize industry contributed to the success of the 1967 Finnish devaluation, and price and wage controls as well as contractionary policies followed the French devaluation of August 1969.

Although the analysis in this chapter has been couched in terms of the devaluation of European currencies relative to the dollar, the same reasoning applies to devaluation of the dollar in terms of other currencies. The two devaluations of the dollar in 1971 and 1973 (see Chapter 9) brought about a sharp improvement in the U.S. balance of payments by 1973. At the same time they contributed to the domestic expansion of 1972–73. And in certain industries, such as machine tools, the export pickup in 1973 was a key factor in pulling the industry out of a slump and nearly doubling its total sales.

It is not possible, nor is it necessarily desirable, for a devaluating country to eliminate all income expansion. An increase in output and employment is, after all, one objective of a devaluation. In an inconsistent situation involving both an external deficit and a domestic recession, such as the United Kingdom faced in our hypothetical example, the devaluation should simply be large enough to allow for some offset to the relative price effect emanating from the real income sources. Only when full employment is approached and the main impact of further expansion will fall on the price level is the policy-maker obligated to slam on the brakes.[8] Considering the possible conflict between output expansion and price stability, the policy-maker is required to walk the tightrope among several objectives: achieving the necessary improvement in the external trade position, maintaining a desirable expansion in employment and output, and containing the domestic price increases. He must also remember that all these influences take time to work their way through the economy.

Redistribution of Domestic Resources

While domestic price and income effects operate against the relative price effect in improving the balance of payments, devaluation also brings about domestic redistribution of resources favorable to its success. It will be recalled that exporters gain a considerable competitive edge abroad, while at the same time the prices of imports increase in terms of the domestic currency. Consequently, British producers can afford to raise the sterling price of both exports and import substitutes to some extent and still remain competitive. In other words, the tendency toward domestic price increases as a result of de-

---

[8] This is an oversimplification. In actual fact there are large gray areas here, calling for different doses of contractionary measures.

valuation is not evenly spread. What occurs is a differential increase, because prices rise more in the foreign-trade industries (exports and import substitutes) than in the purely domestic sectors (construction, services, and so on). This attracts resources to industries that produce internationally traded goods, which in most cases makes the economy more efficient and at the same time promotes the type of production that improves the balance of payments.

Another View of Devaluation—The Absorption Approach

In the previous three sections of this chapter, the effects of devaluation were traced one by one and their possible interactions were analyzed. Specifically the analysis showed that devaluation is likely to help a country's external position while at the same time leading to an expansion of income and employment. Although this was not explicitly stated, domestic expansion is often a prerequisite for improvement in the balance of payments, for the increased production of export goods and import substitutes requires the employment of new resources. Clearly the ready availability of labor and machinery to be put to productive use is of crucial importance to the success of devaluation.

In order to highlight the relationship between the external and internal effects of devaluation, we turn to an alternative approach to the analysis of devaluation—the *absorption approach*. Focusing on the relation between the balance of payments and domestic conditions, this approach complements and sheds additional light on what has been said thus far.

For simplification, consider an economy that produces, consumes, and trades commodities but not services or capital flows. The imbalance of trade is then identical to the imbalance of payments. The following equality between two pairs of magnitudes must hold for all periods. The difference between the value of goods *produced* in the economy (Y) and that of goods *absorbed* domestically by all users (A) must equal the difference between exports (X) and imports (M). In other words,

$$A - Y = M - X \quad \text{or} \quad Y - A = X - M$$

For, if absorption exceeds production, the difference between them must be made up of excess imports over exports; and when production is higher than domestic absorption the difference must be expressed in excess exports over imports.[9] This is the fundamental identity of the absorption approach.

---

[9] The reader having difficulty seeing this should think in terms of a one-good economy—cars, for example. If production is 1000 cars each year and domestic absorption into all uses (including inventories, whether desired or not) is 800, then exports must exceed imports by 200. Exports of 300 and imports of 100 would thus yield an appropriate balance. Alternatively, assume that production is 1500 and imports are 500. Then the total number of cars available for disposition is 2000. If 1700 cars are absorbed by

☐ The more advanced reader will recognize the following derivation of the identity. National income consists of and is equal to four types of expenditure: consumption, net investments, government expenditures on goods and services, and the excess of exports over imports. Symbolically,

$$Y = C + I + G + (X - M) \tag{1}$$

If we omit the import component of C, I, and G and confine these terms to spending on domestically produced goods, we must also delete M. We then obtain:

$$Y = C_d + I_d + G_d + X \tag{2}$$

where d denotes "domestic." Equation (2) states that national product or income consists of what is produced and absorbed domestically ($C_d + I_d + G_d$) plus what is exported (X). The goods and services produced and absorbed domestically are called domestic absorption (A_d). That is, $A_d = C_d + I_d + G_d$. Therefore,

$$Y = A_d + X \tag{3}$$

☐ On the other hand, total absorption (A) consists of what is produced (and absorbed) domestically (A_d) plus imports (M). In our notation:

$$A = A_d + M \quad \tag{4}$$

and therefore $A_d = A - M$. We may combine this with equation (3) to obtain

$$Y = A_d + X = A - M + X = A + X - M \tag{5}$$

Hence,

$$Y - A = X - M$$

This is the fundamental equation of the absorption approach.   ■

Startling from a deficit position where imports (M) exceed exports (X), absorption (A) must exceed production (Y) by the same amount. This is essentially a case of a country living beyond its means (absorbing more than it produces), or a country investing in excess of domestic savings. When the

---

domestic users, then 300 are left over for exports. Hence again:

$$1700 - 1500 = 500 - 300$$
$$(A) \quad\quad (M) \quad\quad (Y) \quad (X)$$

Given three of the four magnitudes, the fourth can be found by using the identity.

currency is devalued, the price and income effects come into force and work their way through the economy. If the relative price effect on the balance of payments is more powerful than the interacting income effect, the final outcome is a reduction in the trade deficit $(M - X)$. But that necessarily implies an equivalent reduction in $A - Y$: either absorption (A) is reduced or domestic production (Y) is increased or a combination of the two occurs.

This is merely another way of looking at what has already been stated. When devaluation occurs under conditions of unemployment, the main impact is on Y: production of exportables and import substitutes rises, and its effect spreads throughout the economy by means of the multiplier mechanism. Resources that were previously unemployed are put to work to produce the goods whose sale was made possible by the improved competitive position.[10] It is for this reason that persistent balance-of-payments deficits combined with unemployed resources in the domestic economy constitute an "ideal" situation to be met by devaluation.

Under full employment, there are no free resources to be put into production to increase Y. Devaluation, which necessarily exerts pressure on scarce resources, is likely to dissipate in domestic inflation. Prices rather than real output would rise. To be sure, there is reason to expect more efficient allocation of resources to follow the devaluation, so that more goods can be produced with existing resources. This is particularly pronounced when the devaluation replaces an assortment of exchange and import controls. In underdeveloped areas it is often the case that countries with overvalued currencies resort to complicated systems of control, inevitably leading to gross misallocation of resources and widespread inefficiences. When devaluation finally comes, economic efficiency can be expected to improve. But this is not the situation in industrial countries, where the effect of improved allocation is not likely to be great.

Thus, under full employment the crucial question revolves around the economy's ability to reduce domestic absorption. Only a reduction in absorption can release otherwise occupied resources for the production of export goods and import substitutes to take advantage of the devaluation. There are reasons to expect some reduction in absorption to follow from the devaluation itself. One of them is the redistribution effect discussed in the previous section. Others result from the alleged reaction of the public to a general increase in domestic prices following devaluation. They involve fine points of economic theory and need not detain us here.[11] In the final analysis, success

---

[10] As a result of the increase in production and income, absorption will also rise, but by less than the rise in income, because part of the increase will leak away into savings. The higher the MPS, the larger will be the difference between ΔY and ΔA, and the more successful the devaluation.

[11] Here are two examples of such effects. (1) Assume that, following a devaluation, money income and prices advance in the same proportion, so that real income remains

depends on the ability of the government to bring about a reduction in absorption through appropriate domestic measures.

It is possible to improve the country's competitive standing by devaluation (when the country is at full employment) only if the devaluation is accompanied by contractionary policies designed to release resources engaged in production for the home market.

☐ A Third Approach—Emphasis on Money

☐ Yet a third approach to the theory of devaluation focuses on monetary balances and can be labeled the *monetary approach*. Assume for simplicity, that the citizens of the home (devaluing) country and those of the rest of the world own either goods or money balances, and that the demand for money balances is positively related to income. Assume, further, that the monetary authorities abstain from changing the money supply except insofar as is necessary to maintain a pegged exchange rate. Accordingly, an increase in the money supply is given by a trade balance surplus, and a decrease by a deficit.

☐ Starting from a position of external equilibrium, devaluation of the home currency raises local prices, primarily because the local prices of traded goods (that is, goods exported and imported) rise; and secondarily because the prices of nontraded goods also rise as some local demand is diverted to them. Consequently the real value of people's monetary balances (and financial assets) declines, inducing them to increase their hoarding in order to restore the real level of the cash balances they desire to hold. To accomplish that they must increase savings or reduce their expenditures relative to income, thereby producing an excess supply of goods (the counterpart of their excess demand for money). Precisely the reverse phenomenon occurs in the rest of the world. Foreigners now experience a reduction in the price of goods imported from the devaluing country, so that the real value of their monetary balances goes up. This induces them to dishoard, or to increase expenditures on goods relative to their income. And among the goods they purchase are imports from the

---

unchanged. Since tax rates are progressive and are based on money (not real) income, this advance places people in higher tax brackets, subjecting them to higher taxes. So, in effect, their real income after taxes declines. To the extent that it is determined by real income, their consumption will be lowered, thereby reducing the major component of absorption. If this is not offset by a rise in government expenditures, total absorption also declines. (2) A general rise in the price level lowers the real value of people's savings inasmuch as these are invested in fixed money-value assets such as bonds and savings accounts. To the extent that people's behavior is governed by a desire to attain some level of real saving, they would try to save more to make up for the loss by building up their monetary balances. They can do that by lowering consumption out of any given income, which in turn means that absorption is reduced.

devaluing country. As a result, the devaluing country develops a balance-of-trade surplus, and the rest of the world, a corresponding deficit.[12]

☐ This approach views devaluation first and foremost as a monetary phenomenon. Its effect derives from the change in the real value of money balances attendant upon a devaluation and the effect of this change on expenditures. Prices in the devaluing country rise, and in the rest of the world they decline, each change (in percentage terms) being less than the percentage devaluation of the currency. This lowers (raises) the real value of money balances in the devaluing country (rest of the world), and induces a reduction (increase) in expenditures on goods, as people attempt to restore the real value of their monetary balances, thereby generating a surplus (deficit) in the balance of trade.

☐ The three approaches to devaluation complement each other, and represent different ways of looking at devaluation. The first (elasticities) approach starts from partial equilibrium analysis (relative price effect), and is supplemented by price and income considerations. The absorption approach emphasizes the fact that given proper (that is, high enough) elasticities, and accounting for the income and price effects, a decline in aggregate expenditures relative to income must take place in order for devaluation to improve the trade balance. The monetary approach brings out a mechanism through which devaluation induces a reduction of expenditures relative to income. ■

Summary

Need for Policy Mixes

By now it should be clear why a change in the exchange rate is recommended for countries in inconsistent situations. Since *devaluation improves the balance of payments and also expands output and employment,* it is well suited for dealing with a combination of domestic unemployment and external deficits. Thus, the 11 percent devaluation of the French franc in August 1969 appeared by mid-1970 to have restored balance-of payments equilibrium and full employment in France.

---

[12] One outcome of the analysis is that the price of nontraded goods in the home country declines relative to that of traded goods. As a result of the devaluation, the citizens of the home country reduce their expenditures on both traded and nontraded goods. But the reduction of spending on traded goods is matched by a corresponding increase in such spending in the rest of the world, maintaining world wide equilibrium in the market for traded goods (hence the trade surplus in the home country). On the other hand, the relative price of nontraded goods must decline in order for equilibrium to be reestablished in the nontraded goods market. For this and other extensions of the analysis, see R. Dornbusch, "Devaluation, Money and Nontraded Goods," *American Economic Review,* December 1973.

Exchange revaluation has the opposite effects (requiring the reader to reverse the thought processes employed above): the deterioration in a country's competitive position lowers inpayments or increases outpayments or both. At the same time, output and employment decline in the export and import-competing industries, and from there the contraction spreads throughout the economy. Consequently, an upward adjustment of the exchange rate is well suited for a country experiencing persistent surpluses in the balance of payments and inflationary booms (overemployment) at one and the same time. *Revaluation removes the surpluses and dampens the inflation.* Thus the successive revaluations of the mark in 1971–1973 appeared by 1973 to have slowed down the rate of inflation as well as the rate of growth in West Germany, and observers forecast a further slowdown in the economic expansion for 1974. Likewise, Japan's balance of payments turned from a surplus to a deficit position over the same period as a result of the revaluation of the yen.

Attainment of the desired results on the external and internal fronts requires that exchange-rate adjustment be accompanied by appropriate domestic measures. In practice, all cases require a mix of policies rather than one measure. The final aim of policy is to satisfy the combined external and internal objectives, including balance-of-payments equilibrium, price stability, full employment, desirable growth rate, and whatever other goals the community agrees upon. Starting from a given situation, any one policy instrument designed to attain one objective is likely to overshoot or undershoot the mark in terms of the other objectives. Such is the nature of the beast. Other instruments must then be brought into play to bring about the necessary adjustments in these areas and put the economy on an even course. It is a rare (perhaps even nonexistent) case indeed when one instrument can properly deal with more than one target. Normally it is necessary to employ as many instruments as there are targets to attain the final objectives.

It cannot be overemphasized, therefore, that in all cases it is a policy mix rather than one policy measure that is called for. The appropriate combination of instruments often necessitates a delicate balancing of the policy doses administered; the nature of the mix depends on the objectives as well as on the circumstances. Thus when Canada unpegged (floated) its exchange rate in June 1970 and attained a 6 percent appreciation of the Canadian dollar, the Bank of Canada saw fit to lower the interest rate, for the appreciation could be relied upon to curb the domestic inflation.

Effectiveness of Policy

So far the proper policy mix has been dealt with only in terms of the situation confronting the country and its policy target. But the optimal mix depends not only on the situation but also on the relative effectiveness of the policy itself, and that varies from country to country.

Consider, for example, the effectiveness of expenditure policies in dealing with a balance-of-payments deficit. A reduction of $1 million in GNP lowers imports and stimulates exports by a fraction of that amount. How big a fraction it is depends on the marginal propensity to import and other variables relating to the degree of openness of the economy, or the degree to which it depends on foreign trade. In an oversimplified fashion it might be stated that the more open the economy is, the greater will be the effectiveness of expenditure policy in dealing with external imbalances, since a given change in GNP would have a greater effect on the balance of trade than in a closed economy. Conversely, in a closed economy such as the United States, with a low marginal propensity to import, a given change in GNP would produce a much smaller change in the trade balance. In other words, it would take a huge reduction in the gross national product to bring about any noticeable improvement in the trade balance.

On the other hand, for a closed economy the cost of engaging in a switching policy, such as devaluation, is likely to be less than for an open economy. "Switching policy" is a catch-all phrase for measures that rely primarily on changes in relative prices (the ratio of import prices to domestic prices) to improve the balance of payments. Switching policies are distinguished from income and expenditure policies, which focus on the income mechanism. An exchange-rate adjustment that affects the ratio of domestic to import prices and causes purchasers to switch to the cheaper goods is a prime example: devaluation induces a switch from imports to domestic substitutes, while revaluation does the reverse.

In a small open economy, the cost of switching can be high. Under the elasticity conditions that normally obtain in the industrial countries, the commodity terms of trade deteriorate as a result of devaluation.[13] When a large share of production and consumption is accounted for by foreign trade, this has a profound effect on domestic economic activity. Foreign imports play an important role in production as well as in the cost of living, and a rise in their prices can cause many dislocations in the economy and reduce real income. The reallocation of resources (as between industries) following devaluation may also be on a large scale. On the other hand, in a closed economy, which is almost totally independent of foreign trade, all these effects are small in size and minor in consequence; it is relatively less costly and less disruptive to adjust by switching than by means of an income policy. Not only that but a large country may need a smaller switching dose to rectify a given imbalance

---

[13] *Commodity terms of trade* are defined as the ratio of the export price index to the import price index. Their deterioration means that the country can obtain less imports for a given quantity of exports, or, equivalently, it must give up more goods by way of export to obtain a given quantity of imports.

than a small country would. Thus the effectiveness of switching policies, or their cost, varies among countries.

In sum, it is not only the situation confronting a country that determines the optimal policy mix. It is also the relative cost or effectiveness of the various policies, and that varies from one country to another depending on how closed or open the economy is or on the magnitude of foreign trade relative to the gross national product. Both the targets and the relative effectiveness of various policies must be considered before the optimal mix can be determined.

Foreign Retaliation

This discussion cannot end without a reminder that devaluation, like domestic policies, has foreign repercussions. When a country devalues its currency, it experiences an increase in output, employment, and income, because exports expand and imports contract. But, by implication, its trading partners suffer a reduction in exports and an increase in imports, with an attendant decline in output and employment. The larger and more important the devaluating country, the greater are the effects elsewhere. If the country devalues in order to get itself out of a domestic recession, then it merely inflicts a recession on other nations. Such a "beggar thy neighbor" policy was fairly common during the worldwide depression of the 1930s. Trading partners can easily retaliate by devaluating their own currencies competitively as they did in the 1930s. This danger is enhanced in a period of managed floats such as we have at the time of writing.

This clearly underscores the need for international harmonization of economic policies. In a multicountry world, it is no longer possible for a country to attain internal and external balance by use of its own policy instruments. Other countries can easily frustrate the balance.[14] In particular, cooperation is needed in the determination of exchange rates, and indeed the IMF charter required that multilateral consultation precede every major devaluation. Under the charter a country could devalue up to a total of 10 percent from the original par value by unilateral action. Any cumulative exchange-rate adjust-

---

[14] Another problem associated with the choice of policy mixes in a multicountry world is known as the "redundancy problem." Since the balance of payments of all countries in the world combined necessarily adds up to zero (shows neither deficit not surplus), external balance can be achieved if all countries *but one* achieve it. Thus, if each of N countries has two policy objectives—internal and external balance—except for one country, which is concerned with only one of these, the total number of objectives, and therefore the total number of policy instruments required, is $2N - 1$. There is, in a sense, a spare policy instrument in the system, giving one country some freedom for maneuverability. The problem is to determine which country should get this freedom. In the 1950s, for example, this freedom belonged to the United States, which did not have to be concerned with its balance-of-payments problem, as foreign countries were content to pile up dollar assets.

ment in excess of that required the prior approval of the Fund, an approval given only in cases of fundamental and persistent disequilibrium in the balance of payments.

Balance-of-Payments Adjustment Under Fluctuating Exchange Rates

Thus far the balance-of-payments adjustment mechanism has been discussed within the context of fixed exchange rates or highly managed floats. In what follows we shall consider some implications this analysis holds for the case of freely fluctuating exchange rates.

What Governs Exchange Variations?

What factors govern the variations of an exchange rate when it is free to respond to market forces? A superficial and general answer would be that anything causing a balance-of-payments deficit under a fixed exchange rate would result in depreciation of a floating currency, while anything causing a surplus would bring about appreciation. But the discussion in the last two chapters showed that practically all economic events and government policies affect the balance of payments, directly or indirectly. It is impossible to provide an exhaustive list of all factors that may come into play, yet it is useful to sort them out under broad headings and emphasize the lines of causation to be observed.

First, there are foreign developments beyond the control of the country in question that bear directly on its balance of payments. An international shift in demand that increased demand for the country's traditional exports would raise the volume and price of these exports and cause its currency to appreciate. Conversely, a shift in demand away from its traditional exports, or an economic slump in its major markets, would harm its export performance and depress the exchange value of its currency. A similar outcome would result from a sharp rise in the price of its imports, other things being equal. Thus the quadrupling of oil prices in 1973 engineered by the OPEC[15] cartel, brought about wide fluctuations in the value of practically all important currencies. Countries possessing no energy sources of their own in whatever form, and therefore depending largely on imported petroleum, witnessed the value of their currencies decline relative to that of countries less dependent on imported petroleum. Toward the end of 1973 the Japanese yen depreciated relative to the dollar, and in January 1974 France was forced to withdraw from the joint float and permit the franc to depreciate. The dollar and the mark, on the other hand, went up in value in late 1973. Likewise, the Dutch guilder appreciated

[15] Organization of Petroleum Exporting Countries.

in mid-1974 because Holland possesses large reserves of natural gas, the price of which went up on world markets. It may be noted that the deterioration in a country's terms of trade that is usually implied in depreciation of its currency (see Appendix II) reflects the added real burden imposed on the country by its need to finance higher oil imports—it now takes more exports to pay for the same volume of imports.

Under the second broad heading we classify all policies of the country's own government that bear directly on the balance of payments. Thus the imposition of import restrictions or limitations on capital outflow raises the value of the currency. The converse of this was illustrated when, following the removal of governmental controls on the outflow of investment capital from the United States on January 30, 1974, the dollar slumped on the foreign exchange markets.

Third, domestic economic events and government policies are likely to *depreciate* the exchange rate *if* they:

(1) Interfere directly with the capacity to produce and export.

(2) Raise money GNP in the country relative to that of the ouside world, thereby stimulating imports more than exports.

(3) Raise domestic prices relative to prices in other countries, thereby impeding the country's ability to compete on both foreign and the domestic markets.

(4) Reduce the country's interest rates relative to those in the outside world, thus stimulating the outflow and discouraging the inflow of short-term capital.

In each case, opposite policies or economic events would *appreciate* the country's currency.

This four-way classification can serve as a useful guide for judging the impact of economic changes on the exchange rate. The linkages involved are as follows:

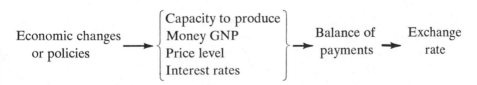

Actual or hypothetical examples under each heading are not difficult to find. The British coal strike in late 1973 and early 1974 deprived industry of its main source of energy and brought large sectors of the British economy to a virtual standstill. As a consequence, the pound sterling slumped on the foreign exchange markets. Conversely, the currency of a country experiencing important technological progress is likely to appreciate. A sharp rise in government expenditures or in the money supply, or both, designed to stimulate the economy and raise money GNP, would lower the exchange value of the currency; a rate of inflation lower at home than abroad would appreciate the country's exchange rate. This last factor has been partly responsible for the continuous strength of the West German mark. On the other hand, should the West German trade unions succeed in winning for themselves massive increases in wage rates and fringe benefits—far in excess of the increases in other countries and not accompanied by commensurate increases in productivity—a depreciation of the mark would be likely to follow. Finally, the reduction in British interest rates in the spring of 1974, designed to stimulate the domestic economy, resulted in depreciation of the pound sterling, while the reverse happened in the summer of 1974. The increase in German interest rates in the spring of 1974, intended to check inflation, caused an appreciation of the mark. In all these cases it is the position of the country *relative* to that in the rest of the world that is important.

While the foregoing factors are fundamental in nature, likely to govern exchange variations in the long run, short-run fluctuations may also result from speculative capital movements that can be triggered by expectations, rumors, and beliefs. Expectations may be based on underlying economic trends, or they may result from sheer confidence factors in the political or sociological arena. The Watergate revelations in mid-1973 fall under the second category; they were held partly responsible for the slumping dollar in that period, and again in mid-May 1974. On the other hand, the dollar gained in July 1974 because of rumors that foreign central banks would start supporting it, and because the U.S. payments deficit in June was not as large as had been expected.

The Role of Fluctuating Rates

Empirical studies suggest that, at least in the industrial countries, elasticities in international trade are generally large enough to meet the conditions for a stable foreign exchange market outlined earlier in this chapter. It is the relatively elastic demand for traded goods that ensures the "normal" slopes of the demand and supply curves for foreign exchange shown in Figure 3-1 (page 28; for further elaboration, see Appendix II). Under stable conditions, the foreign exchange market determines the exchange rate at a level that clears the market for foreign currencies. Automatic exchange fluctuations can be relied upon to ensure equilibrium in the balance of payments: A deficit would cause currency depreciation and a surplus, appreciation. These adjustments contain the equilibrating mechanism that restores equilibrium to the balance of payments. The marketplace, rather than the judgment of government officials, determines the extent of exchange-rate adjustment necessary to restore external equilibrium. *A freely fluctuating exchange rate, therefore, frees the government of direct responsibility for balance-of-payments adjustment; it can rely on the market to provide the necessary equilibrating mechanism.* The government in turn can concentrate on domestic policy goals, and thus the conflict between policy objectives in "inconsistent" situations is removed. Also, *there is no need to accumulate and hold international reserves, for these are only required to maintain a fixed exchange rate.* By contrast, in the case of a managed float, the exchange rate may sometimes be nudged away from its equilibrium level, yielding deficits or surpluses in the balance of payments; for that reason, reserves are required to manage the float.

Exchange fluctuations also affect the domestic economy—affecting money, income, prices, and resource allocation between the production of traded and nontraded goods—in a manner similar to that of a government-sponsored exchange-rate adjustment. Thus, depreciation of the currency raises domestic income and prices and shifts resources from production of nontraded goods to the export and import-competing industries, while appreciation does the reverse. The difference between the two systems is that under fluctuating rates the adjustments occur in small daily intervals rather than in one sizable discrete step (although many small changes in the same direction can add up to a substantial change over a relatively short period) and in response to market forces rather than to a governmental decree.

Because the exchange rate responds to market forces, a fluctuating rate regime is capable of insulating a country from disturbances *originating abroad.* In the section "Foreign Repercussions" of Chapter 4, it was seen that the fixed exchange rate serves as a link between countries. Such a link is absent under fluctuating rates. If country A experiences a depression and lowers its imports from its trading partner, country B, then under a fixed rate the depression would spread to B (via the decline in its exports and the multiplier mechanism), whereas under a fluctuating exchange rate, B's currency would merely depreciate. Likewise, under a fixed rate system, an inflation in country A would spread to B, but under a fluctuating rate regime it would merely cause B's currency to appreciate. Indeed, the Bretton Woods system of fixed exchange rates is often held responsible for the spread of inflation from one country to another in 1971 and 1972.

In a more general way, the discussion of the foreign trade multiplier is not applicable to the fluctuating exchange-rate regime. An autonomous rise in a country's exports or an autonomous decline in its imports will not necessarily expand its income, and certainly not by the amount indicated in the multiplier analysis. Rather, an increase in exports or decrease in imports will appreciate the exchange value of the country's currency until equilibrium is restored in the balance of payments. Depreciation will occur in the cases of an autonomous decline in exports or increase in imports.

However, a floating exchange rate does not completely insulate the economy from the effects of outside fluctuations. For exchange variations produce domestic disturbances via variations in the terms of trade and shifts of resources between industries. Still, some measure of insulation is attained, and as long as countries are unwilling to coordinate their domestic policies, such insulation is important. This is one reason why Canada, fearing economic fluctuations imported from its giant neighbor south of the border, opted for a fluctuating exchange rate during 1951–1964 and again in the 1970s.

From the point of view of the currency system as a whole, it was stated in Chapter 4 that "a combination of fixed exchange rates, currency convertibility, and imperfect harmonization of national economic policies that affect incomes, prices, and interest rates cannot work well. When these features clash, a crisis results." We now see that when domestic policies are not coordinated among countries, each jealously guarding its right for independent economic action, fluctuating exchange rates are more appropriate than fixed rates. However, even with fluctuating rates there is a need for some measure of consultation and coordination. At the very least, it is important to avoid competitive depreciation of currencies when the float is "dirty." This issue was of prime concern in 1974 when each country attempted to protect its balance-of-payments position from the new burden created by the huge increase in oil prices.

Recent Skepticism

☐ There have always been skeptics about the efficacy of the exchange rate adjustment. Traditional skepticism, going all the way back to the 1930s, revolves around the belief that the demand elasticities in international trade are too low and therefore the stability conditions are not met. Some economists hold this view today. But since the adoption of the floating exchange rates in 1973, a new view has emerged, one associated with Professors Mundell and Laffer, which casts a more fundamental doubt on the effectiveness of this policy. Although strictly a minority view, their ideas will be summarized briefly.

☐ It will be recalled that according to the elasticities approach, the immediate impact of exchange rate adjustment is to change relative prices. All else follows from that change. The new view contends that such an effect is impossible for internationally traded commodities. For such products—however heterogeneous or differentiated they may be—must command roughly the same price everywhere. Free international trade would ensure this result. Consequently, a country cannot acquire a competitive advantage by devaluing its currency. If country A devalues relative to country B, then either A's domestic prices must rise or B's domestic prices must decline to compensate for the change in their exchange, rate and to keep relative international prices intact. Since, in the industrial world, domestic prices are rigid in a downward direction, the upshot is that prices in the devaluing country (A) rise roughly in proportion to the devaluation. Consequently, the sole effect of the devaluation is to produce inflation.

☐ A world of floating exchange rates means that some currencies move up and others move down. Because of the asymmetry in domestic price adjustments, this implies inflation in the depreciating countries. But the currencies that appreciate today may depreciate tomorrow; so the inflationary pressures are in fact worldwide. The 1973–74 worldwide inflation was due (in this view) in no small measure to the floating exchange rates. Instead of insulating a country from foreign inflation (as the traditional theory contends), fluctuating rates produce worldwide inflation.

☐ A system of fixed exchange rates avoids this problem. It has the added advantage that inflation and deflation in any one country, caused by an error in the amount of new money supplied by its central bank, could spread around the world, thereby mitigating the (concentrated) impact on that country. The fact that the central bank of each country loses the monopoly on its money supply is therefore a good thing.

☐ The proponents of this view argue for fixed exchange rates as a method of promoting world economic integration, a view held by Professor Kindleberger for a somewhat different reason—that "money" would perform its traditional functions (as a means of exchange and a store of value) best if it were "internationalized." A system based on the dollar as the sole intervention and reserve asset (see Chapter 10) is suggested as an attractive possibility. It bears repeating that this is still very much a minority view.   ■

A further examination of the floating rates system will be undertaken in Chapter 10.

6
Further Analysis of the Adjustment Process and Some Unanswered Questions

Much economic research has been devoted to determining what combinations of policy instruments are most appropriate for moving the economy toward certain targets, and much has been learned about the processes involved. The last two chapters may have left the reader with the erroneous impression that —assuming we can agree upon policy objectives, and conflicts between divergent goals can be resolved politically—our economic instruments can achieve any objective or combination of objectives with a high degree of accuracy. Nothing could be further from the truth; indeed, comments frequently emanate from high quarters to the effect that "fine tuning of the economy" is all but impossible given our present state of knowledge.

Apart from the difficulty of resolving conflicts between objectives, most of what has been said so far has revolved around one main topic: the direction in which the economy moves as a result of the application of various policies. But the direction of change is not a sufficient guide for policy making. Two other interrelated pieces of information are absolutely essential. First, we must know how strong a force is exerted on the economy by each policy measure. This in turn determines how far in the direction of the target the economy moves in response to the policy measure, or, put differently, how great an application of each instrument is required to reach the target. Second, we need to know how long it takes for the full impact of the various instruments to be felt throughout the economy, and what sort of time path the economy follows in its movement toward the target position. The latter information, classified by economists as "economic dynamics," enables public officials and concerned citizens to know roughly what to expect at various intervals after the policy button has been pressed. These two questions are of crucial importance in evaluating not only balance-of-payments policies but also economic policies designed to stabilize the domestic economy. The following discussion is in the context of fixed exchange rates.

Domestic Policies

The Degree of Impact

Consider the internal measures designed to eliminate a balance-of-payments deficit. On the fiscal side the initial instrument at the disposal of the authorities is a reduction in government expenditures or an increase in taxes, or both. Such action lowers the income of the community and is also presumed to reduce the rate of price increase. The reduction in income brings about lower imports and higher exports through the income mechanism, while the improved competitive position operates in the same direction through the price mechanism. In each of these phases the question is: How much?

All that the government can control is the initial fiscal action. That step is *exogenous* to the economy in the sense that it is "arbitrarily" determined at a political level outside the economy. It affects other economic variables, but it is not affected by them. Once the action is taken, however, the government has no further control over the final outcome, unless it wishes to take some other deliberate steps. The initial action sets in motion a sequence of interrelated economic processes, each depending on other economic magnitudes and therefore considered *endogenous* or internal to the economy.

In the case of a reduction in government expenditures, the following sequence of questions can be articulated.

1. By how much does gross national product decline for a given cut in government expeditures? The answer depends on the size of the multiplier, which in turn is determined by the proportion of each round of reduced purchasing power that is withdrawn from the domestic spending stream. These marginal propensities are measurable, and therefore so is the size of the multiplier.

2. What proportion of the total reduction in gross national product is translated into lower imports and higher exports? Again, these have measurable magnitudes, especially the marginal propensity to import. *A priori* reasoning would suggest that the less dependent the economy is on foreign trade, the smaller is the effect on imports of a given change in gross national product. Put differently, the more closed the economy is, the larger is the income adjustment required to achieve a given reduction in imports.

3. Will there be an "unfavorable" side effect to the economic contraction

as long-term capital is encouraged to seek more profitable investment opportunities abroad? If so, how significant is it?

4. To what extent does the reduction in the level of economic activity force producers to curtail the rate of price increase? Here the quantitative estimation can be carried out in terms of the trade-off between the rate of inflation and unemployment.

5. To what extent do lower prices stimulate exports and discourage imports? This depends on various price elasticities.

Similar questions can be asked with respect to an increase in taxes or, if the country wishes to eliminate a balance-of-payments surplus, with respect to an increase in government spending and a reduction in taxes. Such questions were foremost in the minds of economists and politicians when tax rates were reduced early in the 1960s to stimulate the economy and raised again in 1968 to check inflation and help redress the balance-of-payments deficit. It is in estimating these magnitudes that mathematics and statistics have made a significant contribution to economic policy making.

Answering the questions is no mean task. At any given moment a multitude of forces is operating on the economy, and it is necessary to isolate the effect of the policy under investigation. In order to find out the effect of a policy, we need to compare situations with and without the policy, all other things assumed to remain unchanged. It is the validity of this *ceteris paribus* assumption that many laymen often question when they read the writings of economists. How can it be valid if the economy is in fact always in a state of change? The answer is that all other changes take place in the presence or in the absence of the policy under investigation. And making the assumption "other things being equal" is equivalent to comparing the situation with and without the policy. In the physical sciences this is accomplished by controlled laboratory experiments. Since this is not possible in economics, we must use theoretical abstractions and statistical techniques to achieve the same objective.

This is the role of model building in the social sciences. It is often necessary to build a simplified model of the whole economy in order to draw inferences concerning the size of the parameters being estimated. Model construction means the mathematical formulation of the relationships between various economic variables in a manner that lends itself to statistical estimation. The branch of economics concerned with such studies is econometrics. Thanks in no small measure to improved estimation techniques, policy-makers today have at least a rough idea of the magnitudes of the variables involved. For example, we know that the size of the multiplier for the United States is somewhere between 2 and 3, meaning that a $1 million increase in autonomous expenditures by the government, investors, or indeed foreigners (that is, an increase in exports) raises the gross national product by $2–3 million; that the marginal propensity to import[1] is around 0.057, meaning that a $1 million increase in GNP raises imports by $57,000; and that the price elasticity of import demand is 1.2 for all commodities but 4 for finished manufactures, meaning that a 1 percent reduction in import prices raises the volume of manufacturing imports by 4 percent. Similar information is available for some other industrial countries. Although these are merely orders of magnitude, they help determine the optimal dose of each measure that needs to be administered. For the problems outlined above, probably the least light has thus far been shed on question 3, although they all require much additional work.

When it comes to monetary policy, the first instrument in the hands of the central bank is control over the money supply.[2] In the case of an external deficit, the money supply would be contracted—by, say, the Federal Reserve selling government bonds on the open market—and interest rates would be raised. Once administered, the policy must operate through processes internal to the economy and push the economy toward the preassigned target. Whether it would actually get there depends on the answers to the following questions:

1. To what extent does a contraction in the money supply lower the level of economic activity and slow the rate of increase in the price level?

2. By how much do a given economic contraction and price reduction discourage imports and encourage exports?

3. To what extent does an outflow of long-term investment capital occur as an unfavorable side effect to the economic contraction?

4. How sensitive is short-term capital to interest differentials between financial centers, and therefore how strongly is it attracted to the deficit country when its interest rates rise?

Questions 2 and 3 were discussed in connection with fiscal measures. Much econometric work has been done in attempts to answer questions 1 and 4. But, particularly with respect to the last problem, the results of the various studies are inconclusive and at times even contradictory. In a more general way there is still much to be learned about the relative effectiveness

---

[1] Income elasticity (η_Y) of demand for imports differs from the MPM in that it represents a ratio of percentages: the ratio of the percentage change in imports to the percentage change in income. Symbolically,

$$\eta_Y = \frac{\Delta M / M}{\Delta Y / Y} = \frac{\Delta M}{\Delta Y} \times \frac{Y}{M} = \frac{\Delta M / \Delta Y}{M / Y} = \frac{\text{marginal propensity to import}}{\text{average propensity to import}}$$

where the average propensity to import (APM) is the proportion of total income that is spent on imports.

[2] Here we ignore the question of how well the central bank can control the money supply with the policy instruments at its disposal: changes in reserve requirements of commercial banks, open-market operations, and changes in the rediscount rate.

of monetary and fiscal measures in influencing the economy and through it the balance of payments.

The second crucial question concerns the timing of policy and the time path followed by the economy as it moves toward the target position. It certainly makes a great deal of difference whether a policy instrument attains its objective in one year or five years, if for no other reason than because many things can happen in the longer time span to change the course of the economy. Thus the longer the lag is, the greater is the need for further application of policies to maintain the economy on the proper course during the intervening period.

There are two time lags common to practically all policies and exogenous or external to the economy: the lag between the need for action as reflected in the economic conditions and the recognition of that need by the policy-maker, and the lag between the recognition and the point when economic action is initiated. Economists and statisticians can help reduce the recognition lag by speeding up the collection and evaluation of data about the state of the economy and the dissemination of the analytical conclusions and their policy implications. The second lag results from administrative delays and at times from the need for legislative action, as in the case of tax-rate changes. Because they do not require specific legislative approval, expenditure policies and monetary measures can be applied with greater dispatch than tax measures can. To minimize this lag, administration procedures should be improved to speed the decision-making processes.

Next in sequence come the endogenous lags—those that depend on the working process of the economic system itself. Two questions are relevant here. How long does it take for a certain fiscal or monetary action to work its way through the economy before its full impact is realized in terms of changes in gross national product and the price level? (For example, monetary expansion in 1970/71 brought about an expansionary phase of the economy in 1972–73.) And how long is it before the effect of income and price changes on the balance of payments is manifested in whole or in part? These questions call for dynamic studies that specify the time path followed by the economy as it adjusts gradually to the shock of new policy. Such studies, which usually measure the time periods in terms of quarters because the United States collects quarterly data for many variables, are still in their infancy. We know a little about the income adjustment path and therefore the lags involved as gross national product reacts to fiscal and monetary stimuli. We know much less about the price adjustment path and nearly nothing about the reaction path of the balance of payments to changes in prices and income.

Exchange-Rate Adjustment

The Degree of Impact

In the case of persistent balance-of-payments deficits, perhaps coupled with unemployment and excess productive capacity, the economist must determine whether the currency is overvalued and whether the overevaluation is amenable to cure by a downward adjustment in the exchange rate. If so, he must estimate the degree of devaluation required. The same principle applies to revaluation in the case of persistent surpluses. But to arrive at a precise figure is all but impossible. Theoretically, an equilibrium exchange rate between two currencies must in some sense reflect the purchasing power of these currencies in their respective countries; that is, it must reflect their relative price levels. Thus one possible method to determine the degree of adjustment necessary is to select a base period in which equilibrium conditions prevailed in all respects and then measure the changes in price levels of the two countries since that period. If, for example, prices in the United States doubled while prices in the United Kingdom tripled, then sterling would have to be devalued by one-third.

But this method, known as the purchasing-power parity doctrine, leaves many questions unanswered. Where does one find an ideal equilibrium period to serve as a base? Which of the many price or production-cost indexes should be used for the comparison?[3] How can we account for changes in the living and buying habits of the two populations being compared? How do we incorporate the effect of changes in income and employment that might have occurred in the intervening period? How can we allow for the effect of capital flows that are not even reflected in the price levels? All these affect the balance of payments and therefore the exchange rate. They make it impossible to apply a simple rule of thumb in constructing an estimate. They do not render the price comparison operationally irrelevant, however. It must be regarded as a general guide, to be coupled with other considerations and used with discretion.

---

[3] Most widely used in this connection is the wholesale price index, because the consumer price index includes services and other items that never enter international trade. It is interesting to note that the prices of such services (haircuts and dry cleaning, for example) are higher in the United States than in the United Kingdom and higher in Europe than in the less developed countries. One reason for this may be that the prices of internationally traded goods, such as manufactured products, are roughly the same on the two sides of the Atlantic, a phenomenon insured by the free flow of trade. Since labor productivity is two to three times higher in the United States (because of more mechanized production, among other things), American wage rates in the foreign-trade industries are double their European counterparts. Within each economy, mobility of labor exerts a strong pressure toward equalization of wage rates (for equal skills) in all industries. This means that wage rates in the U.S. service industries are double their European counterparts. But since there is no such international productivity difference in these industries, American prices end up being twice the European level. And such price differences can exist in service industries because they are not traded internationally.

The resulting estimate is at best an approximation, subject to considerable error. Indeed, the inability to pinpoint the equilibrium exchange rate is one reason why many economists have been moved to advocate greater exchange flexibility, where market forces can play a role in the precise determination of the exchange rate. That was one reason for widening the band of permissible exchange-rate fluctuation around the dollar from 2 percent to 4½ percent, and for the occasional adoption of *transitional floats* even under the Bretton Woods system. For example, in 1969 the West German government permitted the mark to fluctuate freely for two weeks so that it would settle at a new equilibrium level, at which it was then pegged.

Another way to approach the problem is to turn it around and ask what the impact of a given devaluation would be on the balance of payments and on the gross national product. This too is a rather complex question, because devaluation has several effects that all interact with each other and because the relative price and income effects exert opposite influences on the balance of payments. However, economists have been able to devise mathematical formulas that incorporate the main influences. In such formulas the price effects are measured in terms of price elasticities, while the income effects are shown through various marginal propensities. Estimating the size of these responses is a statistical task to which much effort has been devoted. For countries where such estimates exist, the effect of alternative devaluations of different sizes on the external trade accounts can be roughly approximated. (Even here, however, we know next to nothing about the effect of devaluation on long- and short-term capital flows.)

Thus, the problem of magnitude can be approached from both sides, giving the policy-maker an idea of the degree of adjustment necessary in the exchange rate. What he actually does often depends on political as much as economic considerations. Such questions as how much the currency can be devalued without eliciting retaliation by the country's trading partners or without undue loss of prestige at home and abroad are usually foremost in the minds of any government officials contemplating exchange-rate adjustment. They were certainly prominent considerations in the British decision of 1967 to devalue by less than 15 percent. Peculiar as it may appear, prestige erroneously attached to exchange-rate changes does not seem to be symmetrical. While devaluation is usually associated with loss of prestige, very few observers dwell on possible gain in public esteem emanating from revaluation. But these are matters more properly discussed by psychologists than by economists.

Time Path

Equally important, and much more difficult to determine, is the time path of the economy once its currency has been devalued. After the British devaluation of November 1967, for example, there were several conflicting forecasts, all emanating from responsible and knowledgeable quarters, as to when the salutary effects of the devaluation would become visible. Such conflicting predictions occur in practically every instance of exchange-rate adjustment. The people making the forecasts are not lying; they simply do not know.

Yet such knowledge is important; the sooner the effect takes hold over the economy the less the chance that other forces will set in to alter its course. And accurate time estimates help the policy-makers to determine the need, magnitude, and timing of supplementary measures. The British government, for example, was having trouble in 1969 (nearly two years after the devaluation) in deciding what type of budget to adopt and what its influence was to be on the economy. Indeed, only in 1969 did the British external deficit give way to a moderate surplus—a surplus that was later obliterated by the large wage demands of three and a half million workers and a dock strike. Immediately following the dollar devaluation of 1971, the U.S. balance of payments deteriorated. For the dollar cost of previously contracted U.S. imports went up while the dollar value of American exports remained unchanged. Only when the volume of imports declined in response to higher import prices, and the volume of exports rose in response to lower prices in terms of foreign currencies, did the balance of payments improve. And that did not happen until 1973, when the dollar devaluations of December 1971 and February 1973 converted the U.S. external deficit into a surplus. Adequate time forecasts can allay the fears that devaluation is not working that are based on premature expectations, and forestall speculative activity against the currency.

As before, the time path to be considered involves the mechanisms by which the income and price effects work their way through the economy. Although the price effects of devaluation are more important than those of internal policies, less is known about their time path for two reasons. First, economists have been more derelict in studying the reaction time of the economy to price change than to income change; in most models of the economy, prices are considered endogenous to the system, and there is no need to trace the effect of price change as if it were an outside force exerting its influence on the economy. But devaluation is an exception; it is a price change determined on a political level, by the government, in much the same way as a change in government expenditures or in the money supply. That the impact of such price changes is far from instantaneous can be recognized from the fact that measured response to price changes (elasticity) increases with the time span for which measurements are taken. There is therefore a crucial need to study this time path. Second, price and income changes operate in opposite directions in devaluation. This makes it at once more important and more difficult to determine which impact is felt first and how the two forces interact over time.

The time lag involved in exchange-rate adjustment is also important in a system with fluctuating exchange rates, for in that case it determines the efficiency of the system. If the lag is long and trade flows respond slowly to exchange-rate adjustments, then exchange variations cannot be relied upon to produce equilibrating trade flows with dispatch. Rather, in the short run, equilibrating capital movements will have to be relied upon to bridge the balance-of-payments deficit until the necessary adjustment in trade flows comes about. However, for a variety of reasons, short-term capital may be destabilizing: it may move in the direction opposite to what is desirable. For example, if a currency depreciates as a result of a balance-of-payments deficit, financiers may expect further depreciation and sell the currency rather than buy it. In other words, capital movements may not be a reliable temporary mechanism to bridge a balance-of-payments gap. In that case the efficiency of the system of floating exchange rates must depend on a relatively quick response of trade flows to exchange variations. It is for this reason that economists are showing increased interest in the measurement of this time lag.

7
Exchange Control and Currency Inconvertibility

Exchange Control

Because of the prestige accorded the exchange rate in the popular mind or because the government has debts denominated in foreign currencies, or for a variety of other reasons, a country in persistent deficit may refuse to devalue. It may be driven instead to impose exchange control. For, if foreign currencies are undervalued in price (priced below the equilibrium level) or, equivalently, if the domestic currency is overvalued, the price mechanism cannot clear the market. Rather, it generates excess demand for the undervalued, or "cheap," foreign currencies.

This situation can be met temporarily from reserves or by borrowing. But if it persists over a period of years, the country may be forced to seek an alternative to the market mechanism, by resorting to direct exchange control. Although comprehensive exchange control is of only historical interest for the industrial countries, it is very common in the developing areas. On the other hand, the European countries were subject to such controls until late in the 1950s; the persistent deficits were attributed by some experts to structural causes not curable by devaluation. Even in recent years many industrial nations have been subject to varying degrees of mild government controls over capital movement, and disguised forms of control are at times exercised even on current transactions. In the early 1970s, several European countries imposed restrictions on the inflow of capital, especially when it was considered disruptive of domestic monetary conditions (see Chapter 9). The IMF publishes annually *A Report on Exchange Restrictions* giving a country-by-country account of existing regulations.

In Figure 7-1, French francs are represented as the home currency while

Figure 7-1

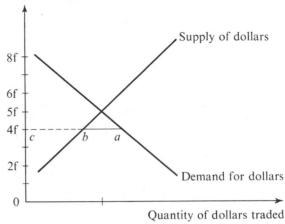

Price of foreign currency (dollar),
in terms of francs

Quantity of dollars traded

foreign currencies are represented by the U.S. dollar. The vertical axis shows the price of one dollar in terms of francs; the horizontal axis indicates the number of dollars traded. Normal supply-and-demand curves for dollars are drawn, the equilibrium price or exchange rate being $1 = 5 francs, or 1 franc = 20¢ This is the price that clears the market. It performs the function of allocating available dollars among competing uses.

Suppose the French government decides to fix the dollar at 4 francs. The dollar will then be *undervalued* compared to its equilibrium price, and the franc, at 25¢ instead of 20¢, will be correspondingly *overvalued* compared to the equilibrium price. This arbitrary exchange rate will not be sustainable for a long period of time, for it creates excess demand for dollars in the amount $\overline{ab}$. If the government refuses to devalue the franc to 20¢, it will be forced to impose exchange control. This makes possible the maintenance of an exchange rate that departs from its equilibrium value. Instead of the market price performing the allocative function, that task is assumed by a government agency. It is that agency that must now determine how to allocate the $\overline{bc}$ available dollars among the larger quantity demanded, $\overline{ac}$.

Under a system of comprehensive exchange control, all earners of foreign currencies must surrender their proceeds to the control authority, be it the central bank or a special division set up in the treasury, while users of such currencies must obtain a government license before engaging in international transactions. This may sound strange to Americans, who are accustomed to exchanging their dollars for any other currency at the bank window without ever needing a license. Most Americans could not imagine their government telling them what they may or may not do with their dollars or how many dollars they may exchange at the border on crossing to Canada or Mexico. This reflects the fortunate experience of inhabitants of the United States. Most other countries have resorted to exchange control at one time or another in their history.

Under an exchange-control system, government officials rather than market forces determine how the available foreign exchange is to be distributed among various goods and services, among sources of supply (supplying countries), and among importers and other users over time. Such decisions are likely to be arbitrary and at times even capricious. Furthermore, since the supply of imported commodities is restricted, their price on the domestic market rises with the imposition of controls. The importers therefore realize more profit per unit than they would have enjoyed in the absence of exchange restrictions. Thus, the foreign exchange license itself assumes a considerable market value, inviting corruption and fraud on the part of the officials issuing the licenses. On occasions, governments practicing exchange control have auctioned import licenses.

☐ An illustration can show the extent of price increase and the consequent monopoly profit. Assume that the Belgian government imposes exchange control and decides to restrict the number of dollars spent on imported automobiles to one-half the free market amount. Since Belgium does not produce cars, the supply-and-demand curves in Figure 7-2 refer to imports. (The sup-

Figure 7-2

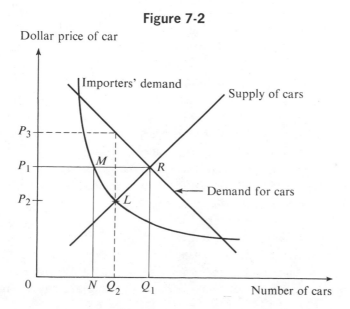

ply curve facing a small country would be horizontal.) Free market price P_1 is established, Q_1 cars being imported at total dollar expenditures of $0P_1RQ_1$. This is the amount that the control authority decides to cut in half. In other words, importers would be allowed to spend only $0P_1MN$ dollars.

□ While the consumer demand curve remains unchanged, the importers' demand curve now diverges from it, because it is governed by the amount of foreign exchange allocation. What characterizes the new importers' demand curve is that the area under it (total dollar expenditures, or price times quantity) is fixed at $0P_1MN$. Such demand conditions are represented by a rectangular hyperbola passing through point M. This curve intersects the foreign-supply function at point L. Thus, the quantity imported is reduced to Q_2 and the import price is set at P_2. Total dollar cost is $0P_2LQ_2$ and is equal to the official allocation.

□ But the demand of domestic consumers has not changed. Quantity Q_2 will command price P_3 on the internal market, $P_3 - P_2$ being the importers' monopoly profit per car. Clearly, the less elastic the local demand is for the product, the higher the profit will be.   ■

Exchange control can be used as a device for limiting commodity imports in much the same way that tariffs or quotas limit imports. It makes little difference whether the authorities restrict the number of cars that may enter the country or limit the quantity of foreign exchange allocated for automobile imports. In either case, the domestic automobile industry obtains protection and the balance-of-payments position improves. An exchange-control system is more effective for dealing with the balance of payments, however, because it encompasses all transactions, including services and capital movement, while tariffs and quotas are restricted to commodity trade. Also, the focus and intent of exchange control is usually to maintain external balance, while that of tariffs is to offer protection to domestic industry from foreign competition.

A government may wish at times to place under control only capital transfers, not current transactions. This was indeed the original intent of exchange control when it was introduced in Europe in the 1930s. The IMF charter permits the imposition of exchange control only to combat severe capital outflow, because under certain conditions, direct control may be the only way to combat speculative flight of short-term funds. Such limited exchange control may succeed as a temporary device, but capital transfers can generally take place under the disguise of regular transactions, thereby evading the regulations. Exporters underbill the foreign importers and instruct them to deposit the difference in a foreign bank account, while importers overpay the foreign exporters, with the difference deposited abroad. It is also easy to see that, like any other rationing system, exchange control generates a black market. That partial evasion by commodity traders gives rises to an undeclared supply of foreign currencies was just illustrated. On the other side of the market are potential users of foreign exchange, such as travelers, who are denied an allocation by the control authority and are willing to pay a higher price than the official exchange rate. They constitute the demand side of the equation. Thus, foreign currencies are traded at a higher price in terms of the domestic currency than the official rate.

From an economic standpoint, exchange control and the attendant rationing of foreign exchange often result in misallocation of resources. Market prices no longer indicate priorities concerning what or how much is needed by producers and desired by consumers. Nor is there a guarantee that the arbitrary decisions of government officials will conform to these priorities.

Furthermore, in attempting to promote exports with an overvalued currency, governments often resort to a *multiple exchange-rate* system that further distorts the structure of the economy (in addition to being complicated to administer). If the official value of the pound is £1 = $4, the British government may place the commodities whose export it desires to encourage and those who import it wishes to discourage at a lower rate of, say, £1 = $3. This amounts to (partial) devaluation of the pound with respect to the specified commodities, for they are traded at a lower exchange value. Exporters obtain one-third more pounds for their foreign-currency proceeds, while importers must pay more pounds for the dollars that they need to buy the merchandise— precisely the same as under devaluation.

Government may adopt a more discriminatory approach and introduce a whole array of exchange rates, with commodities classified according to the degree of encouragement or discouragement attached to their exportation and importation, respectively. By shifting commodities among the various exchange rates, the government has the virtual decision-making power on what is exported and imported. And in an open economy, which is highly dependent on foreign trade, the government can also determine the structure of investments and production by giving hidden subsidies to certain investment goods (through the exchange rate). These decisions do not usually coincide with what is dictated by consideration of comparative advantage (see Chapter 11).

It might be mentioned incidentally that many types of interference with free trade and payments are tantamount to partial and disguised forms of devaluation. Assume that a country tries to combat an external deficit by levying import taxes and providing export subsidies, both to the extent of 10 percent. In terms of government revenue these may roughly balance each other out to effect neutrality. But their effect is really to make imports more expensive and at the same time to cheapen exports—precisely the effect of a 10 percent devaluation. Whereas devaluation affects all balance-of-payments items, however, including service and capital transactions, the trade measures apply only to merchandise.

In general, imports can be discouraged by a whole maze of trade restrictions and exchange controls while exports are encouraged by offering to exchange the foreign-currency proceeds for domestic currency at a more favorable rate, by arranging for cheaper raw materials for the producers of export goods, and by engaging an array of similar measures. Many underdeveloped countries suffer from elaborate systems of control that replace the simple market mechanism and leave a large measure of latitude to government officials in making arbitrary decisions. The result frequently is gross misallocation of resources, which radically distorts the structure of trade, investments, and production and hampers the development process. Overt devaluation quite often comes to replace this disguised devaluation when the controls become so cumbersome as to be unmanageable.

Bilateral Clearing Agreements

If a country is completely devoid of foreign-currency holdings, or nearly so, and still wishes to stimulate private trade, it may impose barter-trade conditions on individual traders. In other words, it may permit an importer to import only if he can team up with a local exporter of some product, who would be paid by the importer in local currency. But this is a rather cumbersome procedure.

To avoid the problems of such barter trade and still stimulate trade, nations use exchange-clearing agreements. These were introduced on a large scale in Europe immediately following World War II, when countries lacked foreign currencies with which to finance foreign trade. Such agreements are designed to permit trade by a multitude of exporters and importers working independently of each other but without the transfer of foreign exchange. A typical agreement between countries A and B would work as follows: Each country's central bank establishes an account for transactions with the other country, as illustrated in Figure 7-3. A's importers from B pay their own currency into B's account, while exporters to B draw payments from the same account. Likewise, B's importers from A make payment in their own currency into A's account in their central bank, while exporters to A are paid out of the same account. If the bilateral trade position balances over the month, then the two accounts will show zero balances. Trade between the two countries is

Figure 7-3

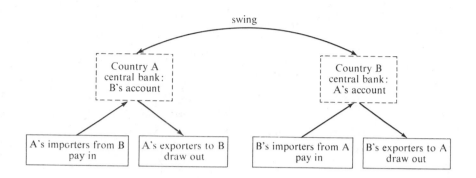

reduced to its barter essentials, and no currency changes hands to finance it.

But complications arise if trade is out of balance. Suppose country A has a surplus with country B and then A's exporters to B draw more out of B's account (in A's central bank) than A's importers pay into it, leaving the account in deficit. Conversely, A's account in B's central bank shows a surplus, for if B has a deficit with A, its importers pay into their account more than B's exporters draw out of it. B could pay up its deficit by transferring the accumulated surplus to A, but that would involve transfer of foreign exchange, which is what the whole system was set up to avoid. Instead, the two countries agree in advance on a mutual line of credit, known as the swing (since it can shift directions), up to a predetermined level. Only if the cumulative deficits exceed the limit is the debtor country obligated to pay up in gold or dollars.

A network of four hundred such agreements covered Western Europe immediately after World War II, as every nation had bilateral agreements with each of the other countries. (These were invariably superimposed upon an exchange-control system.) The economic implications of these agreements derive from the reaction of the participating countries to possible imbalances. In order to avoid paying foreign currencies, deficit country B might halt purchases from its surplus counterpart A and encourage sales there, before the limit of the swing is reached. In fact, much before that point, surplus country A is likely to take action. For, within the limits agreed upon, A is obligated to extend credit to B even if its overall position (with respect to all countries) is weak. Country A cannot use its surplus with B to pay up deficits to other countries C, D, and E. It must grant credit to B, even when A has a deficit with all its trading partners combined. Consequently, A would try to curtail the surplus as soon as it appeared, by encouraging purchases and discouraging sales to B regardless of prices.

The economic implications of this action are adverse on two counts. The volume of trade is reduced to the lowest common denominator. And, since exchange of services is hardly ever covered by the agreement, service and capital transactions are both reduced to a bare minimum. Equally important, the pattern or direction of trade is no longer governed by comparative advantage, as is the case if each trader sells where it is most expensive and buys where it is cheapest. Rather, trade is channeled into lines dictated by the need for bilateral balancing of the accounts. Relative prices in various sources and destinations are relegated to a secondary role, as buyer and seller alike follow government directives concerning their trading partners.

A network of such agreements is an administrative nightmare to finance ministers. Because a surplus with one country cannot be used to pay up a deficit with another, ministers must worry about bilateral balancing of numerous external accounts rather than about one overall position. This leads to some conceptual distinctions often employed in international finance.

Concepts of Currency Convertibility

A currency is considered *fully convertible* if its holders can convert it freely (without government license) to any other currency regardless of either the purpose of conversion or the identity of the holder. The two qualifications provide the distinctions for case of partial convertibility. A currency can be convertible for current transactions but subject to government controls with respect to capital transfers. This is known as *current account convertibility* and was adopted by many European countries in the 1950s as a first step toward full convertibility. A more important distinction (employed on a different plane) relates to the holder of the currency. When a country imposes exchange control, its currency becomes *nonconvertible to its own residents*. But once payment is made to a foreign person or corporation under license by the control authority, the foreigner is free to use it anywhere and convert it to any other currency. In other words, the currency is convertible when held by nonresidents of the country concerned. Such nonresident convertibility disappears if the country enters upon bilateral clearing agreements in addition to exchange control. In our example, the currency of B could not be used by A's citizens (nonresidents of B) to settle deficits with third countries. Since the verdict against bilateralism is more severe than that against exchange control, the attainment of nonresident convertibility was an important step in the European drive toward full convertibility. Table 7-1 summarizes the three possible types of restrictions on currency transfers among countries.

Table 7-1

Effects of Restrictions on Currency Convertibility

Partial convertibility	Comprehensive exchange control	Exchange control with bilateral agreements
Currency inconvertible for capital transactions	Currency convertible for nonresidents only	Currency inconvertible for all transactions for both residents and nonresidents

It is worth noting that, even under the tightest and most comprehensive control discussed here, actual transactions are still in the hands of private traders. The ultimate degree of government intervention is state trading, in which all international trade is conducted by government corporations or trading authorities. This practice is universally adhered to by the Eastern bloc countries.

The European Payments Union (EPU)

How was convertibility attained in post–World War II Europe? The European economy emerged from the war with its productive capacity destroyed, and the network of bilateral clearing agreements is what made possible any trade at all. As an immediate objective, the European countries, organized in the OEEC,[1] wished to attain nonresident convertibility within Europe. This was achieved by the European Payments Union (EPU), which functioned from 1950 to 1958.

Assume that Western Europe consists of three countries, all having exchange-clearing agreements with each other. At the end of each month of transactions they bring their accounts to the central agent for clearing,[2] with the results shown in Figure 7-4 (arrows show the direction of total debts). These figures can be netted out on a bilateral basis with the following results:

Country A	*Country B*	*Country C*
Owes B: 10	Owed by A: 10	Owes A: 5
Owed by C: 5	Owes C: 6	Owed by B: 6

[1] The Organization for European Economic Cooperation was designed to coordinate the reconstruction efforts under the Marshall Plan; it later became the Organization for Economic Cooperation and Development (OECD) with the United States, Canada, Australia, and Japan joining in.

[2] The "agent" in the case of the EPU was the Bank for International Settlement (BIS) in Basel, Switzerland. It was established after World War I to facilitate the transfer of reparations. Today the BIS is used as an instrument of consultation and cooperation among the world's central bankers.

Figure 7-4

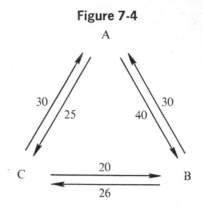

In our hypothetical example, country A has a deficit of 5, while B and C show surpluses of 4 and 1, respectively, but these surpluses do not relieve the two countries of worry. In the absence of nonresident convertibility, B cannot use its surplus with A to pay C, nor can C use its surplus with B to pay A. Each country must concern itself with many bilateral positions, not with its overall balance. The EPU eliminated such anxieties by offering its members unlimited clearing facilities. Instead of owing money to each other, they could shift their debts and credit to the EPU, and all accounts were brought to settlement with the EPU (see Figure 7-5). In the context of our example, the net accounts of Figure 7-5 are reduced to the following magnitudes:

Net positions within Europe

A	−5
B	+4
C	+1

In other words, because of the opportunity for unlimited clearing, member countries can now concentrate on their overall position within Europe and

Figure 7-5

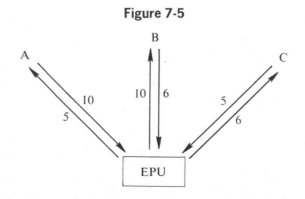

need not concern themselves with a multitude of bilateral accounts. Lest the reader be misled by the smallness of the differences between this tabulation and the preceding one, it should be pointed out that it is a highly oversimplified example. In actual postwar Europe, each of eighteen countries had bilateral agreements with seventeen other countries, so that the net position of each member was a result of 17, not 2, bilateral accounts. Thus the salutory effect of the clearing mechanism is much larger than the example indicates.

A second provision of the EPU was automatic credit. Each member had a quota[3] interpreted as a reference number rather than as a financial contribution. Initially, creditor countries were obligated to extend credit to the EPU amounting to 50 percent of their surpluses, the balance being received in gold or dollars. Debtor countries received full automatic credit of up to 20 percent of their quotas. Beyond that, a sliding scale was agreed upon, with an increasing proportion of the cumulative deficits being paid in gold or dollars. The EPU itself was endowed with a sizable grant from the Marshall Plan to meet deficits.

The main shortcoming of the EPU was that it was restricted to Europe. Creditor countries had an incentive to discriminate in favor of purchases inside the EPU while encouraging exports to non-EPU countries in order to avoid granting automatic credits. Likewise, a member country in an overall balance-of-payments equilibrium consisting of a surplus with the EPU area and an equal deficit with the dollar area could not declare nonresident convertibility (vis-à-vis the world as a whole) because it had to extend credit to the EPU. It is for this reason that the payment rules were gradually revised, reducing the automatic credit component. In 1958, member countries felt sufficiently strong to introduce nonresident convertibility.

Having met its original objective, the EPU was dismantled at the end of 1958 and replaced by another instrument of regional cooperation, the European Monetary Agreement (EMA). The EMA contains provisions for limited financial assistance, but, except for the very short run, such aid is discretionary and not granted automatically.[4]

---

[3] The quota amounted to 15 percent of the country's trade with the EPU areas in 1949, the year before EPU was set up.

[4] Although trade among industrial countries is now financed by transfers of largely convertible currencies, transactions with communist or underdeveloped countries often necessitate barter arrangements. An exchange of Iranian oil for Czechoslovakian power generating stations is a case in point, and a barter of Yugoslavian railroad cars for New Zealand butter is another. More complicated cases arise when there is nothing in the buyer's country that the seller wants. In a typical instance, an American exporter sold some used tiremaking machinery in Eastern Europe for a very attractive price but in a nonconvertible currency. Because of a surplus in a trade agreement between the buying country and Turkey, the money could be used to buy Turkish lira and, with those funds, Turkish chromium. The chromium, in turn, was sold in a fourth country for hard currency.

Historical Survey

In order to place the current international financial scene in proper perspective, it is useful to survey one hundred years of European financial history. If it accomplishes nothing else, such an overview will demonstrate the extent to which present problems are rooted in the more distant past. The century is divided into several periods, distinguished on the basis of major financial events. The dates should be taken as rough approximations rather than precise demarcation points.

The Gold Standard (1870–1914)

These are the years described in economics textbooks as the golden age of the gold standard. Most currencies were pegged either to gold or to a currency (mainly sterling) that was itself on the gold standard (in a manner described in Chapter 3). London was the main financial center of the world. Although exchange-rate adjustments were not unheard of, there was a core of major European currencies whose exchange rates were kept completely fixed. This was allegedly accomplished by the central bankers adhering strictly to the "rules of the game" in their domestic monetary policies (fiscal policies of any kind were not commonly in use). They deflated in times of external deficit and inflated in times of surplus, thereby reinforcing the automatic effects of imbalances on the domestic money supply. (If a central bank pursues reverse policies, contracting during a surplus and expanding in time of deficit, it offsets the automatic tendencies. Such action is therefore known as "offsetting" or "neutralizing" policy.) The attainment and maintenance of external balance was the paramount concern of policy-makers, and domestic stabilization needs were at best secondary in importance. In other words, domestic economic conditions were manipulated to the extent necessary to maintain external equilibrium.

Several factors helped this endeavor. Unlike today, prices and wages were flexible in a downward direction as well as upward. Thus, by deflating the economy in times of deficit, the price and income mechanisms both exerted a powerful balancing pressure. Prices in the deficit country could actually decline while those in the surplus country increased. Consequently, large changes in relative prices in the desired direction could be attained under fixed exchange rates.

Also, wage–price flexibility took some of the sting out of contractionary policies, because a large component of their total effect was on prices rather than income and employment. It will be recalled that the equation of exchange, $MV = PO$, is an identity that holds at all times. It states that the money value (price times volume) of the country's total production of goods and services (GNP) is equal to the money people spend on them, for in fact the two magnitudes are two sides of the same coin. In other words: volume times price equals spending. If total spending on goods and services in the economy declines because of contractionary policies, the impact can be felt either on the price level or on the volume of output (and therefore employment) or on both. To the extent that prices are flexible, variations in them can absorb part of the impact, and the painful effect on output and employment is thereby mitigated. This flexibility must have made central banks during that period more willing than they are now to accept the domestic consequences of the rules of the game whenever they were faced with inconsistent situations defined in Chapter 4. Even so, recent historical research has brought into question the extent to which countries actually followed these "rules."

Furthermore, Europe was at that time reasonably free of direct government controls over trade and payments in the form of import quotas and exchange controls. Even tariffs, although common, did not vary much over the years. Consequently, the price mechanism was permitted to function almost freely in the international arena and exert its stabilizing influence.

Finally, capital movements were generally stabilizing in nature. They responded swiftly to positive interest differentials, making it easy for a country to bridge short-term balance-of-payments deficits by raising interest rates. Even the flow of long-term investment capital and the return flows of repatriated earnings were allegedly timed to suit the needs of the balance of payments.

The gold standard was brought to an abrupt end by World War I. The ravages of war and the differential rates of inflation in various countries destroyed the underlying price–cost relationships on which the prewar exchange rates had been based. For lack of a better alternative, many currencies were left to fluctuate freely as the war ended.

Fluctuating Exchange Rates (1918–23)

Under the system that emerged from World War I, major currencies were not pegged to gold or to each other but were left to fluctuate in response to demand-and-supply conditions. Some of them fluctuated violently. But the arrangement was not viewed as permanent. It was considered to be an interlude until conditions stabilized and countries could go back to the gold standard. Despite the fact that cost and price ratios changed radically during World War I, it was considered a matter of national prestige by every country to restore its prewar parity.

Currency Stabilization (1923–28)

One country after another returned to the gold standard at the prewar exchange rate. The British pound, for example, was stabilized at $5. This was done by unilateral action on the part of the countries concerned; international cooperation, so vitally necessary in these matters, was totally lacking. For the now overvalued currencies, this action contained the seeds of further disturbances. It brought a strain to the balance of payments as well as to domestic economies, which had to bear the brunt of the adjustment process.

The "Devaluation Cycle" (1930–35)

Several countries yielded to pressure and went off the gold standard. The pound sterling in particular became a freely fluctuating currency in 1930. Since the fluctuations were at times violent, a special agency was established in 1931 to help smooth them out. Known as the British Exchange Equalization Account (BEEA),[5] it was to operate secretly in the marketplace by buying and selling foreign and domestic financial assets. If the pound became unduly weak because of the outflow of speculative funds, the BEEA was supposed to offset that trend by buying pounds. An opposite step was to be taken in times of inflow of speculative funds. In addition, through operations in government bonds, the BEEA was supposed to neutralize the effect of short-term capital movements on the domestic money supply. On the other hand, it was not to interfere with long-run trends; that is, with exchange fluctuations resulting from underlying market conditions as reflected in trade in goods and services and long-term capital flows. Its purpose was to moderate but not to eliminate exchange variations. However, some other countries accused it of deliberately depressing the long-run value of the pound to gain competitive advantage.

Other countries, primarily those of the Sterling Area, followed the British example and pegged their currencies to the fluctuating sterling. It was through this action that the Sterling Area first assumed a formal economic status. In most cases devaluations were taken at that time either to bridge balance-of-payments deficits or to help decrease domestic unemployment by raising exports and lowering imports. Since this was done at the expense of the country's trading partners, it was subject to retaliation by competitive devaluation.

Not all countries devalued. The French led a small group of nations that remained on gold at the previous exchange rates and became known as the "gold bloc." France chose to tackle the resulting balance-of-payments deficits by imposing import quotas. Thus, the first time an import quota was used by a major power, it was for the purpose of dealing with balance-of-payments deficits rather than for protection. Germany, on the other hand, imposed exchange control to avoid devaluation and subsequently used its control system to manipulate international power politics. The pound sterling, the franc, and the dollar became the major convertible currencies.

---

[5] Other countries operated similar agencies called exchange stabilization funds, but they were much less successful than the British.

The Tripartite Agreement (1936–39)

As the 1930s approached their midpoint, the pressure on the overvalued franc grew so severe that the French decided to devalue it. To avoid foreign retaliation they commenced negotiations with the United States and England designed to secure cooperation and in particular to obtain a promise that the sterling and the dollar would not be devalued. The resulting tripartite declaration, subsequently adhered to by four additional countries, permitted France to devalue without retaliation and ushered in a period of informal cooperation in international finance—the only such period between the two world wars. Cooperation was short lived, however, being abruptly interrupted by World War II, during which most combatants imposed exchange control. The British operated a "dollar pool," through which they centralized and controlled the dollar dealings of the entire Sterling Area.

Bretton Woods (July 1944)

Immediately after the war, delegates of forty-four nations held a conference in Bretton Woods, New Hampshire, to discuss pressing economic problems. The painful lessons of the 1930s were not lost on the participants, so, unlike the post–World War I period, the aftermath of World War II was characterized by cooperation in international financial matters. Because there had actually been no system functioning since the breakdown of the gold standard, there was a widespread desire to restore fixed exchange rates. But it was also widely recognized that the rules of the game would have to be compromised to some extent, as countries now wished to accord a relatively higher priority to domestic stabilization.

Two plans for an international monetary system were considered at the conference: the British plan authored by Keynes and the American plan of Harry White. Keynes was concerned about the excessive reliance on bilateral payments after the war and about the deflationary bias imparted to the international economy when the responsibility of adjustment rests primarily with deficit countries. He therefore proposed the creation of an international clearing union with unlimited opportunity for clearing of balances, large automatic credit provisions, and the ability to create international reserves (that is, a sort of international EPU). Also, the code of behavior he proposed placed much of the responsibilities of adjustment on the shoulders of the surplus countries.

What emerged from Bretton Woods, the International Monetary Fund (IMF), was akin to the White plan presented on behalf of the American delegation. In fact, the conferees agreed to set up two sister institutions: The

International Bank for Reconstruction and Development (IBRD), which was to help in European reconstruction and later serve as an instrument for financing economic development, and the IMF, which was to become the central international financial institution. The IMF, which is a fund and not a clearing union, provided the framework and determined the ground rules and code of behavior for the postwar financial system. It also serves as an instrument of cooperation and mutual assistance. Since the features of the Bretton Woods system were discussed in Chapter 3, and the IMF will be further analyzed in Chapter 8, there is no need to dwell on it here.

European Reconstruction and Intense Dollar Shortages (1945–50)

The years 1945–50 witnessed intense reconstruction efforts in Europe, with the outpouring of American aid first under the Anglo-American loan agreement and then under the Marshall Plan. Intra-European trade, such as it was, was conducted through a network of bilateral clearing agreements. The continent was starved for dollars, because the United States was the only source of plant and equipment as well as consumer goods. So intense was the dollar shortage that prominent economists suggested that it might become a permanent feature of the financial scene, in defiance of all theoretical expectations. Indeed, it was impossible to believe at the time that twenty years later the shortage would turn into "dollar glut" or at least "dollar adequacy."

The European Payments Union (1950–58)

The EPU was established in 1950 and functioned in Europe until convertibility was restored in 1958. The fact that the European Common Market (see Chapter 16) came into being in the same year is no coincidence, for it makes little sense to set up a common market for the purpose of freeing trade among nations while foreign payments remain restricted and subject to government control. (Regional clearing unions patterned after the EPU are being tried or planned in other areas of the world, such as Central America.)

The "Dollar Glut" (1959–68)

In 1958, the American press became painfully aware of the fact that the United States was running a deficit on its balance of international payments. Although such deficits had occurred in most years of that decade, the problem became acute in the late 1950s for two reasons: First, the average size of the annual deficit rose from $1 billion to $3 billion dollars during the 1950s. Second, whereas European countries had been perfectly content to hold dollar assets and treat them as international reserves, they began to feel saturated with dollar reserves toward the end of the decade and demanded conversion into gold, the more traditional reserve asset.[6]

As the U.S. deficits persisted in the 1960s with foreign countries accumulating (often unwillingly) ever-increasing amounts of dollar assets, the Adminstration attempted to cope with the problem by administrative measures. American tourists were faced with a reduction in the duty-free allowance on goods they brought back to the United States. Foreign aid was tied more closely to purchases in the United States, and efforts were increased to induce our European allies to spend money in the United States for armaments and other purposes and also to accelerate their debt payment to the United States. Congress eliminated the federal gold reserve requirement for all domestic currency except notes, in order to free our gold for foreign transactions, and the Department of Commerce embarked on an export promotion program that includes commercial exhibitions abroad, government guarantees of domestic and foreign bank loans to help finance American exports, exhortation of potential exporters, and the like.

In an attempt to discourage European companies from raising capital in New York, a tax has been imposed on American purchases of European securities. It is known as the *interest-equalization tax,* for in the mid-1960s (when European interest rates were above their American counterparts) it was supposed to equalize the cost of raising funds in the United States and in Europe. The Treasury issued bonds denominated in foreign currencies (known as "Roosa bonds") to be held by foreign central bankers. The exchange-rate guarantee implied in them was designed to discourage foreign central banks from cashing their dollars for gold. And there have been attempts to manipulate the interest-rate structure by raising short-term rates to attract short-term funds to the United States, while at the same time maintaining low long-term interest rates to encourage domestic investment ("Operation Twist"). Finally, the main brunt of government policy was to directly restrict American corporate investments in Europe and limit American bank loans to European borrowers. These controls, as well as the interest-equalization tax were eliminated at the end of January 1974, in view of the improvement in the U.S. balance of payments.

Were there better alternatives to capital controls in the 1960s? Although there were opinions to the contrary,[7] there was considerable evidence of a

---

[6] Some scholars argue that the financial world entered the "crisis zone" when U.S. gold reserves declined below the level of foreign official dollar holdings—in other words, when it became impossible for the United States to meet its obligation to convert foreign official dollar holdings into gold.

[7] For example, Professors Depres, Kindleberger, and Salant held the view that the U.S. deficits were merely a reflection of the role of the dollar as financial intermediary: The United States exports long-term capital and imports short-term capital, thereby accumulating long-term foreign assets and short-term foreign liabilities. Europeans do the reverse. This accommodates the fact that Europeans prefer to hold liquid savings but require long-term investments, while Americans exhibit an opposite set of preferences.

decline in the American competitive position relative to Western Europe and Japan. There were numerous reasons for these phenomena. These included the emergence of discriminatory trading blocs in Europe, nontariff barriers to trade, shifts in the commodity composition of world trade away from traditional American exports and toward those of the other industrial countries, and the increased ability of the latter nations to produce and market effectively. But a reason of overriding importance was the tendency for the currencies of the several competitors to be undervalued relative to the dollar.

In the early to middle 1960s this constituted an inconsistent situation in the United States, for it was accompanied by a domestic recession. And the tax-cut measure of the Kennedy Administration, designed to stimulate the economy, could not help but increase the external deficit. At the same time, Japan and certain European countries faced an inconsistent situation of the opposite variety: domestic booms accompanied by large balance-of-payments surpluses.

Under those circumstances there was a need to realign the exchange rates around the world. However, because of this country's unique position in international finance, that could not be done by devaluation of the dollar. For it was rather difficult to devalue a currency that served as the "standard of value" to which all other currencies were pegged. The only possible way to attempt devaluation was to raise the price of gold, but if all other countries followed suit, the value of the dollar in terms of foreign currencies (and this country's competitive position) would not have been affected at all. Even if it had been possible to devalue the dollar, such a step would not necessarily have represented an optimal solution. Many other countries also had external deficits and were closely dependent on the dollar. They would all have been hurt by devaluation, for it would have improved the U.S. competitive position not only against the few surplus countries, but also against the deficit countries.

On the other hand, since the balance-of-payments surpluses (the counterpart of our deficits) were concentrated in a very few countries, such as West Germany and, later, Japan, it was preferable that these currencies be revalued, making their products less competitive on world markets. A revaluation of the West German mark improves the U.S. competitive position against German products both here and abroad. But other deficit countries are also helped, rather than damaged, competitively (precisely the reverse result of dollar devaluation).

Furthermore, and most emphatically, revaluation was in the best interest of the revaluating countries themselves. West Germany, for example, had not only been "suffering" from huge balance-of-payments surpluses reaching almost embarrassing proportions, but was also experiencing a domestic inflationary boom: an "inconsistent" situation the reverse of that faced by the United States in the early 1960s. Exchange revaluation makes imported commodities less expensive; therefore, it would have raised the standard of living of the West German consumers as their mark wages purchased more foreign goods. It also would have helped to bring inflation under control in West Germany. Moreover, since there is a limit to how much reserves a country is likely to need, it did no good for West Germany to go on piling up reserves indefinitely. Accumulation of reserves beyond a certain point simply denies the population the joy of cheaper imports. Revaluation is merely one way of reaping and distributing the fruits of increased productivity throughout the economy.

Beyond this, placing the burden of adjustment on the surplus countries (revaluation) is highly beneficial to the system as a whole. Traditionally that burden has fallen on the deficit countries. As in the case of family finances, it is not the surplus country that comes under pressure to adjust; nearly always it is the deficit country that must do something because it has run out of reserves. But what can the deficit country do? It can apply contractionary policies at home, which may bring about a recession, or it can impose exchange and trade restrictions. Both methods are unpleasant. Indeed, the whole international financial system was discredited in the interwar period because its net effect was deflationary: The burden of adjustment lay mostly on the deficit countries, which needed to contract, and least on the surplus countries, which needed to expand. If surplus countries were to assume more of the responsibility for adjustment, confidence in the system would be restored.

This analysis invites the obvious question: If it was so beneficial all around, why did West Germany resist revaluation for so long? The answer is that two economic groups were vehemently opposed to revaluation: the big export interests, who wished to maintain their competitive position in foreign markets, and the small farmers, who feared the effects of a reduction in the import prices of foreign farm products.

With the mark undervalued, West Germany was running huge balance-of-payments surpluses and piling up many billions of dollars worth of reserves. But such surpluses imply deficits in other countries, producing an unsettling effect on the international currency system as a whole. The undervaluation of the West German mark figured heavily in every financial crisis in the late 1960s: the sterling crisis of November 1967, the dollar–gold crisis of early 1968, and the French franc crisis of November 1968.

In the fall of 1968, following a series of strikes in France, the weakness of the franc and the strength of the mark became so apparent that a sharp crisis resulted on the European financial markets. Among other things it manifested itself in a massive transfer of speculative funds from France and (to a lesser degree) other countries to West Germany. The pressure on West Germany to revalue intensified. But the West Germans preferred to take another, somewhat equivalent, step. They lowered their export subsidies (which were actually tax rebates to exporters on the domestic value-added tax) from 11 percent to 7 percent, thereby impairing the competitive position of their exports, and at the same time they lowered their border import tax from 11 percent to 7 percent, making imports cheaper. This step was equivalent to a 4 percent revaluation with respect only to the commodity component of the balance of payments. Service and capital transactions were not affected, as they would have been under revaluation. The overall effect of this policy was therefore less than a 4 percent revaluation—all too little by most 1968 calculations and certainly inadequate to eliminate the huge surpluses. The West Germans preferred to press the tax-subsidy button because it is a more flexible policy, capable of being reversed by unilateral administrative action. By contrast, reversal of exchange revaluation, should it become necessary, requires IMF approval. Indeed, the tax-subsidy combination was adopted by the West German government only as a temporary measure.

In May 1969, following the resignation of French President de Gaulle, a new crisis developed, forcing an 11 percent devaluation of the franc on August 8. Following the elections in October, the West German government permitted the mark to float for three weeks (a "transitional" float) and then stabilized it at 9 percent above its September level. Accompanying the revaluation was the abolition of the special border-tax provisions of 1968.

Although the adjustments brought exchange rates into line, stability was not assured under fixed exchange rates as long as the major industrial countries were experiencing widely divergent rates of inflation. This was demonstrated in the Western Hemisphere by the position of Canada. During the first five months of 1970, Canada's international reserves increased by $1.2 billion as a result of a large current account surplus as well as a heavy inflow of funds. To stem this trend the government announced on May 31 that it would cease pegging the Canadian dollar at 92.5 U.S. cents. The floating Canadian dollar appreciated in the subsequent weeks. Considering its proximity to, and dependence upon, the giant U.S. economy, a fluctuating rate is probably the best way for Canada to insulate itself from economic disturbances originating south of its border.

By 1970 another important currency had emerged with considerable strength, namely the Japanese yen. Japan's GNP has grown at the amazing annual rate of 10 to 13 percent in real terms. At the same time Japan rolled up trade surpluses of $3.75 billion and $2.5 billion in 1968 and 1969, respectively, while showing annual balance-of-payments surpluses of around $2.25 billion. Along with the mark, the Japanese yen became a major candidate for revaluation early in the 1970s. Throughout the period under discussion, the United States continued to mount sizeable deficits, with Japan and Europe accumulating large dollar reserves. Confidence in the dollar, the cornerstone of the Bretton Woods system, was continuously eroding, a situation that finally led to the drastic measures of 1971–73 (see below).

The Two-Price System of Gold and Creation of SDRs (1968–   )

The introduction of a "two-price system" for gold in 1968, separating official dealings from private dealings in the yellow metal, marked the first step in downgrading the role of gold in international finance. Accompanying this decision of the world's major central bankers was a decision to introduce, beginning in 1970, a new reserve asset into the international monetary system. By mutual consent of its member nations, the International Monetary Fund created the Special Drawing Rights (abbreviated SDRs and often referred to as "paper gold") and distributed them among its members according to pre-assigned quotas. Both steps will be discussed in Chapter 8.

Two Devaluations of the Dollar (August 1971; February 1973)

President Nixon's "New Economic Policy," announced on August 15, 1971, closed the U.S. gold window to foreign central bankers and ushered in a three-month period of freely fluctuating exchange rates. This was followed by widespread exchange-rate realignment and a devaluation of the dollar in December of that year (the Smithsonian Agreement). After fourteen months of turmoil on the international financial markets, a second devaluation of the dollar took place in February 1973.

The Breakdown of Bretton Woods (March 1973)

But the turmoil continued unabated. In March 1973, nine European currencies inaugurated their "joint float" against the dollar. Together with the floating yen and pound sterling, this development made the dollar a floating currency and effectively spelled the end of the Bretton Woods system. A committee of twenty members of the IMF was established to consider the makeup of a new international financial system.

The period since mid-1971 is covered in detail in Chapter 9.

8
Steps Taken to Increase International Liquidity

Earlier chapters have shown that Europe's main source of international reserves following World War II was the U.S. balance-of-payments deficit, until, because of the gradual decline in confidence in the dollar, the international financial community thought it desirable to develop alternative forms of reserves. This chapter surveys the measures undertaken to date in this field. Proposals for future reform in the international monetary system are reserved for Chapter 10. There is some unavoidable overlapping between the two, however. In particular, this chapter includes a discussion of gold policy which is equally suitable for the later chapter.

Ad Hoc Measures

The measures adopted by the international community before March 1968 were of the ad hoc variety. They included consultation,[1] cooperation, and mutual help among central bankers in the form of loans or commitments to extend loans and advances, currency swaps, and assurances of assistance when needed. Since a country considers convertible foreign currency holdings but not its own currency as reserves, currency swaps[2] increase gross (but not net) reserves of the countries involved. Thus the Federal Reserve Bank of New York, acting as an agent of the United States Treasury and the Federal Reserve System in all foreign-exchange operations, maintains a swap network of $18 billion with fourteen other countries and the Bank for International Settlement.

[1] Regular monthly meetings of the central bankers of the Group of Ten are held under the auspices of the Basel-based Bank for International Settlement (BIS).
[2] A swap transaction between two central banks is a current exchange of currencies with a commitment to reverse the exchange in three months at the same exchange rate.

For an example of what can be achieved by cooperation, consider a case in which France develops a deficit while Germany develops a surplus. The effects on gross global reserves may be many and varied, depending on what the central banks do.

1. If Germany demands and receives payments in marks, gross reserves decline, because marks are considered reserves (convertible foreign currency) by France but not by Germany.

2. If Germany accepts payment in francs, global reserves rise, because francs are reserves to Germany but not to France.

3. Should Germany demand and receive payment in U.S. dollars and keep these dollars (or if it receives payment in gold), global reserves remain unchanged; they are merely redistributed. Of course, the distribution of reserves among countries may be as important as their global availability.

4. However, should Germany obtain payment in dollars and then proceed to exchange them for American gold, global reserves decline, for dollars are not reserves to the United States, whereas gold is a reserve asset in both countries. It is thus of crucial importance whether American dollars fall into the hands of countries with a high ratio of gold to total reserves (that is, countries that prefer to hold much of their reserves in gold form) or a low ratio.

This example abundantly illustrates the vital importance of international collaboration. By agreeing among themselves to pursue the "correct" policy, central bankers can affect the global availability of reserves. Often such actions are tantamount to their extending credit to each other.

A high measure of cooperation among central bankers is not only desirable but absolutely essential. However, such agreements as the swap network are merely contingency planning that provides a buffer against possible attacks on currencies. Used ad hoc they do not constitute a machinery for the orderly creation of universally accepted reserve assets. Reserves *owned* by countries do not increase at a given annual rate to meet desired levels and the needs of the system. Rather, countries are invited to *owe* reserve assets to each other if the need should arise. But central bankers appear to have a distinct preference for owned reserves and would like to see such reserves *rise by some given fraction* every year. In the spring of 1968, the world's central bankers took two important steps to strengthen the international monetary system. These related to the treatment of gold and to the creation of additional reserve assets.

Gold Policy

For many generations now, gold—known to chemists and physicists as element 79—has aroused more passion and emotion than any other natural element, such as copper or lead. Witness the comment of William Jennings Bryan in the last century, during the debate over bimetallism, decrying the crucifixion of mankind on a "cross of gold." More recently, humorist Art Buchwald suggested that gold be replaced by moon rocks as a monetary asset. In an opposite vein, General de Gaulle proclaimed in 1968: "A monetary system based on the foundation of gold, which is alone in having a character of immutability, impartiality, and universality, should therefore be applied." Against such a background, it is no wonder that there exists a significant body of professional and political opinion that considers gold more a blessing than a nuisance and favors return to the pure gold standard.

Indeed this is one of the proposals for basic reform in the system. Under it, foreign currencies would be withdrawn from service as a reserve asset and be replaced entirely by gold. A sizable increase in the price of gold in terms of all currencies is proposed to provide the massive infusion of reserves required for this system. This would immediately increase the monetary value of existing gold stocks in the coffers of central banks, thereby adding considerably to reserves. More importantly, a higher price would induce increased mining and attract privately held gold, to an extent sufficient for the maintenance of the gold standard. Some proponents of the return to a pure gold standard argue that such a system would exercise discipline on the domestic policies of nations, inducing them to avoid inflationary measures which lead to balance-of-payments deficits.

The contrary view is that such a system would be wasteful of resources devoted to gold production; that the benefits from gold revaluation would be unevenly distributed, benefiting mainly the countries that hold their reserves in the form of gold rather than those that very much need additional reserves; that sizable revaluations under this system would have to come at periodic intervals, resulting each time in excess liquidity to be "dissipated" gradually as trade expands; and that the reaction of hoarders and speculators to price increases is far from certain, for it depends on their expectations concerning possible further increases in gold prices.

In this view it is desirable to move in precisely the opposite direction and *demonetize gold*—namely, remove it from its position as an international reserve. Although this step may reduce aggregate reserves in the short run, it would eventually make the system more rational. Within domestic economies, this process has been going on for generations. Gold used to be a circulating currency; then it was withdrawn into national reserves for use in settling international imbalances. A final step in the process is suggested. Just as the management of our internal monetary affairs is subject to the discretion of human managers, so can the international system be managed, although the latter requires much cooperation since it is not backed by an international government. Gold is too expensive (in terms of the resources required to dig it up) and too unreliable a reserve item to occupy such a pivotal role in the currency system.

An example of its capriciousness was the "gold rush" of March 1968. That episode was essentially a sudden spurt of speculative demand for gold on the European markets. It resulted from a general decline of confidence in the ability of the United States to maintain the fixed price of gold at $35 an ounce. Gold buyers expected to benefit if the United States was to be forced to raise the dollar price of the metal. Underlying this deterioration of confidence were the recurring deficits in the American balance of international payments with the attendant accumulation of dollar balances in the hands of foreigners, which constituted a potential claim against our gold reserves.

Clearly it was the U.S. commitment to redeem gold at a fixed price (adhered to only by the United States) that made the gold drain possible. As a matter of fact, the dollar was backed up by the huge productive economy of this country, not gold. Without the price guarantee, gold would be just like any other metal whose price is important only to its users and producers, and a run on it would not have made the news headlines. With gold dethroned, an international financial system could be devised that would function better than the gold-exchange standard.

The "gold rush" made it clear to everyone that official action was necessary to clarify the monetary role of gold. To that end, in March of 1968, the central bankers of the ten major industrialized countries met in Washington. One important decision that emerged from that meeting was a step toward demonetizing gold—to separate the private gold market from the official market. These countries abandoned their joint instrument (known as the London Gold Pool) for buying and selling gold at the fixed price of $35 per ounce on the private market. With governments no longer dealing in the private gold market, private hoarders could no longer bleed the U.S Treasury of its cherished gold stock.

In the ensuing five and a half years, central bankers simply used blocks of gold (at a fixed price and without attachment to the private market) to settle imbalances among themselves, by transferring the metal from one pile to another in the vaults of the New York Federal Reserve Bank, where many European countries store part of their gold supply to avoid shipping it across the Atlantic. Gold thus became a mere bookkeeping unit that could readily be replaced by entries in mutually agreeable bookkeeping operations.

On August 15, 1971, the United States announced that it would no longer redeem in gold (at a fixed price) dollar assets held by foreign central banks. This closing of the gold window made the dollar officially no longer convertible to gold. Thus the fact that the official price of gold was raised twice in the ensuing year and a half—to $38 an ounce in December 1971 and to $42.20 an ounce in February 1973 (see Chapter 9)—was of little consequence. In the words of one U.S. Congressman: "What does it matter if we don't sell gold at $35 or we don't sell gold at $42.20 per ounce?" Also, the large increases in the price of gold on the private market in recent years, at times reaching into the $170–180 per ounce range, made no difference to the official gold holdings of the industrial countries.

On November 13, 1973, seven major central banks[3] including the Federal Reserve, decided to end the agreement not to *sell* gold on the private market. The price of gold on the private market continues to be determined by supply and demand, and official transactions in gold continue at the official price of $42.20 per ounce. But the central bankers now have the additional option of selling gold to private holders, which they may exercise at their discretion.

For the United States, this opened up the possibility of disposing of its entire gold stock on the private market while the price was high, thereby soaking up billions of dollars held by foreigners (this could also be viewed as a way of financing oil imports at the new higher prices). This, of course, can only be done very gradually, for the private gold price may plummet in the face of large sales. But once completed, the United States could lead the way in declaring that its currency is no longer anchored to gold in any way, shape, or form. The opportunity for gradually unloading the official gold stock is, of course, open to the other signatory countries, thereby ridding the financial system of the "cross of gold." Once demonetized, gold would be like any other metal whose price is determined on the marketplace and is of interest only to users and producers. Alternatively, gold could be centralized in the IMF, in return for credit entries. There is certainly no need for gold reserves under a system of fluctuating exchange rates. And should the world decide to return to fixed exchange rates, gold can be replaced by reserves created by the IMF, such as SDRs (see below).

Whether the financial leaders of the world would avail themselves of this opportunity is debatable. Unfortunately, gold still holds a mystical attraction for the minds of men, and tradition-bound central bankers may be loath to dispense with it altogether.[4] But even with the existing official gold stock of $43 billion (of which $36 billion is held by the industrial countries), supplementary sources of reserves may be considered necessary *should fixed exchange rates be restored*. This brings us to the second decision taken by the Group of Ten in March 1968.

---

[3] Belgium, Germany, Italy, the Netherlands, Switzerland, the United Kingdom, and the United States.

[4] In mid-1974, the main central bankers agreed that a country in need (Italy was the first candidate) can secure foreign loans and pledge its gold stock as collateral, at a price close to the market price of the metal. And the Common Market nations expressed a desire to trade gold among themselves at a similar price.

Special Drawing Rights

The assembled central bankers decided to create a new reserve asset, to be known as Special Drawing Rights (SDRs). (These were immediately dubbed "paper gold.") Clearly the most direct route in creating a new reserve asset lies within the framework of an existing organization, such as the International Monetary Fund, but the original charter of the IMF prevented if from becoming a reserve-creating institution. To see this requires an explanation of how the IMF functions.

Regular International Monetary Fund Procedures

There are 126 member countries in the IMF, of which the Group of Ten are the most important in terms of the volume of their international payments and their voting power within the organization. Each member country is assigned a quota, of which it must contribute to the IMF 25 percent in gold and 75 percent in its own currency. (The quota is based on a rather complicated formula that need not be elaborated here.) In turn, the quota determines the voting power of each member as well as the amount of loans it is eligible to receive. The initial resources of the IMF consisted of 25 percent in gold and 75 percent in holdings of a variety of currencies.

Loans granted by the Fund to member countries require approval by the Board of Directors. Furthermore, the loans are given to a country in a specific foreign currency in exchange for an equivalent amount of the borrowing country's own currency. If, for example, France desires supplementary resources, it applies for a loan in the currency it needs, say German marks. If the loan is approved, the Fund provides the marks in return for an equivalent amount of French francs. Thus the Fund does not really make loans in the conventional sense of the word; it sells currencies. The French *purchase* German marks with French francs, and that is the official term used by the Fund for all borrowing activities. When the French wish to repay the loan, they *repurchase* their own currency from the Fund for gold or for such currencies as are acceptable to the Fund at the time.

There are limits to how much a country can "borrow" from the Fund, and these are expressed in terms of how much of a given currency the Fund is permitted to accumulate. If the French continue to borrow from the Fund, that means that they continue to purchase foreign currencies with French francs, which in turn implies that the Fund is accumulating francs. The IMF may do this only to the point at which its franc holdings reach 200 percent of the French quota. Since its initial holdings were 75 percent of the French quota, the total advance that can be made to France in foreign currencies is limited to

125 percent of the French quota. In addition, not more than 25 percent can be drawn in any one year. The same rules apply to all other countries.

It is easy to see that cumulative purchases of a given currency (in this example, the mark), from the IMF would deplete the Fund's holdings of that currency. When these holdings fall below 75 percent of that country's quota, its currency becomes acceptable to the Fund for repayment (repurchase) purposes. It also makes that country eligible for larger future drawings on other currencies, because it increases the shortfall of the Fund's holdings from the 200 percent of quota limit. The fact that in recent years the Fund's holdings of dollars exceeded 75 percent of the American quota has made the dollar ineligible for repurchase purposes. Since many countries owned mainly dollar reserves and wished to use them to make repayments, they had to cash in their dollars for gold to acquire an asset acceptable to the Fund. This created additional pressure on the U.S. gold stock.

In mid-1973, it was mainly the yen and the continental currencies that were acceptable to the Fund for repurchase purposes, with the Fund's holdings of marks at 32 percent of the German quota and its holdings of yen at 54 percent of the Japanese quota. By contrast, the IMF held dollars and pounds at 94 and 96 percent, respectively, of the U.S. and British quotas.

If the Fund runs out of a currency altogether—something that has not happened thus far—that currency can be declared "scarce," permitting other countries to discriminate against it.

Returning to the borrowing country of our example, France, we see that all loans from the Fund are not automatic. Indeed, the larger the cumulative drawings are, the greater the Fund's holdings of francs and the more difficult it becomes for the French to obtain additional loans. Specifically, the 125 percent of quota in total potential drawings is divided into 5 *tranches* (slices) of 25 percent each. The first one is known as the *gold tranche,* since it equals the country's original gold contribution to the Fund. The subsequent four slices are known as the *credit tranches.* Advances within the gold tranche are automatic, as is the right to draw on any credit balance that the country may have built up by having its own currency drawn upon.

Any drawings beyond that are subject to the discretionary decision of the Fund, which may extract pledges from the borrowing country in return for the loan.[5] These pledges usually concern policies to be undertaken by the country to put its international payments situation in order. For example, in return for a half-billion-dollar draw on the IMF in 1969, the British government submitted to the Fund a letter of intent to hold domestic credit expansion to $960

---

[5] The Fund's interest charges, which are levied on any drawings beyond the gold tranche, also increase with the rise in cumulative drawings. In addition to interest, there is a service charge on each transaction and standby commitment.

million for the fiscal year ending April 1970 (compared to $2.9 billion in the previous year) and to strive for a balance-of-payments surplus of three-quarters of a billion dollars. This commitment created quite a stir in the House of Commons.

The automatic-drawing component constitutes the country's reserve position in the Fund. At any given moment, this equals 25 percent of its quota minus its previous drawing plus previous drawings made by other countries on the Fund's holdings of its currency.[6] In other words, a country's reserve position in the IMF is the shortfall in the Fund's holdings of the currency from 100 percent of the country's quota. Even the automatic drawings carry an obligation to repay, usually within three to five years.

Since the gold tranche is equal to the original gold contribution of the member nation, these drawings do not constitute a net increase in reserves. Thus the net effect on global reserves of any increase in the Fund's quotas is at best zero. In particular this applies to the 50 percent general increase in the Fund quotas that took place in 1959, the 25 percent increase in 1966, and a 35 percent increase in the early 1970s—increases that elevated total quotas to $28.9 billion, of which the American share is $6.9 billion. In fact, every increase in quotas brought forth new demand for U.S. gold, because IMF members must make new gold deposits with the Fund. And special bookkeeping arrangements had to be made (between the United States and the Fund) to prevent at least the unfavorable psychological effects of this depletion.

By the late 1960s both the quota positions of some major countries and the Fund's holdings of various strong currencies declined to such a point that any major lending operation necessitated rather complicated transactions. As an example, observe France's drawing on the IMF in September 1969, under its postdevaluation *standby agreement* with the Fund. Under such an arrangement, frequently entered upon by the IMF, the Fund undertakes to sell currencies to the country up to a certain maximum sum and during a fixed period, *should the need arise*. These measures are usually taken in conjunction with devaluation or some internal stabilization policies, and they are designed to assure the country of foreign exchange to fall back on in case of need. The purchase of thirteen currencies totaling the equivalent of $985 million was authorized for France, of which $410 million was to come from the Fund's holdings, $375 million from borrowing from five members under the General Agreement to Borrow, and $200 million from gold sales.

---

[6] Suppose the country's quota is $200,000; its gold tranche would then be $50,000. If its drawings on the Fund amounted to $40,000 while other countries purchased $30,000 of its currency from the Fund, its reserve position would be $40,000 ($50,000 − $40,000 + $30,000). The Fund's holding of its currency would be $160,000, or $40,000 short of 100 percent of its quota.

Special Drawing Rights Procedures

An increase in international liquidity could be accomplished only by making advances within one or more of the credit tranches automatic, which required revision of the IMF charter. In a sense this is the essence of the Special Draw-ing Rights (SDRs), which can be regarded as a natural extension of the regu-lar IMF operating procedures. The IMF membership decided to create a $10 billion special IMF quota to which different rules would apply. These were distributed to the membership in three installments during 1970–72, the allocation being proportional to their regular IMF quota. Thus the United States received roughly 25 percent of the total, and the six original Com-mon Market members combined, over 17 percent.[7] The industrial countries combined received nearly two-thirds of the total allocation. All SDR opera-tions are administered by a special drawing account at the IMF. Each unit of SDR was originally defined in terms of gold to equal one 1970 dollar. But fol-lowing the devaluations of the dollar in 1971–73 (see next chapter), each unit became worth about $1.20. In mid-1974 the IMF adopted a new valua-tion system for the SDRs, one better suited for an era of fluctuating ex-change rates: SDR value is calculated daily as the weighted average value of a "basket" of 16 representative currencies,[8] rather than in terms of gold or dollars. Transactions in SDRs and other vital economic statistics of IMF mem-bers are reported monthly in the IMF's *International Financial Statistics*.

For explanation, let us return to the French and German example and as-sume that each of the two countries receives an allocation of $100 per basic period in SDRs.[9] The allocation is executed by making credit entries for each country on the ledger of the special drawing account, and the country makes no contribution to the Fund. Thus the attractiveness of the SDRs as a reserve asset derives from the obligation of all members to accept them. If France, the deficit country in our example, finds itself in need of convertible foreign

---

[7] Since the agreement required approval by countries having a total of 85 percent of the quota, it gave veto power to the EEC along with the United States.

[8] The relative weights (in percent) are:

United States	33	Belgium	3.5
Germany	12.5	Sweden	2.5
United Kingdom	9	Australia	1.5
France	7.5	Spain	1.5
Japan	7.5	Norway	1.5
Canada	6	Denmark	1.5
Italy	6	Austria	1
Netherlands	4.5	South Africa	1

Total: 100%

These percentage weights were then converted into units of each of the 16 currencies included in the basket. (For details, see *IMF Survey,* July 8, 1974.)

[9] In the first SDR distribution, the basic period was three years. Subsequent basic periods may be between three and five years.

currencies, it can acquire German marks (or any other currency) in exchange for SDRs. The purchase is made directly from Germany (following its designation as the lender by the IMF) and does not affect any of the IMF holdings of the currencies involved. SDR transactions are outside the regular Fund operations, and the IMF role in them is that of intermediary and guarantor. The transaction will deplete France's holdings of SDRs while increasing those of Germany. The French are not required to meet any fixed repayment or "repurchase" schedule, however, as under normal IMF quota operations. Should any other country subsequently require French francs in exchange for SDRs, the French SDR holdings correspondingly would increase. And conversely, should Germany acquire any other currency in exchange for SDRs, its SDR holdings would decline. Thus the only thing that matters is the country's cumulative SDR position in relation to the original allocation. The cumulative position rises any time a country's currency is purchased and declines any time it purchases other currencies for SDRs.

Deficit countries may draw down their entire SDR allocations during the base period, but are encouraged not to draw more than 70 percent of them. They are not bound by a repayment schedule, nor must they repay the entire drawing. Rather, each is obligated to make sure that by the end of the period 30 percent of its cumulative SDR allocation is restored. This can be done either by other countries purchasing its currency for SDRs or by the country exchanging back some convertible currencies for SDRs. The official name of this restoration is not repayment or repurchase but *reconstitution*. Each country must reconstitute at least 30 percent of its allocation. In other words, a member's use of SDRs cannot exceed 70 percent of its average cumulative allocation. And that is the amount of net addition to global reserves.

We now turn to the surplus country (Germany in the present example), whose currency is presumably in great demand. Each participating country is obligated to provide its currency in exchange for SDRs freely, until its total SDR holdings are equal to three times the amount of its allocation. In our example, if Germany (with an initial allocation of $100) uses none of its SDRs, then its acceptance obligation is $200. If it uses the original allocation, its acceptance obligation becomes $300. The plan contains incentives for a country to exceed this limit, in the form of a gold guarantee for SDRs and a moderate interest rate[10] earned on holdings of SDRs, but this is not a requirement.

Special Drawing Rights are held only by central banks. Although they are included in international reserves, they cannot be used for intervention pur-

---

[10] With SDRs carrying interest of only 1.5 percent (way below market rates), the arrangement implies a subsidy by the surplus country to the deficit country. The interest rate was raised in mid-1974.

poses, that is, to peg the value of currencies. Only when commercial banks and other nonofficial institutions are allowed to deal in SDRs as they now deal in dollars will it be possible to use SDRs as an intervention asset.

A country will generally deal in SDRs for one of three principal purposes: (1) To obtain foreign currencies. To meet its balance-of-payments needs, one country may transfer SDRs to another member country designated by the IMF to receive them in exchange for its currency. Such exchanges may not be made solely for the purpose of altering the composition of the first country's reserves. The countries designated by the Fund to receive the SDRs are usually in a strong external position. (2) To redeem a balance of its own currency held by another member country. (3) To pay charges and to "repurchase" its own currency from the General Account of the IMF.[11]

During the four years ended December 31, 1973, there were over 1000 transactions in SDRs, involving close to 5 billion SDRs.

The SDR facility departs from ordinary IMF procedures in two important respects. There is no fixed repayment schedule as under ordinary IMF procedures, where drawings can be made for only three to five years. And, since 70 percent of the allocation can be freely used by the country concerned without requiring any initial deposit of gold, that proportion can be regarded as owned reserves by the participating country. Since 1970, the reserve position of countries has included their SDR holdings, and each country's annual balance-of-payments statement has reflected its allotment of new SDRs whenever such an allocation has been made. The reserve position of all coun-

Table 8-1

Composition of International Reserves ($ billions)

	End of 1970			End of 1973		
	All countries	Industrial countries	United States	All countries	Industrial countries	United States
Gold	37.2	31.1	11.0	43.1	35.9	11.7
SDRs	3.1	2.4	0.9	10.6	8.0	2.2
Reserve position in IMF	7.7	6.1	2.0	7.5	5.4	0.5
Foreign currencies	44.6	26.2	0.6	121.3	65.7	0.0
Total reserves	92.6	65.8	14.5	182.5	115.0	14.4

Note that the changes in reserves between the two dates partly reflect the devaluations of the dollar.

SOURCE: IMF, *International Financial Statistics,* November 1973, and March 1974.

[11] This refers to the regular IMF operations, as distinguished from the Special Drawing Rights Account.

tries and of the United States at the end of 1970 and 1973 is shown in Table 8-1. Most of the increase in international liquidity over the three-year period (and also in 1969–1970) was in the form of foreign currencies, resulting in large part from large U.S. balance-of-payments deficits. The United States experienced no increase in reserves.

Although the SDR facility represented an important advance, it also created a problem, for SDRs now serve as reserves alongside other reserve assets such as gold and convertible currencies, mainly dollars. And a system of international multiple reserve assets cannot work well unless the different reserve assets are equally attractive. Otherwise central bankers may hoard a preferred asset and use a less attractive one in international settlements. Thus the devaluations of the dollar in terms of gold and SDRs in the early 1970s increased the attractiveness of SDRs, inducing central bankers to pay their obligations in dollars rather than SDRs. This problem is illustrated by the British repayment (that is, repurchase) to the IMF of its £479 million ($1,250 million) debt in April 1972.[12] Of course, the relative attractiveness of the various reserve assets is likely to change over time.

To avoid this problem, it has been proposed by E. M. Bernstein that participating countries place all their reserve assets in a single account (called the reserve settlement account) with the IMF.[13] These deposits would be denominated in a *reserve unit* (RU), equal to one U.S. dollar, with a guaranteed gold value. Reserve transactions between any two countries would go through this IMF account and would involve a proportionate use of their different reserve assets. New allocations of SDRs would also be credited to this account. And countries acquiring foreign currencies in excess of their needs for working balances would be required to convert them to RUs, while countries in need of foreign currencies could acquire them for the RUs. Since all international settlements would go through this account, the three types of assets would become equally attractive, and there would be no need for any participating country to limit its acquisition of SDRs to the amount obligated under the agreement. This plan, not now under active consideration by central bankers, would move the system a giant step toward the type of international reserve-creating institution discussed in Chapter 10.

---

[12] Although the United Kingdom had adequate reserves to discharge its IMF obligations, a special problem arose because the Fund was holding its full quota of dollars and could not accept any more in repayment of the British debt.

Besides the British contribution of 400 million gold-linked SDRs, the other feature of the operation was a U.S. drawing on the fund of £83 million, or $217 million. By making this drawing in sterling, the United States reduced the amount the United Kingdom had to repurchase from the Fund to discharge its debt. The difference was made up by eight countries, which purchased (from the United Kingdom) British-held dollars in exchange for their own currencies, acceptable to the Fund. For details, see *The Financial Times,* London, April 27, 1972.

[13] E. M. Bernstein, "The Gold Crisis and the New Gold Standard," *Quarterly Review and Investment Survey* (New York: Model, Roland and Co., Inc., 1968), pp. 1–12.

9

From the Smithsonian Agreement to the Collapse of Bretton Woods

Events Leading to the U.S. Measures of August 15, 1971

In 1968 and 1969 the United States experienced a high rate of inflation, brought about in part by the Vietnam buildup of 1965–1966. Public sentiment against the inflation was widespread, and the government was determined to "cool off" the economy—namely, to reduce the rate of inflation by generating a deliberate reduction in the rate of growth in output and employment. Consequently, in addition to a contractionary fiscal posture, the Federal Reserve stepped on the monetary brakes, and for some months in 1969 the money supply was not permitted to grow at all.

The resultant increase in interest rates in the United States had the effect of attracting short-term funds into dollar assets. Consequently, despite the fact that the U.S. external balance on current account and long-term capital was in deficit to the tune of $2.9 billion in 1969, the dollar was strong on the world currency markets. In fact, the official reserve transactions balance showed a $2.7 billion surplus, as foreign central banks divested themselves of dollars in exchange for local currencies. Because of Regulation Q, which limits the rate of interest that U.S. commercial banks can pay on deposits, much of this short-term capital was invested in the Eurodollar market.

On the U.S. domestic front, a recession set in during 1970, in response to the policy measures pursued in the previous years. But the rate of inflation remained high, failing to respond to the economic slowdown at the desired speed. In part this lag was a result of the cyclical decline in labor productivity (defined as output per worker) during a downswing in the economy,[1] while in another measure it resulted from the ability of large corporations and unions to push up prices and wages even when operating well below capacity. Thus, the inflation continued in 1970, in coincidence with the spreading recession. In the winter of 1970 the Federal Reserve, recognizing the severity of the recession, moved to expand the money supply at an annual rate of approximately 4 percent—a rate sufficient to generate an expansion of output that would maintain unemployment at a constant level. Consequently, following the normal lag of 6 to 9 months, unemployment leveled off at somewhat above the 6 percent mark and remained there in 1971. But the increase in the money supply, coupled with the decline in the demand for money caused by the recession, produced a reduction in interest rates in the United States. This brought about a marked deterioration in the U.S. balance-of-payments position. Not only was there a $3 billion deficit on current account and long-term capital, but the official transactions balance showed a deficit of $10 billion, as short-term dollar funds flowed back into the coffers of foreign central banks.

In 1971, U.S. economic policy had three objectives: to curtail the level of unemployment and speed up the growth rate; to reduce the still unacceptably high rate of inflation; and to curb and reverse the balance-of-payments deficits. Faced with this combination of targets, many economists would have recommended fiscal expansion combined with monetary tightness, perhaps accompanied by "income policy," and also a devaluation of the dollar. But the third option was not available to the United States under the Bretton Woods arrangement, and for one reason or another American politicians (and perhaps the general public) regard high interest rates as highly undesirable. Thus the measures adopted were an expansionary monetary policy, with the money stock rising at an annual rate of 7–10 percent, and an expansionary fiscal posture. These policies helped stimulate economic activity, so that in

---

[1] At the beginning of a downswing, when output declines, corporations do not reduce their labor force by a proportionate amount. Some companies consider the decline in orders and shipments temporary and do not wish to dispense with their trained workers and other personnel. They tend to "hoard" labor in anticipation of a reversal in the situation. In other cases, firms resist laying off workers and executives, simply because it is an unpalatable thing to do. The upshot of this practice is that output per worker declines during the downswing phase of the cycle. Coupled with the fact that overhead costs must now be spread over smaller output, the result is an increase in per-unit production costs, which is reflected in price increases. Not until the downward trend in aggregate demand, output, and economic activity is clearly discernible do the firms make the necessary adjustments in their labor force. This, incidentally, is the reason why changes in employment usually lag behind changes in output.

A reverse phenomenon occurs at the beginning of an upswing. Firms start expanding their output first by making better use of their existing labor force, and second by hiring the most qualified workers out of the unemployed labor pool, hiring the less qualified only when unemployment is down considerably. Couple this with the fact that overhead costs are spread over an expanding output, and the result is an increase in labor productivity. Thus the impact of the expansion on costs and prices is delayed. But coincidentally, the reduction in unemployment also lags behind the rise in output.

1971/72 the economy was undergoing a transformation from a recession to an expansionary phase of the cycle. However, not only did these policies fail to squeeze out the inflation (perhaps they even aggravated it), they caused a further deterioration in the balance of payments. For the first time in this century, a trade deficit appeared in 1971, to the tune of $2.7 billion. And the balance on current account and long-term capital showed a $9.6 billion deficit, while the deficit on official reserve transactions grew to $30 billion. In other words, foreign central banks accumulated huge amounts of dollar reserves.

As these and other indicators imply, the dollar was grossly overvalued in terms of other major currencies. In addition, large amounts of short-term funds flowed from the United States to Europe, in part attracted to higher European interest rates, but also stimulated by a speculative distrust of the dollar, triggered by the U.S. trade deficit. Much of this movement was directed to West Germany, speculating on the possibility of revaluation of the mark, and forcing the West German central bank to absorb large quantities of dollars to prevent the exchange value of the mark from rising about its "ceiling." Over $2 billion were converted into marks in a short period, while hundreds of millions of dollars flowed into the Netherlands, Switzerland, Austria, and Belgium. The premium on ninety days forward (over spot) marks rose by 4 cents in several days as speculators, anticipating revaluation of the mark, were buying forward marks. Such speculation on the forward market created an added inducement to transfer arbitrage funds into West Germany on the spot market, by purchasing spot marks and selling them forward at a premium. Not only was the dollar intake regarded as undesirable because it led to an accumulation of "unwanted" dollar reserves, but the inflow produced inflationary pressures inside West Germany. For the West German central bank had to pay for the dollars in marks, and their infusion into the economy operating on the fractional reserve banking system produced a multiple expansion of the money supply.

Since this inflationary effect was clearly unacceptable to the West Germans, they could have responded by suspending pegging operations and letting the mark float upward or by restricting the inflow of capital. However, they were at first reluctant to do so, primarily because of internal political pressures emanating from the large exporting firms and from the farm sector. Indeed, a chronically undervalued currency (as the mark was in the 1960s) produces artificial incentives to invest in export and import-competing industries, and these industries then constitute a vested interest against exchange adjustment. West Germany would have preferred to see the crisis resolved by an increase in U.S. interest rates, which would have attracted funds to dollar assets. But such a step would have interfered with the American objective of stimulating the domestic economy and was therefore rejected by the Federal Reserve.

Since there was a limit to the volume of dollar inflow that West Germany would absorb, the West German authorities were obliged in May 1971 to stop supporting the exchange rate and set the mark afloat. It gradually rose in value from $0.275 to $0.306 in December 1971. This constellation of events was reenacted several times during the period under review. The Netherlands followed suit, with the guilder rising from $0.278 to $0.305, while Switzerland and Austria revalued their currencies by 7 and 5 percent, respectively.

But the flight from the dollar to other currencies continued, rising to very large proportions in the first half of August 1971. By mid-August, U.S. reserve assets had fallen to $12 billion and official dollar liabilities had risen to $41 billion (from only $20 billion in December 1970). It was this configuration of events that led President Nixon to introduce the new economic measures on August 15, 1971.

Policy Measures Announced on August 15, 1971

Domestic Measures

On the domestic scene, the President announced two measures aimed at further stimulating the still lagging economy: a tax credit on the purchase of equipment for investment purposes, designed to encourage private investment; and the abolition of Federal excise taxes on automobiles, designed to spur consumer spending. As a result of the expansionary monetary policies, aided by these two measures, the economy gained momentum in 1972, with real output expanding at a rapid rate. This expansion continued in 1973. However, the first quarter of 1974 witnessed a 5.8 percent decline in real GNP—the largest single-quarter drop since 1958—and some further decline was expected in the second quarter. This recession appears to have been caused by a general retreat in consumer spending from the previous high level, capped by the energy shortage of 1973–74. However, government policy in 1974 was aimed primarily at curbing the double-digit inflation, and interest rates rose to unprecedented levels.

A second set of domestic measures taken in 1971 was aimed at the persistent inflationary pressures. A three-month freeze was imposed on prices and wage rates, to speed up price stabilization and wring expectations of further price increases out of the economy. The freeze, labeled Phase I, was followed by selective price and wage controls known as Phase II, which lasted for over a year. Early in 1973 these were replaced by the less stringent surveillance procedures of Phase III. Under Phase III, decisions of major corporations and unions to change prices and wages had to be communicated to the government's Cost of Living Council, as did information about corporate profit. The Administration retained the power to force a rollback of "unacceptable" price and wage increases. The rate of inflation in the United States dropped significantly in 1972 (to around 3½ percent) and stood at about one-half its European counterpart. But only some of this decline could be attributed to the direct controls. In large measure it was probably due to the increase in labor productivity during the upswing phase of the cycle; in part it was a delayed reaction on the price front to the previous recession.[2]

However, inflationary pressures reappeared early in 1973, spearheaded by substantial increases in food prices, as rising domestic and foreign demand for food products was hitting a reasonably fixed short-run supply. By mid-1973 these pressures grew so intense that the Administration was forced to reverse its policy of relaxing the direct controls and impose a 60-day price freeze, to be followed again by selective controls (Phase IV). Although these controls were tighter than their Phase III counterpart, the inflation—which now appears to be a worldwide phenomenon—continued unabated through the end of 1973, aided by dislocations produced by the energy shortage. The inflation accelerated to a 10.8 percent annual rate in the first quarter of 1974 (the highest rate since the Korean War), a rate that was expected to continue in the second quarter. Yet the government decided to terminate the wage-price control program at the end of April 1974, viewing it as ineffective at controlling inflation.

International Policies

On the international front, the President announced a series of measures designed to bring about devaluation of the dollar in terms of the major West European currencies and the Japanese yen; or alternatively stated, to induce these countries to revalue their currencies in terms of the dollar. While it had long been recognized that the dollar was overvalued. the devaluation option was not open to the United States becauses of the dollar's dual role in the Bretton Woods system: as the standard of value in terms of which other currencies were effectively defined and as the intervention currency to which they were anchored. The United States played a passive role on the foreign exchange markets, and the value of the dollar in terms of foreign currencies was deter-

---

[2] While it is not possible to split the responsibility for the slowdown in the rate of inflation among the various factors, there is empirical evidence indicating that this and previous price control programs (under the Johnson administration) succeeded in shifting the Phillips curve somewhat to the left; in other words, greater price stability was achieved at a given level of unemployment. This achievement is not costless, however, for the controls interfere with efficient resource allocation in the economy. See O. Eckstein and R. Brinnes, *The Inflationary Process in the United States,* U.S. Congress, Joint Economic Committee (February 22, 1973), and *The Economic Report of the President* (Washington: 1973), p. 61.

mined by other countries, which pegged their currencies to the dollar at a specific rate. Thus the crucial relationship between the dollar and other currencies could be changed only through the consent of other countries.

In terms of their overall economic interest, Japan and Western Europe should have readily given their consent and even welcomed the move. For it makes little sense to mount huge balance-of-payments surpluses, which merely result in the accumulation of unnecessary dollar reserves. More importantly, such an accumulation contributes significantly to domestic inflation, to which some countries—for example, West Germany—are highly sensitive. Beyond that, revaluation of the mark and the yen would raise the standard of living of the West German or Japanese citizenry, as their local currencies would purchase more imported goods and services. Revaluation is one way for them to reap the benefits of higher productivity, and is thus preferable to an accumulation of reserves beyond any reasonable need.

Yet this step, or its counterpart, the devaluation of the dollar, was strongly resisted in Tokyo, Bonn, and other capitals. The reluctance to revalue was partly a result of a deep-seated mercantilist tradition, which places a high value on external trade surpluses. But mainly it can be explained by internal political pressure from the large exporting firms, and in West Germany, also from farm organizations. In some cases, the conflicting pressures led to inconsistent attitudes on the part of European officials, who condemned the United States for the continuing balance-of-payments deficits and at the same time refused to permit the realignment of exchange rates necessary to rectify the situation. It remained for the United States to force their hand, that is, to bring about dollar devaluation, the extent of which would vary with respect to various currencies depending on the assumed degree of undervaluation of each of the currencies concerned. What could have been accomplished by a simple and orderly revaluation of selected currencies had to be achieved with a big "bang," which generated a crisis atmosphere and threatened to disintegrate the world trade and financial systems.

Under the newly announced policy, dollar holdings by foreign central banks would no longer be redeemable in gold by the United States. Although the closing of the gold window was merely a *de jure* recognition of a previously existing situation, in which the U.S. gold stock was only a fraction of foreign official holdings of dollars, it had an important symbolic value. From then on, dollar reserves could not be exchanged for other types of reserve assets, such as gold, so that continued pegging to the dollar by foreign central bankers would place the world on a straight dollar standard. At the same time, foreign countries were invited to revalue their currencies against the dollar.

Believing that these countries would not desire to go on accumulating "nonconvertible" dollars, the President had some reason to hope that this invitation would be accepted. But a hope is not a certainty. And realizing that the European reluctance to permit dollar devaluation was deep-seated, the Administration announced several accompanying measures designed to increase the probability of exchange-rate realignment. Unfortunately, these took the form of trade restrictions, the removal of which would be offered to foreign countries in exchange for currency revaluation. In the trade field, the President imposed a 10 percentage point tariff surcharge on imports into the United States.[3] Excluded from the surcharge were all duty-free goods, which include most raw materials, automobiles, parts manufactured in Canada, and commodities subject to import quotas. The surcharge was less than 10 percentage points for products where the full amount would have raised the duty above the statutory level established by prior trade legislation. Although it was never explicitly stated, the implication was that the surcharge would be removed once exchange-rate adjustments took place. In a similar vein, the 10 percent investment tax credit, part of an earlier attempt to stimulate the domestic economy, was to apply only to purchases of American equipment, not foreign capital goods. Finally, to further stem the outflow of dollars, the President announced a 10 percent reduction in the foreign aid program to developing countries.

The trade measures, clearly in violation of U.S. obligations under GATT (although from the viewpoint of economic efficiency they are superior to quantitative restrictions that are sanctioned by GATT in cases of balance-of-payments deficits), produced a violent reaction in Europe, and the specter of a trans-Atlantic trade war raised its ugly head but fortunately failed to materialize. An additional side effect of the (temporary) import surcharge was that by artificially curbing American imports, it was obscuring the equilibrium exchange rates toward which the major currencies should have been realigned.

The developing countries voiced strong indignation about being penalized in a variety of ways for a currency crisis in which they played no role. Indeed their interests were affected in several ways. The 10 percent cut in foreign aid despite the fact that most American aid is tied to purchases in the United States anyway, hurt them directly. It came at a time when U.S. policy-makers were in an "inward-looking" mood, concerned mainly with domestic problems and unwilling to heed the needs of the less developed world. Secondly, the 10 percent import surcharge affected adversely the less developd countries' exports of manufactured products, precisely at a time when they were pressing for preferential tariff treatment by the industrialized nations and when such treatment was granted them by the EEC and other European countries. It is true that certain products such as cotton textiles were not affected by the order because they are subject to import quotas, and that duty-free raw materials

---

[3] In July 1974 this surcharge was ruled invalid by the U.S. Customs Court, because authority in tariff matters is vested in the Congress. If upheld by the Supreme Court, this decision would require the government to refund the tax proceeds to importers.

were also exempt. But the latter exemption only served to raise the effective rate of protection (that is, protection accorded to domestic value added; see Chapter 13) on the industrial goods covered by the surcharge. It meant a sharp setback to the attempts of the less developed countries to promote the production and export of labor-intensive manufactured goods. Such a setback would have been magnified if the Europeans and Japanese retaliated against the American measures. In general, any trade war among the developed countries would have rather ominous effects on the developing nations. Beyond that, the anticipated exchange-rate adjustments would redirect the trade flows of the less developed nations, inducing them to buy more in the United States and sell more in the revaluating countries. Finally, the composition of their reserves as between gold and various foreign currencies would determine the effect of the exchange-rate realignment on the value of each country's reserve holdings.

Realignment of exchange rates had other repercussions because many international prices are quoted in dollars. Thus, the oil-producing countries moved to renegotiate their prices, as did the various international airlines and shipping conferences.

Post-Announcement Developments

The President's announcement caught the world by surprise. The six members of the European Economic Community were at an impasse, with the West German mark floating and the French insisting that it be stabilized, and with the French and West Germans disagreeing on their future common posture. West Germany wanted to see the currencies of the six EEC nations tightly pegged to each other, with only a narrow band of variations—perhaps a maximum of 1 percent—permitted. This joint bloc of currencies would then float against the dollar. Such a float could be either completely free, with the "dollar–bloc of six" exchange rate being determined by market forces of supply and demand, or it could be a float within a wide band of, say, 8–10 percent. The French, partly fearing the preeminence of the West German mark in this bloc, adamantly opposed the plan. They wished each country to have a two-tier system vis-à-vis the dollar; an officially pegged exchange rate for commercial transactions and a freely floating rate for transfers of capital. The British, who expected to adhere to whatever arrangements were agreed upon when they joined the EEC (on January 1, 1973) appeared at the time to give qualified support to the West German position. In any event, EEC negotiators failed to reach an agreement.

The immediate step taken by most major countries after the President's announcement was to stop pegging their currencies to the dollar and permit them to float, with their exchange rates being determined in the marketplace in response to supply-and-demand conditions. However, the monetary authorities of each country were intervening on the foreign exchange markets by buying and selling their own currencies to control the exchange rate to some extent ("dirty" float). The French, however, adopted a two-tier system: they retained the old, fixed exchange rate to the dollar for commercial transactions but permitted the franc to float freely for capital transfers. Tourist expenditures in France came under the category of capital transfers for this purpose. The Common Market failed to patch up its internal differences, and the West German mark continued to float. Finally, Belgium and Holland pegged their respective currencies to each other and floated jointly vis-à-vis the dollar. This is what West Germany wanted for all six Common Market currencies. Subsequently, however, Belgium opted for a system similar to that of France. Figure 9-1 shows the degree of fluctuations and appreciation of some of the major currencies in the fall of 1971.

Most currencies floated upward (appreciated) 5–8 percent in terms of the dollar, which still remained the most important standard of value and unit of account. The United States did not regard this level of currency appreciation as adequate; and the International Monetary Fund brought forth its own estimates of equilibrium exchange rates, calling for a 13–15 percent revaluation of the yen and lesser revaluations—between 5 and 12 percent—for most European currencies. The IMF also suggested that the price of gold be raised 5 percent in terms of the dollar.

The fact that the various currencies did not appreciate more may have been due to government intervention on the free exchange markets to control the float and to the fact that exchange adjustments require more time, but it was also due to the U.S. import surcharge. In addition to its other drawbacks, the surcharge obscured the true exchange rates by artificially keeping imports out of the United States. Throughout the fall of 1971, when exchange rates were floating, the fluctuations were viewed by most countries as undesirable and transitory phenomena rather than a basic change in the system. They were to last only until an agreement was reached to restabilize exchange rates in some way.

Fortunately, the Europeans and Japanese did not retaliate against the U.S. import surcharge. Rather, they pressed their complaints on trade matters in GATT, while financial negotiations were continued by the IMF and the Group of Ten. It appeared that in return for removing the surcharge, the United States wished to extract from its trading partners not only currency revaluations but also certain concessions in the trade field, as well as a greater contribution to the common defense effort. The desired trade concessions included easing of EEC restrictions on farm imports, limitations on the preferential arrangements contracted by the EEC with other countries that discriminated against American exports, and limitations by intergovernmental agree-

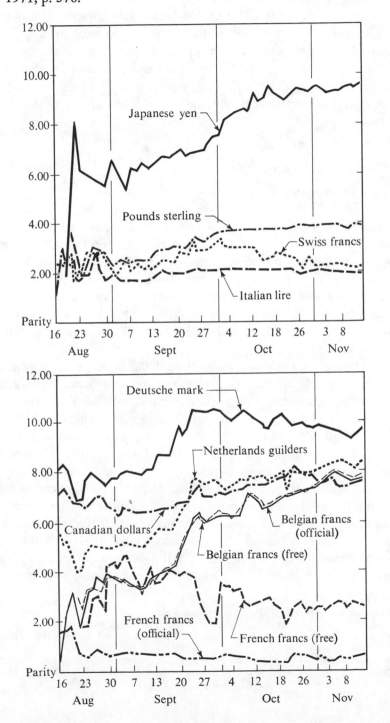

Figure 9-1
Spread of spot rates from par, August 16–November 12, 1971.
Based on noon quotations in New York (in percent).
SOURCE: IMF, *International Financial News Survey,* November 17, 1971, p. 376.

ment on the Japanese penetration into the American market. The fact that trade and financial matters were being discussed at two different forums complicated the negotiating process.

Strictly on the financial side, there evolved a general agreement that exchange rates should be stabilized and the dollar be permitted to devalue. But disagreements persisted, first on the extent of the necessary devaluation, with the United States pressing for 12–15 percent and the Europeans for something like 5–10 percent; and second on whether the price of gold should be raised as a part of the agreement, with the United States saying no and France a resounding yes.

The Smithsonian Agreement

On December 18, 1971, the major financial nations announced an agreement reached at the Smithsonian Institution in Washington, on the realignment of exchange rates and restabilization of currencies. Under it the United States raised the price of gold by 8.57 percent (from $35 to $38 a fine ounce); Japan and West Germany lowered the yen and mark prices of gold by 8.5 and 5 percent, respectively; and in terms of the pound sterling and the French franc the price of gold remained unchanged. Figure 9-2 is a schematic illustration of these changes.

These changes implied that in terms of the dollar the yen was revalued 17.2 percent; the mark, 13.57 percent; and the pound and franc, 8.57 percent. Other European currencies also revalued against the dollar in varying degrees, as did the currencies of about thirty developing countries. Most other developing countries continued to peg their currencies to the dollar at the old rates, while eight countries actually devalued against the dollar.[4] The weighted average devaluation of the dollar in terms of all currencies was around 9 percent. In addition the Japanese yen was revalued vis-à-vis the European currencies, and the mark was revalued vis-à-vis the pound and the franc. The weighted value of gold, and more importantly of the SDRs, in terms of all currencies remained unchanged. But in terms of the dollar, the SDR—originally set to equal one dollar per unit of SDR—went up in value. Although many accounts, such as the U.N. Commodity Trade Statistics, continued to

---

[4] Some representative revaluations against the dollar were: Austria, +11.59 percent; Belgium, the Netherlands, and Luxemburg, +11.57 percent; Norway, +7.49 percent; Sweden, +7.49 percent; Italy, +7.48 percent; Denmark, +7.45 percent; Portugal, +5.50 percent; Finland, +2.44 percent; Mexico, 0.0 percent; Iceland, 0.0 percent; Israel, −16.67 percent. For a detailed listing of all countries' changes and their post-Smithsonian exchange rates, see the IMF, *International Financial News Survey*, December 22–30, 1971 and February 2, 1972.

Figure 9-2

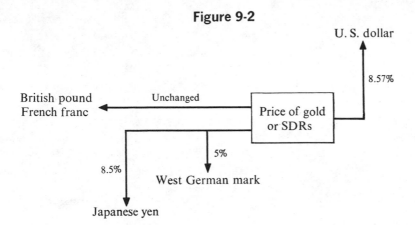

be reported in dollars, the dollar lost some of its status as a unit of value. IMF accounts are now maintained in SDRs ("old" dollars), as is the unit of account used by the EEC in calculating farm subsidies.

As a part of the package, the United States removed the import surcharge and the "Buy American" component of the then-pending tax legislation on investment credit. On the other hand, the dollar remained nonconvertible into gold, and the U.S. "gold window" remained closed. Subsequently, the Administration also introduced legislation permitting the creation of Domestic International Sales Corporations (DISC). Under DISC, companies conducting 95 percent of their business in export trade are allowed to defer one-half of their corporate profit tax obligation. In some cases the deferral becomes a total exemption, because DISC corporations are taxable only when their profits are distributed to shareholders. By mid-1972 it was estimated that 2,000 U.S. companies had set up export subsidiaries to qualify as DISC. The DISC device was intended to offset the European export subsidies granted in the form of export rebates of the domestic value-added tax.

The international financial system itself was hardly changed. The dollar was continued as the intervention currency and the standard of value to which all other currencies were pegged, although they would now be pegged at new exchange rates. One important change, however, was instituted. The range of permissible fluctuations of each currency vis-à-vis the dollar (that is, the "band") was widened from 2 percent to 4½ percent—2¼ percent on either side of the currency's "central rate," namely, the dollar value in which it is defined.[5]

Many countries adopted the wider band. It implied a 9 percent range of fluctuations between each two nondollar currencies. Only the dollar fluctuations

---

[5] For practical purposes the "central rate" and "par value" are identical. The distinction was made by the IMF only for legal reasons, to enable countries to repeg to the dollar at new "central rates" before the dollar price of gold was changed by Congress.

Figure 9-3

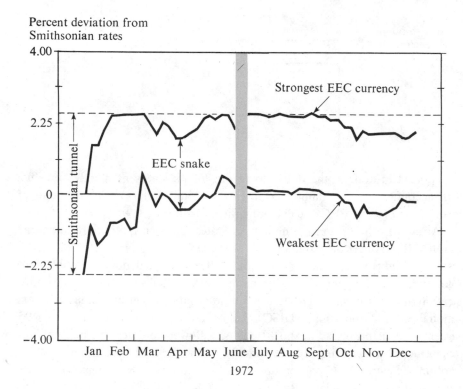

Percent deviation from
Smithsonian rates

against other currencies would be limited to the 4½ percent range because of
the dollar's role as the intervention currency. The United States continued to
be passive in the foreign exchange markets, leaving it to other countries to
stabilize their currencies against the dollar.

One major exception to the 9 percent range of fluctuations between any
two nondollar currencies were the exchange fluctuations among the currencies
of the EEC.[6] Striving to attain or at least display a measure of financial integration, the six members of the Community (France, West Germany, Italy,
and the three Benelux countries) decided in March 1972 to limit the range of
fluctuations between their currencies to only 4½ percent. This meant that
against the dollar their entire range of fluctuations would be only 2¼ percent.
The arrangement, which became known as the "EEC snake in the Smithsonian

[6] The exchange-rate adjustments created problems for the Common Agricultural Policy
of the EEC, for revaluation of the mark meant cheaper farm imports into West Germany and more expensive West German farm exports to its Community partners. To
counteract this, West Germany introduced border tax adjustments—a tax on food imports and a comparable subsidy on farm exports.

tunnel," is best illustrated by Figure 9-3, which relates all currencies to the dollar.

This restricted range of fluctuations was brought about by each central bank intervening in all other EEC currencies to stabilize the rates, that is, by *multiple currency intervention*. Specifically, whenever a member currency came under attack, it was immediately supported by all other member central banks. At the end of each month, the country whose currency had been in difficulty settled up with the other members for the reserves they had used up in supporting the exchange rate. In this settlement the debtor country used gold and gold-guaranteed assets (SDRs and reserve position in the IMF) on the one hand, and foreign currencies on the other, in proportion to its holdings of the two categories of reserve assets. When this decision was made, Great Britain, Ireland, and Denmark were on the verge of joining the Community (they actually acceded on January 1, 1973). Consequently, they decided to adhere to the EEC currency agreement. However, in mid-1972, the United Kingdom was obliged to float the pound (see below), thereby withdrawing from the agreement. The general question of financial integration in the EEC will be discussed in the next chapter.

The Smithsonian conference also set up a committee of twenty countries (The Committee of 20; see Appendix IV) to consider all possible options for international monetary reform and subsequently report to the IMF.

Post-Smithsonian Developments

That the international currency system became increasingly crisis-prone has been abundantly illustrated by the developments of the late 1960s and early 1970s. Even if one had the wisdom of Solomon necessary to fix all exchange rates at their equilibrium levels at a given point of time, such equilibria are unlikely to last. For as long as countries exhibit different rates of growth in productivity, as long as they pursue divergent and uncoordinated monetary and fiscal policies at home, they will have vastly divergent domestic price and income movements, which in turn will change the equilibrium exchange rates. Thus, one or more currencies will begin to show "weakness," while others will become "strong." When that happens, currency speculators move against the "weak" currencies by selling them on the market and purchasing the currencies perceived to be strong; under an adjustable peg system, they can hardly lose and may realize a considerable profit by reacting in the same fashion to market signals.[7] These speculators include the multinational cor-

---

[7] Multinational corporations continuously adjust their liquid assets to take account of expected currency variations. Thus, if revaluation of the mark were expected, a company would make early payments of its debts to West German suppliers and perhaps

porations, the oil-producing countries, and individuals with liquid funds to invest. And it is a feature of the present-day financial scene that private liquid funds, available for such "speculative attacks," are growing by leaps and bounds and have reached into the hundreds of billions of dollars. A recent study[8] estimated that private institutions on the international financial scene controlled $268 billion in short-term funds at the end of 1971, much of it in the hands of multinational corporations. Additional huge sums are owned by the official monetary institutions of the oil-producing countries. Such funds are more than double the total official reserves of the OECD countries. If even a small fraction of these funds moves speculatively from one currency to the other, a genuine crisis can develop. When all speculators react to the same signals, it is exceedingly difficult for any central bank to withstand the assault. Such movements of funds can also be highly disruptive to any domestic economy. In some years, for example, West Germany experienced short-term capital flows amounting to nearly one-tenth of the domestic money supply, which strongly constrained the central bank's ability to carry out the desired monetary policy.

The position of the United States in the world economy has changed from that of a "giant among dwarfs" in the years immediately following World War II to that of "first among equals" today, although the dollar continues to be the most widely used currency for international transactions. During the first twenty postwar years, the American hegemony in international finance was hardly in question. The United States was by far the most productive industrial economy and for a long time was the only source of advanced technology and sophisticated products, for which demand was growing rapidly. It was under these conditions that the dollar, considered "as good as or better than gold," became the intervention currency as well as the reserve currency. For a long time the demand for dollars appeared insatiable. In these circumstances it made sense for the United States to be totally passive on the foreign exchange markets and permit the exchange value of the dollar to be determined by for-

---

even purchase marks to hold. Conversely, rumors of franc devaluation would induce the company to delay payments to Frenchmen and offer a discount for immediate payment of outstanding bills by Frenchmen so as to reduce the amount of francs it was owed. In short, the company would take whatever steps possible to get rid of assets and pile up debts denominated in a threatened currency, while accumulating assets and reducing debts expressed in a strong currency. Such protective steps can be taken either on the spot market or in the forward market. While an individual company would justly claim that it merely adjusts to market conditions, which themselves are beyond its control, when all international corporations act at about the same time and respond to the same (real or imagined) constellation of circumstances, they do *affect* market conditions. Indeed, transfers of funds by these companies account for a large portion of the periodic massive currency swings in Europe.

[8] *Implications of Multinational Firms for World Trade and Investments and for U.S. Trade and Labor,* a Report by the U.S. Tariff Commission to the Senate Finance Committee (Washington: 1973), pp. 8–9.

eign countries in their pegging operations. The United States could relegate the objective of maintaining external equilibrium to a position of "benign neglect." But with the emergence of strong economies in Europe and Japan, who were highly reluctant to see their currencies revalued even when the need arose, the situation became increasingly troublesome for the United States, as it deprived this country of an important policy instrument—exchange-rate adjustment. For that reason, one element of currency reform sought by the United States in the councils of nations was to place the dollar on an equal footing with other currencies—to give it a band of fluctuations of equal width and to permit discrete adjustments in its exchange value. This objective, however, was not easily attained. While the world could agree on using SDRs as the main reserve asset and standard of value, replacing the dollar in that role, SDRs cannot be used for intervention purposes. For only assets held by the general public can be so used; they must be bought and sold on private markets in order to facilitate pegging operations. And SDRs are held only by central banks. This problem could be handled by introducing multiple-currency—instead of dollar—intervention, with the accumulated foreign currencies being converted periodically into SDRs.

Other elements in the American proposals[9] for international currency reform included greater exchange-rate flexibility (including transitional floats), quicker adjustment of exchange rates to market conditions and less reliance on direct controls of capital flows; and a more even or symmetrical sharing of the burden of adjustment between deficit and surplus countries, with penalties imposed on nations whose currencies are undervalued, including a surcharge on their exports or nonallocation of SDRs. A country with persistent surpluses would be expected to lower barriers to import, to reflate domestically (to pursue expansionary domestic policies) or to revalue, once its reserves[10] reach a specified warning point. While there have been no official U.S. ideas on what to do about the huge overhang of dollar assets in the hands of foreign monetary institutions, one private observer has suggested that the U.S. Treasury buy up packages of U.S. corporate securities and offer them at a discount to foreign central banks. Alternatively, the U.S. Treasury could issue special nonmarketable bonds to be sold to foreign central banks.

After several months of post-Smithsonian calm on the international currency markets, the British pound came under severe attack. The high rate of inflation in the United Kingdom coupled with recurrent labor unrest, planted seeds of suspicion in the minds of many that the pound was overvalued. The

[9] See the *Economic Report of the President,* 1973.
[10] The United States proposes the use of a country's reserve position as an indicator of the need for adjustment action. That, of course, includes changes originating in short-term capital flows, which may not reflect the underlying strength or weakness of the currency. The alternative, favored by certain European countries, would be to use the balance on current account and long-term capital.

ensuing flight from the pound to continental currencies coupled with a high rate of unemployment in the United Kingdom forced Britain almost immediately to suspend pegging operations. As of June 1972, the pound was permitted to float. It floated downward from $2.60 to around $2.40.

While short-term funds were flowing out of Britain, they were flowing into Japan, as that country's continuing trade surpluses created expectations of further revaluation of the yen. The Japanese government, resisting such a re-valuation, moved to counter the situation; it tightened control over capital in-flow, liberalized controls over capital outflow, and at the same time loosened import restrictions (but insufficiently) and introduced some measures to dis-courage exports. Switzerland, which also experienced a large influx of capital, imposed an 8 percent annual charge on foreign deposits to discourage the inflow.

In January 1973, the Italian lira came under speculative attack, triggered primarily by internal labor strife. In response, the Italian government decided on January 21, 1973 to adopt the French and Belgian scheme of a two-tier system: an officially fixed exchange rate for commercial transactions (includ-ing, in the case of Italy, trade, shipping revenue, tourist revenue, immigrant remittances, and investment income), and a floating rate for capital trans-actions. The free lira floated downward (628 lire to the dollar compared to 584 for the official lira).

At about the same time, the dollar began to come under pressure. From Italy as well as other sources, dollars began to flow first into Switzerland. After absorbing $250 million, and fearing the domestic inflationary implications of dollar influx in an economy already plagued by inflation, the Swiss central bank decided to let the Swiss franc float. It immediately appreciated by about 3.8 percent. Thus the Swiss franc joined the ranks of the "floaters"—the Cana-dian dollar (floating since May 1970), the British pound, Italy's "financial" lira, and the "financial" francs of France and Belgium. The currency move-ments in 1972 are shown in the chart of Figure 9-4.

The Second Devaluation of the Dollar

But the renewed international financial jitters did not subside. In the first week of February 1973, the United States published its preliminary balance on merchandise trade for 1972. It showed a deficit of over $6.9 billion (up from $2.7 billion in 1971) and created widespread suspicion that the Smithsonian Agreement "was not working." This suggested the possibility of further dollar devaluation and triggered a massive flight from the dollar, mainly toward the West German mark. In one week the West German central bank absorbed

Figure 9-4

Exchange rate trends of major currencies since Smithsonian Agreement (percentage deviations from the central rate or par value). The rates are the midpoint of buying and selling rates for all countries except Switerland, for which buying rate is shown.
SOURCE: IMF *Survey,* March 12, 1973, p. 70.

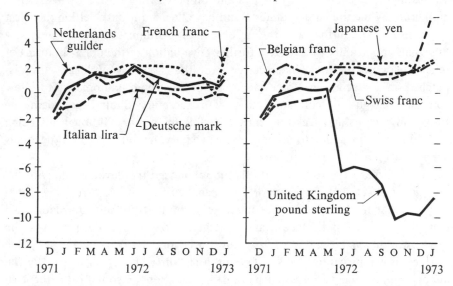

some $6 billion to maintain the peg. So massive was the "run on the dollar," that the Federal Reserve abandoned its traditional policy of nonintervention on the foreign exchange markets and sold $319 million in marks and $20 million in guilders to prop up the dollar. West Germany regarded the influx as highly undesirable, both because it forced its central bank to accumulate further unwanted dollar reserves and because it was highly inflationary.

Although the long-run outlook for the dollar was more favorable than the immediate situation indicated, the speculative activity tended to feed upon itself. Not only did speculators have nothing to lose under the adjustable peg system by switching to marks and yen, but speculative activities can often upset the applecart when there is a long lag in the effect of policy. Suppose devaluation requires two and a half years to have a measurable effect on trade flows, but speculators expect results in six months. If nothing happens in the first year, they begin to suspect that the policy is not effective and speculate against the currency. This can bring about its downfall in the manner of a self-fulfilling prophecy.

In the case at hand, it would have been desirable to permit the mark and the yen to float upward and for Japan to remove completely its remaining restrictions on imports. Japan had an especially urgent need to divert resources from the export industries to domestic needs, and this could be accomplished by currency appreciation. But, for reasons discussed previously, both countries refused to take such a step, and West Germany insisted that it would act only as part of a concerted action by the international financial community. To cope with the immediate siutation, West Germany instituted wide-ranging controls on the import of capital by foreigners and on borrowing abroad by West German firms. While the United States could have "waited it out," letting the West Germans struggle further with their problem, the Administration evidently saw this as an opportunity to achieve a further devaluation of the dollar in terms of other major currencies. Undersecrteary of the Treasury Volcker was dispatched on a special Air Force plane full of electronic equipment (to allow constant and instant communication with Secretary Shultz) to roam the European capitals and seek consent to devalue the dollar. Although his being spotted in Europe added to the speculative activity, he did succeed in negotiating a 10 percent dollar devaluation.

On February 12, 1973, the President announced the devaluation, with the immediate effect that some major European currencies were repegged at a higher rate (the increase in the dollar price of the officially untraded gold from $38 to $42.2 per ounce came later, after Congressional approval). The Japanese yen was permitted to float upward beyond 10 percent, but its value was kept down by central bank intervention (a "dirty" float). A week after the announcement, the yen showed a total appreciation of some 14 percent in terms of the dollar, standing at around 260 yen to the dollar. Thus five major currencies were left floating: the yen, the pound sterling, the Canadian dollar, the Swiss franc, and the Italian lira. In France, the exchange rate governing capital transactions was floating. The floating pound sterling appreciated by a small amount; the currencies of some small European countries were revalued in varying degrees (generally less than 10 percent), and the same applied to some developing countries, such as Brazil; while the currencies of other countries, such as Israel and Mexico, remained unchanged in terms of the dollar. Overall it has been calculated that the trade-weighted average of dollar devaluation in terms of fourteen important currencies was between 5 and 6 percent. Combined with the Smithsonian Agreement, the two devaluations added up to about 15 percent.[11]

The U.S. competitive position improved as a result of the two devaluations, but by a far smaller proportion than the devaluations themselves. In the case of exports, American firms used part of the devaluations to increase profits, particularly in a period of booming demand on the home markets. It has been estimated that about half of the exchange adjustment was passed on to foreign buyers in the form of reduced prices, and at times U.S. companies tried

---

[11] For a detailed listing of the new exchange rates, see *IMF Survey,* February 26, 1973.

to make up in their foreign sales the profits that were denied them on domestic sales by price control. At the same time, foreign exporters often absorbed part of the cost of dollar devaluation.

To underscore the last point, consider the Japanese yen. Over a fourteen-month period it appreciated nearly 30 percent against the dollar, but in no way did that mean that the price of Japanese cars and other goods in the United States rose by 30 percent. First, Japanese producers immediately found that the yen prices of imported raw materials and equipment declined by 30 percent. Since Japan imports most of its raw materials, this substantially reduced production costs in Japan. Secondly, the Japanese producers absorbed part of the devaluation costs out of profit,[12] in an attempt to maintain their share of the U.S. market. At most, increases in U.S. import prices (which may be referred to as the "pass-through" effect of the devaluation) amounted to between one-half and two-thirds of the yen revaluation. For U.S. trade with all countries, it has been estimated that a given dollar devaluation improves the U.S. competitive position by about 70 percent of the devaluation.

March 1973—The Collapse of Bretton Woods

The tranquility following the February 1973 devaluation was short-lived, lasting no more than a few days. Fresh currency jitters erupted on March 1, with West Germany again absorbing $2.7 billion in one day, while smaller amounts flowed into other European countries, including France. This led to the immediate closing of the foreign exchange markets for a two-week period in March, to give central bankers a breathing spell during which a solution could be worked out. Presumably, the European countries found themselves on the horns of a dilemma. By all calculations the dollar was no longer overvalued in a fundamental sense. Yet the huge overhang of short-term dollar assets threatened further pressure on the dollar. This could result in its depreciation, further eroding the European competitive position; but this time the erosion would constitute a departure from long-run equilibrium rather than a movement toward it.

What emerged from the EEC deliberations was a partial "joint float." Under it the currencies of France,[13] West Germany, Belgium, Luxembourg, the Netherlands, and Denmark were pegged closely to each other and floated jointly against the dollar, with a maximum spread of 2¼ percent between the dollar rates of the strongest and weakest participants. Prior to the repegging

---

[12] Note, however, that there is a limit on how much can be absorbed out of profit, for even a huge company can run into financial difficulties, as the experience of Volkswagen has shown.
[13] For the French franc, it is the official exchange rate that was pegged, rather than the one governing capital transactions.

the mark was revalued further by 3 percent. Sweden and Norway (not members of the EEC) adhere to this joint float. The British and Irish pounds float independently, as does the Italian lira. A fund of gold and currencies equivalent to $10 billion was established as a source of credit to EEC countries subscribing to the joint float. Because the resulting movement of the jointly floating currencies produce a "snake-like" pattern, the arrangement continues to be referred to as the "snake" (although now without a "tunnel").

The "joint float" was widely viewed in the EEC as a major step toward the cherished goal of monetary unification. But it contained seeds of trouble. For although the dollar was generally weak, it was weaker against some member currencies (mainly the mark) than against others. And the arrangement contained no machinery for dovetailing policies within the Community to create the conditions necessary for a single currency area. Given the well-known West German aversion to inflation, this could easily result in internal imbalances between members of the floating group, necessitating adjustment in the internal exchange rate or even the abandonment of the joint float. Indeed, the mark and the guilder had to be revalued in the second half of 1973, and on January 20, 1974 France withdrew from the joint float, partly in response to the massive increase in the price of imported petroleum. As the French franc was floated independently, the government also abolished the two-tier market for the franc, and all international transactions are now governed by one floating exchange rate.

The regime inaugurated in March 1973 spelled the end of the Bretton Woods system by placing the industrial countries on a hybrid of fixed and floating exchange rates. The currencies of eight European countries (not coinciding with the membership of the EEC) were pegged to each other and floated jointly, while the pound sterling, the Italian lira, the Irish pound, the Japanese yen, the Canadian dollar, and the Swiss franc floated independently against the U.S. dollar. The U.S. dollar thus effectively became a floating currency, although it retained its reference and intervention roles on the free markets.

There followed a two-month period of relative calm on the foreign exchange markets. Most major exchange rates were reasonably stable in terms of the U.S. dollar through the middle of May 1973. Toward the end of May the dollar came under renewed pressure and its value started sagging against the jointly floating European currencies and the Swiss franc. In the ensuing two months the dollar lost over 15 percent of its value in terms of the continental currencies.[14] This loss is mirrored in the gain of the Swiss franc (used here to represent the continental currencies) shown in Figure 9-5.

---

[14] However, the pound, the yen, and the Italian lira did not appreciate in terms of the dollar.

Figure 9-5
Spot exchange rate, May–July 1973
SOURCE: IMF Survey, July 23, 1973.

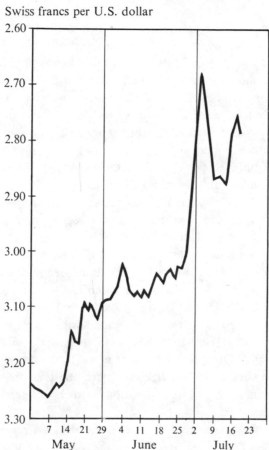

Swiss francs per U.S. dollar

What appeared to have triggered the new wave of dollar sales was renewed demand for gold coming from a variety of quarters, which sent its price soaring from around $90 per ounce in early May 1973 to over $120 in June. But various observers attributed the continued weakness of the dollar to a decline in confidence generated by the Watergate affair, the energy crisis, and similar factors. Considering the huge stock of dollars held in private foreign hands, a decline in confidence can indeed bring about a selling wave unwarranted by underlying economic conditions.

In all, between July 1971 and early July 1973, the trade-weighted devaluation of the dollar against fourteen major currencies amounted to 26 percent. By the end of June, it was widely recognized that the dollar was considerably undervalued. The European governments, fearing a deterioration in their competitive position, were pressuring for resumption of official intervention on the exchange markets, especially by the United States, to stop the decline in the value of the dollar. In early July, the fourteen major industrial nations agreed to increase their swap network to $18 billion and the New York Fed started supporting the dollar on July 10.

At the same time the long-delayed adjustment mechanism in the U.S. balance of payments was making itself felt across a broad front. Feature stories in the financial press told of Sabena (the Belgian airline) switching an order for ten airplanes from the French Dassault-Brequet company to the American Boeing Corporation; of a 33 percent drop in Japanese bicycle exports to the United States; of a decline in U.S. demand for French luxury shoes; of U.S. companies exporting from stateside plants some products they used to manufacture abroad; of small American companies beginning to export for the first time; of the United States regaining competitive advantage in industrial machinery and many textile items; of a 26, 24, and 34 percent climb in 1973 exports of capital goods, cars, and consumer goods, respectively; and of a large increase in the flow of direct foreign investments from Europe and Japan into the United States.[15] This was aided by increased U.S. exports of primary products, by the rise in U.S. interest rates, and by the virtual disappearance of the difference in internal demand pressures between the United States and other industrial countries. In the second and third quarters of 1973, the United States posted the first balance-of-payments surplus since 1969, providing for an external surplus for the full year 1973 (see Table 2-1). This revived confidence in the dollar and initiated an increase in its exchange value. Over the second half of 1973, the dollar recouped much of the loss it had sustained since February (see charts at the end of Chapter 3). However, in the spring of 1974 the dollar was again depreciating relative to the European currencies.

Among the other major trading nations the sharpest reversal occurred in Japan, where the effect of parity changes was reinforced by the rapid recovery of the economy. The large consecutive external surpluses gave way to a sizeable deficit in 1973. For the first seven months of 1973, Japan registered a $4.77 billion deficit compared to a $1.8 billion surplus in 1972. And the Japanese central bank was expending large sums of its dollar reserves to support the yen. The United Kingdom was also experiencing large deficits.

By contrast, the French trade surpluses continued, and the West German trade surpluses increased considerably from their 1972 levels, although there was a deterioration in its service account. It must, however, be remembered

---

[15] Similar changes were occurring between other pairs of countries. For example, the gradual revaluation of the Swiss franc from 165 to 205 Italian lire caused Italians to cease flocking across their border to Swiss towns such as Lugano to purchase gasoline, cigarettes, chocolate, coffee, and other items. In fact, the direction of that border traffic has been reversed, with the Swiss making such purchases in Italy, where these items became cheaper as a result of the lira devaluation.

that 50 percent of West Germany's exports are destined for its Common Market partners, and relative to them the mark was prevented from appreciating as a result of the joint float (save for a 5.5 percent revaluation in June 1973). In fact, the joint float has probably prevented the mark from floating up against noncontinental currencies.

In late 1973 and early 1974, the world financial scene came to be dominated by cutbacks in the supply of Arab oil and by a great increase in the price of oil introduced by the oil-producing cartel (OPEC). During 1973, the price of crude oil quadrupled. Although the new, higher prices may not be sustainable in the long run, they will surely not return to their former level but will remain significantly increased. Several of the international economic implications of these price increases are discussed below.

The industrial countries face a much higher import bill for petroleum, increasing internal inflation and balance-of-payments deficits. The added domestic and external burdens will vary among countries, depending on the degree of their dependence on imported oil; they can be expected to be highest for Japan, be less important for France, and lowest for the United States. While in the long run the United Kingdom may become self-sufficient in petroleum, due to the discoveries in the North Sea, it was severely hit by a coal strike that lasted from December 1973 to March 1974. Since electricity generators are fired by coal, the government was forced to initiate a three-day work week in industry, curtailing both output and exports. As a result, the pound slumped while the dollar advanced on the foreign exchange markets early in 1974.

Translated into bilateral trade, the rise in the price of oil implies an increase in the volume of exports exchangeable for the same quantity of oil imports—a deterioration in the terms of trade of the importing country. Currency depreciation is the mechanism through which this deterioration is brought about. For industrial countries, the burden of increased oil prices, measured as a percent of GNP, is certainly not intolerable.[16]

But the new oil prices also affect the developing countries. These nations can be divided into three groups: oil-producing desert countries with sparse populations, such as Saudi Arabia and Kuwait; oil-producing developing countries, such as Iran, Indonesia, and Nigeria; and oil-importing contries. The main problem facing the first group is that of excess riches: what to do with the immense fortune they amass, and how to ensure accumulation of enough real and financial earning assets to provide a substitute for the oil revenues once the wells run dry. As of mid-1974 they are investing their earnings in the

---

[16] One way of avoiding the burden altogether is for the developed countries gradually to dispose of their gold stock on the private market, at $170 per ounce, and use the proceeds to subsidize oil imports. The gold speculators would then bear most of the burden.

United States and Europe, and contracting with the industrial countries for the establishment of new industries (partly oil-based industries such as petrochemicals) on their soil, in exchange for oil. From the international point of view, it is important that they not use their fortunes to upset the currency markets.[17]

For the second group of oil producers, the new prices constitute an unmitigated boon. Practically all their oil revenues are spent on imported capital equipment. Their economic development is speeded up, and the problem of investment outlets for the additional earnings does not arise.

It is the third group of developing countries that are being subjected to an immense burden. Not only do they lack resources to pay the added cost of oil, but they also encounter increased prices of essential oil-based products such as fertilizers, raising the specter of a setback in farm output. The World Bank singled out twelve countries, with a combined population of more than a billion, for whom the new situation constitutes a life-and-death struggle. They are Bangladesh, Bolivia, Ethiopia, India, Kenya, Mali, Pakistan, Sri Lanka (formerly Ceylon), the Sudan, Tanzania, Uganda, and Zaire. Even for other developing countries, a setback in development is practically assured. Proposals being considered to counteract these dire effects include channeling part of the new oil revenues to the developing countries in the form of loans and grants, increasing economic aid from the industrial countries, and creating a special facility in the IMF to finance oil imports. A special session of the United Nations was called in April 1974 to deal with this and related problems, but no firm proposal has been adopted, let alone implemented, by the spring of 1974.

In the industrial world, floating exchange rates appear to have weathered the oil crisis of 1973 and its aftermath. Contrary to the fears of many central bankers, world trade expanded rapidly during 1973. In view of these developments, the IMF Committee of 20 appears to have shelved for the time being its plan to return to some form of fixed exchange rates. It is also the view of the International Economic Subcommittee of the U.S. Congress that the dollar should be permitted to float indefinitely. The next chapter reviews various plans to reform the international monetary system, culminating with the proposals that are likely to emerge from the Committee of 20.

---

[17] A problem created by the "recycling of petrodollars" in 1974 was that Arab countries preferred to invest their funds in short-term deposits, while the (Eurodollar) banks receiving these deposits were faced with demands for long-term loans. Much of this demand came from countries in balance-of-payments difficulties, such as Italy and France. Prudent banking policy dictates a limitation on such "borrowing short and lending long." Therefore intergovernmental loans were used to supplement the private capital market.

10
Proposals for Reform of the International Monetary System

Over the past decade, economists have developed far-reaching reform plans for the international currency system. The *Wall Street Journal* once noted that any economist can compose such a plan in forty-five minutes and "the trouble is that most of them have done so." Indeed, there is no dearth of proposals and no unanimity on what the next step ought to be. Much of the discussion has been published in four series of pamphlets issued by the International Finance Section of Princeton University.

Four main lines of approach have been selected for discussion in this volume: return to a full-fledged gold standard, establishment of a dollar exchange standard, freely fluctuating exchange rates, and establishment of an international reserve-creating institution or central bank. The selection is not exhaustive, but it serves to delineate the range of possibilities and illustrate some possible combinations. The first of these proposals, calling for an increase in the price of gold, was discussed briefly in Chapter 8, as were the main objections to it. The three others, all involving a considerably reduced role for gold as a monetary asset, will be presented here.

A Dollar Exchange Standard

Under certain conditions the U.S. dollar is in a fairly ideal position to serve as a reserve currency. What accounted for the periodic loss of confidence in the past was the American commitment to convert official foreign dollar holdings into another reserve asset, gold. In order to maintain the credibility of such a commitment, the gold reserves of the reserve center (the United States) had to grow by a certain proportion of the increase in dollar liabilities. This is similar to the position of commercial banks with respect to their deposit liabilities. Having experienced a huge decline in gold reserves over the recent past instead of continuous growth, and with the prospect of any increase in monetary gold stocks being rather dim, the dollar-based system became unstable.

But suppose the United States sold its gold stock on the free market, severed completely the relation between gold and the dollar, and invited all countries to peg their exchange rates to the dollar as well as to maintain the bulk of their reserves in dollars. The price of gold on the free market would be likely to decline, at least in the beginning. But, more important, if an international agreement to that effect could be reached, the trading community would move to a dollar exchange standard.

Reserves would be invested in interest-bearing assets on the New York money market, which is large enough to accommodate them and to withstand disturbances originating from shifts of funds. Countries wishing to increase (or decrease) their rate of reserve accumulation could devalue (or revalue) their currencies vis-à-vis the dollar. But to avoid competitive devaluation, the IMF would have to establish and administer international rules for exchange-rate adjustment. Since foreign trade occupies a very small role in most American industries, changes in its volume resulting from exchange-rate adjustments by foreign nations would not disrupt the domestic economy. The United States would therefore play a relatively passive role. With the dollar serving as the anchor currency, it could maintain complete freedom of international transactions and permit other countries to determine their exchange rates vis-à-vis the dollar and their balance-of-payments positions. The extent of the American external deficit would simply be a by-product of foreign demand for dollar reserves.

Such a system would require central bankers to demonstrate the same confidence in the dollar as was exhibited in the first twenty years after World War II by a multitude of foreign individuals and nongovernmental institutions (the private sectors), who used dollars freely in all international transactions. It also requires central bankers to abide by a reasonable code of behavior and subject themselves to some international surveillance. For example, strong reluctance of the surplus countries to revalue their currencies in terms of the dollar could undermine confidence in the dollar and shatter the system. While the United States can undertake unilaterally to sever the relation between the dollar and gold, smooth operation of a dollar exchange standard requires considerable international cooperation.

Central bankers would, of course, be free to hold some of their reserves in other currencies, such as sterling or marks. But apart from the reluctance of some countries to permit their currencies to serve as reserve currencies, a multiple-reserve-center system is inherently less stable than a single-reserve-center system. Under the latter system, a shift in reserve holdings between any two countries merely involves change in the ownership of assets in the same reserve center. By contrast, under a multiple-reserve-center system, when a country holding its reserves in center A loses some of them to another country holding its reserves in center B, funds are shifted from one reserve center to another, possibly creating disturbances in the centers themselves.

Centralization of Reserves and Establishment of an International Reserve-Creating Institution

Why, asks Robert Triffin of Yale University, should *international* reserves be in the form of a national currency—dollar, sterling, or whatever? Why should the creation of reserves for the system have to depend on balance-of-payments deficits of the center country, with the attendant threat of erosion of confidence in that country lurking in the background? Why not adopt the model of domestic monetary systems and establish some form of an international reserve-creating institution to perform tasks similar to those of domestic central banks? There are several variants of the proposal for an international reserve-creating institution using an expanded version of the IMF.

Under Triffin's proposal, all central banks would be required to maintain a portion (say, one-quarter) of their total international reserves (gold and foreign currencies) on deposit with the expanded IMF (XIMF). The XIMF, in turn, would serve as a clearing house for all intercountry financial transfers, in much the same way as the EPU served the European countries. The XIMF would maintain fractional gold reserves against its deposit liabilities, which are reserves to the member central banks. In turn, member countries could redeem in gold any excess reserves they happened to possess— namely, deposits with the Fund over and above what is required by the agreement. This redemption feature is not essential to the proposal and is designed merely to inspire confidence. But if it were incorporated into its charter, the XIMF might at some future point become short of gold to meet the demand. In that case it could raise the rate of interest it pays so as to attract additional deposits and discourage the demand for gold, or it could increase the proportion of required reserves, thereby eliminating excess reserves.

But the main function of the expanded Fund is to create international reserves in an orderly fashion, to coincide in time and place with the needs of central bankers as indicated by the value of international commerce and other considerations. In a superficial sense this can be viewed as a monetary layer in addition to the credit superstructure built upon the gold held by the Fund. As shown in Figure 10-1 (for a three-country system), central bank deposits with the XIMF are assets and reserves to the member countries and

Figure 10-1

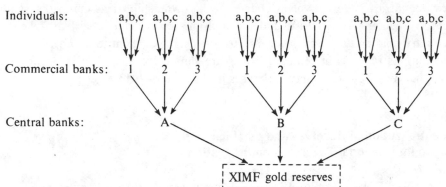

liabilities to the XIMF, in much the same way as commercial bank deposits with their respective central banks are assets and reserves to them and liabilities to the central banks. However, in a more meaningful sense, national currencies are replaced as a reserve instrument by a truly international asset acceptable to all: deposits with the XIMF. And the dangers arising from a multiple-reserve-asset structure are then removed. Excess reserves of central banks can be freely transferred between countries, because the Fund provides unlimited clearing opportunities. They can also be redeemed in gold.

Equally important are the proposed new means for the creation of reserves. Reserves can be created by the Fund extending loans to countries in need. In this case the initiative is taken by the borrowing country, and the loan is made by setting up a deposit on the books of the Fund, against which the country can draw. Such drawings are reserves by virtue of their universal acceptability. To the country receiving the loan these are *owed* reserves. But once transferred to other nations in the form of a Fund deposit, they become *owned* reserves. As a general rule countries prefer owned reserves to owed reserves. Second, reserves can be created through periodic allotments (as under the SDR provisions), where the XIMF distributes reserves among its members by crediting their accounts in accordance with some predetermined ratio. These immediately become owned reserves acceptable to all, and can be used to settle international imbalances.

An equally important way of creating owned reserves on the initiative of the Fund is through open-market operations. With the consent of a country's government, the Fund can go into that country's financial market and purchase national currencies, government bonds, or any other securities, including bonds and obligations of international organizations. Since the Fund pays by check drawn upon itself, the payment, once transmitted through the domestic clearing mechanism, will necessarily end up in the hands of the country's central bank. That bank, in turn, must deposit the payment with the Fund, thereby gaining owned reserves—that is, assets that are a liability of the

XIMF. Since the Fund holds the initiative in such operations, it can control the overall amount of reserves being created and abide by whatever agreement is reached on the annual accretion of reserves. Limits can be imposed on the annual addition to reserves and can be observed as a guard against inflation. The Fund can also determine which countries may obtain the new reserves. Indeed, several variants of the plan center on this determination.

As long as the only purpose of the arrangement is to create reserves, their distribution can follow the present IMF quota allocation or some similar predetermined formula giving the developed countries most of the newly created reserves. But an important body of professional opinion believes that there is nothing sacrosanct about the present quota distribution and that the creation of reserves should be linked to assistance for economic development (this is often referred to as the *link* proposal). In other words, the savings of real resources derived from the creation of fiat reserves (as against the mining of gold) should be assigned in whole or in part to developing countries. Such a combination is particularly desirable in view of the mounting needs for aid coupled with the increasing reluctance of legislatures in industrial nations to allocate funds for that purpose. In a sense, what is proposed is to remove a component of the aid allocation from the political process in the donor countries.

This can be accomplished by the Fund channeling its investments to the securities and currencies of developing countries, thereby giving them the newly created reserves. Most developing countries tend not to accumulate reserves, and they would spend most of the new acquisition on capital goods in the developed countries. Thus the new reserves would end up in the hands of the industrial nations, who pay for them in real resources, but in the process they would provide badly needed developmental assistance. This can also be accomplished under the SDR agreement, by the allocation of a special SDR issue of predetermined size to the developing countries. In addition, the Fund can combine reserve creation with developmental assistance by purchasing the securities of international and regional development institutions, such as the International Bank for Reconstruction and Development, the International Development Association, or any of the regional development banks.

An alternative proposal attempts to combine both of the above-mentioned objectives with the goal of domestic stabilization policies in the developed, aid-giving nations. Under this variant the initiative for reserve creation would lie with the developed country, to be taken when the country faces a combination of balance-of-payment deficit and domestic unemployment. The country would then make a budgetary aid appropriation, to be delivered to the XIMF in the form of national currency or government debt. Using this appropriation as security, the Fund would issue a deposit account to a developing country to finance imports for an approved project from the industrial country. When these imports had been paid for by a check drawn on the Fund, the donor country would obtain owned international reserves, which could then be used anywhere in an unrestricted manner. Thus, the less developed country would receive tied aid, whereas the developed country would obtain reserves in exchange for resources precisely at a time when these resources were abundantly available because of domestic unemployment. The domestic recession would also be alleviated as a result of the transaction. (A danger of the link proposal is that the developed countries would use it to *replace* other forms of aid instead of supplementing them.)

Freely Fluctuating (Floating) Exchange Rates

Embodying the most drastic departure from the Bretton Woods arrangements and nearly always eliciting heated debates, is the proposal to abandon fixed exchange rates permanently and permit the values of all currencies to fluctuate (or float) in terms of each other in response to market conditions of supply and demand. This is the system under which several major currencies function today, although many central bankers advocate return to fixed exchange rates. It seems instructive to present the advantages and disadvantages of this system in the form of a debate between a proponent and an opponent of fluctuation rates. Although such a presentation necessarily reflects a consensus of views on each side (which in fact does not exist), and is therefore oversimplified, it at least captures the essence of the controversy.

PROPONENT   The main advantage of fluctuating exchange rates is that the values of all currencies settle at a price that clears the market for foreign currencies. In a free market, if quantity demanded exceeds quantity supplied at a given price, then the price of the good is bid up until the quantities demanded and supplied are equal. If quantity supplied exceeds quantity demanded, the price is bid down. Similarly, in a free foreign exchange market, changes in the exchange rate equate demand and supply for foreign exchange. We can then rely on exchange fluctuations to maintain continuous equilibrium in the balance of payments, which thereby removes one of the thorniest problems of economic policy—a problem compounded by the fact that countries are often reluctant to assign high priority to external adjustment when it conflicts with the need for domestic stabilization.

Not only does this system solve the adjustment problem, but it also drastically reduces the need for reserves and may even eliminate it.[1] Only when the price is fixed is there a need for reserves. An exchange rate is nothing but a price. Just as we do not fix the prices of manufactured products, so there is no need to fix the price of currencies in terms of each other. The two great issues facing the international financial community—how to improve the

---

[1] On the other hand, fluctuating rates are likely to increase substantially the demand by private traders for foreign currencies to finance international transactions.

balance-of-payments adjustment mechanism and how to generate adequate reserves—would be solved by one act. Balance-of-payments adjustments would be immediate and not postponed for years until action was forced by intense pressure. Economic policy could then concentrate on the domestic objectives of full employment and price stability.

Fluctuating rates would also make monetary policy more effective for domestic stabilization. To see this, assume that a central bank wishes to cope with a depression by lowering interest rates. Under a fixed exchange rate this is supposed to work by encouraging investments that are sensitive to the cost of credit. But that sensitivity, and therefore the effect of the policy, may be limited. With a fluctuating rate, this policy can be expected to operate through an additional channel: the reduction of interest rates induces outflow of short-term capital to other countries where rates are higher. This depreciates the exchange rate and thereby encourages exports and discourages imports. The improvement in the trade balance implies a domestic expansion in employment and output, which spreads through the economy through the multiplier mechanism. The reverse sequence takes place when the central bank combats inflation by raising interest rates. Thus, under fluctuating rates, monetary policy affects the domestic economy through the trade balance in addition to investments.[2]

OPPONENT   Fluctuating exchange rates introduce considerable risk into all international transactions and would therefore lower the volume of foreign trade and investments to the disadvantage of all concerned.

Consider an American couple contemplating a vacation trip to Europe. The normal administrative and financial burdens would be compounded in the case of fluctuating rates by the fact that at no point on their tour would they be able to know in advance the dollar cost of local currencies. They would thus have no way of estimating the cost of their trip, unless they insured against exchange fluctuations or purchased in advance all the foreign currencies they thought they might need. In the latter case they would still face the problem of reconverting to dollars the excess amounts purchased. The same situation holds for investors and traders in general, and it presents an especially difficult problem for international corporations, which produce and sell in more than one country.

Exchange rates are not like any other price, for they involve monetary values, and money is the standard by which everything else is measured. Just

---

[2] On the other hand, fiscal policy is less effective under fluctuating rates. For in recession, fiscal expansion *raises* interest rates, attracts foreign capital, and *appreciates* the currency. The adverse effect on the trade balance operates against the domestic multiplier effect. Thus monetary policy is more effective than fiscal policy for domestic stabilization under flexible exchange rates. If international capital movements are not responsive to interest-rate differentials, both monetary and fiscal policies are more effective under flexible exchange rates than under fixed rates. For flexible rates maintain balance-of-payments equilibrium and prevent leakages through imports, thereby increasing the size of the multiplier.

as it is essential to have a fixed ratio between the New York dollar and the California dollar, so it is useful to have fixed ratios between currencies. Otherwise, commodity traders and investors cannot make advance estimates of costs and prices.

All this is particularly true in open economies, which are highly dependent on foreign trade. Constant exchange fluctuations will introduce continuous variations in the domestic price level as well as in the structure of relative domestic prices. That can result in turn in incessant reallocation of resources and perhaps even loss of confidence in the currency as a store of value. At the very least, such fluctuations can be highly disruptive.

Domestic stabilization of income and employment can be adequately handled by fiscal measures. In fact, under fixed rates the balance of payments constitutes a restraining influence on governments, forcing them to avoid excessive inflation, for it leads to balance-of-payments deficits. With fluctuating rates, all that happens in case of inflation is exchange depreciation, and the anti-inflationary discipline exercised by the balance of payments is lost. Indeed, there is a newly emerging (minority) view that fluctuating exchange rates necessarily lead to inflation.

PROPONENT   The risk introduced by fluctuating exchange rates, and therefore its effect on the volume of transactions, is vastly exaggerated. In reality it depends on the size of the fluctuations, and these are likely to be small, as indicated by Canada's ten years of experience with a fluctuating rate. Consequently, it should be relatively cheap to insure against fluctuations in the forward exchange market.

Theoretically, fluctuating rates can be expected to be reasonably stable because exchange markets are highly competitive, and the underlying demand-and-supply factors involve a high measure of response to price change. Under such conditions, it takes only a small change in price (that is, in the exchange rate) to bring forth whatever quantity response is made necessary by changing circumstances on either side of the market. For example, if for some reason there is an increase in demand, it takes only a small rise in price to bring forth the needed increase in supply to clear the market. Or a decline in demand would require only a small reduction in price to induce suppliers to withdraw from the markets the amounts needed.

This is a general relationship that exists in the market for any commodity: there is a positive correlation between the degree of response to price change (elasticity) and price stability. To see this, compare the effect on prices of a downward shift in the demand schedule under high and low response conditions (Figure 10-2). Starting from equilibrium position at P_1, Q_1, we shift the demand curve from D_1 to D_2. Clearly the price reduction resulting from the same shift in demand (the horizontal distance between D_1 and D_2 is the same in both cases) is much sharper in the low-response (inelastic) case than in the high-response (elastic) case. Precisely the same result may be obtained by

Figure 10-2

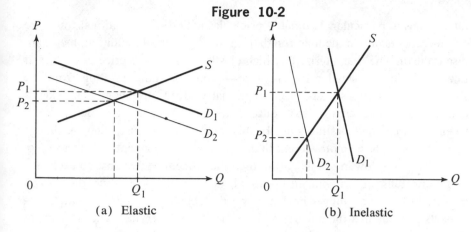

(a) Elastic   (b) Inelastic

shifting the demand curve to the right or by shifting the supply curve in either direction while holding demand unchanged. High elasticities are associated with price stability, low elasticities with sharp price fluctuations.

Exchange rates are nothing but prices. Since the foreign exchange market is characterized by strong responses to price change on both the demand and supply sides, a fluctuating exchange rate can be expected to be relatively stable. The Canadian experience bears out this supposition. Exchange fluctuations as such need not constitute an impediment to trade and investments; this was abundantly illustrated by the growth of both trade and investments during the period of fluctuating rates in 1973. On the other hand, fixed ex-change rates often lead to the imposition of exchange and import controls as a means of coping with deficits in the balance of payments, and these limit international transactions much more than moderate exchange fluctuations.

Furthermore, the analogy to a ratio between New York and California dollars does not hold, for not only are regions of the same country subject to the same monetary and fiscal policies, but factors of production (such as capital and labor) can move between them without government restrictions and compensate for "external" deficits. In other words, the adjustment mechanism under fixed exchange rates works far better interregionally than internationally. This strand of the argument leads to a possible compromise between the two positions, to be discussed later.

If small countries with open economies face especially severe problems under fluctuating rates, the way is always open to them to peg their currencies to the currency of a large country with which they trade a great deal. This indeed is what the sterling countries did in 1930, and what many developing countries do today.

Finally, the monetary authorities can be relied upon to exercise their own anti-inflationary discipline in the management of internal economic affairs.

OPPONENT The view of quick adjustment is contradicted by the time lag in the response of trade flows to price changes in general and to exchange fluctuations in particular. Estimated price elasticities in international trade are considerably higher in the long run than in the short run. In addition, merchandise trade *may* be characterized by high elasticities for large price changes and low elasticities for small price changes[3]—a phenomenon resulting from the significant transactions costs in international trade. Consequently, it takes a considerable price change to induce traders to switch from domestic to foreign sources and destinations. If this were not the case, then exchange fluctuations might be more violent than the previous argument indicates. Also, if elasticities are low in the short run, then the immediate response to exchange variations falls on (stabilizing) capital movements. But depending upon expectations, capital movements may be destabilizing in nature. [Other opponents concede that the underlying factors of goods, services, and investment transfers make for reasonably stable exchange rates, even if these were free to fluctuate, but worry about the nature of capital movements that respond to small exchange fluctuations.]

Even small exchange fluctuations can elicit and feed upon speculative activity; as the value of a currency rises in terms of foreign currencies, speculators may expect it to rise further and therefore *purchase* that currency in large quantities.

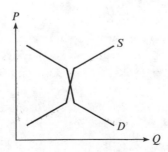

This would indeed bring about the anticipated increase in its value (as self-fulfilling expectations). The reverse would occur in the case of a decline. Thus, speculation superimposed upon the underlying market factors would aggravate fluctuations and be destabilizing in nature. The mild variations shown here by the solid line will be converted by the speculators to the sharper fluctuations illustrated by the dashed line. The Canadian experience is of very limited usefulness, for one cannot generalize from a situation of one fluctuating currency in a world of stable rates to a world in which all rates fluctuate. Al-

---

[3] This supposition would lead to the following demand and supply curves:

P

S

D

Q

though there has not yet been a long enough experience with the latter, the exchange market instability over the period of a few weeks in mid-1973 can be pointed to as an example of destabilizing speculation.

PROPONENT   It is unreasonable to assume that speculation would be destabilizing over the long run. In fact, to be profitable, speculation requires its practitioners to sell when the currency's price is high (not to purchase on the basis of expectations) and to buy when it is low. On the average, therefore, speculation must be a stabilizing phenomenon that has the effect of narrowing rather than aggravating the range of fluctuations. On the other hand, speculation can be highly destabilizing under a regime of fixed rates, as was witnessed in the fall of 1968 when the franc came under attack and in early 1973 when the dollar was attacked. When a currency is weak the speculator knows with reasonable certainty that if it moves at all it can move in only one direction: it can be devalued. He can hardly lose by selling it and buying a strong currency (like the mark or the yen in the late 1960s and early 1970s) that can only be revalued. Indeed, in a regime of fixed exchange rates, speculative activity can bring about changes in the exchange rate when it is superimposed on a certain underlying weakness or strength. Because the risk involved is very low, such speculation is often both destabilizing and excessive. Even the IMF recognizes that fact and permits the imposition of exchange control in cases of speculative attack. By contrast, fluctuating rates may dampen speculative activity by introducing more risk into it. (But even here speculation can be destabilizing, as was the case when the dollar declined in mid-1973).

End of debate. Much of the current and yet unresolved professional discussion centers on the role of speculation in the two exchange-rate systems.

Regardless of the merits of the case, there is still a deeply ingrained belief on the part of many central bankers that complete exchange flexibility on a permanent basis would mean the end of monetary discipline and would be injurious to international transactions. The developing countries also tend to favor fixed exchange rates, partly because such a system would require the creation of new reserves, and they would benefit if some form of a *link* proposal were to be incorporated into the scheme. For these reasons it is important to note that there are a number of compromise positions that enable both sides in this debate to have their cake and eat it too.

One proposal is to establish fixed exchange rates within a group of closely knit countries that together resemble regions of the same country, but to also permit free fluctuations between such blocs of countries. The joint float of six European currencies is a case in point. Such groups of countries are often referred to as "optimum currency areas." While there are no specific rules that define exactly what groups of countries may qualify for inclusion in any one area, some guidelines can be articulated. It is desirable for the countries composing a currency area to have a high measure of coordination in fiscal and, especially, monetary policies, as well as a high level of factor mobility between them. These conditions help lubricate the adjustment mechanism under fixed exchange rates. It will be recalled from Chapter 2 that when resources are highly mobile, as within a country, the adjustment process entails the movement of resources from the deficit (depressed) region to the surplus (prosperous) region. In addition, the currency area ought to be large enough, with most of its international transactions conducted within its own boundaries, that fluctuations between its composite exchange rate and the rates of other areas cannot affect its domestic price levels to any great degree.

Behind these criteria for optimum currency areas is the relative ease of the balance-of-payments adjustment process under the two alternative regimes. A region that is reasonably independent of foreign trade would sustain a lower adjustment cost in a system of flexible rates than in a system of fixed rates, where it takes substantial income adjustment to produce a change in the trade balance. The reverse is true for open economies.[4] For them the cost of balance-of-payments adjustment is lower via the income adjustment mechanism. There is some degree of "closedness" of a country or group of countries for which the costs of adjustment under the income and switching mechanisms are equal. That break-even point can be thought of as determining the size of the optimum currency area.

Adoption of a common currency is the most extreme form of financial integration within an optimum currency area. Money performs its functions (of means of exchange and store of value) best if the same unit covers a wide area. Thus, a worldwide currency is the best from the viewpoint of stimulating saving and economic growth. Barring such a currency, the next best thing would be a currency common to several countries, willing and able to meet the conditions for such an arrangement. In what follows we explore further the issues involved in forming a currency union in the context of the EEC.[5]

□ **Monetary Integration in the EEC** EEC planners have long considered a common currency an essential ingredient of European integration. As a first step in this direction they hope to attain a high measure of "monetary integration" by 1980. This is expected to have two components: permanently fixed

---

[4] The chief disadvantages of floating rates for a small open region are the thinness of the foreign exchange market and therefore the market's vulnerability to the machinations of individual speculators, the sensitivity of the domestic price level to changes in import prices, and the sheer cumbersomeness of the many foreign exchange transactions that are necessary when most goods, and perhaps many services, are bought from and sold to other regions.

[5] The European Economic Community consists of nine countries: West Germany, France, the United Kingdom, Italy, the Netherlands, Belgium, Denmark, Ireland, and Luxembourg. Belgium and Luxembourg have long had a monetary union. The EEC is discussed in Chapter 16.

exchange rates within the EEC, preferably without a band of fluctuations, which may or may not vary jointly relative to other currencies; and the complete absence of exchange control on current or capital transactions within the area.

☐ Three main factors have stimulated the drive toward monetary integration in recent years. The exchange-rate adjustments of the West German mark and the French franc in 1968–69, followed by other currency changes in subsequent years, complicated the operations of the Common Agricultural Policy (see Chapter 16). As farm prices were measured in common units (pre-1971 dollars), revaluation of the mark in relation to other EEC currencies forced West Germany to impose a border tax on farm imports and a subsidy on farm exports equivalent to the revaluation, in order to maintain the income of its farmers. This violated the principles of intra-EEC free trade in food products. With a common currency such problems can be avoided. Second, there was a vague notion that a currency union would force the member states to reach a high measure of economic and even political integration. In other words, if the integration necessary to a currency union could not be attained ahead of its establishment, then its creation might force the EEC members to harmonize their internal economic policies, and in the process further the goal of economic and even political integration. This was perceived to have a symbolic as well as a real value. If the horse cannot be put before the cart, might not placing the cart before the horse achieve the same objective in the long run? The third reason was a desire to set up a major currency or currency bloc that would rival the American dollar on the international financial scene, thereby ending the dollar domination of the international currency system.

☐ Historically, the move toward a common currency received a sharp stimulus from the adoption of the "Barre Plan" in February 1969, which set up a commission to coordinate the members' economic policies, and in particular to harmonize their monetary policies. A further step was taken in the May 1970 "Werner Report," which went into the specifics of monetary integration. As described by Harry G. Johnson,[6]

> the first stage of the Werner Plan called for the establishment of free convertibility among the six currencies; rigid and irrevocable fixation of the parities of the currencies with one another; establishment if possible of a single Community currency . . . (if national currencies were retained, their existence should have no economic significance); centralization of budgetary and monetary policy at the Community level; the adoption of a common external monetary policy; complete integration of members' capital markets by appropriate fiscal and institutional changes; and the establishment of regional policies determined at the Community level. This programme would require the establishment of two new supra-

[6] Harry G. Johnson, "Problems of European Monetary Union," *Journal of World Trade Law,* July/August 1971, p. 380.

national institutions: "a centre of decision for economic policy"—a Community Ministry for Economic Policy, responsible to the European Parliament; and "a community system of central banks", involving coordination of exchange-market interventions, the pooling of international reserves, the adoption of a common representative unit, and the narrowing to zero of the margins of market exchange-rate variations around the official parities.

Although the plan was not formally adopted, it became the cornerstone of European thinking on the subject. Operationally it was reflected in the adoption of narrow exchange-rate margins for EEC currencies after the 1971 Smithsonian agreement (The "snake in the tunnel") and the joint currency float agreed upon in March 1973. As it turned out, however, the joint float does not coincide with EEC membership. The United Kingdom, Ireland, Italy, and now France do not participate in it, while Sweden and Norway—not members of the EEC—do.

□ Is a currency union an attainable or even a desirable objective for the EEC? Alternatively, in terms of our previous discussion, can the EEC be viewed as an "optimum currency area"? It is axiomatic that "money" performs its functions (of medium of exchange and store of value) better the greater the area which it serves. In that sense, a world currency would have been the optimal arrangement, had it been possible for the world to behave like one country. As a second best, similar benefits would be derived from a currency union; and our task is to inquire into the possible composition of such a union.

□ At one extreme, the currency of a mini-country would have no monetary value of its own, and the population would choose to strike bargains and accumulate liquid wealth in terms of foreign currency. Such a country clearly should join a monetary union with other countries, as Luxembourg does with Belgium, Lichtenstein with Austria, and Monaco with France. Advancing to larger states, the same reasoning does not necessarily apply to most of the small European countries. Before a country the size of Norway or the Netherlands joins a currency union, it must weigh the costs of balancing its external accounts through domestic policy, as would be required of a member of the union, and of balancing them through exchange-rate adjustment (remembering that as a member of a customs union the country has already given up its right for independent action on trade controls). The higher the country's marginal propensity to import, the lower are the costs of adjustment via domestic fiscal and monetary policy. For in case of a deficit, the higher the MPM, the more a given reduction in GNP will curtail imports and the less the domestic unemployment necessary to eliminate a given deficit. Likewise the higher the MPM, the smaller the increase in domestic expenditures necessary to eliminate a given external surplus.[7] As a general rule, this implies that the smaller the country and the more open its economy the less the cost of adjustment via domestic policies. The costs of adjusting to external imbalances through variations in the exchange rate are the domestic price instability generated by exchange fluctuations, which would reduce the value of the currency as a store of value, and the domestic economic instability as resources shift between the domestic and foreign trade industries in response to exchange fluctuations. Also, in the case of depreciation there are possible losses in the terms of trade.[8] The costs of adjustment tend to be larger in the case of small open economies, where foreign trade may occupy as much as one-half of GNP, than in large countries. In general, the more important trade is in a country, the greater the potential gain from price certainty in international trade and hence from the assurance of fixed exchange rates. Thus, while the small European countries *may* do well to join a currency union, the same need not apply to the large members of the EEC, such as Italy, France, Germany, or the United Kingdom. There the cost of balancing the external accounts is less via exchange-rate adjustments than via domestic measures.

☐ Are there circumstances under which even the large European countries would benefit, on balance, from a currency union? Two alternative sets of conditions can be so visualized: The first is a set of prerequisites which, if met, would minimize or eliminate external imbalances between members of the currency union so as to minimize the need to adjust. Ideally these countries should have identical growth rates in productivity and identical preferences concerning the unemployment–inflation mix that they consider desirable; their position on the Phillips curve (for example, trade union aggressiveness, industrial concentration, and structural unemployment), should be the same. A difference in any one respect can create problems, unless it is offset by a difference in another respect. Members of the EEC have exhibited nonoffsetting differences in all three respects. Thus, over the 1954–68 period, the cost of living in West Germany rose by 34 percent and in France by 59 percent—a 25 percent differential—with the Benelux countries falling between the two extremes.

☐ Indeed, EEC currencies were unstable vis-à-vis one another in the 1960s. Even the joint float of 1973 did not constitute irrevocably fixed exchange rates, as the mark and the guilder were revalued only a few months after they were anchored to the other five continental currencies. France was forced to withdraw from the joint float in January 1974. And the problems would have certainly been exacerbated had the United Kingdom and Italy been part of the float.

---

[7] More precisely, the inverse of the MPM tells us by how much income would have to be curtailed to reduce imports by one dollar.

[8] Under infinite export supply elasticities, the terms of trade cost of $1 improvement in the balance of payments is $1/(\eta_m + \eta_x + 1)$, where the η's refer to import demand elasticities.

☐ A second set of conditions that would increase the benefits, relative to costs, of a currency union (by minimizing intra-union imbalances) would be for members of the union to behave as though they were regions of one country. This would include a common monetary policy and a common central bank, a high level of capital and labor mobility between members so that the depressed–flourishing area dichotomy would not be translated into unbalanced trade accounts, and an aggressive large-scale "regional policy" that would transfer resources to the depressed areas of the Community and stimulate economic activity in those areas by direct action of the central authorities of the union. This set of conditions is not fulfilled in the case of the EEC, where each country jealously guards its independent monetary policy, where there are cultural and even political obstacles to labor mobility, and where regional policy is still in its infancy. Unless and until the conditions articulated here are met, it may not be in the best interest of the EEC to pursue the objective of a currency union. However, if and when the EEC countries agree to meet these conditions, they can reap the benefits that flow from "money" when it serves a vast and productive area of the world.   ■

A second compromise proposal is to adopt fixed exchange rates but widen the spread within which exchange rates are permitted to fluctuate to, say, 3 or 4 percent on either side of par. This is often referred to as the "wider band" proposal. It would contribute to speeding up balance-of-payments adjustment and at the same time would reduce the need for reserves.

Other ideas bandied about include the so-called crawling peg or sliding parity, which would permit a country in disequilibrium to make preannounced small changes in its parity every month until equilibrium is attained. This would replace the "adjustable peg" system, under which exchange-rate adjustments are large, discrete, "one-shot" affairs. The proposal has the dual advantage of permitting parity adjustments before the pressure on the country has reached a boiling point and of removing some of the political stigma attached to large, discrete exchange variations. On the other hand, preannounced exchange adjustments can stimulate speculative activity, and the country would need to manipulate its interest rates to stem destabilizing capital flows.

An automatic variant of the crawling peg proposal is also being discussed. It would make the parity on any business day a moving average of the exchange rates (or of reserve movements) over a predetermined preceding period. Thus, if the exchange rate bounces along the floor—the lower support limit—for a specified period, the official parity rate along with the entire band would gradually be nudged down. Conversely, it would move upwards should the rate move along the ceiling for a time. In other words, the movements of the par value of each currency (along with its support limits) would depend on the relation between the actual exchange rate and the support limits over a certain past period.

Conclusion

Any international monetary system should contain features that deal with the balance-of-payments adjustment problem, the provision of adequate international reserves, and the maintenance of confidence in the form of reserves (for example, foreign currencies) that countries hold. During the 1960s a disproportionate share of the efforts of professional economists was spent on the problem of liquidity.[9] Only fluctuating exchange rates solve the problems of both liquidity and adjustment in one stroke. Under a regime of fixed rates, reserves only buy time. They only postpone, they do not obviate, the need for adjustment. In the end, equilibrium must be restored to the balance of payments.

Although informal cooperation between central bankers has reached unprecedented proportions since World War II, progress toward a lasting policy solution has been slow. All too often, decisions have been taken under intense pressure, rather than after careful deliberation. The options open to the policy-makers in considering reform of the system are diverse and far-reaching. Furthermore, the plans are not all mutually exclusive. Thus, the idea of "wider bands" might be combined with a central reserve-creating institution, where there is a trade-off between the amount of needed reserves and the width of the band. Or wider bands might be combined with the crawling-peg proposal, resulting in a form of "movable band." Nor does the author propose to advocate one plan over the other. The purpose of this book is to introduce the reader to the maze of problems of international economics and to equip him for making his own choice.

What does the future hold? One possiblity is that central bankers would realize the virtues of the present regime of fluctuating rates (relative to the difficulties of constructing a new system), and leave it intact. They certainly are not likely to tamper with the present arrangements in the immediate future. Another possibility is that the deliberations of the Committee of 20 would yield a new system, to be adopted sometime in the more distant future. Although the Committee's recommendations have not been firmed up, their main features have surfaced in various press reports.

It appears that the Committee would reject floating rates as a permanent

---

[9] This is true also for the time and energy expended by political leaders. But in their case it can be explained by the fact that facing the adjustment issue head on would force into the open an inherent conflict over the distribution of the burden of adjustment between the deficit and surplus countries. On the other hand, the creation of additional reserves eliminates or postpones that conflict.

solution in favor of stable exchange rates subject to frequent adjustments and with floating rates being admissible in particular situations (not necessarily temporary or transitional). Exchange stability would be maintained by multiple currency intervention, in which the U.S. dollar would participate along with other widely traded currencies. SDRs are envisioned as the main reserve asset, with the capital value of each unit related to a basket of currencies, suitably weighted, and its yield related to a group of representative interest rates. The SDR facility would be expanded as the main source of new reserves to be held along with other forms of reserves such as convertible currencies. But SDRs would replace the dollar as the core (numeraire) of the system, and some solution would be proposed for the "overhang of officially held dollar assets." A link *may* be established between reserve creation and development assistance. Currencies would be freely convertible to each other, with capital controls held to absolute minimum. Ground rules would be proposed to improve the balance-of-payments adjustment mechanism, with both surplus and deficit countries "shouldering the burden"; but no one specific indicator would be used to determine the need for adjustment. Instead, international consultation, under IMF auspices, would determine when adjustment action is called for, with the type of policy to be undertaken left to the discretion of the country concerned. But a system of graduated pressure (such as withholding of new SDRs) would be applied if a country is found negligent in its adjustment responsibilities.

But this plan will not be formalized and activated in the foreseeable future. At the time of this writing (the spring of 1974), the Committee appears to have suppressed indefinitely any plan to return to fixed exchange rates. Instead it has turned its attention to the development of guidelines for what it considers an "interim" system of floating rates. These include principles to govern central bank intervention in foreign exchange markets designed to guard against competitive depreciation, a new valuation system for SDRs (basing their value on a "basket" of important currencies), and reconsideration of the interest rates charged on them, and establishment of an "oil facility" to finance oil imports.

2

International Trade Relations

Introduction

Data on International Commodity Trade

Part 1 was devoted to financial problems, covering balance-of-payments adjustment and international liquidity. But a smoothly functioning international financial system is not an end in itself; it merely makes possible an unobstructed trade in goods and services as well as transfers of capital in order that it may serve the interests of the international community. In Part 2, therefore, we turn our attention to the advantages of such unobstructed exchange, and to public policies that affect the flow of trade.

As in Part 1, the emphasis in the chapters that follow is on policy. But the necessary theoretical underpinnings are also explained, in a simple manner. This part of international trade theory is often referred to as the pure theory of international trade to distinguish it from the mechanism of the balance-of-payments adjustment, or monetary trade theory. The word "pure" carries absolutely no moral connotation. It simply underscores the fact that the theory deals with trade in its barter essentials and that monetary phenomena do not occupy a central role in it.

Of the various items in the balance-of-payments statement, merchandise trade is the main concern of Part 2. The only exception is the last chapter, which is devoted to direct foreign investments and labor mobility.

In the balance-of-payments statement, all commodities are lumped together into one item, but there are statistical sources that break this item down into its components and show the sources and destinations of each product. Thus, the United Nations and other international organizations such as the Organization for European Cooperation and Development (OECD) classify all commodities according to the Standard International Trade Classification (SITC). Last revised in 1961, the SITC comprises one-, two-, three-, and four-digit classes. Commodity groups in the one-digit class are fewest in number and least detailed; those in the other classes are greater in number and more detailed, up to the four-digit class, which has the most commodities and is the most refined in detail. Items 5 through 8 of the one-digit class, for example, are manufactures: Item 5 is chemicals, 7 denotes machinery and transport equipment, and 6 and 8 are other manufactures. Each of these items is further subdivided into its components and subcomponents. This is illustrated with respect to SITC number 7. It is divided into categories 71, nonelectrical machinery; 72, electrical machinery; and 73, transport equipment. Category 71 is subdivided into 711, nonelectrical power machinery; 712, agricultural machinery; 714, office machines; and so on. And 714 is even further subdivided into 714.1, typewriters; 714.2, accounting machines; 714.3, statistical machines; and so forth. For certain items, a more refined five-digit breakdown is also available. For example, 711.4 is aircraft engines; two of its subdivisions are 711.41, piston aircraft engines, and 711.42, jet turbines.

The most comprehensive quarterly and annual statistics for all countries, using four-digit (and sometimes five-digit) SITC, are published by the United Nations in *Commodity Trade Statistics*. For Europe and North America, a detailed commodity breakdown appears in the OECD publications *The Network of Intra-European Trade* and *Trade by Commodities, Series B*. These reports are based on data collected by member countries from import and export declarations filed by traders.[1] Information on trade flows as well as on domestic economic variables for the industrialized countries is contained in the OECD's monthly publication *Main Economic Indicators*.

For the United States, a very detailed classification of traded commodities is published quarterly in the U.S. Census Bureau report of exports and imports. Similar national publications exist for other countries. United States international trade may be compared to domestic consumption or production of a given commodity by means of an annual Census Bureau publication, *United States Commodity Imports and Exports as Related to Output*, which converts the U.S. foreign-trade classification to the Standard Industrial Classification of the United States and provides the relevant data for each product category.[2] For other countries, such a comparison may be found in the United Nations publication *The Growth of World Industry*. Finally, the United Nations *Monthly Bulletin of Statistics* offers trade and other information for various nations, and the U.N. regional commissions publish quarterly or annual reviews of economic developments in their areas. Information on East–West trade is contained in surveys published by the U.N. Economic Commission for Europe.

1 "Partner country" statistics contain many sizable discrepancies: a country's export of a given commodity does not always match the importing country's reported import of that commodity. This is true of both volume and value figures. Some of the reasons for the discrepancies are that different countries often categorize the same product differently; there is a time lapse between departure and arrival of goods; traders may under- or over-invoice exports or imports to take advantage of government policies (subsidies, exchange controls); and discrepancies and inaccuracies exist in offical calculations.
2 For conversion tables between the various commodity classifications used domestically and internationally, see the U.S. Bureau of the Census, *U.S. Trade Statistics, Classification and Cross-Classification* (Washington, D.C.: 1968).

Part 2 begins by considering why nations trade and what determines the types of commodities that are imported and exported—that is, the commodity composition of trade. In the process it sheds additional light on the relation between national economic conditions and trade and exchange relations. The discussion then turns to government policies that obstruct the free flow of goods across national boundaries when protection of domestic industry is the foremost objective. It is to be kept in mind, however, that trade and exchange policies are partly interchangeable in their effect, the main distinction between them being the *intent* of a policy: protection in the case of trade measures, and corrections of balance-of-payments disequilibria in the case of exchange restrictions. Subsequent chapters discuss regional and international organizations designed to promote free trade or to advance the interests of a certain group of countries. Chapter 18 is concerned with the reasons for and the effect of international flows of investment capital.

11
Why Nations Trade

Nations trade with each other for fundamentally the same reasons that individuals or regions engage in exchange of goods and services: to obtain the benefits of specialization. Since nations, like individuals, are not equally suited to produce all goods, either because they are differently endowed or for other reasons, all would benefit if each specialized in what it can do best and obtained its other needs through exchange. The point is self-evident, for in a free society communities would not engage in trade if it did not benefit them.

The principles governing the composition and direction of international trade are the same as those governing interregional exchange within a nation. But although a nation can pursue independent foreign trade and exchange policies, its political subdivisions cannot. And only a nation has its own fiscal and monetary policies that in turn affect foreign trade. Countries possess other features unique to national government, which were outlined in Chapter 2. Therefore, the statement that it is in its conduct rather than in its basic purpose that international trade differs from interregional exchange implies a great deal. At the very least this difference confines the entire analysis of trade policies to the examination of independent nations. This chapter focuses on the gains to individual nations from an international exchange of goods; it demonstrates the conditions under which two trading countries may benefit from trade. And in the process it develops a method of determining which goods are exported and which are imported by each country—what economists call the direction of international trade or the commodity compositon of trade. (Although it is interwoven with the reasons for trade and the benefits derived by the trading countries, the question of the direction of trade is subsidiary and will be explored in greater detail in the next chapter.)

The Principle of Comparative Advantage

The Gains from Trade

Asked why he engages in foreign trade, any businessman can promptly offer a superficial, yet correct answer: he purchases a commodity abroad if and when it is cheaper abroad than at home, and he sells a commodity abroad when it fetches a higher price abroad than it does domestically. He buys where it is cheapest and sells where it is dearest in order to maximize his profit. In other words, relative prices at home and abroad determine which goods are exported and which are imported by any given country—the commodity composition of trade.

But what makes some goods cheaper in one country and others cheaper in another? To the businessman this is of no consequence; he simply converts one currency into another at the prevailing exchange rate and compares prices. But to the economist, this is the crux of the matter, for it is only by answering this question that he can determine whether such profit-maximizing behavior on the part of individual traders is beneficial to the country. And, equally important, saying that a commodity is cheaper in one country than in another implies the use of a fixed exchange rate. But in Chapter 3 we indicated that the exchange rate itself must in some way be determined by relative costs and prices as well as by other economic conditions in the two trading countries. Thus, by simply falling back on the businessman's statement, we are, at least in part, explaining relative prices by relative prices. In order to break out of the circular reasoning, it is necessary to investigate what determines the relative cost–price positions of the two countries.

To do this we go to a principle originally enunciated early in the 19th century by the English economist David Ricardo: the principle of comparative advantage or, stated inversely, comparative cost. It is most easily explained by a simplified example similar to the one Ricardo used. Assume that the world consists of two countries, say the United States and the United Kingdom, which produce two commodities, wheat and textiles. Suppose further that the only factor of production employed in producing the two goods is labor in a homogeneous form. This means that the value of each product is determined exclusively by its labor content (yielding the so-called labor theory of value). Goods move freely between the two countries but labor is mobile only domestically, not internationally. Transport costs are also assumed not to exist. Technology is presumed to remain constant, unaffected by trade. Although this is a highly simplified case, it yields considerable insight of general application, as we shall see.

Suppose that the production conditions prevailing in the two countries are those of Scheme 1.

SCHEME 1

In	*One Man-Day of Labor Produces*
United States	60 bushels of wheat *or* 20 yards of textiles
United Kingdom	20 bushels of wheat *or* 10 yards of textiles

Clearly, labor is more productive absolutely in the United States than in the United Kingdom in both the textile and the wheat industries: it produces more of everything in the United States than it does in the United Kingdom. (At a later point it will be shown that the existence of this absolute advantage has important implications with respect to the relative wage rates in the two countries.) It should not be inferred from these figures that because the United States is more efficient in the production of both commodities, it would produce both of them when trade opens up or that the United Kingdom would produce none. To suggest this is to deny the mutual advantage to be derived from international trade. The condition postulated here, that one country is absolutely more productive than another in most of their mutual pursuits, is not uncommon, yet mutually beneficial trade does take place, even between countries as extremely different in productive efficiency as the United States and India.

What is important in the problem at hand is not absolute but comparative advantage. A vertical comparison of the figures in Scheme 1 shows that the degree of American advantage over the United Kingdom is not the same in both industries. The United States has a 3 to 1 advantage in wheat, but only a 2 to 1 advantage in textiles. Comparatively speaking, therefore, the United States has a greater advantage in wheat and least advantage in textiles. The United Kingdom is in the reverse position; it has an absolute disadvantage in both goods, but the extent of disadvantage is most in wheat and least in textiles, because labor can produce only one-third as much wheat as in the United States but it can produce fully one-half as much textiles. Since we are merely comparing the degree of advantage and disadvantage in producing the two goods, the analysis can be expressed by asserting that the United States has a comparative advantage in wheat while the United Kingdom has a comparative advantage in textiles.

This situation is analogous to that of a doctor who is absolutely more efficient than his nurse in the performance of both medical and paramedical duties. But the degree of his advantage is much larger in the first type of duty than in the second. And just as it pays the doctor to concentrate on the former and hire a nurse to do the latter, so it is to America's advantage to specialize in wheat and purchase British textiles.

But this is running somewhat ahead of our story. The productivity comparison between the two countries is possible only because of the existence of an international common denominator—a given quantity of homogeneous labor. Had this been absent, the vertical comparison in Scheme 1 would have been impossible. Consequently, it is more general and meaningful to focus on the horizontal, *within-country,* comparison, although the conclusion is the same in both cases.

What do we see from that vantage point? Domestically, the United States must give up 3 bushels of wheat to obtain 1 yard of textiles. Obviously, wheat is not convertible into textiles in any mechanical sense; but by foregoing 3 bushels of wheat, enough labor (and other resources if present) is released to be put into textile production to produce 1 yard of textiles. This is what the internal cost ratio of 3 to 1 (or 60 bushels of wheat for 20 yards of textiles) means: the resource cost, sometimes called the "opportunity cost," of 1 yard of textiles in the United States is 3 bushels of wheat. The United States would be unwilling to trade 3 bushels of wheat for anything less than 1 yard of textiles, for it can do better at home. But it would be eager to purchase textiles abroad if a yard could be obtained for less than 3 bushels of wheat, because then the resource cost of textiles embodied in the wheat traded is less than that of foregoing wheat production in order to produce the textiles at home.

What is the situation from the British point of view? Domestically, the resource or opportunity cost of 2 bushels of wheat is 1 yard of textiles, because by giving up 1 yard of textiles enough labor is released to produce 2 bushels of wheat. If the United Kingdom is able to obtain through trade more than 2 bushels of wheat per yard of textiles, it will trade, for the resource cost of obtaining wheat by trading away textiles is less than that of giving up textile production to produce wheat at home. But the United Kingdom would be unwilling to trade 1 yard for less than 2 bushels, for it can do better at home.

In sum, the appropriate comparison for each country is between the resource cost of the commodity produced at home and the cost when it is acquired from abroad in exchange for the export good. The figures of Scheme 1 can be transformed into the limits to mutually beneficial trade, as given in Scheme 2.

SCHEME 2   Limits to Mutually Beneficial Trade

1 yard of textiles $\begin{cases} = \text{maximum of 3 bushels of wheat for the United States} \\ = \text{minimum of 2 bushels of wheat for the United Kingdom} \end{cases}$

The United States is willing to purchase 1 yard of textiles for anything less than 3 bushels of wheat, while the United Kingdom is willing to sell 1 yard

Table 11-1

Production and Consumption With and Without Trade,
Where the International Exchange Ratio is 1 Yard = 2½ Bushels

	United States	United Kingdom
Production at full capacity	600 bushels of wheat	200 yards of textiles
Consumption with trade	⎧ 400 bushels of wheat ⎨ 80 yards of textiles	⎧ 200 bushels of wheat ⎨ 120 yards of textiles
Consumption without trade	⎧ 400 bushels of wheat ⎨ 66⅔ yards of textiles	⎧ 160 bushels of wheat ⎨ 120 yards of textiles

of textiles for anything more than 2 bushels of wheat. Trade can take place anywhere between these limits. Stated differently, the domestic cost ratios of the two commodities in the two countries constitute the limits to mutually beneficial trade. Within these limits it is to the advantage of each country to concentrate on the production of the good in which it has a comparative advantage and to obtain the other product through trade.

To see that trade is indeed beneficial to both nations, select any international price ratio within the specified limits, such as 1 yard of textile = 2½ bushels of wheat. Trading at this ratio enables each country to consume more than is possible without trade. Let us say that the United States, employing its entire labor force, produces 600 bushels of wheat, of which it consumes 400 and exchanges 200 for textiles. The United Kingdom at full production manufactures 200 yards of textiles, of which it consumes 120 and exchanges 80 for wheat. With international trade, the 200 bushels of wheat are exchanged for 80 yards of textiles, permitting the United States to consume 400 bushels and 80 yards and the United Kingdom to consume 200 bushels and 120 yards. Without trade the United States can transform (in terms of resource conversion) the 200 bushels into only 66⅔ yards of textiles, making available a total of 400 bushels and 66⅔ yards. The United Kingdom, without trade, can transform the 80 yards of textiles into only 160 bushels of wheat, making available 120 yards and 160 bushels. All this is summarized in Table 11-1, showing clearly that both countries benefit from the exchange.

Demand Considerations

Referring back to Scheme 2, it will be observed that the internal cost ratios provide only the limits to mutually beneficial trade. Within these limits, the actual exchange ratio is determined by the relative strength, or intensity, of each country's demand for the other country's product.

Since the demand for the imported good is expressed in terms of units of the country's own export product—the entire exchange being in barter terms

—it is known as "reciprocal demand." In other words, production costs determine the limits, while reciprocal demand determines what the actual exchange ratio will be within these limits. Clearly, the further apart the two domestic cost ratios are, the more room there is for mutually advantageous trade, and the larger the benefits are that can be derived from trade by both countries, in the sense that the net increase in available goods over the no-trade position is larger. At the other extreme, when the two domestic cost ratios are identical, there are no advantages to trade. Each country is as well off in isolation (without trade) as with trade, so there is no inducement to engage in trade. In the real world, before trade can commence the difference between the two cost ratios must be large enough to compensate for transport costs and artificial barriers to trade.

Finally, in our simple example, the distribution of the benefits between the two countries depends on where the exchange ratio settles. If it ends up near the British cost ratio of 1 yard of textiles = 2 bushels of wheat, the United States derives most of the gain; if it is close to the American cost ratio of 1 yard of textiles = 3 bushels of wheat, the United Kingdom reaps most of the benefits. The reader may wish to verify this by working a couple of simple numerical examples.

The commodity exchange ratio is often referred to as the "commodity terms of trade," for it shows the price of one product in terms of the other. In a multiproduct world these prices must be expressed in terms of composite indexes, and *the terms of trade* of each country become *the export-price index divided by the import-price index*.

Now the link between the commodity terms of trade and the distribution of the benefits from trade among the trading countries occupies a central role in present-day policy debates involving the developing countries (the subject of a later chapter). However, the exchange ratio is a rather superficial barometer of the gains from trade, for several reasons, only one of which is visible in our example. If the ratio ends up near the British domestic ratio (say 1 yard = $2\frac{1}{10}$ bushels), this is a result of the high intensity of British desire for wheat compared to the relatively low level of American eagerness for textiles. Thus, although this trade ratio is more beneficial to Americans in the sense that it increases their available textiles per unit of wheat given up by more than it increases the wheat available to the United Kingdom per unit of textile given up, we must remember that the Americans are much less eager for textiles than the British are for wheat. Consequently, in terms of satisfaction, or utility, reflected in the eagerness of demand, the Americans may not gain more than the British. Once the "commodity gain ratio" is translated into "utility ratio," the gain appears rather equally distributed.

In reality, demand factors often occupy a much more important role than the one ascribed to them here. In the example of Scheme 1, both goods are homogeneous commodities: there is only one universal type of wheat and only one kind of textile. But much of the trade that takes place in the world is in "differentiated products": each commodity has various gradations of quality, size, flavor, and so on, and even differences in packaging and brand names are important. In such circumstances it is no longer true that identical cost ratios would result in no trade. For example, it is reasonable to assume that automobile production has approximately the same rank of comparative advantage in Italy, France, West Germany, and the United Kingdom. And consequently it would be difficult to explain the intense intercountry exchange of Fiats, Renaults, Volkswagens, and Austins on the grounds of cost differentials. A large part of the explanation must lie in consumer preferences for the foreign brand, even when the price equals that of its domestic counterpart. Since these cars are of roughly similar quality and size, the benefit from such trade cannot be quantified as was done in the last section. It is merely a psychic gain in the mind of the consumer, derived from having an option to purchase the foreign brand. The fact that there are such psychic benefits is self-evident; otherwise there would be no exchange of cars. But the size of the gain cannot always be measured.

This example can be generalized to most industrial products. They will be traded even when cost ratios are identical in the countries involved, because consumers may prefer the foreign brands for reasons that have nothing to do with production costs. Since much of world trade is in differentiated products, demand considerations undoubtedly play an important role in determining its composition. They are abstracted from in this exposition only for the sake of simplicity.

Having made this important qualification, we return to the analysis of a world in which all products are homogeneous.

Why Complete Specialization?

A feature of the Ricardian example that may have puzzled the reader is that trade leads each country to specialize completely in the production of the commodity in which it has a comparative advantage. In isolation, of course, every country must produce both goods if it wishes to consume both. Production and consumption are necessarily identical. International trade makes it possible for the production mix to be different from the consumption mix, with the differences being made up by trade. But must the United States get completely out of textile production and devote itself exclusively to wheat? Likewise, must the United Kingdom abandon wheat production altogether and specialize in textiles? Certainly this is not true in the real world, where even the most casual observation shows that countries produce some of the same types of goods as those they import.

Figure 11-1
Wheat and Textiles under Increasing Cost

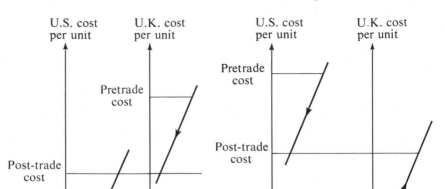

The answer is that "complete specialization" is unique to this type of example and arises from the assumption that production costs per unit of output remain constant as output expands or contracts. When trade opens up, the United States expands its wheat production and contracts its textile production while the reverse happens in the United Kingdom. If the unit cost rises with output (known as "increasing cost" situations), then the American wheat price rises as production expands and the British wheat price declines as production contracts. Precisely the reverse happens to textile prices. Thus, increasing cost conditions constitute a mechanism that forces prices in the two countries to converge. And once prices of the last ("marginal") unit traded are the same in the two countries, there is no inducement for trade to expand further. Equality of prices is the condition for equilibrium between the two countries after international trade opens up. Prices can easily become equal before complete specialization is reached, resulting in equilibrium with trade where production is incompletely specialized, as illustrated in Figure 11-1 (note that prices become equal at the margin; intramarginal units are not equalized in price).

But this mechanism is absent under constant cost. Then production costs remain unchanged as output expands and contracts, and there is no tendency toward price convergence, as is shown in Figure 11-2. Therefore, the process does not stop until complete specialization is reached—until the United Kingdom discontinues wheat production and the United States gets out of textile production. To sum up, production under increasing cost may or may

Figure 11-2
Wheat and Textiles under Constant Cost Conditions

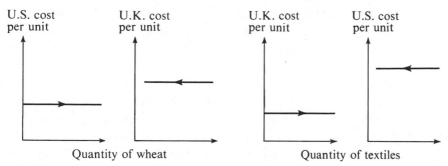

| U.S. cost per unit | U.K. cost per unit | U.K. cost per unit | U.S. cost per unit |

Quantity of wheat   Quantity of textiles

not lead to incomplete specialization, but constant cost conditions necessarily result in complete specialization.[1]

What accounts for the increase in unit production cost as output expands and its decline as output contracts as shown in Figure 11-1? It is what economists call the law of diminishing returns. Suppose it takes land and labor to produce wheat, land being available in fixed quantity while the amount of labor applied to it can be varied. As one increases the number of workers cultivating the fixed acreage of land by successive additions of one worker at a time, the increment of wheat output first rises, but then declines. Stated in technical terms: diminishing returns set in beyond a certain level of output. Concomitantly, the average amount of wheat per worker also begins to decline. This gradual reduction in the average productivity (output per worker) of the variable factor (labor) is a direct result of the fact that successively large quantities of it are employed with a fixed quantity of the fixed factor (land). Why, then, is that not reflected in our Ricardian example? Simply because only one factor of production (labor) is assumed to exist. It need not be combined with any fixed factor and therefore does not result in diminishing returns. Labor productivity, measured as output per worker, remains constant regardless of the level of output. And under constant cost conditions (portrayed in Figure 11-2), there is no mechanism that leads prices to converge as trade expands; hence the necessary outcome of complete specialization.

Comparative Opportunity Cost

Who Exports What

Having disposesd of the puzzle embodied in our example, we are in position to return to the main line of argument. Suppose that labor is not the only factor

---

[1] The only exception occurs if one of the countries is too small to supply its trading partner with all the partner's needs of the commodity.

of production but one of several. Then trade may or may not lead to complete specialization, although at some points in the analysis it helps to assume that it does. Equally important, the common denominator that made it possible to compare productivity between countries is no longer available, for when several productive factors enter into the production process, the productivity of each of them separately is of little consequence. Instead it is necessary to measure their joint productivity.

For convenience we concentrate on the inverse of productivity, or unit production cost, by aggregating the resources that go into the production of one unit of output. But resources or factors are diverse. The only way to aggregate labor, land, and capital is by adding up their money value. Thus, instead of a Ricardian labor-productivity scheme, we end up with a production-cost scheme (Scheme 3), where costs in each country are measured in terms of its currency.[2] We shall presently see that the principle of comparative advantage (or cost) remains inviolate.

SCHEME 3	Production Costs per Unit of Output	
	Wheat per bushel	*Textiles per yard*
United States	$1	$3
United Kingdom	£1	£1

Since we do not know the exchange rate (for there is no exchange rate before trade opens up), there is no way of comparing costs in absolute terms between the two countries. But the intracountry (horizontal) comparison is still possible as before. In the United States, the resource or factor cost of 1 yard of textiles is 3 bushels of wheat. The dollar signs represent composite factor cost—it takes three times as big a resource basket to make 1 yard of textiles as to grow 1 bushel of wheat. It is in this sense that the two goods are interchangeable, but this is the only relevant sense for the economy as a whole.

To restate, the opportunity (or resource) cost of 1 yard of textiles in the United States is 3 bushels of wheat. In the United Kingdom, on the other hand, the resource cost of 1 yard of textiles is 1 bushel of wheat. Comparatively speaking, therefore, textiles are three times as expensive (in terms of wheat) in the United States as in the United Kingdom. More precisely, the textile/ wheat cost ratio in the United States is three times as great as in the United

---

[2] Note that the ratios of Scheme 3 need not be the inverse of those in Scheme 1 because Scheme 3 includes all production costs and is not restricted to labor costs. It would, however, be instructive for the interested reader to work through an example where the production cost ratios are exactly the inverse of the labor productivity ratios postulated in Scheme 1. Scheme 3 would then read

	Wheat	Textiles
United States	$1	$3
United Kingdom	£1	£2

Kingdom. In the same sense, wheat is relatively cheaper in the United States than in the United Kingdom. This establishes the fact that the United States has a comparative advantage in wheat and the United Kingdom, in textiles; they will specialize and trade accordingly.

The Limits to Mutually Beneficial Exchange

Having ascertained the direction of trade should it open up, we next establish the limits to mutually beneficial exchange. Domestically, the United States can obtain 1 yard of textiles for 3 bushels of wheat, for by foregoing 3 bushels of wheat, enough resources are released to produce 1 yard of textiles. It will trade only if it can obtain 1 yard of textiles for less than 3 bushels of wheat. Domestically, the United Kingdom can obtain 1 bushel of wheat per yard of textiles. It would trade only if 1 yard of textiles yielded more than 1 bushel of wheat. As before, the domestic cost ratios set the limits within which the exchange ratio must fall (Scheme 4). If the cost ratios are identical in the two countries, no trade takes place (the limits simply collapse into one point) unless motivated by demand factors as is the case of differentiated products.

SCHEME 4   Limits to Mutually Beneficial Trade

$$1 \text{ yard of textiles} \begin{cases} = \text{maximum of 3 bushels of wheat for the United States} \\ = \text{minimum of 1 bushel of wheat for the United Kingdom} \end{cases}$$

Scheme 4 can be transformed into a simple diagrammatic form. In Figure 11-3, yards of textiles are plotted against bushels of wheat. The U.S. cost ratio of 3 bushels of wheat per yard of textile is represented by a straight line from the origin with a slope of 3. A similar line, but showing a 1 to 1 cost ratio, is drawn for the United Kingdom. All exchange ratios falling between the two lines comprise the region of mutually beneficial trade, where for each country the opportunity cost of acquiring the imported good in exchange for exports is less than that of producing it domestically. Outside this region, one or the other of the two countries will not want to trade, for it can do better at home. The "trade region" is bounded by the cost or supply ratios of the two countries. Thus, cost conditions determine the limits to mutually beneficial trade. (A more advanced analysis of this case is offered later in this chapter.)

Where within these limits trade will take place depends on demand considerations. Because of the barter nature of this presentation, economists had to construct a special tool to demonstrate demand in this context. Whereas the "normal" demand curve shows the price of the goods in question on the vertical axis and the quantity demanded on the horizontal axis, Figure 11-3 has total quantities of the two barter goods on the two axes. To cope with this

Figure 11-3

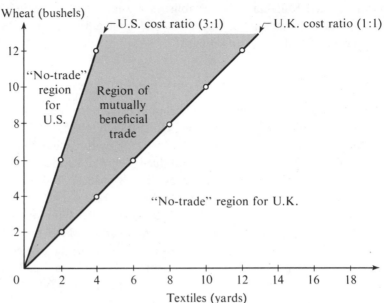

situation, a special tool known as the "reciprocal demand curve" is developed for each country, which shows the respective quantities of the two goods demanded and supplied simultaneously. These curves reflect the intensity of demand on the part of each country for the other country's product. Their intersection determines the precise exchange ratio. If it falls close to the American cost ratio, the United Kingdom reaps most of the benefits from trade; if it falls close to the British cost ratio, the United States reaps most of the benefit. (As articulated on page 222, this commodity-gain ratio does not necessarily correspond to the utility gain ratio.)

☐ Reciprocal Demand or Offer Curve   A highly simplistic way to obtain a reciprocal demand curve from an ordinary demand curve is illustrated in Figure 11-4. Part (a) depicts a negatively sloping British demand for American wheat, where the price of wheat is expressed in terms of textiles. Part (b) shows the same demand curve, but with respect to different axes. The vertical axis of (b) is identical with the horizontal axis of (a); they both show the quantity of American wheat demanded by Britain. However, the horizontal axis of (b) depicts the *total quantity* of textiles offered by Britain in exchange for the American wheat. It is to be distinguished from the vertical axis of (a), which shows a price ratio: units of textiles offered per unit of wheat. Therefore, the horizontal axis of (b), the quantity of textiles offered by Britain, is

Figure 11-4

Price of wheat in terms of textile
(units of textile per unit of wheat)

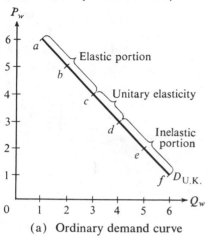

(a) Ordinary demand curve

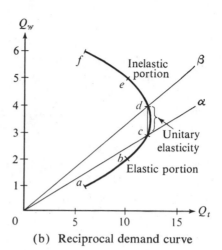

(b) Reciprocal demand curve

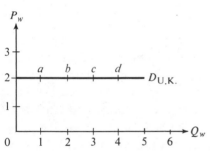

(c) Infinitely elastic demand curve

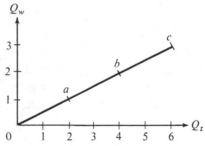

(d) Infinitely elastic reciprocal demand curve

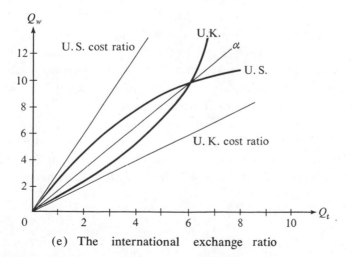

(e) The international exchange ratio

derived from (a) by multiplying the price of wheat in terms of textiles by the quantity of wheat; it is equivalent to the area under the ordinary demand curve. Thus for 1 unit of wheat the British offer $1 \times 6 = 6$ units of textiles (point a); for 2 units of wheat they offer $2 \times 5 = 10$ units of textiles (point b); for 3 units of wheat, $3 \times 4 = 12$ units of textiles (point c); for 4 units of wheat, $4 \times 3 = 12$ units of textiles (point d); for 5 units of wheat, $5 \times 2 = 10$ units of textiles (point e); and for 6 units of wheat, $6 \times 1 = 6$ units of textiles (point f). The resulting curve in (b) is Britain's "reciprocal demand" or "offer" curve.

☐ Unlike the case of an ordinary demand curve, price in Figure 11-4 (b) is not shown explicitly on one of the axes. It can, however, be derived for any point along the reciprocal demand curve by connecting the point with the origin via a straight line, such as line α. The slope of this line shows the quantity of wheat exchanged per unit of textiles. An upward movement along the reciprocal demand curve (from a to b to c and so on) indicates a decline in the price of wheat: fewer units of textiles per unit of wheat or, conversely, more wheat obtainable for a given amount of textiles. This can be easily verified by comparing price lines α and β. Thus the reciprocal demand curve shows at once the quantity of American wheat demanded and of textiles supplied by the United Kingdom at various relative prices.

☐ It was seen in Chapter 5 that elasticity varies along a straight-line demand curve, with the upper part being relatively elastic and the lower part being relatively inelastic. Translated into the reciprocal demand curve configuration, it is seen that the positively sloped part of the curve (lower segment) is relatively elastic; the negatively sloped part (upper segment) is relatively inelastic, while elasticity equals 1 at the bending point. As the price of wheat (in terms of textiles) declines, the quantity of textiles offered (equivalent to total revenue in the case of an ordinary demand curve) rises along the elastic portion, remains constant in the region of unitary elasticity, and declines along the inelastic segment of the curve.

☐ The extreme case of infinitely elastic demand is shown in (c) of Figure 11-4, where the axes are identical to those of (a). The equivalent reciprocal demand curve, shown in (d), is a straight line through the origin. By inference, the flatter the reciprocal demand curve, the more elastic it is. In what follows we restrict ourselves to the elastic portion of the curve.

☐ Each of the two trading countries has a reciprocal demand curve, both curves falling within the region of mutually beneficial trade, for no trade can take place outside that region. These curves are drawn in (e). Their intersection yields price ratio α, at which the international exchange of wheat for textiles takes place.   ■

The Limits to a Sustainable Exchange Rate

This analysis can be carried further. We know from our example that the United States produces and exports wheat and that the United Kingdom produces and exports textiles. Therefore, the limits to the exchange ratio of Scheme 4 (page 227) can be translated from commodities into money by assigning to each commodity the price it commands in the country in which it is produced, in terms of the currency of that country. In other words, 1 yard of textiles costs £1, while 1 bushel of wheat costs $1. The limits of Scheme 4 are thereby converted into the respective currency values illustrated by Scheme 5.

SCHEME 5   The Limits to the Dollar–Pound Exchange Rate

$$1 \text{ yard of textiles} = \pounds 1 = \begin{cases} \$3 \text{ (3 bushels of wheat)} \\ \\ \$1 \text{ (1 bushel of wheat)} \end{cases}$$

Given the production costs of Scheme 3, the values in Scheme 5 must be the limits to the pound–dollar exchange rate. Suppose we arbitrarily select the midpoint of £1 = $2 and apply it to the production-cost example on which this is based (Scheme 3). By converting the pounds sterling cost to dollar cost at this exchange rate, we obtain Scheme 6.[3]

SCHEME 6   Production Costs of Scheme 3 in Terms
of Dollars Where £1 = $2

	Wheat per bushel	Textiles per yard
United States	$1	$3
United Kingdom	$2	$2

Clearly, the United States undersells the United Kingdom in wheat, and the United Kingdom undersells the United States in textiles. This is precisely the answer attributed to the businessman at the beginning of this chapter. But now it is clear that comparative advantage lies behind the statement that one buys where it is cheapest and sells where it is dearest after converting foreign prices to domestic currency at the going exchange rate. It is also clear that the limits to the exchange rate are determined by the cost ratios. Any exchange rate outside these limits is not sustainable, because then one country would undersell the other in both goods, thereby forcing an exchange-rate adjustment "into" these limits. To demonstrate this point, select a value of

[3] The example of footnote 2 yields the following limits to the exchange rate:

$$\pounds 2 = \begin{cases} \$3 \\ \$2 \end{cases} \quad \text{or} \quad \pounds 1 = \begin{cases} \$1\frac{1}{2} \\ \$1 \end{cases}$$

the pound higher than the upper limit, say £1 = $3.50. After conversion of Scheme 3 into one currency, the production costs become those given in Scheme 7.

Clearly, the United States undersells the United Kingdom in both commodities. (However, the degree of underselling is larger in wheat than in textiles, so that the pattern of comparative advantage is preserved.) Not being

SCHEME 7   Production Costs of Scheme 3 in Terms
of Dollars where £1 = $3.50

	Wheat per bushel	Textiles per yard
United States	$1.00	$3.00
United Kingdom	$3.50	$3.50

competitive in any good, the United Kingdom must suffer a fundamental and persistent balance-of-payments deficit, because the pound is overvalued. The $3.50 exchange value of the pound is unsustainable, and the British currency must be devalued.

Conversely, if we select a value for the pound lower than the "floor," say £1 = $0.50, the production cost of Scheme 3 changes to that of Scheme 8. In this case the United Kingdom undersells the United States in both goods (but the pattern of comparative advantage is preserved), with the United States in fundamental and persistent deficits. The sterling is undervalued in terms of the dollar and must be revalued, or the dollar must be devalued.

SCHEME 8   Production Costs of Scheme 3 in Terms
of Dollars where £1 = $0.50

	Wheat per bushel	Textiles per yard
United States	$1.00	$3.00
United Kingdom	$0.50	$0.50

Within the limits specified, the precise exchange rate is determined by considerations of reciprocal demand—demand by each country for the other's product—in such a way as to maintain balance-of-payments equilibrium.

Although this two-commodity case vastly oversimplifies what happens in the real world, it reinforces and illuminates what was said in Chapter 3. The exchange rate of a country cannot be arbitrarily determined; it must reflect the cost–price relationship between the country and its major trading partners. The simplicity of the example makes this relationship rather clear-cut, and this is at once an advantage in terms of clarity and a drawback in terms of realism. (The reader is referred back to Chapter 3 to complete the circle and examine all factors that may come into play.)

More Than Two Commodities

In reality, each country produces many commodities, but the principle of comparative advantage holds nevertheless. All goods produced by a country must be *ranked* in the order of their domstic costs or prices. Each country exports the commodity or commodities in which its advantage is most pronounced or, equivalently, that which ranks lowest on its cost scale. The cutoff point between what is exported and imported depends on reciprocal demand considerations in such a way as to yield a balance-of-payments equilibrium. An example will elucidate the arguments. Suppose the United States and the United Kingdom produce five commodities A, B, C, D, and E with the production costs as given by Scheme 9 (ranked in order of magnitude within each country).

SCHEME 9   Production Costs in Two Countries with Five Goods

Commodity

	A	B	C	D	E
United States	$2	$4	$6	$8	$10
United Kingdom	£1	£2	£3	£4	£5

No trade can take place under these cost conditions, for the relative cost ratios between all commodities are the same in the two countries (the case of differentiated products is assumed not to exist). An exchange rate of £1 = $2 would equalize prices[4] of all commodities between the two countries (as the reader can easily verify by converting British prices to dollars at this exchange rate). Consider, however, the ranked production costs in the two countries as given in Scheme 10.

SCHEME 10   Production Costs in Two Countries with Five Goods

Commodity

	A	B	C	D	E
United States	$1	$4	$9	$15	$20
United Kingdom	£1	£2	£3	£4	£5

Centering attention on the two extremes, A and E, it is immediately apparent that the American comparative advantage is in commodity A, the British in E. The domestic exchange ratios between them set the limits within which the exchange rate must fall (Scheme 11).

---

[4] The words *cost* and *price* are often used interchangeably in this chapter. The reader should think of production costs as including returns to all factors of production, including profits. As such they add up to the price of the product.

SCHEME 11   Limits to the Sterling–Dollar Exchange Rate

$$1E = \text{\pounds}5 \begin{cases} 20A = \$20 \text{ maximum for United States} \\ \\ 5A = \$5 \text{ minimum for United Kingdom} \end{cases}$$

$$\text{or } \text{\pounds}5 = \begin{cases} \$20 \\ \$5 \end{cases} \qquad \text{or } \text{\pounds}1 = \begin{cases} \$4 \\ \$1 \end{cases}$$

If the exchange rate were outside these limits, one country would undersell the other in all five commodities, leading to a fundamental external imbalance, which in turn would necessitate exchange-rate adjustment. Where within these limits the actual exchange rate lies depends on reciprocal demand. In turn, the exchange rate determines the commodity composition of trade. Having ranked the commodities by degree of comparative advantage, we proceed from the two extremes toward the middle to determine where the equilibrium must settle. Assume, for example, that the exchange rate is $\text{\pounds}1 = \$3$. The British cost converted into dollars becomes:

	A	B	C	D	E
U.K. cost ($\text{\pounds}1 = \$3$)	\$3	\$6	\$9	\$12	\$15

The United States exports commodities A and B, while the United Kingdom undersells the United States in D and E and therefore exports them. Commodity C is not traded at all, for its cost is the same in both countries. If this situation balances the accounts, all is well and good. If not, the exchange rate will have to be adjusted. Suppose that the United Kingdom runs a persistent external deficit because its demand for A and B is much more intense than the American demand for D and E. The pound would then have to be devalued to, say, $\text{\pounds}1 = \$2.50$ (or depreciated if exchange rates were flexible). Under the new exchange rate, British costs become:

	A	B	C	D	E
U.K. cost ($\text{\pounds}1 = \$2.50$)	\$2.50	\$5.00	\$7.50	\$10.00	\$12.50

Commodity C now enters trade, to be exported by the United Kingdom where it is cheaper. Such shifts occur whenever the external accounts are fundamentally out of balance, indicating disequilibrium in the exchange rate. The important thing in considering the position of any country is to rank all commodities by degree of comparative advantage, for it is along such ranking that the shifts occur.

This simple illustration should dispel the popular notion that one country can undersell another in every commodity traded. This is not possible.

What is traded and in which direction is determined by the exchange rate. And since underselling in everything means that the balance of payments of the "undersold country" is in fundamental deficit, its currency would have to be devalued (or would depreciate if exchange rates were freely fluctuating) to the point at which it can sell enough goods to balance the accounts. As long as the exchange rate is in long-run equilibrium, the complaints voiced by import-competing industries to the effect that nothing produced at home can withstand foreign competition are baseless. Such competition can affect only the industries that should contract because they rank low in the order of comparative advantage.

In 1970 it was often said in the press that Japan could undersell the United States in everything, generating persistent surpluses in its balance of payments, with the United States experiencing large deficits. But all it took to reverse the situation were the two devaluations of the dollar in 1971 and 1973.

More Than Two Countries

If instead of the previous example we have two commodities but many countries, then the countries must be ranked in terms of the price ratios prevailing in them for the two goods. Suppose goods X and Y have the following price ratios (price of X divided by price of Y in respective currencies) in five countries A–E:

	A	B	C	D	E
X/Y price ratio	1	2	3	4	5

Total world supply and demand determine the worldwide price ratio, somewhere between that in the two "extreme" countries A and E. If that ratio is 3, then country C will not trade, and countries A and B will export X to countries D and E in exchange for good Y. Again the reader may experiment by changing the world price ratio, thereby affecting the direction of trade; the outcome will still be determined by the established ranking of the X/Y price ratio.

In reality, of course, there are many commodities and many countries, and it is rather difficult to demonstrate the principles involved with simple numerical illustrations. But the principles hold nevertheless.

Before proceeding, a note of caution is in order. Thus far this chapter has been devoted to the gains from international trade. It has been shown that when relative production costs or relative prices vary between countries there is room for mutually beneficial trade. Nothing has been said about the causes of the differences in relative costs, a topic to be taken up in the next chapter. Equally important, we have concentrated on the internal ranking of commodities for the purpose of determining comparative advantage *at a given point of time*. But it cannot be overemphasized that the ranking of commodities within each country changes over time, and so does comparative advantage, and countries must adapt to this continuous change. However, these changes are themselves caused by changes in the factors that determine the ranking of industries in the first place—such as the availability of factors of production and technological advancement—and their implications will be analyzed at the end of Chapter 12.

Absolute Advantage and Wage Rates

Let us now return to the Ricardian example of labor productivity used in the first part of this chapter. While comparative advantage held the center of the discussion, it was also noted that absolute advantage in the Ricardian model cannot be disregarded, for it determines the wage level in the two countries. This will be demonstrated presently, with an admittedly over-simplified example. (The model says nothing about what makes American labor more productive in both industries.) Still, the conclusions drawn are useful.

Given the labor-productivity figures of Scheme 1, assume that the wage rate in the United States is $30 per day. Free mobility of labor between industries insures that wages rates within the country are the same in both industries, for if they were not, labor would move from the low-wage to the high-wage industry until wage rates were equalized. The question is: What must the British wage rate be?

Under the productivity conditions postulated in Scheme 1, the answer can be obtained by determining what wage rate, relative to the one assumed for the United States ($30 a day), would enable the United Kingdom to undersell America in textiles and be undersold in wheat. In other words, the relative wage rate must conform to the entire constellation of comparative advantage developed before, to make possible mutually beneficial trade.

Since an American worker produces 60 bushels of wheat per day, the cost of wheat is $0.50 per bushel. Similarly, an American worker can produce 20 yards of textiles a day, and at a daily wage of $30 this yields a price of $1.50 per yard. Because the United Kingdom undersells the United States in textiles, the British price must be $1.50 per yard or less, implying that a British laborer who produces 10 yards a day must earn less than $15 a day. At any higher wage rate the United Kingdom would not remain competitive in textiles. On the other hand, the United States undersells the United Kingdom in wheat, meaning that the British price must be above $0.50 per bushel. Since a British worker produces 20 bushels a day, his minimum wage rate must be $10, for any rate below that level yields a price lower than the American price. Thus if the established pattern of trade is to prevail, the British wage rate must be somewhere between $10 and $15 a day, or between one-half and one-third of the American wage rate. These limits are equal to, and are determined by, the productivity ratios in the two industries.

This result may be used to analyze the frequent complaint of protectionist forces in the United States that they cannot withstand foreign competition because foreign wages are lower than American. Time and again, in hearings before congressional committees, representatives of import-competing industries demand the imposition of a "scientific tariff": a tariff that would equalize wage rates here and abroad. Alternatively stated, their claim is that the tariff level should equal the difference between American wage rates and wage rates prevailing in competing countries. Now we see that this is an untenable position, for if the British wage rate were equal to ours, the United States would undersell the United Kingdom in all commodities. There could be no two-way trade under such conditions. The relative wage rate in two countries is determined by the differences in productive efficiency. And American wages are the highest in the world because this economy is the most efficient. (We defer to the next chapter the question of *why* it is more efficient.) It is true that in our example, American textiles cannot compete. But that is because, in the example, the United States does not possess a comparative advantage in that commodity.

Summary of Policy Implications

To recapitulate, international trade raises the real income of the community by improving the efficiency of resource utilization (the last section of this chapter elaborates on this point). The ranking of industries in the order of their comparative advantage, combined with an equilibrium exchange rate, determines which commodities are to be exported and which are to be imported. The country's resources are most efficiently utilized if they are distributed and employed along this order. Consequently, policies that distort this ranking, such as tariffs and quotas imposed on specific commodities, result in inefficient resource allocation and loss of income to the community.

If the general wage and price level of a country gets out of line in comparison to other countries, its balance of payments gets out of equilibrium. The solution lies in appropriate fiscal and monetary policies or in exchange-rate adjustment. The situation does not call for tariffs, quotas, exchange control, or other interferences with free trade. These latter measures are usually applied on a selective basis, being most restrictive where politically powerful and vocal interests have to be satisfied. Certainly these interests do not include the consumer. As such they distort the aforementioned ranking of industries and result in inefficiencies. The same point applies to multiple exchange rates and bilateral clearing arrangements. By contrast, aggregate domestic policies and exchange-rate adjustments affect all foreign transactions and tend to preserve the ordering of industries by comparative advantage.

As long as the balance of payments is in equilibrium, the demands of import-competing industries for protection—under one guise or another—is often unwarranted. What they are asking for is selective protection or, essentially, tariff protection for themselves. That would distort the industrial ranking and lead to inefficient resource utilization. The claim that they cannot compete, either because their wage rates are "too high" or for other reasons, is essentially correct from their own self-centered point of view. But satisfaction of their demand for protection would be erroneous and injurious to the economy as a whole. The reason they are not competitive is that they rank low in the order of comparative advantage. Allocative efficiency requires that they contract in size and their resources be transferred to the growing industries. Government help in this transfer process—in the form of direct loans, retraining programs, and the like—would contribute to efficiency all around and help alleviate human suffering.

It is in the interest of a country to engage in balanced, mutually beneficial, and market-directed trade. It is contrary to its interest to pursue policies that distort its comparative advantage by providing protection to inefficient industries. There is no particular advantage in being able to undersell other countries in everything. Giving up commodities in exchange for gold, IOUs, or other paper assets simply deprives the nation of the satisfactions derived from consumption, especially if international reserves are already adequate. Under such conditions there is little that is favorable about a huge trade surplus.

Dynamic Gains from International Trade

The foregoing analysis of the benefits from international trade followed the traditional line of emphasizing specialization and reallocation of *existing* resources. In fact, these gains can be outweighed by the impact of trade on the country's growth rate and therefore on the volume of *additional* resources made available to, or employed by, the trading country. These are termed "dynamic" benefits, in contrast to the "static" effects of reallocating an unchanged quantity of resources. The reason for the disproportionately little space devoted to these factors is that they are difficult to measure as well as to theorize upon. But even though they have not become a part of the codified version of received theory, their importance should not be underestimated. The short discourse that follows is intended to be indicative rather than exhaustive.

Consider first a fully employed and highly developed economy. Its growth rate is determined by, among other things, the degree to which the population is willing to abstain from current consumption (their propensity to save, in the economist's parlance), so that resources can be released from production of consumer goods and used for investment purposes. In a Robinson Crusoe economy, production (or output) and income are the number of fish that Crusoe catches each day. If he catches ten fish in a full day's work and consumes ten, his consumption equals output, and his saving is zero. Since he utilizes all his resources (working hours) in producing for consumption, no investment is possible. Should he decide to lower his consumption to five fish a day, he may save the excess of income over consumption (for this is the definition of saving) and be able to utilize his saving for investment purposes—for example, constructing a fishing net. The act of saving, or abstaining from consumption, has freed resources (one-half of his time) for the production of investment goods.

Although these relationships are somewhat obscured in a complex economy, they exist nonetheless. First, income and output are equal and may be considered two sides of the same coin. For what does it imply to state that the price of a desk is $100? It means first that this is its value as a unit of output. But at the same time it means that in the process of producing the desk, a total of $100 in income was generated and paid to productive factors used in the production of the desk, in the following forms: wages and salaries for labor, rental income for the use of natural resources, interest paid on capital, and profit return for entrepreneurial ability. To simplify matters, the last item can be thought of as a residual difference between the price of the desk and the sum of the first three income components. This example can be generalized to all goods and services produced in a given year. Their final value, the gross national product, equals the income generated in the production process.

Second, if in a fully employed economy all income is spent on consumer goods—meaning that the saving rate is nil—then all resources must be occupied in the production of these goods and no investment is possible. On the other hand, should consumers abstain from consuming part of their income, or save, resources would be freed to produce investment goods, making possible economic growth and the attainment of larger streams of output in future years. It is this saving–investment process, and the diversion of resources implied in it, that generates growth and development.

It is an integral part of economic theory, demonstrated time and again in empirical studies, that the level of saving in the community, or abstinence from consumption, is related in a positive way to some measure of the community's income. The higher the income is, the higher the saving is, too, if for no other reason than the fact that it is easier to save out of higher levels of earnings. Thus when the United States gives foreign aid to developing countries, it is in essence doing the saving for them. Since it is difficult to save out of the very low incomes prevailing in the underdeveloped world, and it is much easier for Americans to save out of high incomes, the process of foreign aid involves diversion of American savings, in the form of productive resources, for investment purposes in the recipient countries.

Since it is safe to assume that the marginal propensity to save (the proportion of added income that goes into added savings) is positive, any positive increment to the community's income necessarily results in added savings. In other words, not all the added income will be spent on consumption. Therefore when income is higher the rate of growth possible is higher.

But this is precisely what international trade was shown to do. Income rises because of more efficient utilization of fully employed resources. This raises savings and makes additional resources available for investment purposes. Furthermore, since the opening up of the economy to foreign trade changes relative prices, the tendency toward higher investments is accentuated if investment goods are imported or are made out of imported materials, for the price of imports goes down relative to that of exports and other goods as a result of trade.

An extreme example of this case is that of developing countries in which capital equipment cannot be produced at all, for technical or other reasons. There it is not just a matter of forcing resources toward more efficient uses when the country moves to specialize in "simple" products and import capital goods. The resources could not possibly have manufactured the latter goods because they are totally unsuitable for that purpose. In that case the country must worry not only about the saving rate and the release of resources from current consumption, but also about how to convert these resources into investment goods. Since such transformation is not possible at home, it can be accomplished only by exchange of exportables for imported capital equipment.[5] International trade is the only vehicle by means of which the conversion can be carried out, thereby becoming a main instrument of growth. Indeed, when development is inhibited by insufficient imports of capital goods, underutilization of other factors may occur. Trade (and aid) can break this bottleneck.

This point underscores the fact that international trade does not comprise only flows of finished products intended for the final consumer. Rather, much of it consists of exchange of factors of production in the form of plants and equipment and semiprocessed or raw materials. And since many developing countries do not possess the know-how and ability to produce them at home—even if they were willing to, however inefficiently, devote resources to their production—their importation amounts to much more than specialization

---

[5] This approach has been developed and popularized by H. Chenery and various collaborators and dubbed the "double gap" problem. A developing country must overcome both the saving–investment gap and the foreign-exchange gap.

in production. It enables the country to reach otherwise unattainable horizons in technology and efficiency. A technological gap of centuries may thus be bridged within a generation.

Thus international trade places the economy on a higher growth path, which tends to feed upon itself as continuously rising incomes make possible ever-rising levels of saving and investments. Since in this model the main obstacle to growth is nonavailability of resources, it may be referred to as "supply-propelled growth" made possible by the introduction of trade to an isolated economy or by removal of artificial barriers to trade.

An equally important stimulus to growth occurs when trade is introduced into a somewhat lagging economy not operating at full capacity. In some underdeveloped countries unemployment can assume a disguised form, as where the indigenous farm population is ostensibly at work but for a variety of reasons the output of each worker is only a fraction of his potential. Similar situations, requiring powerful stimuli on the demand side to "get the economy moving" on a rational path, may occur in any country at certain stages of its economic development. Such stimuli can be provided by international trade.

On the export side, the impact of overseas shipments is not confined to the export sector of the economy. Rather, as these industries expand, they require inputs from other sectors and thereby stimulate investments and technological advancement elsewhere. Thus the benefits of specialization are not limited to the expanding industries but tend to spread to the other areas. By the same token, as the standard of living of those engaged in export production rises, the goods and services they require increase in quantity as well as quality, and perhaps change in composition. In turn, this new demand stimulates growth in the industries producing final goods and services, as well as in those supplying the inputs.

Although economists are still studying the various linkages through which the development process spreads, and are still debating the relative merits of unbalanced and balanced growth (whether it is better to concentrate on a few key industries in the country's development plan or to promote development across the board), there is little doubt that export-led growth is an important phenomenon.

On the import side, foreign trade makes it possible for a developing economy to obtain capital equipment and other materials necessary for investment. Without trade such goods may be obtainable not at all or only at prohibitive cost. Again, industrial expansion made possible by such imports tends to spread through the economy, generating growth in many sectors.

The broad implications of the foregoing statements become apparent if one looks at total international economic intercourse rather than just the exchange of commodities. Flows of capital in various forms, not the least of which is direct foreign investments, have come to occupy a prominent share of international transactions. Such transfers of capital embody not only plants and equipment but also technology and managerial skills. They make possible a fast diffusion of all the ingredients necessary for economic growth, highly beneficial to the host countries but with some feedback effects on the donor nation itself.

This is not all. There are important benefits to developed and developing countries alike that arise from the fact that foreign trade increases the size of the national market. Exports enable small and moderately sized countries to establish and operate many plants of efficient size, which would be impossible if production were confined to the domestic market. Not only can firms enjoy "internal economies of scale," but the economy as a whole benefits from the salutary impact of competitive pressure on prices, product improvement, and technological advancement. Innovation is often held back when competition is lacking. Furthermore, expansion of an industry insures the availability of such things as a pool of skilled labor on which individual firms can draw (these benefits are known as economies external to the firm but internal to the industry). And overall industrial expansion usually brings with it the creation and development of the necessary infrastructure, such as transportation and power facilities, on which whole industries can draw (economies external to the industry). In turn, imports assure the existence of competitive pressure on domestic import-competing industries, even those that are internally monopolized. They also dampen inflation in the importing country.

Although this discussion is not exhaustive, it indicates the immense potential of dynamic benefits that can flow from international trade. They are not all restricted to developing countries; some may occur in varying degrees at any stage of a country's growth. That the effect of these benefits is not the same in all countries is due to many causes, some still unknown, not the least of which is the willingness of government to avail itself of such "blessings" through free-trade policies.

☐ More Advanced Analysis of the Static Gains from Trade

☐ Earlier in this chapter we showed that a differential price ratio between two countries gives rise to mutually beneficial trade. The static gains from trade were demonstrated in the case of constant opportunity cost, leading to complete specialization. This section shows the static gains in the context of increasing opportunity cost, where specialization may be incomplete. To do this we must utilize somewhat more advanced analytical tools: indifference maps and transformation curves. Consequently, only students familiar with these

analytical tools should tackle this section. The general reader can skip over
to the next chapter without loss of continuity.

The Consumer Indifference Map

☐ It will be recalled from the theory of consumer demand that the indifference curve represents various combinations of two goods, X and Y, among
which the consumer is indifferent. In Figure 11-5, the consumer presented with
a large number of alternative combinations finds himself indifferent to the
choice among the following combinations of X and Y:

	Quantity of		$\dfrac{\Delta Y}{\Delta X}$
Point	*Y*	*X*	
a	8	1	
			−4
b	4	2	
			−2
c	2	3	
			−½
d	1½	4	

☐ These, as well as all the other combinations lying on the curve, yield equal
amounts of satisfaction to the consumer. Each of the goods is subject to dimin-

Figure 11-5
Consumer Indifference Curve

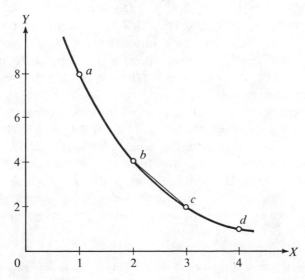

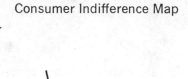

Figure 11-6
Consumer Indifference Map

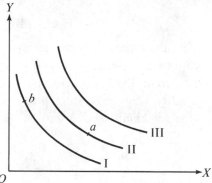

ishing marginal utility, meaning that the more of it that there is in the consumer's possession the less intensely he wants additional units. Thus when he has 8 units of Y and only 1 of X (point a), he is willing to part with 4 of Y to get an extra unit of X. But once the Y in his possession declines to 4 and the X rises to 2 (point b), he is only willing to part with $2Y$ to get an extra unit of X. And beyond that point, an extra unit of X is worth to him only one-half unit of Y.

☐ These substitutions that leave the consumer equally well off are summarized in the third column of the table. Using the Greek letter Δ to denote change or increment (negative for decrement), the ratio $\Delta Y/\Delta X$ stands for what economists call the marginal rate of substitution (MRS) of X for Y. The fact that it is declining is merely a reflection of the law of diminishing marginal utility of each good. And it is this feature that makes the indifference curve convex to the origin. The MRS between any two points along the curve is the slope of the line that connects the two points, such as $\overline{bc}$. It is easy to see that the MRS at a single point is the slope of the tangent to the indifference curve at that point. And that slope (MRS) declines as we move down the curve from a to d.

☐ Each consumer has a whole map of such indifference curves (Figure 11-6), with the higher ones (further away from the origin) indicating higher levels of satisfaction. Because utility cannot be measured, all we can say is that combinations represented by indifference curve III are more satisfactory[6] than those depicted by II, but we cannot say by how much. It is an essential feature of the map that the curves composing it do not intersect. For if I intersects II, then at the point of intersection the two curves yield equal satis-

[6] Note that it is only with the help of the indifference map of the consumer that we can say that he prefers combination a (with more X but less Y) to combination b.

faction, which is clearly inconsistent with the fact that at all preintersection points, II represents a higher level of satisfaction than I. Ordinary demand curves can be derived from the indifference map.

The Community Indifference Map

☐ Can indifference curves of many individuals be aggregated to form the locus of points yielding equal satisfaction to the community or country? In other words, can we scale the axes in millions of units and have indifference curve I show all the combinations of the two goods providing a given level of satisfaction to all citizens combined, and so on for II and III? Strictly speaking the answer is No. For one thing, individual ranking of commodity combinations requires the use of majority rule unless the preferences of all are identical. And this need not result in a harmonious or transitive ranking, making it impossible to draw a community indifference curve.[7]

☐ Even if this were not the case, we must remember that the ranking of situations is done by majority rule, with no "protection" offered to the minority. Indeed, if majority rule prevails, no one knows how strongly members of the "losing" minority feel about the outcome. Translated into real-world situations, any change (free trade, technological advance, or what have you) that improves the position of society as a whole (and should therefore place it on a higher community indifference curve) is also likely to change income distribution, so that even if we increase the total amount of goods available to society, it does not necessarily follow that the amount bestowed upon each member of the community would rise. As long as we are unable to compare the intensity of feelings of the gaining majority with that of the losing minority, we must adhere to the rule that the community as a whole is better off (and should be placed on a higher indifference curve) if and only if some of its members are better off, and *none* is worse off, than before the change. This can occur only when the income distribution remains unaffected by the change in total income, or when the losers are compensated to a point at which they are as well off as before. Diagrammatically it can be shown that any given level of community income can be represented by a large number of intersecting community indifference curves, each corresponding to a different income distribution.

[7] To see what is meant by this possible (though not necessary) outcome, assume that three individuals X, Y, and Z are asked to rank commodity combinations A, B, and C in order of their preferences, and the ranking comes out as follows:

	X	Y	Z
1.	A	B	C
2.	B	C	A
3.	C	A	B

Two of three persons (X and Z) prefer A to B, two of three persons (X and Y) prefer B to C, and two of three persons (Y and Z) prefer C to A. This violates the logical rule that if A is preferred to B and B is preferred to C then A ought to be preferred to C. It is known as lack of transitivity in preference ordering.

☐ In sum, the community indifference curve is not a neat concept. It requires some heroic assumptions, such as permitting one dictator to make decisions (and rank combinations) for the entire community. Alternatively we must assume transitivity in ranking, coupled with unchanged income distribution or compensation of losers. Only then can we generalize from an individual to a country and employ the concept of community indifference curves. For pragmatic reasons economists do make these assumptions and use the concept, as we shall do here. Thus the country will be thought of as having a map of nonintersecting community indifference curves, with the higher ones indicating higher levels of satisfaction.

Transformation Curves

☐ Each country also has a given amount of resources that can be employed to produce two goods X and Y. In Figure 11-7, if all resources are devoted to the production of Y, then 6 million units can be produced. Alternatively, if all resources are employed in producing X, 4 million units of X can be manufactured. In between these two extremes lie all the possible combinations of the two goods that these resources can produce. The locus of these combinations is known as the *transformation function* or curve, for movement along this curve indicates the transformation of one commodity into the other in the sense that resources are transferred from one industry to the other.

☐ If the resources are identically suited for the production of the two goods, they can be shifted back and forth from one industry to another without any loss of efficiency. Certainly this would be the case if there was only one homo-

Figure 11-7
Constant Opportunity Cost (in millions of units)

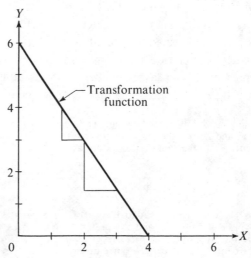

geneous factor (such as labor) or if two or more factors were used in a fixed and identical proportion in the production of both goods and were equally suited for the two industries. This is the constant-opportunity-cost case and can be depicted by a straight-line transformation function. The cost of extra units of X in terms of Y given up (when the resources are transferred from Y to X) does not vary along the function and is equal to the constant slope of the curve. This is the Ricardian case, which leads to complete specialization once trade opens up: the country would produce either 6 million Y or 4 million X, depending on its comparative advantage relative to its trading partner.

☐ But suppose that the country's resources are not equally suited for the production of both goods; some are more efficient in Y production, others in X. In that case the two extreme points of producing only one commodity will exist as before, each point (on one of the two axes) showing how much of a good can be produced if all resources are devoted to its production. But the "transformation" of one good into the other (in the sense of resource transfer) will be different.

☐ Starting, say, from 6 million units of Y, the transformation of Y for X will not be at a fixed ratio yielding a straight line. Instead we encounter a line concave to the origin, depicting increasing opportunity cost (Figure 11-8). At point a all the country's resources, presumably including some resources better suited for the production of X, are employed in production of Y. As we move from a to b to obtain the first million units of X, the resources first trans-

Figure 11-8
Increasing Opportunity Cost (in millions of units)

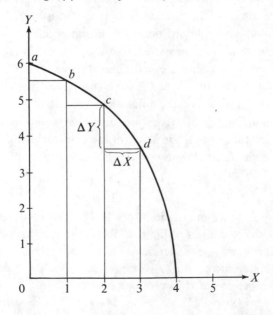

ferred from Y to X are better equipped to manufacture X to begin with. Thus the cost of 1 million X is only 0.5 million units of Y; the ratio of 1 to 2 is depicted by the slope of the straight line connecting a and b. Moving from b to c we begin to transfer from industry Y to X some resources that are better suited to produce Y. Thus it costs nearly 0.75 million of Y to obtain the second million X. By the same token, a move from c to d shows that the third million units of X is obtainable at an opportunity cost of over 1 million units of Y. Finally, to obtain the fourth million units of X implies transferring all resources to industry X, including those that are ideally suited for Y. Thus the cost rises to 3.5 million units of Y.

☐ What the concave opportunity-cost curve depicts is a rising ratio of $\Delta Y / \Delta X$. This ratio is known as the marginal rate of transformation (MRT). At any point on the curve, it is equal to the slope of the curve. This is the case of increasing opportunity cost with which we are presently concerned.

Equilibrium in Isolation without Trade

☐ The transformation function shows all the combinations of the two commodities that the country can produce given its resources. Points inside the curve represent unused resources (for example, unemployment), while points outside the curve represent commodity combinations that cannot be reached. Thus the country will strive to produce somewhere along the curve. But where? That is determined by the pattern of demand, or the community preference scheme for the two goods, as reflected in the community indifference map.

☐ Given its resources, the country attempts to maximize satisfaction—namely, consume on the highest possible community indifference curve. And that indifference curve is the one tangent to the transformation function. In Figure 11-9, P is the equilibrium point of consumption and production, with $0Y_1$ and $0X_1$ produced and consumed. Without international trade, domestic production and consumption are equal. The slope of ML (the common tangent to the indifference curve and the transformation function) is the commodity price ratio prevailing on the domestic market: $\overline{0M}$ of Y is exchangeable for $\overline{0L}$ of X (note that in the constant-cost case depicted in Figure 11-7, the domestic price ratio equals the slope of the transformation function and is independent of demand conditions).

International Trade: Similar Tastes

☐ In order to introduce international trade we must consider two countries. We first assume that the tastes of the two populations, as reflected in the shape of their indifference maps, are identical. On the other hand, their transformation curves are different: country A is better suited to produce commodity Y, and country B is better suited to produce commodity X. The heavy curves in

Figure 11-9
Equilibrium in Isolation

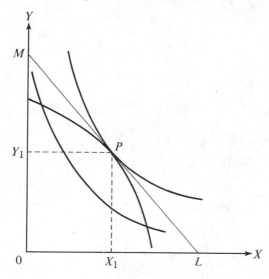

Figure 11-10 depict the two countries in isolation. Given its resource endowment, as represented by its transformation curve, each country gets onto the highest possible indifference curve. Equilibrium production and consumption are obtained from the tangency solution at points E and F for countries A and B, respectively. With equal demand patterns it is the supply conditions that determine relative market prices.

☐ Relative prices of Y and X are different in the two countries, as indicated by the different slopes of price lines MN for A and PR for B. This establishes the fact that there is room for mutually beneficial trade. In particular, commodity Y is relatively cheaper in country A, with $\overline{0M}$ of Y exchangeable for $\overline{0N}$ of X, while commodity X is relatively cheaper in country B, where $\overline{0P}$ of Y are exchangeable for $\overline{0R}$ of X.[8] These relative price ratios establish the fact that country A has a comparative advantage in Y, country B in X. They would move to specialize accordingly.

☐ Each country would move along its transformation curve toward more specialization in production: country A from point E upward, country B from F downward. The slopes of the tangents to the two curves (the respective price lines) change as they move; indeed, the two slopes converge. Post-trade equilibrium is reached when the two price lines become parallel, meaning that the price ratios in the two countries are equal. In other words, after trade opens up, it will proceed to the point at which commodity prices are equalized. The

[8] Ratios of quantities exchanged are employed here to indicate prices.

Figure 11-10
Equilibrium with Trade

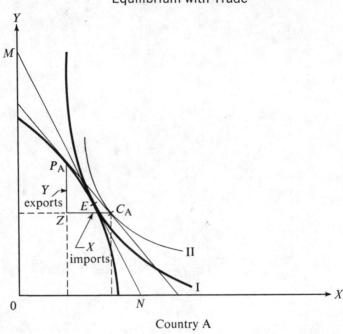

Country A

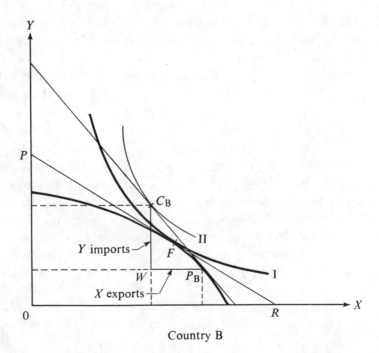

Country B

two lightweight price lines (tangents to curves II at C_A and C_B) meet this requirement. But so do an infinite number of other "pairable" points along the two transformation functions.

☐ To pinpoint the exact equilibrium solution, another condition must be satisfied. In the two-country world depicted here, what one country exports the other must import. The quantity traded by each country is the difference between what is produced and what is consumed domestically. As the production point travels along the transformation curve toward its equilibrium point, the price line tangent to it becomes flatter in country A and steeper in country B. Given the community indifference map of each country, the price lines become tangent to higher and higher indifference curves as this process proceeds. And it is this tangency position that determines the consumption points.

☐ Suppose that consumption point C_A and C_B in the two countries are such that both equilibrium conditions are met. Thus country A produces at P_A and consumes at C_A, while country B produces at P_B and consumes at C_B, each pair of points measured with respect to the axes of the country concerned. The difference between production and consumption is made up by trade. Country A produces more Y than it consumes, and the excess $\overline{P_A Z}$ is exported. It consumes more X than it produces, and the difference $\overline{Z C_A}$ is imported. By similar reasoning, country B imports $\overline{C_B W}$ ($= \overline{P_A Z}$) of Y and exports $\overline{W P_B}$ ($= \overline{C_A Z}$) of X. The "trade triangles" of the two countries are thus identical.

☐ It will be observed that both countries land on a higher indifference curve (II) than they were able to attain in isolation (I). In this case, trade enabled each country to specialize in production according to the "suitability" of its resources and to remain "unspecialized" in consumption. This divergence between production and consumption mixes is not possible without trade. How much the gain is to each country cannot be determined, for there is no way to measure satisfaction. The indifference curves merely tell us the ranking of utility levels in ascending order, as we proceed upward away from the origin. Readers who are uneasy about using community indifference curves in this as well as the subsequent analysis may simply note that trade enables each country to consume outside the region of possible production.

☐ While each country moves to produce more of the commodity in which it has a comparative advantage, specialization in this case is not complete. Commodity prices were equalized before either country got completely out of the production of "the other" product. Thus, the post-trade equilibrium situation finds each country producing some of both products. This is a possible but not necessary result of increasing opportunity cost.[9]

---

[9] To see that it is not a necessary result, the reader might note that not all points along each transformation function are "pairable" with points on the other function in the sense that they have identical slopes.

Factor Endowments

☐ What, it may be asked, makes for the difference between the transformation curves of the two countries? The answers can be many and varied. It could be, for example, that country A has developed a more efficient technique for producing Y, and B employs more efficient means for manufacturing X. Or the two countries may have become equipped by tradition or the skill of their labor forces in the production of their respective products. These as well as other explanations are possible.

☐ But the model that reigned supreme in international trade theory for most of the period after World War II discarded these hypotheses and adopted another explanation of the divergent shape of the transformation curves. (This, as well as other models, will be explored in detail in the next chapter; only a short summary is offered here.) Each commodity is assumed to be produced in the same manner in both countries; economists say that the production function of each commodity is the same in the two countries. By that they mean that, for each possible pair of factor prices, the two countries would use the two factors in the same proportion in the productive process. Another more descriptive way of stating this is to say that the isoquants[10] of each commodity are identical in the two countries.

☐ On the other hand, the isoquants differ between the two commodities, and they differ in a unique and unequivocal way: at all factor prices one commodity (Y) utilizes more of one factor (say, capital) relative to the other commodity (X), which means that the second good (X) utilizes more of the second factor (labor) relative to the first good (Y). It is in that sense that commodity Y is classified as capital intensive and commodity X as labor intensive, and that relation holds in each of the two countries.

☐ Countries differ from each other in their factor endowment—hence the title of the model. Country A is relatively capital-abundant, in the sense that its capital/labor endowment ratio is higher than B's. And that makes country B labor-abundant relative to A. It is now a short step to concluding that country A would have a comparative advantage in producing Y, the commodity requiring relatively more capital in the production process. Conversely, country B would have a comparative advantage in producing X, the commodity requiring relatively more labor, which that country possesses in relative abundance. There are other assumptions attached to the factor-endowment

---

[10] "Isoquant" describes the various combinations of two productive factors that can produce a given quantity of output. Shaped like an indifference curve, it has quantities of factors on the two axes, the isoquant itself labeled for the volume of output it represents.

model that will be described in detail in the next chapter. In the present con-text, however, it can be seen that this model constitutes a very specific ex-planation of the pattern of trade.

□ International trade is brought about by the unequal price ratio existing be-tween the two commodities in the two countries when they produce and consume in isolation. In other words, whenever the price lines are not parallel in the pre-trade equilibrium position, there is room for mutually beneficial trade. The relative slope of the lines represents relative prices and therefore indicates which country has a comparative advantage in each product. The factor-en-dowment model is an attempt to explain what gives rise to comparative advan-tage, and it traces the reason to one specific factor: differences in factor endowments between countries coupled with differences in production func-tions between commodities.

□ Clearly this is one of many possible explanations to the divergent pre-trade commodity price ratios. In the first place there are other reasons that may give rise to divergent transformation curves, which the factor-endowment model dismisses. Second, the model's assumption that demand patterns are identical in the two countries need not hold. Thus, differently shaped maps of community indifference curves can result in unequal price ratios even with identical transformation curves.

Differences in Demand

□ Differences in demand are illustrated in Figure 11-11. The heavy lines rep-resent the pretrade positions; they depict identical transformation functions but different indifference curves. The resulting price lines $\overline{MN}$ and $\overline{PR}$ show that commodity Y is relatively cheaper in country A (where consumers prefer X), and commodity X is relatively cheaper in country B (where consumers prefer Y). This establishes the pattern of comparative advantage and the lines of specialization once trade opens up.

□ As before, the post-trade equilibrium position must satisfy the conditions of equal prices in the two countries (parallel price lines) and equal quantities of each commodity imported and exported. The heavier price lines meet these conditions. Given the difference maps, the two countries will consume at C_A and C_B and produce at P_A and P_B. In this case they move toward less speciali-zation in production and greater specialization in consumption. In other words, trade makes it possible to satisfy divergent wants from identical production conditions. Consequently both countries experience a rise in welfare, as in-dicated by the fact that they find themselves on higher indifference curves. Country A exports $\overrightarrow{P_A Z}$ of Y and imports $\overline{C_A Z}$ of X, while country B exports $\overline{P_B W}$ ($= \overline{C_A Z}$) of X and imports $\overline{C_B W}$ ($= \overline{P_A Z}$) of Y.

Figure 11-11
Equilibrium with Trade

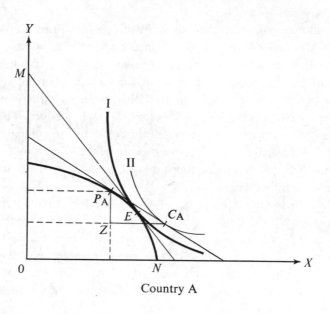

Country A

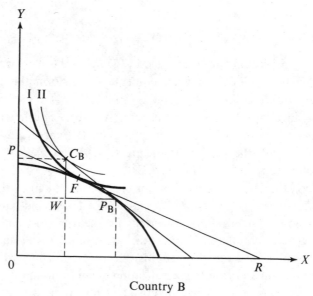

Country B

The General Case

☐ In the general case, both the transformation curves and the indifference maps differ. If the resulting pretrade price lines are not parallel, there is room for mutually beneficial trade. The relative prices established before trade determine the pattern of comparative advantage and the direction of trade. Only when the two pretrade price lines are parallel is there no room for trade. This can come about if both the transformation curves and the indifference maps of the two countries are identical. Alternatively, it can happen when the two sets of curves differ in such a way as to precisely offset each other—in other words, if each country prefers to consume the commodity that it can produce best and that preference exactly compensates for the degree of production advantage so as to produce identical prices.   ■

12
The Commodity Composition of Trade

Introduction

As long as economists were interested merely in demonstrating the gain from international trade, the analysis presented in the previous chapter was adequate. In a nutshell it demonstrates the self-evident proposition that whenever the domestic price (or cost) ratio is different in two countries, there is room for mutually beneficial trade, and the greater the difference is in the price ratios, the greater the static gain will be. Indeed, for a long period in the history of economic doctrine the issue rested here.

During the present century, however, the attention of international trade theorists turned from the gain from trade to the determinants of the commodity composition of trade. In other words, they attempted to unravel the factors that determine which country exports what commodity. To be sure, this question was not ignored in the last chapter. It was treated as a by-product of the focal issue, the gains from international trade. As such the answer was given on two levels. In the context of the "opportunity cost" discussion it was stated that each country exports the commodity that is relatively cheaper in that country, without exploring the reason for this relative cheapness. The Ricardian model with one factor of production (labor) probes a little deeper and hypothesizes that each country exports the commodity that it can produce at lower average labor cost (or higher average labor productivity). In other words, differential labor productivity is said to be the cause of the price differences.

This answer requires no further amplification as long as our concern is with the gains from trade. The very existence of trade under divergent price (or cost) conditions attests to its profitability. But if we wish to focus on the commodity composition of trade, the propositions articulated above may be inaccurate, for in this context they cease to be self-evident and are subject to empirical verification. And even if they are accurate, they are inadequate, for they beg further questions.

With respect to accuracy the answer centering on labor productivity is more specific and therefore more meaningful than the one postulating differential opportunity cost ratios, even though it is based on rather naive assumptions. It attributes the price differential to only one factor: differences in average labor productivity. As applied to the real world, this is a testable hypothesis that can be confirmed or rejected by empirical observations. Labor is not the only cost involved in producing a commodity. Although it is the most important single element, its effect can be swamped by other cost components. Moreover, the flow of manufactured products is not determined by cost and supply considerations alone. Manufactures are characterized by what economists call "product differentiation" or lack of homogeneity. What is essentially the same product appears on the market in a great variety of forms that differ from each other in quality, dimensions, packing, brand names, and what not. The buyer is swayed by many factors other than price. And since industrial goods make up most of world trade, it cannot be concluded *a priori* that costs of production determine the direction of trade flows. The demand side of the equation cannot be ignored.

The Ricardian model, attributing comparative advantage to labor productivity, was tested empirically with reference to U.K. and U.S. exports to third markets (that is, countries other than the United States and the United Kingdom) in both a prewar year and a postwar year. Using a cross section of industries, it was found that American exports to third markets exceeded British exports in industries where U.S. labor productivity (output per worker) was at least two and a half times U.K. labor productivity. Since American wage rates were roughly double the British, this is a successful test of the labor productivity hypothesis. Further cross-section analysis showed that for each one percent rise in the U.S./U.K. output-per-worker ratio, the U.S./U.K. export ratio rises 3 to 4 percent.

But supposing labor productivity were the determining factor of who exports what. It still begs the question of *what determines labor productivity*. In other words, the theorist wishes to go "behind" productivity to find the answer. Over the past several decades, economists have come to believe in a rather specific explanation of the commodity composition of trade, dubbed the *factor proportions* (or *endowment*) *theory*. First introduced by the Swedish economists E. F. Heckscher and B. Ohlin, the theory was refined after World War II by Paul Samuelson and made into a very elegant, though extremely restrictive, construct. Its postulates and the assumptions on which it rests are rather complex. But it can be stripped to its bare essentials by ignoring many of the details and drastically simplifying the economics in-

volved. Stated briefly, this theory is a marriage between the resource endowment of the country, on the one hand, and the economic characteristics of
the commodities traded, on the other. It rests on three fundamental postulates
and several assumptions.

The Factor Proportions Theory

Consider a world of two countries, the United States and the United Kingdom,
producing two commodities, textiles and machinery, with two factors of production, labor and capital. All production is carried on by purely competitive
firms; there are many firms in each industry, none large enough to influence
by its own action the conditions prevailing in the market. Prices of the two
products and of the two factors are determined by supply and demand; each
firm accepts these prices and adjusts its activities to them. In other words,
firms are price takers on both the commodity and factor markets. Also, free
internal mobility of labor and capital between industries insures that the price
of each factor is the same in the two industries within each country. If it were
not, the factor would move from the industry in which it is expensive to the
one in which it is cheaper until its price was equalized. On the other hand,
factors are not free to move between countries, so that pretrade returns to
each factor can differ internationally.

Each producer of a commodity has a range of production methods available to him, from which he selects one. The basic economic feature that distinguishes various production techniques is the labor/capital ratio. The producer
presumably adjusts the factor use ratio to the ratio of factor prices that
he confronts in the marketplace. The more expensive labor is relative to
capital, the less labor and the more capital he would use. Each commodity is
assumed to be produced under identical production conditions[1] in the two
countries, in the sense that *if faced with the same factor prices, producers in
both countries would use the two factors in the same ratio.* In other words, the
processes available in the two countries for the production of a given commodity are the same and, if factor prices were the same, the two countries
would select the identical process—or factor use ratio—to produce the product. Economists summarize this by saying that each commodity has identical
production functions, or isoquants, in the two countries.

On the other hand, the production processes required differ from one

---

[1] An additional assumption is that if a producer increases the use of both factors by a
given proportion, his output will rise by that same proportion. This is known in economics as "constant returns to scale." It is to be sharply distinguished from the law of
diminishing returns in that it allows both factors to vary, while the concept of diminishing returns operates when one factor is variable and the other remains fixed. Thus it is
possible for a firm to function under constant returns to scale and at the same time be
subject to diminishing returns in a sense that the two possibilities coexist.

commodity to the other within each country. And they differ in a definite, unique, and consistent manner: for any given pair of factor prices the production of machinery utilizes a higher capital/labor ratio than the production of textiles.[2] This is expressed technically by saying that machinery is *capital intensive* relative to textiles or, equivalently, that textiles are *labor intensive* relative to machinery. The extension of this relationship to a world of more than two commodities involves the ranking of all goods by their capital/labor ratio. It is a fundamental assumption of the model that this ranking (not necessarily the ratios themselves) is the same in the two trading nations. In other words, machinery is the relatively capital-intensive commodity, textiles the relatively labor-intensive product, in both the United States *and* the United Kingdom. Extension of the model into more than two factors of production creates problems because the concept of "relative factor intensity" loses much of its meaning. For example, textiles can be the relatively capital intensive good on a capital/land scale, while machinery is the relatively capital intensive product on a capital/labor scale. We shall not explore these questions here.

Thus far the discussion has centered on the conditions of production of the two goods. Each commodity is manufactured in the same manner (in the sense described above) in the two countries, but the production method differs between goods. How are countries distinguished from one another? They differ in their resource endowment. In our example, the United States possesses a higher capital/labor ratio than the United Kingdom. We say it is the relatively *capital-abundant* country, while the United Kingdom is the relatively *labor-abundant* country.[3] Note that it is the endowment *ratio,* rather than the absolute amount of each factor available, that is important. If we assume (as this model does) that demand conditions are similar in the two nations, then relative factor prices are determined by their supply as reflected in the resource endowment. Thus capital becomes relatively cheaper in the United States and labor relatively cheaper in the United Kingdom. A more precise way of saying this is that the capital/labor *price* ratio is lower in the United States than in the United Kingdom. Combine this result with the earlier postulates concerning manufacture in the two countries and the following conclusions emerge: the United States specializes in the production of machinery, for that commodity uses much of its relatively cheap factor (capital)—it exports machinery and imports textiles. The United Kingdom

---

[2] Keep in mind that within each country factor prices are the same in both industries. This is guaranteed by the free and unobstructed mobility of factors within each country as assumed in the model. Thus, if the price of labor (wage rates) were higher in the machinery than in the textile industry, labor would move from the latter to the former until wage rates were equal in both.

[3] This explains why labor is more efficient in the United States: it has more capital at its disposal than in Great Britain.

specializes in textiles, the commodity that uses much of the relatively cheap factor there (labor)—it exports textiles and imports machinery.

This result can be translated into the example of the previous chapter. It was shown there that the United States had a comparative advantage in wheat, the United Kingdom in textiles, with comparative labor cost or productivity determining this outcome. Now we can add that U.S. labor is relatively more productive in wheat production because wheat is a relatively capital-intensive commodity and American labor has more capital to work with than British labor, the United States being the relatively capital-abundant country. On the other hand, the United Kingdom, being the relatively labor-abundant country, acquires *comparative* advantage in textiles, a commodity that requires relatively less capital in its production. Translating this into a labor–land (rather than labor–capital) situation may make the example more clear, the United States being the relatively land-abundant country and wheat being the relatively land-intensive product. The results will be the same.

Upon further reflection the reader can convince himself that this statement has general application. Each country exports the commodities that are relatively intensive in the factor with which it is relatively well endowed. In an indirect sense we are saying that each country exports the services of its abundant factor and imports the services of its scarce factor—as embodied in the two bundles of traded goods. All phrases in this general rule are couched in relative terms.

Under this model, specialization may be complete or incomplete, although many manipulations and some interesting results derived from the model involve the further assumption of incomplete specialization—in other words, that each country produces some of both commodities (including the imported one). Economists have worked out the conditions that are likely to lead to complete specialization. It turns out that the more diverse (or different) the resource endowment ratios of the two countries are, and the more similar the factor intensity ratios of the two commodities are, the more likely it is that specialization will be complete. The limiting case of the second condition, where the two products use factors in identical ratios, yields the Ricardian case of constant opportunity cost and complete specialization.

For over twenty years, economists have been practically wedded to this explanation of the pattern of international trade. The model was refined in many ways and used to examine a host of important questions, such as the effect of economic growth on the pattern of trade and on the terms of trade. Even in the face of contrary empirical evidence, to be discussed below, economists were loath to dispense with it as the central theoretical proposition. Appendix V offers a sketchy graphical explanation of the factor proportions model.

It is interesting to speculate on the attraction that the model holds for economic theorists. In the first place it is a logically tight structure, where the conclusions follow uniquely and neatly from the assumptions. Second, it is a very simple explanation (perhaps much too simple) that lends itself readily to geometric and mathematical manipulations—a quality that has fascinated modern economists. Also, despite its limitations and the problems discovered in attempts to test it empirically, it is *highly useful in explaining a wide range of observed phenomena.*

Third, the explanation is in terms of the most elementary properties of the trading countries. Any other explanatory factor that could conceivably be advanced—labor productivity, production cost, or what have you—begs the question "What determines that factor itself?" By embedding the explanation in the bare essentials of the country's economic structure we minimize the need for such questions. The natural resources of the country are determined by nature and not by any economic factors. Immigration policies and sociological factors affecting birth rates, rather than economic variables, are the main determinants of labor supply, although an important qualification is introduced by the fact that the size of the labor force and its level of participation are at least partly related to economic conditions. The point is probably least valid in the case of capital, where it is certainly legitimate to inquire into the economic causes of past investments that led to today's capital stock. These certainly include the saving behavior of past generations that made resources available for investments, natural resources, entrepreneurial ability of the population, and a degree of destruction through wars and other causes. To the extent that technological developments control investments, we can still ask what (besides human genius, which appears in spurts) motivates new technology. But all these are causes of past behavior. Today's capital stock can be taken for granted. Thus despite these important reservations, the model reduces to the bare essentials of the economic structure, at least when considered as of the period under study.

Last but not least, because the model employs the country's economic structure to explain trade, the process can be reversed to inquire into the effect of international trade on the economic structure, especially on the remuneration of factors of production and the distribution of income among factors.[4] Since the model implies that each country exports the *services* of its abundant factor and imports the *services* of its scarce factor, it follows that the introduction of international trade into an otherwise isolated economy raises the demand for the abundant factor, and therefore its remuneration, while lowering returns to the scarce factors. (The opposite result follows

---

[4] The distribution of income among factors of production (the total return to labor, to capital, to natural resources, and to entrepreneurial ability) is known as the *functional distribution of income.* It is to be distinguished from the size distribution, designed to assess the degree of income inequality in the population.

from the imposition of a tariff.) With incomplete specialization, and under the assumption of this model, international trade would lead to the equalization of factor prices between the trading nations.[5]

☐ More specifically, the process of factor price equalization is based on changes in the factor use ratios in the production of the two commodities. In the example used earlier, and under conditions of incomplete specialization, trade causes the United Kingdom to produce more textiles and less machinery. Thus resources are shifted from machinery to textiles. But because of the difference in the factor use ratio in the two industries, resources are released from the machinery industry at a relatively high capital/labor ratio and can be absorbed into the textile industry only at a relatively low capital/labor ratio. Thus the process involves freeing relatively more capital and less labor than can be absorbed. In the market scrambling that ensues, the price of capital falls and that of labor rises. This must be the outcome if (as the model assumes) all factors are fully employed before and after trade. Precisely the reverse holds true in the United States, where resources are released from textiles at a relatively low capital/labor ratio and are absorbed into producing machinery at a relatively high capital/labor ratio. This process entails a rise in the price of capital and a fall in the price of labor.

☐ Two consequences of this transformation are among the topics that have held great fascination for economists since World War II. First, the internal distribution of income in each country has changed, with the relatively abundant factor (capital in the United States and labor in England) gaining from the introduction of trade. These effects occur in both industries as long as specialization is incomplete and both are functioning in the two countries. But in each country the loss to the scarce factor is less than the gain to the abuandant factor, so that the community as a whole gains from the introduction of trade. Conversely, restrictions on trade would benefit the relatively scarce factor. Indeed, Australia, for example, has in the past imposed tariffs in order to affect the internal distribution of income in favor of labor, which is scarce there relative to land. However, there are superior means at the disposal of government to change income distribution without the loss in allocative efficiency that is caused by protection.

☐ Second, in comparing factor remunerations across countries we notice that the introduction of trade lowers the price of capital in the United Kingdom and raises it in the United States. Since capital is the relatively scarce factor in the United Kingdom and was more highly priced there than in the United States before the advent of trade, this constitutes a convergence of the two prices. Simi-

---

[5] These results do not follow the Ricardian model, which immediately leads to complete specialization.

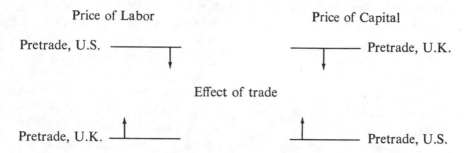

lar convergence occurs in the price of labor as it rises in England and declines in America. Schematically, these movements can be illustrated as in Figure 12-1. This convergence takes place in both industries as long as specialization is incomplete. And under the strict postulates of the Heckscher-Ohlin model, including the assumption of constant returns to scale,[6] factor prices would be equalized completely.   ■

Empirical Testing

With all these virtues, one may ask, is there anything wrong with the model? The answer is that empirical tests to date have failed to verify it. An excellent way to test a theory is by examining its ability to predict real-world phenomena (although another method may be to inquire into the realism of its assumptions). For a long time it was impossible to test the factor proportion theory in that fashion, because commodities entering international trade could not be decomposed into their labor and capital components. The production processes in an industrial economy are rather complex. Each final good, such as automobiles, can be decomposed into its labor, capital, and material inputs. And the last item (such as steel and other metals) also must be decomposed in the same procedure, and so on down the line. Only by working backward through the production processes to the crude material stage, which itself is found in natural form, can one sum up the total labor and capital inputs embodied in each final product. Indeed, for most traded commodities the labor and capital content in the final stage of fabrication is only about half the total.

This procedure presented a monumental obstacle until the impasse was broken in the late 1930s, when mobilization required precise knowledge of the production processes in the economy. If the government decides to in-

---

[6] This implies that the marginal product of each factor depends only on the factor use ratio and is completely independent of the scale of operations.

crease the production of airplanes by one thousand units, to avoid bottlenecks it must also know what inputs from other industries would be required. In fact, any massive shifts in the commodity composition of production, for demobilization or for any other reason, necessitates such knowledge. Smooth transition of the economy is impossible without it. Harvard economist Wassily Leontief was the first to develop a method that provided this information for the United States in the form of "input-output tables." These show the inter-industry flows of goods and services as they work their way through the production processes into final form. This work has been taken over by the U.S. Department of Commerce, and its results are published on occasion in the *Survey of Current Business*. Similar studies are available for numerous other countries.

Once input-output statistics became available, it became possible to de-compose American exports and imports into their labor and capital compo-nents. This Leontief did in the mid-1950s. And lo and behold he discovered that a representative basket of American exports embodied more labor and less capital than one of American imports. Certainly the capital/labor ratio was higher for imports than exports. Since the United States is by far the most capital-abundant country in the world, this result is clearly at variance with the factor proportions theory. His finding caused great consternation among theorists and came to be known as the Leontief scarce-factor paradox.

Since that time similar data from other countries have been subjected to the same analysis, but in many cases they failed to verify the theory. It should be pointed out that the United States occupies an extreme position in the spectrum of countries ranked by capital/labor endowment ratio and there-fore can be considered the relatively capital-abundant country vis-à-vis the rest of the world. This is not true of other nations. Japan, for example, trades with some countries that are capital abundant (in North America) and others that are labor abundant (in Asia) relative to itself. Thus a proper test of the model for Japan requires the breaking up of its trade into two parts according to the nature of the trading partner. In sum, although the tests conducted thus far are not conclusive, such as they are they fail to confirm the accepted doctrine.

These results touched off a heated debate among economists that lasted nearly two decades. Most writers attempted to salvage the factor proportion theory by reconciling it with the empirical findings. Leontief himself pointed to the great effectiveness of American labor, resulting from superior manage-ment, better training, and stronger motivation. He concluded that since Amer-ican labor is three times as effective as its foreign counterpart (even when using the same capital equipment), when labor is measured in efficiency units the United States comes out as the relatively labor-abundant country, and the theory is thus vindicated.

Other economists claimed instead that the U.S. tariff structure so heavily protects labor-intensive industries that the average observed import basket is artificially biased toward capital-intensive products. Still others maintained that the trouble lies in confining the model to two factors of production and ignoring natural resources. In fact, what the United States imports is natural-resource-intensive products, and it happens that these necessitate much capital in their production. Consequently they show up as capital intensive on a capital–labor scale. Finally, some economists emphasized the possibility that strong American demand for capital-intensive goods may have offset the U.S. factor endowment advantage in these goods and raised their relative prices in this country to a point at which they would be imported rather than exported. Other theoretical as well as statistical reconciliations were advanced, and the data were modified and manipulated in various directions.

Although some of the new results were closer to theoretical expectations, it is difficult to overlook the fact that none has yet shown that American exports have a capital-intensity lead over imports. Indeed, in the view of some writers the factor-proportions model should be scrapped altogether or be drastically modified both on the grounds of empirical tests and because it is based on unrealistic assumptions: in a world of free capital movement and integrated capital markets, where the international corporation is becomng a dominant force, and in an era in which technical and managerial talent can be transferred between countries and innovations quickly diffused, can one adhere to the classical assumption of factor immobility between countries? Is it correct to assume constant returns to scale? Is it legitimate to postulate that the ranking of industries by capital/labor ratio is the same in all trading nations? This last assumption was tested directly and was found somewhat lacking, but the evidence to date is inconclusive. Is it legitimate to confine both the analysis and its tests to two factors of production, assumed to be homogeneous in form, when we know that more than two enter the productive process? Is it reasonable to focus almost exclusive attention on supply considerations and assume that demand conditions are largely similar in the trading nations? Both the predictive ability of the theory and the assumptions on which it rests were brought into question. Indeed, relaxation of each of the above assumptions can practically produce a new theory.

Alternative Theories

In the beginning the mainstream of professional opinion refused to abandon or modify the factor-proportions theory, not only for lack of a better substitute but also because the empirical tests do not prove it totally useless. Although the theory cannot explain all international trade, and indeed should not have been expected to do so in the first place, it still has considerable explanatory power. Phenomena such as the stimulus to American investments in Canada provided by the Canadian tariff (which means that Canadians are inconsistent in insisting on a high tariff but complaining about the inflow of American capital) can be explained by reference to the model, as can some of the relationships between economic growth and international trade. But it is unreasonable to expect one simple theory to account fully for such a complex phenomenon as trade in all goods among one hundred nations. It is not surprising, therefore, that during the 1960s and 1970s several alternative explanations appeared in the professional literature. Here are some of the theories that have been advocated by various scholars.

1. *Human skills.* In industrial economies, the training and sophistication of the labor force is the most important characteristic distinguishing one country from another. Therefore, countries that are relatively well endowed with professional personnel and highly trained labor will specialize in and export skill-intensive goods. Conversely, relative abundance of unskilled labor promotes the export of commodities embodying mostly untrained labor. A test of this hypothesis requires information on the skill content of products entering international trade and the matching of this information with the relative abundance (or scarcity) of skill in the trading nations.

The skill content of products can be measured as the ratio of professional and technical manpower in the total labor force of the industry or, alternatively, as average wage rates in the industry, on the assumption that wage rates reflect the degree of training and professionalism. Since interindustry skill differentials are similar the world over, in the sense that the *ranking of industries* by degree of skill used does not vary much between countries,[7] The skill content of each commodity in one country (normally the United States, for which more data are available) is used to represent the skill content of the same commodity in all countries. Of course, the commodity composition of trade, and therefore the "skill mix" embodied in it, varies from country to country. This measure of the skill content of traded goods is matched with the percentage of professional and technical personnel in the labor force of every country, the latter proportion measuring the relative national abundance of trained manpower. The degree of correlation between them indicates whether labor skill is indeed a powerful explanatory variable of the direction of international trade.

2. *Economies of scale.* According to another hypothesis, a large home market is conducive to the export of goods, produced under conditions of increasing returns to scale—that is, where production costs decline as the scale of operations expands. Conversely, a small home market leads to the export

[7] This is referred to as lack of "skill intensity reversals" among industries.

of goods not subject to these conditions. In this case a test would require matching the size of the market with the type of commodities traded, classified by the degree to which their manufacture is subject to economies of scale.

3. *Technological advance.* This hypothesis makes use of the sequence of innovation and imitation as they affect exports. It argues that the industrially sophisticated countries are the early producers of new products; they therefore enjoy easy access to foreign markets at an early stage of manufacture. Later a process of imitation sets in, as other nations start producing and exporting these goods by relying on lower wages or some other factor-cost advantage. An example may be the production of antipollution equipment. Because the United States is the leader in setting up pollution standards, American firms are likely to be the first in developing and producing such equipment. Only later will their manufacture spread to other countries. To test this theory one would need to inquire whether it is indeed the industrially advanced countries that are responsible for the introduction of new products into international trade.

4. *Product cycle.* Instead of emphasizing the time lag involved in the imitation process (as in the technological-advance hypothesis), the product cycle hypothesis stresses the standardization of products. Early manufacture of a new good involves experimentation with both the features of the product and the manufacturing process. Therefore in its beginning stages the good is nonstandardized. As markets grow and the various techniques come to be common knowledge, both the product and the process become more standardized and perhaps even subject to internationally set standards and specifications. At that time, production can begin in less sophisticated nations. The upshot of this hypothesis is that highly sophisticated economies are expected to export nonstandardized goods, while less sophisticated countries specialize in more standardized goods. A test of the theory must relate the degree of standardization (or, conversely, product differentiation) of the country's exports to the level of its industrial sophistication.

5. *Similarity of preferences.* All the explanations mentioned above, along with the factor-endowment theory, have one thing in common. They maintain that international trade compensates for national deficiencies, whether in capital, labor skill, management, or technological sophistication. The gain from trade derives from the fact that it enables countries to specialize in goods that require the factors that they possess in abundance. It is a gain from reallocating resources among different activities. The result is that countries import and export dissimilar goods—dissimilar in terms of one or more of the characteristics outlined above. Presumably the more divergent the countries' endowments are, the more dissimilar will be the commodities exchanged and the greater will be the gain from trade.

The "preference similarity" hypothesis applied to trade in manufactured goods is essentially a different approach. It maintains that a country's export is merely an extension of production for the home market. Such production caters to the needs of the majority, and it is through producing for that market that the country acquires a comparative advantage in the product and then comes to export it. Since the minority of the population has slightly different demands, these can be met with imports from a country where such tastes are those of the majority. Because the type of goods demanded in a country is thought to be uniquely determined by the level of per capita income, most exchange of manufactures takes place between countries of similar industrial structures. And because the trading partners export essentially similar goods, each country's exports are similar to its imports. Thus trade extends the variety of manufactured goods available to the consuming public, and the gain from trade stems from the satisfaction of being offered the precise variety or brand of product the consumer desires. This approach was suggested only as an explanation of international trade in manufactured products. In the case of nonindustrial goods that are high in natural resource content one must certainly rely on the natural resource endowment of the country as an explanatory factor.

International trade theory is now in a state of flux with respect to both formulation and testing. Tests to date have yielded mixed results concerning which of the foregoing hypotheses has the strongest explanatory power. One would hope that some of the explanatory factors can be merged into a composite variable on grounds that make theoretical sense. And each composite variable can perhaps be used to explain a distinct portion of international trade. After all, international commerce is a complex phenomenon, and it is unreasonable to expect one explanation to account for it all.

In order to see what is meant by a composite variable, consider the factor-proportions model based on the capital/labor ratio. Labor is assumed to be a homogeneous factor. Yet we know that it is anything but that. There are different types of labor embodying various degrees of skill and professionalism. In fact, one of the above explanations of the commodity composition of trade that was tested successfully was concerned with human skills—a variable that can be quantified in terms of the education and training needed to acquire them. Education and training are investments in people; they create human capital. And in an economic sense human capital is no different from physical capital. The two can be combined under the heading "capital" and so used in computing the capital content of commodities for the purpose of estimating capital/labor ratios. It even makes sense to merge, under the concept of capital, material capital, human capital, and capital in the form of technological knowledge. The denominator of the capital/labor ratio would then consist only of unskilled or raw labor. Or, instead, capital can be considered an indirect factor of production, to be added to the country's natural endowment of labor and natural resources. As an alternative, one might merge the various technological variables into one and then match the level of technology required to produce various commodities with the degree of technological sophistication of the trading nations. Labor skills can be incorporated into the composite technological variable too, and empirical researchers may indeed discover that technology (so interpreted) is a more important explanation of trade patterns than is factor proportion, however defined.

Economic Adjustment to Changing Circumstances

Having outlined the manifold factors that determine comparative advantage, we hasten to add that these influences are never at a standstill. They change over time, both within and between countries. Technological advance, capital accumulation, acquisition of new skills, and invention of new products are commonplace in all dynamic economies. They occur practically every year and in turn change the ranking of industries in terms of comparative advantage. Industries that could easily meet price competition on world markets at one time may suddenly find themselves shrinking in size because of their inability to compete. Under such circumstances it is important that resources in the economy be mobile enough to shift from sluggish to competitive sectors. The economy itself must be in a process of continuing transformation to meet new circumstances.

Consider, for example, the production of desk calculators. Immediately after World War II this was almost exclusively an American monopoly. But twenty years later—when the technology involved was no longer considered sophisticated—the Burroughs Corporation found it advantageous to move production from Detroit to Scotland where equally qualified but cheaper labor was to be found. Were the Detroit plants shut down? Not at all; they were transformed into the production of more sophisticated electronic computers. While the United States was losing its comparative advantage in calculators, it was gaining a new one in more highly sophisticated equipment.

But at the same time, similar changes were taking place in other countries. Consider the attempts of the developing countries to industrialize. What new industries can they establish? Apart from production based on locally available materials, it is clear that their comparative advantage lies in industries that are both technologically unsophisticated and labor intensive. Textiles and lumber products come immediately to mind as concrete possibilities. Thus, while India, Pakistan, and Taiwan establish textile mills, it is necessary for Great Britain and continental Europe to contract their textile industries and shift to the production of more advanced products, perhaps desk calculators. In terms of their comparative advantage, it pays them to specialize in the latter type of commodities and import the cheaper textiles from abroad.

A reverse change in the structure of comparative advantage may occur if and when developed countries introduce and enforce high antipollution standards. For this may raise the production cost of many synthetic materials above that of their natural substitutes, which are produced mainly in the developing countries. These countries would then regain the competitive advantage that they had previously lost to synthetics.

Perhaps the most dramatic illustration of the dynamic nature of comparative advantage is the recent Japanese concern about textile imports. Toward the end of 1970, in the midst of the American industry's clamor for quota protection from Japanese textile exports, the Japanese mills themselves were becoming increasingly concerned about cheap textile imports from South Korea, Hong Kong, and Taiwan. It can only be hoped that Japan will handle the problem by gradually shifting resources to more sophisticated and capital-intensive industries, and not by the imposition of new restrictions on imports from other Far Eastern countries.

But here comes the hitch. What on paper is a one-paragraph description of economic transformation is in reality a severe problem of human adjustment. Production equipment must be scrapped and new machinery installed. Workers must be retrained in new skills and sometimes relocated. At times, even entire communities are disbanded, and ghost towns appear where once there were thriving cities. In other words, the shift that benefits the entire nation occurs at the expense of considerable hardship to a minority of dislocated people. This problem is common to any type of economic change, such as the introduction of new technology, not only to change brought about by foreign trade. The depressing effect on coal-producing regions of the introduction of oil and natural gas as energy sources is a case in point, but, in view of the energy shortage, that may be reversed again in the 1970s. Public assistance in the adjustment process can help smooth over and speed up the transformation, but hardships remain nonetheless.

Consequently, it is not surprising that the industries directly affected by new import competition strive to protect their interests by demanding tariff or quota production, with the labor unions joining in. The eventual benefit to all, after the transformation has been completed and workers moved to higher paying jobs, is lost sight of. The vested interest of the minority often prevails; certainly little attention is paid to the consuming public that stands to benefit from cheaper imports. The resulting protection of the textile industry in the United States and Europe has become a major grievance of many developing nations.

To all countries, developed and developing alike, inability to transform may spell economic stagnation and continuous difficulties. Difficulties in making the adjustment to new patterns of production as dictated by shifting world demand is one of the problems that have plagued the British economy for the past thirty years. Despite the hardships involved, an economy must maintain the dynamism necessary for continuous change as it adapts to shifts in comparative advantage. The government can help by maintaining a high level of aggregate production and employment so that labor and capital released from declining industries will find alternative employment. It can also provide direct assistance to alleviate the burden of interindustry transfers.

We close this discussion with a pertinent letter (to the *Wall Street Journal,* July 22, 1969), by W. L. Law, president of a leather company that reacted to Japanese imports by switching to other products.

> I have some knowledge of the subject, inasmuch as baseball glove leather was the principal product for our firm until 1957 when Japanese-manufactured ball gloves entered and ultimately captured 70 percent of the United States market. Today we tan no baseball glove leather. Sentiment in the ball glove industry at that time was very strong for protective action and I investigated the matter in some depth but found that I could not in good faith urge protectionist action on my representative. Such action would have been wrong economically, politically, and morally. . . .
>
> Certainly, labor-intensive industries are unable to compete. Give an Italian girl a needle and $20 per week and she will produce lace for one-fourth the cost of the American girl who receives $80 per week. Their productivity must be equal. However, give an American miner a giant mechanical shovel and $150 per week and by mining 100 tons he will produce much cheaper coal than the British miner with less efficient tools who receives $50 per week and only produces 20 tons. So we import handmade lace and we export computers.

13

Protection of Domestic Industries: The Tariff

In light of the gains from international trade that were articulated in Chapter 11, one would expect free trade to be the prevailing rule and artificial barriers to trade the exception. Yet even casual observation may convince the reader that we live in a protection-ridden world, where government interference with the free flow of goods, services, and capital is anything but an exception. As in other areas of national concern, commercial policies do not represent the reasoned opinions of a single decision-maker. They are a product of pressure groups vying for the attention of legislators and policy-makers. The result hardly squares with the dictates of economic theory.

Traditionally, the most common instrument of protection, though by no means the only one, has been the tariff, and it has undergone much economic analysis over the years. It is a highly charged political issue, with import-competing industries clamoring for tariff protection, export industries often favoring free trade, and the consumer who pays the cost of protection being neither vocal nor adequately represented.

Some Institutional Considerations

Export Versus Import Duty

The tariff is a tax levied upon a commodity when it crosses a national boundary. The most common tariff is the import duty, although some countries, primarily exporters of agricultural commodities and raw materials, also employ export taxes. Export taxes may be used to produce government revenue, or they may be designed to curtail exports in order to prop up world prices of a primary commodity, as when Ghana discourages the exportation of cocoa or Brazil the exportation of coffee. It is interesting to note that import and export taxes are symmetrical in their effect on a country's resource allocation. A tax on imports raises their prices in the taxing country relative to the prices of other commodities and draws resources from export industries to import-competing industries. A tax on exports discourages overseas shipment of the taxed commodities and lowers their prices in the taxing country relative to other prices. Consequently, resources are pushed out of the export industries into the import-competing industries. Since export taxes are relatively rare among industrial nations, we shall be concerned mainly with import duties.

In the United States, the Constitution prohibits the imposition of a tax on exports. Consequently, whenever the U.S. government wishes to restrict exports so as to keep down domestic prices (as in the case of soybeans in 1972), it resorts to direct quota restrictions or a complete ban on overseas shipments.

Protection Versus Revenue

In times past, tariffs were imposed mainly as a source of government revenue. They are the easiest taxes to administer, because the collection of them in their entirety can be executed by officers stationed at official points of entry along the border. Many developing nations still rely on tariffs for financing government operations because of this ease of collection. Among industrial countries today, however, tariffs are levied for the protection of domestic industries. The revenue from a protective tariff is a pleasant by-product, not the major objective. A duty is purely for revenue if it does not cause resources to move into industries that produce domestic substitutes for the imported commodities. A tariff levied on a commodity that is not produced at home, such as a U.S. import tax on coffee, or on a commodity whose domestic substitutes bear the same taxation, may serve to illustrate such a duty. At the other extreme, a *prohibitive* tariff—one high enough to keep out all imports—yields only protection and no revenue. For the overwhelming majority of taxed commodities, both the protection and the revenue are present.

Types of Tariff

We distinguish between *ad valorem* duty, specific duty, and compound duty. The *ad valorem* tax is a fixed percentage of the value of the commodity, as when imported cars are taxed at 5 percent of value. A specific duty is a fixed sum of money per physical unit of the commodity, say $100 per imported automobile. A compound duty is a combination of the two, as when a car is taxed at $50 per unit plus 2 percent of value. The United States uses both specific and *ad valorem* duties in roughly equal proportion; European countries rely mainly on *ad valorem* taxes.

What are the advantages and disadvantages of each kind of tax? The *ad valorem* tax is more equitable than the others because it distinguishes among fine gradations of the commodity as they are reflected in its price. The person importing a Cadillac pays more than his counterpart importing a Chevrolet, the result being tantamount to a proportional tax system. On the other hand, under a specific duty each person would pay the same amount, resulting in a higher percentage tax on the cheaper import, which is a form of regressive tax.

In addition, the *ad valorem* tax provides a more constant level of protection to domestic industry in times of inflation than the specific duty does. Since world prices have been rising in recent decades, the level of protection accorded by a fixed sum of money declines as the tax becomes a smaller fraction of value, while the *ad valorem* duty, given as a fixed percentage, is not subject to the same decline. This, incidentally, is a source of frequent complaints by American manufacturers of products subject to specific duties: the level of protection they are accorded gets eroded away by inflation.

On the other side of the ledger, a specific duty is easy to apply and administer, while an *ad valorem* tariff requires evaluation of the price of the commodity by the tax official before the tax can be calculated. Generally speaking there are two bases for such valuation: the f.o.b. price and the c.i.f. price. The first stands for "free on board" and indicates the price of the commodity on board ship at the port of embarkation (if ship-loading costs are excluded we obtain the f.a.s. or "free along side" price). The second designation stands for "cost, insurance, freight" and covers the cost of the commodity up to the port of entry. Essentially it includes ocean freight and other intercountry transportation costs, which the f.o.b. price excludes.

As a general rule the United States and Canada use the f.o.b. price for computing the tariff, while most European countries employ the c.i.f. value. Consequently, a given percentage tariff translates into a level of protection about one-tenth lower in the United States than in Europe.

Certain chemical imports (coal tar products) into the United States that are competitive with homemade merchandise are an exception to this rule. For reasons that need not detain us here, Congress specified in the tariff law that these commodities must be evaluated not at the import price but at the one-fifth higher U.S. selling price of American-made substitutes. This is known as the "American selling price" (ASP) method of valuation. Not only does it mean a much higher rate of protection than is implied by the published tariff rate,[1] but it gives the domestic chemical industry—whose structure is far from

---

[1] Suppose that the cost of producing a unit of a chemical product is $200 in the United States and $100 in Europe. Then a 50 percent tariff calculated by the ASP method will yield $100 and enable U.S. producers to compete in the domestic market. The same tariff rate levied on the foreign export value will yield only $50, making it possible for the European producers to undersell their American competition; a 100 percent duty would be needed to "equalize costs."

competitive—some control over the level of protection it enjoys, through variations in the prices charged on the domestic market. This special provision has been a bone of contention between American and European tariff negotiators for some time; it was a major stumbling block during the Kennedy Round. The chemical industry, of course, is adamantly opposed to the abolition of the ASP method, which gives it such preferential treatment, and the consumer who pays the price and indirectly subsidizes the industry is rarely consulted, let alone adequately represented in the councils of government.

It is apparent that there are advantages and disadvantages to both specific and *ad valorem* duties. A sensible compromise may be to use the specific duty for standardized products and the *ad valorem* duty for goods with a wide range of grade variations.

Since tariff-setting in the United States is a congressional prerogative, the American tariff reflects the influence of a great variety of political pressure groups. This is one reason why the tariff classificaion has traditionally been rather long and complex, compounding the difficulty of administering the tariff. The customs officer must determine the classification within which each imported product falls. Since various categories are subject to different tax rates, this is very important to the importer. Indeed, much tariff litigation revolves around the classification of imported commodities, as well as their valuation (in the cases of *ad valorem* duties). The uncertainty that results from the complexity of the list is in itself a hindrance to international trade. To complicate matters further, a given product may be subject to different rates depending on its source of supply. This reflects the fact that an importing country may accord preferential treatment to certain exporting countries in the form of lower rates, either as a result of trade agreements or because of a general policy such as the imperial preference system of the British Commonwealth. In the case of the United States, the statutory tariff, set by Congress in the 1930s, is much higher than the rates charged on imports from most Western countries (known as the most favored nation rates) after a long succession of reciprocal tariff reductions.

An interesting corollary of the two methods of valuation of commodities for tariff purposes is the way the United Nations, the OECD, and other international organizations report commodity trade statistics. All products entering trade are classified according to the SITC. But the basic sources from which the data are derived are import and export declarations filed by the traders with the respective governments at the time the commodity enters or leaves the country. The declarations include a detailed description of the products to permit further classification, along with quantity and value information. Import declarations usually require more detailed description than their export counterparts, because they are of direct interest not only to the statistician who compiles data but also to the tax assessor. Export values are reported on the f.o.b. basis by all countries. But when it comes to import statistics, the United States and Canada use f.o.b. values, whereas European countries report c.i.f. values, simply because the import declarations are so filed for the purpose of computing the tariff. That is also how they are reported by all data-gathering organizations.

Sources of Data

Tariff rates are published and distributed by individual countries, in their respective languages, but translations of all tariff schedules into the five major languages are printed in the *International Customs Journal,* published by the International Customs Tariff Bureau in Belgium. Tariff systems of foreign countries are also described in various issues of *Overseas Business Reports* published by the U.S. Department of Commerce. And a supplement to the April 1969 issue of *Forum* (published by UNCTAD-GATT International Trade Center in Geneva) gives short descriptions of the import tariff systems of 140 countries on five continents. The American tariff is reported in *The Tariff Schedule of the United States, Annotated* (1969). Virtually all European countries, as well as many of the developing nations, adhere to a standardized classification of commodities know as the Brussels Tariff Nomenclature (BTN) in levying their tariffs, and GATT has compiled tariff averages for each BTN category for all major industrial countries (*Basic Documentation for the Tariff Study,* Geneva, 1971). While the United States and Canada employ their own classification systems, the United States is considering the adoption of the BTN, and the Tariff Commission is in the process of constructing a concordance table between the Tariff Schedule of the United States (TSUS) and the 1100 headings of the BTN.

Economic Effects of the Tariff

Who Pays the Tariff?

It is customary to think of the tariff as being paid by the importer when the commodity enters the country and then passed on in whole or in part to the consumer as a price increase. Because this is the administrative procedure, there is a natural tendency to conclude that the tariff is being paid by the citizens of the country imposing it. Often, however, this is not true.

Consider an extreme example of a two-country world: the United States as a coffee importer and Brazil as the exporter. When the United States imposes a tariff on coffee, its domestic price rises, leading Americans to consume less; they either switch to substitute products such as tea or simply cut down on consumption of hot beverages altogether. But this means that the United States imports less coffee, reducing demand on the world coffee markets and leading to a reduction in its world price. As Brazil's export price declines, the coffee exporters are, in effect, forced to absorb part of the duty. The burden or *incidence* of the duty is divided between the Americans and the Brazilians: the U.S. domestic price rises and the Brazilian export price declines, the two changes adding up to the amount of the tariff. Thus the Brazilian exporter is forced by the market mechanism to absorb and pay part of the U.S.-imposed tax.

From the point of view of the importing country as a whole (the private sector and government combined), the import is now obtained at a lower cost than before (although private consumers pay more). The terms of trade— export prices divided by import prices—have improved. Conversely, the terms of trade of the exporting country deteriorate as its export prices decline.

The distribution of the burden between the importing and exporting countries is not the same in all cases; it depends on the type of commodity and on the countries involved. Consider first the importing country. If it is a small nation, accounting only for an insignificant share of world import of the product, a reduction in the quantity that its citizens consume is unlikely to influence the world price of the commodity. Thus, while the United States is a customer important enough to affect the world price of coffee and consequently shift part of the duty to foreign exporters, the same cannot be said of Luxembourg. The larger the tariff-imposing country is, the more "monopoly power" it can bring to bear on world markets and the better able it is to "tax the exporter" and thereby affect the terms at which it trades. The term "monopoly power" refers to market power. A small country, like a purely competitive firm, is a price taker. It is too small to affect by its own action the conditions prevailing in the market. A large country exercises monopoly power in the sense that it does not accept market prices as given. Its very actions affect them.

A second question on which the ability to shift part of the tax to exporters turns is the extent to which the increase in the domestic price of coffee would lead Americans to curtail consumption. Availability of adequate substitutes, such as tea, or alternative sources of supply of the same product, domestic or foreign, play an influential role here, as does the general willingness to do without coffee. The more readily available the substitutes are, the easier it is to relinquish consumption of Brazilian coffee and thereby depress the export prices and shift the duty to the exporters.

As for the exporting country, the easier it is to find alternative markets for the product, at home or abroad, or to contract production in the face of a price decline, the smaller will be the proportion of the foreign tax it will have to absorb. Instead of taking a price cut, exports simply withdraw from the market in question. In the study of economics all these considerations reduce to various elasticities of supply and demand.

In sum, when a sizable country imposes an import duty, part of it is absorbed by the foreign exporter in the form of a lower export price, part by the home consumer in the form of a higher domestic price. A myriad of country and commodity characteristics determines the division of the tax between the two countries.

Graphic Exposition

A visual demonstration of this analysis requires a simple but useful extension of the tools of demand and supply. What follows pertains to a one-commodity, two-country world in which one country is the importer and the other the exporter.

We begin with the importing country B. Figure 13-1(a) shows supply and demand curves for a single commodity in which country B has a comparative disadvantage compared to country A. P_1 is the equilibrium domestic price, the price that equates domestic supply and demand and thereby clears the market. If the world price is also P_1, country B will not trade in that commodity. But at any price below P_1 country B will import the commodity in question. Figure 13-1(b) describes country B's demand for imports: at price P_1 the demand for imports is zero.

As the price declines to P_2, two things happen on the domestic market: the quantity demanded rises as we move down the (negatively sloped) demand curve, and the quantity supplied declines as we move down the (positively sloped) supply curve. The divergence, or horizontal distance, between the domestic demand and supply at P_2 (distance a) is what the country imports at that price. That distance is plotted in 13-1(b) to obtain another point of the import-demand curve. Likewise, when price drops to P_3, import demand

Figure 13-1
Importing Country B

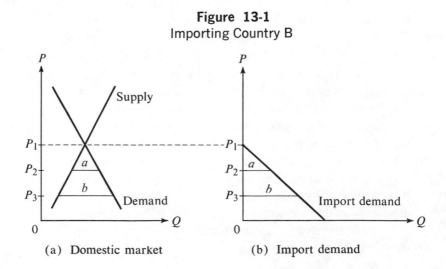

(a) Domestic market   (b) Import demand

increases to b, since domestic demand increases further while domestic supply declines further. Again the divergence (horizontal distance) between demand and supply at P_3 is plotted in (b). By connecting all points in Figure 13-1(b), we obtain the import-demand schedule.

In sum, the import-demand curve shows the quantities that the country stands ready to import at various prices. For each price this quantity equals the horizontal distance between the domestic demand and supply curves. In all cases except when one of the domestic schedules is of zero elasticity (vertical), import demand is flatter and more elastic than domestic demand. This is so because its slope equals the combined slopes of the domestic demand and supply schedules. Thus the demand and supply schedules both affect the shape of the import-demand schedule. (A precise formulation of the relationship is given in Appendix III.) At prices above P_1 domestic supply exceeds domestic demand, and import demand becomes negative. This simply means that at these higher prices the country becomes an exporter of the commodity, and it is a useful reminder of the fact that whether a commodity is exported or imported depends on its domestic price relative to the international price.

An infinitely elastic (horizontal) import-demand schedule is generated when either the domestic demand or the domestic supply curve is infinitely elastic. This the reader can verify by gradually making one of the domestic curves flatter until it approaches the infinitely elastic position, and observing the resulting changes in the import-demand curve.

Next we turn to the exporting country in our configuration, country A. Figure 13-2(a) shows domestic demand and supply, with equilibrium price P_1 being established in isolation. At that price the country will not trade, and therefore zero quantity is shown for export supply in (b). When price rises to P_2, the quantity supplied domestically increases as we move up along the

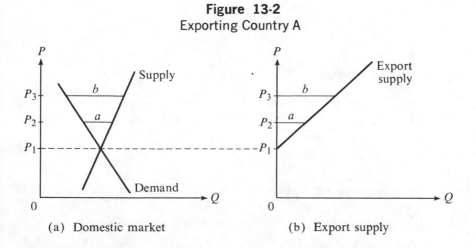

Figure 13-2
Exporting Country A

(a) Domestic market   (b) Export supply

(positively sloped) supply curve, while the quantity demanded internally declines as we move up along the negatively sloped demand curve. The divergence, or horizontal distance, betwen domestic supply and demand at price P_2 is a units of the commodity, the quantity that the country will export at that price. We thus obtain another point on the export-supply curve. By the same token, as price rises to P_3, the quantity exported increases to b. Connecting all the points in (b) yields the export-supply curve.

In sum, the export-supply schedule shows the quantities that the country stands ready to export at various prices. For each price the quantity equals the divergence (horizontal distance) between the internal supply and demand. In all cases except when one of the domestic schedules is of zero elasticity (vertical) export supply is flatter and more elastic than domestic supply, for its slope is made up of the combined slopes of the demand and supply functions. Both domestic supply and demand affect the shape of the export-supply schedule. (A precise formulation of this relation is given in Appendix III.) An infinitely elastic (horizontal) export-supply schedule is generated when either domestic demand or domestic supply is infinitely elastic. This can be verified by making one of the domestic curves flatter in several successive steps, until it approaches the infinitely elastic position, and observing the resulting changes in the export-supply curve. At prices below P_1, domestic demand exceeds supply, export supply is negative, and the country becomes an importer of the commodity.

We are now prepared to illustrate world trade in one commodity. In Figure 13-3, the fact that country A has a lower domestic equilibrium price than B establishes A as the exporter and B as the importer. Indeed, pretrade price in A is P_1 ($20), while that of B is P_2 ($60). From the exporting country we derive the export-supply curve, and from the importing country the import-demand curve, both plotted in Figure 13-3(b).

Figure 13-3

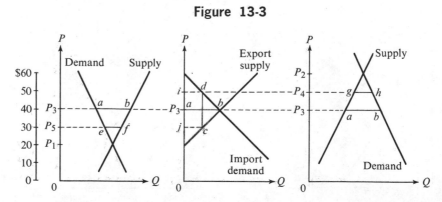

(a) Exporting country A   (b) Foreign trade   (c) Importing country B

Now suppose that trade opens up. Post-trade equilibrium in the absence of transport cost and artificial barriers to trade requires that there be a common price in the two countries and that the quantity exported by one country be equal to the quantity imported by the other. Both conditions are met at price P_3, which is established by the intersection of the export-supply and import-demand curves. Note that the price in the exporting country rises while that in the importing country declines following the opening of trade. Production expands in the exporting country and contracts in the importing country, but the contraction stops short of complete specialization. The importing country continues to produce some of the product.

This free-trade position is now modified by the introduction of a tariff. For simplicity we deal with a specific duty of, say, $20 per unit of the product. Since the vertical axis denotes price, the duty can be measured as a $20 segment on that scale. Starting from the intersection of the export-supply and import-demand curves, we proceed left to where the vertical divergence between the curves equals $20. This occurs at $\overline{cd}$.[2]

As a result of the tariff, the volume of trade declines to $\overline{ef}$ in the exporting country, which equals $\overline{gh}$ in the importing country and $\overline{id}$ $(=\overline{cj})$ in the center sector. Second, the export price declines to P_5 ($30 per unit) in country A, and the import price rises to P_4 ($50) in country B. The difference between the two is the tax per unit levied by the government of B. Government revenue from the duty equals $\overline{gh}$ units of import times $\overline{cd}$ ($20 per unit). Clearly, half of it is paid by the exporters in A and half by the consumers in B. In this example, the incidence of the tariff is divided equally between the two groups —a result of the equal but opposite slopes of the import-demand and export-supply curves. The terms of trade of the importing country have improved, for it now obtains imports from A for $10 per unit less than before. While B's private consumers pay a higher price (P_4) for the commodity than under free trade, the country as a whole (the government and private sectors combined) pays a lower price, P_5. Thus it is the behavior of A's export price that indicates the changes in B's terms of trade.

To demonstrate unequal distribution of the tax burden between the two countries, observe first the case in which supply and demand in country B are more elastic than those in A, so that the import-demand schedule is more elastic than the export-supply schedule. This is shown in Figure 13-4. The free trade equilibrium is determined as before, the resulting price being P_3 (in this case, $50 per unit). A $20 specific duty is introduced, and the divergence equalling that amount, $\overline{cd}$, is shown in the foreign trade sector. Clearly, most of the tax burden is borne by the exporting country, whose export price

[2] Strictly speaking, the introduction of trade and the imposition of tariff involve shifts in the demand and supply schedules. For simplicity, all such shifts are omitted here. Only the post-tariff equilibrium points are shown.

Figure 13-4

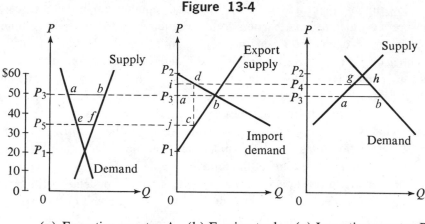

(a) Exporting country A   (b) Foreign trade   (c) Importing country B

declines to $35 ($P_5$), while the consumers in country B pay $55 ($P_4$) per unit. Geometrically, the difference can be traced to the relative size of the "scissors openings" between supply and demand in the two countries. Since the quantity exported by A must equal the quantity imported by B both before and after the tariff, it simply takes a larger drop in A's price to produce a quantity change comparable to the one produced by a small rise in B's price.

But the shape of the curves is merely a representation of economic conditions. Country B does not "tolerate" a large increase in price because its consumers are ready to reduce consumption (elastic demand) or shift to rapidly expanding domestic supply (elastic supply). On the other hand, exporters in A cannot reduce supply fast enough (inelastic supply), cannot expand home sales by much (inelastic demand), and (if this were a multi-country world) have few if any alternative third-market destinations ready to absorb the product. They are therefore forced to take a sharp price cut. Such would be the result of an import tariff on coffee levied by the United States. Most of it would be absorbed by the Brazilian producers in the form of a price reduction. The extreme case occurs when demand or supply in B is infinitely elastic, producing infinitely elastic import demand. The entire tax burden is then borne by the exporters.

The results are the opposite if the domestic demand and supply conditions in the two countries are such that the export-supply is much more elastic than the import-demand. This is shown in Figure 13-5. In this case consumers in importing country B are reluctant to reduce demand (inelastic demand), while domestic producers are unable to expand supply (inelastic supply). On the other hand, exporters in A can easily curtail shipments (elastic supply), expand sales at home (elastic demand), or (if this were a multicountry world) shift to third-market destinations. Consequently, con-

Figure 13-5

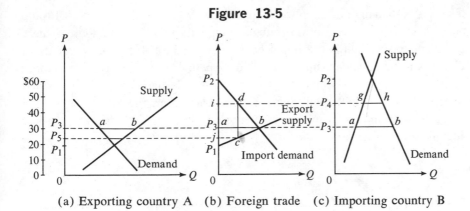

(a) Exporting country A   (b) Foreign trade   (c) Importing country B

sumers in B must absorb most of the tax in the form of a price increase, while producers in A bear only a small share of the burden. Even so, the terms of trade of country B (consumers and government taken as a whole) improve, albeit by a small amount, for B obtains its imports at lower prices. A more precise formulation of the relation between elasticities and the incidence of the tariff is given in Appendix III.

Only in the extreme case of infinitely elastic export supply (caused by infinitely elastic supply or demand in country A) is the full burden of the duty borne by B's consumers. And only then do the importing country's terms of trade remain unaffected (they do not improve). This is not a rare and esoteric case, however. It applies to all countries that are not important enough as importers to affect the terms at which they trade. A small importing nation, like a competitive firm, is a price taker. It is faced with an infinitely elastic export-supply curve, and its domestic price must rise by the full amount of any duty it cares to impose. Only the few large countries can improve their terms of trade by levying import duties.

On the other hand, a small country can improve its terms of trade by imposing an export tax, if it is a major supplier of its export commodities. For example, if Ghana is responsible for one-third of world cocoa supply, then an export tax on cocoa would force marginal producers to withhold supplies from world markets, thereby pushing up the world price of cocoa. Ghana's terms of trade, but not necessarily its economic well-being (see below), would improve as a result. By the same token, when in the fall of 1973 Canada increased its export tax on oil from $0.40 to $1.90, the U.S. consumers had to bear most of the burden, because U.S. demand for Canadian oil was very inelastic in light of the energy shortages prevailing at that time. Similar increases in taxes by other oil-producing countries were also shifted to the consumers.

The foregoing analysis is oversimplified because it deals with only one commodity traded between two countries. This is all that can be handled with the tools of demand and supply. Clearly, the very nature of international trade necessitates one more set of diagrams dealing with another commodity, where B is the exporter and A the importer. Otherwise the balance of payments of B will be in perpetual deficit, that of A in perpetual surplus. Since, in a manner of speaking, the above demonstration portrays only half the story, it is often referred to as "partial equilibrium analysis." However, the same insights can be gleaned from "full equilibrium analysis," through the use of reciprocal demand or offer curves.

☐ In full-equilibrium terms, the imposition of a tariff by Britain can be shown by shifting the U.K. reciprocal demand curve of Figure 11-4(e) (page 229) upward from U.K. to U.K.' as shown in Figure 13-6. For any given quantity of textile exports, Britain will now require the pretariff quantity of wheat imports *plus* the quantity of wheat assessed by the British government in the form of an *ad valorem* tax. As a result of this shift, the British terms of trade (the quantity of wheat imports obtainable for a given amount of textile exports) improve from α to β. Clearly, the United States can *retaliate* by imposing a tariff of its own, shifting its reciprocal demand curve downward and improving its terms of trade.

☐ It is easily verified that if Britain were facing an infinitely elastic U.S. offer curve (that is, a straight line), the terms of trade would remain unchanged following the tariff.   ■

Figure 13-6

International exchange ratio before and after a British tariff

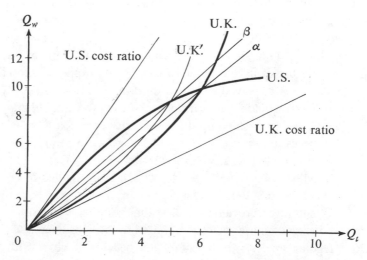

Domestic Effects

To recapitulate, we may say that the imposition of a tariff causes the appearance of two prices in the importing country, where before the tax there was only one. One is the price that the country as a whole (the government and private sectors combined) pays for the product, which equals the foreign country's export price plus transportation costs. This price is generally lower than its pretariff equivalent. The other is the price that the consuming public in the importing country must now pay, which is higher than its pretariff equivalent. The discrepancy between the two prices comprises the import duty, which accrues to the government. Thus, part of that tax is paid by foreign producers and part by domestic consumers. The first component measures the improvement in the importing country's terms of trade, or its equivalent, the deterioration in the exporting country's terms of trade. When it comes to the terms of trade, what one country gains the other loses; the world as a whole is not affected. In our example, Brazil's export/import price ratio declines while that of the United States rises. The second component, the increase in domestic prices, constitutes the protection accorded to domestic producers of import-competing products and is responsible for the changes that occur in the domestic economy of the importing country.

In order to focus attention on the domestic effects in the tariff-imposing country we assume it to be a small one, facing infinitely elastic export supply. The internal price of imports rises by the full amount of the duty, an increase that has several consequences. In the first place, it forces some consumers to curtail consumption of imports and to switch to domestically produced substitutes. The latter are presumably less desirable; otherwise they would have been purchased even in the absence of the tariff. Consequently, this change constitutes a welfare loss to the consumer—a loss that can be measured with the help of the tools of economic theory. In other words, the tariff distorts relative market prices by "artifically" raising the price of imports, thereby inducing the consumer to purchase less desirable products.

Second, production expands in the industries producing substitutes for the tariff-riden imports. Under conditions of full employment this can be accomplished only by drawing resources away from other industries, which presumably rank higher in the order of comparative advantage (otherwise the resources would have been employed there in the first place, even before the tariff). This is a loss in production efficiency for the economy as a whole and is often called "production loss." It is worth emphasizing that the producers of the protected commodity gain from this transformation; the loss occurs in the efficiency of the economy as a whole as these producers are able to attract resources from other sectors. These two losses are partly offset

Figure 13-7

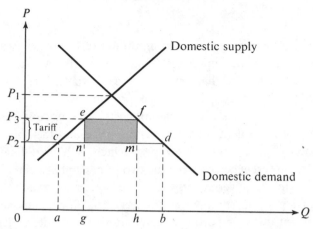

by an increase in government revenue, which under our present assumptions is collected only from domestic sources. Concentrating strictly on what happens within the importing country, we see a net loss in real income coupled with a redistribution of income from the general public to the producers of the protected commodities and to the government. (Because the tariff raises the price to the consumer and gives protection to the domestic producer, its domestic effects are comparable to those of a combined tax on the consumers and subsidy to the producers.)

These changes can be seen in Figure 13-7. The importing country is still assumed to be small enough not to exercise "monopoly power" on world markets, and it faces infinitely elastic export supply. Figure 13-7 depicts the internal supply and demand conditions for a tariff-ridden commodity—say, cars. In the absence of any international trade, domestic price is set at P_1. Under free trade and in the absence of transport cost, the domestic price cannot differ from the world price, assumed here to be P_2. Being a small "price taker," the country has no effect on world price. At P_2 domestic consumption is $\overline{0b}$, production is $\overline{0a}$, and imports, being the difference between the two, are $\overline{ab}$.

A tariff in the amount of $\overline{P_2P_3}$ raises the domestic price to P_3 and produces the following effects. Internal consumption of cars declines by $\overline{hb}$ as demand moves up the curve from d to f. Thus the tariff forces consumers to curtail consumption of the taxed commodity and switch to less desirable subsititutes. Domestic production of cars rises by $\overline{ag}$ as production moves along the supply curve from c to e. These changes are known as, respectively, the consumption and production effects of the tariff. In a general equilibrium context, $\overline{ag}$ represents the resources that the protected car industry was able to bid away from the other, more efficient, industries. Imports decline by *ag* + *hb*. Finally, the shaded rectangle, import volume $\overline{ef}$ (= $\overline{gh}$) times tariff per unit $\overline{P_2P_3}$, represents government revenue from the tariff.

☐ **The Economic Cost of the Tariff—Further Considerations**   The economic cost of the tariff can be delved into in greater detail with the tools of welfare economics. These tools will be developed first.

☐ Consider the demand curve *D* in Figure 13-8. Points on it show the prices that consumers would be willing to pay for various quantities. In conjunction with a supply curve (not shown), a market price is established at $\overline{OP_1}$. Once determined, all buyers pay this uniform price. But in fact it is the price that only the marginal buyer was willing to pay. Other (intramarginal) purchasers, more eager for the product, would have been willing to pay higher prices, as indicated by points on the demand curve above *A*. (Less eager buyers, whose preferences lead to points below *A* on the demand curve, do not purchase the product). Yet despite this differential eagerness, they all pay the same price. The difference between what consumrs would have been willing to pay and the market price that they actually pay is known as *consumers' surplus*. In the diagram it is measured by the area of the triangle P_1AB.[3] If the market price rises to $\overline{OP_2}$, then the consumers' surplus becomes P_2CB. It *declines* by the shaded area P_1P_2CA. Note that the demand curve need not be extended to intersect the price axis in order to determine the *change* in consumers' surplus.

☐ Next consider the supply curve *S* in Figure 13-9. Points on it show the quantities sellers are willing to supply at varying prices. In conjunction with a

Figure 13-8

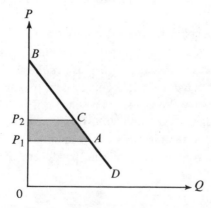

---

[3] The perfect price-discriminating monopolist would charge each consumer what he is willing to pay, instead of one market price for all. He would thereby appropriate the area of the triangle for himself.

Figure 13-9

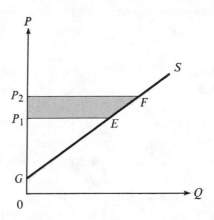

demand curve (not shown), a market price is determined at $\overline{OP_1}$. Once it is established, all sellers receive this uniform price. But in fact only the marginal seller required this price to effect his sale. More eager or efficient (intra-marginal) sellers would have been willing to sell for less, as indicated by points on the supply curve below E (less eager sellers, requiring prices above $\overline{OP_1}$, do not sell). Yet despite this differential eagerness (perhaps reflecting productive efficiency), all sellers obtain the same price. The difference between the price that the sellers would have required to part with the product, as indicated by the supply curve, and the market price they all actually receive is known as *producers' surplus*. In Figure 13-9, it is measured by triangle P_1GE. If the market price rises to $\overline{OP_2}$, then the producers' surplus becomes P_2GF. It *increases* by the shaded area P_1P_2FE. Note that the supply curve need not be extended all the way to the price axis to determine the *change* in producers' surplus.

☐ We are now in position to analyze the welfare effect of the tariff, using Figure 13-7. Tariff P_2P_3 raises the post-trade domestic price from $\overline{OP_2}$ to $\overline{OP_3}$. As a result of this increase, consumers' surplus *declines* by area P_3P_2df; producers' surplus *rises* by area P_3P_2ce; while government revenue *rises* by the shaded rectangle *efmn*. The net welfare loss from the tariff is therefore equal to the sum of the areas of triangles *cen* and *dfm*. It is known as the *deadweight loss*. Apart from this net loss, the tariff results in income redistribution away from the consumers to the government and the producers of the protected commodity.[4]   ■

---

[4] In full-equilibrium terms, the consumption and production effects can be shown with the use of indifference curves. The accompanying diagram portrays a country with a comparative advantage in commodity B. Under free trade, production is at P_1, con-

An important consequence of these effects is that the tariff produces a gain to the factors of production that are heavily utilized in the import-competing industries. The textile workers of America, for example, clearly stand to benefit from a high tariff on imported textiles, in much the same way as resources employed in the export industries gain from free trade. Countries have at times levied tariffs with the objective of helping a certain productive factor at the expense of others in the economy. The total loss to the country of such policy far outweighs the gain to the particular resource. Also, there are better ways to redistribute income in the economy, should such a course be deemed desirable.

Finally, a tariff may have such important indirect consequences as increasing the degree of monopoly in the country, thereby lowering productive efficiency, penalizing consumers, and retarding economic growth. If the country imposing the duty is so small that its internal market can support only one or two firms, foreign competition provides an essential stimulus to innovation and growth and a necessary check on pricing policies. The tariff reduces or bars such stimuli. Even in a large country, imports may provide the major competitive spirit when the industry is monopolized. This may partly explain the clamor for protection by the U.S. steel industry, where oligopolistic practices prevail. It is also a good reason why such protection is contrary to the public interest. This is particularly true in times of inflation, when removal of import restrictions can help cool the economy and hold back price increases.

---

sumption is at C_1, and the level of community welfare is represented by U_1. The international price line is P_1R_1. A prohibitive tariff shifts production and consumption to P_2 and lowers the level of welfare to U_3. This reduction can be viewed as having two components. First, the production mix shifts from P_1 to P_2, but consumers are assumed to continue to face the (more favorable) international price P_2R_2 (parallel to P_1R_1). This represents the production cost, which lowers welfare from U_1 to U_2. Second, the price facing the consumers changes from the international to the domestic (dashed line) price, with the attendant reduction in welfare from U_2 to U_3. This represents the consumer cost of protection.

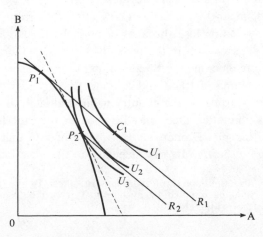

Indeed, countries often liberalize import restrictions as an anti-inflationary device, as the United States did in the case of beef in 1972.

We turn next to the internal repercussions in the exporting country. Nothing happens there if the importing nation is small. But if it is large enough to exercise monopoly power, the price of the export good is depressed, because less of it is now purchased by the country levying the tariff. This leads to a curtailment of production and an increase in consumption of the commodity. Introduction of trade has the opposite effect on the exporting nation; it raises the domestic price of the exported commodity. Thus, it should have surprised nobody that the price of wheat in Canada went up in the mid-1960s when the government concluded an agreement to sell a billion bushels to China, or that it declined when the agreement expired. It merely reflected the increase and subsequent decline in the demand for Canadian wheat. Likewise, the price of wheat in the United States doubled in 1972 after the large sales to Russia.

It is clear that the producers of goods subject to import taxes lose, while the consumers in the exporting country gain. The exporting country as a whole loses, not only because resources are now less efficiently allocated but also because its terms of trade deteriorate. This latter effect merely reflects the fact that the exporting country pays part of the tax collected by the importing country.

Effect of Real Income

The tariff inevitably causes a reduction in the real income of the world as a whole. The effects on the terms of trade in the importing and exporting countries cancel each other out; all that remains is a reduction in the volume of trade compared to what it would have been under free trade conditions. This constitutes a reduction in the world's real income both because the production patterns are distorted and no longer conform to comparative advantage configurations and because consumers are induced to shift from their ideal consumption mix to less desirable substitutes.

This does not mean that every country must lose from the tariff, however. The exporting nation loses because of both the reduction in the volume of trade and the deterioration in the terms of trade. But the importing country is subjected to two conflicting forces: a loss of real income caused by the reduction in the volume of trade and a compensating gain due to improvement in the terms of trade. If the country is large enough to affect the terms at which it trades, the latter effect may be stronger than the first, resulting in a net gain in real income. Economists call the tariff rate that maximizes this net gain the *optimum tariff*.[5] Its size depends on the very factors that deter-

---

[5] Corresponding to the "optimum tariff" on imports, there is an "optimum tax" on capital inflow that could be imposed by a country if it is a big enough borrower to improve the terms of borrowing abroad.

mine the "terms of trade effect." (The section on the "Economic Cost of the Tariff" in Appendix III offers a graphical exposition of the two-country case.)

Developing countries sometimes attempt to justify their complex and cumbersome systems of protection on the grounds that they provide an optimum tariff. But this is not a defensible position. These countries are much too small relative to total world trade in whatever they import to affect the terms at which they trade—to "force" the exporters to pay part of the tariff. Their optimum import tariff is necessarily zero. In their export trade, however, such countries may be able to exploit monopoly power and pass on a tax to outside interests. But only in the case of primary exports can a single developing country be important enough as a supplier to affect world prices. For example, a tax levied by Ghana on cocoa exports, by Brazil on coffee exports, or by Venezuela or Iran on oil exports may restrict world supply of the commodity and raise its price, so that foreign consumers pay part of the tax. As a major exporter of the product it taxes, a country may in this manner improve its terms of trade.

In the case of developing countries the taxed export good is usually an agricultural product or a raw material. Indeed, such export taxes are sometimes hidden in the activities of marketing boards set up by the government to stabilize prices and thereby stabilize the income received by the growers. Ostensibly designed to iron out excessive price fluctuations, the board can also push export prices above long-run equilibrium levels by withholding supplies or by paying farmers a lower price than it receives abroad, inducing them to produce less. And this improves the terms of trade of the exporting country.

Some industrial nations are large enough to benefit from an import levy, and there is little doubt that the United States is one of them. Available evidence suggests that the incidence of the American tariff is about equally divided between the foreign exporters and the domestic consumers. But in many products the height of the American tariff exceeds its "optimum" level in the technical sense of the word. Furthermore, a leading nation like the United States should think twice before using its tariff as a vehicle for taxing other, poorer, nations. It makes little sense to engage in foreign-aid programs and then proceed to nullify part of the aid by imposing import duties. Whatever minor economic gain may accrue could be more than offset by political losses.

Other Effects

Although not purposely designed to deal with balance-of-payments problems, a tariff does have balance-of-payments implications. Since it restricts imports of the products on which it is levied, the duty is generally thought to improve the country's external trade position. This result need not hold if the economy is operating at full employment. Under these circumstances, the shift of consumer demand from imports to domestically produced substitutes requires that labor and machines be shifted from somewhere else in the economy to the import-competing industries. If the factors of production come from the export industries, then exports may decline by as much as imports and there is no improvement in the trade position. Similarly, if the resources come from other import-competing industries, the net effect on imports will be nil. Furthermore, any bidding away of resources through the price mechanism usually contributes to a general increase in the price level, which in turn impairs the country's competitive standing and may nullify the initial gain of reduced imports. These considerations are much less important when the economy is initially at unemployment, for then the resources to produce the import substitutes are abundantly available and need not be attracted from alternative uses.

An immediate implication of the preceding paragraph is that a tariff increases employment if it is imposed during a recession. It is true that unemployed men and machines are put to work to meet the new demand. It does not follow, however, that the tariff should be used for that purpose; not only can the effect be negated easily by foreign retaliation, but also domestic fiscal and monetary measures are far more effective instruments of domestic stabilization. They can increase employment without the loss in economic efficiency caused by the tariff.

Finally, since a tariff restricts competitive imports, it contributes to whatever monopoly power exists in the domestic economy. This further impairs allocative efficiency, technological progress, and economic growth.

Some Empirical Estimates

With the help of theoretical constructs and statistical tools we can approximate the various economic effects of the tariff. Most studies of the subject are based on the *reductions* in tariff rates that have taken place multilaterally since World War II. Also, since more information is available for the United States than for other countries, our discussion pertains mainly to this country. The measurements are usually restricted to the "static" or allocative effect of the tariff. They do not incorporate the damage caused by keeping out foreign competition and thereby promoting internal monopoly.

A possible framework for the analysis of the effect of tariff reduction on the importing country is presented in Figure 13-10. Taking these linkages one at a time, empirical evidence suggests that between one-third and one-half of any reduction in the American tariff accrues to the foreign exporters in the form of increased export prices. The United States is obviously large enough

Figure 13-10

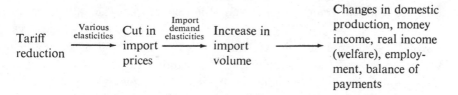

to affect the terms at which it trades. Thus, when it imposes a tariff, foreign exporters are forced to pay part of it by lowering export prices. Conversely when the tariff is lowered (or lifted altogether) these exporters reap part of the benefit.

Although it is difficult to determine the effect of these price changes on the volume of imports, the order of magnitude has been estimated by various investigators. A 50 percent reduction in the American tariff rates prevailing in the early 1960s—as originally contemplated in the Kennedy Round— would raise imports by $1 billion to $1.25 billion. Alternatively, elimination of tariffs on manufactured products would raise imports by $2 billion to $2.25 billion. If tariff reduction were undertaken reciprocally, as is inevitably the case, the respective American exports would rise by somewhat higher amounts. These figures pertain to the 1960 base period and should be compared with total 1960 exports of $17.5 billion and imports of $14.5 billion. When it comes to employment effects, a "representative" $1 billion increase in imports into the United States would lower employment by around 100,000 workers—a small figure compared to a total 1960 labor force of 70 million and to the 16.7 million employed in manufacturing. Even so, under reciprocal tariff reduction, employment in the export industries would rise, so that the expected net loss is virtually nil. Finally, economic theory makes it possible to estimate the welfare effect of the tariff, and the figures arrived at are relatively small— never exceeding 0.5 percent of the gross national product. Estimates for 1971 show a welfare loss from the U.S. tariff of around $1 billion. On the other hand, the losses from import quotas (including the "voluntary export re- straints") were placed at $2.4 billion.

Why does the cost of tariff protection appear to be so small? Three rea- sons come immediately to mind. First, tariff rates (and even effective protec- tion, to be discussed in the next section) in industrial countries are not ex- tremely high, being concentrated in the 10-to-20 percent range. By compari- son, rates upward of 100 percent are common in many developing areas. Second, only a small part of the total production of most industrial econo- mies (particularly the diversified ones) is traded internationally, so compari- son with total GNP is bound to yield a small ratio. Finally, it should be remembered that in a large country most of the benefits from trade are already realized domestically, since trade is always free within the country. It is the *incremental* benefit that accrues from eliminating the moderate level of protection on external trade that is small. Interestingly enough, although this incremental gain is probably much larger for developing countries, because of the small size of their economies, it is they that insist on having high levels of protection. Indeed, recent empirical studies suggest that developing countries often establish new industries behind a protective wall, which results in "negative value added" when their product is measured at world prices. In other words, the amount of foreign exchange saved by domestic production is less than what it would cost to import the merchandise.

How Protective Is the Tariff?

Public discussions of the tariff issue often involve intercountry comparisons of the level of protection, on which policy decisions frequently are based. But protection cannot be measured or compared simply. What the measure of protection purports to convey is *the amount of potential imports kept out of the country by the tariff*. This is a very difficult figure to derive, and the problems of estimating it are often overlooked or side-stepped in public pronouncements. These problems will now be sorted out.

Ad Valorem and Specific Duty

Whenever specific duties are employed they must be converted into their *ad valorem* equivalent to facilitate international or intercommodity comparisons. Only when it is expressed as a percent of price is the tariff rate independent of the unit of the commodity on which it is levied, making duties on diverse commodities comparable. Normally the conversion is made by dividing the duty by the average price of the transactions undertaken over the preceding year.

Nominal Versus Effective Tariff Rates

Even when expressed as a percent of price, the tariff rate published in the country's tariff schedule (known as the "nominal" rate) does not convey the level of protection accorded to the domestic producers. While nominal tariffs apply to the total value of imports, they protect only the portion of that value produced at home. To see this, assume that country A levies a 20 percent import tariff on desks, but imported lumber and other materials that go into the domestic production of desks enter duty-free. Assume further that these imported materials constitute one-half of the final value of the desk, so that the value added in domestic manufacturing is one-half. In other words, if the desk sells for $100, then the manufacturer spends $50 on imported inputs and home production adds another $50 to its value. The 20 percent tax levied on imported desks yields $20 per desk. But this sum protects only that component of the desk's value produced at home, namely half its total value. To that component it accords *effective* protection of 40 percent ($20 as a percentage of $50). If the imported raw materials were taxed at 10 percent, then the effective rate of protection given the desk manufacturer would be 30 percent. It is evident that if the final product entered duty free, while imported raw materials used in domestic production were taxed, then the domestic producer of the final good would be taxed rather than protected.

In essence, the effective protective rate measures the degree of protection given to domestic production activities. It is defined as the percentage increase in *domestic* value added made possible by the tariff structure compared to a situation under free trade, or alternatively as the percentage increase in the price of primary factor inputs resulting from the tariff. The latter definition indicates the ability of the protected producer to pay more for the productive factors he uses. The effective protection for a final product increases as the nominal rate imposed on it increases, and as the nominal rate imposed on imported materials used in the production process decreases. It also varies with the proportion of imported inputs that comprise the final value of the product (a proportion that may itself change as the situation changes from free trade to tariff). These relationships can be derived from a mathematical formula.[6] Alternatively, in what follows they are shown in a series of examples.

[6] A simplified formula for the effective protective rate derived from the above definition is:

$$g_j = \frac{t_j - a_{ij}t_i}{1 - a_{ij}}$$

where g_j is the effective protective rate on final product j, t_j is the nominal tariff rate on final product j, t_i is the nominal tariff rate on imported input i, and a_{ij} is the share of i in the total value of j in the absence of tariffs.

The formula is derived as follows. Value added in industry j, without any tariffs, is

$$v_j = p_j(1 - a_{ij}).$$

Value added in industry j, with tariffs on both the input and the output, is

$$v'_j = p_j(1 + t_j) - p_j a_{ij}(1 + t_i) = p_j[(1 + t_j) - a_{ij}(1 + t_i)]$$

where p_j and p_i are the prices of the output and input, respectively.

$$
\begin{aligned}
g_j &= \frac{v'_j - v_j}{v_j} \\
&= \frac{p_j[(1 + t_j) - a_{ij}(1 + t_i)] - p_j(1 - a_{ij})}{p_j(1 - a_{ij})} \\
&= \frac{(1 + t_j) - a_{ij}(1 + t_i) - (1 - a_{ij})}{1 - a_{ij}} \\
&= \frac{1 + t_j - a_{ij} - a_{ij}t_i - 1 + a_{ij}}{1 - a_{ij}} \\
&= \frac{t_j - a_{ij}t_i}{1 - a_{ij}}
\end{aligned}
$$

Consider a leather wallet whose c.i.f. import price in Belgium *under free trade* is $20. The cost of the leather of which the wallet is made is $10 on the world market, so that a wallet made in Belgium out of imported leather would have a domestic value added of $10 at free trade prices. Translated into Belgian francs at an official exchange rate of $1 = 50 francs, we obtain a product (wallet) price of 1000 francs, a world market cost of inputs (leather) of 500 francs, and a free trade domestic value added of 500 francs.[7]

Case 1.   A 20 percent tariff on wallets and on leather will raise the domestic price of a wallet to 1200 francs and that of the leather input to 600 francs. Protection thus enables the Belgian firm to operate at value added of $1200 - 600 = 600$ francs, compared to $1000 - 500 = 500$ francs, at free trade prices. The difference of 100 francs, equalling 20 percent of the free trade value added, is the effective rate of protection. Thus, when the tariff rate on the input equals the tariff rate on the output, the nominal and effective protection on the output are the same. In the present example they all equal 20 percent.

Case 2.   Consider next a case where the tariff on leather wallets is 40 percent, raising their domestic price to 1400 francs, and the tariff on leather is 20 percent, raising its domestic price to 600 francs. The domestic value added under protection is $1400 - 600 = 800$ francs, compared to 500 francs at free trade prices. The difference of 300 francs constitutes $300/500 = 60$ percent effective protection on leather wallets compared to a 40 percent nominal tariff rate. Thus, when the tariff rate on the final output exceeds the rate levied on the input, the effective protection on the output exceeds the nominal rate imposed on it.

Case 3.   Next, consider a case where the tariff on leather wallets is 30 percent, raising their domestic price to 1300 francs, and the tariff on leather is 40 percent, raising its domestic price to 700 francs. The domestic value added under protection is 600 francs, compared to 500 francs at free trade prices. The difference of 100 francs constitutes a $100/500 = 20$ percent effective protection on wallets compared to 30 percent nominal rate. Thus, when the tariff rate on the input exceeds that on the final output, the effective protection accorded the final output falls short of the nominal rate imposed on it.

Case 4.   Indeed the tariff on the input can be so much in excess of the tariff on the output that the effective protection on the output is negative; the product is taxed rather than protected. For example, suppose that the tariff on leather wallets in Belgium is 10 percent, raising the domestic price

---

[7] A problem that arises in obtaining these figures is that the free trade prices of outputs and inputs, and therefore the value added under free trade, cannot be observed directly in a country under a tariff regime. There are two ways of getting around this problem. The tariff-ridden prices can be deflated by the tariff rates to obtain the implied free trade prices, or the ratio of value added to the final product price can be inferred from that of another country where tariff rates are close to zero.

to 1100 francs, while the duty on leather is 40 percent, raising its domestic price to 700 francs. Value added under protection is then 400 francs, compared to 500 francs under free trade. The result is a *negative* effective protection on wallets of 100 francs or $100/500 = 20$ percent.

In conclusion, the effective protective rate on a product will exceed, be equal to, or fall short of the nominal rate on the product depending on whether this tariff is higher than, equal to, or lower than the tariffs on material inputs. Negative effective protection results when tariffs raise the cost of inputs by a larger absolute amount than they raise the price of the product.[8]

In addition to the tariff rates on the output and input, the effective rate of protection depends also on the share of domestic value added in the product price. This share was assumed to be 0.5 in the above examples. In contrast, assume now that the free-trade c.i.f. import price of a leather wallet in Belgium is $20, but the cost of material input (leather) is $16, so that value added of $4 constitutes only 0.2 of the price of the wallet. Translated into francs, the price is 1000 francs as before, but the imported inputs are 800 francs and the domestic value added under free trade is only 200 francs. Now reconsider Case 2, above. The 40 percent tariff on wallets raises their domestic price to 1400 francs, while the 20 percent tariff on leather raises its price to 960 francs. The domestic value added under protection becomes $1400 - 960 = 440$ francs, compared to only 200 francs under free trade. This constitutes an effective protective rate on wallets of $240/200 = 120$ percent. This result underscores an important fact. If a country establishes a plant for the final processing of a product, importing most inputs at a semifinal stage of fabrication at zero or very low duties, then even moderate nominal protection on the final product translates into a very high effective protection.

The professional economic literature of the late 1960s is replete with articles refining the concept of effective protection and measuring its level in various countries.[9] Several important implications follow from this concept, and they will be considered in turn.

---

[8] In terms of the notation of footnote 6,

If $t_j > t_i$, then $G_j > t_j$.

If $t_j = t_i$, then $G_j = t_j$.

If $t_j < t_i$, then $G_j < t_j$.

If $t_j < a_{ij}t_i$, then $G_j < 0$ (negative protection).

[9] Particular attention has been paid to relaxing the assumptions made in the formula. For example, it was originally assumed that the input coefficient is fixed for each input, as denoted by a_{ij}. But economic theory tells of isoquants that are convex to the origin and along which the firm adjusts its input-use ratio to variations in the relative prices of the inputs. Since tariffs cause such price variations, the fixed a_{ij} should be replaced by a production function in an assumed specified form that allows for price changes. Other assumptions that can be relaxed involve the possibility that some inputs are not traded or that the elasticity of foreign supply of inputs is less than infinite. Finally, a question may be raised about the conformity of this basic concept to general economic theory. Price theory assigns business profits the central role of guiding resource allocation in the economy. By contrast, the theory of effective protection, under which the effec-

First, although the consumer reacts to changes in the final price that reflect the nominal tariff rates, *the producer reacts to changes in the cost of his production processes, and these are affected by the effective rate.* Thus it is the effective rate of protection that indicates the degree of resource misallocation caused by the tariff structure.

A second corollary to this analysis concerns the tariff structure of most industrial countries. They admit raw materials virtually duty free, semi-processed goods at moderate duties, and finished manufactures (especially of the labor-intensive variety) at high duty rates. This structure means that the effective protection on finished manufactures is much higher than the nominal rates indicate. Recent calculations suggest that the effective rates on many finished products are double their nominal counterparts. Developing countries object that this structure encourages the importation of goods into the developed nations in raw or semiprocessed form and therefore discourages industrialization (in the form of final processing) in the developing world.

A third conclusion, applicable to developed and developing countries alike, is that changes in tariff rates on imported inputs have an inverse effect on the level of protection accorded to final products. The significance of this point becomes apparent when we consider a developing country pursuing an import substitution policy as a road to industrialization. Often in such cases the country begins by building up a final assembly plant under a high protective tariff and using untaxed imported inputs. As a second stage, the country begins to "deepen" domestic production by manufacturing the inputs at home and according them high protection. And so it proceeds "backward" through the production process adding new "layers" of inputs. What the government often does not realize is the fact that by imposing tariffs on imported inputs, it actually lowers the level of protection accorded the final product. By that very action it may render the final assembly plant unprofitable.

Fourth, the phenomenon of "negative value added," mentioned previously, was detected in the process of computing effective protective rates. Many industries in Pakistan appear to be functioning under this handicap.[10]

Fifth, this analysis has implications for a country's export position as well. Although export industries must sell at world market prices, they often use imported inputs for which they must pay domestic prices augmented by a

---

tive protective rate determines the "production effect," assigns this role to value added. But value added contains, in addition to profits, domestic primary (labor, for example) and nonprimary inputs. Thus profits and value added may not move in the same direction or by the same amounts, and the two criteria may yield conflicting results. This could occur if we were to relax the assumption of fixed input coefficients a_{ij}.

[10] In Nigeria, it has been shown that in the "important case of printing an imported cloth, the cost of the imported raw materials alone exceeds the value of the imports being replaced." (P. Killy, *Industrialization in an Open Economy: Nigeria 1945–1966,* Cambridge University Press, 1969, p. 126.)

tariff. In Case 2 above, if the Belgian producers had to export their wallets at the world market price of $20, or 1000 francs, apiece, but pay 20 percent tariff on leather, then the tariff would raise the cost of their input from 500 to 600 francs and lower value added from 500 to 400 francs. The producers would thus sustain a negative protection—a tax—of 20 percent. To retain the free trade value added of 500 francs (that is, to compensate the producers for the increased cost of input caused by the tariff) would require that the producers receive an export subsidy of 100 francs, 10 percent of the price of the product. Such subsidies (that is, rebates of the tariff paid on imported materials) are often practiced in developing countries to protect their export position, for in the absence of the subsidy, firms may not have any inducement to export.

Finally, rates of effective protection can be used indirectly as a rough guide to determine comparative advantage. The analysis of Chapter 11 revealed that economic efficiency requires the ranking of industries by degree of comparative advantage. A country would then export the commodities ranked high and import those ranked low on its scale of industries. Under free market competitive conditions, the price mechanism would generate such a ranking, thus bringing about efficient allocation of resources.

But free market conditions hardly ever obtain in the developing countries. Instead, trade is restricted by a variety of policy instruments, such as high tariffs, import quotas, advance deposits for imports, export subsidies, exchange controls, multiple exchange rates, and the like. Not only that, but these restrictions are applied selectively by the government to encourage activities that it perceives to be in the best interest of the country and to discourage others. For example, the government may encourage cheap imports of investment goods (such as machinery) and discourage imports of consumer goods. These restrictions are often coupled with a variety of domestic market distortions, such as artificially high wage rates in certain industries obtained through powerful labor unions. In such cases, not only is the free market ranking distorted beyond recognition, but producers proceed to use capital-intensive processes relative to the country's factor endowments, for factor remunerations are distorted to a point where they no longer reflect the factor endowments. (That is, the prices of imported capital equipment are artificially low and the price of labor artificially high.)

Suppose now that faced with such distorted conditions the government wishes to embark on a new development plan and decide more rationally which industries or projects it should promote; or, alternatively, an international aid organization must determine what projects to support. How can such new resources be allocated optimally? One possible guide is the effective rate of protection. Since that rate measures the inducement to the protected producer to expand his activity, it also reflects the degree of protection that the industry requires to operate on its present scale. The ranking of industries by the level of effective protection[11] indicates their relative incentive to expand output under the existing structure of protection; it would produce a roughly inverse order to the ranking by comparative advantage. The industries at the low end of the scale in terms of effective protection are the ones that should be expanded. (It should be noted that professional opinion is divided on the validity of this use of the effective protection concept.)

A closely related guide to project selection is the domestic cost of foreign exchange earned by exports or saved by import substitution. Every dollar so earned (or saved) by a developing country costs a certain amount in domestic currency expended on processing and other activities. The activities that should be supported are those in which the cost of a dollar earned or saved is least. The ranking of industries from the high to the low domestic currency cost per dollar earned would produce an ordering roughly similar to the ranking from high to low effective protection. In both cases, it is the low-ranking industries that deserve support and encouragement to expand.[12]

This completes the discussion of effective protection. We turn next to other problems encountered in assessing how protective the tariff is.

Aggregation Problems

Suppose we were given the effective rates of protection, expressed in percentage terms, for all commodities and countries. Since countries do not all employ the same tariff classification, it is necessary for comparative purposes to convert all rates into a common classification. Also, because one often wishes to relate tariff rates to trade flows, it is desirable to have this common classification coincide with the SITC, by which all international trade is reported. Indeed the SITC was revised in 1961 to conform more closely to the Brussels Tariff Nomenclature (BTN), by which many countries report their tariff rates. There is now a readily available and easily accessible concordance between the two. It is a common objective of scholars and policy-makers alike to aggregate tariff rates from the highly detailed and divergent commodity classifications by which they are reported

---

[11] In one study of the East African tariff, 34 industries were ranked by their effective protection, with rates ranging all the way from 900 percent to −46 percent.

[12] A widely used manual on industrial cost-benefit analysis suggests the following method for assessing proposed industrial projects: Evaluate all expected costs and benefits at *world prices,* which (in contrast to the often distorted prices prevailing at home) represent the country's real trading opportunities. The resulting streams of annual costs and benefits should then be discounted at a rate of something like 10 percent in real terms (that is, after allowing for inflation, the rate may be 15 to 20 percent), thereby translating future values into their present worth. Finally, the single cost figure should be subtracted from the benefit figure; if there is a surplus, the project is worth undertaking. (See Little and Mirreless, *Manual of Industrial Project Analysis in Developing Countries,* OECD, Paris, 1969.)

into, say, the three-digit SITC. Some people may wish further to aggregate them into one average figure for each country, so as to have a ready-made intercountry comparison of the levels of protection.

But the aggregation of tariff rates is a thorny issue; there is no satisfactory way to average out the rates imposed on diverse commodities. The use of simple unweighted averages of tariff rates implicitly assumes that each commodity is of equal importance in the country's import trade. This, of course, is not realistic. An alternative aggregation procedure is to compute weighted averages, but here the problem is what weights to use. Ideally, one should weigh each rate by what imports would have been in the absence of the tariff. But since this is not known, many investigators employ the country's own tariff-ridden imports as weights. Such a procedure invariably biases the results downward, because the very high tariffs permit fewer imports and therefore receive little weight. At the extreme, a prohibitive tariff excludes all imports and therefore receives no weight and will not be represented at all in the calculation. A better solution is to weigh each tariff by the domestic consumption of the product. But since the two magnitudes are often not available on the same commodity classification basis, a possible compromise is to weigh each tariff by total world (or OECD) trade in the commodity to which the rate applies. Even this procedure incorporates some downward bias because of the similarity in the tariff structures of industrial countries.

It is evident that press reports that use average figures to compare the level of protection of various countries are all subject to errors and biases. To have any value, they should be accompanied by a frequency distribution of the tariff rates as supplementary information or, lacking that, a rough idea of the range within which the country's tariff rates tend to concentrate. Such information is now available in GATT's *Basic Documentation for the Tariff Study* (Geneva, 1971), which presents average tariff rates for the original EEC (6 countries) and the United States, Canada, Japan, Great Britain, Sweden, Denmark, Norway, Finland, Switzerland, and Austria. For each BTN product group, the study presents the unweighted average tariff, an average weighted by the country's own imports, and two averages in which "world" imports are used as weights. A frequency distribution of tariff lines is also presented, as are various trade flows of each product.

The tariff rates for manufactured goods presented in Table 13-1 were arrived at by aggregating weighted averages, where total OECD imports of each commodity were used as weights.

The Response to Price Change

Even in dealing with disaggregative figures, the nominal and effective tariffs do not, in and of themselves, provide a precise indication of the level of pro-

Table 13-1

Nominal and Effective Tariff Rates in Selected Countries

	U.S.	U.K.	EEC	Sweden	Japan
Average tariff rate, %					
Nominal	11.6	15.5	11.9	6.8	16.2
Effective	20.0	27.8	18.6	12.5	29.5

SOURCE: B. Balassa, "Tariff Protection in Industrial Countries: An Evaluation," in R. E. Caves and H. G. Johnson (eds.), *Readings in International Economics* (New York: Irwin, 1968), Ch. 33.

tection. In the final analysis that level refers to the quantity of the imported commodity excluded from the domestic market. And that exclusion operates through the price mechanism; it comes about because the tariff raises the price of imports relative to that of domestic substitutes. But the extent to which the import price rises and the foreign export supply falls depends on various elasticities, as was seen earlier in this chapter. More important, the amount of imports excluded by a given percentage increase in import price depends on the response of the public to the price increase (the elasticity of demand for imports). The higher the response is, the larger will be the exclusion caused by a given percentage rise in price and the more protective a given tariff will be.

This degree of response depends on a variety of factors, not the least of which is the availability of domestic substitutes. But one important variable determining the import-demand elasticity for any commodity is the share of imports in domestic production and consumption. It can be shown that the larger the share of imports the smaller the elasticity (see Appendix III). This relation is important because it permits us to make *a priori* judgments in some cases. Suppose one is comparing the degree of protection afforded by the American tariff to that of a European country, say Italy. Because imports occupy a much smaller share of the United States market than of the Italian, the import-demand elasticity is higher in America and so is the degree of protection embodied in a given percentage price rise. Conversely, when we talk of multilateral tariff reduction, a given percentage reduction in the U.S. import price is translated into a larger increase in the volume of imports than in virtually all other countries.

It is obvious that all pronouncements concerning the degree of protection must be tempered by careful evaluation and sound judgment. After accounting for the factors enumerated here, economists often suggest that by the standards of the United States and Canada the Scandinavian countries have low protection. Before the establishment of the European Common Market,

Germany and the Benelux countries were considered low-tariff countries, while Italy and France were highly protective. British rates were considered to be moderate. Many of the developing countries impose very high duties.

Arguments for Protection

Against the background developed thus far we can briefly evaluate some of the arguments heard in political and economic circles on behalf of the tariff. From the viewpoint of the welfare of the world as a whole, the most popular claim made for tariff protection is the so-called infant-industry argument. It asserts that industries that may benefit from large-scale operations because of the existence of external economies (such as good transport facilities, a well-trained labor force, or the "learning by doing" effect) should be allowed to grow to optimum size under a protective tariff. Once that size is attained, the tariff can be removed, leaving behind a viable and competitive industry. Theoretically this is a valid argument. Indeed, Japan's development is replete with illustrations of how an industry can be developed and fostered under tariff protection until it reaches an optimum size. In its development policy, Japan made effective use of both tariff protection and imported technology in the form of licensing agreements. Today it is one of the world's largest exporters.

Often there are difficulties with the practical application of this theory. First, the argument can be abused, as it has been at times by declining industries that attempt to protect their position in the market and thereby perpetuate inefficiency. Even the American steel industry advanced the argument once in the 1960s in an effort to convince Congress to impose import quotas on steel. Second, once it has been imposed, a tariff is rather difficult to get rid of, regardless of the industry's competitive standing. And finally, even in cases where the infant-industry position applies, it is more efficient to offer a direct subsidy as a means of helping the industry to expand. While the tariff imposes both production and consumption costs on the economy, a subsidy embodies only production costs, not consumption costs. More generally, a tariff is equivalent to a tax on the consumer *plus* a (disguised) subsidy to the producer. By contrast, a direct subsidy does not contain the tax element, and the subsidy component is provided in an overt fashion. It is then open for all interested parties to inspect and evaluate. And when the time comes, it is somewhat easier to discontinue.

From the point of view of an individual nation taken as a whole, the only rational argument for the tariff is the improvement in terms of trade, (the "optimum tariff"). However, this applies only to the major importers that are large enough to exercise monopoly power and affect the terms at which they trade. In a very real sense, such a tariff must be viewed as a transfer of resources from the relatively poor nations to the very large and wealthy nations, a transfer that is undesirable on equity and other grounds and is certainly in conflict with the national objectives embodied in a foreign-aid program. Besides, tariff rates in most industrial countries probably exceed the optimum level. Thus under prevailing circumstances, the loss incurred from the reduced volume of trade is higher than gains from improved terms of trade, even in the absence of foreign retaliation.

Other "national" arguments for protection can be disposed of quickly. Tariffs may at times be used to increase employment or improve the balance of payments. But both objectives can be met more effectively and more efficiently by other means. On the other hand, a period of unemployment in the domestic economy is not a good time to reduce tariffs. After all, the main objective of such a reduction is to increase efficiency by transferring resources to industries in which the country has a comparative advantage, and the existence of widespread unemployment would make such a transfer very difficult if not impossible. (Parenthetically, allocative efficiency matters less when resources are not fully employed.)

Perusal of testimonies before congressional committees on foreign trade reveals a whole array of arguments for protection, only a few of which can be included here. That the perpetual demand for tariffs to equalize wage rates among nations makes no economic sense was already shown in Chapter 11. It was demonstrated that American wages are higher because productivity is higher than in other countries, and that such a wage differential is necessary to the existence of two-way trade. Empirical studies have shown two things. First, within the United States, the import-competing industries —such as textiles—that complain about low foreign wages are themselves low-wage industries by American standards. The export industries, from aircraft to computers, successfully meet foreign competition on both domestic and foreign grounds, despite the fact that their wages far exceed those paid the textile workers. This is not surprising. It is precisely what one would expect on the basis of productivity differences. Foreign competition would force contraction of the textile industry, and the resources released from it could be devoted to products in which this country possesses a comparative advantage, such as electronic computers. These industries can pay the highest wages and still compete effectively. Second, empirical findings do not support the contention that foreign producers gain access to the American market by paying substandard wages, judged by the standards prevailing in these countries.

Industries often claim that their products and the labor skills they utilize are essential to national security, and should therefore be preserved by a tariff. Prior to 1973, the oil-import quota in the United States was justified on these grounds. Whether true or not, this is not a subject on which the economist can pass judgment, except to indicate that if it is true the industry should be directly and overtly subsidized out of the defense budget.

Similarly, the argument that a nation needs the tariff in order to have something to bargain down in tariff negotiations is economically unsound, because the country is better off without the tariff regardless of the level of protection it encounters in the markets of its trading partners. If the argument is modified to suggest that the "bargaining tariff" is used to secure the best of all worlds in which no nation employs a protective tariff, then its validity depends on the effectiveness of the tariff in securing such a situation. And that is more within the purview of the political scientist than of the economist.

A case for protection is sometimes made from the point of view of a single factor of production: through its domestic effects the tariff can be used to redistribute income among factors (in favor of the relatively scarce factors and away from the relatively abundant one) or income groups. But whether desirable or not, there are other, more efficient, means of redistributing income in society.

Finally, many arguments for protection have been advanced in recent years with respect to developing economies. They suggest that the tariff and other means of commercial policy be used to rectify market imperfections existing in the domestic economies of these countries. For example, it has been demonstrated that labor mobility between sectors of the economy is low in many developing countries. This phenomenon is particularly apparent with respect to movement from subsistence agriculture to manufacturing and has its origin in the traditional attachment of the indigenous population to its place of birth and the extended family. But suppose that economic efficiency requires such a move and that the wage differential is not large enough to overcome the inherent obstacles to mobility. The proposed remedy is to impose a protective tariff on manufacturing imports. That would enable industrialists to charge higher prices for their products and thus pay higher wages, inducing labor to move to manufacturing. In other words, where the allocative mechanism in the economy is not sufficiently lubricated in the sense that resources do not respond swiftly or in sufficient quantities to market price differentials, there is a need to artificially accentuate the differential in order to bring about the necessary mobility. The tool suggested for accomplishing this is the protective tariff.

The argument makes sense as far as it goes. It suffers from ignoring the fact that there are far better instruments than tariffs to produce wage differentials and induce mobility. Direct subsidy to labor to help it move, or to the industry itself to help defray the cost of higher wages, comes immediately to mind. The same may be said about the use of tariff policy to eliminate all sorts of domestic distortions,[13] to achieve a desired investment pattern, or to promote rapid growth of certain industries. There is a whole array of instruments at the disposal of the government, and it is usually suboptimal to use international *commercial* policy to influence the *domestic* economy. It is misguided to call upon tariff protection to correct a variety of economic and social ills. But the point is purely academic if the country is so underdeveloped that no policy instruments other than the tariff are available.

In sum, while tariff protection is very common in the present-day world, rational justifications for its use are few and far between. The world as a whole, as well as most individual countries, would be better off if it were dispensed with as an instrument of national policy. The question examined next is whether there has been any progress toward this end.

Approaches to Free Trade

Although it is in the interest of most industrial countries to abolish tariffs, even unilaterally, it is a fact of political and economic life that they are extremely reluctant to do so. There have been instances of unilateral tariff reduction (as in Germany in the mid-1950s), but not many. Either because of prestige attached to diversified industrial production or because of the political pressure of social interest groups, tariff cuts appear to be as painful to the nation as tooth extraction is to the individual.

Any country reducing its level of protection feels that it is giving away something valuable and must obtain something in return from its trading partners. Tariff reduction has come to be regarded as a *concession* to others and is offered only reciprocally. It has also become a subject of tough and prolonged international bargaining, in which each party tries to "extract" as much as possible from its partners and in return to "surrender" as little as possible. Certainly, each delegation returning home from negotiating sessions attempts to convince local politicians that it obtained more and better tariff concessions than it gave away—clearly an impossible outcome for all parties at one and the same time.

---

[13] In developed and developing countries alike, if factors of production are not mobile between industries, then the introduction of trade into an isolated economy will not produce the expected shift in resource allocation and production mix. The resoures that remain "stuck" in the import-competing industries will suffer a reduction in remunerations. But since the consumers will still enjoy the more favorable international prices, society as a whole benefits from the introduction of trade. However, if in addition to factor immobility there is wage rigidity, so that factors refuse to accept a reduction in remunerations, unemployment will result. Under these conditions the economy may be better off without trade than with it. But domestic measures designed to promote factor mobility and wage flexibility are superior to commercial policy for dealing with this situation.

Two main approaches to trade liberalization have evolved over the past thirty years. The first is a succession of small tariff reductions undertaken reciprocally by most trading nations as a result of multilateral negotiations. Under the second approach, a small group of countries agrees to liberalize completely all trade within itself and to attain some measure of economic integration within the region.

The International Approach

The first approach is associated with the General Agreement on Tariffs and Trade (GATT), an international organization with a membership of eighty countries, devoted to the promotion of international trade in general and the reduction of tariff barriers in particular. Its members, known as the contracting parties to GATT, hold periodic negotiating conferences in which tariff "concessions" are exchanged. The reductions agreed upon by any two or more partners are then extended to all member nations. The result is successive rounds of small annual tariff reductions, each applying to all sources of supply on a nondiscriminatory basis. This process and the rules under which GATT operates will be described in Chapter 16.

The approach, although tedious and laborious in the extreme, invariably leads to a worldwide increase in productive efficiency—as the world moves to specialize along lines dictated by comparative advantage—and to more desirable consumption patterns. Although the gains are not equally distributed, and some countries may even lose, there is a gain to the world as a whole. Additionally, small countries may experience important "dynamic" benefits flowing from the increased size of their markets and curtailed monopoly power at home. It can be shown that starting from a certain nonprohibitive tariff level, each round of tariff reduction is less beneficial than the one before, for it applies to lower protection rates (see "Economic Cost of the Tariff," in Appendix III).

The Regional Approach

The regional approach is exemplified by customs unions and free-trade areas. A customs union involves two or more countries, which abolish all or nearly all trade restrictions among themselves and set up a common and uniform tariff against outsiders. The European Economic Community (EEC) or Common Market, is a customs union that originally encompassed West Germany, France, Italy, Belgium, the Netherlands, and Luxembourg, and was enlarged in January 1973 to include Great Britain, Denmark, and Ireland. Trade among members is free of restrictions; nonmembers must pay the common external tariff. An American producer shipping to France is discriminated against in favor of a West German competitor to the extent of the duty.

In a free-trade area, trade among the member countries is also completely liberalized, or nearly so. But there is no common tariff against nonmember countries; each country is free to impose its own duty. The European Free Trade Association (EFTA) is a free-trade area encompassing originally Great Britain, Sweden, Norway, Denmark, Switzerland, Austria, and Portugal; Britain and Denmark withdrew in 1973 to join the European Community. An American exporter to Sweden is discriminated against in favor of his Swiss counterpart by the level of the Swedish duty.

These organizations will be discussed in detail in Chapter 16. It is the approach to trade liberalization that concerns us here. Unlike the international approach, it may or may not lead to an improvement in world allocative efficiency, for it contains an important element of discrimination against nonmember countries.

Indeed the theory of customs unions, developed since World War II, deals mainly with the effect of regional integration on world allocative efficiency. To be sure, other effects of customs unions, such as the impact on the economic welfare or the balance of payments of a single integrating country, have been treated in some detail, but our main concern is with the first effect. Its theoretical interest lies in demonstrating that not every partial movement toward the optimal world of free trade is necessarily beneficial. Each case must be examined on its own merit.

Static Effects   Consider a three-country world in which countries A and B form a customs union to the exclusion of C. In other words, A and B abolish all trade restrictions among themselves, while their imports from C become subject to the common external tariff. The action has two effects. With respect to products in which A and B are competitive, the elimination of tariffs between them causes the replacement of some high-cost production by imports from the partner country. This effect, known as "trade creation," is favorable to world welfare since it rationally reorganizes production within the union. Second, for products in which country C is competitive with one of the integrating countries, A or B begins to import from the other what it earlier imported from C. If C is the most efficient producer, it would be the major supplier as long as its products receive the same tariff treatment as those of its competitor. But the tariff discrimination induces diversion of trade away from C toward a member country. This effect, known as "trade diversion," is unfavorable, because it reorganizes world production less efficiently. Production shifts from the most efficient locations in C to less efficient ones inside the union. Finally, there is a favorable consumption effect, as consumers in each member state benefit from price reduction on imports from the partner country when intraunion tariffs are removed. Indeed, a net un-favorable production effect (when trade diversion exceeds creation) may be more than offset by the consumption effect, yielding a net gain in welfare.

These three effects can be illustrated with the help of a partial equilib-rium diagram pertaining to one commodity imported into country A. For simplicity we assume that A is a small country, facing infinitely elastic (horizontal) supply curves from countries B and C (for a more elaborate presentation, see the last section of Appendix III). Figure 13-11 shows the domestic demand and supply (having the "usual" slopes) in country A for the imported product; it also shows the horizontal supply curves $\overline{P_1C}$ of coun-try C and $\overline{P_2B}$ of country B. Country C is the most efficient and least-cost producer.

Under free trade, price $\overline{OP_1}$ will prevail, and quantity $\overline{Q_1Q_2}$ will be im-ported from country C. Next, if A imposes a nondiscriminatory tariff $\overline{P_1P_3}$, the domestic price rises to $\overline{OP_3}$. Imports decline to $\overline{tT}$, but they come only from the most efficient supplier, country C, for suppliers from B will not be competitive. Finally, when A forms a customs union with B, to the exclu-sion of C, the tariff $\overline{P_1P_3}$ (assumed for simplicity to remain unchanged) is charged only on imports from C, not on those from B. The domestic price declines to $\overline{OP_2}$ and imports rise to $\overline{bB}$, but they will now come exclusively from B (because supply curves are infinitely elastic).

Our concern is in comparing the last two situations. Imports into A in-crease from $\overline{tT}$ to $\overline{bB}$. Trade diversion is represented by $\overline{tT}$, the decline in imports from the most efficient producer, country C. On the other hand, $\overline{br}$,

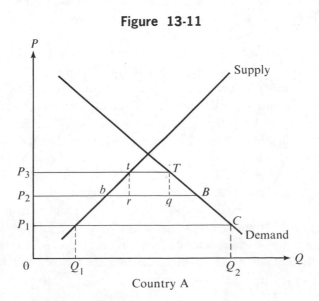

Figure 13-11

Country A

the decrease in domestic output in A and its replacement by imports from B, represents trade creation, while $\overline{qB}$ is the favorable consumption effect.

Although these basic effects need to be modified in various ways to account for such factors as the impact of the customs union on C's trade with D, E, and F in a multicountry world, and for possible balance-of-payments policies in the customs unions, they do constitute the major "static" influences. Their relative magnitude determines whether the customs union is, on balance, favorable to worldwide allocative efficiency. The tools of economic and statistical analysis make it possible to measure or at least approximate these magnitudes. But the estimation is complex. It is not just a matter of looking at the increase in intra-area trade volume: first, because this volume is influenced by many factors other than the formation of the customs union and, second, because even if the "integration effect" were isolated, the observed increase in intra-union trade comprises the trade creation and diversion combined.

The increase in imports into A from B partly reflects a decline in A's own production (trade creation) while in part it is a substitute for imports from C (trade diversion). In order to disentangle the two influences and get at "trade creation" one must subtract from the total increase in imports (adjusted to exclude noncustoms union influences) the decline in imports from nonmember countries (trade diversion) caused by integration. This is a rather complex statistical task, and the reader should not be misled by frequent press reports that identify simple changes in trade values among continental countries with either creation or diversion of trade.

Even without measurement, we can identify some factors that have *a priori* bearing on the relative size of the two effects. The larger the customs union is, the smaller the scope is for trade diversion and the better is the chance that the customs union will have a favorable effect. At the extreme lies a "customs union" encompassing the entire world, where only trade creation and no trade diversion can exist, yielding the optimal situation of universal free trade. Second, the more similar the production patterns are within the integrating countries and the larger the differences are in production costs between them, the greater the scope is for trade creation. One proxy for the differences in production costs is the preintegration tariff rates levied by the individual countries to protect their high-cost producers. Considerable variation in preintegration rates on the same product among the countries might be taken as an indication of large differences in production costs. In general, the higher the pre-union tariff rates are the better are the chances for large trade creation as these rates are dismantled. Finally, the lower the common external tariff of the customs union is, the less will be the degree of discrimination against outsiders and the smaller will be the scope for trade diversion.

Various investigators estimated annual trade creation in manufacturers of the original EEC at $7 to $9 billion for 1969–70, and trade diversion at less than $2 billion.[14] While trade creation was rather widespread, the largest diversion occurred in the chemical, textile and clothing, and processed food industries. It may be noted here that the creation of the EEC has not led to large-scale contraction of entire industries in any one country and their replacement by imports from another member. The tendency toward inter-industry specialization has been very limited. Instead, the main trend is toward intra-industry specialization: the same industry in various member countries moves toward specialization in specific types of subproducts. This eases adjustment to trade liberalization. Such intra-industry specialization is generally characteristic of international trade in manufactured goods. Much of it is an exchange of highly specialized products of the same industries, differing from each other in specifications, packaging, brand names, and similar features. Thus, the exchange of large cars for small cars, Renaults for Fiats, and high-powered machines for low-powered ones is as common as the exchange of industrial machinery for airplanes.

Dynamic Effects   Returning now to the theory of customs unions, there is more to their effect on world welfare than allocative efficiency. At least as important are the dynamic or growth considerations. A customs union expands the size of the market because of both the creation and diversion of trade. This makes production on a larger scale possible and also infuses competition into markets from which it might have been absent. Indeed the United States can be viewed as a large customs union, where the huge size of the market has made possible the establishment of many competitive units, each with large-scale production. This fact is partly responsible for the tremendous productivity of the American economy.

In the case of a new customs union the scale effect is likely to be more powerful in the smaller integrating countries, for large countries enjoy these benefits even in the absence of integration. The favorable growth effect also stimulates imports from nonmember countries, partly offsetting static trade diversion. However, nonmember countries may on balance experience a reduction in their exports to the customs union, and this in turn contracts the size of their market and affects their growth rates adversely. The smaller they are to begin with, the more important this factor is likely to be. Again,

---

[14] A common measure of trade creation is the change in the ratio of total (external plus intra-community) imports to consumption in the EEC between two years before and after integration, allowance being made for the effect on that ratio of factors other than integration. Trade diversion is measured by the change of external imports to consumption over the same period, and with similar allowance for nonintegration effects. See M. E. Kreinin, "Effects of the EEC on Imports of Manufactures," *Economic Journal,* September 1972.

favorable and adverse influences must be weighed against each other to assess the net impact on worldwide growth. The immense difficulties in doing this arise from the fact that a multitude of factors influence the growth rate, and it is not easy to isolate the effect of integration.

Finally, since the elimination of tariffs in the case of a customs union is not reversible, the expansion of the market is certain to last. This stimulates investments, both domestic and foreign, and thereby increases the growth rate. Such "investment creation" can be partly offset by what might be called "investment diversion," when investments are diverted from the most rational location in the world to the integrating region because of the tariff discrimination. Thus, if an American-based company shifts the location of a projected plant from the United States or Canada to the EEC in order to circumvent the tariff wall and gain access to a large market, the outcome is unfavorable to worldwide growth. The same may be said of potential foreign-investment projects in nonmember countries (such as a developing country) that never materialize because they depend too much on export to the customs union; and the possibility of such exports comes into question because they would be discriminated against in the customs union.

In sum, the regional approach has a large number of effects that require individual study. The industrial countries have proceeded along both avenues of trade liberalization since World War II. Under the auspices of GATT, tariffs have been lowered gradually to moderate levels. At the same time, small groups of countries have proceeded to eliminate tariffs altogether, and those in the EEC have taken some further measures to form a cohesive group.

14
U. S. Commercial Policy

A country's commercial policies are those policies which are designed to affect its trade relations with the rest of the world. The main commercial policy instrument employed by the United States has been the tariff. Although in the early years of the republic the tariff was used primarily for raising government revenue, it was later modified to serve exclusively the purpose of protecting domestic industry. Income and profit taxes became the major sources of revenue for the Federal government. Because tariff rates have always been determined by Congress, they have reflected a host of political and economic pressures of diverse groups. Consequently, the level of the American tariff in the first quarter of this century was very high, and the tariff schedule was a long, complicated, and cumbersome document. However, in the mid-1930s the Administration sought and obtained legislation for a gradual reduction in tariff rates subject to limits prescribed by Congress. And in the period following World War II this legislation enabled the United States to be the moving force behind a thirty-year trend of international trade liberalization under the General Agreement on Tariffs and Trade. Following a discussion of the political motivations behind U.S. foreign economic policies this chapter will consider the major strands of that legislation.

Political Considerations in U.S. Commercial Policy

It is important to recognize that political, sociological, and other considerations play a role in economic policies in general and commercial policies in particular. Many countries regard foreign economic policies as a part of foreign policy and assign jurisdiction to their foreign minister in foreign trade matters.

Given the small share of foreign trade in the American economy and the emergence of the United States as the leading Western power, it may not be surprising that political or military rather than economic considerations have often governed our commercial policy decisions in the past twenty-five years. This point can be abundantly illustrated by American attitudes toward European affairs. Immediately after World War II, the United States supported the liberalization of intra-European trade and payments carried out by the OEEC and the EPU, even though both arrangements discriminated against American exports to western Europe. Although the acute dollar shortage then provided an economic rationale for such policy, the real basis for it was a desire to achieve political stability and military viability in Europe.

Likewise, the United States lent its support to the creation of the European Coal and Steel Community under the Schuman Plan, and it subsequently backed the establishment of the European Economic Community and the European Atomic Energy Community. The likelihood that the EEC would unfavorably affect American exports to its six members, primarily in the sale of agricultural products, and the possibly adverse effect of the newly created union on the relative bargaining power of the United States in international economic negotiations were evidently given little weight in the formulation of American policy. The overriding consideration was the presumed political advantage to be drawn from a strong Europe in cold war politics. It goes without saying that the United States expected to remain the unchallenged leader of a stronger western alliance and hoped that the community would be "outward looking" in its commercial policies.

The exclusive emphasis on political considerations changed somewhat in the 1960s and was transformed into what might be called a political-economic mix. In large measure the change can be traced to the emergence of the EEC as a strong bargaining unit in GATT negotiations and as a market whose policy can significantly affect U.S. exports. The fact that the United States is facing an economic power of almost equal strength across the bargaining table for the first time since World War II, coupled with the impending adverse repercussions of EEC discrimination on American exports, has also led to the shift. The fear of trade diversion has been reinforced by serious concern about the U.S. balance-of-payments deficits. The change found its most explicit expression in the Trade Expansion Act of 1962 and has continued into the 1970s. But it cannot be overemphasized that the increasing political strength of the EEC, with the attendant erosion of American leadership in Europe, has also contributed to the transformation of U.S. policies.

The Reciprocal Trade Agreements Legislation

The statements made in the last section relate to behind-the-scenes diplomatic activity and are necessarily conjectural. But similar conclusions concerning the motives underlying American commercial policy can be drawn from actual legislative history. The cornerstone of American commercial policy since 1934 has been the Trade Agreements Act, and it has been continued through a dozen periodic extensions. American participation in GATT's tariff negotiations is implicitly sanctioned by this legislation (although Congress has consistently refused to recognize formally U.S. membership in GATT), as is the extent of duty reduction permissible at any one round of bargaining. The provisions of the act as well as their administration provide the most explicit clues to the motives behind U.S. commercial policies.

Two main lines of thought thread through the successive extensions of the reciprocal trade legislation, although their relative importance has varied from one extension to the next. On the one hand, the legislation has permitted continual though limited tariff reductions on U.S. imports. Since 1945 such reductions have been negotiated within the multilateral framework of GATT, subject to the unconditional most-favored-nation principle. Bargaining has proceeded on a product-by-product basis. On the other hand, most extensions of the law have embodied a "no-injury" philosophy—trade liberalization was to be accomplished with minimum injury to domestic industry. This philosophy found expression in the escape clause, peril point, and national security provisions of the act. The no-injury philosophy was also promoted diplomatically, by inducing Japan "voluntarily" to restrict the export of certain products to the United States.

To the economist, the no-injury approach is clearly inconsistent with the general spirit of the reciprocal trade legislation. He regards tariff reduction first and foremost as a means to improve economic efficiency through increased international specialization. A larger volume of trade is expected to drive domestic resources away from relatively inefficient import-competing industries into industries that have competitive advantage. A similar process would take place abroad with the obvious result of increased efficiency all around. The escape clause is essentially a mechanism for preventing such shifts of resources. By protecting industries from import competition, it perpetuates allocative inefficiency and is therefore in direct conflict with what the act first set out to accomplish. We reduce tariffs and admit larger imports, but the instant such imports begin to have the beneficial effect of driving resources out of inefficient uses, we reverse course. This view of the main purpose of the tariff reduction program is by no means universal. It is certainly not shared by many legislators and public officials. In these circles the program has been regarded as primarily a means of expanding American exports and strengthening the Western Alliance.

The Trade Agreements Act was proposed by the Roosevelt Administration in 1934 as an antidepression measure designed to open up new export markets for American products. The offer of reciprocal tariff concessions was not an end in itself; it was meant to induce foreign countries to open their markets to American products. This view, while still widely held, has been superseded by a political objective. The program has come to be regarded as a means of strengthening the economies of friendly nations by opening the American market to some of their products, as symbolized by the slogan Trade Not Aid. The dollar shortage after 1945 contributed considerably to this objective. Most proponents of the Trade Agreements Program, both administration officials and representatives of other public bodies and private interests, stressed these two purposes when testifying before congressional committees in support of extending the act. The economic end of attaining higher efficiency is usually given some lip service, but it is not held in high regard. To these officials, there exists no real inconsistency between extensive tariff reduction on the one hand and the prevention of injury to domestic interests on the other. If the U.S. goals are to open new export markets and cement the Western Alliance, why not attain them at the least cost in terms of displacement of domestic production?

The 1958 Extension

This indeed has been the major trend in reciprocal trade legislation since the Randall Report of 1954. The Randall Commission, set up by the Eisenhower Administration to study the goals of U.S. foreign economic policies, recommended the continuation of the Trade Agreements Program with appropriate safeguards to domestic industry. The subsequent extensions of the Act during the 1950s—a three-year extension in 1955 and a four-year one in 1958 —contained liberal provisions for tariff reduction averaging 5 percent per year. (All eleven extensions granted before 1958 ranged from one to three years in length.) In 1958, Congress authorized the President to offer tariff concessions of up to 20 percent, to be spread evenly over four years. Alternatively, the President was permitted to cut tariff rates by two percentage points or to reduce to 50 percent *ad valorem* all rates in excess of that level. These two alternatives are significant in cases where the 1958 rates were below 10 percent or above 62.5 percent, respectively. It was under this authority that the so-called Dillon Round was negotiated in GATT in 1961.

At the same time, however, Congress strengthened the protection to domestic interests against import competition. Three avenues of protection were open to domestic industries. Under the peril-point provision, the U.S. Tariff Commission was required to determine *before* negotiations the level to which the tariff rate on each product could be lowered before causing serious injury to any domestic industry. Our delegation is not authorized to offer concessions that would reduce rates below this level, although the peril point is hardly more than an educated guess. Incorporated into the act in 1948, the peril point was repealed in 1949 but reinstated in 1951.

Next, if, after a concession is granted, a domestic industry feels injured by import competition, it can apply for relief under the escape clause. A determination by the Tariff Commission of positive injury may lead to withdrawal of the concession, if the President concurs with the Commission's recommendation. The clause first appeared in the 1951 extension of the act, although it had in fact been incorporated in trade agreements since 1943.

In each escape-clause investigation, the Tariff Commission must make three successive determinations. First, it must define the scope of the industry to be covered by the investigation. Since the impossibility of measuring cross elasticities precludes a precise definition of "industry," it is defined in the act as producers of "like or directly competitive products." More explicit guidance could be provided on this point, but the definition would still leave much of the decision to the discretion of the Commission. The more broadly the industry is defined, the more difficult it is to prove injury, because injury to some segments of the industry may be more than offset by benefits to others (perhaps even from reciprocal expansion of exports), leaving the entire industry thriving. By contrast, the segmentation rule followed by the Commission in the past has been subject to considerable crticism, as it could lead to the use of the escape clause by an "industry" consisting of a few relatively inefficient producers.

Once the industry is defined, the Commission must determine whether serious injury has taken place. In interpreting the act, the Commission tended to follow the "share-of-the-market" concept, requesting only that an industry seeking escape-clause relief prove that its share of the market has declined because of increased imports. Under this criterion even an industry expanding in absolute terms can prove injury if imports have captured a larger share of a rapidly growing market. Finally, there remains the difficult problem of tracing the "decline in share of the market" to the tariff concession. Import-competing industries strongly object to the requirement that they prove such a causal relation; they claim that relief should be granted regardless of whether the increased import is due to an earlier tariff concession.

In the 1958 legislation, escape-clause proceedings were expedited by granting subpoena power to the Tariff Commission, by shortening the time allowed for investigation from nine to six months, and by instructing the Commission to initiate such proceedings whenever it finds in peril-point investigations that more restrictive customs treatment is necessary to prevent injury. (Foreign nations have in the past been reluctant to consent to modifications of American tariff concessions following peril-point findings. Escape-clause relief, on the other hand, is an accepted procedure in international commercial agreements.)

A more restrictive provision is the increase in authority to raise tariffs whenever escape-clause relief is granted. The 1958 Extension Act raised the maximum limit of such increases from 50 percent above the 1945 tariff level to 50 percent above the 1934 level. Within this authority, the President was permitted to convert specific duties existing in July 1934 to their *ad valorem* equivalent in that year and apply the 50 percent increase to the converted figure. This modification restored the effectiveness of specific duties that was impaired by inflation during and after World War II. While permission to use quotas was retained, the President was authorized to impose up to 50 percent duty on commodities on the free list.

With respect to the Tariff Commission's determinations in escape-clause investigations, the legislation permitted a narrow definition of industry, thereby making it possible for a small segment of an industry to demonstrate injury even when the industry as a whole experienced prosperity and growth. It also enabled domestic industries to base their claims for serious injury strictly on a decline in their share of the market even if absolute levels of production and employment were on the increase. Moreover, the 1958 extension introduced for the first time a breach in the President's authority for final decision in escape-clause cases by authorizing a two-thirds majority of both houses of Congress to override the President when he declines to accept a Tariff Commission recommendation.

A final avenue of relief, also strengthened in the 1950s, is the national security clause, which permits withdrawal of concessions in cases where the affected domestic industry is essential to national security.

It is thus abundantly clear that two main threads were woven through the reciprocal trade legislation. One was designed to liberalize imports into the United States, especially of industrial products, while the other was dedicated to the protection of American industry from import competition. It is true that the escape clause has been invoked very sparingly so far. But this may have been a direct result of the noninjurious nature of the concessions and the effective application of the peril-point provisions. However, merely the knowledge that the escape clause exists and may be applied if imports do injure a domestic industry deters foreign exporters from establishing sales outlets in this country, particularly when they require considerable investment capital.

The two general philosophies of the legislation—trade liberalization and no injury to domestic industry—are not reconcilable on economic grounds. But if political considerations are the motivating force behind U.S. commercial policies, they become compatible indeed. The offers of tariff concessions, for whatever political purpose, were designed in such a way as to minimize domestic injury. Product-by-product negotiation, coupled with the aforementioned provisions in the law, made that possible.

It is reasonable to assume that many concessions merely constituted reductions in excess protection. But toward the end of the 1950s the no-injury provisions were becoming increasingly incompatible with the main objective of the legislation even for those who viewed the program strictly as a tool of foreign policy. The concessions granted by the United States during the previous generation had more than halved the level of the tariff, a reduction that practically eliminated all the "excess protection" in the tariff structure. It was no longer possible to grant many concessions without inflicting injury on domestic industries by simply curtailing the amount of "water" in the tariff.

Regardless of its objective, any significant amount of further trade liberalization was likely to be injurious to domestic interests. An effective and strictly enforced escape clause designed to prevent such injury could have jeopardized the entire program. If tariff cuts were needed to strengthen the alliance or to expand American exports, they had to be granted at a sacrifice of some American production. (And inadvertently they would in the long run bring about the salutary economic effect of shifting domestic resources to more competitive industries.) Anything that prevented the influx of foreign products to the American markets would conflict with the policy of tariff liberalization.

Trade Adjustment Assistance

Given an adequate growth rate, the resources displaced by increased imports can shift to industries in which the United States enjoys comparative advantage. But this process takes time. In the short run, a number of workers, employers, and communities might be hurt. And in a society that assumes responsibility for the economic well-being of its members, such an impact of public policy cannot be overlooked.

Legislators and public officials interested in continuing the program began to recognize the need for finding an acceptable substitute for tariff relief under the escape clause. If most Americans stood to benefit from the increased efficiency resulting from trade liberalization, a way had to be found to compensate those who would incur the short-run losses caused by displaced domestic production. Thus, support gathered behind a program for trade-adjustment assistance, which had been advocated by economists for quite some time.

Instead of protecting import-competing industries by the escape clause and thus perpetuating inefficiency, why not promote their transfer to lines of production in which they can compete effectively? The government could facilitate such movement of resources by means of a program designed to aid those who are injured by import competition. Under this program, whenever Tariff Commission investigations revealed that an industry had been injured by import competition generated by a previous tariff concession, its recommendation would not have to be limited to tariff relief. Instead, it could recommend direct assistance. To employers the program would offer low-interest loans, aid in market research, and other assistance in moving to new lines of production. To workers it would provide opportunities for retraining and offer to defray transportation costs to new locations. And to communities injured by import competition, it would offer all assistance necessary to diversify the industrial base and adjust to the new circumstances. This avenue of relief would have the added advantage of making it easier to administer the Trade Agreements Act. Because of the narrow choice of action open to the President under previous legislation, in cases of serious injury (action that involves modification of international obligations) the Tariff Commission had to be very rigid in recommending escape-clause relief. The alternative method would make possible more liberal determinations.

The 1962 Trade Expansion Act

A trade-adjustment program was legislated for the first time in the Trade Expansion Act of 1962. Indeed, this was one of several drastic departures from the earlier reciprocal trade legislation. Under this program, workers made unemployed because of tariff concessions can obtain 65 percent of their weekly wage for 52 weeks plus an additional 26 weeks of pay if they are enrolled in a training program. Eligible firms can obtain technical and managerial assistance to help find new market outlets or develop new products; long-term, low-interest loans; and some minor tax relief. Until late 1969 no firm or group of workers qualified for adjustment assistance, because tariff concessions under the 1962 act did not take effect until 1968, and also because of the narrow interpretation by the Tariff Commission of the criteria[1] justifying such assistance. However, the situation changed, and in the following three years the Commission ruled favorably on 84 out of 203 applications.

Other liberal features of the 1962 act included a vast increase in the President's tariff-cutting authority. Under the new five-year act, the President was permitted to cut duties by up to 50 percent of their July 1962 level, to remove altogether duties that did not exceed 5 percent on that date, and to eliminate duties on articles in which the United States and the EEC were responsible for at least 80 percent of aggregate exports. (The effect of this provision turned out to be minimal, because the 80 percent criterion encompassed very few products as long as Great Britain was not a member of

[1] The adjustment assistance for workers under the Canadian-American automobile pact is more liberal and easier to qualify for.

the EEC.) Also subject to removal were duties on agricultural commodities from the temperate and tropical zones. Tariff negotiations were to be conducted on broad categories rather than product by product.

It was under the authority of this legislation that the United States participated in the Kennedy Round. But the high hopes originally held for that bargaining session gradually gave way to more modest aspirations. What finally emerged from the five years of laborious bargaining (to be described in Chapter 16) was an average reduction of 35 percent on industrial tariff rates. These reductions took effect gradually over the 1967–72 period. No new trade legislation was enacted through 1973, Congress having failed to enact the modest trade liberalization measure submitted by the President in 1969.

The Trade Reform Act of 1973

In 1973 the Nixon Administration submitted to Congress the Trade Reform Act, seeking vast new authority to reduce tariffs and thereby paving the way to a new round of tariff negotiations under GATT. The act would give the President authority for a five-year period to eliminate, reduce, or raise existing tariffs without limit as a part of trade agreements with other countries. Duty reductions would be implemented in a minimum of five equal annual stages, or by a maximum of three percentage points per year. In addition, the President would be granted authority to negotiate away nontariff barriers, but any such agreement may be disapproved by Congress within ninety days of its submission. Unless so disapproved, it becomes effective. Precise peril-point determination by the Tariff Commission in advance of negotiations would no longer be required. But the Tariff Commission would have to investigate and inform the President, within six months of publication of the list of products on which tariff concessions are contemplated, of its judgment of the probable economic effects of such concessions.

Escape-clause relief would continue to be available to domestic industry, but the administration of the clause would be changed. The criteria for determining injury would be liberalized my making it unnecessary to link the injury to the tariff concessions (injury from import competition would be sufficient), and by requiring imports to be the single most important cause ("primary cause") of the injury rather than a cause responsible for at least 51 percent of the injury ("major cause," defined as greater than all other causes combined). The Tariff Commission must make its determination within three months (with a possible two-month extension) after a petition has been filed by a trade association, a firm, or a union.

Within 60 days of an affirmative determination by the Tariff Commission (120 days in case of a tie vote), the President must decide whether to provide import relief, or direct the Secretary of Labor to expedite consideration of workers' petitions for adjustment assistance, or both. Should he decide against any action, he must report to Congress the considerations leading to his negative decision. Import relief can take the form of an increase in duty (without any limit); imposition of a tariff on a duty free item; suspension of the special treatment under provisions 806.3 or 807.0[2] of the tariff schedule; negotiation of orderly marketing arrangements with foreign countries (that is, "voluntary" export quotas); or any combination of the above. In the case where import restrictions are imposed, the President is authorized to negotiate with foreign countries and offer them compensatory concessions. Any import relief is regarded as temporary and must be terminated not later than five years after it is granted, with a possible extension of two years. This phasing-out provision would presumably force the industry to adjust to increased imports.

An alternative avenue of relief would be available to groups of workers hurt by import competition; they may apply to the Secretary of Labor for adjustment assistance. In making his determination, the Secretary need not find a causal link between increased imports and a previous tariff concession; all that would be required is that increased imports "contributed substantially" to workers' separation from employement (rather than be a "major cause"). Qualifying workers would then be eligible for (a) supplementary unemployment insurance, with maximum weekly benefits of two-thirds the average state-wide weekly wage; (b) retraining services; (c) job search allowance of 80 percent of cost and up to $500; and (d) relocation allowance subject to similar limitations as under (c). Despite the easing of the eligibility criteria, these provisions have been criticized because they eliminate adjustment assistance to companies and to trade-impacted communities, and because in most cases they lower the level of benefits to workers.

The bill gives the President authority to impose any type of import restrictions against countries employing unfair import restrictions on American products or those paying export subsidies, including subsidies of foreign supplies to third markets that displace American exports. The antidumping regulations would be changed to conform to GATT's rules, which require, in addition to a finding of price discrimination (see Chapter 15), a determination of injury to domestic producers before countervailing duties can be imposed.

---

[2] These little-noticed provisions in the U.S. tariff code allow the duty free reimportation to the U.S. of semifinished products manufactured abroad out of parts exported from the United States. (More precisely, the American duty is charged only on that part of the value of the imported product that has been added abroad.) As a result, a variety of processing plants have been set up by American corporations in such countries as Mexico and Taiwan, so that suspension of these provisions may harm certain developing countries.

Finally, articles that infringe a U.S. patent would be excluded from entry into the United States.

Next, in the event of a serious balance-of-payments deficit, the President would be authorized to impose a temporary surcharge or temporary quota on imports. In the case of a persistent balance-of-payments surplus or in case of rapid inflation, he would be authorized to reduce temporarily or suspend duties and other import restrictions. Although his actions under this authority must apply uniformly to a broad range of imported products, the President may exempt certain products (for example, duty-free items) or certain countries.

What turned out to be the most controversial title of the bill was the proposal to extend most-favored-nation (MFN) treatment to imports from countries not currently enjoying such treatment (mainly Communist countries), as a part of bilateral agreements. Such agreements would be restricted to a maximum period of three years (renewable once), and their implementation would be subject to a congressional veto procedure. In order to accommodate the trade practices of the socialist states, the Congress has been asked to suspend the imposition of countervailing duties against imports that are from subsidized state-owned industries.

These bilateral commercial agreements might include arrangements to prevent market disruption by imports from the Communist countries; to protect American industrial rights and processes, trademarks, patents, and copyrights; to settle commercial disputes through, for example, arbitration; to establish trade and tourist promotion offices; to establish trade missions; and to facilitate the activities of commercial representatives.

The bill proposes less stringent criteria for the determination of injury from imports from these countries in the event that the Tariff Commission is petitioned for relief from import competition. In the event of a finding of injury, the President would need to impose the import restraint only on exports from Communist countries, thus reestablishing the discrimination that prevailed before.

Finally, the bill offers a Generalized System of Preferences (GSP) to the developing countries. It would authorize the President to grant duty-free entry to the exports of manufactures, semimanufactures, and selected other products from developing countries and territories—with the list of beneficiaries to be determined by the President. While the President may withdraw such treatment for any article or exporting country (for example, in connection with injury finding by the Tariff Commission), he may not establish an intermediate preferential duty between zero and the most-favored-nation rate. The purpose of this program, which is similar to one introduced by other industrial nations, is to help promote the exports and economic development of developing countries. There are, however, several restrictive provisions that severely limit the usefulness of the GSP to the beneficiary countries. These will be discussed in Chapter 17.

After a considerable delay, the House of Representatives approved the bill at the end of 1973. But much to the chagrin of the Administration, it conditioned approval of most-favored-nation treatment and credit extension to Communist countries on the liberalization of their emigration laws. The Senate is expected to take up this legislation in 1974.

15
Other Barriers to Trade

Although the tariff is the most widely used instrument of protection, it is by no means the only one, nor is it the most harmful. Indeed, as tariff rates have come down under programs of multilateral trade liberalization, the nontariff barriers loom increasingly important. Some of these devices will be considered in this chapter. However, it should be remembered that restrictive as these may be, they are only interferences with an otherwise free market system. East European bloc trading, in which international trade is conducted by government corporations and is not subject to the decisions of individuals, goes considerably further in the degree of control it implies than any of the methods discussed here.

Import Quotas

Instead of imposing a tax on the imported commodity, as under the tariff, the government may directly restrict the volume of permissible imports to a certain maximum level. The absolute limit is known as the import quota. For example, the number of cars imported may be limited to 10,000, or the volume of steel to 100,000 tons. In both cases the limits are presumably below what would be imported under free-market conditions, for otherwise there would be no need for the quota. Indeed, if free-market demand for imports falls below the quota, the quota becomes ineffective.

How Common Are Import Quotas?

Although the main purpose of quotas is to protect domestic industries by restricting imports, they have also been employed to cope with balance-of-payments deficits and to raise home employment. Quotas were very common in Western Europe immediately after World War II. Today, international trade in manufactured goods, with the important exception of textiles, is virtually free of such restrictions in all the developed nations (although in 1974 the UAW demanded import quotas on cars to help cope with slumping sales). Of late, whenever the domestic pressure for quotas in this country has become unbearable, the United States has taken to negotiating an alternative device known as the "voluntary export quota." Under it, the exporting country imposes a quota on the export of the good to the United States, as in the case of the steel agreement negotiated with Europe and Japan. Such agreements can be negotiated either with the governments of the exporting countries or with the exporters themselves. The value of U.S. imports covered by voluntary export quotas now exceeds that covered by quantitative import restrictions.[1] (It has been estimated that these agreements cost the American consumer between $1.5 and $3.2 billion annually in higher prices.) The exporting countries agree to this arrangement because the alternative is import controls imposed by the American Congress. Unlike import quotas, these arrangements do not violate the GATT agreement.

On the other hand, trade in agricultural products is subject to a variety of quantitative restrictions in virtually all the industrial countries, including the United States. They all protect their agricultural sectors because the farmers are politically powerful. In the United States as well as in many nations of the European continent, aid to farmers takes the form of price-support programs —the government sets prices somewhere above the free-market level and purchases the food surpluses that result from that fixed price. If imports were allowed in freely, the government would be supporting the prices (and income) of both foreign and domestic farmers. In order to maintain domestic prices above the international level, the United States imposes strict import quotas, while at the same time it often employs export subsidies to dispose of the accumulated surpluses overseas. It will be seen in Chapter 16 that the European Community has devised some new and unique methods of agricultural protection. On the other hand, the United States and other countries have on occasion liberalized or lifted quota restrictions to combat specific shortages or general inflation. Liberalization of the U.S. meat and cheese quotas in 1972–74 is a case in point. Furthermore, during the food "shortages" of 1973, the United States and the European Community resorted to export bans on certain critical products. Indeed, the temporary U.S. restrictions on the export of soybeans to Europe and Japan caused a rift in the Western alliance.

Outside agriculture, the United States maintained an effective quota on oil imports, and several European countries restricted the importation of coal, until 1973, when the controls were liberalized because of the energy shortage.

---

[1] See F. Bergsten, "The Nonequivalence of Import Quotas and Voluntary Export Restraints," in F. Bergsten, ed., *Toward a New World Trade Policy: The Maidenhead Papers.* (Washington, D.C.: The Brookings Institution), 1974.

These programs were set up as a result of intense pressure by domestic interests requesting protection from import competition.

In developing countries, quotas are used in all sectors, for a mixture of reasons. Often, these countries attempt to develop new industries to produce substitutes for imported goods and believe that this can be accomplished only under a protective shield of import quotas. Tariffs, even high ones, do not provide the local manufacturer with the same degree of certainty. No one knows the level of supply and demand response to price change nor, therefore, how much of a foreign commodity would be excluded from the domestic market by a given tariff level. Consumers may prefer imported, internationally known brands even at higher prices. And foreign producers may choose to absorb part of the duty in order to avoid losing sales, although this is unlikely if the duty protects only a small market. None of these uncertainties exists in the case of quotas, where the volume of imports is limited by administrative action.

Economic Effects of Quotas

Since it restricts the volume of imports, the import quota raises the domestic price of the imported commodity in much the same way as the tariff.[2] Consumption declines as consumers switch to less desirable substitutes, while domestic production of substitute products expands under the protection accorded to their producers, with resources drawn from other (presumably more efficient) industries. In contrast to the tariff, however, there is no revenue to the government. In this case it accrues to the importers, who are now able to charge a higher price for each unit of the restricted supply. This is referred to as *monopoly profit,* because a monopolist reaps his profit in the same manner, by curtailing output and thus charging a higher price compared to what would be the case under competition. Only by auctioning off the import licenses can the government recoup this revenue.

But even besides the revenue aspect there are important differences between a tariff and a quota. While the tariff interferes with the market mechanism, a quota replaces it altogether with arbitrary government decisions. With tariffs, domestic price cannot differ from world price by more than the duty. Unlimited quantities of a product may be imported by anyone, provided he is eager enough for the good to pay the tax. Thus, starting from a given tariff-ridden situation, with its attendant level of consumption and production costs, any rise in domestic demand can be satisfied from increased imports at the same price. Domestic production does not rise nor does the cost of protection in terms of misallocated resources and reduced desirability of the consumption

---

[2] The excess of domestic over foreign price can be regarded as the "implicit tariff" equivalent of the nontariff barrier.

mix. This is not so in the case of a quota. Here there is no limit to the differential between domestic and world prices. Since an upward quantity adjustment is not possible, any rise in domestic demand will simply raise the domestic price, leaving admissible imports unaltered. Such an increase raises the production and consumption costs of protection by forcing further misallocation of resources and less desirable consumption patterns.

Figure 15-1 describes the domestic situation in the car market of a small car-importing nation that faces infinitely elastic export supply on world markets. In the absence of international trade, domestic price is P_1, while under free trade the price (world price) is P_2 and $\overline{ab}$ ($=\overline{cd}$) units are imported. A tariff t raises the domestic price to P_3, and imports are reduced to $\overline{gh}$ ($=\overline{ef}$). The same effect on the domestic price and the volume of imports would be produced if the government imposed an import quota of $\overline{gh}$. Indeed, under competitive conditions in all markets, and if the import licenses were auctioned to produce the same government revenue as under the tariff, the initial effects of a tariff and a quota would be identical.

But suppose there is an upward shift in domestic demand to D'. Under a tariff t, the domestic price can never exceed world price (P_2) plus the tariff. It therefore remains at P_3, and the volume of imports rises from $\overline{ef}$ to $\overline{ei}$. In other words, the increase in demand is accommodated by an increase in the volume of trade. On the other hand, in the case of an import quota, quantity adjustment is not possible; the volume of imports is fixed at $\overline{ef}$. Consequently the upward shift in demand will produce a price adjustment. Domestic price rises to P_4, where the quantity imported remains unchanged at $\overline{jk}$ ($=\overline{ef}$). Similarly, if domestic producers become less efficient and the supply curve

Figure 15-1
Domestic Market for Cars in a Small Importing Country

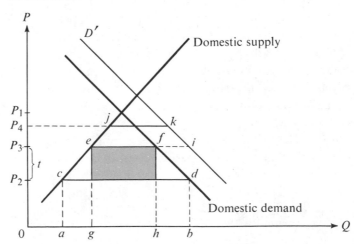

shifts toward the left, a quota would protect them from increased imports, while a tariff would not. In case of a decrease in domestic demand or an increase in domestic supply, the domestic price would decline under a quota, with the quantity imported remaining unchanged; while the volume of imports would decline under a tariff with the price remaining unchanged. The general conclusion is that as long as the quota remains "effective" (the controlled allocation falls short of what would be imported under free-market conditions), the adjustment to any shift in demand or supply occurs in the quantity of imports in the case of a tariff and in the domestic price in the case of a quota.[3]

Another possible difference between a tariff and a quota is suggested by the theory of effective protection. When a quota is imposed on an imported raw material (such as crude oil), it raises the production costs of the final output (such as petroleum products) of which the material is a part. This is the same effect as that of a tariff on inputs. But whereas import duties on raw materials are sometimes rebated when the final product is exported, no such rebate occurs in the case of quotas.

A third important difference between a tariff and a quota concerns the case where the domestic producer of the import substitute is a monopolist. International trade, even with a tariff, imposes severe limitations on his monopoly power. In particular, he cannot charge more than the world price plus the tariff, for consumers can switch to foreign imports in unlimited quantities. There is always a potential (if not actual) threat to his position. In the case of an import quota, all he needs to do is accommodate a certain fixed amount of imports, and beyond that he is the king of the marketplace. He may certainly charge more than with the tariff, he faces less competitive pressure than under the tariff, and in general he can cause greater damage to economic efficiency and growth. (Appendix V-B demonstrates that a profit-maximizing monopolist would indeed charge more under a quota than under a tariff.) He is easily assured of any increase in sales resulting from a rise in domestic demand, because the volume of imports is fixed by decree.

Furthermore, for the competitor and monopolist alike, a tariff does not provide protection with certainty. The foreign exporter may choose to absorb all or most of the duty by reducing export price, leaving the import price virtually unchanged. In fact, under certain conditions some reduction in export price may be expected from the very working of the market mechanism. This means that the volume of imports would decline very little, much to the dismay of the protection-seeking producer. Such an outcome is not possible

---

[3] By the use of consumer and producer surpluses, it can be shown that when import licenses are auctioned by the government, a tariff causes less of a welfare loss than an equivalent quota when domestic demand rises or supply falls, while the reverse is true if demand falls or supply rises.

in the case of a quota, where the volume of admissible imports is prescribed by the government. More generally, domestic producers, lacking precise knowledge of the supply and demand elasticities for their product, can never be sure how much imports would be excluded from the country by a given level of tariff protection. Certainty does obtain in the case of a quota.

All these differences explain the frequent clamor for import quotas in preference to tariffs by the U.S. textile and shoe industries as well as the mammoth oligopolistic steel industry. They also make clear why such demands should be resisted at all cost. In terms of its effect on economic efficiency and consumer sovereignty, a quota is much more harmful than a tariff.

In addition, import quotas require a cumbersome administrative apparatus. The administering government agency must decide how to allocate import licenses among importers as well as among sources of supply (exporting countries) and how to distribute the yearly allocation over time. These decisions can be arbitrary and may bear no relation to consumer choice and producer cost. Furthermore, since sales of the restricted commodity yield monopoly profit to the importer, the import license itself assumes considerable value, so much so that an importer may be willing to bribe government officials to obtain one. Thus the system contains seeds of corruption and fraud.

A final source of inefficiency arises from the fact that the import licenses are usually distributed among the importers who were functioning at the time the control was imposed. The system tends to freeze the situation as it existed at a certain base period. Total sales and profits depend less on current efficiency of operations, forced by competitive markets, than on conditions at some previous base year coupled with arbitrary official judgments. A tax such as a tariff, while distorting relative prices, still permits free-market forces to serve as an allocation mechanism. The importers who are efficient enough to pay the tax get the business. Import quotas displace the market mechanism altogether, and a powerful incentive for business efficiency on the part of importing firms is lost. In sum, while the economic costs of a tariff are bad enough, they pale in comparison to those inflicted by import quotas. Yet today it is the developing countries, precisely those that can least afford to tolerate inefficiency, that insist on using quotas.

International Commodity Agreements

International trade in certain primary commodities is governed by International Commodity Agreements (ICAs), allegedly designed to stabilize the world price of the commodity in question or dispose of surpluses. It is usually the producing nations that press for such agreements, claiming that when the response to price change on the part of consumers and producers is low the market mechanism is too sluggish and cumbersome and needs to be modified by some central direction. After all, the performance of the price system as an allocation mechanism is contingent upon reasonably strong and prompt responses to price change. When the response is weak and tardy, violent price fluctuations frequently occur. If a bumper crop raises the supply of the commodity, it takes a huge decline in price to induce consumers to take even part of that increase. Likewise, a shift in consumer demand, for any reason, produces a large price change because producers cannot respond with sufficient speed and vigor to the new situation. Such circumstances imply large fluctuations in the earnings of growers and in the terms of trade of the countries that produce the primary materials. If a country's economy is largely devoted to the production and exportation of one or two primary products, as many developing countries are, then the entire level of economic activity tends to fluctuate along with these prices. However, in the case of some commodities, the sharp rise in prices in 1972–73 brought about suspension of some of the agreements. Should prices of primary commodities continue to rise, the pressure for commodity agreements might slacken (except for commodities remaining in low demand).

Although the empirical evidence to support the link between price fluctuations and economic growth is lacking, or is at best mixed, several international commodity agreements have been instituted in the past. These agreements have taken one or another of three forms.

Export restriction schemes call for control over the quantity marketed internationally by means of national quotas for the production or export of the supplying countries. A temporary letup in demand would be met by a greater (artificially contrived) reduction in supply, it being hoped that the sharp rise in price would compensate for the decline in quantity, leaving total foreign-exchange earnings unchanged. In Figure 15-2 the original situation is described by schedules D and S, and equilibrium price and quantity are P_1 and Q_1, respectively. Total foreign exchange revenue, which the agreement seeks to maintain, is the area of $0P_1e_1Q_1$. A shift in demand to D' requires the exporting nations to curtail supply to Q_2, so that the price may be raised to P_2, and foreign exchange earnings would be $0P_2e_2Q_2$ $(= 0P_1e_1Q_1)$. The fact that a *reduction* in demand is met by steps designed to *increase* price underscores the perversity of this arrangement.

Buffer stocks set a maximum and a minimum price for the commodity to be maintained by purchases or sales from stocks. In this case, the objective is to maintain equilibrium point e_1 by adding to or substracting from market demand. A reduction in demand from D to D' is met by purchases by the buffer stocks of quantity Q_1Q_3, equalling the decline in demand, thereby maintaining both the quantity and the price of sale. Total revenue remains intact.

Figure 15-2
Effect of International Commodity Agreements

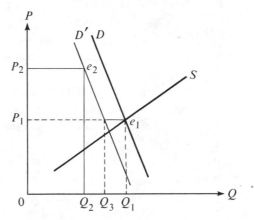

Multilateral contracts specify a maximum price at which producing countries are obliged to sell stipulated quantities to consuming countries and a minimum price at which consuming countries are obliged to purchase stipulated quantities from producing countries. The operations of the contract in each case depend on its provisions.

All three mechanisms interfere with the allocative functions of the market, preventing shifts of resources between industries and thereby causing inefficiencies.

Seven ICAs are in operation today. The International Wheat Agreement, negotiated in 1970 to replace the 1968 Grain Agreement, is in essence a multilateral contract. It involves obligations to buy and sell stipulated quantities at certain prices but calls for no production or export controls nor for central accumulation of stocks. The International Coffee Agreement was first instituted in 1963 and renewed in 1968. It encompasses virtually all sixty-six of the exporting and consuming nations and contains quota restrictions on exports designed to stabilize prices within a certain range. (These provisions were suspended in 1972–74 because of the upswing in coffee prices.) A five-year International Sugar Agreement, which went into effect in 1969, also uses export quotas to regulate trade volume. (The quotas were suspended in 1972–73 because of the rise in prices.) The agreement covers only 40 percent of world trade, since the EEC is not a party to it. An International Tin Agreement between the six major producing countries utilizes buffer stocks to maintain prices. The program is financed by these countries themselves, and it includes provisions for export quotas should the tin supply become overly abundant. The International Cocoa Agreement also has price and export quota provisions, which were rendered ineffective in 1972–73 by high world prices. Finally, there is a largely inoperative agreement on olive oil among the Mediterranean countries, and an agreement concerning trade in powdered milk was concluded in mid-1970. Discussions are under way concerning other commodities such as tea, natural rubber, raw jute, and oils.

All international commodity agreements past and present suffer from attempts to fix and maintain a price different from the long-run equilibrium level. In most cases it is difficult to determine what that price is. Even if it were possible to start at the "correct" level, that level changes over time in response to market forces. While these changes can go in all directions, the continuous pressure of the producing countries is only upward; in other words, they campaign for higher prices, which in turn lead to more production and larger surpluses (except in years of unusually high demand). Thus, agreements become a thinly disguised form of subsidy paid by the consuming nations (whose consumers pay the above-equilibrium prices) to the producing nations. And it is an inefficient method of subsidizing at that, for not only are consumers charged artificially high prices, but the discrepancy between the equilibrium and support prices usually leads to an accumulation of large stocks that are costly to store and maintain.

Besides the problem of financing and storing surpluses, many of the past and present agreements are threatened by noncompliance of small producers with the regulations, each small country thinking that its own action does not affect the world price, and by the incentive offered by high prices to the introduction of synthetic substitutes. In this respect, the most successful of all has been the coffee agreement: production is largely concentrated in a few developing countries, while consumption is mainly in developed countries where demand is not too sensitive to price increases.

Because most agreements have not been particularly successful and are difficult to negotiate to begin with, attempts are being made to find other ways to combat the effects of violent price fluctuations on developing countries. There is a coordinated international effort under way to diversify production of materials, and direct international financial support is available from the IMF to countries that experience a particularly severe decline in export earnings in any given year. Since it does not interfere with the workings of the market mechanism, such compensatory financing is a more efficient method of offsetting fluctuations in commodity prices or export earnings.

Not all international commodity agreements involve primary commodities, and not all are called forth by developing countries. The major exception is textiles. If any sector of the industrial countries should have contracted to make room for imports from developing countries, it is textiles. By reason of simple technology and relative labor intensity in the production process, this industry is the first candidate for introduction into a developing economy attempting to industrialize. Resources in the industrial nations can almost invariably be put to better use elsewhere. Yet well-known economic and political pressures prevail and keep the industry from contracting and imports from expanding. For a long time European countries restricted the importation of cotton textiles from the so-called low-wage countries, primarily in the Far East. Thus Japanese, Taiwanese, and other Asian textiles were diverted to the American market, much to the dismay of the New England and North Carolina textile mills. No wonder that the latter's clamor for protection, strongly supported by the United Textile Workers, grew louder and clearer all the time.

And their claim was partly backed by a valid argument. In addition to the general inefficiency perpetuated by the domestic price support of agricultural products in the United States, the program also subsidizes foreign textile mills by selling them raw cotton at reduced prices. In order to maintain the support price above the market level, the U.S. government is obliged to purchase all the domestic surpluses that are generated. As surpluses accumulate there is pressure to dispose of them on foreign markets at a considerable discount. Thus a Japanese mill can purchase American cotton at a lower price than its New England competitor. And cheaper raw materials constitute a form of subsidy. The domestic industry in the United States wishes to counteract this subsidy by restricting imports of the final product.

But not all the industry's arguments are as logical. For the most part they follow the traditional lines proven invalid in a previous chapter, such as the relatively high wage rate they are obliged to pay compared to those paid by their foreign competitors. In general their demand for import restrictions in the interest of "maintaining orderly markets" or "avoiding market disruptions" is nothing but a disguised request for a subsidy. But as often happens in public affairs, it is not the validity of the argument but the political and economic influence brought to bear by the debater that matters. As a result the United States negotiated an agreement with Japan in the 1950s under which Japan agreed to impose "voluntary export quotas" on shipments of cotton textiles to the United States. Japan agreed to this "voluntary" control because the alternative was the imposition of mandatory import restrictions by the United States. ("Voluntary export quotas" for steel were negotiated with Europe and Japan late in the 1960s and renewed in 1972.) The agreement did not help as much as expected. The newly freed share of the market was not captured by the domestic mills but was partly diverted to imports from other Far Eastern countries, such as Taiwan and Pakistan. The pressure for further restrictions continued unabated.

Since the European countries were interested in similar import limitations, the United States was able in the early 1960s to negotiate a long-term international commodity agreement to govern world trade in cotton textiles. Administered by the General Agreement on Tariffs and Trade (GATT), it now includes most producing and consuming nations and considerably limits the flow of international trade in cotton textiles. On January 1, 1974 a new four-year GATT agreement went into force covering articles of cotton, wool, and man-made fibers. It allows importing countries to restrain textile imports when imports cause "market disruption," but requires that such restrictions be used sparingly and be supervised by an international surveillance body set up under GATT.

Administrative, Technical, and Other Regulations

A myriad of government rules which restrict the free flow of trade and are ostensibly unrelated to protectionism have come to be known as nontariff barriers. It is often difficult to determine whether these are bona fide technical regulations that happen to discriminate against imports or regulations designed primarily to keep out imports.

For example, the French domestic tax on automobiles is graduated on the basis of a car's horsepower and as such raises the prices of American cars relative to domestic cars and can be regarded as discriminatory. The British requirement that importers deposit at the government treasury for six months and at no interest a sum equal to half the value of their imports is certainly a strong barrier to trade. A similar requirement was introduced by Italy in April 1974, to cope with balance-of-payments deficits caused by high oil prices. Although the measure is contrary to the spirit implied in EC membership, EC ministers were unable to persuade Italy to remove or modify it. And the European excise taxes on tropical products that are not produced at home serve merely to discourage imports. On the other hand, many Europeans regard the U.S. laws requiring automotive safety equipment as a protective device. And there is little doubt that the restrictions of minimum size on certain tomatoes sold in the United States discriminate against Mexican imports.

Other examples include complex customs procedures, a French ban on Scotch or bourbon advertising, limitation on the showing of foreign films on British television, and the Buy American Act, which requires the U.S. government to give American contractors a 12 percent edge in bidding for government contracts (50 percent in defense contracts). The list of such regulations staggers the imagination. It ranges from preferences of national industries, such as railroads and airlines, for products of their own country to laws designed to insure that food is produced under hygienic conditions, to safety and other specifications of tractors and electrical equipment, to the labeling requirements for various products. A catalog by GATT of such nontariff restrictions by member nations ran into thousands of items. And a 1963 study by the U.S. Department of Agriculture (Agricultural Protection by

Nontariff Trade Barriers, September 1963) shows that in most developed countries over half of domestic agricultural production is protected by nontariff barriers. As tariff rates among industrial countries come down gradually, these restrictions assume increasing relative importance.

A major form of nontariff barrier that received prominent attention in recent years concerns rebates of domestic taxes to exporters. As a general rule GATT forbids export subsidies in all forms including rebates of domestic taxes, the sole exception to this regulation being the rebate of indirect taxes to exporters. Indirect taxes are those levied on the product at some stage of its manufacture or sale, such as the excise or sales taxes in the United States and the value added taxes in Europe. They are all borne eventually either by the final buyer or by the producer, depending on whether the price of the product goes up by the full amount of the tax or by less than that. In other words, the tax is levied directly on products, and only in an indirect manner is it shifted to individuals or productive resources. If and when the product is exported, GATT's rule permits the government to rebate the tax to the exporter.

This permission does not apply to direct taxes—that is, taxes that are levied directly on people or factors of production, such as the income tax or the corporate profits tax. The implicit rationale for this distinction is based on the poorly founded theory that indirect taxes are "shifted forward" and added in their entirety to the final price charged to the consumer while direct taxes are paid at the source, either out of wages and salaries or out of profit, and do not affect the final price of the product. Consequently, only indirect taxes place the exporter on an unfavorable competitive footing compared to his peers in other countries where such taxes may not exist or may not be as high, and only they need to be rebated.

In discussing tariffs we had occasion to note that the incidence of a tax is a complex matter and cannot be determined merely from the way it is levied. In the case at hand there is no theoretical or empirical justification for the distinction made by GATT. Direct taxes may be shifted to the consumer in precisely the same degree as indirect taxes are, depending on market conditions.

Be that as it may, the distinction has implications for trade between Europe and the United States. The United States relies mainly on direct taxes on income and profits to produce federal government revenue, and these are nonrebatable to exporters. This is not true of most European countries. A major component of their public revenue comes from indirect taxes, particularly the value-added tax, which is a tax levied at each stage of the productive process on the value added at that stage. Being indirect, it is rebatable to exporters.

This provision of GATT permits European countries to levy, in addition to the import duty, a border tax equal to the domestic value-added tax and at the same time rebate the domestic tax to exporters. These two measures together are known as border adjustments for internal taxes. With respect to the products affected they are equivalent to a devaluation of the currency. By contrast, the United States levies a federal indirect tax (excise tax) on very few commodities and only those may qualify for border adjustment under GATT's rule.

In GATT negotiations the United States took the position that this rule is arbitrary and places European exporters at a competitive advantage, and that it should therefore be repealed or altered. Failing this, the Administration considered rebating to American exporters the few indirect taxes levied by the federal government or even substituting a value-added tax for the corporate profits tax. But a country's tax system should be based on considerations of efficiency and equity, and not on the foreign competitive position of its industries. For this and other reasons, the value-added tax was not introduced in the United States. However, in 1971 Congress passed the Domestic International Sales Corporation (DISC) law, under which some 2000 export subsidiaries of U.S. companies enjoy deferrment of the federal profits tax (see Chapter 9).

In fact, while GATT's rule may be arbitrary and unjustified, it is not clear that it discriminates against American exporters or, if it does, what its impact is on trans-Atlantic trade flows. It is quite possible that European producers are subject to the same direct taxes (and other social changes) as their American counterparts and in addition must pay the rebatable indirect taxes. Furthermore, under a floating exchange rate, the discrepancy is adjusted for in the exchange rates. In other words, a thorough examination of the entire tax structure and its impact on trade (as well as of government services received by exporters in return for those taxes) is required to estabilsh the claim of discrimination.

Cartels

Not all trade restrictions originate with governments. Some are rooted in business practices and are extensions of domestic monopolistic behavior into the international arena. When a group of business organizations of the same industry located in different countries agrees to limit competition and to regulate markets and restrict trade in some way, it is known as an international cartel. Thus the International Air Transport Association is a one-hundred-firm cartel incorporating all the major international airlines. Its rate-setting machinery consists of three Traffic Conferences, which correspond to geographical areas of the world. The conferences meet annually to set fares and regulate other matters affecting commercial traffic. Agreements require unanimous ap-

proval, each carrier having one vote regardless of size. Fares are then subject
to the approval of the regulatory agency of each carrier's country, which in the
case of U.S. carriers is the Civil Aeronautics Board. In a similar manner,
freight rates along the major shipping routes are set by conferences that include all the major lines serving a particular route.

The Organization of Petroleum Exporting Countries (OPEC) is a cartel
that in the early 1970s—a period of oil shortages—succeeded in raising substantially the price of crude oil and then, on January 1, 1974, again increased
the posted price from $5.11 to $11.65 per barrel.[4] The Arab members of that
cartel also used an oil embargo as a political weapon. However, in the long
run the power of the cartel to raise prices would be restricted by the operation
of market forces as supply increases outside the cartel and demand declines.
On the one hand, oil production is stimulated elsewhere, such as the continental United States, Alaska, and the North Sea, and at the same time alternative sources of energy such as coal, gas, atomic power, and solar energy
are being developed. On the other hand, energy conservation measures and
consumer response to higher prices will lower demand. However, because the
rise in oil prices was highly precipitous, the normal market response to price
increase—that of discouraging use and encouraging substitutes—had to be
telescoped into an extremely brief period.

The success of OPEC in quadrupling crude oil prices in 1973 has created
a drive among developing countries to form cartels in other commodities. Indeed, OPEC may be a precursor to a host of commodity cartels for copper,
bauxite, tin, rubber, and tropical agricultural products. The question "How
many OPECs in our future?" is certainly important in assessing the future
course of inflation in the industrial world and the export earnings of the
developing countries. Although the move toward cartelization is in earnest,
and a bauxite accord among the seven countries[5] that account for nearly
two-thirds of world output was signed in March 1974, it is doubtful that many
cartels will be formed in the forseeable future. Oil is suited for cartel action
because world export is concentrated in the hands of a very few suppliers with
similar interests, and because no substitutes for oil are readily available *in the
short run*. These conditions do not obtain in the case of other commodities,
and previous attempts to raise prices through international commodity agree-

---

[4] The posted price is merely a bookkeeping reference price used to calculate the tax
and royalty payments to the oil-producing countries. These payments amount to around
60 percent of the posted price, yielding $3.05 a barrel before the last increase, and $7.00
a barrel since. The actual c.i.f. import price at the U.S. East Coast ports in 1974 can
be calculated by adding production cost (12¢ a barrel), taxes and royalties ($7.00 a
barrel), the oil companies' profit (between 40¢ and $1 per barrel), and transportation
costs between the Persian Gulf and the United States (between $1.50 and $2.00 a
barrel), for a total of $9 to $10 per barrel.
[5] Australia, Guyana, Jamaica, Sierra Leone, Surinam, and Yugoslavia.

ments were not crowned with success. Bauxite, which is often cited as the next candidate, has substitute aluminum-bearing ores, and indeed the bauxite accord mentioned earlier does not attempt to raise prices or restrict supplies. Similar limitations hold for other products such as copper.[6]

Even in the case of oil, there is an apparent conflict within the OPEC cartel. Saudi Arabia wishes to keep oil prices below the level that would induce the development of substitute sources of energy in the industrial world. With its huge oil reserves considered the sole foreign currency earner for years to come, Saudi Arabia's interest lies in continued world dependence on oil for as many years as these reserves last. It appears very concerned about the U.S. Project Independence in energy and is pressing within the cartel for some price reduction from present levels. Iran, by contrast, has a much shorter time horizon, since its primary oil reserves are lower. It is industrializing rapidly and would like to maximize short-run oil revenues without regard to the long-run market risks. Thus, Iran would like to see oil prices raised even further. While the outcome of this conflict is far from clear, some retreat of prices from their mid-1974 levels is quite possible.

Overt or illicit agreements often exist among major companies in the manufacturing and extractive industries. Their goals are many and varied, but in most cases they seek to fix prices, allocate world markets among the member firms to avoid competition, control technological research and development, and in other ways limit or alleviate competitive pressure. They may or may not tolerate smaller firms that are not members of the cartel and do not abide by its rules, depending on whether the latter's activities really disrupt the agreement or are merely a nuisance. When a major participant decides to opt out of the agreement, as Alitalia did in 1969, the entire operation of the cartel may be disrupted, much to the dismay of other members but to the joy of the consumers.

It is easy to see that cartel agreements are as harmful to the international economy as monopolies are to the domestic economy. They restrict output, misallocate resources, and extract higher prices from the public compared to conditions prevailing under competition. But international cartel action may even work counter to and negate government policies. If the United States and Canada work out a free-trade arrangement in automobiles and parts, a private auto-marketing agreement can render it effectively void. By the same token, an agreement among the large French, British, German, and Italian

---

[6] In the long run, a shortage of resources may develop. With that in mind the *Law of Sea* Conference was organized by the United Nations in Caracas in 1974 (part of continuing deliberations by the world body), where the nations of the world are attempting to develop laws that will govern the distribution of the immense resources in and under the ocean floor.

auto-makers to allocate markets among themselves and fix prices can easily remove all the salutary effects that the European Community hoped to achieve by eliminating official barriers to trade. The same applies to other major industries on the European continent. It does no good to eliminate tariffs and quotas if firms agree among themselves not to invade each other's territory or in other ways avoid competition. It is for that reason that the European Community found it necessary to adopt and hopefully enforce rules of competition in industry.

It is one thing to realize the harmful effects of cartels and another to decide what to do about them. The United States has a relatively strong domestic antitrust tradition. In Europe, by contrast, that tradition is relatively weak, and monopolistic practices are more acceptable. Lately there has been an increasing realization of their harmful effects, and some attempts are being made to curb them. The question is more complex internationally, where much production and trade is carried on by truly international companies that in an economic sense know no political boundaries. Should legislation be enacted to control these companies? Should governments seek to break up international cartels, or should their activities be permitted but placed under governmental control? These questions have to be answered before effective policy can be formulated. In all probability different solutions will emerge with respect to different industries.

Dumping

Another practice of private industry that may or may not become a subject of government action is dumping. Dumping occurs when a commodity is sold to foreign purchasers at a price lower than the price charged for the identical product on the domestic market. The word "identical" makes it difficult to establish the existence of dumping, because in making international price comparisons full allowance must be made for differences in specifications, including packaging and other superficial features. International standards exist for judging whether a commodity has been "dumped."

Government export subsidies are a form of dumping. With respect to manufactured products such subsidies are prohibited by GATT, except for rebates of indirect taxes (which we discussed in a previous section), yet overt or hidden subsidies are common in many developing countries. When it comes to temperate agricultural products, dumping by governments is a common practice even in industrial countries, including the United States. It is simply a byproduct of the agricultural support program, which seeks to maintain prices above their equilibrium market levels, and the concomitant need to get rid of the accumulated surpluses by selling them abroad at reduced prices. Such practices disappear in years of food shortages, such as 1972.

Our main concern is with dumping by private companies unrelated to government subsidies. It is customary to distinguish among three types of dumping. *Sporadic dumping* is disposal on foreign markets of an occasional surplus or overstock; it is tantamount to a domestic sale, and its effects are negligible. *Predatory dumping* occurs when a large home-based firm sells abroad at a reduced price in order to drive out competitors and gain control over the market, at which time it intends to reintroduce higher prices and use its newly acquired monopoly power to exploit that market. Potential rivals may then be discouraged from entering the field by the fear of a repeat performance on the part of the monopolist. This is the most harmful form of dumping.

Persistent dumping is a direct outgrowth of profit-maximizing behavior by monopolists. Consider a manufacturer who holds a monopoly position on the domestic market, where he is also protected from import competition by transport cost or government restrictions. In foreign markets, on the other hand, he faces the competition of producers from the host country as well as from third countries. Translated into economic terms, this situation implies that the response to price change (elasticity) is lower in the home market, where the consumer cannot turn to competing brands, than on foreign markets, where he can. The availability of close substitutes on foreign markets makes consumers highly responsive to price change in either direction. In other words, in terms of lost sales, the cost to the producer of charging a high price is lower at home than abroad. To maximize his overall net return he would be led to charge a lower price abroad, where he must meet competition, than at home where competitive pressure is lacking. Such dumping is harmful to the producers in the country receiving the dumped product, but this damage may be more than offset by the benefit to its consumers from the lower price. It is the existence of monopoly power, rather than the act of dumping, that is most objectionable.

☐ Dumping can be shown with the geometric tools of economic analysis. Figure 15-3 comprises three sectors. From the demand schedule on the home market we obtain the marginal revenue curve (MR_H). The demand on foreign markets gives the attendant marginal revenue (MR_F). Foreign demand is more elastic than home demand because of the availability of competing brands, which are regarded as close substitutes. The two marginal revenue curves (MR_H and MR_F) are added *horizontally* at each price to obtain the total marginal revenue (MR_T) shown in the right-hand diagram. The firm also has a marginal cost (MC) curve, and its intersection with MR_T deter-

Figure 15-3
A Monopolist Facing Separate Markets

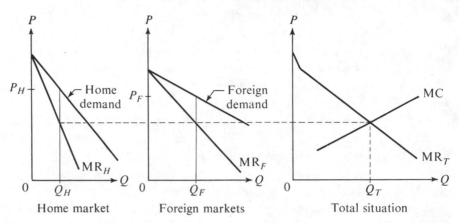

Home market   Foreign markets   Total situation

mines the total quantity (Q_T) to be produced under profit-maximizing conditions.

☐ How will the monopolist divide Q_T between the two separate markets? Profit-maximizing behavior requires the division to be such that the marginal revenue in the two markets is equalized. Marginal revenue is the addition to total revenue derived from an increment of one unit of sales (or subtraction of a unit decrement). If MR_F is greater than MR_H, it would be profitable to shift sales from the home to the foreign market, since the addition to total revenue from the incremental foreign sales is larger than the loss of revenue from the reduced domestic sales. The opposite occurs if MR_H is greater than MR_F. Only equality of the two marginal revenues signals profit-maximizing equilibrium.[7]

☐ This position is shown in Figure 15-3. Quantities Q_H and Q_F are sold on

---

[7] Following is a step-by-step procedure for drawing Figure 15-3:

(a) Draw two separate demand curves in each of the two markets—home market (left-hand diagram) and foreign markets (center diagram). Make the foreign demand curve flatter (more elastic) than the domestic demand schedule.

(b) From each demand schedule, obtain the marginal revenue curve. Graphically this can be done by extending the demand curve to the quantity axis, bisecting the resulting $\overline{0Q}$ distance, and connecting the midpoint with the beginning of the demand curve on the price axis.

(c) For each price, add horizontally the two marginal revenues in the two markets, to obtain total marginal revenue, plotted as MR_T in the right-hand diagram. Its intersection with the marginal cost curve (in the same diagram) yields the total quantity produced.

(d) From the intersection of MC and MR_T draw a straight horizontal broken line to meet the two marginal revenue curves. The points are those at which the marginal revenues in the two markets are equal. They determine the equilibrium division of the output between the two markets: Q_H and Q_F.

(e) Given these quantities, the price in each market is obtained by extending a vertical line from points Q_H and Q_F to the respective demand curves.

the domestic and foreign markets, respectively; by construction they add up to the total quantity Q_T. Given the two quantities, the demand curves (not the marginal revenue) determine the prices prevailing on the two markets P_H and P_F, the domestic price being higher than its foreign counterpart. Indeed, it can be shown mathematically that under profit-maximizing behavior the two prices would be inversely related to the two price elasticities. ∎

One condition necessary for all forms of dumping is separation of the domestic and foreign markets; otherwise, it is always possible for a foreign purchaser to resell the product on the home market and cut into the monopolist's profit. Thus dumping is essentially price discrimination applied to the international arena. Indeed it is easier to practice price discrimination internationally than nationally, because the domestic market cannot be fragmented into separate markets, while both transport costs and government restrictions often form an effective barrier between the domestic and foreign markets. On occasion the pressure of domestic monopolists for import quotas and other restrictions can be traced to their desire to effect such a separation and then practice price discrimination.

In actual practice it is difficult to distinguish the various types of dumping, and government policy, often formulated under pressure from import-competing industries, applies to all of them (although only the predatory variety is demonstrably harmful). The most common measure to counteract dumping in the importing country is the imposition of a countervailing import duty. Such a duty is allowed for in the American tariff legislation, but its imposition requires elaborate proceedings to prove that dumping does in fact exist.

Specifically, antidumping cases involve a two-step investigative procedure. First, the U.S. Treasury Department determines whether an imported product is being sold in the United States at prices below those prevailing in the exporting country ("sales at less than fair value"). In cases of positive findings, the Tariff Commission institutes an investigation to determine whether the American industry "is being or is likely to be injured or is prevented from being established" by reason of such imports. In cases of affirmative determination, an antidumping duty is imposed by the Treasury. Such duties are assessed in addition to the normal tariff, and their size can vary with each shipment, depending on the degree to which the shipment is underpriced. In other words exporters can avoid these duties by raising their export price. Table 15-1 provides a sample of antidumping cases investigated by the Tariff Commission between July 1973 and May 1974, following a Treasury determination of sales at less than "fair value."

Table 15-1

Product	Exporting Country	Was Antidumping Duty Imposed?
Printed vinyl film	Brazil and Argentina	Yes
Concrete reinforcing bars	Mexico	No
Steel wire rope	Japan	Yes
Electronic sorting machines	United Kingdom	No
Stainless steel wire rods	France	Yes
Germanium point contact diodes	Japan	No
Cold-rolled stainless steel sheet and strip	France	No
Elemental sulfur	Canada	Yes
Papermaking machinery and parts	Sweden	No
Calcium pantothenate	Japan	Yes
Expanded metal of base metal	Japan	Yes
Polychloroprene rubber	Japan	Yes
Metal punching machines, single-end type	Japan	No
Primary lead metal	Australia and Canada	Yes
Iron and sponge iron powders	Canada	No
Racing plates	Canada	Yes
Picker sticks	Mexico	Yes

16
International and Regional Trade Organizations among Developed Countries

The thirty years since World War II have witnessed a gradual process of liberalization of international trade of industrial products. The United States, through trade agreements legislation, has been a driving force behind this trend; it induced other countries to offer reciprocal tariff concessions, liberalize quotas, and remove other restrictions. But the institutional framework for multilateral negotiations has been provided by several international organizations that also have established and policed rules of conduct in trade matters and provided a strong impetus to the liberalization process. Internationally they include the General Agreement on Tariffs and Trade (GATT) and the United Nations Conference on Trade and Development (UNCTAD), while regionally they consist of several customs unions and free trade areas. The regional organizations of industrial nations are the European Communities[1] (EC), or Common Market, and the European Free Trade Area Association (EFTA).

These institutions are concerned primarily with trade matters, in contrast to the International Monetary Fund (IMF) and the now defunct European Payments Union, which are, respectively, international and regional organizations dealing with monetary exchange. It is important to recognize, however, that trade and payment restrictions are partly interchangeable in terms of their effect on trade flows if not in their intent. A tariff restricts imports by raising their price, while exchange control lowers imports by limiting

---

[1] Originally called the European Economic Community (EEC), its official name has been changed to the European Communities (EC), since it encompasses the European Economic Community, the European Coal and Steel Community, and Euratom. When discussing its earlier days we refer to it as the EEC, while in current affairs it is called the EC.

the amount of foreign currencies available to finance them. A quota system can discriminate among various commodities and sources of supply by the manner in which the import licenses are issued. But the same end can be accomplished by means of exchange control, multiple exchange rates, and bilateral clearing agreements. Consequently, it is of little value to remove one type of restriction and leave the other intact. A simultaneous attack on both fronts is necessary. This is generally recognized by policy-makers. Thus, members of GATT must belong also to the IMF and must abide by its international currency rules. Similarly, the EEC did not come into existence until the European Payments Union succeeded in abolishing most payment restrictions on the continent.

To place matters in proper perspective, Table 16-1 summarizes the two types of restriction and the organizations set up to deal with them. The distinction is made on the basis of the intent of the policy involved, and even then it is often blurred, as in the case of import quotas. (Institutions set up to foster economic development are not included in our discussion.)

Table 16-1

Trade and Payment Restrictions and the Organizations
that Deal with Them

	Trade restrictions	Payment restrictions
Policy measures	Tariffs, quotas, nontariff barriers, others	Exchange control, multiple exchange rates, bilateral clearing agreements
International organizations	General Agreement on Tariffs and Trade (GATT) U.N. Conference on Trade and Development (UNCTAD)	International Monetary Fund (IMF)
Regional organizations	European Communities (EC) European Free Trade Area Association (EFTA) Customs unions and free trade areas in Central and South America, East and West Africa, and other parts of the world	European Payments Union (EPU) European Monetary Agreements (EMA) The Sterling Area The French franc area

The "payments" side of the scheme was dealt with in Part I. This chapter is concerned with the institutions serving mainly the developed countries that are listed in the "trade" column, although not necessarily in the order in which they are listed. Since proper organization of the material requires certain deviations from chronological order, we begin with the European trade groups and continue with GATT. Discussion of UNCTAD and regional schemes among the developing countries is reserved for Chapter 17.

The European Communities[2]

Perhaps the most significant development in international trade matters after World War II was the establishment in 1958 of the European Economic Community (EEC), sometimes referred to as the European Common Market. Founded by the Treaty of Rome (signed in March 1957), it originally included six countries: West Germany, France, Italy, Belgium, the Netherlands, and Luxembourg. Since the last three nations had already been partly integrated in the Benelux customs union, the original EEC was actually composed of four independent customs areas. In addition, Greece and Turkey hold associate status and expect to become full members. On January 1, 1973, three new members—the United Kingdom, Denmark, and Ireland—acceded to the Community, thereby raising its membership to nine. A five-year transitional period was agreed upon, during which the acceding countries are to adopt all the common rules of the Communities.

The founders of the EEC were motivated by the desire for political integration and considered economic union only a vehicle, albeit an important one, to attain that goal. But as of this writing very little has been accomplished on the political front, and the notes of discord emanating from European capitals are at times stronger than the sounds of cooperation.[3] What meaningful progress there has been has taken place in the economic sphere.

Forerunners

Several organizations whose purpose was to promote economic cooperation in Europe preceded the EEC and in a sense can be considered its forerunners. First, the Organization of European Economic Cooperation (OEEC), encompassing practically all the countries of Western Europe, was established after World War II to coordinate reconstruction plans and channel American aid (under the Marshall Plan) to individual European countries.[4] Head-

---

[2] See footnote 1.
[3] An example of such discord appeared in late 1973 when the Arab oil-producing countries placed an embargo on oil shipments to the Netherlands because of its stance in the Middle East dispute. The other eight members of the European Communities refused to share their oil with the embargoed country, thereby signalling that when a real crunch comes, it is everyone for himself.
[4] The American counterpart organization was the Economic Cooperation Administration. After several metamorphoses, it is now the Agency for International Development (AID) and is engaged in economic aid to developing countries.

quartered in Paris, this organization was also instrumental in bringing about liberalization of intra-European trade by gradually lifting import quotas. The European Payments Union, which led to the elimination of payment restrictions, was an offshoot of the OEEC. Today, with the United States, Canada, Japan, and Australia added to its membership roster, the organization is called the Organization for Economic Cooperation and Development (OECD) and is essentially a coordinative and consultative agency of the industrial nations.[5]

A more direct forerunner of the EEC, and one that eventually merged with it, is the European Coal and Steel Community, established in 1951. Encompassing the original six EEC countries, it abolished trade restrictions and set up a common market for coal and steel products. It laid ground rules such as rules of competition for trade in these products and set up an administrative and judicial machinery to enforce them. In addition, an organization called Euratom provided for cooperation among the same countries in the development of atomic energy for peaceful uses. Finally, mention may be made of the three-nation customs union made up of the Benelux countries, which became part of the EEC, and of various early attempts to integrate the four Scandinavian countries.

This is not to say that the groundwork for the EEC was so well laid that no stumbling blocks needed to be overcome. The obstacles were certainly formidable. But the earlier institutions demonstrated the strong desire for interstate cooperation that existed in Europe. They also provided experience in solving problems and in some sense brought the countries to the brink of an economic union. Perhaps the final push toward integration was given by the realities of international politics, which dictated the need for bigness in international affairs if a country was not to become a "second-rate power" compared to Russia and the United States. To many Europeans this meant regional integration. Indeed, the fact that the European Communities negotiate as one unit in GATT has given them strong leverage in bargaining with the United States. Table 16-2 compares the European Communities with other areas of the world.

Trade Restrictions

The European Communities are first of all a customs union; the member countries abolished all tariffs and other trade restrictions among themselves and set up a common and uniform tariff against outsiders. This was accomplished in several stages during the 1958–68 transitional period. Thus, West German producers have free access to the French market (and vice versa), whereas

---

[5] OECD member governments are Austria, Belgium, Canada, Denmark, Finland, France, the Federal Republic of Germany, Greece, Iceland, Ireland, Italy, Japan, Luxembourg, the Netherlands, Norway, Portugal, Spain, Sweden, Switzerland, Turkey, Australia, the United Kingdom, and the United States.

Table 16-2

GNP and Trade in 1971

	European Communities (9 countries)	U.S.A.	Japan	USSR	Developing Countries
GNP (current prices, in billions $)[a]	644.8[b]	1,000.5	209.0	245.5	410.0
External exports	61.0	44.1	24.1	13.8	60.
Intra-area exports	67.1	—	—	—	—

[a] These dollar figures reflect the official exchange rates prevailing in 1971, grossly over-valuing the dollar. Between July 1971 and mid-1974, the two devaluations of the dollar and its further depreciation as a fluctuating currency vis-à-vis the other Western currencies added up to 18–20 percent. Consequently, in 1974 the European and Japanese GNP's (measured in dollars) would be considerably higher relative to that of the United States than the 1971 figures suggest.
[b] $501.8 billion for the original six members and $143.0 billion for the acceding three.

Japanese and American producers must pay the common external tariff and in this sense are discriminated against. In the case of most industrial products, the common external tariff is the unweighted average of the tariff rates that existed in the constituent countries before integration. An incidental result of this averaging process is that EC tariff rates tend to concentrate around their overall average, with small dispersion. Since France and Italy were relatively high tariff countries while in West Germany and the Benelux countries tariffs were relatively low, the averaging technique meant a decrease for the first two and an increase for the latter. The effect on nonmember countries therefore depended on how their exports to the European Communities were distributed among the constituent customs areas. Those whose exports were traditionally concentrated in Italy and France were harmed less by the creation of the European customs union than those that exported mostly to West Germany and the Benelux countries.

In the 1973–77 period, the three acceding countries are gradually dismantling their tariffs on imports from the original six members (and vice versa) and are adjusting their tariff on imports from nonmember nations to the Common External Tariff of the European Communities. In addition, the expanded EEC has contracted agreements for a free trade area in manufactures with the nonacceding countries of Western Europe so that by mid-1977 free trade in manufactures will prevail throughout Western Europe.

Agricultural Policy

Free trade was established for all products, industrial and agricultural alike. But since all the member countries support their agricultural sector, they needed to develop common farm policies and impose tight and rather unusual import restrictions on many farm products. Not only are the governments directly involved in supporting agriculture, but the farm interests in each country are both deeply entrenched and politically powerful. For this reason, agriculture contained the seeds of the widest diversity of views and the greatest intensity of conflict among the member countries. The farm problem, in fact, presented the most difficult topic in the bargaining process. (This was also the case when the Benelux customs union was formed; Belgium, the most industrially advanced of the three, found it politically necessary to protect its relatively inefficient farm sector from Dutch competition.) It was the subject of numerous and lengthy sessions and twice paralyzed the entire common market. It was on that issue that de Gaulle threatened to withdraw from the EEC and thereby wreck the enterprise.

Consider the case of grains. Before integration, the EEC countries operated independent price-support programs much like those of the United States, and these now had to be merged into one. But their interests with respect to the level of support diverged considerably. The West German farmers, being high-cost producers, campaigned for very high support levels that would keep them in business. The interest of West Germany as a whole would have been served far better by overhauling, rationalizing, and contracting the entire farm economy, transferring the freed resources to the booming industrial sector. But the farm unions exerted powerful political pressure at home, obliging the government to defend their interest. And so the West German official delegation insisted on very high support prices.

The French, on the other hand, pressured for lower support prices: low enough to permit them to undersell their West German competitors but not down to a level that would permit imports from North America, Australia, or Argentina to undercut them. In other words, they wished to reserve for their own grains the great bulk of the EEC market. The United States wanted as low a support price as possible, both to stimulate demand and to lower production inside the EEC, thereby leaving more room for imports. But America was not a party to the negotiations, and as to exerting influence, its moral position was undermined by its own agricultural support and protectionism. As in all cases of diversity, some compromise on the support price was reached after lengthy and laborious bargaining. The system of agricultural protectionism is a byproduct of the internal support system.

Several official terms should be defined for an understanding of the EC import-control program. The *target price* for grains is the support price that the Communities aim to maintain in the major consuming areas within the Communities (the main population centers). Small variations around that target are permitted, and they determine the *intervention prices,* the minimum price at which the Communities buy grains to maintain the floor and the maximum price at which grains are sold out of official stocks to maintain the ceiling. For example, a target price of $4 per bushel and variations of 5 percent around it would produce intervention prices of $3.80 and $4.20. If from the minimum price we subtract the cost of shipping grain overland (say, $0.05) from the port of entry to the main consuming area, we obtain the *threshold price* ($3.75 per bushel for our example). This is the minimum import price that the Communities can tolerate if they are to maintain the minimum intervention price in the main population centers and avoid subsidizing foreign farmers.

In order to protect and preserve the threshold price, the European Communities employ a unique device known as the *variable levy*. It is a tax amounting to the difference between the c.i.f. import price and the threshold price, and it varies with any changes in these two prices. In other words, changes in the internal target price (which indirectly determines the threshold price) or in the world price of grain (which determines c.i.f. import price) would bring about changes in the variable levy.

This levy is more vicious than a fixed tariff as a protective device. Under it, foreign exporters cannot maintain their sales volume by absorbing part of the duty. This would only increase the size of the variable levy. But that is precisely what the customs union wanted. By varying the target price the Communities can regulate the volume of imported grains or the share of domestic consumption satisfied out of imports.

A variable levy is also imposed on imported fruits and vegetables. The equivalent of the target price in this case is the reference price, supposedly based on production costs in the most efficient producing region within the Communities. But this criterion may not be particularly meaningful, since such a producing region may be inefficient by world standards. Also, as a practical matter, the reference price is often determined by intense bargaining between the producing and consuming countries inside the Communities. The variable levy on these imports is the difference between the reference price and the c.i.f. import price exclusive of import duty and domestic turnover taxes. Although the union may impose countervailing duties to prevent the importation of subsidized farm products, it may subsidize its own farm exports and dump accumulated surpluses in foreign countries.

In sum, the common agricultural policy consists of free trade within the Communities, support prices for many products, and highly restrictive import schemes to "validate" the internal prices. In the final analysis, the support price adopted by the Communities determines the level of internal consumption and production and therefore the volume of imports. The interest of foreign exporters such as the United States is served by the lowest support price possible; it is in direct conflict with the interest of producers inside the European Communities.

Figure 16-1

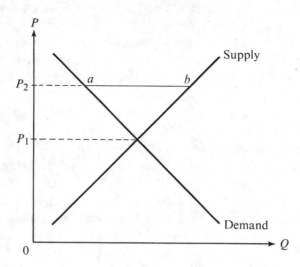

In years of high international prices for food products, such as 1972, the market price rises above the EC target levels, and no Community support is necessary to maintain the price. In that case no variable levy is imposed. Indeed, in 1972 the focus of the European conflict with the United States reversed its "normal" pattern. Large grain purchases by the Soviet Union raised worldwide prices and created shortages, and the European union's interest switched from protection and disposal of surpluses to an attempt to guarantee adequate supply. Thus the quantitative restrictions the United States imposed on the export of soybeans (an important source of protein) brought sharp denunciations from Europe and Japan. But the EEC itself imposed a ban on certain wheat exports at the time. Should the food shortages of 1972–73 prove more than a temporary aberration, the entire emphasis of European Communities policy may shift from protection to stimulation of imports.

Agricultural policy was a major stumbling block to the United Kingdom's entrance into the Communities. To see the problem requires an understanding of the different ways of supporting the farm sector. The Communities operate a price-support program for farm products. In other words, instead of allowing prices to settle at a level that clears the market ($\overline{OP_1}$, Figure 16-1), a higher price $\overline{OP_2}$ is set by administrative decree, and the surpluses ab that are generated are purchased by the authorities. The farmers benefit from the high price and are induced to produce more than would be warranted under free market conditions, while the consumers pay above-equilibrium prices.

By contrast, before they joined the Communities, the British operated a "deficiency payments" system. They let the market price settle at its equilibrium level $\overline{OP_1}$ and made a direct payment to the farmer, the payment amounting to the difference between the equilibrium price and a predetermined price judged to be "fair," say $\overline{OP_2}$. As a consequence, food prices in Britain were much lower than those in the EEC.

Upon accession the United Kingdom had to adopt the Communities price-support system and accept a considerable increase in food prices.[6] Moreover, since the United Kingdom imports a far higher proportion of its food consumption than the rest of Europe, the variable levy collected on these imports would generate a huge contribution to the Communities' agricultural fund and would amount to a large British subsidy of continental farmers.

Also, the increase in food prices and therefore in U.K. production costs (through wage escalator clauses, which attach wage rates to the cost of living) may force a depreciation of the pound sterling. Add to this the damage done to the dominions (such as New Zealand), which depend on the British market for their farm exports (for which some special arrangements had to be negotiated), and the obstacles to an agreement were formidable indeed. Thus, in acceding to the Common Agricultural Policy, Britain has made a considerable sacrifice.

What did Britain gain from entry? First, following the five-year transitional period it is to obtain free access to the Communities market for industrial products, thereby improving its competitive position, and in some industries the resulting expansion of output may also contribute to the lowering of unit cost (that is, economies of scale). Second, at least as important, is the fact that Britain will remove its own protection and open its markets to foreign competition, thereby forcing its industries to operate more efficiently. This, of course, the British could have achieved by unilaterally removing their tariff, but internal political forces prevented such action. In this sense, entry into the union can do for the British what they could actually have done for themselves.

Besides the balancing of economic gains and losses, political and even emotional considerations played an important role in the accession decision. In the final analysis the British government (though not necessarily the majority of the general public), under the Conservative Party leadership, decided that Britain would be better off casting its lot with Europe than maintaining its traditional ties with the Commonwealth. However, when the Labor party came into power in 1974, it sought to renegotiate the terms of the British accession. In particular, it wished to lower Britain's contribution to the EC budget; to reduce food prices and surpluses in the Community; to improve the Commonwealth's and the developing countries' access to EC

---

[6] At least for 1974 the British received special permission from the Communities to subsidize their meat industry to the tune of $53 million, in order to moderate the rise in food prices. In part, this move was designed to dampen the Labor Party's dissatisfaction with the terms of the British accession negotiated by the Conservative Party.

markets; and to reshape the Community's regional policies so as to obtain more help for British industry. The outcome of these negotiations is not known at the time of writing.

Other Rules

The EC agreement goes far beyond trade matters, and thus the Communities are more than a customs union. First they insure free mobility of capital and greater mobility of labor. Workers are free to seek employment anywhere in the Communities, and the number of intra-Communities migrant workers runs into the millions. Second, and this is partly an outcome of the customs union, the treaty provides for coordination of fiscal and monetary policies. For if the member nations give up some measure of independence in commercial policies, such coordination is necessary to minimize balance-of-payments problems. Harmonization of tax and expenditure programs was deemed desirable to place producers in the six countries on an equally competitive footing. Thus, all EC members adopted the value-added tax as the major source of revenue, and the next big push is likely to be for monetary integration.

The Communities hope to attain a monetary union sometime in the 1980s, but the problems involved in reaching this goal are very serious. Thus far, even the "joint float" does not encompass all nine members of the enlarged union, and France had to withdraw from it in January 1974. As of this writing, severe strains are appearing in intermember relations that place in doubt the group's ability to make the political and economic sacrifices necessary for further unity. The problems involved in monetary integration were considered in detail in Chapter 10.

Another feature of the European Communities is that a sizable special fund was set up with the contributions of member countries to help accelerate development in the more backward areas of the union. This aspect of the organization has become known as "regional policy" and is of particular interest to southern Italy and the United Kingdom. In addition, a whole array of rules was promulgated to assure competitive behavior in enterprises within the Communities and to prevent the development of cartels. Finally, a common transportation and energy policy was adopted, and the nine nations cooperate closely (through Euratom) in the development and use of atomic energy.

Political Institutions

A set of political institutions, including a court of justice and a European parliament, were established to deal with Communities matters and to move the EC members closer to political integration.

In the administrative branch of government, there are the Council of Ministers and the European Communities Commission. The council represents the nine constituent governments, while the commission is the supranational decision-making body that presides over the vast bureaucracy at the Brussels headquarters. Although all the day-to-day work is handled by the commission and its staff, the power of final decision is vested in the Council of Ministers, and in important matters decisions must be unanimous.

The relationship between the two bodies can be illustrated by negotiations with foreign powers, as when a nonmember country applies for associate status or a trade agreement with the European Communities. Any such request is initially made to the commission. After study, it is transmitted to the Council of Ministers with the commission's recommendations. The council approves (or disapproves) exploratory talks by the commission within certain terms of reference. Following such talks, the commission returns a recommendation to the council, which also sets terms of reference for the actual negotiations. These are conducted by the commission, with representatives of the member countries as observers. (An exception to this rule was adopted in 1970 with respect to the negotiations for British entry; these were conducted by the foreign ministers themselves.) Any final agreement must be approved by the council. And then there remains the sometimes complicated problem of committing the agreement to writing in all the official languages of the Communities and in the language of the outside negotiating country.

At any one of these stages, individual members of the Council of Ministers are subject to influence exerted through political and economic pressure groups at home. The sum of the EC position is not necessarily limited to a common denominator or reconciled views of nine entities. Each of the nine positions may already be the outcome of political bargaining within each country, and alliances can also be formed across political boundaries. Arriving at a unified stand is no mean feat. During the period in which a foreign request is bounced back and forth between the council and the commission, the applicant has ample opportunity to appeal to political groups in the member states that are sympathetic to its cause for political, economic, or ideological reasons and through them help mold a more favorable decision by the council. In the past, the importance of this leverage was enhanced by the fact that the Community had no coherent foreign policy objectives of its own and did not usually initiate action in foreign affairs. It reacted to foreign requests within the framework of GATT and the rules of other organizations and within the constraints imposed by its own Treaty of Rome.

Any transfer of final decision-making authority from the council to the commission would represent a movement toward supranational power and therefore political integration. A similar movement would be indicated if the commission were given an independent source of revenue (such as all the import duties collected through the common external tariff) to replace the present system of contributions made by member governments. Indeed, the signers of the Treaty of Rome visualized such a gradual transfer of authority. In the 1960s very little was accomplished in this sphere, and the council now makes all final determinations in important matters. Considerable strife within the Communities has indeed centered on the degree of autonomy of the commission. But at the end of 1969 the six member nations agreed that by 1978 the commission would receive all tariff revenue collected on manufacturing imports as well as the levies imposed on agricultural products. It may also call on governments to contribute up to one percent of the internal tax on value added. The final budget of the Communities must also be approved by the European Parliament.

The 1971 budget presented in Table 16-3 shows that the lion's share of the Communities expenditures is devoted to agricultural support, while the bulk of the receipts come from contributions by member states.

Table 16-3

Community Budget, 1971

Receipts (in millions of dollars)		Expenditures (in millions of dollars)	
Euratom research	7.9	Research and investment	
Miscellaneous (e.g.,		(Euratom)	66.6
publications)	12.4	European Social Fund	55.0
ECSC levies allocated to		European Agricultural Fund	2,346.5
administrative expenditure	18.0	Administrative costs of	
Payments by member states		Community institutions	149.2
for Euratom "complementary		Food aid	20.0
programs"	26.7	Reimbursement of member	
Subtotal	65.0	states' costs of collecting	
Community resources and		levies and duties	126.7
direct payments by the			
member states	2,699.0		
Total	2,764.0	Total	2,764.0

The European Free Trade Area Association

Special significance attaches to the EC's relationship with the rest of Europe. At the time of the signing of the Treaty of Rome in 1957, an open invitation was issued to all European countries to join the prospective organization, but for various reasons none except the Six was ready to sign. In particular, Great Britain did not wish to join for three main reasons. The British were generally dubious about the viability of any far-reaching agreement involving both Germany and France. They also did not wish to replace their form of agricultural support with that used on the Continent. Finally, joining the EEC would subject Great Britain to the common external tariff, making it impossible to maintain the imperial tariff preference system within the Commonwealth. More generally, since the avowed purpose of the EEC was political union, the choice was viewed in Great Britain in political and even emotional terms: should it sever the long-standing ties with the Commonwealth and cast its lot with the Continent? Great Britain was not then ready to make the plunge.

Other countries did not join for other reasons. Switzerland, Austria, and Finland felt (or were made to feel) that membership would violate their neutral status in East–West affairs. Switzerland was also reluctant to accept the provision of free factor mobility, fearing an influx of Italian labor. Sweden, Norway, and Denmark did not wish to join and thereby leave Finland "isolated," and in addition they had close economic ties to Great Britain. Only Greece and Turkey later applied for and obtained associate status.

As the EEC moved down the integration road, the British began to view with dismay the prospect of remaining outside. Consequently, they initiated negotiations for membership in the late 1950s. But since it soon became apparent that the obstacles remained unresolved, Great Britain proposed an all-European free trade area in industrial products, which the EEC would join as one unit and all other European countries could join individually. When this proposal was rejected by French President de Gaulle, the British turned their attention to the formation of a smaller trading group, the European Free Trade Area Association (EFTA). Originally consisting of Great Britain, Austria, Switzerland, Portugal, Sweden, Norway, and Denmark (with Finland as an associate member) and headquartered in Geneva, EFTA is in essence a free trade area for industrial goods, with some special provisions for trade in farm products.

A free trade area differs from a customs union in that it does not have a common external tariff, and that difference presents a difficult problem of administration. Since the duty levied on imports from nonmember countries is not the same in all members, while within the area trade is free, there is nothing to prevent imports from the outside from entering the high-duty member nation through a low-duty member, in that way paying only the low rate. Thus the lowest rate in the free trade area on each commodity becomes the effective one for the entire area. This phenomenon is known as "trade deflection." In order to avoid it, the free trade area must retain border checkpoints between its members (unnecessary in the case of a customs union) to investigate the origin of every commodity as it crosses the national boundary. Only if produced within the free trade area is it accorded a duty-free status.

Even this approach can be circumvented. The outside producer can set up a final assembly plant for the product in the member country that has the lowest tariff, with value added accounting for not more than 10 percent of the final product, and ship from there to the entire free trade area. Thus, the integrating nations must decide what portion of the value of each product must be produced within the region in order for it to be accorded duty-free status. In the case of EFTA, the figure is 50 percent, and the rules (known as rules of origin) are enforced through the use of certificates of origin presented at border checkpoints.

The EFTA is a much looser organization than the European Communities. It does not have many of the Communities' institutional features; it has no common economic policies, and unlike the EC, it does not bargain as one unit in GATT negotiations. It was not even conceived of as a permanent organization. Rather it was orginally thought of as a bargaining agent designed to achieve merger with the EEC. For this reason, its schedule of integration closely paralleled that of the EEC. But several rounds of negotiations during the 1960s did not succeed in forming the close link between the two associations that might have ended the division within Europe.

Only in the early 1970s, after de Gaulle passed from the scene, did British Prime Minister Heath succeed in "taking Britain into Europe." On January 1, 1973, the United Kingdom, Denmark, and Ireland acceded to the Communities, with the tariff and other adjustments to take effect over a five-year transitional period. Of the three, Britain and Denmark were former members of the EFTA. Thus, the EFTA was reduced in size from seven to five countries (with Finland as an associate), but the remaining members decided to retain the EFTA as a formal organization. These countries also contracted with the enlarged Community for free-trade arrangements in manufactured products as well as in a few nonmanufactures. Thus by mid-1977 all of Western Europe will have free trade in manufactures.

It is possible to calculate, within a rough order of magnitude, the static effects of EEC enlargement on international trade flows. Accounting for the special arrangements contracted by the EEC (to be described in the next section), it is estimated that intra-area manufacturing trade in the enlarged EEC will be increased by $9.18 billion. This expansion is at the expense of outside exporters as well as of domestic (less efficient) producers inside the Communities. In other words, this figure represents a combination of trade creation and trade diversion. Imports from outsiders are estimated to decline as follows: from the United States, by $2.05 billion; from "other developed countries," by $1.08 billion; and from developing countries, by $0.71 billion. Thus, trade diversion is estimated at $3.84 billion, and trade creation at $5.34 billion.[7] The reduction in imports from the developing countries is concentrated in Asia and Latin America, while the African countries would benefit from a sheltered market in the enlarged European union (see next section).

[7] M. E. Kreinin, "The Static Effects of EEC Enlargement on Trade Flows," *Southern Economic Journal,* April 1973.

For the developing countries, the estimated loss is around 13 percent of their 1970 exports to the nine EC members, while for the non-European developed countries it is over one-fifth. The word "loss" in the present context does not mean actual decline in absolute value. Rather, it implies that outsiders' exports will be less than what they would have been in the absence of EEC enlargement by the indicated amounts. It must be emphasized that this is strictly a "static" analysis, reflecting reallocation of existing resources. Possible dynamic growth effects inside the European Communities may offset in whole or in part the diversionary impact on the exports of nonmember states.

There would also be important changes in the field of agriculture. When the three joiners adopt the Common Agricultural Policy of the Communities, prices of temperate zone products will rise gradually over the transitional period until they reach EEC levels. This will stimulate production and discourage consumption, thereby lowering demand for imports from nonmember countries. Nonmembers will be subject to the variable levies and other import restrictions, while the members of the expanded community, including such agricultural exporters as Ireland, Denmark, and Holland, will have free access. The Food and Agriculture Organization of the United Nations (FAO) estimates a $1.4 billion annual reduction in Europe's import requirements, concentrated in grains, milk, and meat products. The main effect would be felt by exporters of temperate zone products to Western Europe. These estimates assume no lasting worldwide food shortages.

Special Trading Arrangements of the EEC with Developing Countries

Two main factors were responsible for the contracting of special arrangements between the original six-member EEC and groups of developing countries: The preferences previously granted by France and Belgium to their respective colonies in Africa were to be "inherited" by the EEC; and the sheer impact of the integration on certain Mediterranean countries, about half of whose foreign trade is with EEC members, prompted them to negotiate for exemptions from, or reduction of, the Community's external tariff.

The most comprehensive EEC agreement is the one with the nineteen Associated African and Malagasy States,[8] governed by the so-called Yaoundé Convention of 1965, which can be viewed as a natural outgrowth of the Treaty of Rome. The second Yaoundé Convention came into force on January 1, 1970. Under it the associated African countries receive substantial economic

[8] These are: Chad, The Central African Republic, Gabon, Cameroon, and the Congo Republic, which form the Central African (Customs) Union; Dahomey, the Ivory Coast, Mali, Mauritania, Niger, Senegal, and Upper Volta, which form the West African Union; and Togo, Somalia, Zaire, Madagascar, Rwanda, Burundi, and Mauritius.

aid from the EEC ($918 million for five years), through the European Development Fund and the European Investments Bank, and some of this aid is devoted to diversification. Equally important is the special trading relationship between them and the EEC, which has three aspects: preferential access to the EEC for the exports of the African States; preferential access of EEC producers to the markets of the Associated States ("reverse preferences"); and the sanctioning of the creation of regional trading groups among the African countries themselves.

Two regional groupings also emerged among the Yaoundé countries themselves: The Central African and West African Unions (see footnote 8). Members of each group enjoy in each other's market a margin of preferences over those enjoyed by the European Communities (however, even members of the African unions are not placed on equal competitive footing with local producers). In particular, imports from the European Communities are exempt from customs duty but are subject to revenue charges, so that the preferential margin enjoyed by the EC over imports from, say, the United States, is equal to the customs duties. Within the union, members are exempt from part of the revenue charges as well as the customs duties.

A second EEC agreement with countries in sub-Sahara Africa, covering Kenya, Uganda, and Tanzania, was signed in Arusha in 1969 and went into force at the beginning of 1971. This agreement established reciprocal trade preferences on a rather limited scale but contained no provisions for economic aid. The three East African countries thus became associated members of the EEC while retaining their status as members of the British Commonwealth.

Enlargement of the European Communities is likely to bring with it more special arrangements with groups of nonmember countries. In addition to the all-European free trade area discussed previously, the independent commonwealth countries in Africa, the Caribbean, the Indian Ocean, and the Pacific will be offered association treaties or preferential trade agreements with the Communities. Although these "associable states" do not have to make a final choice until 1975, there is considerable resistance among them to accepting the reverse preferences provision of the association treaty, for there is evidence that this provision would force them to pay higher prices for their imports. In addition, the United States exerts pressure against this provision both because it discriminates against American exports to Africa and because it violates the GATT principle of nondiscrimination (see below). Consequently, the European insistence on this component of the association treaty with Africa appears to be weakening.

While the British dependent territories (except for Gibraltar and Hong Kong) are also offered an associate status, no such offer has been made to the major developing members of the Commonwealth—India, Bangladesh, Pakistan, Ceylon, Malaysia, and Singapore. All that is known now is that they will benefit from the Generalized Scheme of Preferences (GSP), which favors all developing countries, and India and Ceylon will enjoy continued suspension of the Community tariff on tea. The GSP will be covered in Chapter 17; the preferences granted under it are more limited in nature than those embodied in the association treaties.

In addition to Africa, the Communities have contracted either association treaties or preferential trading agreements with most countries in the Mediterranean Basin. Trade agreements have also been concluded with Argentina, Uruguay, and Brazil, but these are of a nonpreferential nature.

The General Agreement on Tariff and Trade

Following World War II, the trading nations convened in Havana and agreed to form an International Trade Organization (ITO) based on the charter negotiated there. But since the U.S. Senate failed to ratify ITO it never came into being. As a substitute, the countries decided to set up an informal association, known as the General Agreement on Tariffs and Trade (GATT), to serve as a framework for multilateral tariff negotiations. Since Congress had already ratified the Trade Agreements Legislation, and the new organization could be regarded as merely an instrument to carry out that legislation, the Administration did not consider it necessary to seek special ratification. In fact, despite American participation in all tariff negotiations, Congress has never explicitly recognized the existence of GATT.

Having adopted all the provisions of the defunct ITO, GATT now sets and regulates the code of international trade conduct, which contains three fundamental principles: the principle of nondiscrimination embodied in the most-favored-nation clause (to be discussed below), a general prohibition of nontariff means of protection (such as quotas and export subsidies,[9] except for dealing with balance-of-payments difficulties; and the concept of consultation aimed at avoiding damage to the trade interests of the contracting parties. Special clauses deal with the position and needs of the developing

---

[9] As an interesting aside, it may be noted that subsidies sometimes help rather than hinder economic welfare. In a world with neither agricultural support programs nor other governmental interventions, the United States would be a major exporter of grains. If, under present conditions, the United States removed its export subsidies but retained its price support, it would cease to be an exporter of grains—clearly a move away from the optimal situation. This proposition has general application. In any *piecemeal* removal of the existing maze of governmental interventions, we should be careful that the move is toward rather than away from the best allocation of world resources. For a *partial* movement toward the optimal use of resources is not necessarily an improvement over the existing situation. Each case must be judged on its own merit. This rule applies to a customs union (see Chapter 13), which constitutes a partial movement toward the optimal situation of universal free trade but may result in a reduction in world welfare.

countries. GATT also conducts research into trade matters. But mainly it provides an institutional framework for multilateral negotiations on tariff reduction among the member nations. GATT's membership of eighty nations encompasses all the industrial countries, several East European countries, and forty developing countries, who are responsible in total for 80 percent of world trade. Prior to 1962, member nations conducted five major conferences and several minor ones to negotiate tariff concessions. One lengthy session, which came to be known as the Kennedy Round, was held at GATT's headquarters in Geneva from 1962 to 1967.

The Most-Favored-Nation Principle

All members of GATT are expected to abide by a principle of nondiscrimination in levying tariffs known as the most-favored-nation (MFN) principle. However, such a principle can be conceived of in two forms. Under the conditional interpretation, if country A grants country B a tariff concession, it must also grant it to C (and all other countries), *provided* that C makes A an equivalent concession. The unconditional most-favored-nation principle requires A to apply any concession granted B to all other countries without expecting any equivalent concessions from them.

On the face of it, the conditional MFN appears more equitable. If A and B negotiate mutual tariff concessions, why should these be applied indiscriminately to all other countries that have not conceded anything in return? But in practice the conditional MFN principle poses difficult problems. How does one define an "equivalent concession"? If Belgium and West Germany exchange tariff concessions on cars and bicycles, what should Belgium expect from Great Britain in return for a similar concession on cars? A British concession on bicycles may not be worth much to the Belgians because the British themselves may manufacture bicycles much more efficiently. Thus they will be forced to agree on something else that is in some sense "equivalent." The same would apply to all other members of GATT not party to the original agreement. Translate this to eighty countries negotiating on thousands of products, and the outcome may be total confusion.

Carrying our example further, let us suppose that only countries that come up with equivalent concessions get the Belgian tariff reduction on cars. Belgium would thus be applying differential tariff rates on the same product, depending on its source. By the same token, the countries offering equivalent concessions would charge reduced rates on the products offered only if they originate in Belgium. A multiplicity of rates would prevail there also. And such multiplicity results in unhealthy discrimination between supplying countries and compounds the difficulty of administering the tariff.

It is because of these and other problems that the unconditional MFN principle was adopted by GATT. But since countries do not like to grant what they consider "free concessions," they engage in two practices to skirt the problem. First, each country might offer a tariff concession on a given product only to its major supplier, from whom it receives a reciprocal concession; thus only minor suppliers become "exempt" from the mutual practice. If there is more than one major supplier, the concession is negotiated with all of them, a feasible alternative in the multilateral setting of GATT. Second, countries have adopted a practice of redefining products for tariff purposes. In other words, a product can be broken into several narrow subcategories, the concession applied only to one of them. If supplying countries specialize according to certain features of the product (producing bicycles of a certain size wheel, for example), the concession can be granted only to one supplier and denied to others. In that fashion a country can effectively discriminate against certain suppliers even without a multiplicity of rates on each product. The differential rates charged on product subdivisions are effectively applicable to different sources of supply. But the tariff schedule itself becomes longer and more complicated.

There are several important exceptions to the most-favored-nation rule under GATT. First is a customs union, which involves free trade among members and a common and uniform tariff against outsiders: nonmember countries must pay the common tariff, while member nations pay nothing when crossing into each other's markets, making for discrimination in favor of the members. The EEC was established under this exception. The only proviso attached is that all or most intra-area trade be liberalized and that the post-union common tariff not be more restrictive than the pre-union average tariff of the constituent countries. In 1974 the United States complained that the enlargement of the European Communities had made the Communities' tariff more restrictive for several American export items, such as citrus fruit. After lengthy negotiations the EC agreed to grant compensatory tariff reductions on a variety of agricultural and industrial products of interest to the United States.

The second exception is a free trade area that calls for free trade among members but permits each to levy its own tariff against outsiders. Here the degree of discrimination against nonmember states depends on the tariff levels of the constituent nations, since no common external tariff is introduced. The EFTA, covering all trade in industrial products, was set up under this exception. A third exception allows for preferential treatment on trade between a country and its colonies or dominions. The British imperial tariff system, which grants preferential treatment on intra-Commonwealth trade, was accommodated by this exception, as were the preferences granted in 1957 by the EEC to the African colonies of two of its member states, France and Belgium.

In all cases of deviation from the most-favored-nation clause, the countries involved must seek a GATT waiver to the rule, and a waiver can also be granted under special circumstances not covered by the exceptions above. Outright violations of the principle do occur. Thus, the United States–Canada automobile agreement that liberalized trade in automobiles and their parts between the two nations discriminates against third countries and is in violation of GATT. That is also true of the EC's granting of preferential treatment to the former French colonies (under the Yaoundé convention) when they were no longer under colonial rule and the EC's preferential agreements with Mediterranean countries. Generally, in recent years the nondiscrimination rule has been modified to permit preferences in favor of the developing countries. But even this change cannot justify the reverse preferences embodied in the EC Association treaties.

The Kennedy Round

The major function of GATT is to facilitate periodic multilateral negotiations for tariff reduction, subject to the unconditional most-favored-nation principle. As often as not, the scope of the negotiations is determined by the U.S. trade agreements legislation that prescribed (for the Administration) the degree of latitude in tariff reduction, since the United States is the only major participant that requires prior enabling legislation. Thus the 1961 round, dubbed the Dillon Round after Secretary of the Treasury Douglas Dillon, was made possible by the 1958 four-year extension of the Trade Agreements Act. The latest round, lasting from 1962 to 1967, was negotiated under the authority of the 1962 Trade Expansion Act and was called the Kennedy Round. Since the Trade Expansion Act permitted up to 50 percent tariff reduction on industrial products, the goal of the convening nations was to negotiate such a reduction on broad commodity categories. This seems simple enough. Why, then, did the round last for five years without fully achieving its objective? Although this question is only of historical interest, the answer will shed light on the difficulties that might be encountered in future negotiations.

First, administrative problems were created by the fact that the EEC negotiated as one unit. This placed across the table from the United States a protagonist whose decisions are of major importance simply because of the sheer size of the EEC as a producer, consumer, and trader. No longer could the United States make unilateral decisions with relative impunity, for retaliation by the EEC could be of major consequence. In some sense, therefore, this was a bargaining session between the United States and the European Economic Community.

Of equal importance was the cumbersome decision-making process within the EEC delegation. Ordinarily, each negotiating country, including the United States, goes through a laborious internal process in preparing the list of commodities on which it is prepared to offer concessions and those on which it demands concessions from other participants. Since the economic interests of vast segments of society are involved, this is a lengthy procedure in which conflicting political pressures play an important role. Whereas an individual country can firm up its negotiating position at the end of this line, for the EEC this is just the beginning. The six countries then had to meet at their Brussels headquarters and hammer out a common position that they could take to Geneva. The EEC position already represents substantial compromises following some tough bargaining. It is therefore relatively frozen with respect to further changes. If GATT's sessions require a U.S.–EEC compromise, the change must go back to the EEC headquarters and then to the six capitals for further bargaining and approval. These administrative procedures clearly made any substantive differences difficult to resolve.

What were these substantive differences in 1962–67? The first concerned agricultural products. The European Communities are the major foreign market for U.S. agricultural exports. Consequently, the American delegation insisted at first that there be no industrial agreement without an agricultural one. But the EEC trade position on agriculture was a byproduct of the internal level of support. Since by 1962 the six countries had not yet agreed on the support level, they obviously could not yet negotiate on agricultural trade matters. Internal EEC bargaining over the level of support lasted for over two years, including several months of near paralysis. Once a compromise was reached in Brussels they were in no position to negotiate it away in Geneva. And the United States, with high support prices of its own, was hardly in a strong moral position to castigate others. More than two years of the Kennedy Round were lost in futile attempts in this direction.

With respect to industrial products there was general consensus about the goal of 50 percent tariff reduction. But the EEC delegation balked at the idea of introducing it across the board without exceptions. It contended that because of the so-called tariff disparity, a blanket reduction in tariffs would mean a greater "sacrifice" on the part of Europe than on the part of the United States. In essence it was agreed that the average tariff rates (however measured, and with all the imperfections of that measure) in the United States and the EEC were roughly equal. But while individual rates in the common external tariff are clustered around that average (of, say, 15 percent), the American average is a product of many very high (80 to 100 percent) and many very low (below 5 percent) rates. In other words, the dispersion in the American tariff is much larger than in the EEC. Now the very high rates include considerable "excess protection," and halving them would merely reduce or eliminate this "water" in the tariff but not stimulate imports much. In the case of the very low rates, a 50 percent reduction translates into a mere two or three percentage points—again a cut of minor consequence. By contrast, practically every reduction by the EEC translates into a meaningful decline in the degree of protection.

There are several unsound ingredients in this argument, not the least of which is that it overlooks the likelihood that the American import-demand elasticities are higher than those of the EEC and that therefore any tariff reduction may stimulate imports more in the United States. Be that as it may, the United States conceded the point and the haggling shifted to the definition of disparity and what to do about it. A tariff disparity on a particular commodity was defined to exist if the difference between the American and European rates met two conditions: that one duty was at least double the level of the other and that the difference amounted to at least 10 percentage points. The following example illustrates the double criteria:

| Commodity | Tariff rate (percent) | | Does disparity exist? |
	U.S.	EEC	
A	12	5	No, 10 percentage points criterion not met
B	50	30	No, double criterion not met
C	30	15	Yes, qualifies on both counts

It was agreed that in cases of disparity the low-tariff country would be permitted to reduce duty by one-fourth while the high-tariff country would lower it by one-half. The United States, however, insisted on an exception to this rule when third-country exports are affected most. Assume, for example, that the commodity in question is watches, where the American duty is more than double that of the EEC and exceeds the latter by over 10 percentage points. The EEC would then be permitted to lower the duty by only one-fourth. But the United States is not a major exporter of watches, Switzerland is. The Swiss, who themselves reduce all duties by one-half, would suffer from the U.S.–EEC disparity agreement, which does not involve them directly. Thus this commodity had to be excepted from the exceptions.

In was on this basis that the lists of exceptions to the 50 percent reduction rule were finally developed and negotiated by all participants. And the average reduction finally attained, although substantial, was considerably below 50 percent.

A third bone of contention concerned certain chemicals, the Europeans being adamantly opposed to the American Selling Price (ASP) method of valuation used by the United States for computing duty (see Chapter 13). They demanded that the computation be based on the c.i.f. or f.o.b. import price. But since the valuation procedure had been set by act of Congress, the American delegation had no authority to negotiate it away. What finally emerged on the issue of chemicals was a 50 percent tariff reduction by the United States and a 25 percent reduction by the European countries. However, the Administration undertook to seek legislation for removal of the ASP practice. If and when this was accomplished, the Europeans would lower their tariff by another fourth. But Congress never approved the removal of the ASP.

All this intense bargaining was taking place under the pressure of a deadline emanating from the expiration of the Trade Expansion Act in mid-1967. The end result was an average reduction in tariff rates on manufactured goods of something like 35 percent, which was put into effect by all countries in five equal installments between 1967 and 1972. The American legislation required the agreement to be reached by 1967 but permitted the actual reductions to take place over a subsequent period of time. Developing countries benefited from the concession without having to reciprocate.

What has happened since 1967? Immediately following the conclusion of the Kennedy Round there was considerable enthusiasm, and it was hoped that the trading nations would capitalize on the momentum gained by the agreement and push forward forcefully in the direction of complete freedom of trade. Proposals were discussed in professional and political circles for an Atlantic free trade area, with or without the European Communities, as a fitting culmination to a quarter-century trend of trade liberalization. Also proposed were the elimination of tariffs on manufactured products among all industrial countries and a frontal attack on nontariff barriers. Certainly, very low duties are of nuisance value only and can be dispensed with, and many duties reached such a low level by 1972. The possibility of unilateral concessions on a large scale to developing countries was also widely discussed.

But this optimistic mood gradually gave way to the "facts of life" in the form of increasing protectionist sentiments in the United States. The Trade Expansion Act expired in 1967, and through May 1974 no new trade legislation was enacted; consequently, the Administration lacked authority for any further tariff adjustments. This situation appears to be changing with the submission to Congress of the Trade Reform Act. Should it be enacted into law in 1974, it will clear the way to a new, comprehensive round of negotiations under GATT. Its objectives may go as far as the complete removal of tariffs on all but a few manufactured products or alternatively either an across-the-board reduction or some form of harmonization of rates. Under the harmonization alternative, each of the three major negotiating parties (the United States, the European Communities, and Japan) would lower the tariff rate on every product to the lowest level assessed by any one of the three. Also to be considered is the dismantling of some nontariff barriers to trade and the development of an acceptable safeguard mechanism for domestic industries. Although the agricultural problem may decline in importance because of possible food shortages, the negotiations may prove no less lengthy and laborious than those of the Kennedy Round.

Thus far the discussion has focused on trade relations among the developed Western countries. Before turning to the special trade problems of developing countries, it appears useful to consider East–West trade.

Some Issues in East–West Trade

When it comes to the size and composition of East–West trade, political considerations loom at least as important as economic ones. Judged strictly by population and national income, the potential for trade between the developed market economy countries and the socialist states is vast. The OECD countries occupy one-quarter of the area of the globe, have one-fifth of the world's population, and are responsible for over one-half of the world's industrial production and nearly two-thirds of the world's national income. The socialist countries[10] also occupy a quarter of the globe's area but have one-third of its population, and are responsible for over one-third of the world's industrial output and one-fourth of its national income. Yet East–West trade represents a mere 3 percent of world foreign trade turnover and a like proportion of the Western countries' foreign trade (although it represents a quarter of the socialist states' foreign trade). As can be seen in Table 16-4, Western Europe accounts for most of this trade, while for the United States it is a minuscule share of total trade.

Most of the trade consists of exchange of manufacturing exports from the "West" for the exports of materials from the "East." As such, the commodity composition is similar to that of the trade between the industrialized market economy countries and the developing world.

Political, institutional, and economic forces originating in both East and West, are responsible for the small size of these trade flows and present obstacles to their future growth. Market-oriented economies are generally geared to the satisfaction of consumer wants and permit market-determined prices to govern resource allocation. Even publicly owned enterprises in market economies must function within the market atmosphere. Government economic policies influence the decisions of private units indirectly through the market mechanism, and international trade is an extension of the domestic pricing system to the international arena. By contrast, in centrally planned economies, the economic plan determines resource allocation without regard to market considerations. Often the plan emphasizes the development of heavy industries, with little regard to economic efficiency or comparative cost considerations. Price fixing is largely centralized in the planning commission, and price adjust-

---

[10] Including the USSR, Eastern Europe, Mainland China, Mongolia, North Korea, and North Vietnam.

Table 16-4

Trade[a] of OECD Countries with Communist Countries, 1971
(millions of U.S. dollars)

OECD country or area	Exports to		Imports from	
	World	Communist countries	World	Communist countries
Western Europe[b]	149,233	6,024[c]	155,186	6,243
United States	44,137	384	45,602	228
Japan	24,010	1,147	19,715	944
Canada	17,676	379	15,460	102
Other OECD	5,222	214	9,510	297

[a] Exports are f.o.b.; imports are f.o.b. for U.S.A. and Canada and c.i.f. for Europe and Japan.
[b] Includes intra-EEC and intra-EFTA trade.
[c] Excludes trade between West Germany and East Germany. Estimates for 1970 put West Germany's exports to East Germany at $660.0 million (f.o.b.) and its imports at $545.6 million (c.i.f.).

SOURCE: Committee for Economic Development, *A New Trade Policy Toward Communist Countries*, New York, September 1972, p. 13.

ments are often made to regulate income distribution rather than production. Domestic prices are effectively insulated from external influences.

Foreign trade in centrally planned economies is determined in advance as part of the general economic plan and can generally be described as a residual. This was particularly true in the heyday of autarky, but it also holds true today. First to be determined are the kind and quantity of imports needed to meet the requirements of the plan (for example, to avoid production bottlenecks). Exports are then planned accordingly, as needed, to pay for the desired imports. International trade is carried out within the framework of bilateral agreements. The socialist states do not have convertible currencies and, with the exception of Romania, they are not members of the IMF. Rather, exchange controls are strictly administered, and exchange rates do not relate domestic to foreign prices. The official exchange rate grossly overvalues most socialist countries' currencies. Because domestic prices are insulated from foreign prices and foreign trade is completely monopolized by state trading companies, tariffs lose their conventional significance. The state has direct means of protecting local industry and raising public revenue. The necessary imports are paid for at world prices and are sold domestically at domestic prices, while exports are purchased domestically at the internal prices and are sold abroad at whatever they can fetch on foreign markets. The foreign trade companies need not show profit, and foreign trade prices bear no relation to domestic prices. The state, rather than the relation between domestic and foreign prices, determines what will be traded and in what quantities.

Having decided on the commodity composition and volume of its trade, each socialist state first tries to meet its trading requirements within the socialist bloc. The USSR, Mongolia, and the countries of Eastern Europe[11] are organized in the Council for Mutual Economic Assistance (CMEA or COMECON). Trade among them is governed by bilateral agreements, but imbalances are settled in "transferable rubles." A surplus with one member country can be used to settle a deficit with another; that is, each country needs to balance its exports and imports with the group as a whole and not necessarily bilaterally. The CMEA established the International Bank for Economic Cooperation, which grants limited credit to finance intrabloc trade. Only when the foreign trade requirements cannot be secured within the bloc (for example, because of nonavailability of the products) do the members turn outside. Thus East–West trade is a residual of a residual as far as most socialist states are concerned.

While East–West trade is governed by bilateral trading agreements, the actual conduct of this trade is lodged (in the East) in the hands of state foreign trade corporations that are each responsible for a number of products. It is with them that a private Western company must negotiate. Thus a Western exporter has no direct contact with the final user of his product, be it a store or a factory; nor is a Western importer permitted direct contact with the producers of his goods. This presents an obvious technical complication to the conduct of trade.

While the limitations to trade emanating from the communist bloc are inherent in the nature of its economic system and its preference for autarky and intrabloc trade, the restrictions imposed by the West are essentially political in nature. In 1950, the members of the OECD established the Coordinating Committee on Export Controls (COCOM), which restricts exports of strategic importance to the Eastern countries, and also imposed certain restrictions on the credit terms granted to those countries. While the OECD export restrictions have been liberalized over the years, the United States continued until 1972 to apply its own much stricter controls over trade with the East, and consequently the scope of this trade has been much narrower than that of Western Europe (Table 16-4). Under authorization of the Export Control Act of 1949, succeeded by the somewhat liberalized Export Administration Act of 1969, the President has discretionary authority to impose restrictions on U.S. exports (except for the taxing of exports, which is forbidden by Article I of the Constitution). Operationally, this authority has been used to restrict export to communist countries, while the Trading with the Enemy Act of 1917 was responsible for the embargo the President imposed, until 1971, on trade with China and North Korea.

[11] Bulgaria, Czechoslovakia, East Germany, Hungary, Poland, and Romania.

The main effect of the stricter U.S. controls has been to give an advantage to West European companies, which were subject to the much less restrictive COCOM list. The U.S. embargo on China was lifted by President Nixon in 1971, and in February 1972 the list of restricted export items to China was made comparable to the one applying to the USSR. At that time the President also removed the special restrictions imposed on the exports of foreign subsidiaries of U.S. companies, placing them on the same basis as foreign companies, that is, subject to the laws of their host country. This action was welcomed by foreign governments who had viewed the restrictions on U.S. foreign subsidiaries as an improper intrusion on their sovereignty. Finally, the U.S. control list itself was liberalized and made identical with the COCOM list of the OECD countries. All these actions were taken as a part of a general effort to allay tensions between East and West. But the embargo on North Korea, North Vietnam, and Cuba[12] is still in force. Also in effect are special U.S. restrictions on granting credit to finance exports to the communist countries, despite the fact that their postwar credit rating has been excellent. On the import side, U.S. law forbids granting most-favored-nation treatment to communist countries, except Poland and Yugoslavia. Consequently, most Eastern exports to the United States are subject to the high U.S. statutory tariffs established in 1930,[13] which may be several times as high as the most-favored-nation rates. Depending on the disposition of the issue of Soviet emigration, the Trade Reform Act would change all that if and when it is enacted by Congress.

Eastern bloc countries are very interested in obtaining long-term U.S. credits to finance imports from this country and most-favored-nation treatment for their exports to the United States. With respect to the latter request, a technical question arises concerning the sort of reciprocal concession they can offer. Tariff reduction has no meaning in a centrally planned economy, because the volume of imports and their source are determined by the planning commission and are unrelated to market prices. Thus, when Poland acceded to GATT, a special arrangement was made whereby it undertook to increase its imports from each member of GATT by a given percentage each year, in return for most-favored-nation treatment for its exports and some concessions relating to quantitative restrictions. Romania acceded under a more flexible arrangement, undertaking to increase its imports from GATT members by amounts corresponding to the growth of Romanian exports to those countries. Discussions are currently being held about the accession of Hungary. Some such special arrangement would have to be concluded with any acceding East-

---

[12] However, in 1974, the Ford Motor Company obtained permission to export cars to Cuba from its plants in South America.
[13] Note, however, that this does not apply to much of the present U.S. imports from the USSR, because the duty is zero on raw materials.

ern bloc country. And if and when the U.S. law is eventually changed to permit most-favored-nation treatment for their exports, special arrangements would have to be negotiated with them. By the same token, in the absence of common principles of price formation in the East and the West, a special adaptation of the rules concerning dumping and nondiscriminatory practices would have to be devised.

What trade has taken place between East and West, and where does the common interest lie? The most dramatic transactions in the past between the United States and the Soviet bloc have been the "wheat deals." As long as Eastern Europe and the USSR are unable to meet their grain requirements, they can be expected to continue to display intense interest in importing American and Canadian grain. However, these countries are in the process of expanding their production, with the aim of reaching self-sufficiency. If that target is realized, say by the mid-1970s, large wheat imports would occur only in years of crop failure.

More important is the desire of the socialist states to import sophisticated equipment (such as computers) from the West, as well as Western technology. The technology can be embodied in the imported equipment, or it can be contracted for separately under licensing arrangements or sale of processes and know-how.

Of great importance in recent years have been contracts with Western firms to set up complete plants in the USSR or in Eastern Europe. Since the communist countries do not permit direct equity ownership of such plants (ownership is held by the Eastern European country), these contracts cannot be viewed as direct foreign investments in the normal sense of the word. Rather they have come to be called *coproduction agreements*. While many types or arrangements are covered by this term, in general such an agreement involves a long-term contract under which a Western company agrees to provide capital, technology, and sometimes managerial services for a project in an Eastern country. Ordinarily the contract calls for repayment and a return on investment in the form of products derived from the project, or possibly in foreign currency. Such agreements have been made by West European and Japanese firms in Eastern Europe and the USSR. Thus far, American participation has occurred largely through the European subsidiaries of American companies. But the United States is now exploring the possibility of such agreements for American firms. One field in which the United States is interested is the import of liquefied gas, and two American companies have indicated interest in participating (with Japanese firms) in the exploitation of the Tyumen oil field. The gas would be piped to a port where it would be liquefied and from which it would be exported to the United States.

17
Selected Trade Problems of Developing Countries

We turn now to the interest of developing countries in international trade. It should be emphasized at the outset that foreign trade is not the central issue of the development problem. Exposure to foreign trade does spur development in a variety of ways, but the main impetus must come from within. Economic development requires the generation of a saving–investment process of sizable magnitude within an economic, social, and political environment conducive to growth. However, because of the open nature of their economies, foreign trade is much more important to developing countries than it is to most developed nations. A general discussion of development and its relation to trade policy is beyond the scope of this book; we shall merely be concerned with selected aspects of trade between the developed and developing countries.

Alternative Trade Approaches to Development

Two alternative trade approaches to economic development can be distinguished: import substitution and export-oriented strategies. Under the policy of import substitution, a country imposes high tariffs and nontariff barriers to imports, and behind this shelter it expands domestic production to replace imports. Usually the country starts by producing nondurable consumer goods, which require labor-intensive and unsophisticated techniques. Once this easy stage is completed, further import substitution becomes increasingly difficult. The most usual case is to turn next to the final processing of assembly-type commodities, generating a shift in the composition of imports away from these final products and toward intermediate and capital goods. To do this, the protective structure is escalated by the degree of processing, with final goods being more highly protected than intermediate ones. The effective protection on final goods can at times reach 1000 percent.

This policy can have several results. First, the protective structure has produced many cases in which the foreign exchange costs of the intermediate imported goods are greater than the foreign exchange value of the final products in which they are embodied. This is the "negative value added" phenomenon alluded to in Chapter 13. Second, by restricting the demand for imports, the exchange value of the currency is artificially valued upward as compared to free-market conditions, making it more difficult to export primary or manufactured products. Thus the policy discriminates in favor of import-competing industries and against export industries. Production for domestic consumption is encouraged while production for exports is discouraged. But a unit of foreign exchange saved by import substitution costs more in terms of domestic resources than a unit of foreign exchange earned by exports.

Third, because the domestic market is usually too small to support an optimal-size plant, excess capacity tends to develop. There is empirical evidence that whereas costs per unit in textile and shoe production decline only 10 percent when plant output doubles, in industries such as steel, pulp and paper, and chemicals, optimal-size plants can operate at almost half the per-unit cost of plants of the size that can be sustained by the internal markets of even the large developing countries. Thus the widening of the internal market is one main benefit that accrues from regional integration among the developing countries and the allocation of industries among them (as in the Central American Common Market or in the Andean Group). However, such steps are usually insufficient and must be supplemented by orienting exports toward the developed world. In sum, the fact that specialization and economies of scale cannot be fully exploited raises costs and prices well above the world market level.

Fourth, because the system of protection and other policies subsidize the importation of capital goods (at times coupled with artificially high wage rates brought about by union pressure), there is a strong incentive to use capital-intensive techniques regardless of the country's factor endowments. This is one reason why the rapid growth in industrial production in many developing countries is often not accompanied by a rapid growth in industrial employment. Finally, foreign capital that flows into the protected industries often does not generate export earnings, but instead aggravates the debt-servicing problem.

Because of these problems, several developing countries—for example, Mexico, Taiwan, South Korea, Singapore, and, more recently, Brazil—have opted for an export-oriented strategy. This involves a change in the system of incentives in favor of exports, minimizing or eliminating the discrimination against them. In some countries (such as Mexico and Taiwan), this is done by the establishment of duty-free processing zones, into which inputs are imported duty free and from which final goods are exported after processing. Indeed, it is this policy coupled with the offshore provision in the American tariff law that permits duty-free reimportation of parts processed abroad by American companies (out of U.S. materials) that explains the existence in Mexico of 260 American plants, half of them just south of the California border. Similar extensive operations have been set up in Taiwan. In other cases, tariff rates have been reduced and harmonized, and/or the currency has been devalued (frequent minidevaluations in the case of Brazil). The major effect has been to expand the export of labor-intensive manufactured products and to avoid the establishment of insulated, highly inefficient domestic industries. Although import substitution up to a certain point can be beneficial, the development experience of countries following export-oriented strategy has tended to be more favorable than that of countries developing strictly via import substitution.

However, continued export-oriented growth requires adequate access to the markets of the developed countries, and it is mainly in their demands for freer access to these markets that the developing countries have confronted the developed ones and have thrust their trade problems into the international arena. The focus of this confrontation has been in the United Nations Conference on Trade and Development (UNCTAD).

The United Nations Conference on Trade and Development (UNCTAD)

Most members of the United Nations are developing countries, but the policies of GATT and other organizations have been largely dominated by the score or so industrial nations. On several important grounds the ninety developing countries feel that these policies serve exclusively the interest of developed nations. In order to provide a platform for their demands, in 1964 they initiated an international conference known as the United Nations Conference of Trade and Development (UNCTAD). A second conference was held in New Delhi in 1968, and a third was convened in Santiago, Chile, in 1972. A permanent secretariat of the organization, under United Nations auspices, has headquarters in Geneva. UNCTAD has 141 members. A Trade and Development Board of fifty-five members, which meets twice a year to ensure continuity and implement the work of the conference, has been established as a permanent organ.

Demands Concerning Primary Products

Many of the complaints of the developing nations result from their dependence on the exportation of raw materials and agricultural products, commonly referred to under the heading "primary products." Over three-fourths of their nonpetroleum export earnings are made up of such commodities. Furthermore, in thirty of these countries, over 80 percent of the export earnings are derived from only three leading commodities, and for another thirty-two countries the figure lies between 60 and 80 percent. As a consequence, the price movements of primary commodities are of prime concern to them.

A long-standing complaint of these nations is that their commodity terms of trade, the ratio of the export price index to the import price index, has been declining or deteriorating over the long run. In other words, they can buy fewer imports for a given quantity of their exports. The theories behind the alleged decline in their export prices relative to import prices are many and varied. Much of their trade is an exchange of primary products for manufactured goods. It has been variably claimed that:

1. As world income grows, the demand for manufactured goods expands faster than the demand for primary products, so that the relative price of the latter declines.

2. Because primary products are marketed competitively, their prices are flexible, and any improvement in productivity is partly passed on to the foreign consumers in the form of reduced prices. On the other hand, monopolistic practices in manufacturing make prices rigid in a downward direction, so that the benefits of productivity increases are reaped in the form of high earnings in the producing countries and not in the form of lower prices.

3. The development of synthetic substitutes lowers the demand for many primary materials and thereby depresses their prices.

These and other theoretical arguments were marshalled to support the claim of the developing countries that their commodity terms of trade have deteriorated over the years. But these arguments can be countered by equally convincing propositions on the other side. And more importantly, the legion of empirical studies undertaken since the claim was first advanced early in the 1950s are far from conclusive. (The claim was first advanced as an empirical proposition, and the theoretical rationale for it appeared only later.) The evidence on the problem is at best mixed and fails to substantiate the deterioration thesis. Indeed in the early 1970s there was a sharp rise in the prices of many basic commodities, and in some cases the increase may prove durable, thereby negating the thesis of "secular deterioration in the terms of trade."

Moreover, even a deterioration in the commodity terms of trade is not in itself an indication of decline in economic welfare. It all depends on the cause of the deterioration. To see this, imagine that Brazil achieves a 15 percent productivity improvement in coffee production, thereby increasing the world supply of coffee. If, as a result, world coffee prices decline by 5 percent, Brazil's commodity terms of trade also deteriorate and to the same extent. But the economic lot of Brazilian productive resources still improves by 10 percent. In other words, although Brazil now gets 5 percent fewer imports per unit of exports, it obtains 10 percent more imports per unit of productive services expended on export production.[1]

This alternative concept, the volume of imports obtainable per unit of input employed in the export industries, is known as the "single factoral terms of trade." It is measured by multiplying the commodity terms of trade by the productivity index in the export industries. And in the example at hand it is a better indicator than the commodity terms of trade of the effect of trade on economic welfare. On the other hand, if the price of Brazilian coffee declined because of a shift in world taste from coffee to tea, then the commodity terms of trade would be an adequate indicator.

Economists have developed several concepts of the terms of trade to examine the relationship between trade and economic welfare, and no one term is applicable to all circumstances. It is not sufficient to observe the behavior of the commodity terms of trade in order to determine how a group of countries fares under particular trade conditions.

Additional claims advanced by the developing nations in the area of primary products have to do with agricultural protectionism in the industrial world. Direct quantitative barriers of all sorts are imposed on temperate-zone products, while tropical products are subject to excise taxes in Europe. Both the prices and volume of exports are artificially depressed by such measures. This lowers foreign exchange earnings of the developing countries and seriously handicaps their development efforts, which depend on imported equipment.

Finally, these countries complain of violent short-run fluctuations in their export prices, which in turn generate wide swings in export earnings and in domestic economic activity. Again economic growth is said to be the casualty.

To cope with these real or imagined difficulties, the developing nations press for international commodity agreements to cover most primary products. They wish to have both prices and quantities of traded goods stabilized at as high a level as possible, yielding in essence a disguised subsidy from the developed countries. Even if the developed nations agreed to grant such a subsidy, international commodity agreements are not an efficient way to provide it, for they often result in surpluses, artificially high prices, and misallocation of resources.

Instead, various schemes of compensatory finance have been proposed, under which the developing nations would receive direct monetary compensation whenever their export prices fell below some predetermined level. Administered by an international agency such as the International Bank for Re-

---

[1] The intellectually fascinating case of "immiserizing growth," where technological advance in the export industry increases output and consequently depresses prices by more than the rise in productivity, so as to result in a net loss to society, is more a theoretical novelty than a practical possibility.

construction and Development or the IMF, this would be akin to an income support program and would avoid the pitfalls of price support. Such programs already exist in embryonic form, where the IMF provides special, though limited, "compensatory" drawing facilities to countries suffering temporary export shortfalls due to circumstances beyond their control. Additional facilities are available to finance buffer stocks in connection with international commodity agreements. The International Bank for Reconstruction and Development is also willing to provide assistance in production diversification and commodity stabilization.

Manufactured Products

As for industrial commodities, the main complaint of the developing countries is that the tariff structure of the developed countries discriminates against them. First, rates are high on the labor-intensive simple-technology products in which they are interested. And, while multilateral concessions granted in GATT negotiations are often extended to them without reciprocity, these concessions usually apply to commodities that are too sophisticated for them to manufacture. Indeed, when tariff rates on goods produced in the industrial world were lowered considerably, labor-intensive goods such as textiles were placed under direct quantitative restrictions.

In the second place, the tariff structure of the industrial countries discourages industrialization elewhere. In many cases, rates are low or nonexistent on raw materials and rise gradually with the degree of processing or fabrication to which the product has been subjected. A few examples will illustrate the point. Duties on iron ore are generally negligible, but rates on ingots and other primary steel products are quite steep. Hides and skins are admitted duty free into the developed countries, but tariffs imposed on leather imports are high. The United States admits coconut at 2.5 percent duty but levies rates of up to 20 percent on coconut products. And the European Communities admit raw cocoa at 5.4 percent but charge from 27 to 80 percent duty on chocolate. This means that effective rates of protection on the finished products are much higher (often more than double) than the nominal rates, further accentuating the tariff escalation and reinforcing the incentives of the nonindustrial countries to export goods in their raw form. Certainly the tariff structure they face discourages local processing of the products they export. This effect is abundantly illustrated in the data of Table 17-1. Effective tariff rates in the industrial countries, faced by the main export products of the developing countries, jump from 4.6 percent in their raw form to 22.6 percent in the second stage of fabrication and so on up the line. Imports show a corresponding decline as they move from less to more highly processed goods.

To offset and reverse this structure, the developing countries demanded

Table 17-1

Weighted Averages of Nominal and Effective Tariffs and Imports
from Developing Areas in the Major Industrial Countries
(combined), 1964

Stage of Fabrication	Weighted Averages of Duties		Imports from Developing Countries	
	Nominal	Effective		
1	4.6%	4.6%	$5,663.3 million	71.2%
2	7.9	22.6	1,896.8	23.8
3	16.2	29.7	231.4	2.9
4	22.2	38.4	169.0	2.1

SOURCE: Bela Balassa, "Tariff Protection in Industrial Nations and Its Effect on the Exports of Processed Goods from Developing Countries," *Canadian Journal of Economics,* August 1968, p. 589.

tariff preferences for their manufactured exports in the markets of the industrial countries; they wished to be charged lower rates in the markets of each developed country than competitive products from other industrial countries. Such an arrangement requires a waiver of the nondiscrimination principle of GATT embodied in the most-favored-nation rule.

Analytically, preferences are analogous to customs unions, for they give rise to two static effects on trade flows:

1. *The trade-creation effect:* Tariffs are reduced on imports from the beneficiary countries, which then displace some domestic production in the donor country.

2. *The trade-diversion effect:* The tariff discrimination embodied in the preferences results in imports from third countries being displaced by those from the beneficiary countries in the markets of the donor countries.

A recent study[2] suggests that the structure of effective tariff protection of manufacturing industries in the developed countries is significantly and *positively* correlated with the comparative advantage of the developing countries. Therefore, an across-the-board, duty-free access (without exceptions or limitations) granted to the developing countries' exports could provide them with an incentive to expand industries in which they have a comparative advantage. Conversely, effective protection in the developed countries was shown to be *negatively* correlated with their comparative advantage. Consequently, a truly generalized, limitation-free preference scheme would improve allocative efficiency in the developed countries as well. For insofar as the output displaced is that of

[2] Z. Iqubal, "The Generalized System of Preferences and the Comparative Advantage of Less Developed Countries in Manufactures," (mimeographed), International Monetary Fund, April 1974.

labor-intensive, technologically unsophisticated industries, the resources in the developed countries would be forced to move to industries in which they possess a comparative advantage. But internal political pressures in the donor countries invariably work to limit this effect. As will be seen in what follows, most preferential schemes include restrictions designed to limit the trade-creation effect. The preferences granted by the EC, for example, are most generous on products in which the developing countries have the least comparative advantage.

Since the trade-diversion effect requires that a preferential margin be maintained, once preferences exist the developing countries hold a vested interest in opposing general tariff reduction among the developed countries under GATT.[3]

When preferences were considered in the councils of nations during the 1960s, a host of substantive and administrative problems were raised. Yet sustained pressure from the nonindustrial nations, coupled with East–West politics and the vying for influence in the uncommitted world, kept the issue not only alive but in the forefront of international deliberations. These efforts came to fruition in the early 1970s, when many industrial nations implemented preferential schemes in favor of the developing countries.

The Generalized System of Preferences (GSP)

During 1971–72, Japan and the West European countries introduced preferences in favor of the developing countries under UNCTAD sponsorship,[4] and in the case of the United States such preferences are included in the Trade Reform Bill of 1973. Although it was originally envisaged that all industrial countries would adopt the same scheme in favor of all developing countries (hence the title "Generalized System"), it turned out that the schemes vary greatly in product coverage, list of beneficiary countries, and measures to safeguard domestic output and employment in the donor countries. Because of their importance as major markets, we describe in some detail the EC scheme as revised on January 1, 1974, and the proposed scheme of the United States. It should be noted, however, that the schemes of other European countries are somewhat more liberal in that they place fewer restrictions on the duty-free entry of goods from the developing countries. On the other hand, Canada is likely to introduce its scheme only after the United States has acted.

---

[3] See "The Generalized System of Preferences and the Multilateral Trade Negotiations," UNCTAD, TD/B/C.5/26 (mimeographed), March 29, 1974.
[4] Descriptions of the scheme are available in official UNCTAD documents.

The European Communities GSP

Under the EC scheme, first implemented on July 1, 1971, and revised[5] in 1974, manufacturing imports from developing countries enter the European Communities duty free, while similar goods originating in other developed countries are subject to the most-favored-nation rate, thereby giving a margin of preference to the developing countries equal to the Common External Tariff of the Communities. However, the EC scheme covers only a small part of the Communities' imports from beneficiary countries.

In the case of nonagricultural products (Chapters 25–99 of the Brussels Tariff Nomenclature), the EC system is essentially a duty-free quota. The amount of each product accorded duty-free entry equals the total value of imports in 1971 from the beneficiary countries[6] (basic quota) plus a supplementary quota equalling 5 percent of the 1971 EC imports from nonbeneficiary countries (excluding intra-Communities trade, but including—with the exception of veneered wood and plywood—imports from the Yaoundé countries). In the case of textiles, the two reference years are 1968 and 1970, respectively. Once the ceiling has been reached in any year, further imports from developing countries are charged the full MFN rate of duty, but they revert to duty-free status at the start of the following year. In the case of the "sensitive products" (see below), entry is further restricted by subdividing the ceiling among the EC countries and assigning each member its own quota,[7] so that the quotas effectively become country rather than EC tariff quotas. Because the distribution of the quota among EC members does not match the distribution of EC manufacturing imports from the beneficiary countries, the country quota further restricts the value of the preferences. For the purpose of reimposing the MFN tariff once the quota is exhausted, the EC scheme distinguishes between two types of commodities: sensitive and nonsensitive. "Sensitive" goods are those whose market it is feared will be disrupted by imports from beneficiaries. They constitute over one-half of EC manufacturing imports from the beneficiary countries, and restoration of duty is automatic. For the remaining, "nonsensitive," products; the restoration of the tariff must be ordered by the EC Commission. However, some of the products in the latter category are labelled "semisensitive" and are subject to surveillance. Another

[5] For details, see "Operations and Effects of the GSP of the European Communities" UNCTAD, TD/B/C.5/23 (mimeographed), March 28, 1974.
[6] The beneficiary countries include the 96 developing countries that belong to the "Group of 77" within UNCTAD as well as developing dependent territories, but exclude those countries that have a special tariff arrangement with the Communities (such as the Yaoundé countries). Romania is a beneficiary for certain products.
[7] Benelux, 10.5 percent; Denmark, 5 percent; France, 19 percent; West Germany, 27.5 percent; Ireland, 1 percent; Italy, 15 percent; United Kingdom, 22 percent. The distribution is slightly different in the case of textiles.

restrictive provision is that the preferential imports of each product from any one developing country are not allowed to exceed one-half the total ceiling for that product. For sensitive products this "maximum amount limitation" is often limited to 20 to 30 percent of the total. In the case of textiles thè ceiling is calculated in the same manner, but duty-free entry is accorded only to the seven beneficiary countries[8] subject to the GATT long-term textile agreement (LTA), and to other beneficiaries who undertook, vis-à-vis the EC, bilateral commitments similar to those given in the LTA.[9]

In the agricultural field (Chapters 1–24 of the BTN), the EC grants preferential tariff reduction of 40 percent of the common external tariff on products subject to tariffs, or a similar reduction in the fixed amount of protection for products subject to variable levies. There are, however, many exceptions to this general rule. The average reduction in the MFN duty on all agricultural products covered by the scheme is 6 percentage points.

The quota restrictions severely limit the usefulness of the Generalized System of Preferences in promoting exports of the developing countries, for in many products the normal growth of the developing countries' exports to the EC may soon exceed the prescribed quota. The "rules of origin" governing the GSP further restrict its value to the beneficiary countries. To qualify for duty-free entry, a product must be wholly produced in the preference-receiving country; if imported materials have been used, they must have been subject to "substantial transformation," the general criterion for such a transformation being that it must transfer them to another four-digit BTN heading. However, there are many exceptions to the general rule governing substantial transformation, and a lengthy document explains the industrial transformation that various products must undergo to qualify for duty-free entry. Many developing countries find these specifications difficult to understand and next to impossible to meet. In addition, given the way the program is administered, much of the government tariff revenue given up by the scheme would be absorbed by the European importers rather than transferred to the developing countries' exporters, for in many cases the importers simply offer reduced prices for imports covered by the scheme. Thus, even the so-called revenue transfer is rather limited.

Small as they are, the benefits conferred by the GSP were further diluted by the enlargement of the European customs union from six to nine countries, for two reasons. First, the original British and Danish schemes were relatively liberal; under them, most manufactured imports from developing countries had been admitted duty free. Instead of a system of ceilings designed to limit duty-free imports, they resorted to an escape clause to protect the domestic

[8] Columbia, Egypt, India, Jamaica, Mexico, Pakistan, and South Korea.
[9] Afganistan, Argentina, Bangladesh, El Salvador, Indonesia, Malaysia, Philippines, and Thailand.

industries from "undue disruption." Before joining the Communities, the United Kingdom had offered duty-free access to all but six agricultural products. These provisions were abandoned in 1974 in favor of the more restrictive EC generalized system of preferences. However, to some extent the loss to the developing countries was offset by changes in the EC scheme itself, for the 1974 scheme is somewhat more liberal than the one previously in effect.

A second reason for the erosion in the value of European Communities' preferences is the establishment of a free trade area in Europe. The trade-diversion effect of preferences has value only inasmuch as there are sources of supply over which the developing countries are preferred. After the transitionary period, culminating in mid-1977, the developing countries will no longer be given preference over any West European country. The only nonpreferred suppliers to Europe would be the United States and Japan, with whom the developing nations compete in only a very limited range of products, and the socialist states, who export largely the same products as the developing countries but who are likely to price their exports in such a way as to absorb the preferential margin and remain competitive. Although these statements are subject to several qualifications,[10] the conclusion is inescapable that the EC's contribution to expanding the export market of the developing nations is rather limited. Unfortunately, not much more can be said about the proposed American scheme.

The Proposed U.S. GSP[11]

The Trade Reform Act of 1973 would authorize the President to grant duty-free entry to the exports of manufactures, semimanufactures, and selected other products from developing countries and territories—with the list of beneficiaries to be determined by the President. However, there are several important restrictions in this provision. First, many commodities of particular export interest to the developing countries would probably be excluded by the President, either because they are goods already subject to import relief measures, such as textiles and steel, or because they are politically sensitive items, such as footwear and perhaps watches. The act prohibits the President from designating as eligible for general preference any article subject to import relief measures, and requires withdrawal of preferential treatment from any article that becomes subject to import relief or national security actions. Indeed, in cases where the Tariff Commission determines that injury exists, the President may terminate preferences rather than change the MFN rate to nonbeneficiary countries.

[10] See M. E. Kreinin, *Trade Relations of the EEC—An Empirical Investigation* (New York: Praeger, 1974), Chapter VII.
[11] For further details, see UNCTAD document TD/B/C.5/20 (mimeographed), February 19, 1974.

Second, preferential treatment under the bill would not apply to imports of an article from a particular developing country if that country supplies 50 percent of the total value of U.S. imports *or* $25 million of the article. The $25 million exclusion rule would tend to become more restrictive over time because of inflationary trends. Furthermore, the second restriction makes no distinction between intramarginal and extramarginal exports. Unlike the quota system of the EC, the MFN tariff will apply to all imports of any item excluded by the rule. This constitutes a strong negative incentive for any developing country to export a commodity to the United States, even one dollar beyond the $25 million limit. For that would subject it to MFN duty on all the $25 million plus $1. Also, the two alternative criteria could be made to bite deep if the 50 percent rule were applied to the refined and small commodity subcategories, while the $25 million exclusionary rule was applied to broad commodity categories. The determination of the level of disaggregation would be left up to the Secretary of the Treasury.

A third exclusion states that preferential treatment would not be accorded to any country that discriminates against the United States by granting preferences to other developed countries, unless it provides satisfactory assurances that it will eliminate such preferences before January 1, 1976. This applies to the African states associated with the European Communities[12] and to certain Mediterranean countries that grant preferential treatment to imports from the EC. Countries that do not enjoy MFN treatment (for example, the socialist states) are not eligible for the generalized system of preferences, nor are countries that have expropriated American property. Parenthetically, it might be noted that granting most-favored-nation treatment to the socialist states would be against the interests of the developing countries because the two groups of countries export similar products.

Finally, the U.S. Secretary of the Treasury is empowered to exclude from preferences any article containing less than a specified percentage of value added in the exporting country. It is up to the secretary to determine the percentage of value produced in the exporting country that would qualify a product for preferential treatment, and no legislative guidance is provided.

Regional Integration Among Developing Nations

There is an intense desire on the part of many nonindustrial nations to form regional economic groups among themselves. Customs unions and free trade areas have been established with varying degrees of success in Central America

[12] However, many of these countries may abandon this practice by 1976.

(the Central American Customs Union), South America (the Latin American Free Trade area), and East and West Africa. The main objective in most cases is to enlarge the domestic market.

Many countries adopt an "import substitution" development strategy. Instead of investing in and expanding their export sector, thereby pursuing development along lines dictated by comparative advantage, they impose restrictions on industrial products and set up their own import-substitution industries. This may or may not be justified, depending on the potential viability and competitive standing of these industries once they reach a certain size and become going concerns. They are certainly justified whenever infant-industry conditions prevail. Other arguments advanced on behalf of such "balanced growth" strategy are the interdependence of industries in terms of technology and demand and the unreliability of foreign markets as outlets for surplus products of concentrated production.

But in many cases the developing countries have proceeded on this development course far beyond any conceivable gain and at great cost to their economies in terms of allocative efficiency. Their import-control systems, consisting of tariffs, quotas, exchange controls, and multiple exchange rates, have become correspondingly complicated. Very often the prestige popularly attached to heavy industry is the major force spurring the government to move in this direction. In the end, however, development may be handicapped more than it is helped.

One factor that has an important bearing on the success or failure of such a strategy is the size of the market. The larger the market, the better is the prospect that a new industry can someday reach an efficient size and become viable. Consequently, the small size of the domestic market strongly militates against import substitution. Since it is difficult to gain access to the vast markets of the industrial countries, because of competition from established enterprises and the tariff structure, the developing countries often choose to expand their own markets through regional integration.

In analytical terms there are important differences between European integration and customs unions among developing countries. While in the first case, economic researchers have been mainly concerned with the effect on world welfare, the impact of, say, the Central American Common Market on international trade flows is rather insignificant. The main concern in the latter case is with the effect of integration on the integrating countries themselves, and in that respect, trade creation as well as trade diversion *may* be beneficial. In Europe, trade diversion is considered harmful because it implies misallocation of fully employed resources from more efficient to less efficient pursuits. But in developing countries, the domestic labor drawn into trade-diverting activities may have been formerly unemployed or underemployed, so that its opportunity cost is at or near zero. There is another sense in which trade diversion in a customs union among developing countries may be welcome as "the lesser of two evils"—if the alternative to a trade-diverting, import-substituting customs union is a policy of import substitution pursued individually by the members of the union, each with a small national market. A recent study [12] of the Central American Common Market found the major benefits from integration to be: the savings of scarce foreign exchange (that is, foreign exchange has a scarcity value in excess of its market value), as members trade more with each other and import less from the rest of the world; the utilization of low opportunity cost labor; and the exploration of economics of scale.

An important issue that often crops up with this otherwise desirable approach is the distribution of the gains from integration. Since the integrating area consists of countries at different stages of development, new industries and other economic activity generated by the enlarged markets gravitate toward the most highly developed centers, much to the chagrin of those who represent the more backward regions. In East Africa, the developed center may be the Nairobi area, and in Central America, Guatemala City. This tendency is often referred to as "polarization" of economic activity. The areas that were most advanced to begin with may come to dominate the entire customs union, while the less-advanced areas do not share in the gain from integration. In Central America, Honduras has withdrawn from the customs union, and the entire Central American Common Market has become paralyzed over this issue.[13] To cope with this problem, several customs unions have adopted a scheme of allocating new industries among the nations comprising the union, in the hope of ensuring "equitable" distribution of the gain.

Another common dilemma is the lack of adequate transportation facilities to make the enlarged market economically meaningful. It does little good to establish free trade areas in South America if member countries find it cheaper to ship to North America and Europe than across the Andes. The natural trade orientation of many such members is toward the industrial nations, intracontinental trade constituting only 10 percent of total trade. Without adequate overland transportation facilities, they cannot hope to change that. A final question involves the exchange restrictions with which the developing governments are faced and that are often left intact when trade restrictions are removed. Meaningful integration cannot take place until exchange transactions are freed.

[12] See W. R. Cline, "Benefits and Costs of Economic Integration in Central America," (mimeographed), The Brookings Institution, July 1974.
[13] In the case of the Andean trade bloc (consisting of Chile, Bolivia, Peru, Ecuador, Colombia, and Venezuela), problems arise from the "allocation" of new industries among the member countries. For example, Venezuela is unhappy because it is permitted to produce only heavy trucks and cars.

International Currency Reform

The developing countries are eager for currency reform and for an infusion of new international reserves into the system, for two reasons. They would like a share of the newly created liquidity, for it means additional resources for development. Second, they fear that a shortage of reserves may induce the industrial countries that have balance-of-payments deficits to restrict the outflow of investment capital, which would affect them adversely. Naturally, they endorse the plans for reform that are most responsive to their needs. It is no surprise that the Link proposal, which calls for allocating a large share of newly created reserves to the developing countries, received wide support among them. This is one reason why developing countries generally favor a return to fixed exchange rates; under floating rates there is no need for newly created reserves, and therefore there can be no link between reserve creation and development assistance. Aside from the Link vehicle for obtaining development assistance, they seek a considerable enlargement of financial and technical assistance [14] offered either bilaterally or, preferably, through multilateral channels, and for the untying of the bilateral aid component, thereby increasing its value in real terms.

---

[14] Within UNCTAD, the developing countries also press for more efficient means for obtaining new technology and for technical aid in developing their tourist facilities and shopping services. They are also concerned about the increasing burden of their external debt.

18
International Mobility of Productive Factors

Introduction

Thus far in Part 2 we have dealt only with the merchandise-trade component of the balance of payments. Totally absent from the preceding chapters is an analysis of the capital account. That account was incorporated to some extent in Part 1, where the analysis centered on the implications of capital flows for balance-of-payments policies. Since a country's external position comprises both the current and the capital accounts, both have to be considered in discussing international financial relations. The fact that Part 1 may have been more definitive in treating trade in goods and services than in treating capital flows is merely a reflection of the current state of the art.

By contrast, Part 2 has centered largely on the relation of international transactions to the domestic economy. It deals with the internal factors that motivate trade and the impact of trade (or, conversely, interferences with trade) on a country's well being. Nothing has been said in this context about capital or labor movements. Far from being an accident, this omission is rooted in a long-standing assumption of classical economic theory: In attempting to demonstrate the gains from international trade and explain the commodity composition of trade, it is assumed that factors of production (labor, natural resources, and capital) are free to move only within each country; they cannot move between countries. Despite evidence to the contrary, this assumption lingers on in many a theoretical discourse.

Observing the world around us, we notice a large-scale international mobility of capital. Although much of it is of the portfolio variety, direct investments in foreign countries by multinational enterprises have come to play a dominant role on the world scene. Also, despite social, cultural, and legal obstacles to mobility, people do move across national boundaries, sometimes in great numbers. Finally, while natural resources are obviously attached to their natural location, extracted materials as well as manufactured machinery, both of which are included in merchandise trade, are probably more akin to productive factors (in their economic uses) than to commodities. This, however, is a matter of interpretation.

Productive factors usually move from areas of low remuneration to areas of high remuneration, lowering their supply in the first region and raising it in the latter. The workings of the market then raise the earnings of the migrating factor in the land of departure and lower it in the land of arrival, thus tending to equalize factor rewards the world over. Under the Heckscher-Ohlin theory of international trade, this is what commodity trade is supposed to accomplish. Indeed, under the conditions of that model, commodity trade and factor mobility are substitutes for each other. If factors moved freely to a point where their remunerations were equalized across countries, there would be no international price differentials between commodities and therefore no room for international trade. Only lately have economists begun to develop models that incorporate both commodity and factor mobility,[1] and also to integrate the theory of optimum tariff with the theory of optimum tax on capital flows.[2]

The present chapter takes one rudimentary step in this direction. Relaxing the assumption of immobile capital, it inquires into the costs and benefits of direct foreign investments. Although precise figures are lacking, it is estimated that foreign subsidiaries of American corporations owned $94 billion of direct investments by the end of 1972, while foreign investment holdings in the United States were $14 billion and rising rapidly. Of the total foreign assets owned by American companies, a large share is in petroleum and the extractive industries, but the majority is invested in manufacturing, a large part of it located in Western Europe (see Appendix IV-B).

At the risk of some repetition we shall consider the impact of these in-

---

[1] The following is an example of how the traditional results can change under such conditions: Suppose country A is twice as efficient as country B in the production of two products, so that the price ratio is the same in both countries. Under the Heckscher-Ohlin model, and in the absence of factor mobility, there would be no trade (see Chapters 11 and 12). But with capital mobile, it would flow from B to A to exploit the more efficient environment, thereby raising the capital-labor ratio in A above that of B. Country A would then begin exporting the capital-intensive product and importing the labor-intensive one.

[2] A tariff imposed by a large country (with monopoly power) may affect not only its terms of trade, but also its terms of borrowing. Suppose the EC imports capital-intensive goods from the United States and imposes a tariff on such imports. The terms of trade of the EC would improve and those of the United States, deteriorate. But in addition, U.S. (capital-intensive) exports would decline, reducing the price of capital in the United States. Consequently, the EC's terms of borrowing from the United States would also improve. Similarly, an EC tax on capital imports would improve its terms of trade as well as its terms of borrowing. The optimum tariff on imports would be higher under these conditions than when its indirect effect on capital flows were ignored. (But it would be lower if the capital exporting country exported labor-intensive products.)

vestments on the balance of payments as well as on the economic welfare of the United States. The effect on the welfare of the recipient countries has been widely discussed in the development literature and will be only summarized here. The final section of this chapter discusses briefly the economic implications of labor migration.

Motives for Direct Investments Abroad[3]

Both economic analysis and empirical studies trace the underlying motive for investing abroad to profit expectations. American enterprises invest in foreign countries when the prospects of profit from such investments exceed profits anticipated from alternative uses of the funds. From the viewpoint of the national economy, the "alternative uses" consist of investments in the United States either by the same company or by others that can attain control over real resources by obtaining access to those funds. Thus, when investment funds flow to foreign countries, it may be assumed that, given the investment climate at home and abroad, expected profits (allowing for risk) from an incremental investment in foreign countries exceed the profits expected from such activity in the United States. Factors affecting the relative "investments climate" include the general level of economic activity, existing and anticipated tax and tariff policies, and general institutional arrangements.

But while such a statement lends itself to analysis with the economist's tool kit, it is too superficial for the understanding of business behavior under diverse circumstances. Indeed, when questioned directly about their motives, business organizations may not even mention increased profits. Rather, they tend to emphasize other factors, which in turn have direct or indirect bearing on net earnings. It is important to unravel these basic motivations before one can evaluate the impact of foreign investments.

The factors that contribute to the increased net earnings from foreign investments are so numerous and diverse as to defy an exhaustive survey. At the risk of some oversimplification, I shall lump them into two broad categories. The first category comprises cost or supply considerations that lower the costs of production and distribution, while the second includes market or demand considerations that influence profits by raising total revenue. Since profit is the difference between revenue and cost, whatever factors raise reve-

[3] In recent years, economists have attempted to develop theories that would explain the economic behavior of multinational enterprises. The hypotheses tested have ranged from portfolio diversification (Chapter 4), to sales maximization, to the product cycle theory (Chapter 12), to a desire to maintain a stake in rapidly growing markets, to other factors. However, a cohesive theory of the multinational corporation has not yet emerged and may be years away. For a recent summary of the literature, see J. H. Dunning, "The Determinants of International Production," *Oxford Economic Papers,* November 1973.

nue or lower cost also increase profit. Needless to say, the dichotomy is not clear-cut, and some factors can be classified under either heading.

Cost Considerations

The desire to increase profits by reducing costs certainly plays an important role in foreign investment decisions. It is useful to distinguish between two types of cost-reducing investment. The first arises from the need to obtain raw materials from abroad. Such materials may be either unavailable at home or obtainable only at extremely high costs. But they are essential to the production and sale of final products at home or abroad. Profit opportunities would remain unexploited without them.

Indeed, the vast American foreign investments in the extractive industries are motivated by the fact that the capital must go where the resources are. In a very real sense, the product of such investments is a factor of production *complementary* to the labor and capital employed within the United States. Any diminution in the availability of this resource would directly harm the productivity and remunerations of the other two. This complementary factor includes primary materials, certain agricultural commodities (tropical products), and some semiprocessed goods brought back to the United States for further processing, with the final product marketed either here or abroad. Inclusion of the last item is dictated by the transportation costs of the primary products. When they are prohibitive or very high, the first stage of processing may have to take place at or near the extraction site, with the product brought home in a semiprocessed form. Investments in foreign transportation and communication links, which make possible or cheapen exports from the home country to otherwise isolated regions, can be regarded in the same light. Much of the American investments in developing countries is so motivated.

The second type of cost-reducing investment involves cost other than materials—primarily labor. Although to the company management it makes little difference where costs are cut, the national interest is likely to be differently affected. In the case of extractive industries, the resource whose cost is reduced is complementary to U.S. factors of production, raises the productivity of American labor as well as capital, and often leads to increased production within the United States. In some cases, such as oil, it is essential to the productive process in this country. On the other hand, when foreign investments are designed to lower labor costs, the savings occur in the employment of factors that are competitive with American resources. While such foreign investments raise the productivity of American capital, they tend to lower the productivity of American labor compared to similar investments in the United States.

Perhaps the most potent motive in the second category is the desire to take advantage of lower labor costs in foreign countries. The fact that wage rates in the United States are higher than those abroad is not in itself an indication of higher labor costs. It is simply a reflection of the higher productivity of American labor. But when the wage differentials are not fully offset by productivity differentials, the result is lower labor cost in foreign countries. Industries in which the labor component is high relative to the capital component (the relatively "labor-intensive" industries) would be the first candidates for such cost differentials. But an unfavorable labor-cost differential may appear at times even in capital-intensive industries, when wage rates abroad lag considerably behind increases in productivity. The remarkable wage stability in Europe during the second half of the 1950s certainly contributed to that phenomenon, while a reverse trend may have existed in the early 1960s, as the tight labor market in many European countries had a growing impact on wage rates. Labor-cost differentials can be exploited by producing abroad and selling the final product in the host country, in third countries, and even back in the investing countries.

Another type of saving that can be secured by manufacturing abroad is in transportation costs. When the final product is perishable or has a high weight-to-value ratio, proximity to the main markets becomes very important. It may then be advantageous to replace exports by foreign production.

Government policies often play a direct role in inducing foreign investments. The outflow of capital may be motivated by a desire to take advantage of special tax treatment. More often, tariff policies both here and abroad bring about substantial relocation of plants. Successive reductions of duties by the United States can induce companies to produce abroad for sale in the United States. As the American manufacturer loses his protective tariff he may not be able to compete against lower-cost imports, primarily of labor-intensive products. Consequently, he may set up production facilities in low-cost areas, from which to supply the American market. Likewise, the establishment of the EEC and the EFTA in Europe provided very strong incentives for American companies to invest in the two areas. Such investments enable the producer to circumvent the discriminatory tariff wall he must face when exporting from the United States. And, since each of the two regional groupings provides a large tariff-free market, each facility in one foreign location can supply several national markets. Thus, the plant can be large enough to realize economies of scale and the benefits of specialization. By the same token, there is little doubt that the high Canadian tariff constitutes a powerful inducement for American corporations to invest in Canada. Without it the Canadian market could easily be supplied out of stateside locations.[4]

---

[4] Canadian welfare may either rise or fall from such a policy. The tariff induces a U.S. corporation to set up a subsidiary in Canada. While the subsidiary may yield good profits, the corporation's worldwide profits would presumably fall; otherwise it would

Capital movement has become a substitute for the obstructed commodity movement. The Canadians are clearly inconsistent in proclaiming their dislike of American capital (and the foreign control that comes with it) on the one hand, and erecting a high tariff wall on the other.

Tariff reduction in foreign countries has the opposite effect of making United States exports more competitive abroad, thus lessening the need to produce in foreign countries. In this case, export trade from the United States replaces the potential outward movement of capital. Finally, the devaluation of the dollar in 1971–73 made U.S. investments abroad more expensive, and foreign investments in the United States cheaper.[5] Correspondingly, there occurred a rather substantial increase in the inflow of European and Japanese direct investments into the United States, substantially benefiting the U.S. balance of payments in 1973.

When a large company goes abroad, it sometimes becomes necessary for the enterprises that supply it at home, including banks that provide financial services, to set up overseas branches in order to provide orderly supplies to its foreign subsidiaries.

Marketing Considerations

On an abstract level, there exists a historical pattern according to which firms are induced to set up foreign branches as they become familiar with foreign markets through exports. The general widening of business horizons attendant upon the expansion of international trade leads businessmen to increase their foreign investments. But sheer familiarity is merely an enabling condition. The desire to cater to specific market needs appears to be the real motivation. Initially, dissatisfaction with distribution techniques abroad may stimulate the

---

have set up the subsidiary even without the tariff. Since the corporation's marginal cost of supplying the Canadian market goes up, it would charge higher prices for its products. Hence, the burden of the tariff is split between the corporation and the Canadian consumer. Set against this consumer cost of protection are gains to Canada in the form of higher profit taxes and increased marginal product of labor. The latter gain could be large if prior to the foreign investments Canadian labor were paid more than its marginal social product, due to the existence of underemployment. To these benefits we may add the gain of external economies.

[5] However, the change in the relative price of investments in the United States and abroad is not a satisfactory explanation of the surge in foreign investments in the United States, or of the possible decline in the rate of growth of U.S. investments overseas. For this change is offset by the fact that a given return on U.S. investments abroad is now translated into more dollars, whereas a given dollar return on foreign investments in the United States is translated into smaller amounts of foreign currencies.

Other possible explanations for these phenomena are: (1) Currency overvaluation shrinks the domestic and foreign markets of the firm, resulting in excess capacity, and is an incentive to move redundant capital abroad. (2) If the firm seeks to maximize sales (subject to a minimum profit constraint) rather than profits, overvaluation would lead it to move abroad. Devaluation reverses these trends. (3) Perhaps potential direct investors in the United States have postponed their planned investments in anticipation of dollar devaluation.

establishment of a selling organization, including warehousing and service facilities, to market exports from the United States. As a second stage the company is drawn to set up production or assembly and conversion plants, so as to be close to its customers, provide better services, gear its product lines to local demands in specific markets, and at times satisfy the nationalistic feelings of its customers (or of the local government) and increase their acceptance of the product. However, when mentioning the last factor we should hasten to add that nationalistic feelings also work in the reverse direction. As recent French, Canadian, Mexican, and even British reactions indicate, there is a fairly widespread aversion to American control of foreign-based manufacturing facilities. Such feelings may not apply to minority share holdings, but most American companies strongly prefer majority interest. On balance, however, market and demand considerations constitute a potent factor in stimulating foreign investments. In addition, antitrust legislation in the United States, which often prevents firms from expanding through the acquisition of their competitors, may induce them to purchase such firms overseas.

Foreign Investments and Economic Welfare (Real Income)

World Welfare

It has long been an established proposition of economic theory that free movement of resources is beneficial to the world economy as a whole. When capital is attracted from one country to another by a higher rate of return, it flows from areas where it is relatively abundant and cheap to countries in which it is relatively scarce and expensive, until returns to it are equalized the world over. This flow is bound to be beneficial, because it raises total real output. The contribution of the marginal unit of capital to real output is less in the donor nation than in the host nation; in other words, capital is a relatively more important productive factor where it is scarce than where it is abundant. Thus, the addition to output it brings about in the receiving country exceeds the diminution to output in the giving (or investing) country, causing a net increase in their combined real output.

Host Country

As a general rule, the receiving country benefits considerably from foreign investments. Not only does its real product rise because of the contribution of new capital, but direct foreign investments usually bring with them managerial and technological know-how as well as access to inventions and innovations and to well-developed capital markets. If the level of training of the labor force rises as a result, the foreign capital is said to generate external economies to the benefit of other firms operating in the same industry. Foreign invest-ments help the host country's balance of payments, through both the inflow of capital and the exports of the products produced in the new plants. And finally, as income in the host country rises, so do savings, and the entire economy is consequently placed on a new and higher growth path. In the case of developing countries, an important element in export and growth can be the processing of assembly and component manufactures by vertically integrated multinational companies, who use these components in their opera-tions in other countries.

A partial documentation of host-country benefits is available in a study of the 500 largest U.S. manufacturing affiliates in the United Kingdom. Employ-ing 9.2 percent of the British labor force, their 1970 sales amounted to nearly $6 billion, or 13 percent of the value of total U.K. industrial production. They exported 24 percent of their output (compared with 13 percent for British companies) and were responsible for one-third of the increase in Britain's manufacturing exports over the period 1957–70. The U.S. companies are heavily concentrated in the most technologically advanced sectors of British industry and spend almost twice as much on research and development as their British competitors. Their output per man is one-third higher than the average for all U.K. companies, wages per employee are 23 percent higher than the average, and return on capital has been 50 percent above the average. Finally, less than one in seventy of the personnel in U.S. affiliates in Britain is American, and three out of four U.S. companies are headed by a British managing director.

Against this background, one might puzzle over the strong resentment that American investments generate in various host countries, leading nations like Mexico (in 1972) and Canada (in 1973) to enact laws that, in one way or another, restrict foreign control or takeover of domestic enterprises. To some extent this may be explained by nationalistic or emotional feelings that have little economic foundation.[6] Yet not all charges can be so dismissed; at the very least they should be sorted out and analyzed.

The charge that foreign-owned enterprises exploit labor in the host coun-try and take away natural resources at less than market value is in most cases exaggerated. Exploitation can occur only when monopoly power prevails. When exploration rights for a country's natural resources are sought by many firms, exploitation is unlikely. The host country benefits in terms of taxes, royalties, wages and salaries paid locally, and imported technology. However, when the investing company has monopoly power, "exploitation" is clearly

---

[6] Lest the reader think that such attitudes are uniquely European or Canadian, the huge influx of direct foreign investments into the United States in the 1970s is creating a groundswell of opposition in this country, and demands are heard in the Congress to impose restrictions on such investments.

possible, to the detriment of the terms of trade of the host country. On the other hand, the producing countries can also organize in a cartel and "exploit" the consuming countries, as was done in the case of oil. More serious (and in many cases justified) is the complaint that foreign affiliates of American companies are governed by U.S. policies and laws that conflict with the policies of the host country. The American ban on exports to China until 1972 and the U.S. antitrust legislation that governs American firms are two examples of "justified" complaints. Thus Canada was prevented from exporting potash to China because potash is mined by subsidiaries of U.S. companies, and these could be prosecuted by the U.S. government under the Trading With the Enemy Act.

A third allegation is that the major policy decisions of international companies and their research and development activities are centralized in the home office, leaving only routine work and less technical activities for the employees of foreign subsidiaries. However, in most cases a profit-maximizing company is likely to use local talent to the extent that it is available, especially when the firm is subject to considerable pressure to do so. The charge that American companies are insensitive to local business practices in labor relations and other areas may be correct, but it is often the local practices that contribute to inefficiency and slow down economic growth. Finally, certain countries object to being "dominated" by foreign firms and especially dislike having their high-technology industries controlled by foreign capital. The charge of political domination is probably exaggerated, and in any case it does not fall within the purview of the economist. But the concentration of American capital in the technology- and science-intensive industries is to be expected, because the United States possesses a comparative advantage in these areas. However, far from being injurious, the imported technology is highly beneficial to the host country. In sum, although there are possible losses, on balance the capital-receiving country reaps a considerable gain in most cases.

Investing Country

Such a gain is not the likely outcome for the donor or investing country (for example, the United States). In order to isolate the effect of foreign investments on American real income from its impact on other economic magnitudes, we assume that the economy is operating at full employment and that it is continuously maintained at or about that level by fiscal and monetary means. Also, the balance of payments is assumed to be in equilibrium and to adjust rapidly and smoothly to transfers of capital via a freely fluctuating exchange rate. The question posed under these circumstances is how to distribute the aggregate savings generated by a fully employed economy[7] between domestic and foreign investments so as to maximize real national product (or income). Put differently, will real national product be maximized if the distribution is left strictly to market decisions exercised by a multitude of profit-maximizing enterprises—if the location of each investment project depends on expected after-tax earnings here and abroad?

The answer is that, particularly in the manufacturing sector, foreign investments are likely to proceed considerably beyond what is warranted by the national interest, for several reasons. First, there are several types of risk that the firm may not fully consider before going abroad. The risk of unfavorable public regulations, such as regulations of profits, repudiation of loans, or even confiscation, affect the individual firm whether its investments are at home or abroad. But the national economy suffers only if the investments are abroad.

Second, there is a revenue loss to the U.S. government. In order to avoid double taxation (on grounds of equity), foreign investors are permitted to credit income taxes paid abroad against their domestic tax liability. Only the difference between the host country tax rate and that prevailing in the United States accrues to the American government. In deciding where to invest, the private firm compares expected after-tax profit here and abroad, since it is a matter of indifference to it which government receives the tax. But with corporate taxes ranging up to 48 percent of earnings and constituting a major portion of government revenue, this is of great concern to the national government. A foreign investment yields tax revenue mainly to the host government, while the same investment in the United States yields profits that are taxed by the American government. Under present institutional arrangements, foreign investments benefit the national interest only if after-tax profits abroad exceed net earnings before taxes in the United States. To some extent this fiscal loss is offset by the need for public expenditures to service home investments, a need that is absent in the case of foreign investments.

To recapitulate, for the private investor, the relevant comparison is between net-of-tax returns abroad and net-of-tax returns at home. In terms of world efficiency of resource use, the comparison should be made between gross returns abroad and gross returns at home. But in terms of national interest, the relevant comparison is between returns on investment made abroad after foreign tax and returns on investment made at home before tax. The

---

[7] The full-employment assumption is important at this point. If the economy suffers from considerable unemployment because of insufficient demand, then foreign investments have little or no opportunity cost in terms of forgone domestic investments. All that is important in this case is to channel domestic savings into investments, be they foreign or domestic.

national interest is served only if the former exceeds the latter. For the United States, this national interest criterion was not met in the 1960s, for the return on foreign investments net of foreign taxes fell short of gross domestic return.

Third, investments affect the productivity and remunerations of capital as well as labor and land. An addition to the capital stock, whether here or abroad, has the following effects: (1) Total real output rises as an increasing volume of capital is combined with a relatively stable amount of other resources, mainly labor and land; (2) the productivity of the incremental unit of capital, and therefore the rate of return to existing capital, tends to decline as the capital stock rises in proportion to other factors; and (3) the productivity of labor and land, and their rate of remuneration, tends to increase as each unit of these resources is combined with an increasing volume of capital in the productive process. The private firm is concerned only with the rate of return on capital when deciding where to locate its investment. The national view, on the other hand, cannot overlook the implications to other factors of production. In the case of foreign investments, it is the productivity of foreign labor and land that would rise. If the investments are undertaken at home, these benefits accrue to domestic resources. The point is abundantly illustrated by the American corporations that set up processing plants in Mexico just south of the border with the clear intention of bringing the finished product back to market in the United States. The incentive for doing this is the lower wage cost in Mexico. In the process, Mexican labor gains, and American labor loses as it is deprived of the use of the capital that crosses the border.

Combining the last two criteria, the national interest is served when returns on investments made abroad after foreign taxes exceed the returns on home investments before taxes by more than the loss in productivity of domestic labor.

Furthermore, the expansion of production attendant upon the new investments usually carries with it indirect benefits. These include improvement in the quality of labor, better production methods and techniques, and superior forms of organization. In the case of foreign investments, these benefits would be lost to the domestic economy. Indeed, since foreign investments usually require American technical and managerial talent, the movement of such personnel abroad deprives the U.S. economy of their services.

This loss to the domestic economy may be more than offset in many instances by one important factor: The productivity of domestic capital and other resources depends in some measure on the capital endowment of the rest of the world. This phenomenon is most evident in the case of foreign investments in the extractive industries. The provision of primary materials from foreign sources (when domestic sources are not available) increases the productivity of domestic factors of production, since such materials are complementary to American capital and labor. In this case, there is a gain rather than a loss to domestic factors. Since a large share of U.S. investments in developing countries tends to concentrate in the extractive industries, the foreign policy objective of promoting investments in these areas (either as a substitute for or in addition to foreign aid), happens to coincide with the domestic economic interest.

On the other hand, over half of our investments in developed countries (primarily in Western Europe) is concentrated in manufacturing industries. Here the argument outlined in the previous paragraph holds only to a limited extent. It is therefore suggested that foreign investments, motivated by private profit considerations, would exceed the amount justified by the national interest when that interest is defined as the maximization of real domestic income.

This is a fairly short-run analysis. In the long run, American investments abroad would increase income and output in the receiving countries, inducing increased imports from the United States. American output and employment would thereby be favorably affected. These benefits have not been included in the considerations above.

Finally, and most emphatically, the above argument constitutes a strictly one-sided view of America's stake in international investments. The other side is the rapidly increasing foreign investment in American manufacturing industries. In this case, the indirect benefits accrue to the United States, while the investment process proceeds beyond what is warranted from the foreign national point of view.

Even if the net result of these narrow calculations is unfavorable to the United States, it is not a sufficient reason to tax or otherwise restrict the outflow of investment capital, just as this country can ill afford to impose an "optimum" tariff on imports. It is hardly in keeping with the U.S. position to define its national interest so narrowly. Any interference with the free flow of goods, services, and capital runs counter to our overriding interest in global economic growth and in smoothly functioning international trade and finance. On the other hand, the analysis demonstrates that the assorted complaints emanating from various European quarters that American investments are in some sense harmful to them are unfounded. Far from being damaging, these investments have made a tremendous contribution to the host countries. The international diffusion of technological innovations and managerial knowhow that takes place through the vehicle of the multinational enterprise sufficiently illustrates its contribution to the international economy. Despite these advantages, various governments dislike the idea of large economic entities who know no political boundaries, who can escape governmental regulations, and who can upset the international financial markets. Consequently, suggestions are being put forward for some form of international surveillance over the multinational corporations, and for the establishment of a code of behavior (plus enforcement machinery) to which they would have to adhere.

☐ Taxing the Multinational Corporation   Within the United States, the immediate policy problem is the tax treatment of direct foreign investments. We have seen that if the United States is viewed (wrongly) strictly as the investing country, then the current tax treatment is inconsistent with the national interest. Moreover, it is alleged by the backers of the Hartke-Burke bill (which is supported by labor unions and other organizations) that the federal tax laws discriminate against investments in the United States and in favor of foreign investments and therefore constitute an inducement to invest abroad. Of late these charges have been applied with particular force to the taxation of oil company profits.

☐ Major federal tax concessions granted U.S. investment abroad are the foreign tax credit; tax deferral; and various tax preferences given to Western Hemisphere trade corporations, corporations of the developing countries, and investment in the U.S. possessions. The first two concessions constitute the bulk of the loss in U.S. government revenues; we first consider the foreign tax credit.

☐ Foreign-incorporated subsidiaries and branches of American corporations are entitled to credit against their U.S. income tax the full amount of taxes they pay to foreign governments[8] (at all levels of government). Thus, if the subsidiary earned $1000 and is operating in a country where profits are taxed at the rate of 30 percent, it would pay the host government $300 in taxes. Since the U.S. profit tax is 48 percent, its total tax liability to the American government is $480, from which the corporation is entitled to subtract the full amount of the foreign tax. Its tax obligation to the U.S. government becomes $480 − $300 = $180. If the foreign tax rate were 48 percent, the U.S. tax obligation of the above corporation (on its foreign profit) would be zero. But the credit cannot exceed the U.S. tax of 48 percent, so a corporation operating in a foreign country where the tax exceeds 48 percent has a total foreign and U.S. tax in excess of 48 percent[9] even though it pays no U.S. taxes.

---

[8] This credit is not given on dividend income earned on foreign portfolio investments, that is, where the U.S. corporation own less than 10 percent of the foreign corporations' stock.

[9] However, U.S. corporations operating in more than one foreign country can choose to calculate this credit either on a country-by-country basis or on the overall basis of lumping together taxes paid to all foreign governments. The latter option is advantageous if one foreign country levies a tax in excess of the 48 percent U.S. tax rate and another less than that, for the effective rate of the latter is increased with respect to the tax credit.

☐ The rationale for this tax credit derives from the (public finance) principle of "horizontal equity," which requires equal tax treatment of persons with equal incomes. Applied to the case of foreign investments, the aim is to ensure the same total rate of taxation on domestic and foreign investments; it can be construed as horizontal equity on the international level.[10] An alternative way of interpreting horizontal equity is to apply it on the national level. This would call for treating foreign paid taxes in the same manner as domestically paid state and local taxes. The latter taxes are treated by the federal government as a cost of doing business. Thus, in our example, the $300 tax paid to the foreign government would be subtracted as a *business deduction* from the $1,000 profit, yielding taxable income of $700. The 48 percent U.S. federal tax would then be levied on the $700, resulting in a U.S. tax bill of $336. The total U.S. and foreign tax paid by the company on its overseas profits would then be $300 + $336 = $636, instead of the current $480. This in essence is what the Hartke-Burke bill proposes. Also in 1974, congressional committees were considering some limitations on the foreign tax credit enjoyed by the oil companies, as part of a general program to increase their taxes. An even "tougher" alternative would be to disregard the foreign paid tax altogether and levy the 48 percent U.S. tax on the total foreign profit. The total tax bill of the corporation used in our example would then be $300 + $480 = $780.

☐ The tax deferral provision permits the profits of foreign incorporated subsidiaries of U.S. corporations to enjoy a deferment of U.S. tax until the profit is remitted to the parent corporation.[11] At best, this implies an interest-free loan from the U.S. government to the corporation for the duration of the deferral. But since much of the earnings retained abroad are reinvested in fixed assets, this virtually amounts to a permanent exemption from U.S. tax. Deferral clearly introduces a non-neutral incentive to invest abroad and is difficult to defend on the grounds of either equity or efficiency. No such deferral is available on domestic investments, and the Hartke-Burke bill proposes the elimination of the deferral provision on foreign investments.

☐ It has been estimated that eliminating the deferral provision and switching from the tax credit to the tax deduction principle would have netted the U.S. Treasury an additional income of $3.3 billion on 1970 income flows. Three other types of tax concessions[12] were estimated to cost the U.S. treasury about a quarter of a billion dollars.   ■

---

[10] Carried to its extreme, this principle would require the U.S. government to grant a subsidy to companies paying foreign taxes in excess of 48 percent.

[11] In contrast to the tax credit rule, tax deferral applies also to dividend income on portfolio investments.

[12] The other types of tax concessions are less costly to the U.S. government and can be justified at least in part by the need to foster economic development: Western Hemis-

Effect on the U.S. Balance of Payments

We now drop the assumption of automatic balance-of-payments adjustment to capital outflow and ask what impact foreign investments have on the external accounts of the United States. On the face of it, the balance of payments is affected adversely by the amount of the capital outflow. But this oversimplified statement overlooks the relationship between the various balance-of-payments items and ignores the fact that capital outflow generates "favorable" movements of both goods and funds.

When an American enterprise is established abroad, it immediately generates exports in the form of capital equipment and materials required for plant operations. Available evidence indicates that on the average such sales from the United States constitute about one-fourth of the initial investment. Thus, even in the first year of operation, a $1 million investment requires a payment outflow of only three-fourths that amount. In subsequent years, the export of spare parts, materials, and additional equipment tends to continue, further mitigating the initial impact on the balance of payments.

Next, there is the return inflow of earnings into the United States. In any given year, this inflow represents earnings on investments made in past years. Put differently, an investment made at one time will generate earnings in subsequent years. It has been estimated that on the average, the payback period on the original capital outflow (about three-fourths of the original investment made) is five to ten years.

Finally, we come to the least tangible aspect of foreign investments—the sales of the products of American subsidiaries, most of which are marketed in the host country, the rest being shipped to the United States or to third-country destinations. There are great variations in this mix among different industries and countries, but since we do not know what the situation would be in the absence of foreign investments it is rather difficult to evaluate their effects.

A large portion of the sales of American subsidiaries to the United States consists of raw materials, agricultural products, and semiprocessed goods that cannot be produced at home or that can be produced only at much higher cost here than abroad. Since the United States depends on these materials in whole or in part, their importation from American foreign subsidiaries bene-

---

phere trade corporations are provided a 14 percentage point reduction in their U.S. tax liability, representing a tax preference worth some $115 million. Corporations operating in developing countries were permitted to retain a variety of tax preferences (which were eliminated for other corporations in the 1962 Revenue Act), preferences that account for another $50 million or so. Finally, certain investments in U.S. possessions are treated as foreign corporations for the purpose of the U.S. income tax, at an estimated cost to the treasury of $85 million.

fits the balance of payments. When it comes to manufacturing imports, the answer depends on whether such sales displace domestically produced products or products that would have been imported anyway. In the first case, the effect on the balance of payments is unfavorable, in the second case favorable.

Sales of American subsidiaries in foreign markets (the host country as well as third countries) present a similar problem with respect to American exports. Sales of foreign mining and agricultural enterprises probably do not affect U.S. exports very much because this country is a net importer of these products. Manufactured products, to the extent that they displace exports from the United States, have an adverse effect on the balance of payments, but to the extent that they displace actual or potential foreign sources of supply, their impact on the U.S. balance of payments is favorable. We can only speculate on the relative importance of the two cases. Much of the activities of American subsidiaries in Canada probably fall into the first category, while a large portion of the European operations belong in the second.

Most successful foreign ventures are expanded over the years through the investment of retained earnings and locally borrowed funds. Their book value rises correspondingly. These assets are obviously not available to the American monetary authorities for coping with the balance-of-payments deficit, which is essentially a liquidity problem. But they do strengthen the long-run creditor position of the United States and as such inspire confidence in the dollar as a transaction and reserve currency, thereby increasing the willingness of foreigners to hold and accumulate dollar assets.

Finally, foreign investment is a two-way street, and the 1970s are witnessing a rapid growth of European and Japanese investments in the United States.

International Trade Theory and the Multinational Corporation[13]

The emergence of the multinational corporation (MNC) as a major force on the world economic scene—with MNCs accounting for over one-fifth of all production—raises the fundamental question of whether the traditional theory of international trade still provides an adequate explanation of the economic world. Unfortunately, analytical work on this topic is still in its infancy, and the present exposition is of necessity rudimentary. It attempts to determine which strains of the theory are now the most relevant, and to what extent we need to modify important propositions made earlier in this book.

[13] This section draws heavily on a seminal paper by M. W. Corden, "The Multinational Corporation and International Trade Theory" (mimeographed), University of Reading Paper No. 10, 1974. I am grateful to Professor Corden for permission to use the material.

The Phenomenon of Transfer Pricing

International trade theory assumes that commodities are traded on world markets between independent firms, at market-determined (sometimes referred to as "arm's length") prices. But today, between one-fourth and one-third of world trade in manufactures is conducted *within* firms. MNCs tend to be vertically integrated companies, each producing the intermediate products (for example, components) necessary for its production processes as well as an array of final goods. Various components are manufactured by affiliates or subsidiaries of the corporation located in different countries, while the final assembly plants may be located in still other countries. As components and materials move through the production processes, they are transferred from one subsidiary to another, and therefore become part of international trade. Consequently, a large and growing proportion of international trade is actually intra-firm exchange. And the items entering such trade will be valued according to considerations other than those determining competitive market prices.

In this exchange the corporation is interested in maximizing its overall after-tax profit, rather than the profit of individual subsidiaries. The prices charged by one subsidiary on sales to another (located in a different country) may differ significantly from world prices. In particular, they are designed to minimize overall corporate income taxes and tariff payments. If tax rates differ between the countries in which the corporation's subsidiaries are located, the corporation will shift profits from the high to the low tax country. Thus, if the country into which components are imported has higher tax rates than the components-exporting country, the corporation will artificially *raise* the price of the components; it will underprice them when the opposite is the case. In this fashion it tries to maximize the profit of the subsidiaries in the low tax country and minimize the profit of the subsidiaries in the high tax country. A country raising its profit tax rates may find itself losing rather than gaining tax revenue as MNCs adjust to the new rates.

Secondly, the multinational corporation attempts to minimize its tariff payments to the country that imports components and intermediate goods. This requires underpricing of the exported components and involves shifting profits from the supplying to the importing country subsidiary. If profit tax rates are higher in the former than in the latter, the benefit to the corporation from lower duty reinforces the gain from reduced profit taxes. In the reverse case, the two effects operate in opposite directions. In all cases, the pricing policies of the MNC on intra-firm (but international) trade would be affected by both tariff and tax considerations, and not merely by market forces of supply and demand.

Some implications of this phenomenon may now be considered. If a government imposes a tariff on some intermediate products to protect domestic producers, then the protective effect may be negated by an MNC exporting such products from other countries (to its assembly plant in the said country) at reduced prices. The government can counteract this by fixing component prices for duty purposes at a level close to market prices, by imposing antidumping duties, by converting *ad valorem* into specific tariffs, or by replacing tariffs with import quotas. But if the aim is to raise revenue, the tariff-imposing country may actually gain from the understatement of import values induced by an *ad valorem* tariff. Its loss in customs revenue could be more than offset by a gain in profits taxes. On the other hand, a government wishing to counteract the evasion of profits taxes by MNCs overstating import values can impose or raise tariffs on the imported components. This would encourage the corporation to underprice the components.

Finally, the computed effective rates of protection can be grossly distorted by transfer pricing. In particular, components can be so overpriced by the corporation that they appear to cost more than the value of the final product, when the latter is valued at world market prices. This would give rise to an apparent case of negative value added (see Chapter 13). Even in the absence of such an extreme result, the (erroneous) impression conveyed would be that of high protection for production of the final product in which the imported inputs are used (because the portion of the imported input in the value of the final product would appear artifically high).

The Commodity Composition of Trade

To what extent are the traditional theories (which rest on the assumption of immobile productive factors) still adequate in explaining the pattern of international trade? We can think of the MNC as a huge enclave cutting across national boundaries. It is an independent economic entity that buys and sells factors and goods, makes and receives transfers, and creates various external effects. Its linkages to a country in which it is operating include the employment of local labor and locally raised capital, the purchase of local materials and the sale of final products on the local market, the payment of taxes, and the creation of various externalities.

The corporation employs some productive factors that are immobile between countries—unskilled and skilled labor (and perhaps land)—in conjunction with two factors which move freely within the corporate empire, capital and knowledge. The return to the two mobile factors would be equalized between countries. But the relative factor intensities of the two immobile factors are still relevant in explaining the pattern of trade: skilled-labor-intensive products would be produced in countries relatively well endowed with skilled labor, and unskilled-labor-intensive products, in countries relatively well endowed with unskilled labor. This result underscores the importance of labor skills, as against the simple capital/labor ratio, in explaining the commodity composition of trade, and is consistent with recent empirical findings.

Secondly, the two mobile factors would be attracted to those countries that are generally more efficient because of their physical infrastructure, political stability, and similar conditions. Such countries would therefore tend to produce and export products intensive in capital and knowledge. Thirdly, the existence of transport costs, tariffs, and other import restrictions would induce the corporation to locate close to its main markets and to produce for them. On the other hand, when increasing returns to scale are important, there would be a tendency to limit the number of locations in which any product is produced. The existence of transport costs, along with economies of scale, will confer on countries with large domestic markets a comparative advantage in economies-of-scale-intensive goods.

The skill level of countries can change over time, requiring the MNC to adjust its production configuration. Likewise, knowledge may not be perfectly or instantly mobile within the corporation; it may take time to spread. To that extent, a corporate adjustment may be required, yielding a model similar to the product cycle approach.

This rudimentary discussion demonstrates—however tentatively—that it is possible to use various strains of the traditional theory to explain location and trade in a world in which MNCs play an important role.[14] Explanations are no longer as simple as the Heckscher-Ohlin model and must be adapted to the new circumstances. Labor skill, economies of scale, transport costs, and the product cycle have become important ingredients. As long as some factors are reasonably immobile and others mobile, rather familiar results may be obtained. This takes us one point further. The concern of traditional economic theory with the effect of trade and import restrictions on the welfare of a country remains valid despite the increased mobility of factors in the MNC world. This is so because certain factors—namely labor, human capital embodied in the labor force, and capital embodied in the country's infrastructure—are largely immobile. And it is precisely the welfare of the immobile population that governments often seek to maximize.

---

[14] The multinational corporation, engaged as it is in transfer pricing, also raises questions in connection with the mechanics of the balance-of-payments adjustment. Does the MNC react to currency devaluations, other changes in relative prices, changes in interest rates, and general monetary-fiscal measures in a manner predicted by traditional theory? These questions, still largely unexplored, have implications for the relative efficacy of alternative international financial systems.

International Migration of Labor

People do not move around as freely as capital. Not only are there legal obstacles to migration, but families tend to be socially and culturally rooted in their country of birth, and such attachments are difficult to overcome. Even language is sometimes a formidable obstacle to migration. Yet there are instances of large-scale migration; in particular, the European Communities have provided for free mobility of labor among the member countries. Indeed, highly industrialized areas in Europe (such as West Germany), where labor shortages are common, employ migrant workers on a large scale. Movement of people around the British Commonwealth is another instance of such migration. Such cases are rare enough that they do not negate the proposition that labor is a relatively immobile factor. Yet it is important to examine the welfare implications of labor movements when they do occur.

Under ordinary circumstances people migrate in response to economic incentives; they move from their own country to another where they can command higher remunerations. The consequences of such migration parallel those of capital movements. In most cases migration is beneficial to world welfare. The migrants' marginal productive contribution, which is reflected in the income they command, is generally higher in the new country than in the old. In other words, the loss in production to the country from which they depart falls short of the gain in production to the country in which they settle, resulting in a net gain to the world as a whole. However, if the primary incentive to migration is not financial, the outcome may be different.

Migration also affects the income of factors of production in the two countries. If the migrating population owns no capital, the workers remaining behind in the country of emigration benefit while those in the country of immigration lose from migration, whereas the opposite consequences apply to capital.

So far we have treated labor as a homogeneous factor of production. But in reality it is not, of course. Workers possess varying degrees of skills and training. International migration of highly trained scientific, technical, academic, and medical personnel, notably from the Commonwealth to Great Britain and from the developing countries to Europe and North America, has reached such proportions that it has become a cause for political and intellectual concern in many quarters. It is feared that this "brain drain" deprives developing countries, especially, of badly needed talents, and some concerned politicians have even suggested the imposition of restrictions on the movement of highly trained people.

As was pointed out earlier, when migration takes place in response to economic incentives, it raises the real income of the world as a whole. The developing countries very often simply cannot productively absorb people who are highly trained in certain subjects, because the absorptive capacity of an economy depends on its level of development and degree of industrialization. On the other hand, there may be a crying need for these people in the industrial world. Thus, the difference between their marginal products in the two countries is very large, with migration easily resulting in a net gain to the world. In some cases, however, the country of emigration may justifiably demand compensation against the losses it incurs (even when these fall short of the gain to the receiving country), especially if it has spent resources to train the migrating specialists.

There are only two cases in which the "brain drain" may cause a loss to the world as a whole: first, if diverse taxation (or wage control) systems in the two countries distort the relationship between remunerations and marginal productivity so that educated people move to countries where their marginal productivity is lower than in their native country; second, and more important, when the activity of educated people contributes to the welfare or productivity of others in the country of residence, a contribution known as "externality," and that externality is greater in the country of origin. Contributions such as leadership capacity, originality, creativity, and inventive ability come to mind as examples of "externalities." But it is only when they are not rewarded through the market that externalities may reverse the gain to world welfare that comes from free migration. It is true that on occasion there may be a strong case for compensating the countries of emigration for their losses. But the world as a whole nearly always benefits from unobstructed migration of trained manpower. Moreover, the case against restrictions on international migration goes far beyond economics. It rests upon the cherished principles of personal freedom.

Appendix I

A Formal Proof of the Domestic Multiplier Formula

The successive rounds of increase in consumer expenditures following an exogenous rise in investments can be tabulated with the induced changes in consumption shown as lagging one period behind the changes in income that brought them about. The last column in Table I-1 shows the cumulative effect on national income, where the changes in Y are a convergent series. In order to determine the number toward which this series converges after infinite time periods, we denote the MPC by c and quantify the ΔY for each period in terms of ΔI and c.

Table I-1

The Multiplier Mechanism with Continuous Injection (ΔI)

Period	ΔI	Induced ΔC, lagged one period behind ΔY (MPC $= 0.8$, MPS $= 0.2$)	$\Delta Y = \Delta C + \Delta I$
1	20	0	20
2	20	$20 \times 0.8 = 16$	36
3	20	$36 \times 0.8 = (20 \times 0.8) + (20 \times 0.8^2)$ $= 28.8$	48.8
4	20	$48.8 \times 0.8 = (20 \times 0.8) + (20 \times 0.8^2)$ $+ (20 \times 0.8^3)$ $= 39.04$	59.04
5	20	$59.04 \times 0.8 = (20 \times 0.8) + (20 \times 0.8^2)$ $+ (20 \times 0.8^3) + (20 \times 0.8^4)$ $= 47.232$	67.232

Letting ΔY_i denote the rise in income in period i, the increases in the first five periods become:

(1) $\Delta Y_1 = \Delta I$

(2) $\Delta Y_2 = \Delta I + c\Delta I$

(3) $\Delta Y_3 = \Delta I + c\Delta I + c^2\Delta I$

(4) $\Delta Y_4 = \Delta I + c\Delta I + c^2\Delta I + c^3\Delta I$

(5) $\Delta Y_5 = \Delta I + c\Delta I + c^2\Delta I + c^3\Delta I + c^4\Delta I$

Extrapolating to the final period, *n,* we obtain the equation

(6) $\Delta Y_n = \Delta I + c\Delta I + c^2\Delta I + c^3\Delta I + c^4\Delta I + \cdots + c^{n-1}\Delta I$

To solve equation (6), we multiply both sides by c and obtain

(7) $c\Delta Y_n = c\Delta I + c^2\Delta I + c^3\Delta I + c^4\Delta I + c^5\Delta I + \cdots + c^{n-1}\Delta I + c^n\Delta I$

Next we subtract (7) from (6):

$$\Delta Y_n - c\Delta Y_n = \Delta I - c^n\Delta I$$

$$\Delta Y_n(1 - c) = \Delta I(1 - c^n)$$

And the multiplier is

$$k = \frac{\Delta Y_n}{\Delta I} = \frac{1 - c^n}{1 - c}$$

Since $c < 1$, as n grows very large, c^n becomes very small and approaches zero at the limit. Therefore,

$$k = \frac{1}{1 - c} = \frac{1}{1 - \text{MPC}} = \frac{1}{\text{MPS}} = \frac{1}{\text{leakage}}$$

Foreign-Trade Multiplier with Foreign Repercussions

It is possible to derive foreign-trade multiplier formulas that allow for foreign repercussions. Consider a two-country world in which country A and country B trade with each other. (In all notations, then, subscripts A and B denote country.) Any change in exports or imports of one country necessarily constitutes an equivalent change in imports or exports of the other. Each country's total income or production (Y) consists of consumption (C), investment (I), government purchases (G) of domestically produced goods and services, and exports (X):

$$Y = C + I + G + X \tag{1}$$

Changes in national income, brought about by any autonomous change in expenditures, are made up of changes in these four expenditure components:

$$\Delta Y = \Delta C + \Delta I + \Delta G + \Delta X \tag{2}$$

For simplicity, assume that I and G are strictly autonomous. While a change in them generates changes in income, the reverse is not true; changes in Y do not induce changes in I or G. On the other hand, consumption and imports (that is, exports of the other country) have both autonomous and induced components. All autonomous changes in expenditures, from what-ever source (investments, government expenditures, or the autonomous part of consumption) will be lumped under the term "exogenous shock" and labeled A. They are not affected by income changes.

By contrast, changes in income do induce changes in consumption, sav-ings, and imports, the extent of which is determined respectively by the marginal propensities to consume (denoted by c), to save (s), and to import (m). In notational form:

$$\Delta C = \text{MPC} \times \Delta Y = c\Delta Y$$
$$\Delta S = \text{MPS} \times \Delta Y = s\Delta Y$$
$$\Delta M = \text{MPM} \times \Delta Y = m\Delta Y$$

where for each country $c + s + m = 1$. Remembering that the ΔX of each country equals the ΔM of its trading partner, we can now rewrite equation (2) for each of the two countries, incorporating the above assumptions:

$$\Delta Y_A = c_A\Delta Y_A + m_B\Delta Y_B + A_A \tag{3}$$

$$\Delta Y_B = c_B\Delta Y_B + m_A\Delta Y_A + A_B \tag{4}$$

That is, the change in income of each country is made up of the antonomous change in expenditures (A), an induced change in consumption, and a change in exports equaling the induced change in imports in the other country. It is the last item that forms the link between the two countries and reflects the foreign repercussions.

Given equations (3) and (4), our aim is to find an expression for ΔY resulting from an exogenous shock in terms of the marginal propensities and the autonomous change. From (4) we obtain:

$$\Delta Y_B - c_B\Delta Y_B = A_B + m_A\Delta Y_A$$
$$\Delta Y_B(1 - c_B) = A_B + m_A\Delta Y_A$$

$$\Delta Y_B = \frac{A_B + m_A\Delta Y_A}{1 - c_B} \tag{5}$$

Next, we substitute (5) into (3) to obtain:

$$\Delta Y_A = c_A\Delta Y_A + m_B\frac{A_B + m_A\Delta Y_A}{1 - c_B} + A_A \tag{6}$$

$$\Delta Y_A(1 - c_A) = A_A + m_B\frac{A_B + m_A\Delta Y_A}{1 - c_B}$$

Multiplying through by $(1 - c_B)$:

$$\Delta Y_A(1 - c_A)(1 - c_B) = A_A(1 - c_B) + m_BA_B + m_Bm_A\Delta Y_A$$

Then,

$$\Delta Y_A[(1 - c_A)(1 - c_B) - m_B m_A] = A_A(1 - c_B) + m_B A_B$$

Remembering that $c + s + m = 1$, we obtain

$$\Delta Y_A = \frac{A_A(1 - c_B) + m_B A_B}{(1 - c_A)(1 - c_B) - m_B m_A} = \frac{A_A(s_B + m_B) + m_B A_B}{(s_A + m_A)(s_B + m_B) - m_B m_A} \quad (7)$$

By similar procedures, we can solve the equations for the second country and obtain ΔY_B. Notice that $1 - c = m + s$ is the inverse of the domestic multiplier. Given an increase in autonomous expenditures (A) in whatever form in one or both countries, equation (7) tells us the resultant change in A's income.

Consider now the case in which the autonomous increase occurs in country A's exports to country B, arising from, say, a shift in B's taste for A's products. In other words, starting from an equilibrium position, A's exports to B (and B's imports from A) suddenly rise to a new annual level, higher than the old one by amount A. This produces a "shock" in A equal to A_A. But in country B, the autonomous increase in imports may or may not produce an equivalent negative shock.

At one extreme we may assume that all the new imports into B substitute for domestically produced goods. Thus the effect of the increase in imports is to reduce the autonomous component of domestic consumption (lower the consumption function) by the same amount. This is likely to approximate reality in a large diversified economy (such as the United States) that produces close substitutes for all its manufacturing imports. In terms of our notation, this means that $A_A = -A_B$. Formula (7) then reduces to

$$\Delta Y_A = \frac{s_B A_A + m_B A_A - m_B A_A}{s_A s_B + s_A m_B + m_A s_B + m_A m_B - m_A m_B} \quad (8)$$

and the foreign-trade multiplier of A is

$$k = \frac{\Delta Y_A}{A_A} = \frac{s_B}{s_A s_B + s_A m_B + m_A s_B} \quad (9)$$

or, dividing by s_B,

$$k = \frac{1}{s_A + m_A + m_B(s_A/s_B)}$$

At the other extreme, assume that country B absorbs the entire increase in imports out of savings, so that there is no autonomous reduction in the consumption of domestic goods. In that case $A_B = 0$, and equation (7) becomes

$$\Delta Y_A = \frac{A_A(s_B + m_B)}{(s_A + m_A)(s_B + m_B) - m_B m_A} \quad (10)$$

The multiplier is

$$k = \frac{\Delta Y_A}{A} = \frac{s_B + m_B}{s_A s_B + s_A m_B + m_A s_B} \tag{11}$$

or, dividing by s_B,

$$k = \frac{1 + (m_B/s_B)}{s_A + m_A + m_B(s_A/s_B)}$$

Between the two extremes fall any number of cases where the impact of the increased imports in B is absorbed partly out of savings and partly out of consumption of domestic goods. Clearly the assumptions embodied in equation (9) constitute the most dampening effect that country B can have on the multiplier of country A through foreign repercussions.

Appendix II

Stability of the Foreign Exchange Market

Chapter 5 analyzed the "stability conditions" of the commodity markets on the assumption of infinite supply elasticities. Its first section developed the conditions under which devaluation of the home currency (pound sterling in our example) would improve (or revaluation would worsen) the balance of payments; that is, move the balance of payments in the desired *direction*. These elasticity conditions are directly related to the stability of the foreign exchange market, and here we shall move from the "commodity space" to the "foreign exchange space" to demonstrate the relationship.

The foreign exchange market is said to be *stable* if changes in the exchange rate induce a movement in the balance of payments in the "right" or desired direction. Devaluation is expected to improve and revaluation to worsen the country's external payments position. In other words, stability requires that devaluation of the currency (pound sterling in our example) increase the difference *inpayments minus outpayments,* both expressed in terms of dollars. It was seen in Chapter 5 that, in terms of the foreign currency, outpayments necessarily decline while inpayments may move in either direction. But even when inpayments decline, stability may obtain if the decline is outpaced by a greater reduction in outpayments.

Figures 5-6 and 5-7 in Chapter 5, which demonstrated these relationships with respect to commodity trade, can be transformed into a chart that deals directly in foreign currency flows. Consider Figure II-1. The horizontal axis measures the quantity of foreign exchange demanded (outpayments) or supplied (inpayments). It is equivalent to the area under the $S_{\text{U.S.}}$ or $D_{\text{U.S.}}$ curves in the upper part of Figures 5-6 and 5-7, respectively—that is, the quantity of merchandise traded times its dollar price. Movements along the vertical axis (the exchange rate) are equivalent to shifts in, say, the supply curves in the commodity space as the exchange rate changes. The exchange rate is defined in such a way that devaluation is portrayed as moving upward along the vertical axis; that is, as a great number of domestic currency units per dollar.

414

Figure II-1

The U.K. Foreign Exchange Market

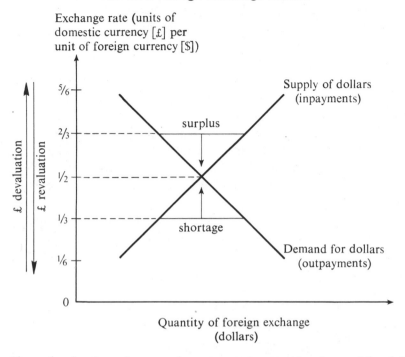

Exchange rate (units of
domestic currency [£] per
unit of foreign currency [$])

£ devaluation

£ revaluation

⁵⁄₆

²⁄₃

½

⅓

⅙

0

Supply of dollars
(inpayments)

surplus

shortage

Demand for dollars
(outpayments)

Quantity of foreign exchange
(dollars)

Since devaluation always reduces outpayments, the demand-for-dollars curve is of necessity negatively sloped. It is derived from Figure 5-6 by relating changes in the exchange rate to changes in the area under $S_{\text{U.S.}}$ at points of equilibrium (quantity times dollar price). The inpayments line is derived from the upper panel of Figure 5-7 by relating the areas under the equilibrium points on $D_{\text{U.S.}}$ to changes in the exchange rate as reflected in shifts of $S_{\text{U.K.}}$. The inpayments line can slope in either direction, depending on the elasticity of $D_{\text{U.S.}}$ In Figure II-1 it is positively sloped, showing a rise in the supply of dollars in case of devaluation and reflecting a relatively elastic $D_{\text{U.S.}}$. In other words, this case shows the outpayments line negatively sloped and the inpayments positively sloped, so that the slope (or elasticity) of inpayments exceeds that of outpayments. In sum, Figure II-1 shows the foreign exchange market when devaluation lowers outpayments and raises inpayments and when revaluation does the reverse. On both counts, devaluation improves and revaluation worsens the balance of payments, and the foreign exchange market is clearly stable. In Figure II-1 the dollar is undervalued and the pound is overvalued at $1 = £⅓, resulting in excess demand for dollars (a dollar shortage). A devaluation of the pound is indicated, which would push the exchange rate toward the equilibrium point of $1 = £½ (or £ = $2). Conversely, at an exchange rate of $1 = £⅔, the dollar is overvalued and the pound is undervalued, resulting in an excess supply of dollars (a dollar surplus). A revaluation of the pound is indicated, which would push the exchange rate toward equilibrium. In both cases the movement is in the "right" direction, indicating a stable foreign exchange market.

While the outpayments line must be negatively sloped, the inpayments line can slope either way, depending on the U.S. import-demand elasticity.

In Figure II-2, the inpayment curve is negatively sloped, indicating relatively inelastic U.S. import demand, but it is steeper than the outpayment line (cuts it from above). Although both slopes are negative, the slope of the inpayment line is greater than that of the outpayment line. This is still a stable situation, for it represents the case where the adjustment in outpayments exceeds that in inpayments. As before, at $1 = £⅓ (or £1 = $3) the dollar is undervalued and the pound overvalued, creating excess demand (shortage) for dollars. Devaluation of the pound sterling reduces inpayments, but it lowers outpayments by a greater amount, so that the quantity *inpayments minus outpayments* increases, and the market moves toward equilibrium. Conversely, at $1 = £⅔, the dollar is overvalued (and the pound is undervalued), creating excess supply of dollars. Revaluation of the sterling pushes the market toward the equilibrium exchange rate of £1 = $2.

Finally, consider the case where both lines are negatively sloped, but the outpayments line is steeper than the inpayment line (Figure II-3). In other words, the slope of the inpayments line is less (has a higher negative number)

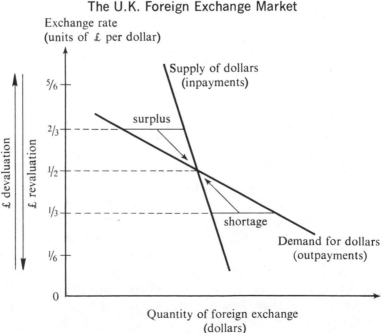

Figure II-2

The U.K. Foreign Exchange Market

Figure II-3
The U.K. Foreign Exchange Market

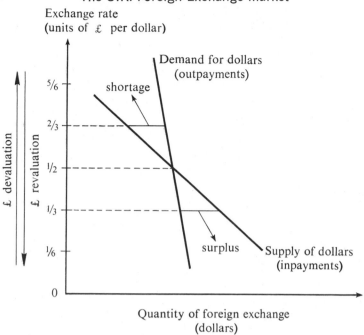

Quantity of foreign exchange
(dollars)

than that of the outpayments line. Devaluation reduces both inpayments and outpayments, but the decline in inpayments is greater for any given devaluation, so that the difference *inpayments minus outpayments* declines rather than rises. This is the foreign exchange equivalent of the case where the sum of the demand elasticities is below 1 (in absolute value), with supply elasticities being infinite. In this case when $1 = £⅓ there is excess supply (surplus) of dollars and revaluation is indicated, while at $1 = £⅔ there is excess demand for dollars (a dollar shortage), which calls for devaluation of the pound. In both cases the indicated action drives the market away from, rather than toward, equilibrium. This is an unstable foreign exchange market, and it occurs when the inpayment line has a lower slope than the outpayment line.

Cases of multiple equilibria are also possible. Figure II-4 shows an example of an unstable equilibrium and two stable equilibria on either side of it.

Elasticity Conditions with Less Than Infinite Supply Elasticities

In terms of foreign exchange, stability occurs when devaluation increases *inpayments minus outpayments*. On the assumption that all foreign currency

Figure II-4
The U.K. Foreign Exchange Market

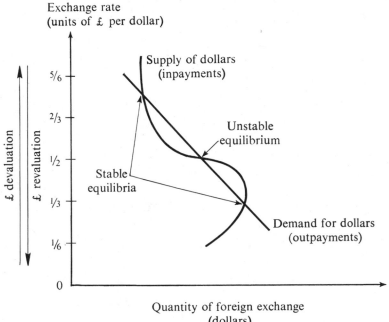

Quantity of foreign exchange
(dollars)

dealings are a result of commodity transactions, this condition can be trans-lated back into the commodity markets by algebraic manipulations of the various elasticity concepts.

Such an algebraic derivation of the general elasticity conditions, where export-supply elasticities can assume any value, is offered by Leland B. Yea-ger in his book *International Monetary Relations.*[1] The following is adapted from his presentation.

Starting from conditions of external balance, *a 1 percent devaluation* of the currency will *increase* inpayments (exports) by Σ_f percent and *lower* out-payments (imports) by η_f percent. In turn, Σ_f is made up of three compo-nents:

(a) the percentage increase in the home currency price of exports *plus*[2]

(b) the percentage increase in the quantity of exports *minus*

(c) 1.

Since items (a) and (b) combined give the percentage increase in the home currency value of exports, and since that currency was devalued by 1 percent, the subtraction of 1 converts that increase into foreign currency terms.

[1] (New York: Harper & Row, 1966), pp. 158–60.
[2] Notice that we are dealing in percentages and that these are additive.

Similarly, the percentage decrease in outpayments η_f equals

(a) the percentage decrease in the quantity of imports

plus

(b) the percentage decrease in the foreign currency price of imports.

Each one of these components is expressed in terms of export-supply and import-demand elasticities. Denoting η_m as the import-demand elasticity of the home (devaluing) country, η_x as the foreign demand elasticity for its exports, e_x as the home (devaluing) country export-supply elasticity, and e_m as the foreign elasticity of export supply facing that country (each elasticity is expressed with respect to price in the country's currency), we obtain the following percentage improvement in the balance of trade resulting from a 1 percent devaluation:[3]

$$\Sigma_f + \eta_f = \frac{e_x(\eta_x - 1)}{e_x + \eta_x} + \frac{\eta_m(e_m + 1)}{e_m + \eta_m}$$

The condition necessary for devaluation to improve the balance of payments is that this expression be positive ($\Sigma_f + \eta_f > 0$).[4]

To obtain the special case of infinite supply elasticities, divide the left-hand component by e_x and the right-hand component by e_m:

$$\Sigma_f + \eta_f = \frac{\eta_x - 1}{1 + \eta_x/e_x} + \frac{\eta_m + \eta_m/e_m}{1 + \eta_m/e_m}$$

For $e_m = e_x = \infty$ this reduces to

$$\Sigma_f + \eta_f = \eta_x - 1 + \eta_m$$

which tells us that under infinite export-supply elasticities a 1 percent devaluation improves the balance of payment by ($\eta_x + \eta_m - 1$) percent. The condition necessary for the success of devaluation is that this expression be larger than zero or that $\eta_x + \eta_m > 1$.[5]

---

[3] An alternative formulation is obtained by combining the two components of the expression over a common denominator:

$$\Sigma_f + \eta_f = \frac{e_m e_x(\eta_m + \eta_x - 1) + \eta_m \eta_x(e_m + e_x + 1)}{(e_x + \eta_x)(e_m + \eta_m)}$$

[4] This condition holds only if the devaluation occurs at an initial condition of external balance. If a country devalues from a deficit position, the stability condition is less exacting (the sum $\Sigma_f + \eta_f$ can be somewhat smaller than zero), because the η_f is applied to a higher base than the Σ_f. For example, assume that $\Sigma_f = 1$ percent and $\eta_f = 1$ percent, so their sum assumes the critical number of zero. If the predevaluation inpayments and outpayments equal 100 (external balance), then the changes resulting from the devaluation are ΔInpayments $= 1$, and ΔOutpayments $= 1$, for a net improvement of zero. But if we start from a deficit position—for example, if predevaluation inpayments equal 100 and outpayments equal 110—then the devaluation would raise inpayments by $.01 \times 100 = 1$ and lower outpayments by $.01 \times 110 = 1.1$, for a net improvement of 0.1 in the balance of payments. Hence, the aforementioned condition of "starting from an external balance . . . .".

[5] This condition is derived directly, with the help of simple calculus, by Anne Kreuger in "Balance of Payments Theory," *The Review of Economic Literature* (March 1969), p. 6*n*.

Returning to the general case, the stability condition is

$$\frac{\eta_x - 1}{1 + \eta_x/e_x} + \frac{\eta_m + \eta_m/e_m}{1 + \eta_m/e_m} > 0 \tag{1}$$

where each elasticity is expressed with respect to price in the country's own currency. The first term of the expression refers to the *country's inpayments* (value of exports), while the second term refers to its *outpayments* (value of imports). The expression shows that when supply is less than infinitely elastic, the stability conditions depend on the interaction between export supply and import demand. Our interest lies in interpreting the economic meaning of the above expression: What is the algebra trying to tell us? We interpret it with the aid of supply and demand curves, where "supply" refers to "export supply" and "demand" to "import demand."

Consider a devaluation of the British pound sterling from £1 = $3 to £1 = $2, where the United Kingdom is interested in increasing the difference between inpayments and outpayments, both expressed in terms of dollars. Since inpayments may move in either direction, the British interest lies in maximizing the increase or minimizing the decline. In the case of dollar outpayments, it lies in maximizing their decline.

Dollar Inpayments

The impact of devaluation on the dollar value of British exports depends on the elasticities of American demand and British supply. This is shown in the left-hand part of expression (1), to which we turn first.

When U.S. demand for British exports is relatively elastic ($|\eta_x| > 1$), the first term of expression (1) is positive; in other words, inpayments would rise. Since, to achieve stability, it is desirable to maximize the gain in inpayments, we wish the term to be as large as possible, which is to say that the denominator should be as small as possible. For that to occur, e_x (the U.K. export-supply elasticity) should be as large as possible. In other words, when $|\eta_x| > 1$, we want e_x to be as large as possible, for elastic supply conditions would enable Britain to capitalize on the high American demand elasticity. This can be seen with the help of supply-and-demand analysis. On the pair of panels comprising Figure II-5(a), the quantity axes are identical, showing both British exports and American imports in volume terms; but the price is expressed in dollars on the upper panel and in pounds on the lower panel. A relatively elastic American demand for British products, $D_{U.S.}$, is shown on the upper panel, while British supply, $S_{U.K.}$, is shown on the lower panel. For the sake of simplicity we do not translate $S_{U.K.}$ into dollars, so that the upper panel does not include the two British supply curves at the pre- and post-devaluation exchange rates. However, the points of intersection of these two

Figure II-5
A Geometric Demonstration of the Stability Conditions

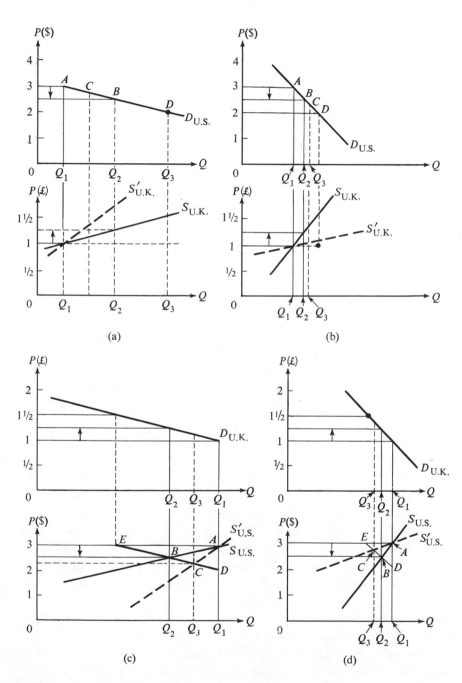

(a)

(b)

(c)

(d)

curves with $D_{\text{U.S.}}$ are shown as A and B, respectively. At the predevaluation exchange rate of £1 = $3, quantity $0Q_1$ is exported from Britain to the United States, with the area under point A on $D_{\text{U.S.}}$ constituting dollar inpayments. Devaluation of the pound to £1 = $2 shifts $S_{\text{U.K.}}$ on the upper panel so that its intersection with $D_{\text{U.S.}}$ is at point B (£1¼ = $2½). Note that dollar prices decline and sterling prices rise as a result of the devaluation, both changes adding up to the degree of devaluation. Since $D_{\text{U.S.}}$ is assumed here to be elastic, this means an *increase* in dollar inpayments to the area under point B. Had $S_{\text{U.K.}}$ been less elastic, as represented by the broken line $S'_{\text{U.K.}}$, the post-devaluation (£1 = $2) equilibrium solution would have been point C (where £1⅜ = $2¾), with a smaller increase in dollar inpayments. The maximum gain in dollar inpayments would occur under an infinitely elastic British supply (not shown), where the post-devaluation quantity is $0Q_3$, with dollar inpayments being the area under point D. Conversely, had $S_{\text{U.K.}}$ been vertical (zero elasticity), the quantity exported would have remained $0Q_1$, with no increase in dollar inpayments. The only change would have been a 50 percent rise in sterling prices (commensurate with the devaluation), so as to leave dollar prices unchanged.

On the other hand, were American demand for British products relatively inelastic, ($|\eta_x| < 1$), the first term of expression (1) would be negative, and stability requires that it be as small as possible. In that case, devaluation would reduce dollar inpayments, and the British interest lies in *minimizing* this reduction. This would occur if e_x were as small as possible. In other words, under inelastic U.S. demand for British products, stability requires the U.K. supply elasticity to be low. In Figure II-5(b), $D_{\text{U.S.}}$ and $S_{\text{U.K.}}$ represent demand and supply, respectively. Point A represents equilibrium at the pre-devaluation exchange rate of £1 = $3, with quantity $0Q_1$ being exported; and the area under point A in the upper panel shows total dollar inpayments into Britain. Devaluation of the pound to £1 = $2 moves the equilibrium to point B (where £1¼ = $2½), with $0Q_2$ being exported. (Again note that dollar prices decline and pound prices rise as a result of the devaluation.) Since American demand is assumed to be inelastic, the area under point B is smaller than that under A, so that dollar inpayments decline as a result of the devaluation. With inelastic British supply, sterling prices would tend to rise, nullifying much of the decline in dollar prices, thereby restricting the movement of the equilibrium point downward along the demand curve $D_{\text{U.S.}}$. The limiting case is a vertical $S_{\text{U.K.}}$ (zero elasticity), which would leave dollar prices unchanged by forcing sterling prices up in proportion to the devaluation. Equilibrium would then remain at A, and inpayments would not decline. On the other hand, a highly elastic British supply, represented by the broken line $S'_{\text{U.K.}}$, leads to equilibrium point C, with a greater reduction in dollar payments. The limiting case is an infinitely elastic $S_{U.K.}$ (not shown) with post-devaluation equilibrium at point D.

To summarize: With relatively elastic U.S. demand, the more elastic British supply, the greater the increase in inpayments; with relatively inelastic U.S. demand, the less elastic British supply, the smaller the decrease in inpayments; with U.S. demand of unitary elasticity, dollar inpayments remain unchanged regardless of British supply elasticity, because the area under $D_{U.S.}$ does not vary.

Dollar Outpayments

The British interest lies in maximizing the reduction in dollar outpayments, which is the volume of imports times their dollar price. The conditions for that are shown in the second term of expression (1).

If the British demand for imports was relatively elastic, ($|\eta_m| > 1$), then the smaller the ratio η_m/e_m the larger the value of this term, because the same ratio (η_m/e_m) is added to 1 in the denominator and to a number greater than 1 in the numerator. In other words, for stability it would then be desirable to have the U.S. supply elasticity (e_m) as large as possible. Under elastic British demand, the increase in sterling prices of imports following the devaluation would lead to a large shrinkage in the volume of imports. It would then be useful to have American supply highly elastic so that suppliers would withdraw from the British market as a result of the decline in dollar prices. This is shown in Figure II-5c, where prices are expressed in pounds in the upper panel and in dollars in the lower panel. British demand for American products is assumed to be elastic, and at the predevaluation exchange rate of £1 = $3, the volume of imports is $0Q_1$; and British dollar outpayments are represented by the area under point A. Devaluation to £1 = $2 raises prices in terms of pounds and lowers them in terms of dollars. Given $D_{U.K.}$ and $S_{U.S.}$, the new equilibrium point is at B, where £1¼ = $2½. Dollar outpayments *decline* to the area under B. Had American supply been less elastic, as represented by the broken line $S'_{U.S.}$, the new equilibrium would have been at point C, where £1⅛ = $2¼. The area under point C (dollar outpayments) is greater than that under point B. Maximum reduction in outpayments would be achieved under infinitely elastic U.S. supply, where dollar prices would remain $3 and sterling prices at £1½. Equilibrium outpayments would be the area under point E. Conversely, minimum reduction would occur under zero U.S. supply elasticity, where the new equilibrium position is at point D (£1 = $2). The volume of imports and their sterling price remain at their predevaluation levels of $0Q_1$ and £1, respectively, but outpayments decline because of the reduction in dollar price to $2. The line $\overline{EBCD}$ is the locus of the post-devaluation points of equilibria under alternative U.S. supply elasticities, given $D_{U.K.}$ and the degree of pound devaluation. In fact, this line represents the British demand curve translated into dollars at the post-devaluation exchange rate. Only the relevant range of it is shown: between its intersections with U.S. export-supply curves of zero and infinite elasticities. Since it is relatively elastic, the area under point B is less than that under point C, which in turn is less than that under point D. The more elastic $S_{U.S.}$, the greater the decline in outpayments, with maximum decline reached at point E.

Conversely, under inelastic British import demand ($|\eta_m| < 1$), the second term of the expression—the reduction in dollar outpayments—would be greater the smaller the U.S. supply elasticity (e_m). This is shown in Figure II-5d, where an inelastic $D_{U.K.}$ is portrayed on the upper panel and $S_{U.S.}$ on the lower panel. With American supply represented by $S_{U.S.}$, the predevaluation equilibrium (at £1 = $3) is at point A, with the volume of imports $0Q_1$ and dollar outpayments represented by the area under point A. The post-devaluation equilibrium is at point B (£1¼ = $2½). Import volume declines to $0Q_2$ and dollar outpayments to the area under B. Had American supply been more elastic, as represented by the broken line $S'_{U.K.}$, the post-devaluation equilibrium point would be at C (£1⅜ = $2¾), with import volume $0Q_3$ and dollar outpayments the area under point C. Given $D_{U.K.}$ and the extent of devaluation, we can rotate $S_{U.S.}$ around point A to represent various supply elasticities, and the locus of the points of equilibrium is shown by the line $\overline{ECBD}$. It stretches from zero to infinite U.S. supply elasticity and is also the relevant segment of the British import-demand curve translated into dollars at the post-devaluation exchange rate. Since it is relatively inelastic (by construction), minimum outpayments are reached under point D, where $S_{U.S.}$ is of zero elasticity. Note that at all points, $\overline{ECBD}$ outpayments are below their predevaluation level (point A). The same holds true for Figure II-5c, indicating that dollar outpayments are invariably reduced by devaluation. The only exception, in which they remain unchanged, is the case of zero U.K. demand elasticity.

To summarize: Outpayments decline as a result of devaluation, and the question is, what elasticity conditions would maximize the reduction? With relatively elastic British demand, the more elastic the U.S. supply, the greater the reduction. With relatively inelastic British demand, the less elastic the U.S. supply, the greater the reduction.

Effect of Devaluation on the Terms of Trade

A problem that has occupied economists for a long time is the effect of devaluation on the commodity terms of trade—that is, on the ratio of the export-price index to the import-price index. It was long believed that devaluation must worsen the country's terms of trade: It causes export prices to decline and import prices to rise, so that their ratio necessarily declines. This change in the price ratio implies a reduction in the country's real income, for it means that less imports are obtainable for a given quantity of exports or, alternatively, that more exports are required to obtain a given volume of imports.

But there is a flaw in the argument concerning the effect of devaluation on the terms of trade. Export prices decline in terms of the foreign currency, while import prices rise in terms of the domestic currency. Proper comparison requires that both prices be expressed in terms of the same currency.

What actually happens in the case of devaluation is that both export and import prices decline in terms of the foreign currency and rise in terms of the domestic currency. To see this, consider a British devaluation from £1 = $3 to £1 = $2, and observe the two sets of diagrams in Figure II-6.

Figure II-6

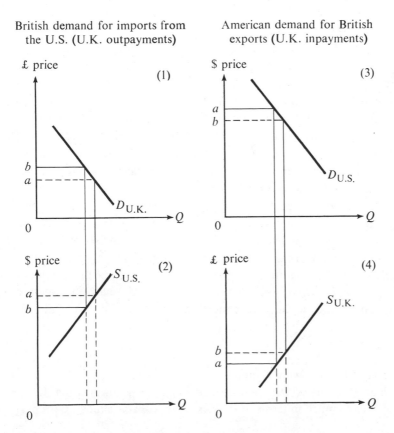

British demand for imports from the U.S. (U.K. outpayments)

American demand for British exports (U.K. inpayments)

The left-hand charts (parts 1 and 2) refer to British import demand for and American (foreign) export supply of U.K. imports, where each schedule is shown with respect to prices expressed in terms of the country's own currency. Thus, while the price axes of 1 and 2 are different, for they show different currencies, the quantity axes are common to both. What the United Kingdom imports the United States exports, and vice versa. The predevaluation price is $\overline{0a}$ on both diagrams, reflecting the ratio £1 = $3, while the post-devaluation price $\overline{0b}$ reflects the ratio of £1 = $2. British import prices rise in terms of sterling and decline in terms of dollars, the two changes adding up to the degree of devaluation. Clearly, the size of the two changes depends on the relative elasticities of the export-supply and import-demand schedules. With infinitely elastic U.S. export supply, the sterling import price rises by the amount of the devaluation and the dollar export price is unaffected.

The right-hand set (parts 3 and 4) refers to American (foreign) demand for and British supply of exports, where each schedule is expressed in terms of the country's own currency. The quantity axes are common to both. As a result of the devaluation, the price changes from the pair of values $\overline{0a}$ (reflecting a £1 = $3 exchange rate) to $\overline{0b}$ (reflecting a £1 = $2 exchange rate). Dollar import prices decline while sterling export prices rise, the two changes adding up to the degree of devaluation. The size of the two changes depends on the relative elasticities of the export-supply and import-demand schedules. With infinitely elastic British export supply, the dollar import price declines by the amount of the devaluation.

To assess the effect of devaluation on the terms of trade, we must properly compare diagrams 1 and 4, which show, respectively, the rise in British import and export prices (by $\overline{ab}$), both expressed in terms of sterling. Alternatively, we can compare diagrams 2 and 3, which show, respectively, the decline ($\overline{ab}$) in British import and export prices, both expressed in terms of dollars. In each case export prices can change by more or by less than import prices, and the effect of devaluation on the terms of trade is indeterminate. It all depends on the constellation of the four elasticities in question. In his algebraic derivation, Yeager[6] shows that devaluation improves the terms of trade if the product of the demand elasticities exceeds the product of the supply elasticities ($\eta_m \eta_x > e_m e_x$) and vice versa. Alternatively stated, given a devaluation of the pound, the condition for improved terms of trade are

$$\frac{\eta_x}{e_x} > \frac{e_m}{\eta_m}$$

which carries the following meaning:

A high elasticity of U.S. demand for imports, η_x, ensures that U.K. prices will not decline much in terms of dollars; they will rise almost in proportion to

[6] *Op. cit.*, pp. 168–69.

the devaluation in terms of pounds. A low U.K. supply elasticity, e_x, ensures that British prices will rise (in terms of pounds) almost in proportion to the devaluation. These are the conditions that ensure a high η_x/e_x ratio.

A high U.K. import-demand elasticity, η_m, ensures that British imports will decline considerably, depressing their dollar prices. A low U.S. export-supply elasticity, e_m, ensures that as British demand for American products declines, U.S. export prices also come down. These are the conditions for a small e_m/η_m ratio.

Clearly, if supply elasticities are assumed to be infinite, then $e_m e_x > \eta_m \eta_x$, and the terms of trade of the devaluating country deteriorate. In fact, in this case they deteriorate by precisely the degree of devaluation. For, in terms of sterling, British import prices rise by the degree of devaluation while export prices remain unchanged. In terms of dollars, British export prices decline by the extent of the devaluation and import prices remain unchanged.

We can use charts a through d of Figure II-5 for an intuitive demonstration that in the unstable case—that is, when the balance of trade deteriorates as a result of devaluation—the terms of trade must deteriorate.

Consider first the case of no change in either inpayments or outpayments; $D_{\text{U.S.}}$ in chart a is of unitary elasticity, and $D_{\text{U.K.}}$ in chart d is of zero elasticity. In that case, devaluation reduces the dollar price of exports and leaves the dollar price of imports unchanged. The terms of trade deteriorate. For the unstable case, first make $D_{\text{U.S.}}$ relatively inelastic (chart b) and retain $D_{\text{U.K.}}$ at zero elasticity. The terms of trade deteriorate. Next allow $D_{\text{U.K.}}$ to be somewhat elastic. Dollar outpayments decline, but instability requires a greater reduction in inpayments than in outpayments. A "large" reduction in inpayments would obtain under inelastic $D_{\text{U.S.}}$ and elastic $S_{\text{U.K.}}$—precisely the conditions that lead to a "large" reduction in the dollar price of exports. On the other hand, a "small" decline in outpayments obtains when a low-elasticity $D_{\text{U.K.}}$ is accompanied by a highly elastic $S_{\text{U.S.}}$—conditions that give rise to a "small" reduction in the dollar price of imports. Thus the terms of trade tend to deteriorate.

Appendix III

Elasticity of Import Demand and the Domestic Demand and Supply Elasticities

The elasticity of import demand for a given product is positively (and uniquely) related to the domestic demand and supply elasticities, negatively related to the share of imports in domestic consumption and production.

Remembering that the volume of imports (Q_m) is the difference between the quantities demanded (Q_d) and supplied (Q_s) at home, we can derive the import-demand elasticity (η_m) from the definition of elasticity, as follows:

$$\eta_m = \frac{-P}{Q_m} \times \frac{\Delta Q_m}{\Delta P} = \frac{-P}{Q_m} \times \frac{\Delta(Q_d - Q_s)}{\Delta P}$$

$$= \frac{-P}{Q_m} \times \frac{\Delta Q_d}{\Delta P} + \frac{P}{Q_m} \times \frac{\Delta Q_s}{\Delta P}$$

Next, we multiply and divide the first term of the last expression by Q_d and the second term by Q_s:

$$\eta_m = \frac{\dfrac{-P}{Q_d} \times \dfrac{\Delta Q_d}{\Delta P} \times Q_d}{Q_m} + \frac{\dfrac{P}{Q_s} \times \dfrac{\Delta Q_s}{\Delta P} \times Q_s}{Q_m}$$

$$= \frac{\epsilon_d \times Q_d}{Q_m} + \frac{\epsilon_s \times Q_s}{Q_m}$$

where ϵ_d and ϵ_s represent domestic demand and supply elasticities, respectively. Thus,

$$\eta_m = \frac{Q_d}{Q_m} \times \epsilon_d + \frac{Q_s}{Q_m} \times \epsilon_s$$

Elasticity of Export Supply and the Domestic Demand and Supply Elasticities

The export-supply elasticity of a given product is positively related to the domestic demand and supply elasticities and negatively related to the share of exports in domestic production and consumption. Remembering that the

428

volume of exports (Q_e) is the difference between the quantities supplied and demanded domestically (Q_s and Q_d), we can derive the export-supply elasticity (Σ_x) from the definition of elasticity, as follows:

$$\Sigma_x = \frac{P}{Q_e} \times \frac{\Delta Q_e}{\Delta P} = \frac{P}{Q_e} \times \frac{\Delta(Q_s - Q_d)}{\Delta P} = \frac{P}{Q_e} \times \frac{\Delta Q_s}{\Delta P} - \frac{P}{Q_e} \times \frac{\Delta Q_d}{\Delta P}$$

Next, we multiply and divide the first term by Q_s and the second term by Q_d:

$$\Sigma_x = \frac{\frac{P}{Q_s} \times \frac{\Delta Q_s}{\Delta P} \times Q_s}{Q_e} - \frac{\frac{P}{Q_d} \times \frac{\Delta Q_d}{\Delta P} \times Q_d}{Q_e} = \frac{\epsilon_s \times Q_s}{Q_e} + \frac{\epsilon_d \times Q_d}{Q_e}$$

where ϵ_s and ϵ_d represent domestic supply and demand elasticities, recalling that the demand elasticity is negative. Thus:

$$\Sigma_x = \frac{Q_s}{Q_e} \times \epsilon_s + \frac{Q_d}{Q_e} \times \epsilon_d$$

A Country's Share in World Export Markets and the Elasticity of Demand for Its Exports

The elasticity of demand for a country's exports of a given product is inversely related to its share in the world market.

If W is the world demand for imports of a given product and C is the quantity exported by competing sources (other countries), then $W - C$ is the quantity exported by the country in question. Let η_x be the elasticity of demand for the country's exports of the product; then

$$\eta_x = \frac{-P}{W - C} \times \frac{\Delta(W - C)}{\Delta P} = -\frac{P}{W - C}\left(\frac{\Delta W}{\Delta P}\right) - \frac{P}{W - C}\left(-\frac{\Delta C}{\Delta P}\right)$$

$$= \frac{-P(\Delta W/\Delta P)}{W - C} + \frac{P(\Delta C/\Delta P)}{W - C}$$

Multiply and divide the first term by W and the second term by C:

$$\eta_x = \frac{W(-P/W)(\Delta W/\Delta P)}{W - C} + \frac{C(P/C)(\Delta C/\Delta P)}{W - C} = \frac{W}{W - C}\eta_w + \frac{C}{W - C}e_c$$

where η_w is the world demand elasticity for the product and e_c is the supply elasticity from competing sources.

One important implication of this relation is that even if the demand for a certain product is relatively inelastic, the demand for a particular country's exports of the product can be highly elastic if it has only a small share in total world markets. Applying this to the domestic market we can see how the demand for wheat can be inelastic but the demand for a single farmer's wheat infinitely elastic, when he accounts for a very small share in the total supply.

Import-Demand and Export-Supply Elasticities
and the Incidence of a Tariff

In Figure III-1 the pretariff international price is $\overline{OP}$ and the quantity traded is $\overline{OQ}$, as determined by the intersection of the import-demand and export-supply curves. A specific tariff of size t is then imposed, shifting export supply upward to the broken line. Domestic price in the importing country rises by fraction s of the tariff, while its terms of trade improve by a fraction $(1 - s)$. The quantity traded declines by ΔQ. Our objective is to find an expression for s.

The elasticity of the import-demand curve at point E is

$$|\Sigma_D| = \frac{\Delta Q}{Q} \times \frac{P}{\Delta P} = \frac{\Delta Q}{\overline{0Q}} \times \frac{\overline{OP}}{st} \tag{1}$$

From that we obtain:

$$\frac{\Delta Q}{\overline{0Q}} = |\Sigma_D| \frac{st}{\overline{OP}} \tag{2}$$

The elasticity of the export-supply curve at point E is

$$\Sigma_S = \frac{\Delta Q}{\overline{0Q}} \times \frac{\overline{OP}}{\Delta P} = \frac{\Delta Q}{\overline{0Q}} \times \frac{\overline{OP}}{(1 - s)t} \tag{3}$$

Substituting (2) into (3) gives

$$\Sigma_S = |\Sigma_D| \frac{st}{\overline{OP}} \times \frac{\overline{OP}}{(1 - s)t} = |\Sigma_D| \frac{s}{1 - s} \tag{4}$$

Figure III-1

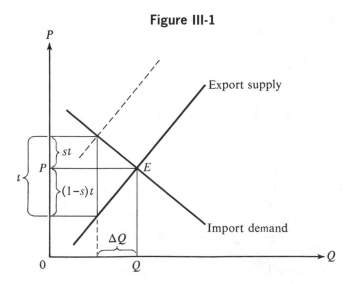

Therefore,

$$\frac{s}{1-s} = \frac{\Sigma_S}{|\Sigma_D|}$$

and

$$\Sigma_S - s\Sigma_S = s \times |\Sigma_D|$$

$$s(|\Sigma_D| + \Sigma_S) = \Sigma_S$$

$$s = \frac{\Sigma_S}{|\Sigma_D| + \Sigma_S}$$

Dividing through by Σ_S, we obtain

$$s = \frac{1}{|\Sigma_D|/\Sigma_S + 1}$$

$$(1 - s) = \frac{|\Sigma_D| + \Sigma_S - \Sigma_S}{|\Sigma_D| + \Sigma_S}$$

$$= \frac{|\Sigma_D|}{|\Sigma_D| + \Sigma_S}$$

$$= \frac{1}{1 + \Sigma_S/|\Sigma_D|}$$

Clearly it is the *relative* size of the import-demand and export-supply elasticities that determines the incidence of the tariff. In turn, these elasticities are related to the domestic supply and demand elasticities in the respective countries (as spelled out in the previous sections of this appendix).

The expressions above assume that the government does nothing with the tariff revenue. If, however, we assume that these funds are distributed to the population in the form of a general income subsidy, the expressions must be modified to take into account the added demand for imports arising from the added income (the marginal propensity to import). Also, this is a partial equilibrium formula, which refers only to a tax on a single product. A different, full-equilibrium formula would apply when analyzing the incidence of a tariff levied across the board on all products.

Similar formulas apply to the incidence of domestic indirect taxes, except that domestic rather than international elasticities are involved.

Economic Cost of the Tariff

In Chapter 13 the economic cost of the tariff was analyzed with the use of producers' and consumers' surpluses and changes in government revenue. But the analysis was restricted to a small country whose terms of trade remain unaffected, so that all the effects of the tariff are visible inside the importing

Figure III-2

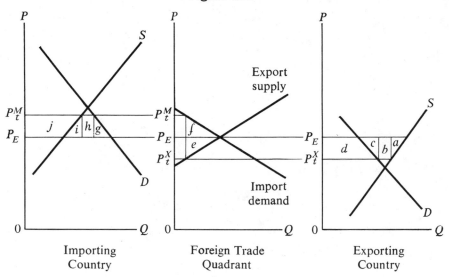

country. This can be extended to the more general case of a two-country world, where the terms of trade are affected by the tariff.

Figure III-2 is similar to Figure 13-3. The free-trade price is P_E, while the tariff-ridden price in the importing country is P_t^M and that in the exporting country is P_t^X. The following changes occur in the importing country:

Consumers' surplus declines by the area $g + h + i + j$.

Producers' surplus increases by area j.

Government revenue increases by area h.

Figure III-3

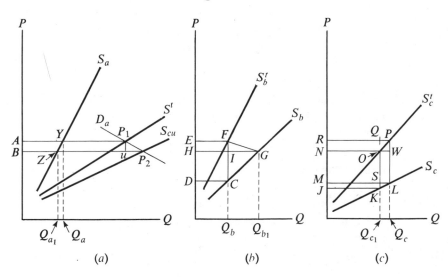

• The net deadweight loss equals the sum of the triangular areas $i + g$. The following changes take place in the exporting country:

Producers' surplus declines by area $a + b + c + d$.

Consumers' surplus increases by area d.

Government revenue accruing to the *importing* country increases by area b. (Area b is a transfer from the exporting to the importing country. It does not affect worldwide welfare because whereas it is a loss to the exporting country, it is an equal gain to the importing country.)

The net deadweight loss equals the areas of triangles $a + c$.

The net loss to the importing country is triangles i and g, while the net gain is rectangle b. Its *optimum tariff* is the tariff rate that would maximize the net gain, the area $[b - (g + i)]$. The exporting country sustains a net loss measured by the area $a + b + c$, of which b is a transfer to the importing country. To the world taken as a whole, the *net* deadweight *loss* from the tariff is triangles $a + c + i + g$. Geometrically, we have $i + g = f$, because their height is the same, and the base of f equals the combined bases of i and g, both being the difference between the free-trade imports and the tariff-ridden imports. By identical reasoning, areas $a + c = e$. Thus, in the foreign trade quadrant, the net welfare cost of the tariff to the world taken as a whole (that is, disregarding distributional effects) is area $e + f$. Without further marking of the diagram, it can be seen that if the tariff is removed in two successive steps of equal size, the first 50 percent reduction would improve world welfare by a far greater amount (trapezoid area) than the second and final reduction (remaining triangle).

Static Effects of a Customs Union[1]

In Figure III-3 assume that S_a and D_a are the internal supply and demand curves in country A for a given product. S_b and S_c are the export-supply curves of countries B and C to country A, with C being a more efficient producer than B. S_b^t and S_c^t are the same two supply curves subject to 100 percent tariff imposed by country A. Curve S^t indicates total supply of the commodity in country A ($S_a + S_b^t + S_c^t$). Price P_1 is established. Country A produces Q_a domestically and imports Q_b and Q_c from countries B and C, respectively.

When countries A and B form a customs union to the exclusion of C, the relevant supply curve in country B becomes S_b, while S_c^t remains in effect in country C.[2] Total supply in country A's market becomes S_{CU}, consisting of

[1] Reprinted with permission from M. E. Kreinin, *Kyklos*, December 1973.
[2] This assumes that A's tariff against outsiders remains unchanged, which is characteristic of a free trade area rather than of a customs union. But the diagram can be adjusted to account for any modification in that tariff rate.

$S_a + S_b + S_c^t$. The price in country A drops to P_2; domestic supply declines to Q_{a1}; imports from country B rise to Q_{b1}; and imports from country C diminish to Q_{c1}. These changes can be quantified in terms of their effect on producers' surpluses in all three countries, and on consumers' surpluses and government tariff revenue of country A. The following observations relate to each section of the diagram:

(a) Country A enjoys an increase of consumers' surpluses of BAP_1P_2 and suffers a reduction of producers' surpluses amounting to $BAYZ$. There is a *gain of* ZYP_1P_2.

(b) Country B enjoys a gain in producers' surplus of $HGCD$. Country A faces a loss in government tariff revenue of $CDEF$. Since area $DCHI$ is common to both, we obtain in part (b) *a loss of* $EHIF$ *and a gain of* ICG.

(c) Tariff revenue of country A declines from $RPLM$ to $NOKJ$. Subtracting the area $NOSM$, common to both, we get a loss of $RNOP + POSL$ and a gain of $MJKS$. At the same time, producers' surpluses of country C decline by $MJKL$. Thus Figure III-3c yields the *following loss:* $RNOP + POSL - MJKS + MJKL = RNOP + POSL + LSK = RNOP + POKL$.

Area ZYP_1P_2 [the net gain in (a)] is equal by construction to areas $EFGH$ in (b) plus $RNOP$ in (c). Subtracting from this net gain in (a) the losses $EHIF$ in (b) and $RNOP$ in (c), we are left with a net gain of FIG in (b). Adding it to the earlier gain CIG, we obtain a *net gain of* CFG in part (b), to be weighed against the *net loss of* $POKL$ in part (c). The net effect on world welfare depends on the relative size of the two areas.

Appendix IV

Table IV-1

U.S. Balance of Payments, 1972 and 1973

Line	(Credits +; debits −)	1972	1973[g]
1	Merchandise trade balance[a]	−6,912	688
2	Exports	48,769	70,255
3	Imports	−55,681	−69,567
4	Military transactions, net	−3,558	−2,171
5	Travel and transportation, net	−2,853	−2,312
6	Investment income, net[b]	7,863	9,723
7	U.S. direct investments abroad	10,433	13,974
8	Other U.S. investments abroad	3,492	4,576
9	Foreign investments in the United States	−6,062	−8,827
10	Other services, net	851	972
11	Balance on goods and services[c]	−4,610	6,900
12	Remittances, pensions and other transfers	−1,570	−1,913
13	Balance on goods, services and remittances	−6,180	4,987
14	U.S. government grants (excluding military)	−2,174	−1,947
15	Balance on current accounts[d]	−8,353	3,041
16	U.S. government capital flows excluding nonscheduled repayments, net[e]	−1,714	−2,894
17	Nonscheduled repayments of U.S. government assets	137	289
18	U.S. government nonliquid liabilities to other than foreign official reserve agencies	238	1,136
19	Long-term private capital flows, net	−152	−357
20	U.S. direct investments abroad	−3,404	−4,855
21	Foreign direct investments in the United States	160	2,068
22	Foreign securities	−614	−791
23	U.S. securities other than Treasury issues	4,335	4,093
24	Other, reported by U.S. banks	−1,120	−596
25	Other, reported by U.S. nonbanking concerns	492	−276
26	Balance on current account and long-term capital[e]	−9,843	1,214
27	Nonliquid short-term private capital flows, net	−1,637	−4,210

Table IV-1 (continued)

Line	(Credits +; debits —)	1972	1973ᵍ
28	Claims reported by U.S. banks	−1,495	−3,953
29	Claims reported by U.S. nonbanking concerns	−315	−735
30	Liabilities reported by U.S. nonbanking concerns	173	478
31	Allocations of special drawing rights (SDRs)ᵈ	710	
32	Errors and ommissions, net	−3,112	−4,793
33	Net liquidity balance	−13,882	−7,789
34	Liquid private capital flows, net	3,542	2,503
35	Liquid claims	−1,234	−1,933
36	Reported by U.S. banks	−742	−1,100
37	Reported by U.S. nonbanking concerns	−492	−833
38	Liquid liabilities	4,776	4,436
39	To foreign commercial banks	3,862	2,863
40	To international and regional organizations	104	373
41	To other foreigners	810	1,200
42	Official reserve transactions balance	−10,340	−5,286
	Financed by changes in:		
43	Liquid liabilities to foreign official agencies	9,720	4,434
44	Other readily marketable liabilities to foreign official agenciesᶠ	399	1,118
45	Nonliquid liabilities to foreign official reserve agencies reported by U.S. government	189	−475
46	U.S. official reserve assets, net	32	209
	Memoranda:		
47	Transfers under military grant programs (excluded from lines 2, 4, and 14)	4,200	2,558
48	Reinvested earnings of foreign incorporated affiliates of U.S. firms (excluded from lines 7 and 20)	4,521	n.a.
49	Reinvested earnings of U.S. incorporated affiliates of foreign firms (excluded from lines 9 and 21)	548	n.a.
50	Gross liquidity balance, excluding allocations of SDRs	−15,826	−9,722

[a] Adjusted to balance of payments basis; excludes exports under U.S. military agency sales contracts and imports of U.S. military agencies.
[b] Includes fees and royalties from U.S. direct investments abroad or from foreign direct investments in the United States.
[c] Equal to net exports of goods and services in national income and product accounts of the United States.
[d] The sum of lines 15 and 31 is equal to "net foreign investment" in the national income and product accounts of the United States.
[e] Includes some short-term U.S. government assets.
[f] Includes changes in nonliquid liabilities reported by U.S. banks and in investments by foreign official agencies in debt securities of U.S. government corporations and agencies, private corporations, and state and local governments.
[g] Data for 1973 are preliminary.
Note: Details may not add to totals because of rounding.
SOURCE: *Survey of Current Business,* March 1974.

Table IV-2

U.S. International Investment Position in Selected Years,
1950–72 ($ Billions)

	1950	1960	1971	1972P
U.S. assets and investments abroad[a]	31.5	68.1	170.1	188.8
Private investments	19.0	49.5	134.5	150.0
Total long-term	17.5	44.5	115.9	128.4
Direct	11.8	31.9	86.2	94.0
Securities	4.3	9.5	21.7	24.9
Banking claims and other	1.4	3.1	8.0	9.4
Total short-term	1.5	5.0	18.6	21.6
Reported by banks	0.9	3.6	10.9	12.4
Other	0.6	1.4	3.8	4.1
U.S. government credits and claims[b]	11.1	17.0	34.1	36.1
U.S. monetary reserve assets[a]	1.4	1.6	2.0	2.7
Foreign assets and investments in United States	17.7	41.2	123.1	148.7
Nonliquid obligations	8.8	19.7	55.3	65.7
Total private	8.7	19.4	53.7	63.9
Direct	3.4	6.9	13.7	14.4
U.S. corporate stocks	2.9	9.3	21.4	27.6
Other long-term	1.7	2.2	14.7	17.8
Short-term reported by nonbanks	0.7	1.0	3.9	4.1
Total U.S. government	0.1	0.3	5.0	5.5
Liquid liabilities	8.9	21.5	67.8	82.9
Total to private foreigners	4.3	9.1	16.6	21.4
Foreign banks (including U.S. bank branches)	2.1	4.8	10.9	14.8
Others	2.2	4.3	5.7	6.6
Total to official accounts[c]	4.6	12.4	51.2	61.5
Liabilities of U.S. banks	2.4	4.0	7.4P	n.a.
U.S. government obligations	2.2	8.4	44.4P	n.a.
Memo U.S. monetary gold	22.8	17.8	10.2	10.5

[a] Excludes U.S. monetary gold.
[b] Other than U.S. monetary reserve assets.
[c] Includes, in addition to foreign reserve holders, other foreign government agencies.
P = preliminary
SOURCES: *Federal Reserve Bulletin,* April 1970, p. 325, and *Survey of Current Business,* August 1973.

Appendix V

Forums for Trade and Monetary Talks

The principal organizations and groups of countries that are discussing or are proposing to hold discussions on reforms in the world's trading and monetary system are described in brief below.

The Six   the original members of the European Economic Community (EEC), that is, Belgium, France, West Germany, Italy, Luxembourg, and the Netherlands.

The Nine   the enlarged EEC, or European Community—that is, the Six plus Denmark, Ireland, and the United Kingdom.

Group of Ten   the ten major industrial countries (the Six less Luxembourg plus Canada, Japan, Sweden, the United Kingdom, and the United States) that agreed in October 1962 to stand ready to lend their currencies to the IMF under the General Agreement to Borrow. The Group of Ten finance ministers and central bank governors (and their deputies) have met from time to time over the past decade to discuss the international monetary system.

Bank for International Settlement (BIS)   originally set up in 1930 to promote cooperation between European central banks and to provide additional facilities for international financial transactions. In addition, it acts as agent for the European Monetary Agreement and organizes regular meetings in Basel attended by the central bank governors of the major industrial nations. Representatives of the IMF, the OECD, and the Commission of the EEC may attend these meetings.

Group of Twenty   a committee of the Board of Governors of the IMF considering international monetary reform. Membership is based on the pattern of the executive board of the IMF (see IMF) with provision for attendance, on the invitation of the Committee, of persons designated by other international organizations or by nonmembers of the Fund.

438

Organization for Economic Cooperation and Development (OECD)   established in 1961 as successor to the Organization for European Economic Cooperation. Consists of 23 developed countries: the Group of Ten plus Australia, Austria, Denmark, Finland, Greece, Iceland, Ireland, Luxembourg, Norway, Portugal, Spain, Switzerland, and Turkey. Yugoslavia is an associate member. The OECD is concerned with a wide variety of economic matters.

Group of 24   made up of eight countries each in Africa, Asia, and Latin America deputed by the Group of 77 to consider monetary matters. The 24 countries are as follows:

Algeria	Ghana	Pakistan
Argentina	Guatemala	Peru
Brazil	India	Philippines
Ceylon	Iran	Syrian Arab Republic
Colombia	Ivory Coast	Trinidad and Tobago
Egypt	Lebanon	Venezuela
Ethiopia	Mexico	Yugoslavia
Gabon	Nigeria	Zaïre

Group of 77   a group of developing countries within the United Nations Conference on Trade and Development (UNCTAD). Originally numbering 77, the Group now has 96 members. The full membership of UNCTAD, which was established under a UN General Assembly resolution of December 30, 1964, is 141 (of which 132 are members of the United Nations).

General Agreement on Tariffs and Trade (GATT)   a multilateral trade treaty among governments, made up of 80 full contracting parties and one provisional member, as well as 15 other countries applying the General Agreement on a *de facto* basis.

International Monetary Fund (IMF)   established in December 1945. The international organization with prime responsibility for international monetary matters. It operates on the basis of weighted voting power for its 120 members. The Fund's highest authority is the board of governors (consisting of a governor and an alternate governor appointed by each member), which normally meets once a year but otherwise votes by mail. The general operations of the Fund are the responsibility of 20 executive directors, of which currently 6 are appointed by France, West Germany, India, Japan, the United Kingdom, and the United States and 14 are elected by groups of members.

Appendix VI

The Factor Proportions Theory

Students thoroughly familiar with advanced price theory will recognize that the transformation curve of a country can be derived from its contract curve, which in turn is the locus of points of tangency between two sets of isoquants, each set pertaining to one of the country's two industries. The Edgeworth-Bowley box diagram is used to delineate the country's fixed amount of resources, made up of two productive factors (for example, labor and capital), and the contract curve is drawn inside the box. That curve is the locus of points of efficient allocation of the two productive factors between the two industries; from any point off the contract curve one can move to *certain points* on that curve and increase the output produced by the given quantity of the two factors. We can thus show the contract curves for countries A and B from which the respective transformation curves in Figure 11-9 (page 249) can be derived.

The assumptions of the factor proportions model, outlined on p. 252 and

Figure VI-1

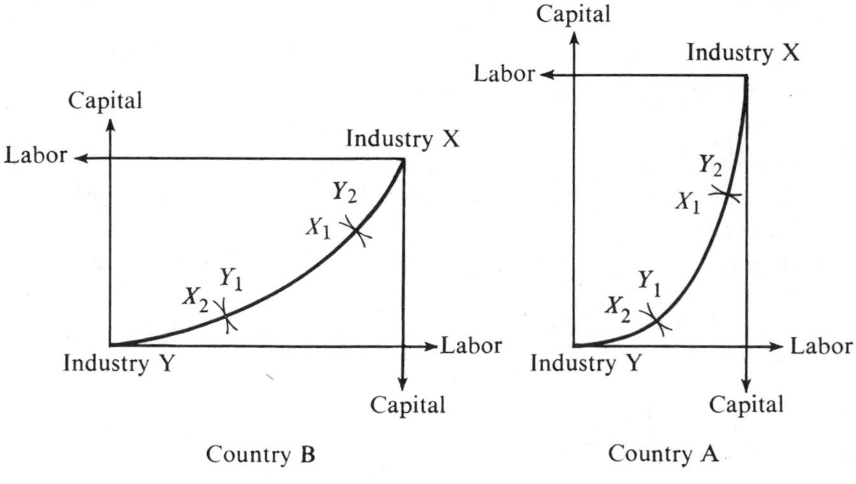

Country B

Country A

pp. 258–263, are built into the two diagrams (Figure VI-1). Besides pure competition and perfect internal factor mobility, the model's assumptions are as follows.

(a) The isoquants of industry X are identical in both countries; so are the isoquants of industry Y.

(b) Industry Y is labor intensive relative to industry X and X is capital intensive relative to industry Y, and this relationship holds for both countries. Translated into a multicommodity world, this assumption means that the *ranking* of industries by the labor/capital ratio required for production (that is, the factor-use ratio) would be the same in both countries even if the factor-price ratio varied. This assumption is known as the nonreversibility of factor intensities.

(c) Both commodities are produced under diminishing returns but constant returns to scale. The latter assumption implies that any straight ray from each origin (say of industry Y) will intersect the isoquants of the industry depicted on that origin (for example, the Y isoquants) at points of equal slopes. The economic meaning of this is that all such points of intersection show equal ratios between the marginal physical productivities of the two factors in the given industry. In other words, under constant returns to scale, the marginal productivity of a factor in a given industry is independent of the scale of operations and depends only on its ratio to the other factor in use (that is, on the factor-use ratio). And the factor-use ratio is identical along a straight line from the origin; it is equal to the constant slope of that line.

(d) Country A is capital-abundant relative to country B, while B is labor-abundant relative to country A. This is indicated by the relative size of the two boxes.

As a next step, place the box diagram of country A on top of the one of country B, in such a way that their origins for industry Y will coincide. This is shown in Figure VI-2, where the isoquants are deleted for the sake of clarity. The identical Y isoquants for both countries coincide exactly, while the identical X isoquants start at two different points of origin. Any ray from the (joint) origin of Y, such as $\overline{YMN}$, intersects the contract curves of the two countries at points M and N, where the Y isoquants common to the two countries have equal slopes. In other words, the ratio of the marginal products of the two factors in industry Y is the same in both countries. Since within each country, factor mobility ensures that the ratio of the marginal products of the two factors is the same in industries Y and X, that ratio must also be the same in industry X of the two countries. Geometrically this means that the straight line connecting M with the origin of industry X in country A is parallel to the straight line connecting N with the origin of industry X in country B.

Equality of the marginal products ensures that the output mixes at point

Figure VI-2

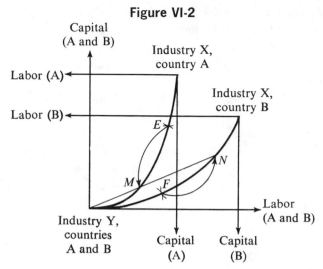

M for country A and at point N for country B would result in identical product prices (or price ratios) in the two countries. And this is the requirement
for post-trade equilibrium. Depending on demand patterns (which are shown
by indifference curves in Figure 11-9 but cannot be shown on a box diagram),
the pretrade output mix was E in country A and F in country B. The opening
of trade moved that mix to points M and N, respectively. The relatively
capital-abundant country A moved to specialize more in the relatively capital-
intensive product X; and the relatively labor-abundant country B moved to
specialize more in the relatively labor-intensive product Y. Specialization is
incomplete in both countries as is the case in Figure 11-9. Thus there is one-
to-one correspondence between the output mix in the factor "space" and in
the commodity "space." *As long as specialization is incomplete* (that is, each
country produces some of both products), not only would commodity prices
be equalized between the two countries at the post-trade production equilibrium points such as M and N, but factor prices would also.

But the number of such post-trade production equilibrium points is unlimited, as there are unlimited rays from the joint origin Y that would intersect the two contract curves. Which one would prevail depends on the relative international prices of the two products. If Y's price rises relative to X,
the ray shifts upward and more Y is produced in both countries, while if the
price of X rises relative to Y, the ray shifts downward, and more X is produced in both countries. Thus the "relevant" ray must depend on conditions
of demand as well as supply; it must be derived from Figure 11-9, where
demand is also depicted, in a way that ensures the identity of the two trade
triangles. Only then is the final equilibrium uniquely determined.

Not all points on the two contract curves are "pairable" in the sense of
intersecting a straight ray from origin Y, in much the same way that not all

points along the two transformation curves are pairable in the sense of having equal slopes. Thus the price of Y relative to that of X can rise to a point where the *ray from the joint origin Y becomes the diagonal of country B's box diagram.* Here country B completely specializes in industry Y, and further increases in the relative price of Y can lead only country A to move upward along its contract curve to produce more Y and less X. Conversely, if the price of X relative to that of Y rises to a point where the *ray from the joint origin Y becomes tangent to country A's contract curve,* then country A is completely specialized in X and produces no Y. Further increases in the relative price of X would lead only country B to move downward along its contract curve toward greater specialization in X.

Thus the two rays whose descriptions are italicized in the previous paragraph delineate the limits to incomplete specialization. All rays falling within these limits indicate incomplete specialization and correspond to points of equal slopes of the two transformation functions in the commodity space (Figure 11-9). The size of *the range of incomplete specialization* depends on two factors:

(a) It varies directly with the similarity of relative factor endowments of the two countries. The more the factor endowment ratios differ the more the shapes of the two box diagrams differ (this can be readily seen by adding labor to country B, leaving all else unchanged) and the smaller the range of pairable points along a ray from joint origin Y.

(b) It varies inversely with the similarity of the production isoquants of X and Y. The more alike they are, the less the "belly" of the two contract curves and the smaller the range of "pairable" points along a ray from origin Y. The extreme case, which corresponds to the Ricardian model of constant opportunity costs, is the one of identical isoquants of the two commodities. The contract curve of each country becomes the diagonal of its box diagram, and there is no range of incomplete specialization. Once trade opens up, country A moves to specialize completely in product X, and country B in product Y.

A Domestic Monopolist Under a Tariff and a Quota

In this section we shall formally demonstrate the proposition that when domestic production is carried on by a monopolist, a tariff would curtail his monopoly power by more than an "equivalent" quota—a quota that allows the same volume of imports as under the tariff. In Figure VI-3, assume that domestic demand is represented by average revenue curve AR, yielding marginal revenue MR, and that the monopolist's marginal cost is represented by MC. In the absence of international trade, the quantity produced and sold

Figure VI-3

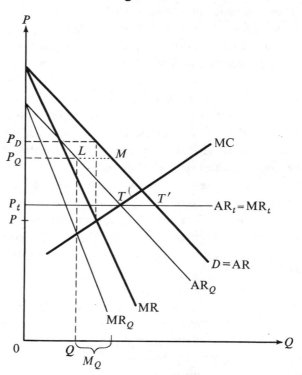

domestically is shown by the intersection of MR and MC, with the resulting price $\overline{OP_D}$.

Assume now that the international price of the commodity is $\overline{OP}$. If the economy is opened up to international trade, with a tariff $\overline{PP_t}$ imposed on the commodity, then the domestic price cannot rise above $\overline{OP_t}$. In fact, the demand curve would then become kinked: $\overline{P_t TT'D}$. Along its flat portion it coincides with the marginal revenue, MR_t. Domestic output would then be $\overline{P_t T}$, where point T is the intersection of the MC and the MR_t curves, while imports would equal $\overline{TT'}$, all sold at price $\overline{OP_t}$.

If the import volume under the tariff regime, $\overline{TT'}$ is converted into a quota, then we have a dominant supplier model, under which the monopolist need only accommodate himself to a fixed amount of imports. Graphically, the market demand curve remains unaffected, but the demand curve facing the monopolist is AR_Q, obtained by shifting the market AR leftward (horizontally) by the amount of the quota. The corresponding marginal revenue curve, MR_Q, is then generated. Domestic output is determined by the intersection of MC and MR_Q, yielding price $\overline{OP_Q}$. The quantity imported, LM (shown as M_Q on the horizontal axis) is the same as that under a tariff regime, but the price charged, and therefore monopoly profit accruing to the importers, is higher.

Bibliography

General References

Instructors wishing to supplement the text with relevant articles, will find no shortage of reading volumes (paperbacks) on which to draw. A selected, though far from exhaustive list, is offered below:

Balassa, Bela (ed.). *The Changing Patterns in Foreign Trade and Payments*. New York: W.W. Norton, 1970. Covers selected policy issues.

Baldwin, R.E., and J.O. Richardson (eds.). *International Trade and Finance*. Boston: Little Brown, 1974. Readings covering both trade and finance; theory as well as policy.

Cohen, Benjamin (ed.). *American Foreign Economic Policy*. New York: Harper and Row, 1968. Covers a variety of policy issues.

Kapoor, A., and P. Drab (eds.). *The Multinational Enterprise In Transition*. Princeton: The Darwin Press, 1972.

Krause, W., and F.J. Mathis, *International Economics and Business*. Boston: Houghton Mifflin, 1968. Covers a wide range of policy issues.

Meier, Gerald M. *Problems of Trade Policy*. New York: Oxford University Press, 1973. Covers commercial policy.

Officer, L., and T. Willet (eds.). *The International Currency System*. Columbia, Missouri: Lucas Brothers, 1973.

For more advanced theoretical topics, see

Caves, R., and H. Johnson (eds.). *Readings in International Economics*. Homewood, Illinois: R.D. Irwin, 1968.

Survey Articles

Over the past decade, numerous articles and monographs have appeared, each surveying a portion of the field of international economics. These in-depth surveys may or may not be at a higher level of sophistication than this textbook. They are usually accompanied by extensive bibliographies that are useful to students pursuing further work in a specific area. A selected list of such surveys is offered below. Except for the first three entries, the list is divided into two parts (following the organization of the book): contributions dealing with international finance and contributions dealing with international trade. The title of each article describes

445

adequately the specific area that it covers. The first three publications cover both finance and trade.

Clement, M.O., R.L. Pfister, and K.J. Rothwell. *Theoretical Issues in International Economics.* Boston: Houghton Mifflin, 1967.

Corden, W.M., "Recent Developments In The Theory of International Trade," *Special Papers in International Economics,* No. 7 (March 1965), International Finance Section, Princeton University.

Haberler, Gottfried. "A Survey of International Trade Theory," *Special Papers In International Economics,* No. 1 (July 1961), International Finance Section, Princeton University.

Finance

Fellner, William, "The Dollar's Place in the International System: Suggested Criteria for The Appraisal of Emerging Views," *Journal of Economic Literature,* Sept. 1972, pp. 735–54.

Grubel, Herbert G., "The Demand for International Reserves: A Critical Review of The Literature," *Journal of Economic Literature,* Dec. 1971, pp. 1148–66.

Krueger, Anne O., "Balance of Payments Theory," *Journal of Economic Literature,* Mar. 1969, pp. 1–26.

Machlup, Fritz, "Plans for Reform of the International Monetary System," *Special Papers in International Economics,* No. 3 (August 1962), International Finance Section, Princeton University.

Whitman, Marina V.N., "Policies for Internal and External Balance," *Special Papers in International Economics,* No. 9 (Dec. 1970), International Finance Section, Princeton University.

Williamson, J., "International Liquidity—A Survey," *Economic Journal,* September 1973.

Trade

Bhagwati, Jadish, "The Pure Theory of International Trade," *Economic Journal,* Mar. 1964.

Corden, W.M. *The Theory of Protection.* New York: Oxford University Press, 1971.

Krauss, Melvyn B., "Recent Developments in Customs Union Theory: An Interpretive Survey," *Journal of Economic Literature,* June 1972, pp. 413–36.

Meier, G.M. *International Trade and Development.* Evanston, Ill.: Harper and Row, 1963.

Stern, Robert, "Tariffs and Other Measures of Trade Control: A Survey of Recent Developments," *Journal of Economic Literature,* September 1973, pp. 857–88.

Selected Readings

Chapters 1–3

Cooper, R.N. *The Economics of Inter-Dependence: Economic Policy in the Atlantic Community.* New York: McGraw-Hill, 1968.

Friedman, I., "The International Monetary System," *IMF Staff Papers,* July 1963, pp. 221–34. Reprinted in R.A. Ward (ed.). *Monetary Theory and Policy.* Scranton, Pa.: International Textbook Co., 1966.

Gold, J. *Interpretation by the Fund.* Washington, D.C.: IMF Pamphlet Series, No. 11, 1968; *The Reform of the Fund.* IMF Pamphlet Series, No. 12, 1969.

Grubel, H.G. *Foreign Exchange, Speculation, and the International Flow of Capital.* Stanford, Cal.: Stanford University Press, 1966.

Heller, R. *International Trade: Theory and Empirical Evidence.* 2nd ed. Englewood Cliffs, N.J.: Prentice-Hall, 1973, Chapter 1.

Holmes, A.R., and F.H. Schoot. *The New Foreign Exchange Market.* New York: Federal Reserve Bank of New York, 1965, pp. 9–17. Reprinted in R.A. Ward (ed.). *Monetary Theory and Policy.* Scranton, Pa.: International Textbook Co., 1966.

Host-Madsen, P. *Balance of Payments—Its Meaning and Uses.* Washington, D.C.: IMF Pamphlet Series, No. 9, 1967.

International Monetary Fund. *Balance of Payments Concepts and Definitions.* Washington, D.C.: IMF Pamphlet Series, No. 10, 1969.

————, "Terms Used in Balance of Payments Analysis," *IMF Survey,* Nov. 12, 23 and Dec. 17, 1973.

Klopstock, F., "The Euro-dollar Market: Some Unresolved Issues," Princeton *Essays in International Finance,* No. 65, 1968.

Pizer, S., and E. Cutler, "U.S. Business Investments in Foreign Countries," *Survey of Current Business* (supplement), 1960.

Rivlin, D.T., "The U.S. Balance of Payments: Revised Presentation," *Survey of Current Business,* June 1971, pp. 24–57.

Schott, F.H., "The Evolution of Latin American Exchange Rate Policies Since World War II," Princeton *Essays in International Finance,* No. 32, 1959.

Sergeyer, V.P., "Economic Principles of the Foreign Trade of the Socialist States." In R. Harrod and D.C. Hague (eds.), *International Trade Theory in a Developing World.* New York: St. Martins Press, 1963, Chapter 12.

Tew, B., "The International Monetary Fund: Its Present Role and Future Prospects," Princeton *Essays in International Finance,* No. 36, 1961.

Weston, F., and B. Sorge, *International Managerial Finance.* Homewood, Ill.: R.D. Irwin, 1972.

Chapter 4

Caterbery, E.R., "Foreign Exchange, Capital Flows and Monetary Policy," *Princeton Studies in International Finance,* No. 15, 1965.

Cooper, R.N., "Macroeconomic Policy Adjustment in Interdependent Economies," *Quarterly Journal of Economics.* Feb. 1969.

Corden, M., "Geometrical Representation of Policies to Attain Internal and External Balance," *Review of Economic Studies,* Oct. 1960.

Corden, M., and M. Hemming, "Import Restrictions as an Instrument of Balance of Payments Policy," *Economic Journal,* Sept. 1958.

Helliwell, J., "Monetary and Fiscal Policies for an Open Economy," *Oxford Economic Papers,* Mar. 1969.

Metzler, L.A., "The Transfer Problem Reconsidered." In H.S. Ellis and L.A. Metzler (eds.). *Readings in the Theory of International Trade.* Homewood, Ill.: Irwin, 1949.

Michaeli, M., *Balance of Payments Adjustment Policies*. New York: National Bureau of Economic Research, 1968.

Neisser, H., and F. Modigliani. *National Income and International Trade*. Urbana: University of Illinois, 1953.

Officer, L., and T. Willett, "The Covered Arbitrage Schedule: A Critical Survey of Recent Developments," *Journal of Money Credit and Banking,* May 1970.

Robinson, R., "A Graphical Analysis of the Foreign Trade Multiplier," *Economic Journal,* Sept. 1952.

Stein, J.S., "The Nature and Efficiency of the Foreign Exchange Market," Princeton *Essays in International Finance,* No. 40, 1962.

Stolper, W., "The Volume of Trade and the Level of Living," *Quarterly Journal of Economics,* Feb. 1942.

Swan, T.W., "Longer Run Problems of the Balance of Payments." In R.E. Caves and H.G. Johnson (eds.). *Readings in International Economics*. Homewood, Ill.: Irwin, 1968.

Vanek, J., *International Trade*. Homewood, Ill.: Irwin, 1962, Chapters 4, 6.

White, W.H., "Interest Rate Differential and Capital Movements," *IMF Staff Papers,* Nov. 1963.

Chapter 5

Alexander, S.S., "The Effects of a Devaluation on the Trade Balance," *IMF Staff Papers,* April 1952.

————, "Devaluation vs. Import Restrictions," *IMF Staff Papers,* April 1958.

Cooper, R., "Currency Devaluation in Developing Countries," Princeton *Essays in International Finance,* No. 86, 1971.

Diaz Alejandro, C.F. *Exchange Rate Devaluation in a Semi-Industrialized Country —the Experience of Argentina 1955–1961*. Boston: MIT Press, 1965.

Gillespie, R., and P. Rushing, "Expenditure Switching vs. Altering Absorption: An Empirical Approach," *Southern Economic Journal,* Jul. 1973.

Haberler, G., "The Market for Foreign Exchange and the Stability of the Balance of Payments," *Kyklos* Fasc. 3, 1949.

Harberger, A., "Currency Depreciation, Income and the Balance of Trade," *Journal of Political Economy,* February 1950.

Johnson, H.G., "Towards a General Theory of the Balance of Payments." In R.E. Caves and H.G. Johnson (eds.). *Readings in International Economics*. Homewood, Ill.: Irwin, 1968, Chapter 23.

Laursen, S., and L.A. Metzler, "Flexible Exchange Rates and the Theory of Employment," *Review of Economics and Statistics,* Nov. 1950.

Machlup, F., "The Terms of Trade Effects of Devaluation Upon Real Income and the Balance of Trade," *Kyklos,* Fasc. 4, 1956.

Magee, S.P., "Currency Contracts, Pass-through, and Devaluation," *Brookings Papers on Economic Activity,* No. 1, 1973.

Mundell, R.A., "The Appropriate Use of Monetary and Fiscal Policy for Internal and External Stability," *IMF Staff Papers,* Mar. 1962.

————, "Capital Mobility and Stabilization Policy Under Fixed and Flexible Exchange Rates," *Canadian Journal of Economics and Political Science,* Nov. 1963.

Officer, L., "The Effect of Monopoly in Commodity Markets Upon the Foreign Exchange Market," *Quarterly Journal of Economics,* May 1966.

———, "A Comparison of the Effects of Monopoly and Competition in Commodity Markets Upon the Foreign Exchange Market," *Western Economic Journal,* Dec. 1969.

Smith, W., "Effects of Exchange Rate Adjustment on the Standard of Living," *American Economic Review,* Dec. 1954.

Yeager, L.B., *International Monetary Relations.* New York: Harper and Row, 1966, Chapters 8, 9.

Chapter 6

Balassa, B., "The Purchasing Power Parity Doctrine," *Journal of Political Economy,* Dec. 1964.

Ball, R.J. (ed.). *The International Linkage of National Econometric Models.* Amsterdam: North-Holland Publishing Co., 1973.

Harberger, A., "Some Evidence on the International Price Mechanism," *Review of Economics and Statistics* (supplement), Feb. 1958.

Houthakker, H., and S. Magee, "Income and Price Elasticities in World Trade," *Review of Economics and Statistics,* May 1969.

Junz, H.B., and R.R. Rhomberg, "Prices and Export Performance of Industrial Countries," *IMF Staff Papers,* Jul. 1965.

———, "Price Competitiveness in Export Trade Among Industrial Countries," *American Economic Review,* May 1973.

Krause, L., "United States Imports, 1947–1958," *Econometrica,* April 1962.

Kreinin, M., "Price Elasticities in International Trade," *Review of Economics and Statistics,* Nov. 1967.

———, "Disaggregated Import Demand Functions," *Southern Journal of Economics,* Jul. 1973.

———, "A Further Note on the Elasticity of Substitution," *Canadian Journal of Economics,* Nov. 1973.

Leamer, E., and R. Stern. *Quantitative International Economics.* Boston: Allyn and Bacon, 1969.

Orcutt, G., "Measurement of Elasticities in International Trade," *Review of Economics and Statistics,* May 1950.

Chapters 7–9

Branson, W., "Trade Effects of the 1971 Currency Realignments," *Brookings Papers on Economic Activity,* No. 1, 1972.

Cooper, R.C., "The Balance of Payments in Review," *Journal of Political Economy,* Aug. 1966.

Depres, E. *International Economic Reform.* New York: Oxford University Press, 1973, Chapters 13–16.

Dunn, R.M., "Exchange Rigidities, Investments Distortions and the Failure of Bretton Woods," *Princeton Essays in International Finance,* No. 97, Feb. 1973.

Fleming, R., "The SDR: Some Problems and Possibilities," *IMF Staff Papers,* Mar. 1971.

Floyd, J.E., "The Overvaluation of the Dollar," *American Economic Review,* Mar. 1965.

Frisch, R., "On the Need for Forecasting a Multilateral Balance of Payments," *American Economic Review,* Sept. 1947.

Furth, H., "The U.S. Balance of Payments and the Recession," *Quarterly Journal of Economics,* May 1959.

Hause, J.C., "The Welfare Cost of Disequilibrium Exchange Rates," *Journal of Political Economy,* Aug. 1966.

Herring R., and T. Willett, "The Capital Control Program and U.S. Investments Activity Abroad," *Southern Economic Journal,* Jul. 1972.

Hinshaw, R., "Towards European Convertibility," *Princeton Series in International Finance,* No. 31, November 1968.

International Monetary Fund, *Special Drawing Rights: Character and Use,* Pamphlet No. 13 (Washington), 1970.

Kindleberger, C., "The Dollar Shortage Revisited," *American Economic Review,* June 1958.

Kindleberger, C., W. Salant, and E. Depres. "The Dollar and World Liquidity: A Minority View," *The Economist* (London), February 5, 1966. Reprinted in E. Depres. *International Economic Reform.* New York: Oxford University Press, 1973, Chapter 17.

Krause, L., "Private International Finance," *Brookings Institution Reprint Series,* No. 223, 1972.

Kreinin, M., "Needed—A Super-Agency for International Finance, Trade and Aid," *Journal of Economic Issues,* Dec. 1972.

Kreinin, M., and R. Gilbert, "The Demand for Foreign Currency Holdings by European Banks," *Southern Economic Journal,* Jul. 1971.

Krueger, A., "Some Economic Costs of Exchange Control: The Turkish Case," *Journal of Political Economy,* Oct. 1966.

Machlup, F., *Remaking the International Currency System.* Baltimore: Johns Hopkins Press, 1968.

Makin, J.H., "The Composition of International Reserve Holdings," *American Economic Review,* Dec. 1971.

Mundell, R., "The Dollar and the Policy Mix: 1971," Princeton *Essays in International Finance,* No. 85, 1971.

Salant, W., "The Post-Devaluation Weakness of the Dollar," *Brookings Papers in Economic Activity,* No. 2, 1973.

Scaperlanda, and Mauer, "Impact of U.S. Foreign Investments Control Program," *Southern Economic Journal,* Jan. 1973.

Triffin, R., *Europe and the Money Muddle.* New Haven, Conn.: Yale University Press, 1957.

Yeager, L.B., *International Monetary Relations.* New York: Harper and Row, 1966.

Chapter 10

Aliber, R., "National Preferences and the Scope for International Monetary Reform," Princeton *Essays in International Finance,* No. 101, 1973.

Corden, M., "Monetary Integration," Princeton *Essays in International Finance,* No. 93, 1972.

Flanders, J., "The Demand for International Reserves," *Princeton Studies in International Finance,* No. 27, 1971.

Friedman, M., "The Case for Flexible Exchange Rates." In R.E. Caves and H. G. Johnson (eds.). *Readings in International Economics.* Homewood, Ill.: Irwin, 1968, Chapter 25.

Friedman, M., and R. Roosa, *The Balance of Payments: Free Versus Fixed Exchange Rates.* Washington, D.C.: American Enterprise Institute, 1967.

Halm, G., "The Band Proposal: The Limits of Permissible Exchange Rate Variations," Princeton *Special Papers in International Economics,* No. 6, 1965.

———, "Toward Limited Exchange Rate Flexibility," Princeton *Essays in International Finance,* No. 73, 1969.

Heller, R., "Optimal International Reserves," *Economic Journal,* June 1966.

Ingram, J., "The Case for European Monetary Integration," Princeton *Essays in International Finance,* No. 98, 1973.

Johnson, H., "Theoretical Problems of the International Monetary System," *Pakistan Development Review,* 1967.

Kenen, P., "International Liquidity and the Balance of Payments of a Reserve Currency Area," *Quarterly Journal of Economics,* Nov. 1960.

———, "Reserve Asset Preferences of Central Banks and Stability of the Gold Exchange Standard," *Princeton Studies in International Finance,* No. 10, 1963.

———, "The Theory of Optimum Currency Areas: An Eclectic View." In R. A. Mundell and A. K. Swoboda (eds.). *Monetary Problems of the International Economy,* University of Chicago Press, 1969.

Kenen, P., P. McCracken, J. Holliwell, and R. Heller, "The Costs and Benefits of the Dollar as a Reserve Currency," *American Economic Review,* May 1973.

Kenen, P., and Yudin, "The Demand for International Reserves," *Review of Economics and Statistics,* Aug. 1965.

Kreinin M., and R. Heller, "Adjustment Costs, Currency Areas and Reserves." In W. Sellekarts (ed.). *Essays in Honor of Ian Tinbergen,* New York: Macmillan, 1974.

Lanyi, A., "The Case for Floating Exchange Rates Reconsidered," *Princeton Essays in International Finance,* No. 72, 1969.

Machlup, F., "On Terms, Concepts, Theories and Strategies in the Discussion of Greater Flexibility of Exchange Rates," *Princeton Reprints in International Finance,* No. 14, 1970.

———, "The Cloakroom Rule of International Reserves," *Quarterly Journal of Economics,* Aug. 1965.

McKinnon, R., "Private and Official Money: The Case for the Dollar," Princeton *Essays in International Finance,* No. 74, 1969.

———, "Optimum Currency Areas," *American Economic Review,* Sept. 1963.

Magnifico, G., *European Monetary Unification.* London: McMillan, 1973.

Meade, J., "The Belgium-Luxembourg Economic Union," Princeton *Essays in International Finance,* No. 25, 1956.

Mundell, R.A., "A Theory of Optimum Currency Areas," *American Economic Review,* September 1961.

Mundell, R.A., and A.K. Swoboda (eds.). *Monetary Problems of the International Economy.* Chicago: University of Chicago Press, 1969.

Park, Y.S., "The Link Between Special Drawing Rights and Development Finance," Princeton *Essays in International Finance,* No. 100, Sept. 1973.

Sohmen, E., "International Monetary Problems and the Foreign Exchanges," Princeton *Special Papers in International Economics,* No. 4, 1963.

Symposium on International Liquidity, summarized by J. Letiche, *American Economic Review,* May 1968.

Symposium on the International Monetary System. Papers by J. Bhagwati, R. Cooper, J. Fleming, R. Triffin, H. Johnson, C. Kindleberger, and P. Samuelson, in the *Journal of International Economics,* Sept. 1972.

Thomas, L., "The Behavior of Flexible Exchange Rates," *Southern Economic Journal,* Oct. 1973.

Triffin, R., *Gold and the Dollar Crisis.* New Haven, Conn.: Yale University Press, 1961.

Williamson, J., "The Crawling Peg," Princeton *Essays in International Finance,* No. 50, 1965.

Chapter 11

Chenery, H.B., "Comparative Advantage and Development Policy," *American Economic Review,* Mar. 1961.

GATT, *International Trade,* Annual Reports, Geneva.

Graham, F., "The Theory of International Values Re-examined," in H. Ellis and L. Metzler (eds.). *Readings in the Theory of International Trade.* Homewood, Ill.: Irwin, 1949, Chapter 14.

Haberler, G., *The Theory of International Trade.* New York: Macmillan, 1950, Chapters IX–XII.

Leontief, V., "The Use of Indifference Curves in the Analysis of Foreign Trade." In H. Ellis and L. Metzler (eds.). *Readings in the Theory of International Trade.* Homewood, Ill.: Irwin, 1949, Chapter 10.

Meade, J.E., *A Geometry of International Trade.* London: Allen & Unwin, 1951.

Samuelson, P.A., "The Gains from International Trade." In H. Ellis and L. Metzler (eds.). *Readings in the Theory of International Trade.* Homewood Ill.: Irwin, 1949, Chapter 11.

Viner, J., *Studies in the Theory of International Trade,* New York: Harper & Brothers, 1937, Chapters VIII, IX.

Chapter 12

Arrow, K., H. Chenery, Minhas, and R. Solow, "Capital-Labor Substitution and Economic Efficiency," *Review of Economics and Statistics,* Aug. 1961.

Balassa, B., "An Empirical Demonstration of Classical Comparative Cost Theory," *Review of Economics and Statistics,* Aug. 1965.

Baldwin, R., "Determinants of the Commodity Structure of U.S. Trade," *American Economic Review,* Mar. 1971.

Bhagwati J., and H. Johnson, "Notes on Some Controversies in the Theory of International Trade," *Economic Journal,* Mar. 1960.

Blumenthal, T., "Export and Economic Growth: The Case of Japan," *Quarterly Journal of Economics,* November 1972.

Branson W., and H. Junz, "Trends in U.S. Trade and Comparative Advantage," *Brookings Papers in Economic Activity,* 1971, No. 2 and 3.

Caves, R., *Trade and the Economic Structure.* Cambridge, Mass.: Harvard University Press, 1963.

Chenery, H., "Patterns of Industrial Growth," *American Economic Review,* Sept. 1960.

Diab, A., *The U.S. Capital Position and the Structure of Its Foreign Trade*, Amsterdam: North-Holland Publishing Co., 1956.

Flatters, F., "Commodity Price Equalization: A Note on Factor Mobility and Trade," *American Economic Review*, June 1972.

Heckscher, E., "The Effect of Foreign Trade on the Distribution of Income." In H. Ellis and L. Metzler (eds.). *Readings in the Theory of International Trade*. Homewood, Ill.: Irwin, 1949, Chapter 13.

Hicks, J.R., "The Long-Run Dollar Problem." In R.E. Caves and H.G. Johnson (eds.). *Readings in International Economics*. Homewood, Ill.: Irwin, 1968, Chapter 26.

Hufbauer, G., "The Commodity Composition of Trade in Manufactured Goods." In R. Vernon (ed.). *The Technology Factor in International Trade*. New York: National Bureau of Economic Research, 1970, pp. 145–232.

Johnson, H., "Economic Expansion and International Trade," *Manchester School*, May 1955.

————, "Factor Endowments, International Trade, and Factor Prices," *Manchester School*, Sept. 1957.

————. *International Trade and Economic Growth*. Cambridge, Mass.: Harvard University Press, 1961.

Jones, R., "Factor Proportions and the Heckscher-Ohlin Model," *Review of Economic Studies*, 1956–57.

Keesing, D., "Labor Skills and International Trade," *Review of Economics and Statistics*, August 1965.

————, "Labor Skills and Comparative Advantage," *American Economic Review*, May 1966.

Kenen, P., "Nature, Capital and Trade," *Journal of Political Economy*, October 1965.

Kindleberger, C., *Foreign Trade and the National Economy*. New Haven, Conn.: Yale University Press, 1962.

Kravis, I., "Wages and Foreign Trade," *Review of Economics and Statistics*, February 1956.

————, "Availability and Other Influences on the Commodity Composition of Trade," *Journal of Political Economy*, Apr. 1956.

Kreinin, M., "The Leontief Paradox," *American Economic Review*, Mar. 1965.

————, "The Theory of Comparative Cost—Further Evidence," *Economia Internazionale*, Nov. 1969.

Lancaster, K., "The Heckscher-Ohlin Model—A Geometric Treatment," *Economica*, Feb. 1957.

Leontief, V., "Domestic Production and Foreign Trade; The American Capital Position Re-examined." In R.E. Caves and H.G. Johnson, (eds.). Readings in International Economics. Homewood Ill.: Irwin, 1968, Chapter 30.

————. "Factor Proportions and the Structure of American Foreign Trade," *Review of Economics and Statistics*, Nov. 1956.

————, "The Structure of the U.S. Economy," *Scientific American*, Apr. 1965.

Lerner, A., "Factor Prices and International Trade," *Economica*, Feb. 1952.

Linder, S., *An Essay On Trade and Transformation*. New York: John Wiley & Sons, 1961.

MacDougall, G.D.A., "British and American Exports: A Study Suggested by the Theory of Comparative Costs," *Economic Journal*, Dec. 1951 and Sept. 1952.

Michaels, M., "Factor Proportions in International Trade: Current State of the Theory," *Kyklos,* 1964.

Mundell, A., "International Trade and Factor Mobility." In R.E. Caves and H.G. Johnson (eds.). *Readings in International Economics.* Homewood, Ill.: Irwin, 1968, Chapter 7.

Ohlin, B., *International and Interregional Trade.* Cambridge, Mass.: Harvard Economic Studies, 1933; revised ed., 1967.

Posner, M., "International Trade and Technological Change," *Oxford Economic Papers,* Oct. 1961.

Robinson, R., "Factor Proportions and Comparative Advantage," *Quarterly Journal of Economics,* May 1956 and Aug. 1956.

Rosefield, S., "Factor Proportions and Economic Rationality in Soviet International Trade, 1955–1968," *American Economic Review,* September 1974.

Rybczynski, T.M., "Factor Endowment and Relative Commodity Prices." In R.E. Caves and H.G. Johnson (eds.). *Readings in International Economics.* Homewood, Ill.: Irwin, 1968, Chapter 4.

Samuelson, P., "International Factor Price Equalization," *Economic Journal,* June 1948.

———. "International Factor Price Equalization Once Again," *Economic Journal,* June 1949.

Stern, R., "British and American Productivity and Comparative Costs in International Trade," *Oxford Economic Papers,* October 1962.

Stolper, W., and P. Samuelson, "Protection and Real Wages," *Review of Economic Studies,* Nov. 1941.

Travis, W., *The Theory of Trade and Protection.* Cambridge, Mass.: Harvard University Press, 1964.

Vanek, J., *The Natural Resource Content of United States Foreign Trade 1870–1955,* Cambridge, Mass.: MIT Press, 1963.

———, "Variable Factor Proportions and Interindustry Flows in Trade Theory," *Quarterly Journal of Economics,* Feb. 1963.

Vernon, R., "International Investment and International Trade in the Product Cycle," *Quarterly Journal of Economics,* May 1966.

Chapter 13

Balassa, B., "Tariff Protection in Industrial Countries: An Evaluation." In R.E. Caves and H.G. Johnson (eds.). *Readings in International Economics.* Homewood, Ill.: Irwin, 1968, Chapter 33.

———. *The Structure of Protection in Developing Countries.* Baltimore: The Johns Hopkins Press, 1971.

———, "Tariff Protection in Industrial Nations and Its Effects on the Exports of Processed Goods from Developing Countries," *Canadian Journal of Economics,* Aug. 1968.

Balassa B., and D. Schydlowsky, "Effective Tariffs, Domestic Cost of Foreign Exchange, and the Equilibrium Exchange Rate," *Journal of Political Economy,* May, June 1968; and Jan., Feb. 1972.

Barker, T., and S. Han, "Effective Rate of Protection for United Kingdom Production," *Economic Journal,* June 1971.

Basevi, G., "The United States Tariff Structure: Estimates of Effective Rates of Protection of U.S. Industries and Industrial Labor, *Review of Economics and Statistics,* May 1966.

Bhagwati J., and H. Johnson, "A Generalized Theory of the Effects of Tariffs on the Terms of Trade," *Oxford Economic Papers,* Oct. 1961.

Black, J., "Arguments for Tariffs," *Oxford Economic Papers,* June 1959.

Corden, M., *The Theory of Protection.* New York: Oxford University Press, 1971.

———, "The Structure of a Tariff System and the Effective Protective Rate," *Journal of Political Economy,* June 1966.

———, "Protection and Growth," *International Economics and Development.* New York: Academic Press, 1972.

DeVries, M., "Trade and Exchange Policy and Economic Development," *Oxford Economic Papers,* Mar. 1960.

Grubel H., and H. Johnson (eds.). *Effective Tariff Protection.* Geneva, Switzerland: GATT and the Graduate Institute for International Studies, 1971.

———, "Nominal Tariffs, Indirect Taxes, and Effective Rates of Protection: The Common Market Countries 1959," *Economic Journal,* Dec. 1967.

———, "Nominal Tariff Rates and United States Valuation Practices: Two Case Studies," *Review of Economics and Statistics,* May 1967.

Haberler, G., "Some Problems in the Pure Theory of International Trade." In R.E. Caves and H.G. Johnson, (eds.). *Readings in International Economics.* Homewood, Ill.: Irwin, 1968, Chapter 13.

Johnson, H., "Optimum Tariffs and Retaliation," *Review of Economic Studies,* 1953–54, pp. 142–9.

———, "Effective Protection and Preferences," *Economica,* May 1969.

———, "The Cost of Protection and the Scientific Tariff," *Journal of Political Economy,* August 1960; "The Cost of Protection and Self Sufficiency," *Quarterly Journal of Economics,* Aug. 1965.

Kreinin, M., "On the Dynamic Effects of a Customs Union," *Journal of Political Economy,* Apr. 1964.

———, "Trade Creation and Diversion in a Customs Union: A Graphical Presentation," *Kyklos,* Fasc. 4, 1963.

Kreinin, M., J. Ramsey, and J. Kmenta, "Factor Substitution and Effective Protection Reconsidered," *American Economic Review,* Dec. 1971.

Leith, C., "Substitution and Supply Elasticities in Calculating the Effective Protective Rate," *Quarterly Journal of Economics,* Nov. 1968.

———, "The Effect of Tariffs on Production, Consumption, and Trade: A Revised Analysis," *American Economic Review,* Mar. 1971.

Leith, C., and G. Reuber, "The Impact of the Industrial Countries' Tariff Structure on their Imports of Manufactures from the Less Developed Areas," *Economica,* February 1969.

Lewis, S., and S. Guisinger, "Measuring Protection in a Developing Country: The Case of Pakistan," *Journal of Political Economy,* Nov., Dec. 1968.

Lipsey, R., "The Theory of Customs Unions—A General Survey." In R.E. Caves and H.G. Johnson (eds.). *Readings in International Economics.* Homewood, Ill.: Irwin, 1968, Chapter 16.

Magee, S., "The Welfare Effects of Restrictions on U.S. Trade," *Brookings Papers on Economic Activity,* No. 3, 1972.

Meade, J., *Trade and Welfare.* London: Oxford University Press, 1955.

Meade, J., *The Theory of Customs Unions*. Amsterdam: North-Holland Publishing Co., 1955.

Metzler, L., "Tariffs, The Terms of Trade and the Distribution of National Income." In R.E. Caves and H.G. Johnson (eds.). *Readings in International Economics*. Homewood, Ill.: Irwin, 1968, Chapter 2.

Myint, H., "Infant Industry Arguments for Assistance to Industries in the Setting of Dynamic Trade Theory." In R. Harrod and D. Hague (eds.). *International Trade Theory in a Developing World*. New York: St. Martins Press, 1963. Chapter 7.

Nagui, S., "Protection and Economic Development," *Kyklos,* Winter 1969.

Reimer, R., "Effective Rates of Protection in East Africa," *East African Economic Review,* Dec. 1971.

Vanek, J., "Tariff, Economic Welfare and Development Potential," *Economic Journal,* Dec. 1971.

Wipf, L., "Tariffs, Nontariff Distortions, and Effective Protection in U.S. Agriculture," *American Journal of Agricultural Economics,* Aug. 1971.

Chapter 14

Humphrey, D., *The United States and the Common Market*. New York: Praeger, 1962.

Jonish, J., "Adjustment Assistance Under the U.S.—Canadian Automotive Agreement," *Industrial and Labor Relations Review,* July 1970.

Kelly, W., "The Expanded Trade Agreements Escape Clause, 1955–61," *Journal of Political Economy*, Feb. 1961.

Kravis, I., "The Trade Agreements Escape Clause," *American Economic Review,* June 1954.

Kreinin, M., *Alternative Commercial Policies*. East Lansing, Mich.: MSU Bureau of Economic and Business Research, 1967.

Murray, T., and M. Edgmand, "Full Employment Trade Expansion and Adjustment Assistance," *Southern Economic Journal,* April 1970.

U.S. Department of State, "How a Trade Agreement is Made," Washington, D.C.: Department of State Bulletin, Feb. 24, 1958.

U.S. Tariff Commission, *Operation of The Trade Agreements Program*, Annual Reports, Washington, D.C.

Chapter 15

Balassa, B., and associates, *Studies in Trade Liberalization*. Baltimore: Johns Hopkins Press, 1967 (especially Chapters 8, 9).

Baldwin, R., *Nontariff Distortions of International Trade*. Washington D.C.: The Brookings Institution, 1970.

Bergsten, F., "On The Non-Equivalence of Import Quotas and 'Voluntary' Export Restraints." In F. Bergsten (ed.). *Toward A New Trade Policy: The Maidenhead Papers*. Washington, D.C.: Brookings Institution, 1974.

Bhagwati, J., "The Theory and Practice of Commercial Policy: Departures from Unified Exchange Rates," Princeton *Special Papers in International Economics,* No. 8, 1968.

————, "On the Equivalence of Tariffs and Quotas." In R. Baldwin (ed.). *Trade Growth and the Balance of Payments*. Chicago: Rand McNally, 1965.

Grubel, H., and H. Johnson, "Nominal Tariff Rates and United States Valuation Practices: Two Case Studies," *Review of Economics and Statistics,* May 1967.

Haberler, G., "Import Taxes and Export Subsidies: A Substitute for Realignment of Exchange Rates?", *Kyklos,* 1967.

Holzman, F., "Comparison of Different Forms of Trade Barriers," *Review of Economics and Statistics,* May 1969.

Patterson, G., *Discrimination in International Trade, 1945–1965.* Princeton, N.J.: Princeton University Press, 1966.

Rom, M., "National Tariff Quotas in the Common Market," *Aussenwirtschaft,* Mar. 1972.

Shibata, A., "On the Equivalence of Tariffs and Quotas," *American Economic Review,* Mar. 1968.

Shoup, C. (ed.). *Fiscal Harmonization in Common Markets.* New York: Columbia University Press, 1967.

Viner, J., *Dumping: A Problem in International Trade,* Chicago, Ill.: University of Chicago Press, 1923.

Walter, I., *Trade Policy for the 1970's: The Free Trade Area Alternative.* New York: New York University Press, 1969, Chapter 8.

Walter, I., and J. Chung, "Non-Tariff Distortions and Trade Preferences For Developing Countries, *Kyklos,* Fasc. 4, 1971.

Weaver, J., "The Impact of U.S. Cotton Textile Quotas on the LDC," *Southern Economic Journal,* Jul. 1968.

Chapter 16

Aitkin, N.D., "The Effect of the EEC and EFTA On European Trade," *American Economic Review,* Dec. 1973.

Balassa, B., *The Theory of Economic Integration.* Homewood, Ill.: Irwin, 1961.

———, *Trade Liberalization Among Industrial Countries.* New York: McGraw-Hill, 1967.

Balassa, B., and M. Kreinin, "Trade Liberalization Under the Kennedy Round— The Static Effects," *Review of Economics and Statistics,* May 1967.

Dell, S., *Trade Blocs and Common Markets.* New York: Knopf, 1963.

General Agreement on Tariffs and Trade. *GATT—What is It, How it Works.* Geneva, 1965.

Krause, L.B., *European Economic Integration and the United States.* Washington D.C.: The Brookings Institution, 1968.

Kreinin, M., "Effect of Tariff Changes on the Prices and Volume of Imports," *American Economic Review,* June 1961.

———, "Effect of the EEC On Imports of Manufactures," *Economic Journal,* Sept. 1972.

———, "Effect of EEC Enlargement on Trade Flows," *Southern Economic Journal,* Apr. 1973.

———, "Israel and the EEC," *Quarterly Journal of Economics,* May 1968.

Jelacic, J.E., "Impact of Granting MFN Treatment to the Countries of Eastern Europe and the People's Republic of China," U.S. Tariff Commission, Staff Research Studies, No. 6, Washington, D.C., 1974.

Preeg, E., *Traders and Diplomats.* Washington, D.C.: The Brookings Institution, 1970.

Resnick, S., and E. Truman, "The Distribution of West European Trade Under Alternative Tariff Policies," *Review of Economics and Statistics,* Feb. 1974.

Salant, W., and B. Vaccara. *Import Liberalization and Employment.* Washington, D.C.: The Brookings Institution, 1961.

Wilczynski, J., *The Economics and Politics of East-West Trade.* New York: Praeger, 1969.

Wolf, T., "A Note on the Restrictive Effect of Unilateral U.S. Export Control," *Journal of Political Economy,* Jan., Feb. 1973.

Chapter 17

Balassa, B., C. Clague, and I. Walter, "Commercial Policy and Less Developed Countries," *American Economic Review,* May 1971.

Balassa, B., "Regional Integration and Trade Liberalization In Latin America," *Journal of Common Market Studies,* Sept. 1971.

Bhagwati, J., and A. Krueger, "Exchange Control, Liberalization, and Economic Development," *American Economic Review,* May 1973.

Cooper, R., "The European Community's System of Generalized Preferences: A Criticue," *Journal of Development Studies,* Jul. 1973.

Iqbal, Z., "The Generalized System of Preferences and the Comparative Advantage of Less Developed Countries in Manufactures," *IMF Research Papers,* Apr. 12, 1974.

Johnson, H., *Economic Policies Toward Less Developed Countries.* Washington, D.C.: The Brookings Institution, 1966.

Kreinin, M., *EEC Trade Relations—An Empirical Investigation.* New York: Praeger, 1974, Chapter 7.

————, "Generalized Tariff Preferences—A Proposed Variant," *Journal of World Trade Law,* Summer 1973.

Lary, H., *Imports of Manufactures from Less Developed Countries.* New York: National Bureau of Economic Research, 1968.

Melvin, J., "The Effects of Tariff Preferences on Canadian Imports," *Canadian Journal of Economics,* Jan., Feb. 1972.

Murray, T., "How Helpful is the Generalized System of Preferences to Developing Countries," *Economic Journal,* June 1973.

————, "Preferential Tariffs for the LDCs," *Southern Economic Journal,* Jul. 1973.

Myint, H., "Economic Theory and Development Policy," *Economica,* May 1967.

————, "International Trade and the Developing Countries," in *Proceedings of the International Economic Association Meetings,* Montreal, Canada, Sept. 1968.

Nagui, S., "Protection and Economic Development," *Kyklos,* Fasc. 1, 1969.

Chapter 18

Baldwin, R., J. Baranson, and S. Hymer, "The International Firm and Efficient Economic Allocation," *American Economic Review,* May 1970.

Berry, R., and R. Soligo, "Some Welfare Aspects of International Migration," *Journal of Political Economy,* 1969.

Caves, R., "International Corporations: The Industrial Economics of Foreign Investments," *Economica,* Feb. 1971.

Helleiner, G., "Manufactured Exports from LDC and Multinational Firms," *Economic Journal,* Mar. 1973.

Kindleberger, C., *American Business Abroad.* New Haven, Conn.: Yale University Press, 1969.

―――― (ed.). *The International Corporation.* Cambridge, Mass.: MIT Press, 1970.

Kreinin, M., "Freedom of Trade and Capital Movement—Empirical Evidence," *Economic Journal,* Dec. 1965.

Mikesell, R., *U.S. Private and Government Investments Abroad.* Eugene, Ore: University of Oregon Press, 1962.

Musgrave, P., "Tax Preferences to Foreign Investments," in Joint Economic Committee, U.S. Congress, *The Economics of Federal Subsidy Programs,* June 11, 1972.

Parry, T., "The International Firm and National Economic Policy," *Economic Journal,* Dec. 1973.

Streeten, P., "The Multinational Enterprise and the Theory of Development Policy," *World Development,* Vol. 1, No. 10, Oct. 1973.

Vernon, R., *Sovereignty at Bay.* New York: Basic Books, 1971.

Index

Index

Absolute advantage, wage rates and, 219, 236–37

Absorption approach to devaluation, 112–15

Accommodating (balancing) items, 14–15

Ad valorem duty, 273–75, 294, 318, 405

Adjustable peg system, 44, 181, 185, 208

Agency for International Development (AID), 347

Agriculture: dumping, 340–41; EEC and, 326, 349–54, 365; in Great Britain, 352–53; prices, 205, 291, 326, 350; in West Germany, 205, 350

Agriculture, U.S. Department of, 335–36

American selling price (ASP), 274–75, 366–67

Antidumping duty, 343–44, 405

Appreciation, 27, 117, 120–23, 186, 187; defined, 98

Arbitrage, 38, 42; triangular, 39

Associated African and Malagasy States, 359

Atomic energy, 354

Australia: in OECD, 348; tariffs, 262

Austria, 206, 357; in EFTA, 308, 357, 358; in OECD, 348; revaluation, 171

Automatic credit, 145

Automatic processes in balance of payments adjustment, 58–80; monetary mechanism, impact of, 74–79; private expenditures, effect on, 58–74

Autonomous items, 13–15

Average propensity to consume (APC), 66

Average propensity to import (APM), 69

Average propensity to save (APS), 66

Balance of goods and services, 15, 16

Balance of international payments, 11–25, 28–29; accommodating items, 14–15; adjustment under fixed exchange rates, 56–96; adjustment under fluctuating exchange rates, 120–25; automatic adjustment processes, 58–80; autonomous items, 14–15; capital outflow, 402–03; in context of general policy objectives, 91–96; deficit and surplus, 11–18; devaluation and, *see* Devaluation; government policy, 80, 82–87; interdependence of nations and, 87–91; interrelationships among items, 18–19; limitations of information, 23–24; long-run shifts in merchandise trade balance, 19–21; monetary mechanism and, 74–79; private expenditure, effects on, 58–74; proper perspective on, 22–23; short-run imbalances, 56–58; statistics, uses and misuses of, 18–25; switching policies, 118; tariffs and, 291–92

Balance of Payments Yearbook, 18

Balance of trade, 11, 15, 16, 82–83
Bangladesh, 192, 360
Bank for International Settlement (BIS), 156
Barre Plan, 205
Barter trade, 110
Basic balance, 15, 16
Basic Documentation for the Tariff Study (GATT), 276, 301
Belgium, 206; in EEC, 307, 347; in OECD, 348; *see also* Franc (Belgian)
Benelux customs union, 347, 350
Bernstein, E. M., 167
Bilateral clearing agreements, 140–42, 143, 150, 238, 323, 346, 370
Black market, 138–39
Bolivia, 192
Bonds, 83, 91, 151
Border adjustments for internal taxes, 336–37
Brain drain, 407–08
Brazil, 186; export-oriented strategy, 273, 374, 375; tariffs, 276–77
Bretton Woods system, 33–35, 123, 132, 149–50, 169, 172; collapse of, 89, 155, 187–92; role of dollar, 44–50
British Commonwealth, 275, 360, 363
British Exchange Equalization Account (BEEA), 148
Brussels Tariff Nomenclature (BTN), 276, 300, 381, 382
Bryan, William Jennings, 158
Buchwald, Art, 158
Buffer stocks, 331–32
Buy American Act, 335

c.i.f. (cost, insurance, freight) price, 274, 276, 351, 366
Canada: export taxes, 283; international reserves, 154; in OECD, 348; tariffs, 266, 392–93; U.S. investments, 392–93, 395, 403; wheat prices, 290; *see also* Dollar (Canadian)
Capital: destabilizing movements, 57; direct investment, 83; exchange control, 135–40; and interest differentials, 83–87; long-term, 12; portfolio, 83; restrictions on flow of, 90–91; short-term, 13, 43, 83–87, 95, 134; stabilization movements, 57; transfer, 11, 13; *see also* Foreign investments
Capital-abundant country, 259, 264
Capital-intensive commodity, 259

Cartels, 337–40, 396
Central African (Customs) Union, 359, 360
Central American Common Market, 385, 386
Central American Customs Union, 385
Central banks: gold standard and, 146–47; joint floats, 51; managed floats, 50–51; offsetting policies, 77; *see also* Exchange rates; International reserves
Chemical industry (U.S.), 274–75
Chenery, H., 240
China, U.S. ban on exports, 370, 371, 396
Civil Aeronautics Board, 338
Classical economic doctrine, 76–77, 388
Closed economy, defined, 1–2
Commerce, U.S. Department of, 11, 15, 24, 151, 264, 276
Commercial paper, 83
Commercial policy (U.S.), 313–24; political considerations, 313–14; reciprocal trade agreements legislation, 314–19; trade adjustment assistance, 319–20; Trade Expansion Act (1962), 314, 320–21, 364; Trade Reform Act (1973), 321–24, 367, 371, 380, 383–84
Committee of 20, 181, 192, 209–10
Commodity composition of trade, 215, 217, 218, 234, 256–71, 405–06; economic adjustment to change, 269–71; economies of scale, 266–67; factor proportions (endowment) theory, 252–53, 257–65; human skills theory, 266, 268; preference similarity, 267–68; product cycle, 267; technological advance, 267
Commodity gain ratio, 222, 228
Commodity terms of trade, 118, 222
Commodity Trade Statistics (United Nations), 23, 178, 214
Common Agricultural Policy, 205
Common currency, 204–08
Common Market, *see* European Economic Community (EEC)
Community indifference maps, 245–46, 248
Comparative advantage, principle of, 139, 218–25, 231, 233, 236, 238, 253, 255, 257, 260, 269, 270, 299; complete specialization, 223–25; de-

mand considerations, 221–23; gains from trade, 218–21

Comparative opportunity cost, 225–26

Complete specialization, 223–25, 242, 260

Composite variable, 268–69

Compound duty, 273

Consistent economic situations, 91–92

Consumer indifference maps, 243–45

Consumer's surplus, 287

Constant cost conditions, 224–25

Constant opportunity cost, 242, 260

Consumption, income and, 61, 64–66

Coordinating Committee on Export Controls (COCOM), 370, 371

Coproduction agreements, 372

Corporate profit tax, 336

Corporations, 93–94, 169, 171; multi-national, 181–82, 400–01, 403–06

Cost-price relationship, 232

Cost-push inflation, 93

Council for Mutual Economic Assistance (CMEA or COMECON), 370

Crawling peg proposal, 208

Credit, automatic, 145

Credit *tranches,* 162

Cuba, 371

Currencies, *see* Bretton Woods system; Devaluation; Exchange rates; Gold standard; International reserves; names of currencies

Currency convertibility, 14, 24, 89, 210; concepts of, 142–43; European Payments Union (EPU), 143–45

Currency stabilization, 147–48

Currency swaps, 156

Currency union, 204–08

Current account balance, 15, 16

Current account convertibility, 142

Customs unions, 307–08, 363, 384–86; dynamic effects, 311–12; static effects, 308–11

De Gaulle, Charles, 158

Deadweight loss, 288

Deficit, 7–8; meaning of, 11–18; on merchandise trade, 20–21

Demand: comparative advantage and, 221–23; differences in, 253; price elasticity of, 100, 103; reciprocal, 222, 228–30, 232, 234; relatively elastic, 100; relatively inelastic, 100; unitary elasticity, 100

Denmark, 91; EEC and, 307, 347, 358; in EFTA, 308, 357, 358; in OECD, 348

Depreciation, 108–09, 120–24, 134; defined, 98

Devaluation, 97–134, 139–40; absorption approach, 112–15; defined, 30–31, 97; degree of impact, 131–32; dollar (U.S.), 7, 97–99, 111, 133, 155, 172–76, 178, 184–87, 235, 393; domestic income and price effects, 109–11; effectiveness of policy, 117–19; foreign retaliation, 119–20; franc (French), 97, 110–11, 116, 149, 154; inflation and, 110, 114, 125; mark (Finnish), 97, 111; monetary approach, 115–16; pound sterling, 7, 97–98, 103–08, 110, 132, 133; recent skepticism, 124–25; redistribution of domestic resources, 111–12; relative price effect, 98–109; time path, 133

Devaluation cycle (1930–35), 148

Developing countries, 222; double gap problem, 240; EEC trading agreements with, 359–61; export-oriented strategy, 374–75; fixed exchange rates, 203; foreign aid, 239–40; Generalized System of Preferences, 323–24, 380–84; import substitution, 373–75, 385; industrialization, 269; international currency reform, 387; Link proposal, 387; migration of labor, 407; oil prices, 191–92; quotas, 327, 330; regional integration among, 384–86; reserves and, 197; tariffs, 273, 291, 298, 303; trade problems of, 373–87; UNCTAD, 375–80; U.S. investments in, 399

Dillon, Douglas, 364

Dillon Round, 316, 364

Diminishing returns, law of, 225

Direct taxes, 336

Dirty floats, 50–51, 124, 176, 186

Dollar (Canadian): appreciation, 117; floating, 7, 27, 50, 184, 186, 188, 200, 202

Dollar (U.S.), 26, 54–55; appreciation, 120; depreciation, 122; devaluation, 7, 97–99, 111, 133, 155, 172–76, 178, 184–87, 235, 393; floating, 27, 155; gold exchange standard, 33–35; as intervention currency, 33–36, 44; shortages, 150, 314, 316; supply and demand, 27–30

Dollar adequacy, 150
Dollar exchange standard, 193–95
Dollar glut, 150–55
Dollar pool, 149
Dollar selling and buying points, 34
Domestic International Sales Corporations (DISC), 179, 337
Domestic multipliers, 66–68
Double gap problem, 240
Dumping, 340–44, 372
Dynamic benefits of international trade, 238–42

East-West trade, 368–72
Econometrics, 128–29
Economic dynamics, 126
Economic Report of the President, 18
Economic welfare, foreign investments and, 394–401
Economies of scale, 266–67
EEC, *see* European Economic Community (EEC)
Effective protection, theory of, 329
Effective tariff rates, 294–300, 301–02
EFTA, *see* European Free Trade Area Association (EFTA)
Employment: balance of payments deficit, 58–59; surplus and, 59–60; tariffs and, 292
Energy crisis, 189, 270, 326
EPU, *see* European Payments Union (EPU)
Equation of exchange, 76
Equilibrium exchange rate, 38
Equilibrium in isolation, 248–49
Escalator clause, 110
Escape clause, 315, 317–20, 321
Ethiopia, 192
Euratom, 345, 348, 354
Eurobonds, 45
Eurodollars, 45–46, 54, 89–90, 168
European Atomic Energy Community, 314
European Coal and Steel Community, 314, 345, 348
European Communities (EC), *see* European Economic Community (EEC)
European Development Fund, 360
European Economic Community (EEC), 51, 55, 88, 174, 175, 176, 345, 392; agricultural policy, 326, 349–54, 365; beginnings of, 150; Common External Tariff, 349; enlargement, effects of, 358–59, 360; forerunners of, 347–48; Generalized System of Preferences,

380–83; joint float, 187–88; Kennedy Round and, 364–67; membership, 307, 347; monetary integration in, 204–08, 354; political institutions, 354–56; political strength, 314; Smithsonian Agreement, 180–81; tariffs, 307–08, 312; trade creation, 311; trade restrictions, 348–49; trading with developing countries, 359–61; U.S. imports and, 314
European Free Trade Area Association (EFTA), 308, 345, 356–58, 392
European Investment Bank, 360
European Monetary Agreement (EMA), 145
European Payments Union (EPU), 143–45, 150, 195, 314, 345
Exchange clearing agreements, *see* Bilateral clearing agreements
Exchange control, 44, 48, 135–40, 141, 147, 203, 237, 299, 346, 385
Exchange rates, 26–38; adjustable peg system, 44, 181, 185, 208; defined, 26; fixed, *see* Fixed exchange rates; forward, 41–42; freely fluctuating (floating), *see* Freely fluctuating (floating) exchange rates; market-determined, 27–31; multiple, 139, 238, 299, 346, 385; spot, 41–42, 52–53
Exchange stabilization, 97; under Bretton Woods system, 33–35; under gold standard, 31–32
Exchange-rate adjustment, *see* Devaluation; Revaluation
Excise tax, 337
Exploitation, 395
Export Administration Act (1969), 370
Export Control Act (1949), 370
Export restriction schemes, 331
Export subsidies, 299, 340
Export taxes, 272–73, 283
Export-price index, 222
Exports, 2–3, 11–12; balance of payments deficit and, 58–59; supply and demand, 278–84; surplus and, 59–60; *see also* Tariffs

f.a.s. (free along side) price, 274
f.o.b. (free on board) price, 274, 276, 366
Factor mobility, 389
Factor proportions (endowment) theory, 252–53, 257–65; empirical testing, 263–65

Farm prices, *see* Agriculture

Federal Reserve Bank of New York, 156, 159

Federal Reserve Board, 90, 93, 95–96, 129, 168–70

Federal Reserve Bulletin, 18

Federal Reserve System, 156

Finland: in EFTA, 357, 358; in OECD, 348; *see also* Mark (Finnish)

Fixed exchange rates, 27, 30–38, 47, 55, 198, 203, 209–10; balance of payments adjustment policies under, 56–96; inflation and, 123; interdependence of nations, 87–91; market forces and determination of, 35, 36–38; wider band proposal, 208, 209; *see also* Devaluation; Revaluation

Floating exchange rates, *see* Freely fluctuating (floating) exchange rates

Food and Agriculture Organization of the United Nations (FAO), 359

Foreign aid programs, 12, 19, 22, 151, 174, 239

Foreign exchange market, 38–44; forward exchange market, 40–44, 58; organization, 38–39; speculation, 43–44

Foreign investments, 12, 13, 19, 242; cost considerations, 391–93; economic welfare (real income), 394–401; marketing considerations, 393–94; motives for direct, 390–94; U.S., 12, 13, 19, 24, 389–403

Foreign trade, *see* International trade

Foreign-trade multiplier, 68–71, 123

Forum, 276

Forward exchange market, 40–44, 58

Forward exchange rates, 41–42

Franc (Belgian), 26; floating, 51, 176

Franc (French), 26; depreciation, 120; devaluation, 97, 110–11, 116, 149, 154; floating, 51, 53, 54, 176, 187, 188; revaluation, 178; weakening of, 88–89

Franc (Swiss), floating, 50, 184, 186, 188

France, 153, 206; EEC and, 206, 207, 307, 347; farm prices, 350; gold bloc and, 148; in OECD, 348; oil prices and, 191; trade surpluses, 190; Tripartite agreement, 149; *see also* Franc (French)

Free floats, 50–51

Free trade, 242, 272, 349, 357, 363, 383–86; approaches to, 306–12

Freely fluctuating (floating) exchange rates, 27–30, 50–55, 98, 147, 155, 209–10; advantages and disadvantages, 198–204; balance of payments adjustments, 120–25; role of, 122–23; time lag, 134

Functional distribution of income, 261

General Agreement to Borrow, 163

General Agreement on Tariffs and Trade (GATT), 174, 176, 276, 301, 307, 312, 313, 315, 326, 345, 355, 361–67; antidumping regulations, 322; border adjustments for internal taxes, 336–37, 340; Dillon Round, 316; export subsidies, 340; functions of, 361–62; Kennedy Round, 364–67; most-favored-nation principle, 360, 362–64; textile trade and, 334–35, 382

General Theory of Employment, Interest, and Money (Keynes), 76

Generalized System of Preferences (GSP), 323–24, 361, 380–84; EEC and, 380–83; proposed U.S., 383–84

Germany: war reparations, 77; *see also* West Germany

Ghana, export taxes, 273, 283

Gold, 14; demonetization of, 158–60; price of, 152, 158–60, 178, 189; two-price system, 155

Gold bloc, 148

Gold exchange standard, 33

Gold rush (March 1968), 159

Gold standard, 44, 77, 93, 146–47; exchange stabilization under, 31–32

Gold *tranche,* 162, 163

Grain Agreement, 332

Great Britain: agricultural policy, 352–53; EEC and, 206, 207, 307, 347, 352–54, 356–57, 358; in EFTA, 308, 357, 358; in OECD, 348; U.S. investments in, 395; *see also* Pound sterling

Greece: EEC and, 347, 357; in OECD, 348

Gross national product (GNP), 1, 2, 118, 127, 129, 154, 206

Group of Ten, 156, 161, 176

Growth of World Industry, The (United Nations), 214

Guilder (Netherlands): appreciation, 120–21; floating, 51, 171, 176; revaluation, 53, 97, 207

Hartke-Burke bill, 400, 401
Heath, Edward, 358
Heckscher, E. F., 257
Heckscher-Ohlin theory of international trade, 389, 406
Hedging, 41
Historical survey of international financial relations, 146–55
Honduras, 386
Horizontal equity, principle of, 401
Hot money, 43
Human skills theory, 266, 268
Hungary, 371

Iceland, 348
Imperial tariff system, 275, 363
Import duty, 272–73
Import licenses, 330
Import quotas, 147, 174, 299, 325–30, 405; commonness of, 325–27; economic effects of, 327–30
Import substitution, 373–75, 385
Import surcharge, 174–76, 179
Import-price index, 222
Imports, 2–3, 11–12; balance of payments deficit and, 58–59; supply and demand, 278–84; surplus and, 60; *see also* Tariffs
Income: determination of domestic, 61–66; devaluation and, 109–111; domestic multiplier, 66–68; foreign-trade multiplier, 68–71, 123, limitation of, 48; monetary mechanism effect on, 74–79; real, 290–91; reversal factors, 110
Income tax, 336
Incomplete specialization, 260, 262
Inconsistent economic situations, 92–93, 147
Increasing cost situations, 224–25
India, 192, 269, 360, 361
Indifference maps, 242, 253, 255; community, 245–46, 248; consumer, 243–45
Indirect taxes, 336–37
Indonesia, 191
Industry, *see* Tariffs
Infant-industry argument, 303, 385
Inflation, 3, 49, 80, 88, 91–95; cost-push, 93; devaluation and, 110, 114, 125; fixed exchange rates and, 123; import restrictions and, 289–90; revaluation and, 117; Swiss, 86; U.S., 49, 168–70; West German, 88, 152–53

Input-output statistics, 264–65
Interdependence of nations, balance of payments and, 87–91
Interest, differentials, 83–87, 147
Interest rates, 48, 75, 78; Operation Twist, 95–96, 151; in U.S., 168–72, 190
Interest-equalization tax, 151
International Air Transport Association, 337–38
International Bank for Economic Cooperation, 370
International Bank for Reconstruction and Development (IBRD), 150, 197, 377–78
International Cocoa Agreement, 332
International Coffee Agreement, 332
International Commodity Agreements (ICAs), 330–35, 377, 378
International Customs Journal, 276
International Customs Tariff Bureau, 276
International Development Association, 197
International Finance Section, Princeton University, 193
International financial relations, 7–210; alleged mystique of, 7–9; balance of payments, *see* Balance of international payments; bilateral clearing agreements, 140–42, 143, 150, 238, 323, 346, 370; Bretton Woods system, *see* Bretton Woods system; currency convertibility, 14, 24, 89, 142–45, 210; exchange control, 44, 48, 141, 147, 203, 237, 299, 346, 385; exchange rates, *see* Exchange rates; exchange-rate adjustment, 97–125; foreign exchange market, 38–44; historical survey, 146–55; liquidity, 156–67; post-Smithsonian developments, 181–87; reform proposals, 193–210; reserves, *see* International reserves; Smithsonian Agreement, 155, 178–81, 184, 186, 206; U.S. measures of March 1971, 168–78
International Financial Statistics (IMF), 18, 47, 164
International Monetary Fund (IMF), 16, 18, 55, 58, 93, 97, 135, 149–50, 160, 176, 181, 203, 333, 345, 369, 378; charter, 119–20, 138; establishment of, 33, 44; expanded (XIMF), 195–98; functions of, 44–45; official reserves, 14; procedures, 161–63;

quotas, 161–63; Special Drawing Rights, 155, 160, 164–67; *tranches,* 162
International reserves, 58, 123, 150–51; centralization of, 195–98; dollar exchange standard, 193–95; freely fluctuating exchange rates, 198–204; reasons for, 47–48; reserve-creating institution, establishment of, 195–98; shortage of, 48; *see also* Liquidity
International Sugar Agreement, 332
International Tin Agreement, 332
International trade, 213–408; absolute advantage and wage rates, 219, 236–37; cartels, 337–40, 396; commercial policy (U.S.), *see* Commercial policy (U.S.); commodity composition of, *see* Commodity composition of trade; comparative advantage, *see* Comparative advantage, principle of; comparative opportunity cost, 225–36; developing countries, 337–87; dumping, 340–44, 372; dynamic gains from, 238–42; East-West, 368–72; import quotas, 299, 325–30, 405; International Commodity Agreements, 330–35, 377, 378; international and regional organizations, 345–72; mobility of productive factors, 388–408; nontariff barriers, 335–37; pure theory of, 213; reasons for, 217–55; reciprocal trade agreements legislation, 314–19; static gains from, 242–55; traiffs, *see* Tariffs
International Trade Organization (ITO), 361
International trade theory, 403–06
International Wheat Agreement, 332
Intervention prices, 350–51
Investments: direct, 83, 242; foreign, *see* Foreign investments; planned and realized, 61–64; portfolio, 84–87
Invisible items, 11
Iran, 191
Ireland: EEC and, 307, 347, 358; in OECD, 348
Israel, 186
Italy: EEC and, 206, 207, 307, 347; in OECD, 348; *see also* Lira (Italian)

Japan, 264; balance-of-payment surpluses, 152; deficit (1973), 190; dollar devaluation and, 173, 185–86; GNP, 154; inconsistent economic situations, 92; in OECD, 348; oil

prices, 191; tariffs, 303; textile industry, 270, 334; trade surpluses, 154, 184
Johnson, Harry G., 205–06
Joint float, 51, 53, 155, 187, 191, 203, 206, 207, 354

Kennedy Round, 275, 293, 321, 364–67
Kenya, 192, 360
Keynes, John Maynard, 60, 76–78, 149
Keynesian economics, 76–79, 93
Kindleberger, C. P., 125
Kroner (Danish), 51
Kroner (Norwegian), 51
Kronor (Swedish), 51
Kuwait, 191

Labor, international migration of, 406–08
Labor productivity, 218–25, 236, 256–61
Labor theory of value, 218
Labor unions, 93–94, 110, 169, 171, 270, 299
Labor-abundant country, 259, 264
Labor-intensive commodity, 259
Laffer, Arthur, 124
Latin American Free Trade area, 385
Law, W. L., 271
Leontief, Wassily, 264
Leontief scarce-factor paradox, 264
Lichtenstein, 206
Link proposal, 197, 387
Liquidity, 47, 156–67, 209; ad hoc measures, 156–57; gold policy, 157–61; Special Drawing Rights, 161–67; *see also* International reserves
Lira (Italian), floating, 50, 184, 186, 188
London Gold Pool, 159
Luxembourg, 206; EEC and, 307, 347; in OECD, 348

Majority rule, 245
Malaysia, 360
Mali, 192
Managed floats, 50–51, 55, 98, 123
Marginal propensity to consume (MPC), 59, 66, 67, 70–73
Marginal propensity to import (MPM), 69–73, 80, 118, 129, 206
Marginal propensity to save (MPS), 66, 67, 70–74, 240

Marginal rate of substitution (MRS), 244

Marginal rate of transformation (MRT), 248

Mark (Finnish), devaluation, 97, 111

Mark (German), 26–28; appreciation, 120, 122; floating, 51, 132, 154, 171, 176, 187, 191; revaluation, 7, 97, 117, 152–54, 178, 188, 205, 207

Marshall Plan, 145, 150, 347

Merchandise trade, 11, 12; long-run shifts in the balance on, 19–21

Mexico, 186, 374; U.S. investments in, 375, 395, 398

Migration of labor, 406–08

Model building, 128

Monaco, 206

Monetary approach to devaluation, 115–16

Monetary integration, in EEC, 204–08, 354

Monetary mechanism, impact on income and prices, 74–79

Money-supply–price-change mechanism, 76–78

Monopoly power, 277, 286, 290, 341, 395

Monopoly profit, 327

Monthly Bulletin of Statistics (United Nations), 214

Most-favored-nation (MFN) principle, 275, 315, 323, 360, 362–64, 371, 372, 381–84

Multilateral contracts, 332

Multinational corporations, 181–82; international trade theory and, 403–06; taxing, 400–01

Multiple currency intervention, 51, 181, 183

Multiple exchange rates, 139, 238, 299, 346, 385

Multiple-reserve-center system, 194–95

Multiplier, 79, 127, 128; defined, 60; domestic, 66–68; foreign-trade, 68–71, 123; implications of formula, 71–74

Mundell, Robert, 124

National security provisions, 315, 318

Negative value added, 294, 298, 374

Net liquidity balance, 15, 16, 18

Netherlands: EEC and, 307, 347; in OECD, 348; restrictions of inflow of funds, 90; see also Guilder (Netherlands)

Network of Intra-European Trade, The (OECD), 214

Neutralizing policy, 146

New Economic Policy, 155, 171–78

New York foreign exchange market, 46

Nigeria, 191

Nixon, Richard M., 155, 171, 371

No-injury philosophy, 315, 318–19

Nominal tariff rates, 294–300, 301–02

Nontariff trade barriers, 335–37

North Korea, 371

North Vietnam, 371

Norway, 188, 206; in EFTA, 308, 357, 358; in OECD, 348

OECD, see Organization for Economic Cooperation and Development (OECD)

OEEC, see Organization of European Economic Cooperation (OEEC)

Official reserve transactions balance, 15, 16, 18

Offsetting policies, 77, 146

Ohlin, Bertil, 77, 257

Oil prices, 12, 29–30, 51, 55, 120, 338

Open-market operations, 82, 196–97

Operation Twist, 95–96, 151

Opportunity costs, 220, 256; comparative, 225–36; constant, 242, 260; increasing, 224–25

Optimum currency areas, 203–04, 206

Optimum tariff, 290–91, 303–04, 399

Orderly cross rates, 39

Organization for European Cooperation and Development (OECD), 1, 95, 213, 214, 275, 301, 348, 370

Organization of European Economic Cooperation (OEEC), 314, 347–48

Organization of Petroleum Exporting Countries, (OPEC), 120, 191, 338

Outpayments, 75

Overseas Business Reports, 276

Pakistan, 192, 269, 298, 360

Paper gold, 7, 155, 161

Par value, 31

Partial equilibrium analysis, 284

Peril point, 315, 316–17, 321

Persistent dumping, 341

Poland, 371

Portfolio capital, 83

Portugal: in EFTA, 308, 357, 358; in OECD, 348

Pound sterling, 26; depreciation, 121, 122; devaluation, 7, 97–98, 103–08,

110, 132, 133; floating, 27, 50, 148, 155, 178, 181, 183–84, 186; gold exchange standard, 33–35; revaluation, 178
Predatory dumping, 341
Preference similarity hypothesis, 267–68
Price elasticity, 80, 94; of demand, 100, 103
Price and wage controls, 111, 171–72
Prices: agriculture, 205, 291, 326, 350; change, 74, 99–102, 301–03; cost-push inflation, 93; devaluation and, 109–11; gold standard and, 146–47; monetary mechanism effect on, 74–79
Price-support programs, 326
Primary products, 375–78
Private expenditures, balance of payments adjustment policies and, 58–74
Producer's surplus, 288
Product cycle hypothesis, 267
Product differentiation, 257
Production: balance of payments deficit, 58–59; costs, 233; loss, 285; surplus and, 59–60
Purchasing-power parity doctrine, 131
Pure theory of international trade, defined, 213

Quota restrictions, 48, 273
Quotas, 237, 385; differences between tariffs and, 327–30; export, 326, 334; import, see Import quotas; in International Monetary Fund, 161–63; see also Tariffs

Randall Commission, 316
Randall Report of 1954, 316
Real income, tariffs and, 290–91
Reciprocal demand, 222, 228–30, 232, 234
Reciprocal trade agreements legislation, 314–19
Reconstitution, 165
Redundancy problem, 119
Reform proposals, 193–210, 387; centralization of reserves, 195–98; dollar exchange standard, 193–95; freely fluctuating exchange rates, 198–204; monetary integration in EEC, 204–08; reserve-creating institution, establishment of, 195–98
Regulation Q, 90, 168

Relative factor intensity, concept of, 259
Report on Exchange Restrictions, A (IMF), 135
Reserve settlement account, 167
Reserve unit (RU), 167
Reserves, see International reserves; Liquidity
Resource cost, 220
Revaluation, 57, 118, 131, 173; defined, 31, 97; franc (French), 178; guilder (Netherlands), 53, 97, 207; inflation and, 117; mark (German), 7, 97, 117, 152–54, 178, 188, 205, 207; pound sterling, 178; yen, 178
Reversal factors, 108, 110
Ricardo, David, 218
Robinson Crusoe economy, 61, 62
Romania, 369, 371
Roosa bonds, 151
Rules of the game, 77, 93, 146–47, 149
Rules of origin, 358, 382

Sales at less than fair value, 343
Samuelson, Paul, 257
Saudi Arabia, 191
Savings, planned and realized, 61–64
Savings function, 65–66
Scandinavia, see names of countries
Schuman Plan, 314
Scientific tariff, 237
Services, exchange of, 11
Share-of-the-market concept, 317
Short-run imbalances of balance of payments, 56–58
Shultz, George P., 186
Singapore, 360, 374
Single factoral terms of trade, 377
Single-reserve-center system, 194–95
Skill intensity reversals, 266
Sliding parity, 208
Smithsonian Agreement, 155, 178–81, 184, 186, 206
South Korea, 374
Spain, 348
Special Drawing Rights (SDRs), 7, 14, 16, 45, 55, 155, 160, 178–79, 183, 197, 210; creation of, 161; procedures, 164–67
Specialization, 241; complete, 223–25, 242, 260; incomplete, 260, 262
Specie-flow mechanism, 76–79
Specific duty, 273–75, 294, 318, 405
Speculation, 43–44, 57, 77–78, 181–82, 185, 203

Sporadic dumping, 341
Spot exchange rates, 41–42, 52–53
Sri Lanka, 192, 360, 361
Standard International Trade Classification (SITC), 23, 213, 275, 300
Statutory tariff, 275, 371
Sterling Area, 148
Stock, 83
Sudan, 192
Supply and demand: exchange rate, 27–30, 37; exports and imports, 278–84; of gold, 31; *see also* Demand
Supply-propelled growth, 241
Surplus, 59–60; meaning of, 11–18; on merchandise trade, 20–21
Survey of Current Business, 18
Sweden, 188, 206; in EFTA, 308, 357, 358; in OECD, 348
Switching policy, 118–19
Switzerland, 171; capital inflow, 90, 184; in EFTA, 308, 357, 358; inflation, 86; in OECD, 348; *see also* Franc (Swiss)

Taiwan, 269, 374, 375
Tanzania, 192, 360
Target price, 350–51
Tariff Schedule of the United States (TSUS), 276
Tariff Schedule of the United States, Annotated (1969), The, 276
Tariffs, 147, 237, 272–312, 385; *ad valorem* duty, 273–75, 294, 318, 405; aggregation problems, 300–01; Australian, 262; balance of payments and, 291–92; Brazilian, 276–77; Canadian, 266, 392–93; of developing countries, 273, 291, 298, 303; differences between quotas and, 327–30; Dillon Round, 316, 364; domestic effects, 284–90; economic effects, 276–94; export versus import duty, 272–73; imperial system, 275, 363; infant-industry argument, 303; institutional considerations, 272–76; Japanese, 303; Kennedy Round, 275, 293, 321, 364–67; nominal versus effective rates, 294–300, 301–02; optimum, 290–91, 303–04, 399; price change, response to, 301–03; protection, arguments for, 303–06; protection, levels of, 294–303; protection versus revenue, 273; real income, effects of, 290–91; reduction

and elimination, 306–12; scientific, 237; sources of data, 276; specific, 273–75, 294, 318, 405; statutory, 275, 371; types of, 273–76; U.S., 289–93, 303; *see also* Commercial policy (U.S.)
Taxes: border adjustment for internal, 336–37; corporate profit, 336; direct, 336; excise, 337; export, 272–73, 283; foreign investments, 400–01; income, 336; indirect, 336–37
Technological advance hypothesis, 267
Textile industry, 270, 289, 304, 333–35
Threshold price, 351
Tied aid, 19
Time lags, 130, 134, 202
Time path, 132–33
Trade, *see* International trade
Trade adjustment assistance, 319–20
Trade Agreements Act (1934), 315, 320; 1958 extension, 364
Trade Agreements Legislation, 361
Trade Agreements Program, 316
Trade by Commodities, Series B (OECD), 214
Trade creation, 308–11, 358, 379
Trade deflection, 357
Trade diversion, 308–11, 358, 379, 385–86
Trade Expansion Act (1962), 314, 320–21, 364
Trade Not Aid, 316
Trade organizations, 345–72
Trade Reform Act (1973), 321–24, 367, 371, 380, 383–84
Trading with the Enemy Act (1917), 370
Tranches, 162
Transfer pricing, 404–05
Transformation curves, 242, 246–55
Transitional floats, 132, 183
Transportation costs, 391, 392
Treaty of Rome, 347, 355–56, 359
Triangular arbitrage, 39
Triffin, Robert, 195
Tripartite agreement, 149
Turkey: EEC and, 347, 357; in OECD, 348

Uganda, 192, 360
Underdeveloped countries, *see* Developing countries
Unemployment, 91–96, 169, 241
United Automobile Workers, 326

United Nations, 192, 213, 214, 275

United Nations Conference on Trade and Development (UNCTAD), 345, 375–80

UNCTAD-GATT International Trade Center, 276

United States of America: antitrust legislation, 396; balance of payments, 11–24, 49, 50, 169, 170, 190, 402–03; as closed economy, 1–2; commercial policy, *see* Commercial policy (U.S.); consistent economic situations, 91, 92; East-West trade, 370–72, 396; events leading to measures of August 1971, 168–71; farm prices, 350; foreign aid programs, 12, 19, 174, 239–40; foreign investments, 12, 13, 19, 24, 389–403; Generalized System of Preferences (proposed), 383–84; GNP, 1, 2; inflation, 49, 168–70; interest rates, 168–72, 190; New Economic Policy, 155, 171–78; in OECD, 348; oil prices, 191; post-Smithsonian developments, 182–87; price and wage controls, 171–72; restrictions on outflow of funds, 90; Smithsonian Agreement, 178–81; tariffs, 289–93, 303; *see also* Dollar (U.S.)

United States Census Bureau, 214

United States Commodity Imports and Exports as Related to Output (Census Bureau), 214

United States government bonds, 91

United States Tariff Commission, 316–18, 319–21, 343, 383

United States Treasury, 156, 183, 343

United Textile Workers, 334

Utility gain ratio, 228

Value-added tax, 336, 337, 354

Variable levy, 351

Volcker, Paul, 186

Voluntary export quotas, 326, 334

Wage rates, 304, 392; absolute advantage and, 219, 236–37; gold standard and, 146–47

Wage-price control program, 171–72

Wall Street Journal, 193

War reparations, 21, 77

Watergate affair, 122, 189

Welfare effect of the tariff, 287–89

Werner Report, 205–06

West African Union, 359, 360

West Germany, 170; balance-of-payment surpluses, 152; dollar devaluation and, 173, 184–86; EEC and, 307, 347; exchange control, 148; farm prices, 205, 350; inconsistent economic situations, 92; inflation, 88, 152–53; in OECD, 348; restrictions of inflow of funds, 90; short-term capital flows, 182; trade surpluses, 190

Western Alliance, 315, 316

Wheat, price of, 290

White, Harry, 149

Wholesale price index, 131

Wider band proposal, 208, 209

World Bank, 192

XIMF, 195–98

Yaoundé Convention (1965), 359

Yen (Japanese), 26, 154; appreciation, 186, 187; depreciation, 120; floating, 27, 50, 155, 186, 188; revaluation, 178

Yugoslavia, 371

Zaire, 192